ECONOMIC THOUGHT SINCE KEYNES

To Calliope

To Marielle

Economic Thought Since Keynes

A History and Dictionary of Major Economists

Michel Beaud

Professor of Economics
University of Paris 7-Jussieu
France

and

Gilles Dostaler

Professor of Economics
University of Quebec at Montreal
Canada

Translated from French by Valérie Cauchemez
with the participation of Eric Litwack

London and New York

Originally published in French as *La pensée économique depuis Keynes: Historique et dictionnaire des principaux auteurs* by Seuil, Paris, 1993

First published 1995 by
Edward Elgar Publishing Limited

First published in paperback 1997
by Routledge
11 New Fetter Lane, London EC4P 4EE

Simultaneously published in the USA and Canada
by Routledge
29 West 35th Street, New York, NY 10001

Typeset by Manton Typesetters, Louth, Lincolnshire, UK
Printed and bound in Great Britain by
Clays, Ltd, St Ives PLC

British Library Cataloguing in Publication Data
Beaud, Michel
Economic Thought Since Keynes: A History
and Dictionary of Major Economists
I. Title II. Dostaler, Gilles
330.0922

Library of Congress Cataloguing in Publication Data
Beaud, Michel.
[Pensée économique depuis Keynes. English]
Economic thought since Keynes: a history and dictionary of major economists / Michel Beaud and Gilles Dostaler.
p. cm.
Includes bibliographical references.
1. Economics—History—20th century. 2. Economists—Biography—Dictionaries. I. Dostaler, Gilles. II. Title.
HB87.B4313 1994
330'.092'2—dc20 93–50629

ISBN 0–415–16454–0

Contents

Introduction

This book is concerned with the evolution of economic ideas since Keynes's *The General Theory of Employment, Interest and Money*. It is addressed to all those who wish to acquaint themselves with the complex evolution of contemporary economic thought. One has in mind here students and teachers of economics and social sciences, in particular, but also specialists, professional economists, whether academics or not, who, while familiar with the authors and debates in their domain of specialization, will find here a working tool, a reference for other fields of research.

Nearly all histories of economic thought stop at Keynes or the Keynesian revolution. They devote at most a chapter, conclusion or epilogue to subsequent developments. Since *The General Theory*, a half century has passed, one rich in developments and debates, with marked transformations of the landscape of economic theory: first, based on interventionism, the consolidation and spread of Keynesianism, then, after a form of apotheosis, a retreat corresponding to the rise of liberalism and new schools of thought. Also witnessed throughout this period was the growing formalization and mathematicization of economic theory.

During the last half century, the total production of books and articles in economics has greatly surpassed the sum of publications from the beginning of economic thought to the publication of Keynes's book.[1] Old tendencies and schools have been renewed, new ones have appeared, while regroupings, fusions and separations have occurred. The fields of specialization – the elaboration and deepening of theory or applications to particular areas – have multiplied. With the movement towards formalization and mathematicization, the very nature of the theoretical literature has been transformed.

Whilst it was relatively easy to find one's way amidst the diversity of doctrines and theories up to the Second World War and the immediate postwar period, this became increasingly difficult in the 1960s. Obviously, there are many books and articles dealing with one or another aspect of the development of contemporary economic thought.[2] There also exist, in diverse forms, presentations of the ideas of important authors of this period. This book aims to present the various trends which have marked the evolution of economic thought since the Keynesian revolution. Concerned mainly with the central corpus of contemporary economics, the analyses, themes and fundamental questions, it strives to present a thorough, systematic account with a view to making the material accessible to the general public, providing specialists with rigorously verified information and describing new approaches to the comprehension of economics.

Among the difficulties raised by a work of this type, the following elements dictated the choice of form which we adopted: the period studied is characterized by the diversity of schools of thought, but also by convergence, overlap and shift – sometimes partial, sometimes temporary – which make the borders fuzzy or mobile. In addition, authors evolve in the 30, 40 or 50 years during which they are active: many authors have followed very special itineraries, some not belonging to any school, others following paths which lead them successively to a variety of different schools. As for those whose tendencies have linked them to a single school, their place on the economic scene and the manner in which they are perceived have also changed.

The same applies to the cleavage, as old as economic thought itself, between liberals and interventionists.[3] Here, simple reductionism must be avoided. On the one hand, while many economists hold the same doctrinal position as long as they live, others have been able to change, in some cases, as with Hansen or Robbins, from liberalism to interventionism, or, inversely, like the former young Keynesians converting to liberalism in the 1980s. On the other hand, this doctrinal opposition overlaps many groups: that of formalist and mathematical economists as well as those of a literary bent, those inclined to pure theory and economists working on more concrete realities.

To present the evolution of contemporary economic thought, it is imperative to put in perspective the various schools of thought, their evolution and the debates between them, along with the authors, their specificity and their evolution. This book will offer: (1) a historical account, indicating the major advances and shifts, the schools and trends, the debates involved in economics, and the authors who played significant roles; (2) a dictionary of 150 authors, for each of whom are given biographical details, a list of major published works, an analysis of contributions to economic thought and a selection of studies devoted to the author; and (3) a bibliography and a comprehensive index of subjects and of all the names mentioned in the historical account and the dictionary.[4]

Historical account

There is no reading of facts and there is no research without a framework. One such framework, long predominant, may be summarized in the following manner. With the publication of *The General Theory of Employment, Interest and Money*, Keynes marked the beginning of a major mutation of economics. Keynesianism and interventionism attained their peak in the 1960s but then the first signs and generalization of economic crisis facilitated the onset of a liberal counter-offensive, which benefited from diverse theoretical support.

This framework appears somewhat inadequate. First of all, *The General Theory* includes intuitions, analyses and interpretations which other authors had produced, sometimes independently of Keynes, during the 1920s and 1930s. Very different systems of analysis and thought, sometimes divergent, were developed under the same rubric of Keynesianism with interference and sometimes very diverse combinations involving other currents and schools. In the background of the Keynesian mutation, another one developed: the mathematicization of economics with the development of econometric research and modelling, and with the reinforcement of axiomatization and formalization. Also a bipolarization took on major importance: on the one hand, a corpus devoted to theoretical elaboration, at the heart of which the pole of general equilibrium and neoclassical theory – rationality and equilibrium – occupies a crucial place; and on the other, an approach devoted to understanding and interpreting economic phenomena and dynamics largely focused on Keynes's vision and on Keynesian macroeconomics.

Our reading of the evolution of contemporary economic thought can, therefore, be schematized as follows. Despite its ambiguities, the importance of *The General Theory* is twofold: as a theoretical construction claiming to replace the old English classical approach, and as a theoretical justification of interventionism (Chapter 1). At least as much as the work of a man and the group surrounding him, it was the expression of the dominant ideas and research in the period of its publication, in the context of the Great Depression (Chapter 2). Very quickly, made concrete by the renewal of approaches, tools of analysis and economic policies, one saw a victory for Keynesianism, although it was mainly interventionism which triumphed (Chapter 3).

Parallel to this mutation, another shift, perhaps a more fundamental one, was produced with the development of econometrics and new techniques of mathematical analysis, the mathematicization of economics and the reformulation of general equilibrium theory (Chapter 4). This mathematicization affected the nature of economic thought. It contributed to the recasting of Keynesian macroeconomics in terms of equilibrium, the 'neoclassical synthesis', and to the construction of large macroeconomic models which left no place for some of Keynes's essential intuitions and hypotheses (Chapter 5).

In the postwar period, with the development of general equilibrium theory and pre-eminence of the neoclassical synthesis, there was a resurgence of heterodoxy, often aimed at a better accounting for actual contemporary economies in accord with the post-Keynesian, institutionalist and Marxist traditions, and with other novel approaches (Chapter 6). Soon recession and inflation revealed the limits of an interventionism regarded as Keynesian and liberal traditions re-emerged. The critics of the state and of active economic policy multiplied, with various forms of theoretical support, most notably from the work of Milton Friedman and the monetarists (Chapter 7) and from the 'new classical' macroeconomics, which claimed to succeed several types of macroeconomics of Keynesian inspiration, itself challenged by disequilibrium theories and new Keynesian economics (Chapter 8). Today, whilst the neoclassical approach has, once again, asserted itself as the unavoidable point of reference in economic theory, new avenues of escape from its lack of realism are open: new reflections on the market, the firm, organization and rationality, and new attempts to construct approaches to economics with historical, social and ethical dimensions (Chapter 9).

The dictionary of authors

As sufficient distance is necessary to take into account the reaction of the profession to published work, we have considered for the dictionary those economists who produced their essential ideas, or at least published an important work, between the publication of Keynes's *General Theory* in 1936 and 1980.[5]

With respect to economists who were active both before and after 1936, we distinguished those who produced their key work before that date and those who wrote their most important work after the publication of *The General Theory*. The former are absent from the dictionary and include, for example, Hawtrey, Knight, Lindahl, Mises, Robertson, Rueff, Schumpeter, Simons and Viner. For the economists corresponding to the chosen period, 1936–1980, we had to decide which should be included. The criterion used was the publication of at least one important work between 1936 and 1980; that is to say a book or an article which constituted a major contribution to theory, analysis or an important debate in the field of economics. Thus are excluded teachers who played a crucial role in training generations of students, authors who published very successful works of popularization, and the political and public figures who contributed to economic thought and action. Problems arise in the case of specialists in adjacent areas overlapping the field of economics, such as demographers, sociologists, historians, anthropologists or philosophers, for example Fernand Braudel, Karl Polanyi or Alfred Sauvy. We chose not to open this door, for fear that we might not be able to close it.

Our choices reflect the localization of the profession at the present time. At one time or other Spanish, Italian, French and English, political economy has now become in large part American, so it is reasonable that American economists should be amply represented in our selection. Nonetheless, more than a third of those American economists are of foreign origin, coming in particular from Eastern Europe. Many contemporary economists fled totalitarianism in Germany or the Soviet Union, which led to an impoverishment of economic thought in the countries concerned. After the United States, Western Europe is best represented and, at the forefront, Great Britain, which continued to play a dominant role at the beginning of the period that concerns us. Clearly we will have forgotten some of our eminent colleagues. That is inevitable in such an undertaking as the present work.

Questions of method

The history of thought is an undertaking both complex and riddled with difficulties. Can one judge past works in the light of present truth? Should one emphasize the coherence of schools and currents of thought, or focus on the works of authors? Should we try to understand why an author produced a particular work by reconstructing its historical genesis, or rather should we evaluate its logical and rational coherence? Should this coherence be evaluated on the basis of world views prevalent at the moment of its production, or of theories accepted at the present time? This issue is linked to essential questions concerning the relationships between the psychological bases of individual creation and the evolution of ideas, and those between this evolution and history, which have haunted philosophical thought since its beginnings.

The problems are certainly aggravated in the area of economic thought by the nature of the subject, concerned with money, power and conflicts between individuals and social groups. This is a question of the relationship between theory and politics, sometimes a question of violence and war. Therefore, it is not surprising that, from its beginnings, political economy should have been an area of intense debate, in which rational discussion often turns to fierce fighting. We do not claim to have surmounted these difficulties or to have escaped the effects of our own intellectual positions, but we tried to minimize their influence by adopting certain guiding principles. First, we refused to judge the material in the light of any orthodoxy. Then we used a combination of the history of thought and the history of ideas, best expressed by the German term *Geistesgeschichte*, 'history of the spirit'.[6] We tried to identify the central questions and logical coherence of the theoretical landscape throughout the various periods studied.

We were careful to present the authors studied in their specificity and to situate them relative to the main axes and lines of development of economic thought, which led us to adopt the method of 'historical reconstruction'. This led us to observe how the multiple classifications and taxonomies used in the contemporary period are fragile, uncertain and open to debate. It is exceptional for an author to identify himself strictly and unequivocally with one school of thought.

Semantic questions

One difficulty we encountered in writing this book was a semantic one. The words required to speak about contemporary economic thought are used in diverse ways, to such an extent that confusion often reigns supreme in discussion. Such is the case, for example, with the term 'Keynesian', which is used in at least three very different ways: to describe the work and thought of Keynes, to characterize that which refers to the central corpus of the Keynesian revolution and (most frequently, by political scientists, sociologists and other analysts, as well as by economists) to refer to every theoretical development, every economic policy or measure, bearing even a very weak relationship to this or that contribution of Keynes or of the Keynesian revolution. But, as we will show, Keynes's work has been interpreted very diversely, and the Keynesian revolution covers multiple, sometimes disparate, ideas.

The same difficulties emerge with the term 'neoclassical'. For some, it is associated with the marginalist revolution, seen by its authors as breaking with classical thought; but the term was coined, on the contrary, to mark the continuity between classical thought and the marginalist revolution. More generally, 'neoclassical theory' is a vast, eclectic corpus containing the theory of price determination by supply and demand, the quantity theory of money, and Say's Law. Keynes attacked the last two elements, which he described as 'classical'. Also described as the 'neoclassical synthesis' was the reconciliation between the marginalist microeconomic tradition and Keynesian macroeconomics. For some, the term neoclassical is used as a 'catch-all' reflecting all that is more liberal than interventionist, which leads, for example, to the inclusion of such authors as Friedrich Hayek, who rejects several of the basic assumptions of neoclassical theory. For others, it implies particular assumptions such as the rationality of agents and market equilibrium. In the latter sense, the Walrasian general equilibrium model, perfected by Arrow and Debreu, constitutes the quintessence of the neoclassical approach; but Walras, no more than Arrow or Debreu, never claimed to draw from the model any political conclusion justifying liberalism rather than interventionism. The term 'liberal' itself takes different meanings, often being used in the sense of interventionist in the United States, contrary to the European tradition where liberal is opposed to social-democrat. Keynes is himself sometimes described as a social liberal, or as a liberal socialist.

In the following pages we take into account the different uses that various authors make of these words, and the manner in which they describe themselves or in which they are described by their peers, their critics and historians of thought. When an expression is crucial, we seek to determine a precise meaning and to specify, whenever possible, how it is used: in the current meaning, the sense in which the authors considered used it, or in the precise sense which we will have defined.

Bibliographies

Bibliographical details obviously constitute an essential element of this work. It was our aim to create a useful tool and we tried to be coherent, clear and as complete as possible, without claiming to be exhaustive. At the end of the book we provide a bibliography of the main works of reference, dictionaries, encyclopaedias, textbooks, monographs and main issues of journals devoted to the period studied, in its entirety or on some special topic. Also, for each author treated in the dictionary, there is a bibliographical selection of his main books and articles and a selection of relevant publications about him. Among the latter, some are given with complete references and others in abbreviated form directing the reader to a reference work mentioned in the final bibliography. When the author has published an autobiographical work, we mention it in this section with an abridged reference. When the author has received the Nobel Memorial Prize in Economics, we cite the issue of the *Swedish* (from 1976 *Scandinavian*) *Journal of Economics* containing the jury's proclamation, one or more articles concerning him, and a bibliography.

Other works and articles of lesser importance or by authors not featured in the dictionary are cited only at the point in the text where we mention them, with complete references. For yet others, cited in the text, we give just the name of the author and date of publication.[7] The complete reference may be found either by turning to the bibliography of the author or by consulting the bibliography at the end of the book.

Acknowledgements

We thank the Social Science and Humanities Research Council of Canada, the Programme d'aide financière aux chercheurs et créateurs (PAFACC) of Université du Québec à Montréal and the Comité d'aide à la publication of Université du Québec à Montréal for financial support which helped us to carry out our work and made the publication of this book possible. A grant from the PAFACC covered part of the cost of translating our manuscript from French to English.

We are grateful to the Royal Economic Society, Macmillan and Cambridge University Press for permission to quote from *The Collected Writings of John Maynard Keynes*, edited by Austin Robinson and Donald Moggridge, and Keynes's *The General Theory of Employment, Interest and Money*; to the Econometric Society for permission to reprint a graph published in the February 1937 issue of *Econometrica*; to Basil Blackwell for permission to reproduce two tables published by *Economica*. We thank Professor Paul A. Samuelson who kindly granted us the permission to reproduce a figure from his *Economics*, and Professors Samuelson and Robert Solow for permission to reproduce a figure from their *American Economic Review* (1960) paper.

Many authors provided us with biographical and bibliographical information which was very useful to us. Some of them pointed out mistakes in the French version of this book. For their collaboration we thank Irma Adelman, Armen Alchian, Maurice Allais, Samir Amin, Kenneth Arrow, Athanasios Asimakopulos, Joe S. Bain, Bela Balassa, Alain Barrère, Robert Barro, William Baumol, Gary Becker, Abram Bergson, Charles Bettleheim, Mark Blaug, Marcel Boiteux, Kenneth Boulding, Sam Bowles, Andras Brody, Martin Bronfenbrenner, Suzanne de Brunhoff, James Buchanan, Hollis B. Chenery, Robert Clower, Ronald Coase, Paul Davidson, Gérard Debreu, Harold Demsetz, Edward F. Denison, Evsey Domar, Anthony Downs, John Eatwell, Robert Eisner, Robert Fogel, André Gunder Frank, Milton Friedman, Celso Furtado, John Kenneth Galbraith, Pierangelo Garegnani, Nicholas Georgescu-Roegen, Richard M. Goodwin, Claude Gruson, Trygve Haavelmo, Gottfried Haberler, Frank Hahn, Geoffrey Harcourt, Friedrich A. Hayek, Robert Heilbroner, Albert Hirschman, Terence Hutchison, Walter Isard, Dale Jorgenson, Charles Kindleberger, Lawrence Klein, Janos Kornai, Jan Kregel, Harvey Leibenstein, Axel Leijonhufvud, Wassily Leontief, William Arthur Lewis, Richard Lipsey, Ian M. Little, Robert Lucas, Edmond Malinvaud, Ernest Mandel, Thomas Mayer, Donald McCloskey, James Meade, Jacob Mincer, Hyman P. Minsky, Franco Modigliani, Michio Morishima, Douglass C. North, Alec Nove, Luigi Pasinetti, Don Patinkin, Edmund Phelps, Henry Phelps Brown, Richard A. Posner, Walt Rostow, Paul A. Samuelson, Thomas Sargent, Anna Schwartz, Tibor Scitovsky, Amartya Sen, Herbert Simon, Hans Singer, Robert Solow, Michael A. Spence, George Stigler, Joseph Stiglitz, Paul M. Sweezy, Lorie Tarshis, James Tobin, Robert Triffin, Shigeto Tsuru, Gordon Tullock, Jaroslav Vanek, Raymond Vernon, Oliver E. Williamson and Arnold Zellner.

We thank those who read, either wholly or in part, our manuscript in its several stages of preparation, who suggested corrections or offered advice as to how to bring the whole effort to fruition: Edmond Blanc, Mark Blaug, Gilles Bourque, Marielle Cauchy, Antoine del Busso, Edward Elgar, Robert Leonard and Robin Rowley. We are obviously solely responsible for the final product. At the final stage of the preparation of the manuscript, we benefited from the research assistance of Ianik Marcil, and we thank him for his efficient work. We also thank Isabelle Bruston and François Plourde for their assistance in the first stages of our research. Valérie Cauchemez carried out the major part of the translation of this book, the French version of which was published as *La Pensée économique depuis Keynes: historique et dictionnaire des principaux auteurs* by Les Éditions du Seuil (Paris, 1993). Eric Litwack translated 60 dictionary entries. Marielle Cauchy and Marguerite Mendell also translated some entries. We are very grateful to Venant Cauchy, Robert Leonard and Robin Rowley, who extensively revised the translation. We would finally like to thank Julie Leppard and the staff of

Edward Elgar Publishing for the courteous efficiency with which they helped bring the manuscript to publication. The preparation of the English version of this work was supervised by Gilles Dostaler.

Notes

1. Some estimate that this period's production represents 14 times the stock of existing works in economics in 1936. See G. Stigler, 'The Literature of Economics: The Case of the Kinked Oligopoly Demand Curve', *Economic Inquiry*, vol. 16, 1978, 185–204.
2. See the Bibliography at the end of the book.
3. We use here and throughout the term 'liberal' in its traditional, European sense of partisan of laissez-faire, instead of its usual American sense of partisan of state intervention.
4. When there is an entry on the author in the dictionary, the corresponding pages are printed in bold characters.
5. Obviously, in the historical section, it was, at various points, necessary for us to recall previous developments.
6. See M. Blaug, 'On the Historiography of Economics', *Journal of the History of Economic Thought*, vol. 12, 1990, 27–37. Adopting the categories proposed by Richard Rorty ('The Historiography of Philosophy: Four Genres', in *Philosophy in History: Essays on the Historiography of Philosophy*, edited by R. Rorty, J.B. Schneewind and Q. Skinner, Cambridge, England, Cambridge University Press, 1984, 49–75), Blaug distinguishes four characteristic approaches to the history of economic thought: *Geistesgeschichte*, historical reconstruction, rational reconstruction and doxography. *Geistesgeschichte* seeks to identify the central questions posed by thinkers of the past, so as to situate them in the context of their own thought worlds. Historical reconstruction seeks to take account of the thinking of these authors, in the terms in which they formulated them and in ways they would find acceptable. As for rational reconstruction, it attempts to present the ideas of authors in modern idiom, with a view to showing their errors, contributions and lacunae relative to the contemporary state of knowledge. Finally, doxography reformulates the thought of past authors with the aim of evaluating them in the light of modern orthodoxy.
7. When there is more than one publication for a given date, the latter is followed by the indication of the book's title or the journal in abridged form. When a quote is taken from a later reprint, the original date is given in square brackets before the date of the quotation's source, as for example: Hayek [1937] 1948.

PART I

OUTLINE OF A HISTORY OF ECONOMIC THOUGHT SINCE KEYNES

Prologue

The General Theory of Employment, Interest and Money by John Maynard Keynes was published in 1936, a little over a century and a half after Adam Smith's *An Inquiry into the Nature and Causes of the Wealth of Nations*.[1] In his well known book, Smith offers a synthesis of several earlier currents of thought, including French physiocracy, and this new comprehensive theoretical system constitutes the point of departure of classical political economy. Criticizing what he called mercantilism, which, dominating economic thought during the two previous centuries, advocated protectionism as well as an active intervention, as much economic as military, by the newly constituted Nation States, Adam Smith expressed the well known allegory in which the individual is 'led by an invisible hand to promote an end which was no part of his intention ... By pursuing his own interest he frequently promotes that of the society more effectually than when he really intends to promote it'.[2] For Smith, the 'expences of the sovereign or commonwealth'[3] must be limited to those necessitated by defence and justice, and to 'erecting and maintaining those public institutions and those public works, which, though they may be in the highest degree advantageous to a great society, are, however, of such a nature, that the profit could never repay the expence to any individual or small number of individuals, and which it therefore cannot be expected that any individual or small number of individuals should erect or maintain'.[4] Smith's work played an essential role in the development of the economic liberalism, emergent with the triumph of nineteenth-century capitalism, in an England which had become a dominant world power. Codified by David Ricardo[5] and John Stuart Mill,[6] political economy became, for the most part, an English science. But it was a French economist, Jean-Baptiste Say, who enunciated in 1803 the law of markets,[7] according to which, considering the neutrality of money in the economy, supply creates its own demand, and, therefore, there could be no question of having general gluts in a free market economy and thus no chance of the phenomenon which Keynes would call involuntary unemployment. Economic reality, with its regular succession of crises generating simultaneously masses of unsold commodities and misery, contradicted the theory, as was stressed by, among others, Malthus,[8] Sismondi[9] and then Marx.[10] Paradoxically, it was by constructing his system from Ricardian political economy that Marx, in his major work, *Capital*, attempted to give a theoretical foundation to what he believed to be the ineluctable fate of the capitalist societies, namely their transformation into socialist societies.

In the last quarter of the nineteenth century, while Marxism imposed itself on the European workers' organizations and came to dominate a socialist movement which had, of course, preceded it, political economy underwent an important transformation under what is now called the marginalist revolution. Linked to the names of Jevons,[11] Menger[12] and Walras,[13] it made a clean sweep of the classical, and especially Ricardian, vision of value and distribution. The new theory of prices, primarily based on the principle of decreasing marginal utility, found its development and codification in Walras's system of general equilibrium, which subsequently dominated economic thought. There, society is perceived as a natural mechanism, similar in nature to the solar system or a biological organism, in which the interaction of free agents ensures the best allocation of resources and economic optimum.

Critical in some respects of classical theory, the marginalist revolution improved Smith's parable of the invisible hand, giving it a mathematical formulation. Its upholders remained faithful to Say's law of markets, developing under the form of Walras's law the dichotomy between real data and monetary data. The quantity theory of money, whose history goes back to at least the sixteenth century, links the general level of price to the quantity of money in circulation. The expression of neoclassical theory was soon forged to express continuity, rather than rupture, between the classical vision and that which succeeded it in the twentieth century. The *Principles of Political Economy* by Alfred Marshall (whose first edition dates back to 1890[14] and which would dominate the teaching of economics, at least in the English-speaking world, for several decades) symbolizes this continuity, illustrated moreover by the phrase in the epigraph on the title page: '*Natura non facit saltum*'. Economic science, which is, according to Marshall, 'of slow and continuous growth',[15] constitutes 'a study of mankind in the ordinary business of life'.[16] Born in 1842, dying in 1924, Alfred Marshall supported his economic vision with the political and ethical conceptions which characterized the Victorian era in England.

Throughout these various developments, reality never stopped contradicting the vision, shared by several classical and neoclassical economists, according to which the free play of markets is enough to ensure the full employment of resources and their optimal allocation. The economic crises succeeded one another during the entire nineteenth century and up to the great war of 1914–18. The workers' uprisings in the nineteenth century (in particular the events of 1848 and the Paris Commune of 1871), the Russian revolution in 1917, and then the workers' insurrections experienced by several European capitals as the war drew to a close seemed to confirm, for several, the vision of Marx and his disciples. The crises went on after the war. The stock market euphoria, evident in particular in the United States in the second half of the 1920s, may be compared to a maniacal upsurge, the prelude to a depressive episode which, triggered one day in October 1929, became increasingly severe. The entire world was then ravaged by the Great Depression, which manifested itself in plummeting economic activity, rising unemployment and the broadening of poverty and misery. For some, especially in the labour movement in Europe, the USSR appeared to be a country bearing immense hope: the construction of socialism was under way. For others, nationalism, isolationism or national expansion constituted the principal factors of cohesion and strength. Developing, in particular, the second of these in the form of rearmament, the assertion of national greatness and military expansion, Hitler made National Socialism triumph in Germany.

The world of economists was affected in several ways by this situation. First, the crisis deeply marked the consciences and the lives of those born at the beginning of the century. Numerous were those who, enrolled in courses in literature, law or mathematics, became economists in an attempt to understand the causes of the ills they observed around them, and to look for solutions to contribute towards fighting them. Then, at the beginning of the 1930s, many economists (as did so many intellectuals and artists, especially Jews) left Hitler's Germany and the European countries where his ideas flourished. This migration followed that which occurred from the USSR, after the October revolution; it would be prolonged by that from the countries of Eastern Europe after the Yalta agreements. Western Europe often ensured the first reception, but it was almost always the United States which ultimately received these emigrants. Grants, subsidies and support from diverse institutions helped cope with the more urgent cases; then, very rapidly, positions were offered in universities, research institutes and, from the beginning of the Second World War, in administration and in bodies devoted to military activity. Finally, the crisis accentuated the uneasiness in economic theory by stirring up the debate which brought into opposition those who believed that a market economy had at its disposal the mechanisms necessary to adjust automatically to exogenous shocks and those, descended from very diverse currents of thought, who believed on the contrary that liberal capitalism was suffering from serious illnesses, that it had to be overturned or profoundly transformed, or that, at least, an active and even massive intervention by public authorities was necessary in order to avoid its collapse, and to ease the sufferings of those who were the casualties of growth.

Well before the publication, in 1936, of *The General Theory* by Keynes, a very broad range of critiques and counter-positions was heard, defying the liberal orthodoxy, which came down, in several cases, to advocating monetary rigour and price flexibility, particularly that of wages, as the only means to boost employment. Often of pragmatic inspiration, with both national and social concerns, these critiques and counter-positions put forward the ideas of large public projects and employment programmes, of anticyclical budgets;

one immediately thinks of Schacht in Germany, the proposals of the founders of the Stockholm School[17] which inspired the Swedish Social Democratic politicians, the ideas of the English Fabian socialists, the work of Frisch in Norway on economies depressed by a lack of effective demand, that of Tinbergen in Holland which defined the basis of a full employment policy, of the research in France of the 'X-crise' group, and the great debate which arose in the United States during the 1930s.[18]

In this context, *The General Theory* constituted a crucial contribution. Indeed, on the double basis of its author's reputation and of a text of great intellectual ambition, it appeared as both a critique of classical thought, which for Keynes included neoclassical thought, and a new theoretical construction attacking (itself in the name of political liberalism) the liberal economists' dogmatism, justifying active economic policies and suggesting some essential levers for action. And it is not diminishing its merit to note that, for example, with the package of new policies called the New Deal, President Roosevelt of the United States, elected on 8 November 1932, at the height of the Depression, and assuming office on 4 March 1933, had largely opened the way for those modern economic policies which would, later on, often be labelled Keynesian.[19] In this general movement, the publication of *The General Theory* played a major role. This is why we devote to it the first chapter of this text.

Notes

1. London, W. Straham and T. Cadell, 1776.
2. *An Inquiry into the Nature and Causes of the Wealth of Nations*, Homewood, Illinois, Richard D. Irwin, 1963, vol. 2, p. 23.
3. Ibid., p. 215.
4. Ibid., p. 239.
5. *On the Principles of Political Economy and Taxation*, London, John Murray, 1817.
6. *Principles of Political Economy, with Some of their Applications to Social Philosophy*, London, John W. Parker, 1848.
7. *Traité d'économie politique*, Paris, Deterville, 1803; Engl. transl., *Treatise on Political Economy*, Philadelphia, Claxton, Remsen and Haggelsinder, 1880.
8. *Principles of Political Economy: Considered with a View to Their Practical Application*, London, John Murray, 1820.
9. *Nouveaux principes d'économie politique ou De la richesse dans ses rapports avec la population*, Paris, Delaunay, 1819.
10. *Das Kapital: Kritik der politischen Ökonomie*, Hamburg, Otto Meissner, vol. 1, 1867, vol. 2, 1885, vol. 3, 1894; Engl. transl., *Capital: A Critique of Political Economy*, Chicago, Charles H. Kerr, 1887, 1907, 1909.
11. *The Theory of Political Economy*, London, Macmillan, 1871.
12. *Grundsätze der Volkswirtschaftslehre*, Vienna, Wilhelm Braumüller, 1871; Engl. transl., *Principles of Economics*, Glencoe, Illinois, Free Press, 1950.
13. *Éléments d'économie politique pure ou théorie de la richesse sociale*, Lausanne, Imprimerie L. Corbaz, 1874–7; Engl. transl., *Elements of Pure Economics or the Theory of Social Wealth*, Homewood, Illinois, Richard D. Irwin; London, Allen & Unwin, 1954.
14. *Principles of Economics: An Introductory Volume*, London, Macmillan; 8th edn, 1920.
15. Ibid., p. v.

16. Ibid., p. 1.
17. See below, Chapter 2.
18. See below, Chapter 3.
19. Keynes, who met President Roosevelt in 1934, had written an 'Open Letter to the President', published in the *New York Times* on 31 December 1933: 'You have made yourself the trustee for those in every country who seek to mend the evils of our condition by reasoned experiment within the framework of the existing social system. If you fail, rational change will be gravely prejudiced throughout the world, leaving orthodoxy and revolution to fight it out. But if you succeed, new and bolder methods will be tried everywhere, and we may date the first chapter of a new economic era from your accession to office' (*The Collected Writings of John Maynard Keynes*, edited by Sir Austin Robinson and Donald Moggridge, London, Macmillan and New York, Cambridge University Press, for the Royal Economic Society, vol. XXI, p. 289; hereafter we will refer to this edition of Keynes's works, published in 30 volumes between 1971 and 1989, as *JMK*, followed by the volume's number).

1 Keynes and *The General Theory of Employment, Interest and Money*

From ethics to politics

John Maynard Keynes was born in Cambridge on 5 June 1883.[1] His father, John Neville, was an academic there and taught logic and political economy. He was also the author of one of the first books devoted to the methodology of economics, a volume which remains an important reference and a useful synthesis. By trying to define a median path between political economy conceived as a 'positive, abstract and deductive science' and his own vision based on an 'ethical, realistic, and inductive method',[2] John Neville Keynes expressed the distinction between positive and normative science, in terms still referred to by Milton Friedman at the beginning of his well known text on 'The Methodology of Positive Economics' (Friedman 1953). He was a conservative, adhering, like his friend Alfred Marshall, to the ideals of Victorian England.[3] John Maynard, who early revealed exceptional intellectual faculties, soon departed from these ideals, especially under the intellectual influence of the milieux in which he was educated: first Eton (1897–1902) and then Cambridge (1902–6).

In February 1903, Keynes was admitted, at the suggestion of Lytton Strachey and Leonard Woolf, to the Cambridge Conversazione Society, also known as the Apostles, a secret society founded in 1820, devoted, in the words of one of its well known members, Henry Sidgwick, to 'the pursuit of truth with absolute devotion and unreserve by a group of intimate friends'.[4] The Apostles included the philosopher George Edward Moore, who in the autumn of 1903 published his *Principia Ethica*, a book which had a deep and lasting influence on Keynes. The ethical conceptions and the political philosophy which would remain with Keynes until the end of his life took shape at this time, as revealed for example by 'My Early Beliefs', a paper read by Keynes to his friends at the Bloomsbury Memoir Club in 1938 and published posthumously, according to his wishes, in 1949 (*JMK*, X, 433–50).[5] In this memoir, Keynes writes that Moore's philosophy helped him to escape from the Benthamite tradition and from Victorian morality, while contributing 'to protect the whole lot of us from the final *reductio ad absurdum* of Benthamism known as Marxism' (ibid., p. 446). For Keynes and his friends, who proclaimed themselves to be nonconformists and even 'immoralists',[6] the pursuit of beauty and truth, and the relationships of friendship and love, constituted the ultimate goals of human existence. Political and economic organization, Keynes always believed, should be subordinate to these ends: aims which technical progress appeared to have rendered accessible to the greater part of society, for the first time in the history of humanity.[7]

The convictions acquired at Eton and Cambridge would subsequently strengthen in the Bloomsbury group,[8] an informal community with which Keynes would remain closely associated until the end of his life. In a certain sense, Keynes always led a double life, the private and artistic dimension being associated with Bloomsbury and the public one linked to his activities as an economist and political adviser. Consisting of artists and writers, the Bloomsbury group played an important part in the transformation of the Victorian world view. This revolution was reflected in the challenges to prevailing thinking launched by Roger Fry, Virginia Woolf and Lytton Strachey in the areas of art criticism, the novel and biography, and by Keynes himself in the area of economics. All shared the conviction that deterministic logic had little to do with human action, propelled as it was for the most part by irrational motives. Freud's influence was also then making itself felt, and his work was translated and published by Lytton Strachey's brother, James. This Keynes himself read attentively and referred to on several occasions, particularly in his criticism of the gold standard system, a fundamental element of Great Britain's economic and monetary dominance during the nineteenth century.[9] More generally, it was a condemnation of enrichment seen as an end unto itself, the 'chrematistics' condemned by Aristotle that was, ironically, penned by a man who would later acquire considerable wealth through speculation. About 'love of money as a possession – as distinguished from the love of money as a means to the enjoyments and realities of life' Keynes indeed claimed it was 'one of those semi-criminal, semi-pathological propensities which one hands over with a shudder to the specialists in mental disease' (*JMK*, IX, p. 329).[10]

From the beginning of his career, Keynes engaged in intense reflection on the bases of human action and, in particular, on its links with imperfect and uncertain knowledge. For two years from 1906, his reflections centred upon the preparation of a dissertation on the foundations of probability, written while working as a civil servant in the India Office. This work earned him in 1909 a fellowship at King's College, where he began his academic career. Until 1911, a great part of Keynes's time was devoted to revising this dissertation, which was finally published in 1921 with the title *A Treatise on Probability* (*JMK*, VIII). In this book, which is an important contribution to the analysis of the logical foundations of the theory of probability, Keynes appeals to an intellectual tradition which, beginning with Leibniz and Pascal, passes through Locke, Berkeley and Hume to W.E. Johnson, Moore and Bertrand Russell. In one section, dealing with 'some philosophical applications of probability', he further elaborates upon his scepticism towards

Benthamite utilitarianism, claiming that the theory of mathematical expectation, developed for the study of games, was not suitable in the field of probability as applied to human conduct. The degrees of probability were not subject to the laws of arithmetic:

> The hope, which sustained many investigators in the course of the nineteenth century, of gradually bringing the moral sciences under the sway of mathematical reasoning, steadily recedes – if we mean, as they meant, by mathematics the introduction of precise numerical method. ... I, at any rate, have not the same lively hope as Concorcet, or even as Edgeworth, 'éclairer les Sciences morales et politiques par le flambeau de l'algèbre'. (JMK, VIII, p. 349; quotation in French in the original)

Keynes was 30 years old when the First World War broke out. Hired by the British Treasury, he became an important figure in the negotiations which marked the end of that war. Disagreeing with the nature of the reparations imposed on Germany as part of the Treaty of Versailles, he resigned from the British delegation and wrote *The Economic Consequences of the Peace*[11] in three months. Rapidly translated into several languages, this book achieved great success and instantaneously won international notoriety for its author. Bearing witness to the end of an era, Keynes's report sketched the outline for a new liberalism, of which he would thereafter become a tireless advocate, both as a member of the English Liberal Party and through other activities.[12] In a 1926 pamphlet entitled *The End of Laissez-Faire*,[13] originating in lectures given in Oxford in 1924 and in Berlin in 1926, Keynes strongly denounced what he called elsewhere the 'principle of diffusion' (*JMK*, XIX, p. 440), the belief in the myth of the automatic adjustment of prices and quantities: 'It is *not* a correct deduction from the principles of economics that enlightened self-interest always operates in the public interest' (*JMK*, IX, p. 288).

Hence Keynes did not believe in Adam Smith's parable of the invisible hand, and even less in the mathematical formalization of it given by Walras. He rejected this vision not only because it was based on an intellectual mistake, but also because it constituted a dangerous illusion when it informed one's political vision. Indeed, the inaction it implied regarding the economic problems of the times entailed the risk of a collapse of the system, which could give rise to Bolshevism or Fascism. Although sympathetic towards certain ideals expressed by the Russian Revolution, and particularly its attempt to displace the goal of enrichment as life's primary aim, Keynes was nonetheless very critical of totalitarianism, and especially opposed to the sometimes violent methods of radical transformation advocated by some of its supporters.[14] He thus felt a most profound repugnance for the systems established in Mussolini's Italy or Hitler's Germany. Besides, the rise of

Nazism could be linked to the worsening of economic difficulties, which itself was one of the consequences of the Treaty condemned by Keynes in *The Economic Consequences of the Peace*.

For Keynes, 'the political problem of mankind is to combine three things: economic efficiency, social justice, and individual liberty' (*JMK*, IX, p. 311). Only thorough reforms would allow the accomplishment of these objectives. The pursuit of conservative policies, based on the illusion of laissez-faire, constituted the seedbed of revolution. Keynes's bitter struggle against the return of the gold standard to prewar parity in Great Britain well illustrated this preoccupation.[15] After this decision was announed by Churchill in April 1925, Keynes wrote *The Economic Consequences of Mr Churchill*,[16] a virulent pamphlet against classical liberalism.[17] The coal miners' strike and the general strike of May 1926 were some of these consequences.

It was largely in the 1920s that Keynes developed the collection of propositions later called Keynesian policies in a form which, furthermore, was more radical than the form that would prevail after the war (insisting, for example, on the importance of public investment). A presentation of these policies can be found in a document published by the English Liberal Party in 1928, entitled *Britain's Industrial Future*, to which Keynes was one of the principal contributors. These ideas were elaborated during the electoral campaign of 1929 in *We Can Conquer Unemployment* and in a pamphlet that Keynes wrote with Hubert Henderson, *Can Lloyd George Do It?* (*JMK*, IX, 86–125). Recommending a substantial programme of public spending to fight unemployment, Keynes and Henderson led a vigorous attack against the policy of inaction of the Conservatives in power. The Liberal Party sustained a painful setback in this election that swept the Labour Party to power. In November 1929, the new government named Keynes as a member of the Committee on Finance and Industry (the Macmillan Committee) that was set up by the Chancellor of the Exchequer to study the economic situation. There, Keynes continued his crusade in favour of active state intervention in the economy, as he did as a member of an Economic Advisory Council set up to advise the government in 1930.

Assault on the citadel

The problem Keynes had to confront was that his economic analysis, based in part on an orthodox tradition which he had helped develop in his early writings, lagged behind his own political vision. Between the propositions of reform suggested in *Can Lloyd George Do It?* and the analysis developed in *A Treatise on Money*, published in 1930 (*JMK*, V and VI) there was a distance that led Keynes to begin, as soon as the book was published, a thorough reappraisal of his economic conceptions. This would result, six years later, in *The General Theory,* whose objective he described in a letter to his friend George Bernard Shaw, who was more sympathetic than Keynes towards both the Labour Party and Marxism:

> To understand *my* state of mind, however, you have to know that I believe myself to be writing a book on economic theory which will largely revolutionise – not, I suppose, at once but in the course of the next ten years – the way the world thinks about economic problems. When my new theory has been duly assimilated and mixed with politics and feelings and passions, I can't predict what the final upshot will be in its effect on action and affairs. But there will be a great change, and, in particular, the Ricardian foundations of Marxism will be knocked away.
>
> I can't expect you, or anyone else, to believe this at the present stage. But for myself I don't merely hope what I say, in my own mind I'm quite sure. (Keynes, letter to George Bernard Shaw, 1 January 1935, *JMK*, XIII, pp. 492–3)

The elaboration of this new theory constituted a long and complex process, as one can note by reading the documents in the thirteenth volume of Keynes's *Collected Writings.*[18] Keynes described this process to Roy Harrod, who received the proofs of *The General Theory* and with whom Keynes corresponded regularly during the elaboration of his work:

> I have been much pre-occupied with the causation, so to speak, of my own progress of mind from the classical position to my present views, – with the order in which the problem developed in my mind. What some people treat as an unnecessarily controversial tone is really due to the importance in my own mind of what I used to believe, and of the moments of transitions which were for me personally moments of illumination. You don't feel the weight of the past as I do. One cannot shake off a pack one has never properly worn. ... The portholes of light seen in escaping from a tunnel are interesting neither to those who mean to stay there nor to those who have never been there! (Keynes, letter to R.F. Harrod, 30 August 1936, in *JMK*, XIV, pp. 84–5)

Keynes's words illustrate well the process which, beginning with *Indian Currency and Finance* (1913; *JMK*, I), passing through *A Tract on Monetary Reform* (1923; *JMK*, IV) and *A Treatise on Money* (1930; *JMK*, V and VI), leads to *The General Theory* (1936, *JMK*, VII) and the articles succeeding it. Keynes began his career as an economist under Marshall's guidance as a 'classical' economist. Indeed, in *The General Theory*, he claims to include not only Ricardo and his immediate successors in the classical school, but also 'those, that it so say, who adopted and perfected the theory of the Ricardian economics, including (for example) J.S. Mill, Marshall, Edgeworth and Prof. Pigou'.[19] In doing this, Keynes chose to differ from a tradition which held there to be a rupture between the classical school, ending with Mill, and the neoclassical school, beginning with Jevons, Menger and Walras. But obviously, as far as Keynes was concerned, there was a continuity between these authors. In particular, they unanimously accepted Say's Law, the determination of investment by saving, the dichotomy between monetary and real sectors, and the quantity theory of money.

These are precisely the conceptions from which Keynes gradually freed himself in order to develop the analysis revealed in *The General Theory*. This process of liberation, which appears to have been difficult, was at its most intense between 1932 and 1934. Keynes understood his task as the destruction of a citadel, a task made even more difficult by the fact that the demolition had to be done from within. It was on the occasion of a radio broadcast in 1934, later published, that he expressed himself most clearly on the subject.[20] Here he distinguished among economists two groups, between which the gulf was greater than was typically assumed. The first group, in the majority by and large, included those who 'believe that it [the existing economic system] has an inherent tendency towards self-adjustment, if it is not interfered with and if the action of change and chance is not too rapid' (*JMK*, XIII, p. 487). Keynes described this as the orthodox view, according to which there could not be any general overproduction or involuntary unemployment. The orthodox theory was thus unable to explain the most significant contemporary economic problems: unemployment and business cycles. Keynes added that the essential elements of orthodoxy were accepted by the Marxists in such a way that the laissez-faire school and Marxism had to be considered the twin offspring of Say and Ricardo. They were in the same citadel. On the other side of the gulf were 'those who reject the idea that the existing economic system is, in any significant sense, self-adjusting. They believe that the failure of effective demand to reach the full potentialities of supply, in spite of human psychological demand being immensely far from satisfied for the vast majority of individuals, is due to much more fundamental causes' (*JMK*, XIII, p. 487). These economists had diverse opinions as to these causes. Keynes called them heretics and stressed the fact that there was a long line of heretics in the history of economic thought. But, since the eighteenth century, the dominant orthodoxy was Ricardianism, which had the support of the economic elite and, in turn, upheld established economic interests.

Keynes regarded himself as one of the heretics: 'Now *I* range myself with the heretics' (ibid., p. 489). His problem, however, came from the fact that he had been raised in the citadel whose strength and power he recognized. His evolution, since the beginning of his career as an economist, consisted of gradually extricating himself from the influence of orthodoxy, and successively discovering its shortcomings. This long effort did not result in a perfect achievement in *The General Theory*, because the rupture with the classical and orthodox tradition involved maintaining a number of elements of this theory. Undoubtedly, Keynes was aware of this himself: as soon as his book was published, he began considering a revision of his theory, as he did with *A Treatise on Money*. In the preface to the French translation of *The General Theory* he wrote:

> For a hundred years or longer English Political Economy has been dominated by an orthodoxy. ... In that orthodoxy, in that continuous transition, I was brought up. I learned it, I taught it, I wrote it. To those looking from outside I probably still belong to it. Subsequent historians of doctrine will regard this book as in essentially the same tradition. But I myself in writing it, and in other recent work which has led up to it, I felt myself to be breaking away from this orthodoxy, to be in strong reaction against it, to be escaping from something, to be gaining an emancipation. (*JMK*, VII, p. xxxi)

Breaking away

The points of rupture with orthodoxy, the cracks in the citadel, are the elements of Keynes's vision which cannot be reconciled with the classical view. They are not necessarily explicitly formulated in *The General Theory*, for which, nonetheless, they constitute the keys to interpretation. It is often in later articles, in particular the answer to his critics entitled 'The General Theory of Employment',[21] that Keynes is most clear on the subject.

The first fissure concerns method. Several critics, underlining the difficulties of interpretation involved in Keynes's book, blame its author for not using a mathematical language that perhaps he had not mastered. Others go further and describe him as a less than meticulous theoretician, more inclined towards intuition than rigour. It is obvious that Keynes granted intuition an important role in the process of economic analysis. On several occasions he also wrote that the economist should be endowed with good sense, and base his analysis on a thorough knowledge of real processes as well as institutions. Such was precisely his own case. Among economic theorists, Keynes was one of those who had the most concrete knowledge of the matters with which he dealt. When he describes speculation or the evolution of the price of raw materials or currencies, he deals with a subject he knows at first hand. The fact that from the beginning of his career he met decision makers in all fields, whether it be in politics, trades unions, banking or business, led him to describe what he himself knew. And Keynes considered that economic theory should describe reality. He criticized classical theory not for its lack of rigour, but for the fact that 'the characteristics of the special case assumed by the classical theory happen not to be those of the economic society in which we actually live' (*GT*, p. 3), the classical economists being 'as Candides, who, having left this world for the cultivation of their gardens, teach that all is for the best in the best of all possible worlds provided we will let well alone ... It may well be that the classical theory represents the way in which we should like our Economy to behave' (*GT*, pp. 33–4). It is thus clear that Keynes could not view economic theory as a general theory of optimization, the way Robbins or Samuelson did, nor accept Friedman's thesis, widely accepted by today's economists, concerning the unimportance of the realism of hypotheses.

As to the use of mathematics, it is certainly hazardous to make the hypothesis that the author of *A Treatise on Probability* lacked competence. Moreover, it is in the light of this book that one can understand Keynes's deliberate will not to use mathematical formalization in *The General Theory*, and his negative reaction to Tinbergen's attempt to make a statistical testing of business cycle theories.[22] In his *Treatise on Probability*, Keynes explained the reasons why, according to him, social sciences could not be dealt with using the same quantitative methods used for natural sciences. In this book, he deals with the 'atomic' character of natural law, to which is opposed an approach labelled 'organic' (*JMK*, VIII, pp. 276–8).[23]

Following a tradition dating back to Aristotle and the Scholastics and which was reaffirmed by Sidgwick, Marshall and his own father John Neville Keynes, Keynes considered economics a moral science. On 4 July 1938, he wrote to Harrod that 'economics is essentially a moral science and not a natural science. That is to say, it employs introspection and judgments of value' (*JMK*, XIV, p. 297). In his criticism of Tinbergen, and referring explicitly to his *Treatise on Probability*, Keynes showed his scepticism as to the use of statistics in a field, that of business cycles, in which time and uncertainty play such an important role. Tinbergen's method, Keynes suggests, supposes that all factors are measurable, which renders it inapplicable for 'all those economic problems where political, social and psychological factors, including such things as government policy, the progress of invention and the state of expectation, may be significant. In particular, it is inapplicable to the problem of the business cycle' (*JMK*, XIV, p. 309). Thus, for Keynes, economics is not a mathematical science closed unto itself. It must open up to other disciplines. Nonetheless, the statistical modelling that Keynes rejected would later develop on the basis provided by his theory. More generally, contemporary economics has developed in a direction entirely different from the one envisaged by Keynes.[24]

The role of time in the analysis might be regarded as a second point of rupture. For his disciple and colleague, Joan Robinson, it is the main break with orthodoxy: 'Thirdly, Keynes brought back *time* into economic theory. He woke the Sleeping Princess from the long oblivion to which "equilibrium" and "perfect foresight" had condemned her and led her out into the world here and now' (Robinson 1962 *Economic Philosophy*, p. 73). But this is not a matter of just any time. It is historic and irreversible time which is opposed to the logical time of general equilibrium models and neoclassical theory.

However, it is from the Marshallian tradition that Keynes borrowed the distinction between short run and long run, although he gives it a direction and meaning different from those found in Marshall's analysis. It is in *A Tract on Monetary Reform* of Keynes that can be found the oft-quoted passage according to which '*In the long run* we are all dead.' This is not a jest. This sentence was pronounced on the occasion of an analysis of the quantity theory of money, which Keynes accepted at the time but later rejected in *The General Theory*. By 1923, this acceptance was already much qualified. Indeed, it is only in the long run that this theory is valid, which eventually renders it useless to understand current problems: 'But this *long run* is a misleading guide to current affairs. *In the long run* we are all dead. Economists set themselves too easy, too useless a task if in tempestuous seasons they can only tell us that when the storm is long past the ocean is flat again' (*JMK*, III, p. 65). It was precisely during a turbulent period that Keynes elaborated *The General Theory*. In the short run, in which he places his analysis, there is a past gone by, which constitutes a point of departure and which is indicated, in particular, by a stock and composition of capital, inventories, labour with its diverse qualifications, income distribution, and also political and social institutions, diverse events, moods and values. There is also an unknown future. The treatment of expectations in the context of uncertainty is one of the major elements of Keynes's rupture with orthodoxy. It seemed to be in Keynes's mind since it was his principal theme in his article in the February 1937 issue of the *Quarterly Journal of Economics*. For Keynes, uncertain and more or less probable should not be confused. A number, the expression of a probability, cannot be assigned to a future event. Uncertainty cannot be calculated. In economics there is no scientific basis on which a mathematical probability could be established. Such is one of the principal faults of the theory he combats: 'I accuse the classical economic theory of being itself one of these pretty, polite techniques which tries to deal with the present by abstracting from the fact that we know very little about the future' (*JMK*, XIV, p. 115).

To the perception of time and uncertainty is closely linked a conception of money, by means of which Keynes, once more, dissociates himself from orthodoxy. The orthodox conception distinguishes a real sector in which relative prices are set, and a monetary sector in which the general level of price is determined according to the mechanism of the quantity theory of money. The abandonment of this theory by Keynes runs parallel with that of Say's Law. The words 'money' or 'monetary' are mentioned in the titles of all of his main theoretical books. The path to *The General Theory* consists of integrating the real and the monetary. In a text published in 1933, Keynes explains himself clearly.[25] In it he announces that he is writing a 'monetary theory of production', the title of some of the first drafts of his forthcoming book. He writes that the classical theory is a theory which deals with a real exchange economy. Elsewhere, he speaks of a cooperative economy or else of a barter economy to which he opposes a monetary economy or an economy of entrepreneurs. In Keynes's view, money is intimately linked to uncertainty and in this way to unemployment. Keynes says in *The General Theory* that money is a bridge between past and future:

> This book, on the other hand, has evolved into what is primarily a study of the forces which determine changes in the scale of output and employment as a whole; and, whilst it is found that money enters into the economic scheme in an essential and peculiar manner, technical monetary detail falls into the background. A monetary economy, we shall find, is essentially one in which changing views about the future are capable of influencing the quantity of employment and not merely its direction. (*GT*, p. vii)

Keynes blamed classical theory for not having an explanation of what determines the aggregate level of employment, production and income. Or indeed, if they have, it is one according to which the equilibrium between supply and demand on the labour market sets, simultaneously, the equilibrium real wage and an employment level which can then only be that of full employment. And the latter is defined by the fact that all those who wish to work at such a real wage, in view of their preference function for leisure, find employment. In a similar manner, the real interest rate and level of investment are determined in the capital market, with equilibrium represented by the intersection of the investment demand and supply schedules. The latter corresponds to saving, which itself is linked to the intertemporal preferences of agents. In *A Treatise on Money*, Keynes already broke with the conception which had prevailed in classical thought since Smith, who borrowed it himself from Turgot before him, and according to which the investment is limited by the fund of preliminary savings.

Like all economists, Keynes considers that saving, defined as the difference between income and consumption spending, always equals investment. But this is an accounting identity that one notices *ex post*. Indeed, saving is a residue while investment is the motor of economic activity. More precisely, the decision to invest is the main determinant of production, employment and income. In no way is this decision limited by preliminary saving. Investment ensues from the expectations of entrepreneurs, whose decisions, as with any human decision, 'can only be taken as a result of animal spirits – of a spontaneous urge to action rather than inaction, and not as the outcome of a weighted average of quantitative benefits multiplied by quantitative probabilities. ... In estimating the prospects of investment, we must have regard, therefore, to the nerves and hysteria and even the digestions and reactions to the weather of those upon whose spontaneous activity it largely depends' (*GT*, pp. 161–2).

Not only is investment not limited by a preliminary saving fund, it induces saving equivalent to itself through the variations of production it provokes.

This idea is sometimes presented as the central paradox of *The General Theory*: when all the individuals decide to save more, effective demand, investment, income and therefore final aggregate saving are reduced.[26] Such is one of the principal results of the construction that Keynes substitutes for classical analysis. This approach is based on what he calls 'the three fundamental psychological factors, namely, the psychological propensity to consume, the psychological attitude to liquidity and the psychological expectation of future yield from capital-assets' (*GT*, pp. 246–7). He thus describes the way these concepts appeared to him, allowing him to reconstruct his own theory of employment in place of the citadel he has dismantled:

> You don't mention *effective demand* or, more precisely, the demand schedule for output as a whole, except in so far as it is implicit in the multiplier. To me, regarded historically, the most extraordinary thing is the complete disappearance of the theory of the demand and supply for output as a whole, i.e. the theory of employment, *after* it had been for a quarter of a century the most discussed thing in economics. One of the most important transitions for me, after my *Treatise on Money* had been published, was suddenly realising this. It only came after I had enunciated to myself the psychological law that, when income increases, the gap between income and consumption will increase, – a conclusion of vast importance to my own thinking but not apparently, expressed just like that, to anyone else's. Then, appreciably later, came the notion of interest as being the measure of liquidity preference, which became quite clear in my mind the moment I thought of it. And last of all, after an immense lot of muddling and many drafts, the proper definition of the marginal efficiency of capital linked up one thing with another. (Keynes, letter to R.F. Harrod, 30 August 1936, JMK, XIV, p. 85)[27]

A detailed description of these concepts and of Keynes's theoretical construction would be out of place here. We refer the reader to Keynes's book and the countless interpretations it has been given. But we may say that these presentations are numerous and contradictory, and this ensues in part from Keynes's exposition, for reasons we will now briefly evoke as a conclusion to this chapter.

Continuity

Although attacking it, Keynes nonetheless used elements from the classical theory for his own reconstruction. Here lies the origin of innumerable subsequent debates and exegetical quarrels. Keynes's text, because of its multifaceted and ambiguous nature, can be read through in the light of the orthodoxy that Keynes himself condemned. This is to say that it can be read without taking into consideration, or erasing, the points of rupture examined earlier.

The first and principal ambiguity of Keynes's work has to do with the role assigned to the classical theory. According to Keynes, the main fault with the latter lies in its incapacity to determine the aggregate level of employment and production. It supposes that market forces naturally push the economy towards full employment. For Keynes, classical theory only applies when full employment is achieved. More generally, this theory is valid when it is a matter of studying the allocation of determined resources. This leads him to accept the classical theory of prices and distribution. Having criticized the classical theory of the determination of real wage and employment, he nonetheless accepted the idea according to which, employment being given, the real wage equals the marginal productivity of labour. It is this position that subsequently permitted an attempted synthesis between what would henceforth be called macroeconomics (Keynesian) and microeconomics (neoclassical).

Another ambiguity concerns macroeconomics itself. Keynes wants to avoid what he calls the crystallization of his system. But some of his developments lend themselves to it, in particular the multiplier, as well as the concept of marginal efficiency of capital. It is not the formalization in itself that poses a problem, but the possibility of carrying it out, while forgetting about uncertainty and the irreversibility of time. The complex causal links, brought to light by Keynes, can be transformed into functional relationships between variables which can be dealt with in a manner that Keynes had, in fact, criticized in his debate with Tinbergen. Moreover, the fact that the analysis is anchored in the short run and the absence of a theory of growth constitute for several interpreters another limitation, if not indeed a major weakness, of *The General Theory*. Besides, it is significant to note that Keynes would subsequently be very critical of Harrod's attempt to dynamize his theory and extend it to the long run (*JMK,* XIV, p. 320). Yet Harrod's growth theory would be one of the fundamental underpinnings of post-Keynesian theory.

A final ambiguity relates to the status of money, an ambiguity which is all the more important given the fundamental role played by money in the Keynesian analysis. While the idea that the quantity of money is determined by the monetary authorities suggests a conception of the money supply as exogenous, Keynes implies (elsewhere) that the money supply might be considered as endogenous, determined by the needs of the economy. In the end, it is the banking and financial system that creates money according to the enterprises's needs. Keynes would later develop this vision in some articles, subsequent to the publication of *The General Theory*, especially when he adds what he calls the 'finance motive' to the motives for the demand for liquidity listed in his book. When theorists of a post-Keynesian persuasion would subsequently insist on the latter interpretation, neoclassical theorists would retain the conception of an exogenous money supply, compatible with the quantity theory of money. Later, one would see Friedman, the leader of monetarism, assert that Keynes, resolutely quantity theorist in his *Tract on Monetary Reform*, had remained so for the most part in *The General Theory*!

Notes

1. On the life of Keynes, see Harrod 1951; C.H. Hession, *John Maynard Keynes: A Personal Biography of the Man who Revolutionized Capitalism and the Way we Lived*, New York, Macmillan, 1984; M. Keynes (ed.), *Essays on John Maynard Keynes*, Cambridge, England, Cambridge University Press, 1975; D.E. Moggridge, *Maynard Keynes: An Economist's Biography*, London and New York, Routledge, 1992; E.A.G. Robinson, 'John Maynard Keynes 1883–1946', *Economic Journal*, vol. 57, 1947, 1–68; R. Skidelsky, *John Maynard Keynes*, vol.1, *Hopes Betrayed, 1883–1920*, London, Macmillan, 1983, New York, Viking, 1986; vol.2, *The Economist as Saviour 1920–37*, London, Macmillan, 1992.
2. *The Scope and Method of Political Economy*, London, Macmillan, 1891, pp. 9, 20.
3. More progressist than her husband, socially and politically very active, the mother of John Maynard, Florence Ada, was mayor of Cambridge in 1932–3. Keynes's parents, his sister Margaret and his brother Geoffrey, respectively born in 1885 and 1887, survived him. In 1925, John Maynard married Lydia Lopokova, a ballerina of Russian origin and member of the renowned Diaghilev company.
4. A. Sidgwick and E.M. Sidgwick, *Henry Sidgwick: A Memoir*, London, Macmillan, 1906, pp. 34–5, quoted by D.E. Moggridge, *Maynard Keynes*, op. cit., p. 66.
5. A number of recent works emphasized the primordial importance of Keynes's philosophical views and their relations with his political vision and his economic theory. In particular, see: B.W. Bateman and J.B. Davis (eds), *Keynes and Philosophy: Essays on the Origin of Keynes's Thought*, Aldershot, Hants, Edward Elgar, 1991; A.M. Carabelli, *On Keynes's Method*, London, Macmillan and New York, St Martin's Press, 1988; J.B. Davis, *Keynes's Philosophical Development*, Cambridge, England, Cambridge University Press, 1994; A. Fitzgibbons, *Keynes's Vision: A New Political Economy*, Oxford, Clarendon Press, 1988; B. Gerrard and J. Hillard (eds), *The Philosophy and Economics of J.M. Keynes*, Aldershot, Hants, Edward Elgar, 1992; T. Lawson and H. Pesaran (eds), *Keynes' Economics: Methodological Issues*, London and New York, Routledge, 1985; R.O'Donnell, *Keynes: Philosophy, Economics and Politics. The Philosophical Foundations of Keynes's Thought and their Influence on his Economics and Politics*, London, Macmillan, 1989; id. (ed.), *Keynes as Philosopher-Economist*, London, Macmillan, 1991. From these volumes there emerges a picture of a radical thinker, who once wrote: 'The republic of my imagination lies on the extreme left of celestial space' (*JMK*, IX, p. 309).
6. 'Yet so far as I am concerned, it is too late to change. I remain and always will remain, an immoralist' (*JMK*, X, p. 447). Hayek, among others, sees in Keynes's self-proclaimed immoralism one source of the perversity of his economic vision (see, for example, Hayek 1978, p. 16; 1988, pp. 57–8).
7. Nevertheless, Keynes always professed a Platonic form of elitism which led him to believe that some social categories perhaps lacked the qualities necessary for an appreciation of the most subtle refinements of civilization.
8. Named after a district in London where, among others, Vanessa and Clive Bell, Leonard and Virginia Woolf, Duncan Grant, Roger Fry and Lytton Strachey lived and met. See, among others: Q. Bell, *Bloomsbury*, New York, Basic Books, 1969; D. Crabtree and A.P. Thirwall (eds), *Keynes and the Bloomsbury Group*, London, Macmillan and New York, Holmes and Meier, 1980; D. Gadd, *The Loving Friends: A Portrait of Bloomsbury*, New York, Harcourt Brace Jovanovich, 1975; P.V. Mini, *Keynes, Bloomsbury and The General Theory*, New York, St Martin's Press, 1991; S.P. Rosenbaum (ed.), *The Bloomsbury Group: A Collection of Memoirs, Commentary and Criticism*, University of Toronto Press, 1975.
9. See P. Meisel and W. Rendick (eds), *Bloomsbury-Freud: The Lettters of James and Alix Strachey, 1924–25*, New York, Basic Books, 1985. The following is what Keynes wrote about Freud in the August 29 1925 issue of *The Nation & the Athenaeum*, a weekly publication of which he had been chairman of the board of directors since 1923: 'Professor Freud seems to me to be endowed, to the degree of genius, with the scientific imagination which can body forth an abundance of innovating ideas, shattering possibilities, working hypotheses, which have sufficient foundation in intuition and common

experience to deserve the most patient and unprejudiced examination, and which contain, in all probability, both theories which will have to be discarded or altered out of recognition and also theories of great and permanent significance' ('Freudian Psycho Analysis', *The Nation & the Athenaeum*, 29 August 1925, p. 643).

10. This is extracted from an essay entitled 'Economic Possibilities for our Grandchildren', first read in 1928 and published in *The Nation & the Athenaeum* on 11 and 18 October 1930, subsequently included in *Essays in Persuasion*, formed of excerpts from books and articles published between 1919 and 1931 and collected by Keynes in 1931 (London, Macmillan; augmented version, *JMK*, IX). These texts, which are very accessible, constitute an excellent introduction to Keynes's economic and political thought, and an illustration of his art of convincing, such as it is used in very diverse communicative forms, from the abstract treatise to speaking on radio. Here is how Keynes himself presented them: 'Here are collected the croakings of twelve years – the croakings of a Cassandra who could never influence the course of events in time. ... But it was in a spirit of persuasion that most of these essays were written, in an attempt to influence opinion' (*JMK*, IX, p. xvii).
11. London, Macmillan, 1919; *JMK*, II.
12. From his years of studies at Cambridge, where he was member of the Liberal Club, to the end of his life, when he sat on the Liberal benches of the House of Lords, Keynes was always closely linked to the English Liberal Party, for which, for example, he gave speeches during electoral campaigns. Nevertheless, he was also close to the Labour Party and on several occasions tried to establish bridges between the two parties (see the first editorial of *The Nation & the Athenaeum*, 5 May 1923). Among other things, he reproached the Labour Party for both tolerating within its ranks partisans of the violent revolution and not taking monetary problems seriously. To some extent, he considered himself to be to the left of the Labour Party, but what prevented him from joining the 'great party of the proletariat' (*JMK*, IX, p. 311) was the fact that it was 'a class party, and the class is not my class. ...but the *class* war will find me on the side of the educated *bourgeoisie*' (*JMK*, IX, p. 297). Having said that, all of Keynes's political action aimed at creating the conditions which would ensure that this war did not break out. On Keynes's political adherence, see 'Am I a Liberal?' (1925, in *JMK*, IX, 295–306) and 'Liberalism and Labour'(1926, ibid., 307–11).
13. London, Hogarth; *JMK*, IX, 272–94.
14. See, in particular 'A Short View of Russia' (London, Hogarth, 1925; in *JMK*, IX, 253–71), where he defined Leninism as being 'a combination of two things which Europeans have kept for some centuries in different compartments of the soul – religion and business. We are shocked because the religion is new, and contemptuous because the business, being subordinated to the religion instead of the other way round, is highly inefficient' (*JMK*, IX, p. 256). At the end of a conference delivered in the USSR in 1925, Keynes had written: 'We in the West will watch what you do with sympathy and lively attention, in the hope that we may find something which we can learn from you' (*JMK*, XIX, p. 441–2).
15. On this subject, see D. Moggridge, *British Monetary Policy 1924–1931*, Cambridge, England, Cambridge University Press, 1972. See also G. Dostaler, 'Le Retour à l'étalon-or en Grande-Bretagne: une fâcheuse illusion', in F. Poulon (ed.), *Les Écrits de Keynes,* Paris, Dunod, 1985, 176–94.
16. London, Hogarth, 1925; first published as 'Unemployment and Monetary Policy', *Evening Standard*, 22, 23 and 24 July 1925; condensed version prepared by Keynes for his *Essays in Persuasion* (*JMK*, IX, 207–30). See also *JMK*, XIX, 357–453.
17. In 1983, Nicholas Kaldor would publish a book with the same title, replacing the name of Churchill with that of Mrs Thatcher.
18. On the evolution of Keynes's economic thought, see in particular P. Clarke, *The Keynesian Revolution in the Making, 1924–1936*, Oxford, Clarendon Press and New York, Oxford University Press, 1988; Robert W. Dimand, *The Origins of the Keynesian Revolution: The Development of Keynes' Theory of Employment and Output*, Aldershot, Hants, Edward Elgar, 1988; D. Moggridge, *John Maynard Keynes*, London, Macmillan, 1976; R.F. Kahn, *The Making of Keynes' General Theory*, Cambridge, England, Cambridge

University Press, 1984; Patinkin 1976, 1978, 1982; T.K. Rymes (ed.), *Keynes' Lectures 1932–35: Notes of a Representative Student*, London, Macmillan and Ann Arbor, University of Michigan Press, 1989.

19. J.M. Keynes, *The General Theory of Employment, Interest and Money* [hereafter *GT*], London, Macmillan, 1936, p. 3.
20. 'Poverty in Plenty: Is the Economic System Self-Adjusting?', *The Listener*, 21 November 1934; in *JMK*, XIII, 485–92.
21. *Quarterly Journal of Economics*, vol. 51, 1937, 209–23; *JMK*, XIV, 109–23.
22. 'Professor Tinbergen's Method', *Economic Journal*, vol. 49, 1939, 558–70, taken up with other documents regarding this controversy in *JMK*, XIV, 285–320.
23. We can find the analysis of this atomic–organic dichotomy in some of Keynes's papers read to the Apostles, such as 'Ethics in Relation to Conduct' (1904), 'Miscellanea Ethica' (1905), 'On the Principle of Organic Unity' (1910). They shed light on the Keynesian vision of a macroeconomics, irreducible to the sum of its individual elements. On this, see R.X. Chase, 'Keynes's Dichotomy: A Methodological Escape for a Theoretic Revolution', *Methodus*, vol. 3, no. 2, 1991, 79–85.
24. On the debate between Keynes and Tinbergen, see T. Lawson, 'Keynes, Prediction and Econometrics', and H. Pesaran and R. Smith, 'Keynes on Econometrics', both in T. Lawson and H. Pesaran (eds), *Keynes' Economics: Methodological Issues*, London and New York, Routledge, 1985, 116–33 and 134–50, as well as Stone 1978 *PBA* and Zellner 1984.
25. 'A Monetary Theory of Production', in G. Clausing (ed.), *Der Stand und die nächste Zukunft der Konjunkturforschung. Festschrift für Arthur Spiethoff*, Munich, Duncker & Humblot; *JMK*, XIII, 408–11.
26. This well illustrates the methodological conception specific to Keynesian macroeconomics, according to which the global processes are not the additive resultant of all the elementary processes.
27. Also see the letter to Abba Lerner, 16 June 1936, in *JMK*, XXIX, 214–16.

2 The Keynesian revolution

Keynes and the Keynesian revolution

When *The General Theory of Employment, Interest and Money* was published on 4 February 1936, its author, John Maynard Keynes, then 52 years old, was Britain's most famous and influential economist. This book would secure his rise to the first rank among twentieth-century economists, and ultimately his eminence among the other great names in the history of political economy such as Smith, Ricardo and Marx. Ten years after the publication of his book, on Easter Sunday 21 April 1946, Keynes died, laid low by the last of a series of heart attacks which had first struck him in 1937. He lived to see the partial achievement of the prophecy made to his friend George Bernard Shaw on 1 January 1935. Indeed, in 1946, *The General Theory* had already made an impression as a book 'which will largely revolutionise – not, I suppose, at once but in the course of the next ten years – the way the world thinks about economic problems' (*JMK*, XIII, p. 492). Thus Keynes used the expression 'revolutionise' to characterize the impact of his work. The 'Keynesian revolution' formula would appear in the title of a book by Lawrence Klein (1947) which played an important role in the diffusion of Keynesian ideas in the United States.

However, what one calls the Keynesian revolution is a phenomenon whose extent goes beyond the publication and impact of *The General Theory*. In the course of his life, Keynes witnessed important transformations at political, social, economic and cultural levels. In a significant book published in 1944, Karl Polanyi labelled as 'the great transformation' the collapse between 1900 and 1940 of an international system which had triumphed in the nineteenth century, based on four institutions: the balance of powers, the international gold standard, the self-regulating market and the liberal state. This system was based on a utopia, on the idea of a self-regulating market, including gold, land and labour: 'the origins of the cataclysm lay in the utopian endeavor of economic liberalism to set up a self-regulating market system'.[1] The rise of socialism, Nazism and Fascism, and also the search for a 'third way' in the capitalist countries, are consequences of this cataclysm: 'Its landmarks were the abandonment of the gold standard by Great Britain; the Five-Year Plans in Russia; the launching of the New Deal; the National Socialist Revolution in Germany; the collapse of the League in favour of autarchist empires.'[2] The path was narrow for a reform of the system that would emerge neither as authoritarianism nor as barbarity. The search for this path was the direction given by Keynes to his struggle, a fight he led with a fierceness that was no doubt partly responsible for his premature death.[3]

What we call Keynesian revolution was one moment in this great transformation. The expression, however, is ambiguous. The word 'revolution', in the first place, needs to be handled with care. In the world of ideas (as much as in the social, political and economic domains) what appears to be an abrupt rupture is often the fruit of a long evolution. Furthermore, history often repeats itself. Moreover, revolutions, in the primary meaning of the term, leave us at our point of departure. So the Keynesian theory takes up again certain currents that classical theory was believed to have eliminated. It even planted its roots in a remote past, to which the author himself refers in *The General Theory*.[4] Thus he speaks highly of the true intuition of the Scholastics in their condemnation of usurious lending, specifying that the first steps towards a distinction between interest rate and the marginal efficiency of capital were already to be found there. He rehabilitates the mercantilists who had understood the problem of employment much better than the classical economists. He indicates that Malthus, to whom he had already devoted a significant study,[5] had well perceived the faults of the Ricardian theory. For the French readers of his book he underlines the fact that, regarding the theory of interest, he comes back to the doctrine of Montesquieu, 'who was the real French equivalent of Adam Smith, the greatest of your economists, head and shoulders above the physiocrats in penetration, clear headedness and good sense (which are the qualities an economist should have)' (*JMK*, VII, p. xxxiv).

Nor is the word 'Keynesian' without some ambiguity. Indeed, it could lead us to believe that Keynes was the sole author of this revolution, a revolution for which his work served as a catalyst. This is not the case. Keynes was, of course, the principal architect of the Keynesian revolution but, as we will see, others also developed, at the same time or even before, some significant elements of what is now known as 'Keynesian' theory. In 1948, Joan Robinson presented what she termed the 'General Theory' as the collective product of a theoretical transformation of which Keynes's book only represented one part among others:

> But by general theory, I do not mean the celebrated book of that author [Keynes]. Of course, that work is very important, but it is neither complete nor definitive. It constituted, when it was published, a sort of provisional account of a movement of ideas in the course of its development. … What I mean by general theory is rather a method of analysis. It is a living body of ideas that is developing and producing quite different results when it is applied in different circumstances by such or such person. (Robinson 1948, p. 185; translated from French)

But it is fair that Keynes's name be ranked first. If the revolution referred to is called Keynesian, it is indeed due to John Maynard Keynes's personal qualities, as well as a complex combination of circumstances. Keynes was an exceptional person and, besides, he wrote at the right time, in the right place and in the right language. Polish, Swedish, Norwegian and Dutch were not as effective vehicles as English, the long dominant language in the field of political economy. Finally, Keynes always knew how to publish his works at key moments and to ensure that, when they did appear, they were eagerly awaited. It is difficult to know the respective parts played by chance and calculation in all of this, but it is undeniable that each publication by Keynes, at least since *The Economic Consequences of the Peace*, constituted a public event. In any case, what was a matter of calculation was the effective post-publication campaigns designed to publicize and discuss the works. For Keynes was a man of power. An influential adviser and a dreaded critic of governmental policies, he played important roles at different levels of the state apparatus until the end of his life. As we have seen, he was an influential and active member of the Liberal Party, while being carefully listened to by the Labour Party. Within the economic profession, Keynes, at the age of 28, took control of *The Economic Journal* in 1911, thus occupying a central position. He also knew how to surround himself with loyal and dedicated disciples.

A powerful figure, Keynes was also an intellectual endowed with great qualities. His intelligence, culture and working capacities were exceptional. He was a prolific writer whose style was much livelier than that of most of his colleagues. And far from confining himself to economics, he became involved in numerous areas. His reputation went far beyond the restricted circle of the economic profession or of the political world. Furthermore, it included the area of the arts, in which Keynes played an important role. Even the ambiguities of his writings and teachings contributed to Keynes's success. Many could read in them what they wanted. It is beyond doubt that Keynes revelled in the role of provocateur and card shuffler, which allowed him to remain in the foreground. The force of his convictions did not prevent him, on several occasions, from showing an opportunism that was at times surprising. Keynes was not one to hesitate before difficult turns in the road nor to flinch before challenges to his sincerely held beliefs. This was the struggle in which Keynes was involved throughout his career, a fight in which, however, he preferred the pen to the sword. In this combat, he had tough opponents who occasionally admired him and would in some cases even rally round him, and had committed, at times almost cumbersome, disciples. Let us look first at his principal opponents.

From Vienna to London[6]

For Keynes and his friends, all that counted, on a scientific level, was taking place within a triangle whose vertices were Cambridge, Oxford and London

– Cambridge of course being the most important one. There was indeed a so-called 'continental' economic literature to which one sometimes alluded, but it was relatively unknown, especially in Cambridge. In London, on the other hand, scholars at the London School of Economics,[7] which published *Economica*, rival of the *Economic Journal*, the journal of the Royal Economic Society and controlled with an iron fist by Keynes,[8] were more open to these foreign influences. It was through London that both the Walras–Pareto school and the Austrian school entered the English-speaking world. The first was finally to lead to the neoclassical synthesis of which we will speak later. The second, due to Hayek in particular, would engender one of the sharpest poles of resistance to interventionism and Keynesianism.

In relation to the two other branches of the marginalist revolution, the Austrian School, initiated by Carl Menger, always constituted an autonomous stream of thought. Today, it has even undergone a vigorous rebirth under the name of the neo-Austrian School.[9] While the traditions stemming from Walras and Jevons led to the emergence of neoclassical theory, the Austrian School distinguished itself by rather specific methodological positions, which it made explicit.[10] As opposed to a general equilibrium view of the world, the Austrian approach prefers a causal vision which leads, for example to the reduction of capital to time and labour. The ultimate cause in social and economic fields lies, for this approach, in the economic subject. Indeed, the perceptions of the subject constitute the prime reality on which one needs to base economic theory. For the Austrian School, it is through introspection that one elaborates the hypotheses of economic theory. Methodological individualism, subjectivism and even a radical apriorism are among the expressions used to characterize this approach. By insisting on the importance of time and uncertainty in human affairs, the Austrian School critically distrusts the hypnotizing effect on economists of the natural sciences and mathematics.

Analogies exist between the Austrian vision and that of Keynes. Hayek developed a critique of the Walras–Pareto vision of general equilibrium, which is not unlike Keynes's critique of classical theory. As early as his first works, in the 1920s, he blamed economists for neglecting time in their analysis and questioned the possibility of constructing an economic theory, formal and mathematical in character, along the lines of the natural sciences. His 'Economics and Knowledge' (Hayek 1937) includes a critique of equilibrium analysis which resembles the article published by Keynes that same year in the *Quarterly Journal of Economics.* It is possible to imagine that, on the occasion of his controversy with Hayek, Keynes might have been partly influenced by the latter. Despite these parental links, the Austrian school is characterized by a radical liberalism which was to lead to one of the most vigorous criticisms of Keynesianism. This liberalism does not come from the founders. On the political plane, Menger, Böhm-Bawerk and Wieser espoused rather progressive ideas, as did Jevons and Walras. It was with Ludwig von Mises and Friedrich Hayek that an intransigent liberalism became one of the principal characteristics of the Austrian School. While Pareto or Barone claimed that the Walrasian general equilibrium could constitute the rational foundation of socialist planning, Mises claimed to demonstrate that such planning is impossible. This impossibility is based on methodological and epistemological arguments. Planning is impossible because no human brain could hold all the knowledge necessary to secure the optimal organization of production. For Hayek, Keynesian interventionism shares the same illusion. It has its roots in an intellectual tradition that includes, among others, Marx, Comte, Rousseau, Voltaire and Descartes, arguably going as far back as Plato, and is based on the belief that it is possible to organize society rationally. For Hayek, on the contrary, society constitutes a spontaneous order, the fruit of a long evolution.

Parallel to Keynes, in the 1920s, Hayek developed a theory of the business cycle which gives a theoretical foundation to his rejection of interventionism.[11] He wrote under the influences of Wicksell, founder of the Swedish tradition,[12] and of Böhm-Bawerk.[13] From the first, he borrowed the idea of the disequilibrium between the natural rate of interest, linked to the productivity of capital and to agents' temporal preferences, and the monetary rate determined by the banking system, disequilibrium beginning a cumulative process of rising or falling prices. From the second, he took the conception of investment as the lengthening of the production process, whose basic factors are labour and natural resources. In both cases, the conception of time is fundamental. Money also plays a significant role, for Hayek considered, as did Keynes, that a monetary economy is different from a real-exchange economy. Far from acting solely on the general level of prices, as the traditional quantity theory of money explains it, the variation of the quantity of money has an impact on the structure of relative prices. Thus an increase in the money supply, for example through increased credit facilities, lowers the monetary rate of interest below the natural rate. This provokes a lengthening of the production process and a disequilibrium between investment and the saving intended by agents. A subsequent increase of the consumer goods prices releases the supplementary saving, called 'forced saving', necessary to finance the overinvestment. From then on, there begins a shortening of the production process, a cause of increased unemployment in the sector producing consumer goods and then gradually throughout the whole economy. Thus, for Hayek, the 1929 crisis was provoked by overinvestment stemming from an easy monetary policy, based on the illusion of stimulating the economy through inflation. From this point, he criticized the underconsumptionist illusions propagated by such authors as Foster and Catchings and, in a more sophisticated manner, by Keynes.[14]

Such are the theses developed by Hayek, on the occasion of a series of lectures presented in February 1931 at the London School of Economics, at the invitation of Lionel Robbins, just a few months after the publication of Keynes's *Treatise on Money*. Hayek's lectures, published in September 1931 and entitled *Prices and Production*, aroused enthusiasm and earned their author a professorial position at the London School of Economics, where he soon established himself as the leader of the opposition to Keynes and his disciples. Then a young lecturer at the London School of Economics, Hicks described years later, in 'The Hayek Story', how the conflict between the ideas of Keynes and Hayek put several young economists of the time in a difficult position.

> When the definitive history of economic analysis during the nineteen-thirties comes to be written, a leading character in the drama (it was quite a drama) will be Professor Hayek. ... it is hardly remembered that there was a time when the new theories of Hayek were the principal rival of the new theories of Keynes. Which was right, Keynes or Hayek? There are many still living teachers of economics, and practical economists, who have passed through a time when they had to make up their minds on that question; and there are many of them (including the present writer) who took quite a time to make up their mind. (Hicks 1967, p. 203)

This difficulty was further accentuated by political differences among some of them. While for Keynes and his disciples the collapse of investment was the ultimate cause of the Great Depression, for Hayek, Robbins and their colleagues, on the contrary, it was overinvestment provoked by an easy monetary policy. While some called for vigorous public intervention to stimulate consumption and investment, others spoke for the 'Treasury View', according to which public intervention simply diverted funds destined for private use. For one, it was necessary to raise wages in order to stimulate consumption. For another, only a drop in wages could re-establish full employment.[15]

Besides Hicks, the London School of Economics assembled within its walls other young economists who were to have a significant role in the development of economic thought after Keynes, including Kaldor, Lerner and Shackle. Led to distance themselves from Robbins and Hayek for political reasons, these authors would nonetheless be significantly affected by the London School. It is here that we can find the roots of a certain *rapprochement*, odd at first glance, between the Austrian world and that of Keynes's radical disciples, who would later be named post-Keynesians. As for Hicks, besides the Austrian influence and that of Walras and Pareto, he met along the way the Swedes, independent explorers, whom we will discuss in the next section. Then lecturer at the London School, Kaldor made contact with

Keynes in 1931 and offered to bridge the gap between Cambridge and the London School of Economics, like Lerner, who would later become one of the principal initiators of the Keynesian revolution in the United States. Kaldor, Hayek's translator, would become, after moving to Cambridge, one of his most severe critics.[16] Himself a new disciple of Keynes, Shackle, for his part, would nonetheless remain close to Hayek, his first thesis adviser. In one of his first published texts (Shackle 1933), he tried to achieve a synthesis between the approaches of Keynes and Hayek. Drawing attention to the similarities found in Keynes's article published in 1937 in the *Quarterly Journal of Economics* and that of Hayek published the same year in *Economica*, he has since devoted his career to deepening what he considers to be their common contributions, namely the taking into account of uncertainty and expectations and placing the analysis in time. Shackle is also one of the first to have drawn attention to the Swedish contribution, and particularly that of Myrdal. He considers Myrdal and Kalecki independent explorers who arrived, before Keynes, at the same conclusions as the latter (Shackle 1967).

Precursors and independent explorers

In his *Monetary Equilibrium*, the first version of which (in Swedish) was released in 1932,[17] Gunnar Myrdal wrote: 'J.M. Keynes' new, brilliant, though not always clear, work, *A Treatise on Money*, is completely permeated by Wicksell's influence. Nevertheless Keynes' work, too, suffers somewhat from the attractive Anglo-Saxon kind of unnecessary originality, which has its roots in certain systematic gaps in the knowledge of the German language on the part of the majority of English economists' (Myrdal [1931] 1939, pp. 8–9). Beginning with neoclassical theory, of which he was one of the principal theoreticians,[18] Wicksell tried to integrate the real and the monetary, which he did with his well-known distinction between the natural and the monetary rate of interest. The disequilibrium between these two rates generates a cumulative process of either a rise or a fall in prices. Not only do we find in Wicksell the idea of the necessity of aggregate monetary demand for stimulating production, but also that of a disequilibrium between saving and investment, which result from independent decisions. In fact, Keynes acknowledged the relationship between some of his theses and those of Wicksell, even claiming in *A Treatise on Money* to be close to a German and a neo-Austrian/neo-Wicksellian school to which Hayek belonged. Besides, Myrdal himself wrote, in his *Monetary Equilibrium* (presented as an 'immanent criticism' of Wicksell's theory): 'I hope, however, to complement the present positive presentation later in another connection by a criticism, particularly of Keynes and Hayek, whose works are naturally nearest to mine' (Myrdal [1931] 1939, p. 32). In *The General Theory*, however, Keynes only made a brief allusion to the fact that he had developed, at the time of the *Treatise*, the concept of Wicksell's natural rate, but that this concept now appeared to be erroneous.

As for the Swedish, they would see little new in *The General Theory* and more generally, in the so-called revolution that Keynes claimed to have led against the classical theory, compared to the theses that first Wicksell and then his young disciples (ranking first among whom were Erik Lindahl, Gunnar Myrdal and Bertil Ohlin) had developed in the 1920s and 1930s. Lindahl,[19] the eldest of this group, not only elaborated ideas very close to Keynes's theory of effective demand, describing, at the end of the 1920s, the possibility of an underemployment equilibrium or clarifying the paradox of saving, but he also started to develop, at the same time, a dynamic analysis which constitutes one of the characteristics of the Swedish approach, an analysis which moreover exerted an important influence on the Hicks of *Value and Capital* (Hicks 1939). The approach in terms of *ex ante* and *ex post* put forward by Myrdal in the German version of his *Monetary Equilibrium*, published in 1933, constitutes, from this point of view, one of the outstanding contributions of the Swedish School. Furthermore, Lindahl and, especially, Myrdal in his doctoral dissertation published in 1927, explicitly introduced the role of expectations in economic analysis, and in particular in the analysis of price formation. Some economists see here one of the intellectual origins of the present approach in terms of rational expectations, while others see in the most recent developments of general equilibrium a return to the concept of temporary equilibrium first put forward by Lindahl.

In the 1920s and 1930s, Ohlin developed analyses designed to underpin state intervention against unemployment. A resident in Cambridge in the 1920s, he met Keynes with whom he remained in contact thereafter. In 1929, in a controversy with him over the matter of transfers, he developed positions more 'Keynesian' than those defended by Keynes at that time. It was Ohlin who, in two articles published in the 1937 issue of *The Economic Journal*, coined the term 'Stockholm School' and revealed its theses for the first time to an English-speaking public. In the same year there appeared *Studies in the Theory of Economic Expansion* by Erik Lundberg, a member of the second generation of the Stockholm School, along with Dag Hammarksjöld[20] and Bent Hansen.[21] It was only two years later that the major contributions of Myrdal and Lindahl would finally come out in English. Among the authors of a report of Sweden's 1927 Committee on Unemployment, published in 1934, along with Myrdal, Ohlin and Hammarkjöld one also finds Gösta Bagge, a more conservative economist. It is clear that the members of the Stockholm School played an important role in the setting up, by the Social-Democrat government elected in 1932, of stimulative policies which one can *ex post* call Keynesian.[22] Having said that, the desire to ascertain the extent to which the Stockholm School anticipated the Keynesian revolution, as well as the degree of convergence between their theses and those developed in *The General Theory*, has since 1937 been the object of a debate which does not seem to be near a conclusion.[23]

There are similar features in the links between Keynes and Kalecki. It is not a matter this time of a school but of an individual, and an isolated one. While Myrdal and his Swedish colleagues began with Wicksell, Michal Kalecki found his inspiration in Marx and Rosa Luxemburg, to elaborate the first of a series of models in which he integrated a theory of effective demand comparable to Keynes's, an analysis of distribution of classical type, a theory of prices integrating monopolies and, finally, a theory of growth. As Klein, Joan Robinson and several others underlined, Kalecki's model – first published in Polish in 1933 – appeared to be more general than Keynes's. In October 1933, it was also the subject of a presentation at the meeting of the Econometric Society at Leyden, and the text presented on this occasion was published in the society's journal, *Econometrica*, in 1935. The same year, Kalecki also made his ideas known to a French public in the *Revue d'économie politique*. The very succinct style of these texts, characteristic of Kalecki, and their mathematical character meant that they went almost unnoticed. Some economists who were to play a major role in the evolution of twentieth-century economic thought nonetheless saw their importance from the beginning. In particular, there were Ragnar Frisch and Jan Tinbergen. In a long survey of business cycle theory published in the same *Econometrica* issue as Kalecki's article, Tinbergen contrasted Keynes's and Hayek's 'non and semi-mathematical' theories to the mathematical ones of Kalecki and Frisch (Tinbergen 1933). The same year, Frisch created the expression 'macrodynamics'. Frisch and Tinbergen, who would be the first recipients of the Nobel Memorial Prize in Economics in 1969, must be included, in the same way as Kalecki or the Swedes, among the independent explorers of what would later be called the Keynesian revolution. The creators of econometrics, they are also among the major initiators of the movement to mathematize economics, which began in the 1930s, independently of the Keynesian revolution, and of which we will speak again in Chapter 4.

These independent explorers thus made contact with the others. In 1936, having a grant from the Rockefeller Foundation at his disposal, Kalecki went to Stockholm where he met the Swedish economists. This is where he read *The General Theory*. He then went to Cambridge, where Keynes's disciples were amazed at Kalecki's speed and facility in assimilating and then explaining the theory of their mentor! From then on, Kalecki was to exert a determinant influence on Keynes's disciples, especially on Joan Robinson and Kaldor, which made him one of the initiators of the post-Keynesian school. It was Kalecki who introduced Joan Robinson to Marx's work. The author of the first book favourable to Marx in the English-speaking academic world

(Robinson 1942), Joan Robinson then discovered that Kahn, in order to explain the operation of the multiplier, had simply rediscovered Marx's reproduction schemas. But this leads us to Keynes's Cambridge disciples.

Disciples and fellow-travellers

The attack against the orthodox citadel was a collective work. Keynes was helped by students and faithful disciples who, younger than himself, did not have to endure so intensely the weight of the past. The critique of *A Treatise on Money*, then the development of the central theses of *The General Theory*, was not the work of Keynes alone, as is clearly shown in the documents included in volumes XIII and XXIX of Keynes's *Collected Writings*. Kahn, Keynes's student, friend and finally executor, was certainly his closest collaborator. Schumpeter considered he should be recognized as virtual co-author of *The General Theory*, as he corrected and discussed all of Keynes's drafts.[24] Kahn himself developed the concept of the multiplier.[25] He was also the messenger who linked Keynes with the 'Circus' which met in Cambridge in 1931. The group in question was formed by Keynes's young disciples. Their initial objective, the discussion of *A Treatise on Money,* soon turned into a critique, then into the elaboration of theoretical propositions that Kahn passed on to Keynes, and that the latter integrated, after transforming them in his lectures and preparatory works, into what was to become *The General Theory*. The core of the Circus comprised, besides Kahn, several economists who would subsequently play an important role in the development of economic thought after Keynes: James Meade, Austin and Joan Robinson, and Piero Sraffa.[26]

These authors were also associated with another significant transformation of economic theory in the inter-war period, independent of the Keynesian revolution and resulting in the emergence of the theory of monopolistic competition. Arriving at Cambridge from Italy in the mid-1920s, Sraffa can be considered one of this movement's first initiators through his severe critique of the Marshallian theory of supply and demand (1925, 1926). However, it was not he, but Chamberlin, Harrod, Kahn and Joan Robinson, who would attempt in the late 1920s and early 1930s to reconcile orthodox theory with the existence of monopolies. Later very critical of this first work (Robinson 1933 *The Economics*), Joan Robinson and more generally the post-Keynesian theorists would adopt the positions already articulated by Kalecki in the mid-1930s, according to which one must consider monetary prices as being determined by the addition of a margin (depending on the degree of monopoly of the firm or industry in question) to average variable cost, whose most important component is the money wage, itself resulting from the balance of power between employers and employees. Sraffa, for his part, would advocate a return to the classical vision of value, which he would formulate again in a later book (Sraffa 1960), giving birth to a school of thought subsequently called neo-Ricardian. It was with the encouragement of Keynes himself that Sraffa, in the 1930s, began the lengthy task of publishing the complete works and correspondence of Ricardo (Sraffa 1951–73).

Keynes had disciples outside Cambridge too. Besides his supporters at the London School of Economics, some of his intellectual allies were to be found at Oxford. A member of the Circus following a stay at Cambridge, Meade was attached to Oxford. Another ally was Roy Harrod, who had been sent to Cambridge in the early 1920s to be initiated into political economy by Keynes in order to teach this subject at Oxford. Harrod became a friend and collaborator to whom Keynes sent the proofs of *The General Theory*. Harrod attempted, in vain, to tone down the harshness of Keynes's attacks upon the classical economists and would play an essential part in making the Keynesian analysis dynamic and in the birth of modern growth theory (Harrod 1939, 1948). He was also asked by Keynes's family to write his first biography (Harrod 1951). Those just named belong to the group which, to borrow Keynes's imagery, never really had to 'feel the weight of the past' or dwell in the dark tunnel of classicism. This explains the more radical version of Keynesianism which they would develop. Others, including Hawtrey[27] and Robertson,[28] had to undergo an exorcism, like Keynes. Not only did Keynes not consider them as classical but indeed he was heard to say that it was they who showed him the way to salvation in the mid-1920s. However, the relationships between them were to be more and more difficult the closer Keynes came to finalizing his ideas. Neither Hawtrey nor Robertson were able to follow him to the end. Acrimonious controversy was to separate Keynes and Robertson after the publication of *The General Theory*.[29]

From theory to politics

For Keynes, as for the authors to whom we have just referred, the links between economic theory and policy are very complex. It is too simple to consider an economic policy as resulting automatically from a particular theory. One might even reverse the traditional causal link and assert, for example, that *The General Theory* was written to give a theoretical foundation to the policy proposals which Keynes and several other economists had formulated in the 1920s. The political vision often precedes the theoretical one. On the other hand, there is no strict linkage between political position and choice of theory. Thus several of the economists whom Keynes considered classical supported, as early as the 1920s, positions in economic policy very close to Keynes's. Such is the case with Pigou, in particular, himself the main target of *The General Theory*. It is also the case, as we have seen, with several economists of the London School of Economics, considered nonetheless the bastion of conservatism.

Finally, Keynes himself opened up several perspectives. His diagnosis is clear. The two major faults of capitalism, 'its failure to provide for full employment and its arbitrary and inequitable distribution of wealth and incomes' (*GT*, p. 372) could destroy social cohesion and favour sedition and revolution, resulting in Fascism or Bolshevism. The persistence of high unemployment and cyclical fluctuations of the economy are not inevitable economic phenomena, but rather the unavoidable results of laissez-faire capitalism. They result from the combination of a marginal propensity to consume which is too low and instability of investment, itself the consequence of excessive liquidity preference and insufficient marginal efficiency of capital. The latter two phenomena result from the expectations of the agents facing an uncertain future. *The General Theory* offers a diagnosis of this complex and dangerous illness, but this diagnosis can lead to several types of cure:

> This that I offer is, therefore, a theory of why output and employment are so liable to fluctuation. It does not offer a ready-made remedy as to how to avoid these fluctuations and to maintain output at a steady optimum level. But it is, properly speaking, a theory of employment because it explains *why*, in any given circumstances, employment is what it is. Naturally I am interested not only in the diagnosis, but also in the cure; and many pages of my book are devoted to the latter. But I consider that my suggestions for a cure, which, avowedly, are not worked out completely, are on a different plane from the diagnosis. They are not meant to be definitive; they are subject to all sorts of special assumptions and are necessarily related to the particular conditions of the time. (Keynes, 'The General Theory of Employment', *Quarterly Journal of Economics*, vol. 51, 1937; *JMK*, XIV, pp. 121–2)

The options for economic policy thus remain open. Between herbal medicine and outright surgery, there are several possible remedies! While Keynes himself in the last chapter of his book describes the implications of his theory as 'moderately conservative' (*GT*, p. 377), since it implies the maintenance of a system of private enterprise with income inequality which one should not aim to remove entirely, the interventionism he promotes throughout his career has some very radical characteristics. Thus does he sometimes assert that only the state is capable of undertaking necessary investment, not only to stimulate effective demand, but also to ensure its social utility. Besides the socialization of investment, planning and even the 'semi-socialism' or 'liberal socialism' implied by this vision, Keynes also appealed for a radical social transformation when he evoked the necessary euthanasia of the rentier, to which a gradual decline in the interest rate can contribute. It is remarkable to see Keynes attack the same parasitical social class, non-productive and living on rentier income, that Ricardo had attacked in his own time.

At the time when the Soviet system appeared to many as an alternative to capitalism – hope for some, threat for others; when some showed confidence in central planning (Bettleheim 1939; Dobb 1928) and others, such as Lerner (1934–5) and Lange (1936–7) asserted, in opposition to Mises, the theoretical possibility of socialism; when Hansen (1938, 1939) considered stagnation an enduring feature of capitalism; when Schumpeter expressed his pessimistic views on the future of capitalism,[30] and when Colin Clark analysed the sources of economic progress, Keynes, on the basis of his diagnosis, sketched out several types of policy which should allow capitalism to overcome its own contradictions and thus safeguard liberal society. And in the postwar period, it was to an extremely diverse range of economic policies that the term 'Keynesian' could be applied.

Notes

1. K. Polanyi, *The Great Transformation*, New York, Rinehart, 1944, p. 29.
2. Ibid., p. 23.
3. It was indeed against all caution and despite his doctors' opinions that, during and immediately after the Second World War, Keynes was one of the principal architects of complex negotiations aimed at ensuring the economic and political conditions of a pacified world, in which one could at last devote oneself to the quest of beauty, knowledge, love and friendship. Besides his exhausting functions as a negotiator, which led him to cross the Atlantic many times, Keynes, from 1942, devoted much energy to the activities of the Committee for the Encouragement of Music and the Arts (CEMA, which after the war would become the Arts Council), which he chaired and whose activities he oversaw constantly, even during his stays in the United States, requiring that the minutes of the meetings be sent to him.
4. See in particular Chapter 23, 'Notes on Mercantilism, the Usury Laws, Stamped Money and Theories of Under-consumption'. On the theory of effective demand before Adam Smith, consult in particular H. Brems, *Pioneering Economic Theory, 1630–1980 – A Mathematical Restatement*, Baltimore, Johns Hopkins Press, 1986 and Hutchison 1988.
5. Sketched out in 1914, developed in 1922 and 1924 on the occasion of several presentations, this study was completed in 1933, to be integrated in *Essays in Biography*, published by Keynes that same year (London, Macmillan); see *JMK*, X, 71–108.
6. Some elements in this section are taken from G. Dostaler, 'The Debate Between Hayek and Keynes', in W. Barber (ed.), *Perspectives on the History of Economic Thought*, vol. 6, *Themes in Keynesian Criticism and Supplementary Modern Topics*, Aldershot, Hants, Edward Elgar, 1991, 77–101.
7. On the London School of Economics in the 1930s, see A.W. Coats, 'The L.S.E. Ethos in the Inter-War Years', *Atlantic Economic Journal*, vol. 10, 1982, 18–30; J.R. Hicks, 'LSE and the Robbins Circle', in *Money, Interest and Wages, Collected Essays on Economic Theory*, vol. 2, Oxford, Basil Blackwell, 1982, 3–10; C. Ménard, 'Le keynésianisme: naissance d'une illusion', *Economies et sociétés*, vol. 19, série *Oeconomia*, no. 3, 1985, 3–27; L.C. Robbins, *Autobiography of An Economist*, London, Macmillan, 1971.
8. In 1933, a group of young economists from Cambridge and London set up the *Review of Economic Studies* with the aim, *inter alia*, of going beyond the divisions between rival schools. Their elder colleagues called it the 'Children's Journal'!
9. See below, Chapter 9.
10. This can no doubt be explained by the fact that it was the Austrian founders of marginalism who crossed swords both with the German historical school, in the context of the *Methodenstreit* [war of methods] and with a Marxist movement strongly established in Germany and Austria. Menger, Böhm-Bawerk and Wieser thus had to oppose these streams of thought with a coherent alternative vision.
11. See the texts, then published in German, translated and collected in Hayek 1984 (*Money, Capital*), as well as Hayek 1929, 1931 and 1939. On this, see M. Colonna, H. Hagemann

and O. Hamouda (eds), *The Economics of F.A. Hayek*, vol. 1, *Money and Business Cycles*, Aldershot, Hants, Edward Elgar, 1994.

12. See following section.
13. To which it is certainly necessary to add those American institutionalist economists Hayek met during his trip to the United States in 1923 and 1924.
14. In a series of books, generally ignored by economists, but which have been widely circulated (*Money*, Boston, Houghton Mifflin, 1923; *Profits*, Boston, Houghton Mifflin, 1925; *Business Without a Buyer*, Boston, Houghton Mifflin, 1927; *The Road to Plenty*, Boston, Houghton Mifflin, 1928, which in fact is a novel!), William Trufant Foster and Waddill Catchings developed the thesis according to which insufficient demand, provoked by excessive saving, constitutes one of the major causes of economic difficulties. See Hayek, 'The "Paradox" of Saving', *Economica*, vol. 11, 1931, 125–69.
15. For example, see the letter in which Keynes, Pigou and other economists denounced the orthodoxy, in the 17 October 1932 issue of *The Times*, and the response of Hayek, Robbins and their friends, on 19 October.
16. See his 'Professor Hayek and the Concertina-Effect', *Economica*, vol. 9, 1942, 359–82.
17. The *Ekonomisk Tidskrift* issue in which the first version of Myrdal's text was published was dated 1931, but was in fact released in the summer of 1932.
18. This fact, among others, illustrates well the idea according to which there is no necessary congruence between the adhesion to neoclassical theory and faith in liberalism. Wicksell was a proponent of state intervention to correct an equilibrium unfavourable to workers. Born in 1851, dying in 1926, Wicksell is the author of, among others: *Value, Capital and Rent*, London, George Allen & Unwin, 1954; 1st German edn, 1893; *Interest and Prices: A Study of the Causes Regulating the Value of Money*, London, Macmillan, 1936; 1st German edn, 1898 and *Lectures on Political Economy*, 2 vols, London, Macmillan, 1934–5; 1st Swedish edn, 1901–6.
19. Born in 1891, dying in 1960, Erik Lindahl wrote most of his major contributions before the publication of *The General Theory*, although they would only be revealed to an English-speaking readership in 1939, with the publication of *Studies in the Theory of Money and Capital*, London, George Allen & Unwin.
20. See, for example, 'The Swedish Discussion on the Aims of Monetary Policy', *International Economic Papers*, no. 5, 1955, 145–54.
21. *A Study in the Theory of Inflation*, London, George Allen & Unwin, 1951; *The Economic Theory of Fiscal Policy*, London, Allen & Unwin, 1958; 1st Swedish edn, 1955.
22. Written by Myrdal, the annex to the budget speech delivered by the Social-Democratic Minister of finance Ernst Wigforss, on 2 January 1933, includes the theoretical justification of an expansionary policy which one could call Keynesian. As early as 1912, Wigforss and the leaders of the Swedish Social-Democratic Party had started to propose policies of this type.
23. On this subject, see among others: B.J. Hansson, *The Stockholm School and the Development of Dynamic Method*, London, Croom Helm, 1982 (by the same author, see also the entry 'Stockholm School' in the *New Palgrave*, vol. 4, 503–7); L. Jonung (ed.), *The Stockholm School of Economics Revisited*, Cambridge, England, Cambridge University Press, 1991; K.-G. Landgren, *Economics in Modern Sweden*, Washington, Library of Congress, Reference Department, 1957; id., *Den 'nya ekonomien' i Sverige. J.M. Keynes, E. Wigforss, B. Ohlin och utvecklingen 1927–39* [The 'new economics' in Sweden: J.M. Keynes, E. Wigforss, B. Ohlin and developments 1927–39], Stockholm, Almqvist & Wiksell, 1960; O. Steiger, *Studien zur Entstehung der Neuen Wirtschaftslehre in Schweden: Eine Anti-Kritik* [Studies in the development of the new economics in Sweden: A counter-critique], Berlin, Duncker und Humblot, 1971.
24. 'Next, we must record Keynes's acknowledgments of indebtedness, which in all cases can be independently established, to Mrs. Joan Robinson, Mr. R.G. Hawtrey, Mr. R.F. Harrod, but especially to Mr. R.F. Kahn, whose share in the historic achievement cannot have fallen very far short of co-authorship' (Schumpeter 1954, p. 1172).
25. 'The Relation of Home Investment to Unemployment', *Economic Journal*, vol. 41, 1931, 173–98. One can find Kahn's principal theoretical contributions gathered in *Selected*

Essays on Employment and Growth, Cambridge, England, Cambridge University Press, 1972. Defended in 1929, his doctoral thesis was published 60 years later (*The Economics of the Short Period*, London, Macmillan, 1989). One may read, first hand, his testimony on the genesis of *The General Theory* in *The Making of Keynes' General Theory* Cambridge, England, Cambridge University Press, 1984. On Kahn (1905–1989), see G.C. Harcourt, 'R.F. Kahn: A Tribute', *Quarterly Review, Banca Nazionale del Lavoro*, no. 176, 1991, pp. 15–30.

26. On the Circus, see the editor's notes in Keynes, *JMK*, XIII, 202–11 and 337–43; and especially the accounts of Richard Kahn and Austin Robinson in Harcourt 1985.
27. See his *Good and Bad Trade: An Inquiry into the Causes of Trade Fluctuations*, London, Macmillan, 1913; *Currency and Credit*, London, Macmillan, 1919; *The Art of Central Banking*, London, Macmillan, 1932.
28. Robertson's dissertation (*A Study of Industrial Fluctuations*, London, P.S. King & Sons, 1915) was written in Cambridge where Keynes was his tutor. The latter was influenced by this work as well as by Robertson's *Banking Policy and the Price Level* (London, P.S. King & Sons, 1926). Keynes once wrote him: 'I certainly date all my emancipation from the discussions between us which preceded your *Banking Policy and the Price Level.* The last thing I should accuse you of is being classical or orthodox' (letter to Robertson, 13 December 1936, *JMK*, XIV, p. 94). On Robertson's work, see J.R. Presley, *Robertsonian Economics. An Examination of the Work of Sir D.H. Robertson on Industrial Fluctuations*, London, Macmillan, 1979.
29. On the critique of Keynes's theory by Robertson, see his *Essays in Monetary Theory*, London, Staple Press, 1940; see also *Essays in Money and Interest*, edited by J.R. Hicks, Manchester, Collins, 1966.
30. *Capitalism, Socialism and Democracy*, New York, Harper & Brothers; London, George Allen & Unwin, 1942. Joseph Schumpeter, born the same year as Keynes, 1883, dying in 1950, leaving unfinished his monumental *History of Economic Analysis* (1954), is one of the twentieth century's greatest economists (see below, Chapters 6 and 9). Born in Vienna, he was finance minister of the Austrian government in 1919–20. He left Hitler's Germany in 1932 and took a position at Harvard, where he had a profound influence on many of the economists that we mention in this work. His major work, *Business Cycles: A Theoretical, Historical and Statistical Analysis of the Capitalist Process*, 2 vols, New York and London, McGraw-Hill, 1939, in which he tried to integrate in a coherent ensemble analyses of cyclical fluctuations of various durations, growth and long-term development, was unfortunately published at a time when discussion was dominated by *The General Theory*. Very far away from Marx ideologically and politically, Schumpeter nonetheless accepted some essential elements of the former's vision of the dynamics of capitalism, in which crises play an essential role. He first presented his theses, in particular his theory of innovations, in *The Theory of Economic Development: An Inquiry into Profits, Capital, Credit, Interest, and the Business Cycle*, Cambridge, Massachusetts, Harvard University Press, 1934; 1st German edn, 1912. Overshadowed for a long time, Schumpeter's thought is now more and more referred to. On Schumpeter, see, among many works: R.V. Clemence and F.S. Doody, *The Schumpeterian System*, New York, A.M. Kelley, 1950; E. Marz, *Joseph Schumpeter. Scholar, Teacher, and Politician*, New Haven and London, Connecticut, Yale University Press, 1991; A. Oakley, *Schumpeter's Theory of Capitalist Motion: A Critical Exposition and Reassessment*, Aldershot, Hants, Edward Elgar, 1990; R. Swedberg, *Schumpeter: His Life and Work*, Princeton University Press; Oxford, Polity Press, 1991.

3 The triumph of interventionism

From 1936 onward, Keynesianism developed in a more and more autonomous way, independent of its founder. However, for a further ten years, Keynes continued to play an important role in its evolution. His views, with their variations and, sometimes, contradictions, helped shed light on the ambiguities characterizing the development of that body of doctrine and theory subsequently labelled 'Keynesian'.

Keynes's views after 1936

As was predictable, the publication of *The General Theory* gave rise to lively debate.[1] Keynes took part in this, through articles and conferences, correspondence and discussions, evidence of which can be found in various places.[2] What emerges from them is that Keynes shifted on the subject of the interpretation his work should be given. The article published in the February 1937 issue of the *Quarterly Journal of Economics*, to which we have already referred, obviously aimed at a total rupture with orthodoxy. But when Hicks sent him the manuscript of the article, 'Mr Keynes and the "Classics": A Suggested Interpretation' (Hicks 1937), which proposed a common grid, the IS–LL scheme, for reading both the classical theory and *The General Theory* – thereby opening the way to the neoclassical synthesis – Keynes replied on 31 March 1937: 'I found it very interesting and really have next to nothing to say by way of criticism' (*JMK*, XIV, p. 79). To Joan Robinson, who offered to write a 'children's version of *The General Theory*', Keynes had written on 2 December 1936:

> So far as I myself am concerned, I am trying to prevent my mind from crystallising too much on the precise lines of the *General Theory*. I am attentive to criticisms and to what raises difficulties and catches people's attention – in which there are a good many surprises. I think that the best popular version may have to be approached along lines of its own. I think about it all a good deal, but I do not feel ready. There is a considerable difference between more or less formal theory, which my existing book purports to be, and something which is meant to be applied to current events without too much qualification by people who do not fully comprehend the theory. So I am against hurry and in favour of gestation. (*JMK*, XXIX, pp. 185–6)

On 20 April 1937, he wrote to her: 'I am gradually getting myself into an outside position towards the book, and am feeling my way to new lines of exposition' (*JMK*, XIV, p. 150). Incidentally, Keynes also revealed his intention of publishing explanatory notes to his book. On another occasion, in the context of a critical discussion of the Swedish economists' conception of the interest rate, he announced his intention of examining the relations between his concepts and the *ex ante* and *ex post* analysis of the Stockholm School.[3]

As to the place of classical theory in *The General Theory*, we also note an evolution on Keynes's part. To a letter from Gerald Shove, a professor at Cambridge who agreed with his critique of the classics but was critical of Keynes's generosity towards this theory in its application to individual industry and firm, Keynes answered on 15 April 1936: 'What you say about the classical analysis as applied to the individual industry and firm is probably right. I have been concentrating on the other problem, and have not, like you, thought very much about the elements of the system' (*JMK*, XIV, p. 2). Then, in an article published three years later, Keynes reconsidered his acceptance of the first postulate of the classical theory, that of the equality of the real wage and the marginal physical product of labour.[4]

Also noticeable are variations in Keynes's position concerning economic policy. For example, at times, he warned against taking a full employment policy too far.[5] While Beveridge chose 3 per cent unemployment as the level below which an active policy of full employment was likely to induce an inflationary process, Keynes set it at around 4.5 per cent. But, during the war, Keynes took the clearest positions in favour of the socialization of investment and of significant state control of economic activity. He had even proposed precise mechanisms for the public management of investment. After the publication in 1944 of *The Road to Serfdom*, Hayek's virulent denunciation of socialism, in which he affirmed that any form of planning could ultimately only lead to totalitarianism, Keynes had written to him to tell him that he totally agreed, morally and philosophically, in his condemnation of totalitarianism and his praise of freedom. Nevertheless, he broke with this critique on the matter of economic policy: it was not less but more planning that was needed to avoid the shift towards totalitarianism. At the end of his letter, Keynes said that he feared the consequences of the application of extreme versions of theses such as Hayek's in a country such as the United States (*JMK*, XXVII, p. 382). But, according to Hayek's testimony, during the last conversation they had, shortly before Keynes's death, the latter indicated he was ready to set out on a policy pilgrimage to encourage governments to fight inflation first and foremost, if it emerged that this was becoming the main danger (Hayek 1978, pp. 286–7).

Thus Keynes's views varied between the publication of *The General Theory* in 1936 and his death in 1946. His books and articles were the object of diverse readings and interpretations. Whatever their importance, his contributions are inscribed in a broad intellectual transformation taking place in the 1930s and 1940s. That is to say, if what was called the Keynesian revolution constituted a profound reconstitution of the intellectual world of the economists and policy makers, this transformation is not easily reduced to the simplistic form that it has all too often been given.

The ambiguous Keynesian tidal wave

In his review of Harrod's book, *The Life of John Maynard Keynes*, published in the 26 January 1951 issue of *The Times*, Lionel Robbins wrote: 'The future historian of social thought may well call this period the period of John Maynard Keynes. Yet it is not at all easy to find any simple formula to describe wherein this ascendancy consisted' (Robbins 1970, p. 244). This account is perfectly applicable to the developments of economic thought and to the economic policies of the postwar period. Almost everybody agrees in emphasizing its Keynesian nature, but one is forced to recognize that, more often, the Keynesian character is related less to a deep coherence with the hard core of Keynes's theory than to continuities or convergences in relation to different aspects of his thinking.

The success of *The General Theory* was affirmed in several stages. First, some of Keynes's intimates and followers adopted this book as a 'warhorse'. American economists, notably Hansen in his Harvard seminar, found in it a theoretical coherence, which at that time appealed to a number of students and young researchers, including Samuelson, Galbraith and Tobin. In France, while Pierre Mendès-France was acquainted with Keynes's ideas as early as 1938, F. Perroux, C. Gruson, P. Uri and A. Barrère discovered *The General Theory* during the Second World War,[6] as did R. Prebisch in Argentina. Then, in the changing intellectual world which came with the end of the war, simple ideas were imposed which were not unrelated to *The General Theory* but went beyond it, and may be linked to many other sources of inspiration: the duty of governments to ensure full employment (and later growth); a renewed and, at the same time, simple reading of national economies, with the large macroeconomic aggregates and the functional relations which linked them, which the national accounts would subsequently provide with a coherent structure and increasingly reliable data; and finally, on these bases, an improved understanding of economic policies.

After the war, these ideas were equally embraced by English-speaking liberals and radicals, by British Labour Party members, European social-democrats and socialist reformers, and also Christian democrats, social reformers, supporters of national economic development, heirs of Colbert, List or Carey. That is to say, these ideas were widely spread among the milieux which came to power at the end of the Second World War; and it is only in a very broad sense that they can be described as Keynesian. But Keynesianism had other, different aspects. Parallel to the publication of *The General Theory* and the circulation of its ideas, a radical mutation was taking place: the mathematicization and formalization of economics, which we shall deal with in the next chapter. Like other theories, Keynes's was rewritten in mathematical language, appropriate to some simple functional relations between macroeconomic magnitudes; this formalization was often carried out at the expense of simplifications, which erased insights or essential aspects of Keynes's thinking. Thus was facilitated the development of a descriptive macroeconomics, commonly described as Keynesian and nourished by the increased postwar availability of data, especially from the national accounts.

These simplifications also rendered possible the development, begun as we have seen by Hicks in 1937, of the combination of tools of analysis suggested by Keynes with other tools offered by approaches to which he himself had been opposed. This syncretism received the name of 'neoclassical synthesis'. It became predominant in the 1950s and 1960s and provided the theoretical basis on which the large econometric models, themselves rendered operational by the progress of computer science and data bases, were conceived and constructed. Economists thus had at their disposal the possibility of establishing the theoretical foundations of economic policies, as well as the powerful tools of macroeconomic analysis to facilitate their guidance.

Thus the revolution conceived by Keynes – the elaboration of a theory breaking with the classical approach – and the large movement of ideas in the 1930s of which it was part produced several developments, which under one guise or another have been called Keynesian. They marked the postwar period, as much in the field of economic policy as in that of applied economics and theory. But was it, perhaps, the groundswell of formalization and mathematicization, long obscured by this theoretical revival, which constituted the decisive transformation of the discipline during this period?[7] Later on, we will examine the progressions and steps which led to the *rapprochement* of those theoretical elements belonging, in some cases, to the neoclassical tradition and, in others, to the Keynesian theory,[8] and then the works of Keynes's intimates, followers and disciples who, in the spirit of Keynes, took it upon themselves to develop an analysis at odds with the neoclassical theory.[9] We will therefore limit ourselves here to presenting some fields in which approaches and visions were transformed between the end of the 1930s and the end of the 1950s: full employment as a priority objective; the broad consensus concerning economic policy; and the setting up of systems of national accounts. In each of these fields one can find the influence of Keynes's thinking, even if none of these advances can be explained by his contributions alone.

The acceptance of full employment as a priority objective

Even in its third edition, published in 1941, the book written by Gottfried Haberler for the League of Nations, *Prosperity and Depression* (Haberler

1937), remains principally devoted to debates antecedent to *The General Theory* and barely makes space for Keynes's ideas. But as early as 1943, a report of the League of Nations delegation in charge of studying economic depressions promoted the right to work with the aim of simultaneously ensuring freedom and possibility of employment.[10]

In Great Britain, William Beveridge extended his report on Social Insurance and Allied Services (1942) with a second one on full employment.[11] The latter was at the printers when the government published, in May 1944, a white paper in which it took on the responsibility to maintain a high and stable level of employment by means of policies designed to stabilize aggregate demand. In his report, *Full Employment in a Free Society* (1944), Beveridge explicitly refers to Keynes:

> A new era of economic theorizing about employment and unemployment was inaugurated by the publication in 1936 of *The General Theory of Employment, Interest and Money* by J.M. Keynes, now Lord Keynes. No account, however brief, of all the changes of economic thought and language induced by this epoch-making work can be attempted here.[12]

Beveridge was ready to go very far to ensure full employment: if, he wrote, 'it should be shown by experience or by argument that abolition of private property in the means of production was necessary for full employment, this abolition would have to be undertaken'.[13] However, his propositions came within the context of a less radical interventionism, with, in particular, a new budgetary policy, where the 'Budget is made with reference to available man-power, not to money'[14] and, more widely, 'a policy of socializing demand rather than production'.[15]

The affirmation of full employment as a priority objective spread quickly. In April 1945, the Canadian government published a white paper which emphasized that one of the main objectives of Canadian policy was to guarantee a high and stable level of employment and income and thus to uphold the standard of living. Similarly, Australia published a white paper on full employment and New Zealand adopted an employment law. In various forms, similar stances affirming the full employment objective were adopted in many European countries, such as Belgium, France, the Netherlands and Norway.

In the United States, the preamble to the Employment Act of 1946 affirmed that it is the 'responsibility of the Federal Government to use all practicable means ... in a manner calculated to foster and promote free competitive enterprise and the general welfare to promote maximum employment, production and purchasing power' (quoted in Lerner 1947, p. 331). More widely, the United Nations conference on trade and employment, held in Havana in

February 1948, underlined the importance of achieving and maintaining productive full employment.

A victory for Keynes's ideas, certainly, but also for all those who had sought, and suggested measures for, full employment in the 1930s and 1940s: in Europe, among many others, Ohlin, Myrdal, and Tinbergen; in the United States, the numerous economists who, as early as the beginning of the 1930s, had called for a new policy in order to fight the massive unemployment: from Sumner Slichter and Virgil Jordan to the Chicago academics who had signed a memorandum claiming that the only remaining choice was between a waiting period (which might well be long) for a sufficient decline in costs and a public policy stimulating substantial new purchasing power;[16] and also John Maurice Clark[17] and Paul H. Douglas,[18] whose ideas and propositions in this field, published in 1934 and 1935, preceded those of *The General Theory*.

Paradoxically, by the time political leaders were adopting the objective of full employment, with or without reference to Keynes, it had already been several years since Keynes had begun to worry about the difficulties which would emerge with the approach of full employment. For their part, Fellner (1946) and Lerner (1951) were concerned with the risks to price stability of policies led without the necessary caution. And, writing the foreword to the French translation of her *Introduction to the Theory of Employment* (1937), Robinson, in 1948, expressed a similar concern:

> The very success of an employment policy creates new problems. In a private enterprise system, the existence of an unemployed workers' reserve played an important role. ... Unemployment maintained discipline in industry ... gave to the production system enough flexibility to adapt itself to technological change and demand fluctuation ... [and] by slowing down the tendency to rise of nominal wages ... ensured a sufficient stability in the value of money. To obtain all this, unemployment was a cruel and costly method. But if it must be abolished, other means have to be found to fulfil the same functions. (Robinson, *Introduction à la théorie de l'emploi*, Paris, Presses Universitaires de France, 1948, p. 10; translated from French)

Of course, Joan Robinson was not advocating the abandonment of the Keynesian project; but, facing a new situation, she urged maintaining theoretical analysis and applying it to economic policies to be set up in the new postwar circumstances. This is what was done by Weintraub, among others, who very early became aware of the possible risk that unemployment and inflation could coexist, underlined the importance of the money wage rate and suggested completing the policy of demand management with an incomes policy (Weintraub 1940, 1946).

The golden age of interventionism and economic policy

In his book published in 1947, *Economic Policy and Full Employment*, Alvin Hansen rejected the position put forward by Hayek in *The Road to Serfdom* (1944). Warning against the progression which leads from intervention to planning and from socialism to Nazism, in short to totalitarianism and serfdom, Hayek's book was widely circulated. Witnessing the collapse of the old order, Hansen pleaded for the reconstruction of a market economy, as much at the national as the international level, on the basis of new institutions. Capitalism's new characteristics had made necessary economic policy; and the management of aggregate demand and of its major elements was to be the principal instrument: 'Planning for full employment and maximum production involves, among other things, planning for stability' (Hansen 1947, p. 3). In 1950, a paper on the problem of economic instability, written by a committee of the American Economic Association,[19] placed the objectives of full employment and price stability on virtually the same level; it advocated a rather wide variety of measures ranging from public finance to monetary policy. Among the five authors of this study, we find two young economists whose paths would subsequently diverge: Milton Friedman and Paul Samuelson.

More generally, the voices of Hayek and other opponents to interventionism were largely muffled in the postwar period by those advocating economic policy, whether the latter referred to Keynes or not. To politicians and their advisers, the rejuvenation and modernization of their national economies was viewed as a primary responsibility. Other objectives were also pursued: the broadening and improvement of social protection, housing, health, education, raising the standard of living; in short, growth. In all industrial countries, it was the age of economic policy.[20] To the extent that they contained, at the heart of their operation, the management of demand as the main lever for increasing or slowing down economic activity, these policies were frequently described as Keynesian. But they were also inspired by other sources: liberal corporatism in Japan and Germany, the social-democrat tradition in Northern Europe, interventionism and Colbertism in France, where Jean Monnet[21] had laid the basis for indicative planning with Etienne Hirsch, F. Gaillard, Robert Marjolin and Pierre Uri.

In West Germany, Ludwig Erhard conceived and set in motion the social market economy, characterized by a general confidence in the market mechanism, the state being required to ensure that progress was to the benefit of the society as a whole; Wilhelm Röpke, the main representative of the Freiburg School after the death of Walter Euken in 1950, gave it his support.[22] In Great Britain, Meade, who had already given his support to Keynes's propositions before the war, advocated the 'lib-lab policy' in 1948: a liberal policy in the sense that it must respect the market but also a social one, concerned for the interests of labour. In Scandinavian countries, contemporaneous policies were inspired by the writings and analyses of Frisch in Norway and Ohlin, Myrdal and Lundberg in Sweden.

In Holland, although his influence extended beyond this country, Tinbergen played an active role in the construction of a model of the Dutch economy and the implementation of national accounting but also, in the 1950s, in the planning and design of economic policy; criticizing the simultaneous implementation of several economic policies, each seeking one or more objectives, he asserted the necessary unity of economic policy, and set forth the principle according to which it is possible to pursue several major objectives, as long as one implements an equal number of major instruments. For that matter, he ascribed heavy responsibilities to economic policy, ranging from 'maximum real expenditure per capita with "full" employment and monetary equilibrium' to 'improvement of distribution of real income or expenditure over social groups and countries' and from 'emancipation of certain underprivileged groups' to 'maintenance of international peace' (Tinbergen 1956, 15–16). Very early, Meade (1951–5) and Tinbergen (1952) took the external environment into consideration and conceived the tools and the actions of policy for an open economy.

With the developments of economic analysis, progress of statistical methods and the implementation of macroeconometric models, the knowledge of national economies was simultaneously solidified and refined. The deterioration in the US economic situation towards the end of the 1950s gave rise to a strong demand for growth.[23] And John F. Kennedy's election gave American economists, partisans of state intervention, the opportunity to prove the validity and efficacy of their new knowledge. Besides the advice given him by Samuelson and Galbraith, the president was also counselled by a solid team of official advisers, including, in particular, Walter Heller, James Tobin, Kermit Gordon, Robert Solow and Arthur Okun; together they prepared and suggested a new economic policy: the 'new economics'.[24] This, according to Tobin, was based on three principles: the first consisting in 'the explicit dedication of macroeconomic policy instruments to real economic goals, in particular full employment and real growth of national output'; the second is the activist demand management 'responsive to the actually observed state of the economy'; the third is 'to put both fiscal and monetary policies in consistent and coordinated harness in the pursuit of macroeconomic objectives'. Finally, inasmuch as the implementation of these two types of policies was not sufficient to ensure full employment and price stability together, a third type of policy, embryonic in *The General Theory,* proved necessary: income policy.[25]

W. Heller, who headed the Council of Economic Advisers under Kennedy's presidency, emphasizes the importance of the policies led by Kennedy and his successor:

> Economics has come of age in the 1960's. Two Presidents have recognized and drawn on modern economics as a source of national strength and Presidential power. Their willingness to use, for the first time, the full range of modern economic tools underlies the unbroken U. S. expansion since early 1961 – an expansion that in its first five years created over seven million new jobs, doubled profits, increased the nation's real output by a third, and closed the $50-billion gap between actual and potential production that plagued the American economy in 1961. (Heller 1966, p. 1)

Thus economic science triumphed. But also, from then on, the responsibility of government for economic matters was recognized:

> We at last accept in fact what was accepted in law twenty years ago (in the Employment Act of 1946), namely, that the Federal government has an overarching responsibility for the nation's economic stability and growth. And we have at last unleashed fiscal and monetary policy for the aggressive pursuit of those objectives.
>
> These are profound changes. What they have wrought is not the creation of a 'new economics', but the completion of the Keynesian Revolution – thirty years after John Maynard Keynes fired the opening salvo. (Ibid., p. 2)

The Keynesian revolution thus appears to lie at the origin of the view that, at last, it was possible to control economic activity. Heller enumerates all the advances in economics which, according to him, rendered possible this new management of economies: the new economics:

> – Lord Keynes' spectacular rescue (via the *General Theory of Employment, Interest, and Money* in 1936) of economics from the wilderness of classical equilibrium ...
> – Alvin Hansen's Americanization of Keynes ...
> – Simon Kuznets' seminal work on the concepts of national income and gross national product ...
> – Paul Samuelson's 'neoclassical synthesis' which ranges the contributions of the classical economist side-by-side with those of Keynes in balanced policy for full employment and efficient resource allocation.
> – The contributions of a new generation of computer-oriented economists ... (Ibid., p. 4)

W. Heller indicates here the triple entrenchment of the 'new economics': in Keynes's thought, in the American tradition and in the 'modernity' of the 1950s and 1960s. He thus issues a declaration of faith, characteristic of the mid-1960s: 'But we do agree that the economy cannot regulate itself. We now take for granted that the government must step in to provide the essential stability at high levels of employment and growth that the market mechanism, left alone, cannot deliver' (ibid., p. 9). But this agreement was not general. Persistent supporters of laissez-faire, such as F.A. Hayek and A.F.

Burns, who was the chairman of President Eisenhower's Council of Economic Advisers and who directed the National Bureau of Economic Research from 1957 to 1967, M. Friedman, who published *Capitalism and Freedom* in 1962, and Jacques Rueff in France, all affirmed their radically opposed positions.

Nevertheless, the 1950s and 1960s constitute the golden age of economic policies. With or without reference to Keynes, more or less interventionist, based on the structural transformations or more centred on the subtle management of economic fluctuations, it is indisputable that these policies had Keynesian components. The strategic variables were the aggregate quantities; the stress was on demand and its components (investment, consumption, government spending), with intervention on public investment and the determinants of private investment, income distribution (in particular through budgeting and redistribution) and public finance.

This was the time of certainty. The economists knew, thanks to an increasingly precise knowledge of reality, how to play on a more and more varied range of instruments in order to allow governments to achieve diverse objectives, while ensuring balanced growth. At least, this is what many of them firmly believed!

The implementation of national accounts

Essential instruments for the knowledge of economic reality, the national accounts were put in place in the immediate postwar period. Without referring to the precursors of past centuries, their conception and elaboration were prepared by the inter-war efforts to measure production and income by the statistical services of many countries: in particular Canada, Denmark, the United States, Germany, Japan, New Zealand and Turkey. They were also prepared by the pioneering works of economists such as S. Kuznets (1934, 1938, 1941), C. Clark (1937, 1938 with Crawford, 1939), and also R. Frisch, M. Kalecki, E. Lindahl, E. Varga, C. Colson, A. Sauvy and many others.

It was in Great Britain, in connection with the war effort, that the decisive initiative was taken, with the support of Keynes and the assistance of the government. A first white paper, published by the British Treasury in 1941,[26] includes both a series of estimates by the Treasury staff and another, developed by academic economists including R. Stone and J.E. Meade, which was based on three accounts: national income, household income and expenditure, and the sources and uses of saving. From this point on, the British national accounts were developed, serving as a model for all English-speaking countries. Simultaneously, on the basis of previous work,[27] new paths were cleared: in Holland under the influence of Tinbergen, and in France under L.A. Vincent and C. Gruson.[28] Efforts to bring these different systems closer together were conducted in the context of the League of Nations, and then the United Nations, and also at the Organisation for European Economic Cooperation. They resulted, under the influence of R. Stone, O. Aukrust and J. Marczewski, in a simplified system of accounts, subsequently standardized according to, first, the OEEC,[29] and then, under R. Stone's supervision, the United Nations[30] normalized accounts system. In the postwar period, each country adopted a national accounts system. And very quickly, other improvements were seen, such as the integration of input–output tables, of which W. Leontief had been the untiring inventor, craftsman and promoter since the 1930s (1936, 1941).

Between the national accounts measuring the main annual global fluctuations and Keynesian macroeconomic analysis describing the relations and interactions between the principal aggregates of a national economic system, there was clearly reciprocal support and enrichment. Keynesian analysis offered a conceptual framework for the design, construction and use of national accounts. And these in turn provided the statistical data necessary for measuring or estimating the principal Keynesian aggregates, relations and functions: the investment multiplier, the marginal propensity to consume, the link between production and employment. During the entire postwar period, there was mutual stimulation of, and interaction between, the improvements in national accounting, progress in macroeconomic analysis and advances in econometrics. The whole culminated in the construction of national econometric models which permitted the analysis of the economic situation, carrying out simulations and projections, and thus the enlightenment of economic policy and planning. These models, often described as Keynesian, fall into the general category of Keynesian macroeconomics, but have increasingly integrated the results of work conducted in the context of the neoclassical synthesis.

Hydraulic Keynesianism

Simultaneously, there circulated a simplified form of Keynesianism reduced to a mechanics of aggregate quantities or to hydraulics of flows and devoid of the essence of Keynes's thought: time, non-probabilistic uncertainty, anticipations and the inclusion of monetary phenomena as essential to production and, more largely, to economic activity and dynamics. As well as in countless textbooks and popularizations, this is well illustrated (see Figure 3.1) in P. Samuelson's textbook, *Economics*, first published in 1948, whose numerous subsequent editions have turned it into the greatest best-seller in the history of economics.

At the same time, A.W. Phillips, an engineer by training, devised a system of pipes and tanks (see Figure 3.2) which was meant to put in concrete form the relations between macroeconomic stocks, flows and price levels (Phillips 1950, p. 285).

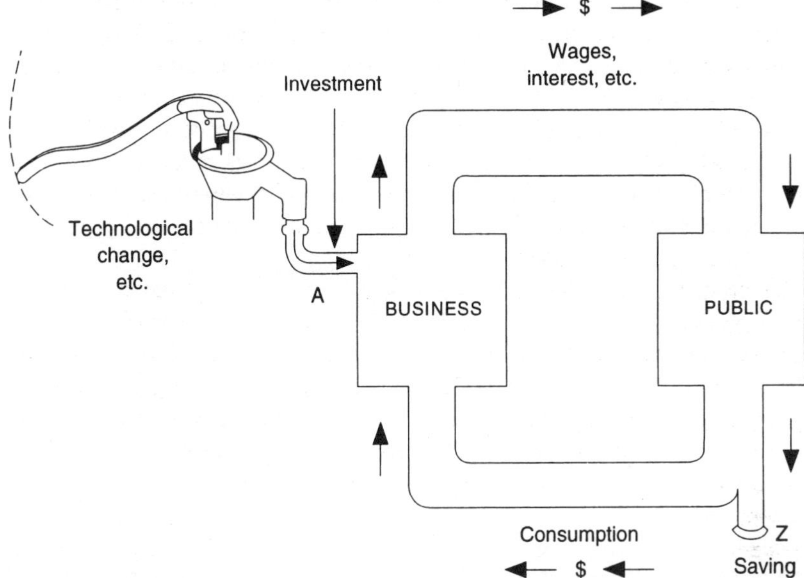

Technological change, population growth, and other dynamic factors keep the investment pump handle going. Income rises and falls with changes in investment, its equilibrium level, at any time, being realized only when intended saving at Z matches intended investment at A.

Source: SAMUELSON P., *Economics: An Introductory Analysis*, New York, McGraw-Hill, 4th edn, 1958, p. 231.

Figure 3.1 Dynamic investment pumps national income up and down

The construction remained a curiosity, but a related curve, ten years later, made him famous.

The transformations discussed in this chapter profoundly affected the post-war landscape of economic thought. Fitting in, one way or another, with the continuation of Keynes's work or views, they legitimately illustrated those features of the Keynesian revolution most accessible to the general public. They benefited from an exceptional conjunction of circumstances, political choices and the theoretical work of a bevy of economists, by no means confined to Keynes's intimates and disciples.

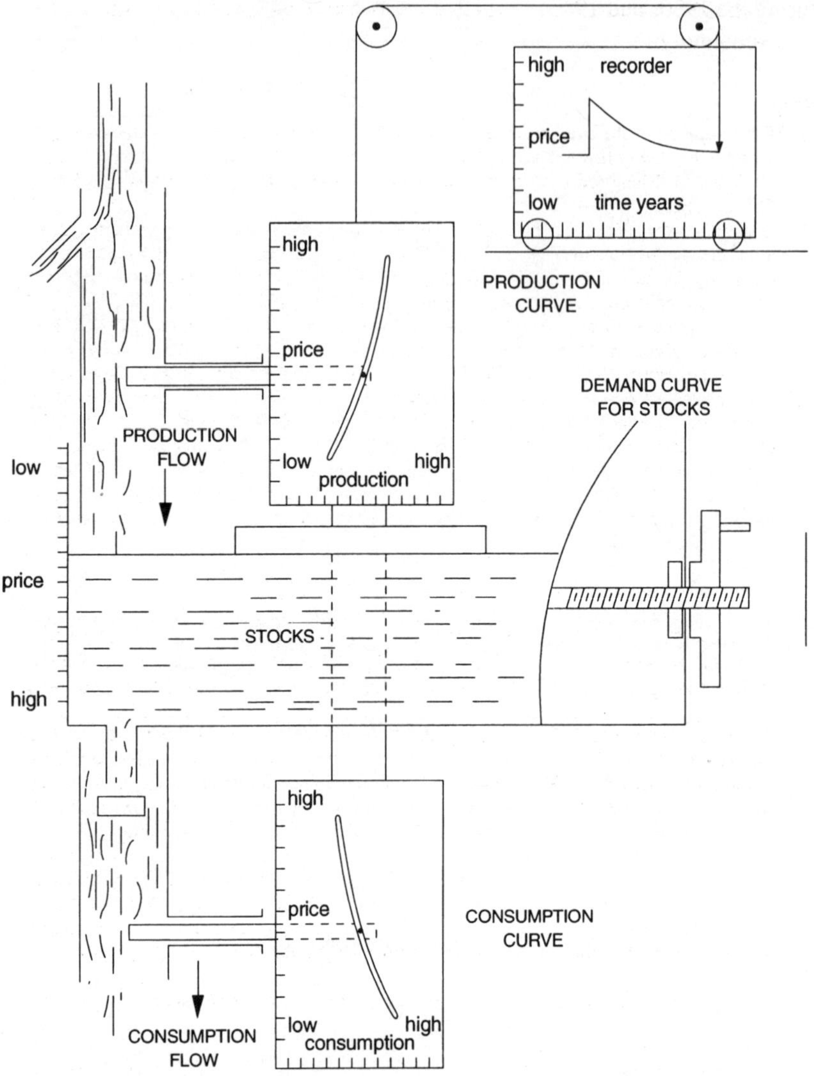

Source: PHILLIPS A.W., 'Mechanical Models in Economic Dynamics', *Economica*, vol. 17, 1950, p. 285.

Figure 3.2 Stocks, flows and price levels

So, if it undoubtedly deserves to be called Keynesian, the revolution which took place crystallized several shifts in thought which were in gestation during the 1930s and 1940s – which contributed to its success, but also added to its ambiguity.

Notes

1. For an *aperçu* of the ever-growing Keynesian literature, see the articles collected in J.C. Wood (ed.), *John Maynard Keynes: Critical Assessments*, 4 vols, London, Croom Helm, 1983 and M. Blaug (ed.), *John Maynard Keynes (1883–1946)*, 2 vols, Aldershot, Hants, Edward Elgar, 1991.
2. In particular, see *JMK*, XIV and XXIX. There follows a list of Keynes's important articles after the publication of *The General Theory*: 'The General Theory of Employment', *Quarterly Journal of Economics*, vol. 51, February 1937, 209–23; 'Alternative Theories of the Rate of Interest', *Economic Journal*, vol. 47, June 1937, 241–52; 'The "Ex Ante" Theory of the Rate of Interest', *Economic Journal*, vol. 47, December 1937, 663–9; 'Professor Pigou on Money Wages in Relation to Unemployment', *Economic Journal*, vol. 47, December 1937, 743–5; 'The Theory of the Rate of Interest', in A.D. Gayer (ed.), *The Lessons of Monetary Experience: Essays in Honour of Irving Fisher*, New York, Farrar and Rinehart; London, George Allen & Unwin, 145–52; 'Mr Keynes and "Finance"', *Economic Journal*, vol. 48, June 1938, 318–22; 'Mr Keynes's Consumption Function: Reply', *Quarterly Journal of Economics*, vol. 52, August 1938, 708–9 and November 1938, 160; 'Relative Movements of Real Wages and Output', *Economic Journal*, vol. 49, March 1939, 34–51; 'Professor Tinbergen's Method', *Economic Journal*, vol. 49, September 1939, 558–70.
3. 'The "Ex Ante" Theory of the Rate of Interest', 1937, in *JMK*, XIV, p. 216.
4. 'Relative Movements of Real Wages and Output', 1939.
5. See, for example, 'How to Avoid a Slump', *The Times*, 12 January 1937. Also see the collection of articles in *JMK*, XXVII. The comments that these texts inspired in Hutchison (1977 *Keynes versus the 'Keynesians'*) and A.H. Meltzer ('Keynes's *General Theory*: A Different Perspective', *Journal of Economic Literature*, vol. 19, 1981, 34–64) provoked lively controversies. See the debate with J. Crotty, P. Davidson, D. Patinkin and S. Weintraub in the March 1983 issue of the *Journal of Economic Literature*, as well as Meltzer, *Keynes's Monetary Theory: A Different Interpretation*, Cambridge, England, Cambridge University Press, 1988; D. Patinkin, 'On Different Interpretations of the *General Theory*', *Journal of Monetary Economics*, vol. 26, 1990, 205–43; Meltzer's answer to Patinkin in the same journal (vol. 29, 1992, 151–62); and Patinkin, 'Meltzer and Keynes', *Journal of Monetary Economics*, vol. 32, 1993, 347–56. For Hutchison, 'The doctrines of Keynes set out in his articles of 1937 obviously conflict very seriously with the Pseudo-Keynesian views regarding employment policy and its objective developed in the 1950s and 1960s' ([1977] 1981, p. 119). Adopting Joan Robinson's taxonomy, he even adds in the same text that Keynes was himself rather a bastard Keynesian (id., p. 123)!
6. See F. Fourquet, *Les Comptes de la puissance*, Paris, Ed. Recherches, 1980, pp. 28, 42, 47, 71.
7. See below, Chapter 4.
8. See below, Chapter 5
9. See below, Chapter 6.
10. Société des nations, *Le Passage de l'économie de guerre à l'économie de paix*, Geneva, 1943, pp. 17, 20.
11. The first report was governmental, but the second was the result of an independent enquiry by Beveridge, who was not considered as author of an official report on full employment.
12. *Full Employment in a Free Society*, London, George Allen & Unwin, 1944, p. 93.
13. Ibid., p. 23.
14. Ibid., p. 136.
15. Ibid., p. 190.

16. Among those signing were Paul H. Douglas, Frank H. Knight, Henry Schultz, Henry C. Simons and Jacob Viner. See J.R. Davis, *The New Economics and the Old Economists*, Ames, Iowa State University Press, 1971, pp. 12 ff. and 25 ff.
17. *Strategic Factors in Business Cycles*, New York, National Bureau of Economic Research, 1934; *Economics of Planning Public Works*, Washington, DC, US Government Printing Office, 1935. See Davis, op. cit., pp. 64 ff.
18. *Controlling Depressions*, New York, W.W. Norton, 1935. See Davis, op. cit., pp. 47 ff.
19. 'The Problem of Economic Instability', *American Economic Review*, vol. 40, 1950, 501–38.
20. The following collective work bears witness to their closeness and diversity: *Economic Policy in Our Time*, 3 vols, Amsterdam, North-Holland, 1964. This book includes contributions by E.S. Kirschen, J. Bénard, H. Besters, F. Blackaby, O. Eckstein, J. Faaland, F. Hartog, L. Morissens and E. Tosco.
21. Jean Monnet, first commissioner at the *Plan*, left this position in 1950 to head the European Coal and Steel Community. He was replaced by E. Hirsch, whom Pierre Massé would later succeed. These two were engineers by training. Cf. Pierre Bauchet, *La Planification française*, Paris, Seuil, 1962, p. 16. See also Gruson 1968; Pierre Massé, *Le Plan ou l'anti-hasard*, Paris, Gallimard, 1965.
22. See L. Erhard, *Deutsche Wirtschaftspolitik*, Düsseldorf, Econ-Verlag, 1962.
23. In 1959, the AFL-CIO published *Policies for Economic Growth* and the CED (Committee for Economic Development) *The Budget and Economic Growth*; in 1960, the Joint Economic Committee of Congress published *Employment, Growth and Price Levels*, the United States Chamber of Commerce *The Promise of Economic Growth*, and the National Planning Association *Long-Range Projections for Economic Growth*; see H.W. Arndt, *The Rise and Fall of Economic Growth*, University of Chicago Press [1978] 1984, p. 57.
24. In 1988, J. Tobin and M.L. Weidenbaum edited the first economic report prepared by the advisers to President Kennedy in 1961 and that, written 20 years later, by the advisers to President Reagan, under the significant title, *Two Revolutions in Economic Policy* (Tobin 1988). The following is a passage from President Kennedy's advisers' report: 'The unfinished business of economic policy includes (1) the achievement of full employment and sustained prosperity without inflation, (2) the acceleration of economic growth, (3) the extension of equality of opportunity, and (4) the restoration of balance of payments equilibrium. Economic policy thus confronts a demanding assignment, but one which can and will be met within the framework of a free economy' (pp. 93–4).
25. 'Keynes's Policies in Theory and Practice', in H.L. Wattel (ed.), *The Policy Consequences of John Maynard Keynes*, Armonk, New York, M.E. Sharpe, 1985, pp. 18–19.
26. *An Analysis of the Sources of War Finance and an Estimate of the National Income and Expenditure in 1938 and 1940*, Cmd 6261, London, HMSO.
27. In Holland, E. van Cleeff, National Bœkhouding, 'Prœve van een Jaaroverzicht Nederland, 1938', *De Economist*, Harlem, 1941; in France, L.A. Vincent, *L'Organisation dans l'entreprise et la nation*, Nancy, Société industrielle de l'Est, 1941.
28. As with planning, one of the characteristics of national accounting in France is the fact that it was a collective creation. Through diverse sections of the administration, contributions were made by J. Dumontier, R. Froment, P. Gavanier, J. Sérisé and S. Nora and, in the context of the Institut de sciences économiques appliquées (ISEA) – university research centre – F. Perroux, J. Marczewski and P. Uri. See J. Marczewski, *Comptabilité nationale*, Paris, Dalloz, 1965; A. Sauvy, 'Historique de la comptabilité nationale' and 'Les organisations internationales de comptabilité économique', *Economie et statistique*, 1970, no. 15 and 17; F. Fourquet 1980, op. cit.
29. OEEC, *A Simplified System of National Accounts*, Paris, 1950; OEEC, *Standardised System of National Accounts*, Paris, 1952.
30. Nations Unies, *Le Système de comptabilité nationale et tableaux connexes: Etudes méthodologiques*, série F, no. 2, New York, 1953.

4 Axiomatization, formalization, mathematicization

One scientific revolution in fact concealed another. While Keynes was preparing and publishing *The General Theory*, a radical change was beginning, the full effect of which would not be felt until much later: the mathematicization of the discipline. The use of mathematics in the area of economic thought was well established: in the seventeenth century, William Petty, Charles Davenant, Gregory King and others in England created what they called 'political arithmetick',[1] and made the first inroads in the area of national accounting. King is considered to be the author of the first quantitative estimation of a demand function. In 1738, mathematician Daniel Bernoulli formulated the hypothesis of the individual's diminishing marginal utility of wealth, illustrating it in a diagram showing, on the abscissa, gains in wealth and, on the ordinate, corresponding utilities.[2]

It was a philosopher, Augustin Cournot, who in 1838 published the first important work in mathematical economics, *Researches into the Mathematical Principles of the Theory of Wealth*.[3] This book, which first went unnoticed, is today recognized as an important step towards the formalization of economic theory. This evolution took off with the marginalist revolution, in particular under the impulse of the founder of general equilibrium theory, Léon Walras, who declared at the beginning of his *Elements of Pure Economics*: 'If the pure theory of economics or the theory of exchange and value in exchange, that is, the theory of social wealth considered by itself, is a physico-mathematical science like mechanics or hydrodynamics, then economists should not be afraid to use the methods and language of mathematics'.[4] Jevons, for his part, declared of the new science which he aimed to found that it 'must be a mathematical science in matter if not in language. ... The theory of economy, thus treated, presents a close analogy to the science of statical mechanics'.[5]

In spite of the enthusiasm of the architects of the marginalist revolution for mathematical economics, the discipline remained largely literary until the Second World War. Walras, who went into exile in Switzerland, was ignored in France and elsewhere. Marshall, who codified the new science in England, warned against the proliferation of mathematical formulation, which he confined to an appendix.[6] He preferred the analogy with biology rather than physics. It was in the 1930s that economists, principally European, and often with backgrounds in mathematics, physics or engineering,[7] prepared the transformation of the discipline.

The birth and development of econometrics[8]

It was under a certain amount of isolation that the founding fathers of econometrics worked at the beginning of the century, as much in the United States as in Europe. The word itself was not yet then in use, although it was to be found as early as 1910 under the signature of Pawel Ciompa.[9] The economist Henry L. Moore was one of the first systematically to use statistics to test economic relations empirically, for example the theory linking wages to marginal productivity of labour, and even the hypotheses linking business cycles to climatic variations, themselves linked to the movements of the planet Venus.[10] At the same time, several other economists, some of them forgotten nowadays, sought ways to formulate economic hypotheses in the form of mathematical models, to gather enough data and to estimate the models' parameters so as to evaluate the influence of independent variables.[11]

Better known economists, such as Irving Fisher and Wesley Clair Mitchell, also had an interest in mathematical economics and the use of statistics. As early as 1912, Fisher, Mitchell and Moore had attempted without success to set up a society devoted to the promotion of research in mathematical and quantitative economics. In 1917, the Harvard Committee for Economic Research was created. This organization founded in 1919 the *Review of Economic Statistics*, whose name was changed in 1948 to the *Review of Economics and Statistics*. In 1920, Mitchell and other economists who, like himself, were linked with the institutionalist current, set up the National Bureau of Economic Research which would become one of the principal institutions devoted to empirical research in the United States. According to the first article of a resolution adopted on 25 October 1926 and revised on 6 February 1933, the aim of the National Bureau of Economic Research was 'to ascertain and to present to the public important economic facts and their interpretation in a scientific and impartial manner'. Mitchell was director of research of the Bureau from its foundation until 1945, when he was succeeded by his collaborator, Arthur Burns.

It was an economist of European origin, Ragnar Frisch, first recipient of the Nobel Memorial Prize in Economics,[12] who played a determining role in the birth and organization of the new discipline he named 'econometrics'. Having already published, in Europe, works in mathematical economics, in particular on consumer theory, Frisch arrived in the United States in 1928. With Charles Roos he tried to persuade Irving Fisher to set up a society devoted to the unification of economics, mathematics and statistics. A foundational meeting of the Econometric Society was held in Cleveland on 29 December 1930. Chaired by Joseph Schumpeter, it brought together 12 Americans and four Europeans, who elected Irving Fisher as their first president. The first article of the constitution then adopted stipulates that: 'The Econometric Society is an international society for the advancement of economic theory in its relation to statistics and mathematics. ... Its main object shall be to promote studies that aim at a unification of the theoretical–quantitative and the empirical–quantitative approach to economic problems and that are penetrated by constructive and rigorous thinking similar to that which has come to dominate in the natural sciences.'[13] The first meeting of the new association was held in Lausanne the following year. In January 1933, there appeared the first issue of *Econometrica*, the Society's journal, with an editorial written by Ragnar Frisch, who would remain editor until 1954, and an introductory article by Joseph Schumpeter, discussing the origins of mathematical economics.[14] Here is how Frisch defines econometrics:

> Thus, econometrics is by no means the same as economic statistics. Nor is it identical with what we call general economic theory, although a considerable portion of this theory has a definitely quantitative character. Nor should econometrics be taken as synonymous with the application of mathematics to economics. Experience has shown that each of these three view-points, that of statistics, economic theory, and mathematics, is a necessary, but not by itself a sufficient, condition for a real understanding of the quantitative relations in modern economic life. It is the *unification* of all three that is powerful. And it is this unification that constitutes econometrics. ('Editorial', *Econometrica*, vol. 1, 1933, p. 2)

So it is the union of economic theory, mathematics and statistics which defines econometrics according to Frisch and the discipline's founders. Thus they were as much opposed to pure theoretical speculation as to the empirical inductivism which, in their view, characterized the works of institutionalist economists and, in particular, the founders and central figures of the National Bureau of Economic Research. Indeed, very sharp conflicts subsequently developed between econometricians and those espousing the research methods of the National Bureau of Economic Research. Through one of those strange coincidences of history, Gunnar Myrdal, who joined the institutionalist camp, was among the guests of Irving Fisher at a Sunday luncheon when they discussed the creation of the Econometric Society, conceived, among other things, as a strike against institutionalism, then very powerful in the United States.[15]

The year of the founding of *Econometrica* was also that of the publication of an important paper in which Frisch created the term 'macrodynamics' (Frisch 1933). Relying on a study published in Russian, in 1927, by the Conjuncture Institute of Moscow, under the signature of Eugen Slutzky,[16] Frisch constructed a mathematical model of the trade cycle, in which oscillations are caused by exogenous shocks. Also in 1933, Kalecki presented to the Econometric Society his model of the business cycle, the Polish version of which was published in the same year, shortened versions in French and English coming out in 1935. In *Econometrica*, in 1935, Tinbergen published an important survey on quantitative business cycle theory, in which he opposed the open and non-mathematical models of Keynes and Hayek to the closed and mathematical models developed by Frisch, Kalecki and himself. Tinbergen, joint Nobel laureate with Frisch, also played a major role in the progress of econometrics. In 1936, the very year Keynes's *General Theory* was released, he published the first global macroeconomic model of a national economy, that of his own country, the Netherlands.

At the behest of the League of Nations, Tinbergen then devoted himself to the empirical verification of business cycle theory, which resulted in the publication of a major work in two volumes (1939), the second of which contained the first macroeconomic model of the American economy. These two volumes were criticized by Keynes[17] and Friedman.[18] Keynes's critique is far better known than Friedman's, but it is interesting to note that they developed some similar themes. Both express much scepticism regarding the possibility of constructing mathematical models of business cycles and, in particular, of making precise macroeconomic predictions. Nonetheless, the scepticism shown by Keynes regarding the practice of econometrics did not prevent him from being part of *Econometrica*'s editorial committee and from sitting on the Council of the Econometric Society, of which he would be elected president in 1944. Furthermore, he encouraged the creation of a department of applied economics at Cambridge of which he was the first director. Stone succeeded him in this position and turned the department of applied economics into one of the principal centres of econometric research in postwar Britain.[19]

In the United States, it was a private institution, closely linked to the Econometric Society, that became the principal promoter of econometric research: the Cowles Commission for Research in Economics, founded in 1932 in Colorado Springs by Alfred Cowles.[20] The foundation of the commission followed a budget offer of $12,000 a year, proposed by Cowles to Fisher in his capacity as president of the Econometric Society, for the setting up of a research centre in econometrics. Initially met with suspicion, the offer was finally accepted. The Cowles Commission was established with the Econometric Society retaining the power to nominate its consultative council. The agreement also provided that Cowles, who became treasurer–secretary of the Society in 1937, would financially support the establishment of the journal, *Econometrica*. The statutes of the Commission stipulate that 'The particular purpose and business for which said corporation is formed is to educate and benefit its members and mankind, and to advance the scientific study and development ... of economic theory in its relation to mathematics and statistics.'[21] The dynamism of Cowles, first director of the Commission bearing his name,[22] led him to attract to Commission activities, in particular to its summer conferences, such names as R.G.D. Allen, Fisher, Frisch,

Hotelling, Marschak, Karl Menger,[23] Schumpeter, Abraham Wald and T. Yntema.[24] The Commission quickly began to publish its famous monographs, which, for 20 years bore as an epigraph Lord Kelvin's words, 'Science is measurement'. In 1939, the Commission moved to Chicago,[25] where, until 1955, it would be affiliated with the University of Chicago,[26] before settling at Yale and changing its name to the Cowles Foundation.

In 1942, Cowles persuaded Jacob Marschak to take over as director of the Commission. Gifted in drawing other theorists to work together, Marschak, who directed the Commission until 1948, attracted, among others, Kenneth Arrow, Trygve Haavelmo, George Katona, Lawrence Klein, Tjalling Koopmans, Oskar Lange, Don Patinkin and Herbert Simon.[27] Haavelmo, who had participated with Marschak in an econometric seminar in 1941 in New York, had started to circulate there a dissertation which advocated the use of a probability approach in economics, against the opinion of many economists, including Frisch. Haavelmo considered that probability theory was the basis of the statistical analysis which formed the methodological content of econometrics. The variables economics deals with are of a stochastic nature. Marschak and the other members of the Commission were quickly convinced of the richness and accuracy of the approach of Haavelmo, whose text was finally published in 1944. Some go so far as to characterize this development as a 'probabilistic revolution'.[28]

Also coming from physics, Marschak's successor as director of the Commission, Tjalling Koopmans, was one of the principal improvers and promoters of the new techniques. Among other things, he was editor of some of the famous books published by the Commission at the beginning of the 1950s (Koopmans 1950, 1951). A theorist, but also an administrator and publicist, he responded more severely than Tinbergen to Keynes (Koopmans 1941), before going on to cross swords, at the end of the 1940s, with the practitioners of what he called 'measurement without theory' at the National Bureau of Economic Research.[29] Marschak, moreover, had himself written, with Oskar Lange, a response to Keynes, which the latter did not accept for the *Economic Journal*.[30] Haavelmo joined the fray in 1943, and one may consider his 1944 text as, among other things, a reply to Keynes's objections to econometrics. The postwar period saw the birth and development of large macroeconomic models, of which Klein was the first architect. We will discuss this in the next chapter.

Games and war

One of the most famous mathematicians of our century, John von Neumann, played an essential role, as much in the construction of the theory of games, which eventually grew to play a major role in economic theory, as in the development of mathematical instruments central to the improvement of general equilibrium theory. In 1928, he demonstrated the minimax theorem, according to which any two-person zero-sum game, such as chess, with a finite number of strategies for each player, has a determinate solution. There is a rational strategy which grants a player the maximal advantage, whatever his opponent's choice of strategy. However, von Neumann did not invent game theory. In 1913, Zermelo had formulated a theorem which showed the game of chess to be strictly determined.[31] Zermelo's theorem was limited to a situation of perfect knowledge. The mathematician E. Borel developed some elements of the minimax before von Neumann.[32]

But it was von Neumann who perceived the richness of this approach. Once game theory is considered as applying to any situation in which the choices of agents affect each other, one notices that this can apply not only to chess and cards, but to politics, war, diplomacy and economics. And in a perspective, such as the neoclassical one, which sees the functioning of the economy as the result of the interaction between rational agents, game theory appears as a potentially fruitful tool. In any case, this was the conviction of von Neumann, as well as that of the economist Oskar Morgenstern, who criticized economists for using primitive mathematical techniques. In a book published in 1928, based on his doctoral thesis and devoted to economic prediction, Morgenstern himself had implicitly suggested the application of game theory to social behaviour. The two men began to collaborate in 1939, at Princeton. This collaboration resulted in a major book, *Theory of Games and Economic Behavior*, published in 1944, the same year as Haavelmo's *The Probability Approach in Econometrics*. Besides the development of game theory, it is a very rigorous axiomatization of economic theory that von Neumann and Morgenstern's book offers, with the aim of finding 'the mathematically complete principles which define "rational behavior" for the participants in a social economy, and to derive from them the general characteristics of that behavior' (von Neumann and Morgenstern [1944] 1953, p. 31). However, it was not economic theory but rather war which constituted game theory's first field of application and driving developmental force.

Moreover, several of those who contributed to the development of mathematical economics found themselves closely linked on the occasion of war.[33] As early as 1937, von Neumann himself had started to work for the American government on military issues. Present at Los Alamos, in the context of the development of the atomic bomb,[34] he had become, at the time of his premature death in 1957, one of the most important scientists in the United States. During the Second World War, the Research and Analysis Branch of the Office of Strategic Services (OSS), forerunner of the Central Intelligence Agency, was one of the privileged places of contact between men from diverse academic backgrounds. This agency was itself constituted on the model of analogous groups set up in Great Britain in the mid-1930s with the aim of using scientific and technological progress to reinforce the country's military capability: the Statistics Branch, run by F.A. Lindemann, later Lord Cherwell, employed, among others, Roy Harrod[35] and G.L.S. Shackle. As for the OSS, among the 50 or so economists it recruited, one might have found Moses Abramowitz, Sidney Alexander, Paul Baran, Abram Bergson, Carl Kaysen, Charles Kindleberger, Walt Rostow, William Salant and Paul Sweezy.[36] Another body closely linked to military research, in particular to air battles, the Statistical Research Group at Columbia, was run by Allen Wallis and Harold Hotelling, who recruited, among others, Milton Friedman, John Savage, George Stigler and Abraham Wald. At the end of the war, the Rand (Research and Development) Corporation was set up, a private research institution whose sole client in the beginning was the US Air Force. Armen Alchian was the first economist recruited by this institution, which ultimately supported, either directly or indirectly, the research of a great number of well known economists.

Systems analysis, activity analysis, game theory, operations research, linear programming: such were the research techniques, equally applicable to economic and to military activity, which stemmed from the activities of these institutions. Developed by Russian émigré, Wassily Leontief, input–output theory was also a powerful instrument developed and used in this context. At the same time, similar techniques were developed in the USSR by economists, such as Kantorovich and Novozilov, working for military production. In their textbook on linear programming, presented as 'one of the most important postwar developments in economic theory', Dorfman, Samuelson and Solow wrote that its creation was the fruit of 'the joint efforts of mathematicians, business and defense administrators, statisticians, and economists' (Samuelson 1958 with Dorfman and Solow, p. vii). This textbook, incidentally, was produced by the Rand Corporation. The first book devoted to the presentation of linear programming techniques, *Activity Analysis of Production and Allocation* (Koopmans 1951), was the fruit of a joint effort of the Rand Corporation and the Cowles Commission.

General equilibrium

These developments had an effect in return on pure economic theory, in particular on the theory of general equilibrium. It was the French economist Walras who suggested the classical formulation of what became the central nucleus of not only contemporary microeconomics, but also macroeconomics in its most recent developments. The model of general equilibrium aims at answering a question which has haunted economic thought at least since Smith's parable of the invisible hand: how can an order be born from the interactions within a multitude of agents, taking independent decisions, each agent being motivated by his own interest? The market system's efficiency, viability and optimality are at stake. The development is based on the hypothesis that society is composed of rational agents, that is to say consumers who maximize their utility and producers who act so as to maximize their profits. From Walras to the most recent formulations, it is here that the foundation of the neoclassical research programme lies. It is also, as we have seen, a basic element of game theory, so that it is not surprising that the two theoretical issues join in the postwar period.

It is a matter of determining the equilibrium prices and quantities of all commodities, given the agents' endowments and preferences, assuming furthermore that prices fluctuate in such a way as to balance supply and demand for each good, in a context of perfect competition where prices are given for each agent. The term 'general equilibrium', as opposed to the analysis in terms of partial equilibrium developed by Marshall, refers to the fact that it is considered that supply and demand for each good depends, not only on this good's price, but on all the other prices. Walras merely counted the number of equations and unknowns to assert, without proof, the existence of a general equilibrium. To simplify, one can say that the history of the general equilibrium theory since that date has consisted of trying to prove the existence of a general equilibrium, in which all prices are positive and, if possible, unique and stable.[37]

Following the efforts of G. Cassell,[38] H. Neisser,[39] K. Schlesinger,[40] H. von Stackelberg[41] and F. Zeuthen,[42] it was the mathematician Abraham Wald who gave, in two articles published in 1935 and 1936,[43] the first solution to the problem of the existence of a general equilibrium. His articles, mathematically very complex, went unnoticed. In 1932, John von Neumann, in a seminar at Princeton University, presented a model of economic growth (which was published in German in 1937 and in English in 1945–6 as 'A Model of General Economic Equilibrium'). This text contained a mathematical instrument that would serve to give the theory of general equilibrium its modern formulation. It is the fixed point theorem, itself linked to the minimax concept, and falling within the mathematical field of algebraic topology, which was proved in 1911 by the mathematician Brouwer and used in the field of physics, among others. Extended in 1941 by the mathematician S. Kakutani,[44] it serves as a basis as much for the improvement of game theory as for that of the theory of general equilibrium. In the first case, we are referring to the contribution of mathematician John Nash, in which, in a short note published in 1950,[45] he proves the existence of an equilibrium in the case of a game said to be 'non-cooperative', that is to say a game in which there is no communication or contracting among the players. Nash's non-cooperative equilibrium, in which each of the participants adopts the best strategy possible given the strategies of all the other participants, is one of the concepts most commonly found in contemporary economic literature.

Going beyond geometry and the differential and integral calculus, mainly used until then in mathematical economics, it was by drawing on topology and particularly the theory of convex sets that, more or less at the same time, Arrow and Debreu (1954) and McKenzie[46] proved the existence of a general equilibrium from a limited number of hypotheses relating to the rationality of consumers' and firms' behaviour. Debreu developed this study in a short monograph published by the Cowles Commission in 1959, meant to present 'an axiomatic analysis of economic equilibrium', according to the criteria of formalist rigour achieved in von Neumann and Morgenstern (1944). In comparison with Wald's model, beyond the reduction of the number of hypotheses relative to technologies and preferences, one of the achievements consists in presenting 'an integrated system of production and consumption which takes account of the circular flow of income' (Arrow and Debreu 1954, p. 266). Arrow and Debreu prove that 'if every individual has initially some positive quantity of every commodity available for sale, then a competitive equilibrium will exist' (ibid.): this is what they call the theorem of the existence of a competitive equilibrium. They consider that 'Descriptively, the view that the competitive model is a reasonably accurate description of reality, at least for certain purposes, presupposes that the equations describing the model are consistent with each other' (ibid.). However, neither stability nor uniqueness of this equilibrium are proved.

This model has important implications concerning 'the problems of normative or welfare economics' (ibid., p. 265). Independent of each other, Arrow (1951 'An Extension') and Debreu (1952) had already established the equivalence of general equilibrium and Pareto optimum. Thus the parable of the invisible hand received a rigorous mathematical proof, demonstrating the efficiency and optimality of competitive equilibrium. For the authors of this argument, there is no follow-up of a demonstration of the free market over planning: 'Foes of state intervention read in those two theorems [establishing the equivalence between competitive equilibrium and Pareto optimum] a mathematical demonstration of the unqualified superiority of market economies, while advocates of state intervention welcome the same theorems because the explicitness of their assumptions emphasizes discrepancies between the theoretic model and the economies that they observe' (Debreu [1986] 1987, p. 402). In fact, following Pareto and Barone, the demonstration that perfectly informed planning can also lead an economy to the optimum was also perfected.

Not only partisans of state intervention and those who reject the neoclassical approach, but more generally those economists distrustful of sophisticated mathematical instruments, have, on numerous occasions, criticized the lack of realism of the hypotheses essential to the construction of these models.[47] This distrust, of course, did not prevent the proliferation of a very rich literature, relying on Kakutani's theorem, among other things, to improve, develop and render more complex Walras's model of general equilibrium.[48] But the first to draw attention to the models' limits and to warn against drawing conclusions from them were the architects of these sophisticated constructions themselves. Debreu stressed the fact that the demonstration of the uniqueness and stability of the general equilibrium requires hypotheses that are far too restrictive.[49] In an important textbook on the theory of general equilibrium, more accessible to the average reader than the founder's works, Arrow and Hahn draw attention to the unrealistic nature of a theory which excludes, among other things, money and uncertainty, fundamental features of the contemporary economy: 'in a world with a past as well as a future in which contracts are made in terms of money, no equilibrium may exist' (Arrow and Hahn 1971, p. 361). There is, indeed, no money in Arrow–Debreu's model of general equilibrium, where all the transactions take place at the beginning of a given time interval. Neither is there asymmetrical information. It is difficult to integrate both the government and monopoly in the model. Hahn and several others have worked at enriching the theory of general equilibrium by trying to integrate into it some of these elements, as well as trying to make it dynamic.

Triumph and limits of mathematics

Econometrics constitutes a field of specialization in economics; and whilst, most of the time, academic programmes require attendance at classes in econometrics, one can be an economist without being an econometrician. Similarly, neither are all academic economists required to master the topological subtleties of modern general equilibrium theory. But today no student of economics can escape mathematicization. The professional economist can neither understand his colleagues nor read the academic journals without a minimal stock of mathematical knowledge.

This development also started in the 1930s, with the reformulation in mathematical language of all the sectors of the economic science. The theory of international trade, for example, lent itself to mathematical formulation, and business cycle theory, beginning in the early 1930s, became increasingly the object of mathematical treatment. At the same time, consumption theory and the theory of value were the object of formalizations, for example by Frisch, as early as 1928. Then, after the publication of *The General Theory*, it was Keynesian macroeconomics which was to be increasingly recast in a mathematical mould, in spite of the author's warnings against 'recent "mathematical" economics ... which allow the author to lose sight of the complexities and interdependencies of the real world in a maze of pretentious and unhelpful symbols' (Keynes, *GT*, p. 298).

Three authors, in particular, played a key role in this mathematical reformulation of the different domains of economic theory, which was to be integrated into textbooks. In Great Britain, John Hicks initiated the English-speaking world into the approach of Walras, whose founding work, *Eléments d'économie politique pure* was translated into English only in 1954. More generally, in various articles published in the 1930s, in particular the reformulation of the theory of value written with R.G.D. Allen (1934), but especially in his *Value and Capital* (1939), Hicks developed a great number of the analytical instruments which nowadays have become an integral part of orthodox economic theory, to such an extent indeed that their origin is no longer seen very clearly in Hicks – even more so given that their author gradually moved away from both the neoclassical tradition and mathematical economics.

Such is not the case of the economist Maurice Allais, who today remains convinced of the fecundity of the path which he opened in 1943, with the monumental book, *A la recherche d'une discipline économique*, which he wrote in relative isolation, with only Walras, Pareto and mathematics at his disposal. A physicist and an engineer, as much as an economist, Allais tried to reconstruct the entire science of economics on a basis similar to that of physics. His work, in which he demonstrated among others a theorem of equivalence analogous to Arrow and Debreu's demonstration of the equivalence between competitive equilibrium and Pareto optimum, was long to remain unknown.

The American economist Paul Samuelson was more favoured. He published in English, in the United States, and he invaded all the journals with articles mathematically reformulating almost all of the economic knowledge of the time. He wrote mainly in 1937 a doctoral thesis submitted in 1941, in which he tried to prove the existence in all fields of economic research of meaningful theorems, issuing for the most part from the hypothesis that 'the conditions of equilibrium are equivalent to the maximization (minimization) of some magnitude' (Samuelson 1947, p. 5). This thesis appeared in print in 1947 under the title *Foundations of Economic Analysis*; the war and the mathematical character of the manuscript contributing to the delay in its publication. Yet it played a significant role in the transformation of the discipline which would take place in the postwar period. This transformation was characterized not only by the creation of new mathematical economics journals (adding to *Econometrica*, *Review of Economic Studies* and *Review of Economics and Statistics*), such as *International Economic Review* (1960), *Journal of Economic Theory* (1969) and *Journal of Mathematical Economics* (1974), but also by the fact that, in journals such as the *American Economic Review*, the pages containing mathematical expressions went from less than 3 per cent of total pages in 1940 to 40 per cent in 1990 (Debreu 1991 *AER*, p. 1). Many think that economic science has simply provided itself with new tools. In fact, these mathematical tools, which have appeared *en masse* in economic theory and analysis, have changed the nature of this discipline.

The neoclassical synthesis (see next Chapter), of which Hicks was one of the initial architects, is probably the first indication of this change. Indeed, the neoclassical synthesis is largely the reformulation in a context of common formalization, which allowed the *rapprochement* of the Keynesian approach and that which Keynes himself had chosen to fight. The mathematical formalization led to the erasure of non-probabilistic uncertainty, a key element of Keynes's critique of classical theory. Such an exclusion permitted the restatement in terms of equilibrium of the principal elements of Keynesian analysis. More generally, the invasion of economic science by technique and mathematical language contributed to the fact that economics became more and more difficult to define in terms of its object. Of course, the object of study of economists has certainly changed since the birth of their discipline: wealth of the prince, then that of the nation (mercantilism), circulation of the net product (physiocrats), production and distribution of wealth (classical school), capitalist mode of production (Marx), real exchange economy (marginalists), monetary exchange economy (Wicksell) and monetary production economy (Keynes). These objects differ, but all concern the material conditions of the reproduction of human society. Formalized economic science of the postwar period took up more or less all of this inheritance, although it arguably transformed it into more abstract terms, while adding market equilibrium and optimization. Progressively, the object of formalized economic science broadened to encompass all behaviour of any agent in the situation of evaluating, deciding and acting.

The most disparate processes and projects were about to develop within what would continue to be called economic science. With the passage of time, it is possible to perceive the formation of two galaxies, one with an axiomatic predominance (where the diverse theoretical approaches are reconstructed, principally concerned with formal logical coherence), the other (based on different theoretical approaches) mainly devoted to the knowledge and interpretation of processes and observable phenomena. Consisting less and less in the uniqueness of the object studied, the unity of the whole from then on would reside in the sharing of common tools and language, both elements being increasingly mathematical.

Among the social sciences, economic science would subsequently distinguish itself by the development of its formalized methods, creating new distances and differentiation and provoking complex reactions of both fascination and repulsion. And all the more so since followers of this new formalized economics were, sometimes without much caution, about to apply their tools to fields traditionally dealt with by other disciplines: the analysis of family and fertility (G. Becker), of political ballots and bureaucracy (A. Downs) and criminality and judicial procedure (G. Tullock). R. Fogel went so far as to claim to replace the old 'traditional history', with a new 'scientific history', cliometrics. In a strong position because of practical successes (national accounting, economic policy, and planning) and formal capabilities (which the works on general equilibrium symbolize), economic science enjoys exceptional prestige. Its cohesion very largely comes about through procedures of reciprocal recognition, in which international associations, such as the Econometric Society and, more and more, the American Economic Association, with its annual conference and its publications, play a major role.

The third important mutation of the period was the shift of the geographic pole of economic science from Great Britain to the United States. This was where the most dynamic community of economists was formed, benefiting from an exceptional system of interrelations among worlds often separated in Europe: university, banking, business, and foundations and research institutions (the Cowles Foundation, Brookings Institution, National Science Foundation, National Bureau of Economic Research, among others). With an amazing ability to set the theoretical tone – to such an extent that one may have the feeling that there is a real management of the profession – the United States has shown itself adept at both absorbing conventional talent from other countries[50] and attracting dissidents, protesters and unconventional minds.

Notes

1. Here is the definition given of it by Davenant: 'By Political Arithmetick we mean the art of reasoning by figures upon things relating to government ... The art itself is undoubtedly very ancient' (*The Politics and Commercial Works of James Davenant*, edited by Sir Charles Whitworth, London, R. Horsfield 1771, I, p. 128, quoted by Schumpeter 1954, pp. 210–11).
2. 'Specimen Theoriae Novae de Mensura Sortis', *Papers of the Imperial Academy of Sciences in Petersburg*, vol. 5, 1738, 175–92; Engl. transl., 'Exposition of a New Theory on the Measurement of Risk', *Econometrica*, vol. 22, 1954, 23–36.
3. *Recherches sur les principes mathématiques de la théorie des richesses*, Paris, Hachette; Engl. transl., London, Macmillan, 1927.
4. *Elements of Pure Economics*, Homewood, Illinois, Richard D. Irwin; London, George Allen & Unwin, p. 71.
5. *The Theory of Political Economy*, Harmondsworth, Penguin, 1971 [1st edn, 1871], p. 44.
6. *Principles of Economics*, London, Macmillan, 1966 [1st edn, 1890], p. ix.
7. Such as Marschak, Kalecki, von Neumann, Frisch, Tinbergen, Georgescu-Roegen and Kantorovich. They were followed by Allais, Koopmans, Arrow, Debreu, Malinvaud, Domar and many others.
8. On this theme, see De Marchi and Gilbert 1989, Epstein 1987, Morgan 1990 and M.H. Pesaran,'Econometrics', *New Palgrave*, 1987, vol. 2, 8–22.
9. Pesaran, op. cit., p. 8.
10. See, among other works: 'The Statistical Complement of Pure Economics', *Quarterly Journal of Economics*, vol. 23, 1908, 1–33; *Laws of Wages*, New York, Macmillan, 1911; *Economic Cycles – Their Law and Cause*, New York, Macmillan, 1914; *Generating Economic Cycles*, New York, Macmillan, 1923. Jevons had already suggested a theory linking business cycles to the recurrence of sunspots ('The Solar Period and the Price of Corn', in *Investigations in Currency and Finance*, London, Macmillan, 1884, 194–205).
11. One might mention, among others, Paul Douglas, Mordecai Ezekiel, Marcel Lenoir,

Robert Lehfeldt, Warren Persons, Charles Roos, Henry Schultz, Elmar and Holbrook Working, Fred Waugh, Sewall Wright, George Yule. Details on these authors' contributions will be found in Epstein 1987, Morgan 1990 and Stigler 1954, among others.

12. He was its co-recipient with Jan Tinbergen, who would also play a significant part in this story.
13. Quoted in the editorial of the first issue of *Econometrica* (vol. 1, 1933, p. 1).
14. See C.F. Christ, 'The Founding of the Econometric Society and *Econometrica*', *Econometrica*, vol. 51, 1983, 3–6.
15. See Myrdal, 'Institutional Economics', *Journal of Economic Issues*, vol. 12, 1978, pp. 771–2.
16. Engl. transl.: 'The Summation of Random Causes as the Source of Cyclic Processes', *Econometrica*, vol. 5, 1937, 105–46.
17. *Economic Journal*, vol. 49, 1939, 306–18; see above, Chapter 1.
18. *American Economic Review*, vol. 30, 1940, 657–60.
19. On this subject, see Stone 1978 *Proceedings*.
20. Alfred Cowles, a member of a wealthy family involved in the publishing business, ran a stock market forecasting company in Colorado Springs. It was the failure of predictions made in the context of the 1929 crash which prompted him to discontinue his forecasting service in 1931 and devote himself to the study of the forces determining the fluctuations of stocks and shares and, more generally, to the study of business cycles. On the foundation and history of the Cowles Commission, see C.F. Christ, *Economic Theory and Measurement: A Twenty-Year Research Report, 1932–52*, Chicago, Cowles Commission for Research in Economics, 1952; C. Hildreth, *The Cowles Commission in Chicago, 1939–1955*, Berlin and New York, Springer-Verlag, 1986; E. Malinvaud, 'Econometric Methodology at the Cowles Commission: Rise and Maturity', *Econometric Theory*, vol. 4, 1988, 187–209.
21. Quoted by Malinvaud, op. cit., p. 188.
22. The first consultative council was made up of Frisch, Fisher, A. L. Bowley and Carl Snyder. In 1934, Charles F. Roos became research director.
23. Son of the Austrian School founder, Carl Menger.
24. It is interesting to note that the 1938 summer conference was devoted to the celebration of *Researches* by Cournot.
25. At the same time, the Econometric Society also moved its headquarters to Chicago.
26. It was in Chicago that very sharp tension developed between the researchers and teachers linked with the Cowles Commission and those attached to the National Bureau of Economic Research and, in the same manner, between those two groups and such individuals as Knight, who were resolutely hostile to any form of mathematical economics. On this subject, see in particular, Klein, Bodkin and Marwah 1991, and J. Lodewijks, 'Macroeconometric Models and the Methodology of Macroeconomics', *History of Economics Society Bulletin*, vol. 11, 1989, 33–58.
27. Other future Nobel Prize winners, such as Gerard Debreu and Franco Modigliani, were to join the Commission later.
28. On the probabilistic revolution in sciences, as much natural as social, which took place between 1830 and 1950, see L. Krüger, L. Daston and M. Heidelberger (eds), *The Probabilistic Revolution*, 2 vols, Cambridge, Massachusetts, MIT Press, 1987.
29. Such is the title that Koopmans actually gave to his long, very critical, review of Burns and Mitchell's book on the measure of business cycles (1946). R. Vining would reply, equally harshly, in the name of the Bureau's researchers, in 'Koopmans on the Choice of Variables to be Studied and of Methods of Measurement' (*Review of Economics and Statistics*, vol. 31, 1949, 77–86, followed by a reply by Koopmans, 86–91 and a rejoinder by Vining, 91–4).
30. See Morgan 1990, p. 128.
31. 'Über eine Anwendung der Mengenlehre auf die Theorie des Schachspiels', *Proceedings of the Fifth International Congress of Mathematicians*, vol. 2, 1913, 501–4.
32. See in particular E. Borel, 'Sur les jeux où interviennent le hasard et l'habileté des joueurs', in J. Hermann (ed.), *Éléments de la théorie des probabilités*, Paris, Librairie

scientifique, 1924, 204–24. It is to be noted that Borel published, that same year, a review of Keynes's *Treatise on Probability*: 'A propos d'un traité de probabilités', *Revue philosophique*, vol. 98, 1924, 321–6. On Borel, see Maurice Fréchet, 'Emile Borel, Initiator of the Theory of Psychological Games and its Application', *Econometrica*, vol. 21, 1953, 118–27.

33. On this question, see R. Leonard, 'War as a "Simple Economic Problem" – the Rise of an Economics of Defense', *History of Political Economy*, vol. 23, 1991, annual supplement, 261–83, from which we draw some of the following material. By the same author, see also 'Creating a Context for Game Theory', *History of Political Economy*, vol. 24, 1992, annual supplement, 29–76; and P. Mirowski, 'When Games Grow Deadly Serious: The Military Influence on the Evolution of Game Theory', *History of Political Economy*, vol. 23, 1991, annual supplement, 227–55. One may also consult the other texts gathered in these special editions, the first of which is devoted to economics and national security and the second to the history of game theory.
34. Einstein and von Neumann were colleagues, neighbours and friends at Princeton, which was, at one time, one of the most extraordinary concentrations of minds driven out of Europe by the rise of Nazism.
35. Who, moreover, wrote a biography of Lord Cherwell (Harrod 1959).
36. As we can see, the ideological range was very large: Franz Horkheimer and Herbert Marcuse were also part of it! (See Leonard, 'War as a Simple Economic Problem', op. cit., p. 264).
37. On this see Ingrao and Israel 1987; E.R. Weintraub, 'On the Existence of a Competitive Equilibrium; 1930–1954', *Journal of Economic Literature*, vol. 21, 1983, 1–39; id., *General Equilibrium Analysis*, Cambridge, England, Cambridge University Press, 1985.
38. *Theoretische Sozialökonomie*, Leipzig, C.F. Winter, 1918; Engl. transl., *The Theory of Social Economy*, New York, Harcourt Brace, 1932.
39. 'Lohnöhe und Beschäftigungsgrad im Marktgleichgewicht', *Weltwirtschaftliches Archiv*, vol. 36, 1932, 415–55.
40. 'Über die Produktionsgleichungen der ökonomischen Wertlehre', *Ergebnisse eines mathematischen Kolloquiums*, vol. 6, 1935, 10–11; Engl. transl. in W.J. Baumol and S.M. Goldfeld, *Precursors in Mathematical Economics: An Anthology*, London, London School of Economics and Political Science, 1968, 278–80.
41. 'Zwei kritische Bemerkungen zur Preistheorie Gustav Cassels', *Zeitschrift für Natinalökonomie*, vol. 4, 1933, 456–72.
42. 'Das Prinzip der Knappheit, technische Kombination und ökonomische Qualität', *Zeitschrift für Nationalökonomie*, vol. 4, 1932, 1–24.
43. 'Über die eindeutige positive Lösbarkeit der neuen Produktionsgleichungen', *Ergebnisse eines mathematischen Kolloquiums*, vol. 6, 1935, 12–20; Engl. transl., 'On the Unique Non-Negative Solvability of the New Production Equations, Part I', in Baumol and Goldfeld, op. cit., 281–8; 'Über die Produktionsgleichungen der ökonomischen Wertlehre', *Ergebnisse eines mathematischen Kolloquiums*, vol. 7, 1936, 1-6; Engl. transl., 'On the Production Equations of Economic Value Theory (Part II)' in Baumol and Goldfeld, op. cit., 289–93. For a less technical presentation see 'Über einige Gleichungssysteme der mathematischen Ökonomie', *Zeitschrift für Nationalökonomie*, vol. 7, 1936, 637–70; Engl. transl., 'On Some Systems of Equations of Mathematical Economics', *Econometrica*, vol. 19, 1951, 368–403.
44. 'A Generalization of Brouwer's Fixed Point Theorem', *Duke Mathematical Journal*, vol. 8, 1941, 457–9. Another important development of this theorem is due to Herbert E. Scarf, 'The Approximation of Fixed Points of a Continuous Mapping', *SIAM Journal of Applied Mathematics*, vol. 15, 1967, 1328–43.
45. 'Equilibrium Points in N-Person Games', *Proceedings of the National Academy of Science of the USA*, vol. 36, 1950, 48–9.
46. 'On Equilibrium in Graham's Model of World Trade and Other Competitive Systems', *Econometrica*, vol. 22, 1954, 147–61; see also id., 'On the Existence of General Equilibrium for a Competitive Market', *Econometrica*, vol. 27, 1959, 54–71.
47. Among the critiques of the theory of general equilibrium and its assumptions, one notes,

for example, those of the institutionalists (including Galbraith) and of the post-Keynesians, among the foremost of whose ranks we find Joan Robinson, as well as other 'unclassifiable' authors such as Georgescu-Roegen and Kornai.

48. One may find a detailed bibliography of these contributions in Debreu 1982.
49. See Debreu 1974. For a demonstration of the conditions for stability of the equilibrium, which with Walras took the form of the mechanism of '*tâtonnement*' with the auctioneer, one may consult K. Arrow and L. Hurwicz, 'On the Stability of the Competitive Equilibrium I', *Econometrica*, vol. 26, 1958, 522–52 and K. Arrow, J. Block and L. Hurwicz, 'On the Stability of the Competitive Equilibrium II', *Econometrica*, vol. 27, 1959, 82–109.
50. Among the authors studied in our dictionary, some were born of families which had emigrated to the United States at the beginning of the century: Arrow, Burns, Friedman, Stigler. In the same way, Nove, Singer and Hahn's families had emigrated to Great Britain. A good 20 economists emigrated to the United States: from Russia, Marschak in 1919 and Kuznets in 1921; at the beginning of the 1930s, from Germany, von Neumann and Katona (born in Budapest), Baran and Leontief (born in Russia), Hirschman and, from Austria, Machlup; in the second part of the 1930s, Domar (from Russia), Boulding (from Great Britain), Morgenstern (from Vienna), Modigliani (from Italy), Scitovsky and Fellner (from Hungary), Lerner (from Great Britain, but he was born in Bessarabiea); during the Second World War, Koopmans (from Holland) and Nurkse (from Estonia); and after the war, Georgescu-Roegen (from Romania, 1948), I. Adelman (born in Romania , emigrating from Israel in 1949), Debreu (from France, 1950), Coase (from Great Britain, 1951), Vanek (from Czechoslovakia, 1955), Balassa (from Hungary, 1956), Leijonhufvud (from Sweden, 1960–61). Moves in the opposite direction were seldom seen.

5 A new orthodoxy: the neoclassical synthesis

The path towards a reconciliation of some of the contributions of *The General Theory* with certain elements from the neoclassical tradition was left open by Keynes's ambiguities. John Hicks was one of the first to enter this arena, soon after the appearance of *The General Theory*. Then numerous works contributed to the development of a macroeconomics, within which the main economic relations put forward in Keynes's work were re-examined and reformulated. It was chiefly in this analytical context that a revised version of what would still be called Keynesianism – running the risk of a misunderstanding – would be taught to generations of students. In this context, the first large macroeconometric models, allowing the simulation of the functioning and dynamics of the principal industrialized economies, would be constructed, thanks to progress in the system of economic accounts, econometrics and computer science.

Macroeconomics reconceived in terms of equilibrium

Hicks cannot be accused of misreading *The General Theory*; in his account of the book, published in the June 1936 issue of *The Economic Journal*, he brought out the importance of taking expectations and disequilibrium into account. He reminded his readers that the discovery was not entirely new and that the Swedish economists, in particular Lindahl and Myrdal, had preceded Keynes by several years on the subject. But he asserted: 'From the standpoint of pure theory, the use of the method of expectations is perhaps the most revolutionary thing about this book' (Hicks 1936, p. 240).

The following year, in his article, published in *Econometrica*, 'Mr. Keynes and the "Classics": A Suggested Interpretation', Hicks no longer spoke of expectations. His aim, it is true, was different. First, it was to evaluate in what measure there is a real conflict between Keynes's theory and the classical theory, which he had explicitly attacked. In order to do this, he reduced the two theories to three equations: one for the demand for money M, the second for investment I_x considered as demand for capital, and the third taking investment as equal to saving S. Reformulated in this manner, the two theories hardly conflict any more.[1] With both the classical economists and Keynes, the three magnitudes are functions of either income, I, or interest rate, i, or both I and i. Hicks then suggests, being concerned with mathematical elegance, to take I and i as variables in the three equations, which gives:[2]

$$M = L(I, i) \quad I_x = C(I, i) \quad I_x = S(I, i)$$

This is then presented by Hicks as the nucleus of a 'Generalized General Theory'. This he turned into a graphic presentation in a diagram (Figure 5.1) with i on the ordinate and I on the abcissa, on which he drew (1) the *IS* curve: the locus of points where there is equality of I_x and S, for pairs (I, i), i representing here the 'investment interest rate' which is very close, according to Hicks, to Wicksell's natural rate; and (2) the *LL* curve: the locus of points where there is equilibrium in the money market for pairs (I, i), i here representing the 'monetary interest rate'.

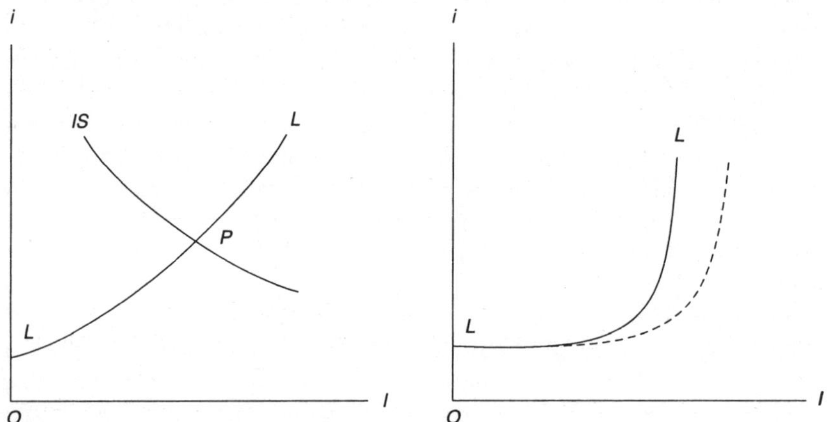

Source: HICKS, J.R., 'Mr. Keynes and the "Classics": A Suggested Interpretation', *Econometrica*, vol. 5, 1937, p. 153.

Figure 5.1 The ancestor of the IS–LM model, Hicks's IS–LL diagram

The point of intersection of the two curves, P, is the equilibrium point of the economy, since there is, at the same time, equilibrium in the money market, equality of investment and saving, and equality of the 'investment interest rate' and of the 'monetary interest rate'. It thus permits one to know the (I, i) pair corresponding to equilibrium. Arriving at this point, Hicks cannot help but remark: 'When generalized in this way, Mr. Keynes' theory begins to look very like Wicksell's' (ibid., p. 158).

Was Keynes seduced by the elegance of the argument? Or did he lack vigilance? The fact is that he did not refute this interpretation, which remained nonetheless quite incompatible with some of the main ideas of *The General Theory*, as we can see from his letter to Hicks of 31 March 1937,[3] about a preliminary version of Hicks's text, which had first been presented at a meeting of the Econometric Society in Oxford in September 1936. However, Keynes wrote to Hicks, concerning the concept of income appearing in his equations: 'The objection to this is that it overemphasises current income. In the case of the inducement to invest, expected income for the period of the investment is the relevant variable. This I have attempted to take account of in the definition of the marginal efficiency of capital' (*JMK*, XIV, p. 80). But, above all, he ended his letter by announcing an article dealing with the fundamental differences between his theory of interest and that of the Swedish, adding that he did not understand Hicks's position on this subject. In a letter dated 11 April 1937 (*JMK*, XIV, p. 83), he wrote that, in this article, he would have to accuse Hicks of being in the same camp as the Swedes. For Keynes, both the Swedish theory of interest and the classical one, which are linked, radically conflicted with his own monetary theory of interest, which he increasingly regarded as his major contribution. However, the *IS–LL* model makes no distinction between the classical and the Keynesian ideas of interest, which precisely leads to consider both models as specific cases of a more general model, which could be described as Hicksian.

It so happened that Hicks was then working on *Value and Capital* (1939),[4] with the aim of offering a global explanation of the functioning of modern economies. It was thus natural for him to look for a common context for the classical theory and *General Theory* macroeconomics relations. It remains true that his 1937 article would often be read as a particularly concise, synthetic, reformulation of the Keynesian theory. Standing back, it is clear that this is a particular reading, distinguished by its taking into consideration neither uncertainty nor expectations in face of an unknown and unknowable future, and the insertion of certain Keynesian functions, formalized in the context of an intellectual framework entirely different from that of *The General Theory*, since the principal aim is to define the conditions of equilibrium.

Besides Hicks, Harrod and Meade, at the September 1936 meeting of the Econometric Society, also presented very similar readings of *The General Theory*, which were published the following year in *Econometrica* and *The Review of Economic Studies*, respectively. In fact, they lack only the geometrical presentation which constitutes the originality and is certainly at the origin of Hicks's version's success. Hicks was also the only one to present Keynesian and the classical frameworks as specific cases of a more general model. Harrod compared a traditional theory of interest reduced to two equations to Keynes's theory translated into three equations, and wrote: 'In my judgement Mr. Keynes has not affected [*sic*] a revolution in fundamental economic theory but a re-adjustment and a shift of emphasis' (1937, p. 85).[5] Meade presented a model of the Keynesian system in eight equations. Before the publication of *The General Theory*, David Champernowne submitted to *The Review of Economic Studies* a paper whose aim was to model the difference between the classical and the Keynesian approaches, by constructing a system which includes both.[6]

Numerous other authors, despite often dissimilar concerns and perspectives, participated in this search for a systematized and simplified version of Keynes's theory. In 1937, in a review of *The General Theory* published by *The Economic Record*, W.B. Reddaway developed, independently of Champernowne, Harrod, Hicks and Meade, an analysis very similar to that which underlies the *IS–LL* model.[7] The same year, Nicholas Kaldor, who would later assert himself as one of the principal theorists of the post-Keynesian current, was the first to apply the *IS–LL* diagram in a critique of the article in which Pigou enunciates the existence of the effect that would subsequently bear his name.[8] In 1938, in an article based on the intuition that the traditional and the Keynes theories are both specific cases of a more general theory, O. Lange, in turn, used a diagram of the *IS–LL* type, as well as others suggestive of the forthcoming '45° diagram'.[9] He was one of few authors to construct his model using the wage units advocated by Keynes in *The General Theory*. Author of a review of *The General Theory* published in 1936, Abba Lerner soon became one the most passionate propagators of the *IS–LL* geometry,[10] thus playing an important part in the popularization of Keynesianism in the United States.

In 1944, Franco Modigliani published, in *Econometrica*, an article, initiated in a doctoral thesis written under the supervision of Marschak, which had an influence on the formation of the neoclassical synthesis as important as that of Hicks's article, published in the same journal seven years earlier. Several years later, Modigliani recalled that one of his principal research objectives was 'integrating the main building blocks of the *General theory* with the more traditional and established methodology of economics that rests on the basic postulate of rational maximizing behavior on the part of economic agents' (Modigliani 1980, p. xi). In his article he presented the Keynesian system in such a manner as to render possible its comparison with both a 'basic classical' system and a 'generalized classical' system, each being described through 12 equations, and in a form which made their empirical verification easy. He used a diagram of the *IS–LL* type (pp. 58–9) and showed that the hypothesis of wage stickiness was essential to explain underemployment equilibrium. He became interested in the problem of the dichotomy between real and monetary sectors, a theme he would deal with again in another article in which, in 1963, he made his own 1944 model more complex, describing the Keynesian system through 14 equations.

Modigliani's model had a significant influence on those building macroeconometric models. Among them, L. Klein himself contributed to the development of the Keynesian model, in, *inter alia*, a 1947 article in *The Journal of Political Economy*, and in his book published the same year, entitled *The Keynesian Revolution* and stemming from his doctoral thesis. In the former, translating them into equations, he compared the classical, Keynesian and – unusual at the time – Marxist systems. In the fifth chapter of his book, he gave a simplified version, in eight fundamental relations, of Keynes's system and analysed its interdependencies with the help of several diagrams, among which one of the *IS–LL* type (p. 88). The year Klein's book was released, the *Foundations of Economic Analysis* was published, in which Samuelson also proposed a mathematical presentation of *The General Theory*, along the same lines as Hicks, Lange and Meade.

The *IS–LL* diagram was to be the object of new developments and of a more systematic presentation by A. Hansen, in particular in two significant books published in 1949 (especially Chapter 5) and in 1953 (Chapter 7) which played a determining role in the popularization of this approach. The second, *A Guide to Keynes*, although written essentially in mathematical terms, is at the same time very accessible and, as an interpretation of *The General Theory*, ultimately imposed itself as a possible substitute for reading Keynes's book. Like his predecessors, Hansen attempted to reconcile Keynes and his adversaries, such as Pigou, Robertson or the Swedes. He was certainly one of the first to distinguish Keynes's economic theory from Keynesian economic theory, emphasizing, for example, the fact that 'considering the Keynesian system as a whole without concentrating too narrowly on certain passages in the *General Theory* there is much more agreement between Robertson and Keynes than appears on the surface' (Hansen 1949, p. 81). In *A Guide to Keynes*, to obtain the *IS* curve, Hansen combined Keynes's investment demand function with the neoclassical loanable funds theory. He obtained the *LL* curve by bringing together the supply of money with a family of money demand curves for different levels of wages: he thus constructed the curve of the points where there is equality of supply and demand of money for (Y, i) pairs. (Hansen chose the more usual symbol Y for income and I for investment.) He called this curve *LM*,[11] and it was henceforth the term *IS–LM* which was used to describe the model initially presented by Hicks. The *IS–LM* model, progressively systematized,[12] constituted the principal framework for the teaching[13] and development of Keynesian macroeconomics in the 1950s and 1960s, in the version of the neoclassical synthesis,[14] and in the construction of econometric models.

In the same way that, for microeconomics, the supply and demand curves illustrate the analysis of prices and quantities equilibrium in markets, for macroeconomics, *IS–LM* symbolizes global quantity equilibrium; more precisely, it permits one to determine the income and interest levels for which equilibrium is achieved in both goods and money markets. Whereas Keynes's functions and analyses were intended to explain the dysfunctions of economic systems, and particularly the persistence of underemployment, the *IS–*

LM diagram enables economists to find their favoured point of reference: equilibrium.

Of course, it was criticized as being non-Keynesian, notably by Weintraub (1961), Clower (1963) and Leijonhufvud (1968). Hicks himself expressed scepticism, as he moved away, in the postwar period, from the new orthodoxy and became increasingly critical in face of a mathematical economics which simplifies reality by ignoring time and uncertainty. Thus, of the diagram he had created and which had already been used to initiate innumerable students into Keynesian theory, he wrote that it 'reduces the *General Theory* to equilibrium economics; it is not really *in* time' (1976, p. 141). In 1981, he engaged in self-criticism in the *Journal of Post Keynesian Economics*, the organ of a school of thought which continued to attack the debased Keynesianism symbolized by the *IS–LM* model, underlining the fact that this model was far from containing all the contributions provided by *The General Theory*. Nonetheless, for generations of students and therefore of economists, there took place a clear association between *IS–LM*, macroeconomics and Keynesianism.

At the same time as the *IS–LM* model, with its clearly distinct real and monetary sectors, was adopted as the favoured analytic framework, there occurred a renewed separation of works devoted to real equilibria and those dealing with monetary phenomena. Despite their relative abundance, the latter contributed to the creation of neither a set of hypotheses, a definite analytical approach, nor a dominant vision. After debates on the question of the national debt, the Radcliffe Report (1959) in Great Britain and the Report of the Budget and Credit Commission of the Committee for Economic Development (1961) in the United States dealt mainly with institutions and instruments of monetary policy.[15] In the theoretical field, several authors, including W. Baumol (1952 *QJE*), R. Kahn,[16] and J. Tobin (1955, 1958, 1961) integrated the theory of the demand for money in an analysis enlarged to include assets of different types.

D. Patinkin's works (1948, 1949, 1956), for their part, constitute an effort to integrate monetary theory and 'real' theory. Moreover, from his first published text, Patinkin proved to be very critical regarding what he called the classical dichotomy, found in the models of the *IS–LM* type, which he criticized for, *inter alia*, their absence of satisfactory microeconomic foundations. Patinkin's works were themselves the object of very divergent interpretations, his contribution appearing to some as directly linked to *The General Theory*, to others as misrepresenting its central message, and to still others as the accomplishment of the neoclassical synthesis. His 1956 book deals successively with the microeconomic approach, particularly with the real balance effect, and the macroeconomic approach, searching, in a Keynesian framework and with neoclassical behavioural hypotheses, the conditions of money neutrality.[17] The same year, Milton Friedman published his modern restatement of the quantity theory of money (Friedman 1956).

The fact that the works devoted to real economic flows and their interrelations and those devoted to monetary phenomena have, on the whole, been separated, with the former being predominant relative to the latter, led to a paradox. While Keynes's project, with *The General Theory*, was to construct a monetary theory of production, Keynesianism of the 1950s and 1960s appeared to neglect money; and it was in a complex reaction simultaneously against Keynes, Keynesian economic policies and this non-monetary Keynesianism that monetarism affirmed itself from the end of the 1960s with the simple idea that 'money matters'.[18] Keynesianism must indeed have been a distortion of Keynes if it had become possible to counter it with the radical critique that money really mattered!

Reappraisal of the principal Keynesian functions

The Keynesian functions lent themselves to statistical testing, to critique and to new developments in the 1940s and 1950s by economists mainly trained in the neoclassical tradition. Whether it concerned the consumption function, the determinants of investment or the unemployment–inflation trade-off, there was a profusion of research, publications, debates and, at times, conflicts. Standing back, what emerges from it, beyond revisions and additions, is a certain denaturation of the founding intuition or intention of Keynes.

This effect was particularly clear in the case of the consumption function. Keynes's position was not overly sophisticated: a stable relationship between consumption and income, measured by the propensity to consume; the importance of this propensity for determining the level of activity through the multiplier effect; a decrease of the propensity to consume as income rises, which justifies a fiscal policy aiming at reducing inequality. J. Duesenberry was among the first to try to test statistically, using time series, the link between income and consumption; his observations did not confirm the Keynesian hypothesis, either in the cycle or in the trend. He then suggested a modified function, in which he included not only current available income, but also the highest income obtained in the past (Duesenberry 1948). He took up this hypothesis, still for the analysis of time series, in his 1949 book, and completed it, for the interpretation of results dealing with family budgets in a given time period, with another, that the share of income saved is a function, not of current income but of the relative family position in the scale of incomes.

Modigliani went further in his revision of the Keynesian consumption function, as much in his 1954 study, published with R. Brumberg, as in his 1963 article, written in collaboration with A. Ando. In the 1954 study, Modigliani and Brumberg again started off from the theory of consumer's choice and the individual consumption function. Their aim was not only to explain the results observed in the surveys of family budgets, but also to bridge the gap between this type of investigation and those dealing with time series in such a way as to obtain a coherent explanation. They arrived at the idea that the proportion of income saved was essentially independent of income, but explained by the choices made at different phases of one's life cycle. No hostility towards Keynes marked their work; on the contrary, they wrote:

> The results of our labor basically confirm the propositions put forward by Keynes in *The General Theory*. At the same time, we take some satisfaction in having been able to tie this aspect of his analysis into the mainstream of economic theory. ...
>
> We may, nonetheless, point out, as an example, that our new understanding of the determinants of saving behavior casts some doubts on the effectiveness of a policy of income redistribution for the purpose of reducing the average propensity to save. (Modigliani 1954, pp. 430–31)

This quotation, combining tribute to Keynes with doubts and concern about how to integrate his theory into the mainstream, are characteristic of the period. Ando and Modigliani placed the life-cycle hypothesis at the heart of their 1963 article. Its point of departure was the article published nine years earlier with Brumberg. Taking into account three variables – the period's current income, the total net worth transmitted from the former period and the expected future annual average income – they derived individual consumption functions which they aggregated according to age group, from which they deducted the global consumption function. They thus carried on with their effort to bridge the gap between the analysis of individual behaviour and the work done on aggregate quantities. And they reached empirical results which, to them, appeared to corroborate those of Duesenberry, Modigliani and Modigliani–Brumberg: if the Keynesian function is modified, it is not fundamentally called into question.

Such was not the case with the book published by Milton Friedman in 1957. Straight away, Keynes, *The General Theory* and the key role played in it by the consumption function became targets. Friedman underlined the fact that several empirical analyses invalidated the ideas put forward by Keynes on the determinants of consumption. He was not satisfied by the studies mentioned above and went even further:

> The doubts about the adequacy of the Keynesian consumption function raised by the empirical evidence were reinforced by the theoretical controversy about Keynes's proposition that there is no automatic force in a monetary economy to assure the existence of a full-employment equilibrium position. (Friedman 1957, p. 5)

Starting again from the pure theory of consumption, putting forward the 'permanent income hypothesis', supported by empirical research and statistical tests, he set up the elements of a new theory of the consumption function. The latter breaks away from Keynes's theory less because of the permanent income hypothesis than by taking into account, in the function itself, such elements as the interest rate, the wealth–income ratio and other factors likely to explain the choice by consumption units between current consumption and the accumulation of assets. With this book, it is no longer a question of verifying or improving Keynes's contribution. We have now reached an era of calling it into question.[19]

The works on the investment function did not result in such marked revision. Here one notes principally the efforts of, on the one hand, E. Kuh,[20] R. Eisner (1967) and D. Jorgenson and C. Siebert (1968), to improve knowledge of firm behaviour and, on the other, R. Eisner (1962, 1965), D. Jorgenson (1963), M.K. Evans[21] and D. Jorgenson and J.A. Stephenson (1967), to refine the aggregate investment function, particularly by taking into consideration a more diversified range of explanatory variables: level or variation of sales, rate of capacity utilization, price of investment goods, rate of output, level or variation of profits and the tax structure. T. Haavelmo (1960) questioned the link between investment and interest rate. J. Tobin, for his part, tried to explain investment patterns through the relations between financial and real sectors of economy. His famous index, 'Tobin *q*', the relationship between the market evaluation of an asset and its real cost of replacement, determined the rate of investment (1968 *AER*, 1969).

The invention of the Phillips curve

The analysis of the wage rate–unemployment relationship constituted another major question. In a sense, Keynes's position was clear. All of *The General Theory* might appear as the refutation of the explanation of unemployment through the high levels of the wage rate, and as the demonstration that wage reduction would not reduce massive unemployment. But Keynes's position was not entirely unambiguous. He was well aware of the fact that, as full employment drew near, the rise in wages, nominal or real, could contribute to the increase of prices, to inflation.[22] Of course, this was not the problem of the 1930s. It became the problem of the 1940s and 1950s and a key question for those who recommended or implemented the policies of full employment, as for those who called them into question.

Very early, some of those close to Keynes, such as J. Robinson,[23] as well as other authors, such as Fellner (1946), Patinkin (1948), Lerner (1951) and Friedman (1951), were concerned about the subject. However, the debate was rather muted, because it was difficult just after the war and about 20 years after the Great Depression, not to assert one's attachment to full employement.

It was in December 1959 that P. Samuelson and R. Solow set the cat among the pigeons. At the seventy-second annual meeting of the American Economic Association, they presented their paper, 'Analytical Aspects of Anti-Inflation Policy', published in the May 1960 issue of *The American Economic Review*, in a section devoted to the question of the maintenance of a stable price level. After formulating the problem of the best possible way to fight inflation and examining the different existing positions – quantity theory of money, demand–pull inflation *à la* Keynes, cost–push inflation – they put forward the Phillips diagram linking unemployment and wages variation.

A year and a half earlier, Phillips had published, in *Economica*, an article on this matter, based on statistics from the United Kingdom covering the 1861–1957 period (Phillips 1958). In it, he was attempting 'to see whether statistical evidence supports the hypothesis that the rate of change of money wage rates in the United Kingdom can be explained by the level of unemployment and the rate of change of unemployment' (p. 284). Several diagrams covering the 1861–1913 (Figure 5.2), 1913–48 and 1948–57 periods suggested the association of low increases of the money wage rate (as well as decreases until 1932) with situations of high unemployment; and noticeable increases of the money wage rate with situations of low unemployment.

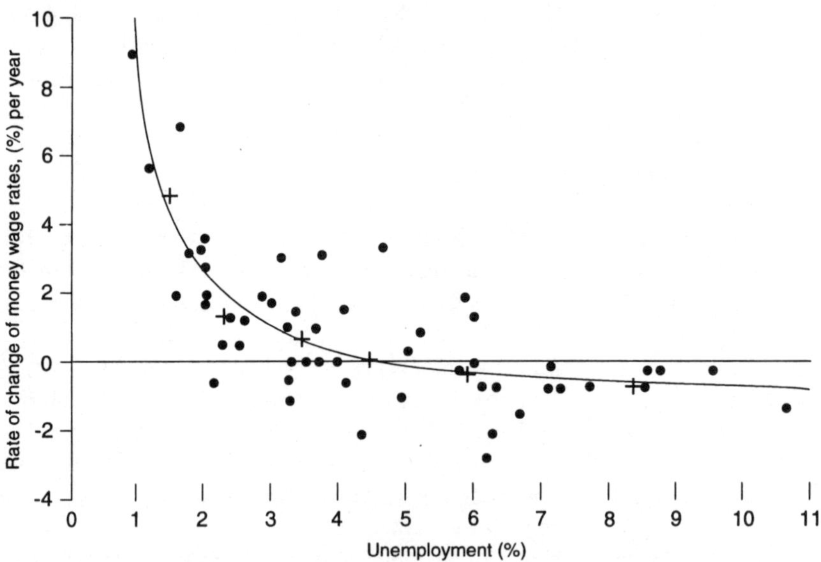

Source: PHILLIPS, A.W., 'The Relation Between Unemployment and the Rate of Change of Money Wage Rates in the United Kingdom, 1861–1957', *Economica*, vol. 25, 1958, p. 285.

Figure 5.2 The Phillips curve

Thus Phillips was answering positively the question he had formulated at the beginning of the article; he estimated at 5.5 per cent the unemployment rate likely to ensure the stability of the wage rate. But he ended with a wise warning: 'These conclusions are of course tentative. There is need for much more detailed research into the relations between unemployment, wage rates, prices and productivity' (p. 299).

After expounding the results arrived at by Phillips, Samuelson and Solow presented, following his model, a diagram (Figure 5.3) concerning the United States for the 1900–45 and 1945–58 periods: the cloud of points is rather scattered and of little significance. Our authors then started again from the curve established by Phillips, modifying it in a double way: on the one hand,

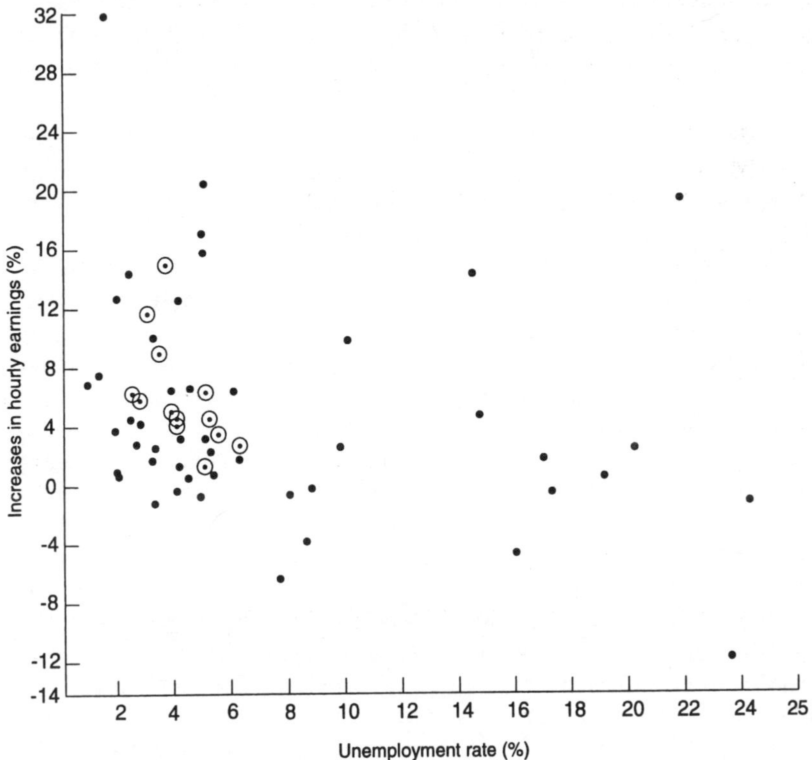

Note: The circled points are for recent years.

Source: SAMUELSON, P.A. and SOLOW, R.M., 'Analytical Aspects of Anti-Inflation Policy', *American Economic Review*, vol. 50, 1960, *Papers and Proceedings*, p. 188.

Figure 5.3 Phillips scatter diagram for US

they replaced the variation of wage rate with the the annual rise in prices; on the other, they modified the nature of the diagram, converted it into a 'diagram showing the differents levels of unemployment that would be "needed" for each degree of price level change' (1960, p. 192).

The diagram may thus be read in two different ways:

> 1. In order to have wages increase at no more than the 2½ per cent per annum characteristic of our productivity growth, the American economy would seem on the basis of twentieth-century and postwar experience to have to undergo something like 5 to 6 per cent of the civilian labor force's being unemployed. That much unemployment would appear to be the cost of price stability in the years immediately ahead.
> 2. In order to achieve the nonperfectionist's goal of high enough output to give us no more than 3 per cent unemployment, the price index might have to rise by as much as 4 to 5 per cent per year. That much price rise would seem to be the necessary cost of high employment and production in the years immediately ahead. (Samuelson and Solow 1960, p. 192)

The modified Phillips curve, because it filled a gap in the *IS–LM* model, entered the arsenal of 1960s Keynesian macroeconomics. Apart from Samuelson and Solow's paper, the article published the same year by R. Lipsey played an important role in the popularization of the Phillips curve. Lipsey attempted, in particular, to give theoretical microeconomic foundations to a relationship whose existence Phillips had merely observed without really explaining it. It must be emphasized that here, as elsewhere, entirely new ideas are very rare. As early as 1926, Irving Fisher published an article entitled 'A Statistical Relation between Unemployment and Price Changes',[24] which makes him an important precursor of Phillips.

Where Keynes asserted the choice, both ethical and political, of fighting massive unemployment, and looked for a way of acting in this sense on the economic system, the economists using Keynesianism as their authority introduced 'Phillips relations' in their analyses and models, as instruments permitting us to choose between unemployment and inflation, considered as two alternative ills, or to choose the least noxious inflation–unemployment pair. It is not surprising that this vision, according to which the price to be paid in inflation for the realization of full employment can be known, was criticized by the supporters of a more radical interpretation of Keynes's vision, such as Weintraub,[25] and more generally by the economists of the post-Keynesian school of thought.[26] Paradoxically, it was with the 'expectations augmented' Phillips curve that monetarists and new classical economists attacked the Keynesianism of the neoclassical synthesis, developing in particular the concept of the natural rate of unemployment. To Friedman, who would first affirm that, in the long run, the Phillips curve is vertical, if not even of positive slope, Lucas and his disciples retorted that it is positive even in the short run. The true trademark of the Keynesians resistant to monetarism, and to the new classical macroeconomics, was their persistent faith in a Phillips curve of negative slope.[27]

The development of the large macroeconomic models

With the background of progress in econometrics, the mathematicization of economics and controversies about how to treat data, especially between researchers associated with the National Bureau of Economic Research and those of the Cowles Commission,[28] the macroeconomics of the neoclassical synthesis yielded a context where the revised, corrected and completed Keynesian functions constituted the basic relations; the development of national accounting and the statistical apparatus provided the material; the computers, increasingly powerful, were the instruments.

It was, as we have also mentioned, L. Klein who played a major role in the development of the macroeconometric models. As early as 1947 (*Econometrica*), he understood the importance of these models for economic policies. His first model, developed from 1946, was estimated in 1953 (presented in a book published with Goldberger in 1955); it was used as a prototype for the Wharton model, on which he worked with M.K. Evans. This model, which in 1983 had 1600 equations, was, in 1953, based on 12 equations. Klein also worked with D.B. Suits in relation with the University of Michigan Research Seminar of Quantitative Economics on the Michigan Model, set up in 1950. At the same time, further related efforts were associated with the Cowles Commission, as well as with the Chase Econometrics Model, on which M.K. Evans worked, and the Data Resources Inc. Model, led by O. Eckstein from Harvard and J. Duesenberry. Progressively, the macroeconometric models left the administrative and academic worlds. They elicited the increased interest of banks, financial organizations and big firms: constructing them and making them work also became a new branch of activity.

The end of the 1950s ushered in the era of the great models. Thus the Brookings SSRC (Social Science Research Council) Model was set up, beginning in 1959. It was coordinated by L. Klein and J. Duesenberry. Numerous specialists participated: D. Jorgenson and R. Eisner for the investment equations, S. Maisel and D.B. Suits for consumption, E. Kuh for the distribution of income and employment, C.L. Schultze for prices and wages, F. de Leeuw for the financial sector;[29] the model, functioning with six sectors and 100 equations, was progressively developed, to reach 32 sectors and more than 350 equations. For the first time, it integrated an input–output trade table and sought to take into account financial flows. Similarly, the MPS Model (MIT-Penn-Social Science Research Council) was developed, beginning in 1962, with F. Modigliani from MIT and A. Ando from the University of Pennsylvania participating.

In the 1960s, most of the large models referred to a structure of the *IS–LM* type, with equations estimated or inspired by other studies, in particular by the work of Modigliani–Brumberg and Ando–Modigliani on consumption, Jorgensen on investment and de Leeuw on the financial markets. They thus constituted the outcome in macroeconomics of the neoclassical synthesis which indisputably prevailed in the community of economists of this period. They became the essential instruments, not only for the definition and the evaluation of economic policies, but more broadly for the knowledge of the economy and of economic perspectives, which all sectors of activity henceforth needed.

The practice of econometrics gave rise to acrimonious debate in the 1970s and 1980s, linked to the controversy between Keynesianism, monetarism and new classical macroeconomics. Friedman criticized the Keynesian macroeconometric models for, among other things, their size and their complexity, and he advocated the return to simple, even naïve models, of which, according to him, Keynes himself was a follower. In his 1976 critique, Lucas, for his part, criticized traditional econometrics for not taking into account the fact that the parameters of the models were changed by the economic policies put forward to influence the evolution of such variables as the unemployment rate.

Thus, in a certain manner, Keynesianism triumphed once more. But not Keynes, in any case not the Keynes who was trying to break with classical tradition. In the increasingly sophisticated and powerful equipment of computerized models, instruments and formal relations were the sole survivors. This Keynesianism is usually labelled 'the neoclassical synthesis'. Is this term not deceptive? Was there a synthesis between the strong elements of classical theory and the significant contributions of Keynes? Certainly not. Rather, there was a bringing closer, of a syncretic type, of elements – classical and Keynesian – compatible or so rendered, and an insertion of these elements in formalized frameworks, theoretical and econometric models.

However, what would henceforth be called neoclassical synthesis became the new orthodoxy, which dominated economic thought for much of the postwar period. Orthodoxy is defined in reference to a dogma considered to be a truth; we have presented the content of this dogma. But it also exists as a structured social force. In the field which concerns us, it first includes education: the textbooks exude this orthodoxy which constitutes the content of teaching at all levels; the necessity for the students to conform to the mould ensures the dogma's durability. Journals are also a powerful medium of orthodoxy propagation: more and more, the competence and reputation of an economist is measured by the number of published articles, which become the basis for hiring, promotion and obtaining research contracts and grants. In short, a powerful system is set up which discourages dissent, according to a mechanism which was described by, among others, Kuhn in his book on scientific revolutions.[30]

Nonetheless, dissension still exists. Heterodoxies never die. We will notice this in the following chapter, as we examine, in particular, the opposition to the neoclassical synthesis led by post-Keynesians, who claim to be the true heirs to Keynes's radicalism. For its part, orthodoxy, like any orthodoxy, is itself in evolution. It formed and consolidated in the 1940s and 1950s, to triumph in the 1960s under the label of 'new economics'.[31] The new economic problems of the 1970s started to shake several certainties. In addition to the questioning from the left, criticism of interventionism on the right never ceased. It was found, for example, in the Mont-Pèlerin Society organized by Friedrich Hayek. In the 1960s, Milton Friedman established himself as the leader of the opposition to Keynesianism. What he himself called the monetarist counter-revolution aimed at no less than the reversal of the orthodoxy we have just described, in the same way that Keynes had tried to overthrow what he called the classical orthodoxy.

Notes

1. In both, investment depends on interest rate ($I_x = C\ (i)$); as for the demand for money, M, it depends, for the classical theory, on income ($M = k\ I$), and, for Keynes, on income and the interest rate ($M = L\ (I, i)$) ; finally, for the classical theory, saving depends on the interest rate and income ($I_x = S\ (I, i)$) whilst, for Keynes, it depends only on income ($I_x = S(I)$).
2. Ibid., p. 156.
3. See above, Chapter 3.
4. Which might explain the concluding sentence of his article: '*The General Theory of Employment* is a useful book; but it is neither the beginning nor the end of Dynamic Economics' (p. 159). Schumpeter, whose *Business Cycles* was also released three years after Keynes's book, had a similar reaction, writing, about *The General Theory*, in his *History of Economic Analysis* 'that the leading Swedish economists, in particular Lindahl, Myrdal, and Ohlin, developing certain pointers of Wicksell's, build with similar materials according to a similar plan' (Schumpeter 1954, p. 1173).
5. As a reader of *The General Theory*'s proofs, Harrod advised Keynes to soften his attacks against the classical economists. Keynes answered that, on the contrary, it was necessary to accentuate them so as to bring out fully the essence of his message (letter dated 27 August 1935 in *JMK*, XIII, 547–53; see pp. 526–65 for the correspondence between Harrod and Keynes relating to *The General Theory*'s proofs). About his text, Keynes wrote to Harrod, as he did to Hicks: 'I like your paper ... more than I can say. I have found it instructive and illuminating, and I really have no criticisms' (*JMK*, XIV, p. 84), but this preliminary statement was followed by a section in which Keynes insisted on his rupture with the classical vision, which he compared to moments of illumination and to the escape from a tunnel. He also blamed Harrod for not mentioning effective demand.
6. 'Unemployment, Basic and Monetary: the Classical Analysis and the Keynesian', *Review of Economic Studies*, vol. 3, 1935–6, 201–16. Each model includes six equations and Champernowne, who was an undergraduate enrolled in Keynes's classes at the time he wrote this paper, also used a graphic illustration which prefigured that of Hicks.

7. 'The General Theory of Employment, Interest, and Money', *Economic Record*, vol. 12, 1937, 28–36.
8. 'Prof. Pigou on Money Wages in Relation to Unemployment', *Economic Journal*, vol. 47, 1937, 743–53. See Pigou, 'Real and Money Wage Rates in Relation to Unemployment', *Economic Journal*, vol. 47, 1937, 405–22.
9. Of Lange's article, Keynes wrote, in the context of a controversy with Robertson, that it 'follows very closely and accurately my line of thought', adding that the analysis given in his book was the same as that of the 'general theory' presented by Lange ('Mr. Keynes and "Finance"', *Economic Journal*, vol. 48, 1938, p. 321).
10. See in particular Lerner 1938, 1939, in which he used this model to study the theory of the Swedes, of whom, in another paper, he questioned both the priority of discovery and the superiority of analysis in relation to Keynes's (1940).
11. In fact, it was in his 1949 book (pp. 77–8) that Hansen proceeded to replace the label *LL* with that of *LM*.
12. On the abundant literature provoked by the *IS–LM* diagram, one may refer to, besides Young 1987; I. Maes, '*IS–LM*: The Hicksian Journey', *De Economist*, 137, no. 1, 1989, 91–104; D. Patinkin, 'In Defense of *IS–LM*', *Quarterly Review, Banca Nazionale del Lavoro*, no. 172, March 1990, 119–34; G.L.S. Shackle, 'Sir John Hicks's "*IS–LM*: An Explanation": A Comment', *Journal of Post Keynesian Economics*, vol. 4, 1982, 435–8; H. Zajdela, '*IS–LM*: la controverse Hicks–Keynes', *Économie appliquée*, vol. 41, no. 2, 1988, 225–46.
13. In this context, several books played an essential part: Klein's *The Keynesian Revolution* (1947), Hansen's *A Guide to Keynes* (1953) and above all Samuelson's *Economics* (1948), which has sold more than four million copies and has been translated into more than forty languages.
14. Indeed, we will see in the next chapter that another Keynesian macroeconomics would develop at this time, partly under the inspiration of Kalecki's works.
15. Johnson 1962 *AER*, pp. 336, 365.
16. 'Some Notes on Liquidity Preference', *Manchester School of Economic and Social Studies*, vol. 22, 1954, 229–57.
17. His analysis was criticized by, among others, J. Gurley and E. Shaw, *Money in a Theory of Finance*, Washington, Brookings Institution, 1960. It also gave rise to a debate with Hicks: see Hicks, 'A Rehabilitation of "Classical" Economics', *Economic Journal*, vol. 67, 1957, 278–89 and Patinkin 1959 *EJ*.
18. On monetarism, see below, Chapter 7.
19. On consumption, one should also note the books by Stone 1954–66 and Katona 1960, 1964, 1968.
20. *Capital and Growth: a Micro-Economic Approach*, Amsterdam, North-Holland, 1963.
21. 'A Study of Industry Investment Decisions', *Review of Economics and Statistics*, vol. 49, 1967, 151–64.
22. See above, Chapter 3.
23. Foreword to the French translation of her 1937 book (*Introduction à la théorie de l'emploi*, Paris, Presses Universitaires de France, 1947).
24. *International Labour Review*, vol. 13, 1926, 785–92; reprinted in *Journal of Political Economy*, vol. 81, 1973, 496–502.
25. See the texts gathered in his 1973 book.
26. See the following chapter.
27. On these points, see below, Chapters 7 and 8. On Phillips Curve, see, among others: G.C. Archibald, 'Wage-Price Dynamics, Inflation, and Unemployment: The Phillips Curve and the Distribution of Unemployment', *American Economic Review*, vol. 59, 1959, *Papers and Proceedings*, 124–34; K. Brunner and A. H. Meltzer (eds), *The Phillips Curve and Labor Markets*, Amsterdam, North-Holland, 1976; P. Fortin, 'The Phillips Curve, Macroeconomic Policy, and the Welfare of Canadians', *Canadian Journal of Economics*, vol. 24, 1991, 774–803; M.C. Sawyer, *The Political Economy of the Phillips Curve*, Aldershot, Hants, Edward Elgar, 1991.
28. See preceding chapter.

29. See J. Duesenberry *et al.* (eds) 1965 and L. Klein *et al.* (eds) 1969.
30. *The Structure of Scientific Revolutions*, University of Chicago Press, 1962; 2nd edn, 1970.
31. See above, Chapter 3.

6 Heterodoxies: permanence and renewal

In the postwar period, concealed in part by the pre-eminence of Keynesianism, the ascent of neoclassical economics began, solidly based in rejuvenated general equilibrium theory and strong in both its theoretical coherence and its foundation in the academic tradition. This orthodoxy, rooted in some aspects of classical economics but generated by the marginalist revolution, privileges *homo economicus*, and therefore, a general conception of rationality revolving around a few elementary choices, market, optimum and equilibrium. It does not claim to give a direct account of the real world, but it imposes itself as the theoretical benchmark for all economists and in particular for those in academia. The paradox is that none of the classical economists, none of the fathers of the marginalist revolution, and none of the great economists of the twentieth century who have contributed to the development of neoclassical analysis, limited his thinking or writing to this theoretical development within its unrealistic framework. Nevertheless, the indestructible neoclassical edifice continues to dominate both theoretical debate and the teaching of economics.

In each period, heterodoxies are born or revived: after Marx and his critique of classical political economy, Veblen and his account of social behaviour and institutions, Schumpeter and his explanations of long economic cycles, and Keynes with his explanation of unemployment. Schumpeter's influence was diffuse, but the three other heterodoxies took root: that of Marx, with a profusion of Marxisms, sometimes in bitter conflict one with another; that of Veblen, with the institutionalist tradition; that of Keynes, with the post-Keynesian current. The postwar era was marked by the affirmation of the post-Keynesian heterodoxy, the perpetuation of institutionalism – enriched by the contributions of such original thinkers as Myrdal, Perroux and Galbraith, but also Coase and Simon – and the revival of Marxism. The principal debates were started around the analysis of growth and capital, the transformation of contemporary capitalism and the question of development.

New Keynesian developments

After Keynes's death, those close to him and many in the rising tide of authors referring to him were attached to the major elements of the rupture he had effected: theory conceived so as to take reality into account and to aid the formulation of economic policy; time considered in its historical dimension; expectations formed and decisions taken under uncertainty; and money, the bridge between past and future, viewed as a constitutive element of the economic process. It was through a wide selection of diverse works that the post-Keynesian body of analysis was progressively set up.

The first of these deal with growth and distribution. The macroeconomics of *The General Theory* is situated for the most part in the short run, sometimes even in a static framework. On this point, Keynes stands apart from the classical tradition, to which consideration of the dynamics of the capitalist economy was fundamental. From the end of the 1920s, sketches of formalized analyses, as much of business cycles as of growth, were published, in particular by Frisch, Kalecki and Tinbergen. The members of the Stockholm School contributed also to this theoretical effort. For his part, Schumpeter endeavoured to construct a global explanation of the dynamics of capitalism. In the second half of the 1930s, Harrod (1936) and Lundberg (1937) presented analyses combining the multiplier and the accelerator, permitting Harrod to explain the business cycle, and Lundberg growth instability. Samuelson made this combination the key to the explanation of short-run fluctuations (1939 *REStat*; 1939 *JPE*).

Harrod (1939, 1948) remained faithful to this process by placing, at the centre of his model, the equation $GC = s$, which links the growth rate G and the capital coefficient C, the key variable of the accelerator with the propensity to save s, central to the multiplier: a mathematical tautology which transforms, in a dynamic setting, the equality between saving and investment necessarily obtained *ex post* in static analysis.[1] At the same time, he opened a new path, giving a dynamic extension to the theory of effective demand. Next to G, the actual rate of growth, he took into account G_w, the warranted rate of growth,[2] that which is consistent with entrepreneurs' expectations; finally, he took into account a third rate, G_n, the natural rate of growth which is the maximum rate allowed by population growth and technical progress.

With the barrier constituted in the long run by the natural rate of growth and by the fact that, as soon as one departs from the stable growth path, forces come into action that induce even further departure, this model allows one to take into account instability in growth: what Solow would call in 1956 the 'knife-edge equilibrium'. The gaps between the three growth rates allow Harrod to explain situations of overheating and of chronic unemployment as well as those of cyclical fluctuation. Thus became available an approach to economic changes, based largely on the incorporation of investment and expectations. When Solow raised, in 1956, the 'Harrod–Domar model of economic growth' or 'line of thought', he reduced it to the relation $GC = s$ and presented the constancy of the capital coefficient as the essential source of growth instability.[3] However, here one is as far from Harrod's analysis as from that of Domar.[4] But it was this simplified 'Harrod–Domar model' that was accepted by the textbooks, and to which generations of future economists were initiated. Very few had a chance to know, therefore to understand, the original economic analysis undertaken by both Harrod and Domar.

Along with Solow, T.W. Swan,[5] Tobin (1955), Meade (1961) and others worked to show that Harrod's growth instability stemmed from unrealist hypotheses, the removal of which permitted stable growth. Thus, according to the neoclassical postulates, once one considers the capital coefficient to be flexible and that it is such depending on the relative remuneration of factors, then there are no barriers to growth stability. Such was the core of the construction Solow suggested in 1956. Growth analysis was one of the objects of the fierce controversy which then developed between two Cambridges: the American Cambridge, centre of the neoclassical synthesis, and the British Cambridge, loyal to Keynes the radical theorist.[6]

Besides those of Harrod, Kalecki's and Kaldor's contributions were decisive for the post-Keynesian movement. As early as 1933, on the basis of a formulation of the theory of effective demand and taking income distribution into account, Kalecki had paved the way for an explanation of the instability of capitalist economies; in his approach to distribution, inspired by Marx and the classical economists, society is divided into two classes, one of which has profits as income, and the other, wages. He also developed an analysis of prices, centring on the notion of the mark-up, linked to the degree of monopoly.[7] At the same time, in 1940, Kaldor suggested a model of the business cycle which fitted in with Keynes's macroeconomic analysis, while extending the work of Kalecki and Harrod. There lay the seeds of the principal ideas he would develop later: taking into account the income distribution to explain economic dynamics, which constituted the core of the Cantabrigian theory; the importance of expected profit, on which depends the level of production; the observation that the multiplier and the relation between saving and income vary with changes in income distribution. In this same vein, after the war, Kaldor developed his analyses of growth. In his 1956 article, the sharing of incomes between profits and wages became the major element of explanation. The driving feature resides in the spending of entrepreneurs, whether it be on consumption or investment goods: this spending determines both the level of activity and the incomes of the entrepreneurs. Thus the share of profits in national income depends on the ratio of investment to product. If one supposes that the workers do not save, we obtain the Cambridge equation, in which the profit rate in economy is equal to the growth rate divided by the propensity to save of the capitalists; it is not linked to technological considerations, marginal productivity or production functions. This model, and the one proposed by Robinson, also in 1956, are in total contradiction to the neoclassical theses and thus gave rise to animated debate.[8]

Robinson explicitly set herself the task, in her *Accumulation of Capital*, of 'the generalisation of the General Theory' through an extension of the analysis to the long run, to the 'over-all movements of an economy through time, involving changes in population, capital accumulation and technical change' (Robinson 1956, pp. v–vi). Concerned with the consideration of historical time, expectations and the institutions of contemporary capitalism, she was suspicious of mathematical formalization which favours static equilibrium and empties the analysis of its historical and institutional content. The heart of her model, whose most clear presentation is found in *Essays in the Theory of Economic Growth* (1962), consists of a double relationship (which Kalecki had already brought to light) between the profit rate and the accumulation rate. On one hand, the investment rate is linked to expected profit, while, on the other, the actual profit rate is determined by investment. The problem is that of the relation between these two rates linked by inverse causalities. Robinson showed, in particular, how a rise of saving reduces the growth rate, thus projecting onto the long run analysis what is sometimes called the central paradox of *The General Theory*.

Robinson was also one of the most intransigent critics of the neoclassical synthesis. Besides growth theory, the theory of capital was another field of controversy between the two Cambridges. Initiated by the 1953–4 article of Robinson, 'The Production Function and the Theory of Capital', the debate was sustained in the camp of the British Cambridge with the publication of Sraffa's *Production of Commodities by Means of Commodities* in 1960 and by subsequent contributions of, among others, Kaldor, Pasinetti and Garegnani. The controversy on the phenomenon of reswitching constituted one of its crucial moments. According to this process, analysed by Sraffa, but already brought to light by Wicksell at the end of the last century,[9] a given technique of production, characterized by a certain capital intensity, may become more profitable than another at two different levels of the wage–profit ratio. This is linked to the fact, shown by Sraffa, that it is impossible to measure the capital without knowledge of prices and profit rate. For this reason, the aggregate production function, based on a 'real', impossible-to-measure capital, which is at the heart of the adjustment to equilibrium in the neoclassical models of growth, collapses and with it the theory of distribution based on the marginal productivity of the factors. With Samuelson as spokesperson, the neoclassical theoreticians recognized, following a symposium of the *Quarterly Journal of Economics,*[10] the rightness of the Anglo-Cantabrigian[11] positions on the switching of techniques. This did not prevent the development and the proliferation of neoclassical models of growth, more and more formalized and mathematicized, as the outcome of the 'dialogue of the deaf' between the two Cambridges. After a respite linked to the slowing down of growth in the 1970s and 1980s, we are now seeing the resurgence of a 'new growth theory', which attempts to go past the controversy just mentioned and revives in part the approaches of authors such as Schumpeter and Spiethoff.[12]

The constitution of the post-Keynesian current[13]

The extension in a dynamic setting of the Keynesian analysis, and its connection with the Kaleckian approach to distribution,[14] revealed the willingness to continue Keynes's work of rupture; they were at the heart of the constitution, facing the neoclassical sphere of influence, of a 'post-Keynesian' school of thought, carrier of an alternative analysis. In a large part, this current, diversified and heterogeneous, translates as a return to the origins of classical thought, essentially to Ricardo and, for some, to Marx. Even though the post-Keynesian school was born well before, the christening certificate of this current was an article by Eichner and Kregel in 1975.[15] According to them, the post-Keynesian theory constitutes the real 'generalization of the *General Theory*' sought by Joan Robinson: 'This generalization may be said to represent, in Thomas Kuhn's sense, a new paradigm; and since it extends the analysis set forth in Keynes's *Treatise on Money* (1930) and *The General Theory*, it can be termed post-Keynesian' (Eichner and Kregel 1975, p. 1293).

This current of thought has expressed itself, in Great Britain, through the *Cambridge Journal of Economics*, founded by Richard Goodwin, Luigi Pasinetti and Joan Robinson in 1977, and in the United States through the *Journal of Post Keynesian Economics*, founded in 1978 by Paul Davidson and Sidney Weintraub. From the end of the 1940s, independently of the economists of the British Cambridge, Weintraub started a radical critique of the neoclassical synthesis Keynesianism, a form of Keynesianism which he called classical,[16] Joan Robinson called bastard,[17] and Coddington (1976, 1983) hydraulic. Conversely, Coddington described as fundamentalist the interpretation of Keynes found as much in post-Keynesians as in authors not easily classified, such as Shackle – who devoted most of his career to the development of a theory of decision making under uncertainty. While some of its adversaries readily present the post-Keynesian analysis as essentially critical, this current is characterized by its efforts to advance knowledge of contemporary economies. First, there is the body, already mentioned, of works on growth and distribution. Inspired by these works, models have been constructed, for example for Great Britain by Eichner (1979 *JPKE*, 1987) and for France by Jacques Mazier[18] in his work for the Forecasting Department of the Ministry of Economy.

Then there were convergent efforts aimed at constructing a non-neoclassical analysis of prices. At its origin stood the interest which Sraffa and Robinson showed in the analysis of imperfect competition. But it was Kalecki's analysis which was recognized as being the founding one: for him, the prices of most manufactured goods are determined by variable costs (wages and raw material) to which a mark-up linked to the degree of monopoly is applied. With this line of analysis, Eichner's works fit in as well as Weintraub's. They lead to recommending, in order to control inflation, the completion of Keynesian policies of demand management by an incomes policy. This theory of prices makes the rupture with the neoclassical approach complete: and from the moment it is admitted that the determination of wages depends principally on the firms' decisions and the wage agreements, one has a microeconomic approach coherent with post-Keynesian macroeconomics.

Also characteristic is the position of the post-Keynesians on money. The latter is active; it is indissociable from all the various economic processes; created by credit, it is one of the vectors through which historical time, uncertainty and expectations play a role. The book published by Davidson in 1972, in which he blamed the Cantabrigians for neglecting the role of money, played an important part in this development. But well before, Alain Barrère (1952)[19] had drawn attention to this dimension of Keynes's effort: the construction of the theory of a monetary economy of production, in radical rupture with the classical and neoclassical visions of a real exchange economy. The theoreticians of the circuit, in France (in particular, A. Parguez,[20] F. Poulon,[21] and B. Schmitt[22]) developed an approach which was in certain respects analagous.[23] For his part, having led the analysis of financial relations and complex financial institutions in modern economies, Minsky showed that there was here a source of instability which needed to be combated (Minsky 1977, 1982, 1986). In contradistinction to both the neoclassical synthesis and monetarism, the post-Keynesians offer a conception of an endogenous money supply, which Keynes had himself developed in his reflections after *The General Theory*, focused on a finance motive for liquidity holding.[24]

The publication by Sraffa, in 1960, of a brief book on which he had worked since the end of the 1920s, *Production of Commodities by Means of Commodities*, played a role that was both important and complex in the evolution of the post-Keynesian movement. This book solves a problem left in abeyance by Ricardo and suggests a model of price determination and distribution which took up the classical approach. Subtitled 'prelude to a critique of economic theory', it played a major role in the quarrel between the two Cambridges. Greeted by some as a new revolution, it is at the origin of a current described as neo-Ricardian.[25] The relations between Sraffa's and Keynes's theses (as, moreover, between those of Sraffa and Marx[26]) raised intense debates. For several, such as Eatwell, Garegnani, Milgate, Nell[27] and Pasinetti, Sraffa's work provided the microeconomic bases missing from the Keynesian theory. But others considered that there was a radical rupture between Sraffa's static model, based on an analysis in terms of equilibrium, and an authentically Keynesian approach: such was, for example, the position towards which Robinson, who had always been very close to Sraffa, evolved at the end of her life; and such was also that of A. Asimakopulos. Some post-Keynesians also opposed Sraffa's 'real' analysis and Keynes's monetary theory. The 1980s saw the accentuation of splits and acrimonious debates between post-Keynesians and neo-Ricardians. Some took place during summer school in Trieste, which drew together over a number of years the principal protagonists of these two schools.[28]

But if one stands back a little, there remains a core of authors, identifiable as post-Keynesians, who put the accent on the rupture between Keynes and the neoclassical theory, and who thus reject the neoclassical synthesis, and many of whom advocate economic policies which are not limited to 'fine-tuning', but imply heavy intervention and structural changes.

Around institutionalism

Over the same period, other authors, outside the mainstream, strove to lay the foundations of a non-neoclassical alternative; like Keynes, facing the unemployment of the 1930s, they were concerned to alleviate the world's problems (poverty, inequality, unequal growth, access to non-renewable resources and the environment) by constructing an adequate explanational structure.

Thus Gunnar Myrdal, having established himself with his work on monetary theory, increasingly distanced himself from pure economic theory. From the study of the racial problems of the United States (1944) to that of underdevelopment in South Asia (1968), from his deep involvement in the Swedish social-democratic party to his work as an expert adviser on questions of economic development, he came increasingly to consider that the economy cannot be separated from its social, cultural and political dimensions; and his analysis of circular and cumulative causality, which he used to explain equally the situation of Black Americans and underdevelopment (Myrdal 1957), belongs to a universe which has nothing to do with that of equilibria and optima. He drew closer to the institutionalist current, which he ultimately embraced.

In France, François Perroux criticized the lack of realism of the neoclassical postulates – especially that of identical actors – and the reference framework, the equilibrium, of the neoclassical theory. He devoted a great part of his work to constructing an alternative vision on two levels. First, from 1948, he constructed a new analytical apparatus, at the heart of which he located the domination effect, which applies to the relations between nations, sectors, regions and firms and allows the study of the inequalities' dynamics and their structuring and destructuring effects. Then he pleaded for a 'humane economy' in which man would occupy the centre (1961). Perroux had an influence and disciples in France in particular,[29] in the Latin world and in some of the Third World countries. In the United States, John K. Galbraith also attempted to establish the bases of an alternative approach, analysing the role of the big firm in the industrial system and delimiting crucial phenomena to which he gave expressions which enjoyed great vogue: 'countervailing powers' (1952 *American Capitalism*) and 'technostructure' (1967 *The New Industrial*). Even if, later in life, he drew closer to institutionalism – or maybe was it institutionalism which drew nearer to him? – Galbraith, unlike Myrdal, refused the prize of the Association for Evolutionary Economics, which grouped together the partisans of this approach.

Many other authors, among them Boulding, Furtado, Georgescu-Roegen, Hirschman, Kornai, Prebisch, Sen and Tinbergen attempted to escape the yoke of the neoclassical approach and some of them have explicitly criticized it. From many aspects, their approach came close to that of institutionalism:[30] the latter developed, after Veblen, the founder, with Commons and his 'collective economics', J.M. Clark and his 'social economics', Tugwell and his 'experimental economics', Mitchell and his 'quantitative economics',[31] Ayres[32] and his 'instrumentalism',[33] and Gruchy,[34] who was at the origin of the creation in 1958 of the Association for Evolutionary Economics. In spite of their obvious difficulty in defining themselves under the same emblematic word, all these authors have in common a holistic approach – refusing to cut the economic field off from the rest of the social reality or to reduce economics solely to the market – a pluridisciplinary approach, taking into account values, institutions, technologies and evolution and, often, revealing an attitude favourable to active economic policy.

But such a programme allows the inclusion of virtually all of the heterodoxes. Thus, in his 1972 book on contemporary economic thought and what he calls the 'neo-institutionalism', Gruchy devotes chapters not only to Gerhard Colm and Ayres, but also to Galbraith and Myrdal, calling to mind on several occasions, and at some length, Perroux; but he clearly dissociates himself from Keynes, whom he blames for the short-run setting of his analysis (p. 5), from the Keynesians whose process is 'static and non-interdisciplinary' (p. 334) and especially from the radicals of the Union for Radical Political Economics (URPE), accused variously of anarchism, socialism and of a lack of a clear vision of what they would like to establish instead of the existing social system (pp. viii–ix).

In its diversity, the institutionalist movement principally expresses itself through the *Journal of Economic Issues*, from the Association for Evolutionary Economics, created in 1967. Of course, it does not lack common points with behavioural economics; marked by the contributions of Coase, H. Simon and Arrow, its members gather into more restricted circles including behavioural, new institutional economics, neo-institutional economics and even industrial economics.[35] Beyond, one can find links between institutionalism and the German historical school and Sombart – Kuznets being somewhere between the two – and with the British Fabians and their successors, with Polanyi, as well as with Hayek and the modern Austrian School. Besides, the Nobel Memorial Prize in 1974 was awarded jointly to Myrdal and Hayek; the choice of Myrdal might have been interpreted as a form of acknowledgement of institutionalism, and it is remarkable that the jury mentioned, in its comment about the two authors, multidisciplinarity.

On the Marxism side

The other great heterodox tradition was that of Marxism, which broadened, especially in the United States, to what is called 'radical economics' or 'radical political economy'. However, the stamp 'radical' covers extremely different fields: thus, for Sherman,[36] and many others, the radical current embraces post-Keynesians, neo-Ricardians, institutionalists and Marxists; in short, all of the heterodoxies. On the contrary, for Bronfenbrenner (1970), Appelbaum[37] and Flaherty,[38] it appears principally as a label for the Marxists of the United States in the 1950s and 1960s; but for Bowles and Edwards (1990), the radical current which formed in the 1970s and 1980s 'is distinct from both neoclassical economics and classical Marxism' (vol. 1, p. 1) ; this new radical current finds its roots in the United States in postwar Marxism, in the Union for Radical Political Economics where a broad range of radical dissidents met, libertarians as well as Marxists,[39] as well as in the vigorous debate, research and criticism of the 1960s.

So there remains Marxism. But this is a world in itself, and a world deeply marked by history and its rifts (Lenin against Bernstein, Kautsky and others; Stalin against Trotsky and others; Mao Tse-tung against Stalin), by philosophy and its debates (Lukacs, Gramsci, Korsch, Bloch, Habermas and, more recently, Marcuse, Lefebvre, Althusser, Kosik), by the political stakes and cleavages and, under the rationale of theoretical formulations, by the beliefs – for example that such a country is socialist or initiated the construction of socialism. And then, between Marx and Marxism, relations are even more complex and muddled than those between Keynes and Keynesianism,[40] and the quarrels of inheritance even more merciless, all the more so since they involve violence.

In the English-speaking world, postwar Marxist economic thought[41] has been dominated by three names: Paul Baran, Maurice Dobb and Paul Sweezy. It expresses itself through journals such as the *Review of Radical Political Economy*, the *Socialist Review*, the *New Left Review*, *Capital and Class* and the *Monthly Review* founded in 1949 by Sweezy and Leo Huberman, and which Sweezy ran with Harry Magdoff after Huberman's death in 1968. In the French-speaking world, the names of Charles Bettelheim, Henri Denis[42] and Ernest Mandel emerged. After the war, von Mises's theses on the impossibility of socialism, which Lange and Lerner opposed in the 1930s, seemed invalid. With its centralized planning, the USSR – studied early by Bettelheim (1939 and 1950) and Dobb (1948) – asserted itself both as a great power and as a socialist one. For many, socialism made decisive progress in the USSR, China and the Third World;[43] but self-censorship marks many writings: does one have the right to formulate doubts or critiques when men sacrifice their lives for socialism and revolution? Illustrative of this trouble is Bettelheim's long evolution in the face of the Soviet reality, from the 1939 and 1950 descriptive studies showing progress, to an analysis in terms of state capitalism (1964, 1968, 1970 *Calcul*), to arrive at the end of a powerful historical fresco (1974–82) at the conclusion that the 1917 revolution was not a socialist revolution but a capitalist one.

As for capitalism, despite Hansen's analyses (1938, 1939, 1941) which pointed to a long period of economic stagnation, and Schumpeter's judgement in *Capitalism, Socialism and Democracy* (1942) according to which the decline of capitalism was ineluctable, there was, after the war, one of the longest periods of prosperity in the history of capitalism. Noticing that the Marxian law of the declining profit rate no longer held for a capitalism in which monopolies fixed their prices, Baran (1957) and Baran and Sweezy (1966) noted the rising trend of the potential surplus, the major origin of the tendency to stagnation of modern capitalism. But it was in the tendency of the declining profit rate and the Kondratiev long waves that Mandel (1962, 1972) saw the roots of contemporary capitalist crises.

But Marxism is not only a matter of intellectuals and of individual choices. It was, from 1917, the ideology of the USSR, of its leading party and of all the communist parties linked to it:[44] after Lenin, and even more so after Stalin, an orthodox Marxism asserted itself. As early as 1936, Stalin ordered the writing of a textbook of political economy: the latter, after a difficult gestation,[45] would only be published in 1954. It gives a linear vision of history, with a succession of modes of production leading to the socialist mode, and develops in a scholastic way the political economy of socialism; it affirms the two dogmas of socialism's superiority and capitalism's collapse. These ideas mark directly all of the works from communist parties linked to the USSR[46] and indirectly all thinking linked to workers' organizations and national liberation movements. The Soviet reality, nevertheless, was soon the object of critiques coming either from the Trotskyite camp or from other revolutionary groups.[47] In the socialist camp itself, a major gap opened between the USSR and China; from 1937, Mao Tse-tung had presented a Marxism in which the analysis of contradictions plays a key role;[48] later, he criticized Stalin's economism; the rupture with the USSR in 1960, then the 'Great cultural proletarian revolution' (1966–71) would put in concrete form, after the schism of Tito, the questioning of the orthodoxy inherited from Stalin, who died in 1953.

The very difficulties of centralized planning and of the system of state control set up in the name of socialism led, in successive waves, to proposals of reforms from I. Birman, V. Nemchinov and E. Liberman in the USSR, W. Brus in Poland, O. Sik in Czechoslovakia and J. Kornai in Hungary. Kornai, who brought to light the hypercentralization of planning as early as 1957, contributed for more than 30 years to enlightenment and sketches of ways for possible reforms. If the movements of May 1968 led to a certain renewal of Marxist thinking, the fall of the Soviet and Eastern European regimes at the end of the 1980s would drastically change the ideological and intellectual landscape.

Debates on development

The questions of economic retardation, then of development and underdevelopment, have, since the Second World War, been the object of numerous works, written in particular by heterodox economists.[49] The first contemporary reflections on the problems of economic arrears concerned South-east and Eastern Europe. Paul Rosenstein-Rodan[50] put forward the necessity of the 'big push'.[51] Kurt Mandelbaum emphasized 'the vicious circle of demographic pressures, of poverty and of the absence of industry',[52] pleading for industrialization, while finding that the principal obstacles are due to demand inadequacy on the one hand and the scarcity of capital on the other.

Nominated in 1950 as executive secretary of the Economic Commission for Latin America (ECLA), which had been created in 1948, R. Prebisch pleaded for the programming of economic development. From flexible programming, such as was advocated by Meade (1948) or as set in place in France after the war, to Soviet planning (which authors such as Bettelheim (1939, 1950) and Dobb (1948) contributed to publicizing outside the USSR sphere of influence) to the multiple efforts (in particular of Tinbergen and Myrdal) to establish simple and sturdy models, planning was to be the almost undisputed tool of industrialization and modernization for poor countries: just as economic policy was then, for wealthy countries, the essential instrument of growth. But, at the same time, divisions were revealed. Prebisch, along with Singer, in 1950, called into question the worsening of the terms of trade, a thesis criticized by Viner.[53] For many, whether Marxists of the North or new leaders of the South, the Soviet path towards industrialization appeared as the model to be adopted: which is what communist China did after 1949, and then, in its own manner, India, whose choices were influenced by the 'Mahalanobis model', as well as many other newly independent countries. But how could the United States accept the whole of the underdeveloped world swinging into the Soviet camp?

In 1951, under the auspices of the United Nations, a report on *Measures for the Economic Development of Under-Developed Countries* was published. This had been prepared by A. Baltra Cortez (Chile), D.R. Gadgil (India), G. Hakim (Lebanon), A. Lewis (Great Britain) and T.W. Schultz (United States). It noticed the existence of excess labour and the small part of national income devoted to capital formation, and it advocated the implementation of development programmes, including the necessary investment budgets. Rostow (1952 *The Process*) sketched a description of the development which would lead to a reassuring vision of the growth stages (1960 *The Stages*): stages which the developed countries passed through, and which the still-developing countries would traverse one day, providing that they put together the conditions for the 'take-off'. If Viner worried about the risk that development would favour demographic growth, Lewis, on the contrary, saw in his 1954 article the existence of an unlimited supply of labour in the traditional sector and an opportunity for the expansion of the capitalist sector. And if Nurkse (1953) brought out the doubly vicious circle of poverty, simultaneously the cause of weak demand and of insufficient financing capacity, Schultz (1945 ed., 1964) brought to light the importance of the farming potential. Finally, their liberal beliefs would lead economists such as Viner and Haberler (1988) to criticize the restrictions on international business advocated, or adopted, in favour of development. If Rostow's stages and Viners's views were clearly liberal, it was necessary to simplify Lewis's analysis to turn it into the caricature of a dualistic approach. Facing these positions, two standpoints asserted themselves.

In the first place, Marxist economists used their analyses to shed light on the situation and on the choices to be made. Dobb (1951), agreeing with Nurkse on this point, considered that the most important factor governing a country's productivity is its fixed factors of production and that the accumulation of capital, the quantitative and qualitative growth of the stock of means of production is at the centre of the developmental process.[54] But, as Baran (1957) showed, in the developing countries, stuck between feudalism and the capitalism of the developed countries, the surplus is not put to productive ends, rather it is partly wasted for the ruling classes' consumption, military spending and the maintenance of bureaucracy, and partly captured by foreign capital. For all Marxists, development goes through socialism; this is how Sweezy and Huberman (1969) saw a model for Latin America in Cuba. In the second place, different authors whose common point is not to leave development to the market (at the national as well as at the international level) attempted to identify the rigidities and distortions and the sources of backwardness stemming from the poor countries' structures (as much in their economies and their societies as in their relations with industrialized countries); this approach, nourished by several sources, may be called structuralist in the very wide sense of the term.

F. Perroux develops tools for the analysis of underdevelopment and pleads, in the tradition of Christian humanism (in which the works by Father Lebret and of *Économie et Humanisme* also lie), that the 'costs of man' be covered and that development be that 'of the whole man' and 'of all men' (1961, pp. 17, 511, 512). Myrdal (1957, 1968) applies to underdevelopment his analysis in terms of circular and cumulative causality and invites the young economists of the Third World to reject doctrines and theories devoid of significance and pertinence and to engage in a new reflection starting from their own needs and problems (Myrdal 1957, pp. 103–4). Likewise, Hirschman (1958), in the face of the partisans of balanced development, underlines the necessarily unbalanced nature of any developmental process; he takes into account (1963, 1967), as Schultz does, the hidden rationalities and, as does Perroux, the driving effects.

In Latin America, the dependency school[55] covers a broad spectrum of combinations involving the structural approach and the Marxist analysis. With Prebisch, and supporting him in particular O. Sunkel and A. Pinto in the context of ECLA, it constituted an active focus of research, thinking and propositions. At the beginning of the 1950s, it led the analysis of the structures of production and exchange which bring about inflation as well as deterioration in the terms of trade, and it suggested the strategies of industrialization through import substitution. It then analysed centre–periphery relations and the characteristics specific to peripheral capitalism. It led to a very broad range of positions, from the moderate and reformist propositions of C. Furtado (1967 *Teoria*, 1972, 1974) to the analyses of Marxist inspiration of F.H. Cardoso and E. Faletto,[56] to that, radical Marxist, of A.G. Frank (1967, 1969, 1972), R.M. Marini and T. Dos Santos. These latter, along with Samir Amin, were, in the 1970s, representative of a movement of Third World economists with a dominant anti-imperialist theme.

While the unequal relations worldwide were increasingly indicted, in 1972, Robert McNamara, president of the World Bank,[57] put the accent on the worsening of inequalities within each country as the major obstacle to development;[58] also carried out at this time was the work of I. Adelman, of the World Bank, linking growth with income inequality.[59] Then the analysis focused on the necessary minimum, on basic needs, whilst around the mid-1970s the necessities of self-reliance and a new international economic order were put forward. But the oil crisis, the end of the growth of the rich countries, and the debt trap soon submitted a number of Third World countries to urgent pressures, and then to the need for structural adjustment.

Notes

1. If Y is national income, K the stock of capital and S saving, G is defined by $\Delta Y/Y$, C by $\Delta K/\Delta Y$ and s by S/Y. The investment I being defined by ΔK, one deduces Harrod's equation from the equality between I and S.
2. For a desired capital coefficient C_r and a propensity to save s, the warranted rate of growth G_w is defined by the relation: $G_w = s/C_r$; this relation expresses the conditions of a stable growth.
3. Solow recognizes the improper simplification which he had undertaken there in his 1970 book, admitting that it is 'with some injustice' that he speaks of the 'Harrod–Domar version' of what he calls a 'parable' (Solow 1970, p. 11).

4. Domar was preoccupied, above all, with defining the conditions of full employment. He brought to light that investment has not only an effect of income creation but also on increasing the capacity of production. While the support of productive investment can, at first, contribute to full employment, it may afterwards be a cause of unemployment (Domar 1947).
5. 'Economic Growth and Capital Accumulation', *Economic Record*, vol. 32, 1956, 334–43.
6. Harcourt offered a living chronicle of this 'war of the two Cambridges', of which Joan Robinson and Robert Solow were the leaders, and which was characterized by its virulence as well as its high level of abstraction (Harcourt 1969, 1972, 1976). See also Blaug 1974, Kregel 1971 and Kregel 1972, who present quite different points of view. Also see the texts gathered in Hahn 1971 (ed.); Harcourt and Laing 1971; E.K. Hunt and J. G. Schwartz (eds), *A Critique of Economic Theory*, Harmondsworth, Penguin Books, 1972; Stiglitz and Uzawa 1969; A. Weintraub, E. Schwartz and J.R. Aronson (eds), *The Economic Growth Controversy*, White Plains, New York, International Arts and Sciences Press, 1973.
7. Joan Robinson called this latter theory the Keynesian theory of prices. Kaldor (1956) named Keynesian the Kaleckian theory of distribution. Thus a Keynesianism progressively constituted itself – largely Kaleckian, with an at least partial return to the classical vision, Ricardian or Marxist, of distribution – breaking radically with neoclassical theory.
8. One of the neoclassical critiques is based on the fact that workers save more than is supposed by Kaldor, and that they can have at their disposal revenues other than those strictly from wages. The model offered by Pasinetti in 1962 aims at answering this objection.
9. On this, see Garegnani 1960.
10. Samuelson, 'A Summing Up', *Quarterly Journal of Economics*, vol. 80, 1966, 568–83.
11. It is sometimes spoken of as an Italo-Cambridgian school, owing to the large number of economists of Italian origin in the post-Keynesian camp.
12. In the growth literature, see, among others, the texts gathered in E. Burmeister and R. Becker (eds), *Growth Theory*, 3 vols, Aldershot, Hants, Edward Elgar, 1990. Besides the authors mentioned in this section, several other well-known economists contributed to growth theory, with views often very different from those we have just put forward; they include Duesenberry 1958, Goodwin 1955, 1967, 1982, Hicks 1965, Johnson 1962 *Money*, Kuznets 1968, and several other titles given in the dictionary, Lewis 1955 and Morishima 1964, 1969.
13. On the post-Keynesian current, see, among others Arestis 1991, Arestis and Skouras 1985, Blaug 1974, Eichner 1979, Eichner and Kregel 1975, Harcourt 1987, Lavoie 1992 and Sawyer 1989.
14. M. Sawyer, emphasizing in 1982 the importance of the Kaleckian inheritance, spoke of a post-Kaleckian macroeconomics (see 'Towards a Post-Kaleckian Macroeconomics', in Arestis and Skouras 1985, 146–79). See G. Dostaler, 'La théorie post-keynésienne, la *Théorie générale* et Kalecki', in P. Maurisson (ed.), *La 'Théorie générale' de John Maynard Keynes: Un Cinquantenaire'*, Paris, L'Harmattan, 1988, 123–42.
15. Kregel has continuously attempted to give synthetic presentations of the theses of the post-Keynesian current, as an author (1971, 1972, 1973 and 1976 *Theory*) and as editor of collective works (1983, 1988 and 1989), while Eichner, who supervised, in 1978, the publication *A Guide to Post-Keynesian Economics*, also contributed to the development and affirmation of a body of post-Keynesian analyses (1985, 1987).
16. See his articles gathered in the 1961 book.
17. Review of *Money, Trade and Economic Growth* by H.G. Johnson, *Economic Journal*, vol. 72, 1962, 690–92.
18. *La Macroéconomie appliquée*, Paris, Presses Universitaires de France, 1978.
19. See also Barrère 1979 and 1990, in which this perspective is deepened in the light of the most recent debates.
20. *Monnaie et macroéconomie*, Paris, Économica, 1975.
21. *Macroéconomie approfondie: équilibre, déséquilibre, circuit*, Paris, Cujas, 1982.
22. *Monnaie, salaires et profits*, Paris, Presses Universitaires de France, 1966; *L'analyse macro-économique des revenus*, Paris, Dalloz, 1971.

23. See also R. Arena and A. Graziani (eds), *Production, circulation et monnaie*, Paris, Presses Universitaires de France, 1985; G. Deleplace and E. Nell (eds), *Money in Motion: The Post-Keynesian and Circulation Approaches*, London, Macmillan, 1994; E. Nell, *Transformational Growth and Effective Demand*, London, Macmillan and New York University Press, 1992.
24. See Asimakopulos 1983; A. Graziani,'The Debate on Keynes's Finance Motive', *Economic Notes*, no. 1, 1984, 5–33; B. Moore, 'The Endogeneous Money Supply', *Journal of Post Keynesian Economics*, vol. 2, 1979, 49–70; id., *Horizontalists and Verticalists: The Macrotheory of Credit Money*, Cambridge, England, Cambridge University Press, 1988.
25. Steedman (1989) reproduced the main articles relating to this current of thought. One may refer to the dictionary entry on Sraffa to discover part of the rich bibliography stimulated by his work.
26. See on this subject G. Dostaler, 'Marx et Sraffa', *L'Actualité économique*, vol. 58, 1982, 95–114; ibid., 'From Marx to Sraffa: Comments on an Article by P.L. Porta', *History of Political Economy*, vol. 18, 1986, 463–9. See also below Chapter 9.
27. *Keynes After Sraffa*, London, Unwin Hyman, 1977.
28. See on this subject R. Arena, 'L'école internationale d'été de Trieste (1981–1985): Vers une synthèse classico-keynésienne?', *Économies et sociétés*, vol. 21, série *Oeconomia*, n° 7, 1987, 205–38; id., 'La dynamique économique: nouveaux débats, nouvelles perspectives', *L'Actualité économique*, vol. 63, 1987, 77–117.
29. Particularly, in international economics, Maurice Byé and Jean Weiller.
30. See Adams 1980, Gruchy 1947 and 1972, Samuels 1989 and Tool 1988.
31. See P.A. Klein, 'A Reconsideration of Holistic Economics', in Adams 1980, 45–7.
32. *The Problem of Economic Order*, New York, Farrar and Rinehart, 1938; *The Theory of Economic Progress*, Chapel Hill, University of North Carolina Press, 1944; *The Industrial Economy*, Boston, Houghton Mifflin, 1952; *Toward a Reasonable Society*, Austin, University of Texas Press, 1961.
33. See Gruchy 1972, 97–132.
34. Besides Gruchy 1947 and 1972, quoted above, see *Comparative Economic Systems, Competing ways to Stability and Growth*, Boston, Houghton Mifflin, 1966; *The Reconstruction of Economics – An Analysis of the Fundamentals of Institutional Economics*, New York, Greenwood Press, 1987.
35. See below, Chapter 9.
36. *Radical Political Economy: Capitalism and Socialism from a Marxist–Humanist Perspective*, New York and London, Basic Books, 1972; id., *Foundations of Radical Political Economy*, Armonk, New York, M.E. Sharpe, 1987.
37. 'Radical Economics', in Weintraub 1977, 559–74.
38. 'Radical Political Economy', *New Palgrave* 1987, vol. 4, 36–9. In the *New Palgrave* there is, moreover, a wide cross-reference between the authors taken into account by D. Flaherty in his article and those whom A. Glynn deals with in his article, 'Marxist Economics', vol. 3, 390–95.
39. Flaherty, op. cit., p. 36.
40. It has been said of Keynes that he declared himself non-Keynesian, and of Marx that he was not a Marxist.
41. See also Chapter 9. We will limit ourselves here to the most typical representatives; we have already shown above the influence of Kalecki, particularly on the post-Keynesian movement. One should also mention Ricardian Marxism (following Sraffa, Dobb and Meek) and also neoclassical, even Walrasian, interpretations of Marxism, as well as the case of Lange, whose work falls within both Marxist and neoclassical tradition.
42. *La Monnaie*, Paris, Editions sociales, 1951; *Valeur et capitalisme*, Paris, Edition Sociales, 1957; *Histoire de la pensée économique*, Paris, Presses Universitaires de France, 1966 (several later editions). More recently, following a thorough reinterpretation of Hegel, Denis was led to modify his evaluation of Marx and especially of Marxian economics (*L'économie de Marx. Histoire d'un échec*, Paris, Presses Universitaires de France, 1980; *Logiques hégélienne et systèmes économique*, Paris, Presses Universitaires de France, 1984).

43. See Bettelheim 1965 on China; Sweezy and Huberman 1969 on Cuba; Sweezy and Bettelheim 1970.
44. Which, of course, does not prevent numerous other parties and organizations also claiming to go back, in one form or another, to Marxism.
45. Stalin himself found it necessary to intervene to settle some points of doctrine, with, in particular, 'The Economic Problems of Socialism in URSS' (*Bolshevik*, 1952). See R.L. Meek, 'Stalin as an Economist', *Review of Economic Studies*, vol. 21, 1953–4, 232–9.
46. See works by Lange (1953, 1957, 1959). In France, see the book written, under the direction of Philippe Herzog and Paul Boccara, by the economists of the French Communist Party, *Traité marxiste d'économie politique. Le capitalisme monopoliste d'Etat*, 2 vols, Paris, Editions sociales, 1971.
47. Thus, in the 1930s, the writings of the group 'Living Marxism' (see K. Korsch, P. Mattick and A. Pannekoek, *La Contre-révolution bureaucratique*, Paris, Union générale d'édition, 1973); Bruno Rizzi, *La Bureaucratisation du monde*, published by the author, held in the Hachette distributing service, 1939; Engl. transl., *The Bureaucratization of the World. The USSR: Bureaucratic Collectivism*, London, Tavistock, 1985; and after the war, the writings of 'Socialisme ou Barbarie' (see C. Castoriadis, *La Société bureaucratique*, 2 vols, Paris, Union générale d'édition, 1973); and more recently, R. Bahro, *The Alternative in Eastern Europe*, London, New Left Books, 1978. See M. Beaud, *Le Socialisme à l'épreuve de l'histoire*, Paris, Seuil, 1982; Engl. transl., *Socialism in the Crucible of History*, Atlantic Highlands, New Jersey, Humanities Press, 1993.
48. *On Contradiction*, New York, International Publishers, 1953.
49. See Meier and Seers 1984; Arndt, *Economic Development. History of an Idea*, University of Chicago Press, 1987; Hirschman, 'The Rise and Decline of Development Economics', in Hirschman 1981. For access to a vast bibliography, refer to Lal 1992, Omman and Wignaraja 1991, and Stern 1989.
50. 'Problems of Industrialization of Eastern and South-Eastern Europe', *Economic Journal*, vol. 53, 1943, 202–11.
51. Gerschenkron's 'big spurt', Leibenstein's critical threshold, and Rostow's take-off echo this formula.
52. *Industrialization of Backward Areas*, Oxford, Basil Blackwell, 1947, p. iii.
53. *International Trade and Economic Development*, Oxford, Clarendon Press, 1953.
54. Dobb 1951, p.7.
55. See F.H. Cardoso, *As Ideas e seu lugar*, Vozes and CEBRAP, 1980; O. Rodriguez, *'La Teoria' del Subdesarrollo de la CEPAL*, Mexico, Siglo XXI, 1980.
56. F.H. Cardoso and E. Faletto, *Dependencia y desarrollo en America Latina*, Mexico, Siglo XXI, 1967; Engl. transl., *Dependency and Development in Latin America*, Berkeley, University of California Press, 1979.
57. At the head of the Economic Department of the World Bank, from 1970 to 1972, Hollis B. Chenery had launched, in the spirit of S. Kuznets's work (1959), a broad programme of quantitative research on underdeveloped countries.
58. Hirschman, 'The Rise and Decline of Development Economics', in Hirschman 1981, p. 13.
59. See Adelman and Morris 1973, Chenery *et al.* 1974.

7 The liberal resurgence

The triumph of Keynesianism may have given the illusion that it dominated the stage, that *The General Theory* had effectively dethroned classical theory. The acknowledgement, by Pigou,[1] of the validity of Keynes's theory constituted, in a way, a symbol of this triumph on the theoretical level, as the new economic policy, implemented at the beginning of the 1960s under the presidency of John F. Kennedy, seemed to mark its political victory. But Keynesianism, as we saw above, constitutes a vast nebula, crossed by currents and sub-currents; economists with very diverse theoretical or political orientations were there able to find substance to nourish or back up their theses.

For its part, the classical liberalism attacked by Keynes and several others in the 1920s and 1930s, and apparently undone in the 1940s and 1950s, is, in fact, far from having disappeared. In the shadow of Keynesianism, it has even developed, keeping what might be called a low profile. Several of its partisans even seemed to have become Keynesian. Among them, some contributed from the interior to the deconstruction of Keynesianism, just as Keynes himself had undertaken from the interior his deconstruction of the orthodox citadel. Others never accepted Keynes's theses, and never rallied to Keynesianism. Some met in the Mont Pèlerin Society which, founded in 1947 on Hayek's initiative, played an important role in preserving and developing classical liberalism.[2] Some made at least part of their career at the University of Chicago.[3] One can thus speak of a Chicago School[4] to describe the work carried out in very diverse fields of specialization, but united by a solid faith in the neoclassical theory of prices, the conviction that the free market is the most efficient mechanism to allocate resources and a fundamental scepticism about state intervention in the economy. Milton Friedman, who studied at, and continued his academic career in this university (before joining the Hoover Institution in 1977) was the most reputable spokesman of this school in the 1960s and 1970s.[5]

It was thus a resurgence of liberalism that was witnessed during this period, while the euphoria linked to growth started to disappear. In advanced capitalist economies the end of the 1960s and the beginning of the 1970s were characterized by breaks in productivity growth, rising unemployment, inflationist tendencies, dysfunctions of the international monetary system. Part of what is called the 'Third World' was sinking beneath insuperable difficulties. There was also deadlock for Eastern countries, which were confronted by problems and aspirations to which their system could not respond. Gradually, from the beginning of the 1970s, Keynesianism began to be questioned. The coexistence of inflation and a rising unemployment rate challenged the certainties associated with the Phillips curve and symbolized the failure of Keynesian policies. For lack of explanation, a word was created: stagflation. And some started to explain the more and more serious difficulties of the 1970s by the secondary effects of the dangerous Keynesian medicine, the source of ever-growing inflation.

Alternative theories already existed. In the first rank among the candidates, monetarism rapidly asserted itself as a major pole of the opposition to Keynesianism, as much on the political as on the theoretical level. Supply-side economics and diverse other liberal currents also competed with each other as suppliers of recipes for economies in difficulty. At the same time, on the theoretical side, neoclassical microeconomics was used as a way to shed light not only onto the economic issues, but also onto all the social phenomena. Like the theoreticians of monetarism or the supply-side economists, the followers of economics' new imperialism appeared as resolute adversaries of interventionism. It was by reasserting the necessity of this interventionism that the Keynesians would launch their counter-attack against these new currents of thought, while accepting some of their contributions.

Milton Friedman and monetarism[6]

The term 'monetarism' was coined in 1968 by Karl Brunner.[7] He described as the 'monetarist revolution'[8] what Harry Johnson (1971 *AER*) called the 'monetarist counter-revolution'. Friedman himself does not like the word monetarism but explained why he cannot avoid it in a text in which he described 'the counter-revolution in monetary theory', which he claimed to have predicted as early as 1958, and whose victory was now clear, at the end of the 1960s (Friedman 1970). This counter-revolution was characterized by 'the renewed emphasis on the role of the quantity of money' (ibid., pp. 7–8).

This new appellation covers an ancient, complex and diverse reality. It designates as much a global political vision as a theoretical construction, the latter varying from one author to the next. The global vision in the case of monetarism is the faith in the inherent stability of market economies and, therefore, the mistrust of interventionism. The theoretical core is the quantity theory of money. Generally attributed to Jean Bodin,[9] in the sixteenth century, this theory received from the philosopher David Hume, in the middle of the eighteenth century,[10] the formulation which, taken up again by classical economists, was formalized at the beginning of the twentieth century in Irving Fisher's transactions equations and Marshall's and Pigou's cash-balance approach. According to this theory, a variation of the stock of money translates, in the long run, into a variation in the same direction and in the same proportion of the general level of prices. Keynes, during the early part of his career, accepted this theory, the surrender of which constituted an important moment in the development of *The General Theory*. He nonetheless affirmed in the latter book that the quantity theory of money, like the classical theory of which it constitutes a major element, is valid when full employment is reached. Friedman even considers that Keynes remained fundamentally a quantity theorist in *The General Theory* (Friedman 1970, p. 8).

It was in 1956, 20 years after the publication of *The General Theory*, that Friedman offered a rehabilitation and a reformulation of the quantity theory of money in the introductory text of a collective book stemming from work done at the University of Chicago, in the context of a workshop on money and banking. Echoing Bodin's conviction, he wrote:

> there is perhaps no other empirical relation in economics that has been observed to recur so uniformly under so wide a variety of circumstances as the relation between substantial changes over short periods in the stock of money and in prices; the one is invariably linked with the other and is in the same direction; this uniformity is, I suspect, of the same order as many of the uniformities that form the basis of the physical sciences. (Friedman 1956, pp. 20–21)

The principal characteristic of Friedman's reformulation consists in presenting the quantity theory as a theory of the demand for money. The total demand for money is aggregated from the individual demands for real cash balances, money being one of the forms in which one chooses to hold wealth. The real quantity of money is equal to its nominal quantity weighted by the price index. The demand for money is a relatively stable function of a few key variables. These variables include the interest rate. Friedman thus admitted an important aspect of Keynes's approach, and he considered the liquidity preference theory a positive contribution of the Keynesian revolution which the monetarist counter-revolution should retain. It was the same with the perception of money as an asset among others, such as bonds.[11] Like Keynes, and contrary to the orthodox quantity theory tradition, he also considered the velocity of the circulation of money to be variable. But, unlike Keynes, he deemed this variability unimportant and, above all, predictable, reacting in turn to changes in the key variables. It was on this basis, and from the alleged weakness of the interest elasticity of money demand, that Friedman drew his principal conclusion.

For him, money supply, determined by the monetary authorities, is much more volatile than demand, which stems from consumers' behaviour. It follows that changes in the value of money, and therefore in the general level of prices, are fundamentally determined by money supply. The variations of the nominal quantity of money act in the short run on quantities and employment, and in the long run their effects are purely nominal. It is on this argumentation that Friedman's declaration is based, according to which 'inflation is always and everywhere a monetary phenomenon' (Friedman 1968 *Dollars*, p. 105).

The question of the relationship between money supply and macroeconomic aggregates was raised before the 1956 publication by Friedman himself, but also by other authors. From the end of the 1940s, Friedman began to affirm the superiority of the quantity of money approach over the Keynesian one, based on autonomous expenditures, in accounting for the level and fluctuation of national income. It was at this time that Friedman and Schwartz started, at the National Bureau of Economic Research, a study of the relationship between business cycles and the variations of the stock of money.[12] This long research generated three major books co-authored by Friedman and Schwartz (1963, 1970 and 1982) and a study by Cagan,[13] in which the authors claim to have empirically demonstrated that the variations in the quantity of money play a determining role in accounting for economic fluctuations. Thus the depth of the crisis of the 1930s could be explained by monetary contractions, for which the Federal Reserve System was responsible. It is clear that this conclusion conflicts with the analyses of Keynes and his disciples.

In a study co-authored with Meiselman and also carried out at the National Bureau of Economic Research, Friedman claimed that he had definitely shown the superiority of his analysis over that of Keynesianism, on the basis of a comparative study, for the period from 1897 to 1958, of the stability of the multiplier and that of the velocity of money:

> The income velocity of circulation of money is consistently and decidedly stabler than the investment multiplier except only during the early years of the Great Depression after 1929. ...
>
> In other words, the simple version of the income–expenditure theory to which we have deliberately restricted ourselves in this paper is almost completely useless as a description of stable empirical relationships, as judged by six decades of experience in the United States. (Friedman and Meiselman 1963, pp. 186–7)

This publication gave rise to intense controversies, instituting one of the important phases of the debate between Keynesianism and monetarism.[14] Among these controversies, which often took a very technical turn, radically different conceptions conflicted over the functioning of economies and state intervention: the debate turned fundamentally on the stability of market economies. For Friedman and the other partisans of monetarism, modern economies are stable, and the market's free functioning is enough to ensure an optimal allocation of resources and the full employment of the productive capabilities. For Keynes and his disciples, economies are unstable and the market mechanism is not enough to ensure full employment. For each, the conviction is antecedent to the theoretical analysis: what we call monetarist policies, therefore, are not, despite appearances, the result of the rehabilitation of the quantity theory of money, just as Keynesian policies were not conceived on the basis of the theses developed in *The General Theory*.

Moreover, Friedman's economic policy programme is, in large measure, contained in his 'A Monetary and Fiscal Framework for Economic Stability' (1948), itself inspired by the theses put forward by Simons in the same year *The General Theory* was published.[15] The state must limit itself to ensuring a stable framework for the functioning of the market. This implies that an objective such as the realization of full employment at all costs must be questioned, the more so since the policies implemented to bring it about may increase economic instability. For the Keynesian policies of managing the economic situation, in particular through taxation and public spending, it is necessary to substitute the automatic reactions of a fiscal and monetary framework which is stable in the face of variations in national income. It is necessary merely to fix some global objectives and to leave free of intervention the only mechanism capable of effectively managing the allocation of resources: the market. This framework includes, in addition to monetary discipline, the stability of government spending and transfer payments, which must not be used as a way of stabilizing the economy, and that of taxation rates, whose objective must be budgetary equilibrium. To these rules Friedman added in 1960 his well known monetary rule which has become, for many, the symbol of monetarism: the only way to obtain price stability is to remove the variations in the stock of money from the arbitrary decision of political authorities. The growth rate of the stock of money must be stabilized, according to the long-term growth rate of the real national product. Friedman even suggested that this rule be inscribed in the constitution, so as to separate it from the arbitrariness of political decision.

The critique of the theoretical basis of the Phillips relationship, one of the most popular instruments of Keynesian economic management, led by Friedman (1968 *AER*) and Phelps (1967), added a new concept to the monetarists' baggage: the hypothesis of the natural rate of unemployment, defined as that towards which an economy tends in a state of equilibrium. This rate depends on the structural characteristics of the economy and on the preferences of the agents who constitute it, in brief on what are called the 'real forces at play'. Market imperfections, institutional arrangements such as unemployment-insurance systems, the nature of the job market and trade union characteristics are among the realities which determine the level of this natural rate. The existence of a natural rate has important consequences. Indeed, it implies that the policies, fiscal as well as monetary, to reduce the rate of unemployment below the natural rate are ineffective in the long run;

they generate an accelerating inflation. Thus the Phillips curve is vertical in the long run. There is thus no trade-off between inflation and unemployment. The trade-off disappears because agents adapt to the inflation rate which they notice in the economy. One cannot deceive them indefinitely. A monetary policy aimed at stimulating effective demand, therefore, can only have a real effect on the economy in the short run, at the price of an increase in inflation. In the long run, agents adapt and the economy reaches the natural rate of unemployment.

The rehabilitation of the quantity theory of money and the 'discovery' of the natural rate of unemployment, therefore, theoretically justified monetarist policies. But the liberal counter-offensive was to take many other forms too. Moreover, monetarism itself is as diversified as Keynesianism. Here we have favoured the Friedmanian version, on account of the impact it had. But there are other authors to whom we have not done justice, like Brunner and Meltzer,[16] whose monetarism is sometimes contrasted with that of Friedman, and David Laidler,[17] among others.

Supply-side economics and other liberal currents[18]

Keynesian theory is often presented as a theory of effective demand, and Keynesian policies as those of demand stimulation. The monetarists criticize the conception, attributed to Keynes, of an infinitely elastic supply. They insist that it is necessary to take into account aggregate supply. But what is called supply-side economics is a more specific current, sometimes identified with what has been called 'Reaganomics'. Before he was elected President of the United States, Ronald Reagan was Governor of the State of California. A movement of revolt against taxation resulted in the Californian vote of Proposition Thirteen in 1978, which anticipated an important reduction on land tax. This wind of revolt amongst taxpayers spread through the United States. The following year, Arthur Laffer and Jan P. Seymour published *The Economics of the Tax Revolt* (1979).

In this book can be found the curve bearing Laffer's name, which suggests the tax yield initially increases and then decreases as the tax rate increases. Taxes on income and on profit that are too high discourage initiative, saving, investment and productive effort. Too oppressive a fiscal regime provokes the emergence and expansion of the underground economy, as well as the proliferation of jobs exclusively linked to tax evasion. The supply-side economists suggest a substantial cut in direct taxation and an appreciable dilution of its progressive aspect, since the wealthy are those who save and, therefore, invest most. To back up their argument, the supply-side economists use the law enunciated in 1803 by Jean-Baptiste Say, according to which global supply creates its own demand in such a way that any macroeconomic disequilibrium, in particular the existence of unemployment, can only be born from exogenous shocks or bad functioning of markets. The Keynesian solution of demand stimulation is not only ineffective, but can also have an effect opposite to the one desired.

Close to the monetarists in many respects, the supply-siders criticize them, however, for focusing all their interest on the money supply. It is necessary, according to them, to deal with the processes of production, productivity and innovation. They insist on the creation of money demand through the production of goods rather than on the control of money supply. The fundamental problem for them, therefore, is not that of inflation, but a stagnation of productivity, caused in great part by a fiscal system which ruins initiative and provokes distortions in relative prices and, therefore, in decisions concerning the level of production, the supply of productive factors and, more generally, the allocation of resources.

Tax reductions must go with a reduction of state spending. Given faith in the inherent stability of market economies, supply-side economics believes in the existence of the crowding-out effect, a modern version of the 'Treasury View' against which Keynes had fought at the turn of the 1930s, by which government spending diverts funds otherwise available for the private sector.[19] The resources necessary for production need to be procured by diversion from an omnipresent welfare state. This diversion makes it necessary to cut state social spending. This goal was the subject of an attempt at justification in *Wealth and Poverty*, by Georges Gilder.[20] For him, social policies constitute the main obstacle, not only to economic growth, but even to the survival of civilization, which is threatened by dreams of a stationary state, alternative and immoral ways of life, and the claims of the ecologists. Reminding one of some emphases of Malthus, Townsend and DeFoe in their critiques of the poor laws and their praise of the stimulus of hunger, Gilder writes that help provided to the unemployed, divorced people, deviants and prodigals can only encourage them to multiply and thus constitute a threat of social disintegration: 'Welfare now erodes work and family and thus keeps poor people poor' (ibid., p. 127).

Supply-side economics thus participates in a greater movement, inspired by a conservative philosophy, and in which can be found currents such as that of the libertarians, sometimes called anarcho-capitalists. The theoretical content of these diverse schools of thought is reduced to the reaffirmation of the virtues of the market and of competition, against state intervention and all forms of social regulation. The excessive level of the natural rate of unemployment is considered to be the result of the laws on minimum wages, unemployment insurance and the militancy of the unions whose power must be reduced. The libertarians go the furthest in calling into question the role of the state, since they deprive it of the functions recognized by Adam Smith and his liberal successors – army, police, justice, education and production of some essential infrastructure such as the transport system – transforming liberalism into a panacea. One of the driving forces behind this current is David Friedman, who blames Milton Friedman and Hayek for not being sufficiently radical in their opposition to the state.[21] Ultimately, the state should disappear; in this the libertarians declare themselves in accord with the anarchists. But contrary to Proudhon, Bakunin and even Marx who also was considering the dissolution of the state, the libertarians place their confidence in the market; for them, anarchism is the ultimate form of liberal capitalism.

The imperialism of neoclassical economics

Even if they overlap considerably, liberalism and neoclassical theory must not be confused. Neoclassical economics can coexist with several ideological and political orientations. However, since the end of the 1950s, the renewal and generalization of the neoclassical approach has gone hand-in-hand with the resurgence of liberalism, with the encouragement, in particular, of economists bound to the Chicago School. Whilst the neoclassical theory had been criticized (for a very long time) for the reductionism which prevents it from accounting for the complex realities of the world in which we live,[22] some neoclassical theoreticians still push this reduction to the extreme, and turn the theory into the key to knowledge of all social phenomena.

According to this view, society is considered as a sum of independent agents (individuals, households, firms); each is endowed with free will, and the interaction of individual decisions is at the origin of economic, social and political phenomena; each agent is submitted to constraints, both cognitive and material; the resources at his disposal, goods and services, productive factors and information, are limited; and his behaviour can be predicted from the hypothesis of rationality. This last hypothesis constitutes the central core of the neoclassical theory.

One of the most important forms of the generalization of the neoclassical approach is the theory of human capital, closely associated with the Chicago School. Indeed, of the four main theoreticians of this new field, Mincer, Schultz, Becker and Stigler, only the first does not teach at Chicago. Mincer is regarded as its initiator, since the expression 'human capital' appears in the title of an article he published in 1958; however, it is the 1961 article by Schultz, 'Investment in Human Capital', which is considered as the first presentation of the new theory, to which Becker would in turn devote an important monograph (Becker 1964). In addition to the material goods used for the production of other goods, henceforth, human resources are also considered as capital, managed according to the same principles as physical resources. The novelty here does not lie in the importance given to the capacities of human beings, which Schultz's *Investing in People* (1980) illustrates.[23] In a situation where health care and education have become both expensive and profitable, one understands that investment in human capital must be taken into account; and that, for developing countries, Schultz was criticizing physical investment at the expense of human investment which he claimed must have priority. But this analysis may also be applied at the level of the individual. Thus education spending may be analysed as an investment in capital, an operation in which the rational agent compares the flow of future benefits with a present cost. Applied to education, training and health, this new approach permits the analysis of individual choices in those fields on the basis of the agent's rationality. And income disparities may thus be analysed as the result of the choice of a rational consumer, endowed with specific preferences.

Stigler applied this approach to the acquisition of information which also constitutes a costly activity: one which will be continued as long as the marginal benefit exceeds its marginal cost (Stigler 1961). Applied, amongst other fields, to that of job search, this extension of the neoclassical theory plays an important role in some recent developments of labour economics and macroeconomics. The major step was taken by Becker and Mincer, who apply the rationality postulate to all human behaviour. This allows them to explain virtually any human acts, including, for example, criminal activities. The approach was generalized by Becker and his colleagues to decisions such as those to marry, to have children and to divorce, as well as to share tasks within a household. In all cases, it is a matter of comparing, rationally, costs and benefits.[24] The development of specializations, such as the 'new family economics' (Becker 1981) or crime and punishment economics (Becker 1968, Becker and Landes 1974),[25] illustrates the broadening of the field of analysis in terms of *homo economicus* and of rational choice.

Both the terms 'revolutionary' and 'imperialist' have been used in characterizing these new developments (Stigler 1984). Once the approach of Becker and his colleagues has been adopted, one is unsure what is left to investigate in anthropology, psychology, political science, sociology and other human sciences, when economics is conceived as the general theory of human behaviour:

> *There is only one social science.* What gives economics its imperialist invasive power is that our analytical categories – scarcity, cost, preferences, opportunities, etc. – are truly universal in applicability. ... Thus economics really does constitute the universal grammar of social science. (J. Hirshleifer, 'The Expanding Domain of Economics', *American Economic Review*, vol. 75, no. 6, 1985, p. 53, emphasis in original)

Thus conceived, economics may, for example, apply to politics. As soon as one postulates that the same rationality determines the behaviour of the agents in all their activities, the path is open to develop an economic analysis of political processes. Such is the domain opened by the theory of public choice. As the former is associated with the Chicago School, the latter is associated with the Virginia School, in view of the institutional membership of its main leaders, James Buchanan and Gordon Tullock, who founded the Public Choice Society in 1963, following the publication of their 1962 book.

But it was Anthony Downs (1957) who for the first time suggested using the tools of microeconomics to analyse the behaviour of electors and the elected, and subsequently applied them (1967) to the study of bureaucracy. As the theory of human capital had done for the choices of the individual in his private life, the theory of public choices uses microeconomic tools to study the behaviour of individuals in administration and in political life, as citizens and decision makers, and to analyse public finances and public economics. As in the goods market, agents (who may be interest groups) for example, meet in a political market, each trying to maximize their private interests, here with governmental means. On these bases, while Buchanan (1980, 1985) endeavoured to elaborate an explanation of the sharing out between the field of the market and that of political power, and to produce an objective theory of the institutional structure and of the constitutional context, Tullock, joining Becker's process, was applying the microeconomic approach to numerous fields: judiciary procedure, crime and its sanction, charity and altruism, and pollution.

Closely linked to these developments, the application of microeconomic theory to the analysis of the effects of laws is one of the constituent elements of the new branch of specialization known under the name of 'Law and Economics'.[26] The *Journal of Law of Economics*, established at the University of Chicago, and directed from 1964 to 1982 by Ronald Coase, is one of its important pillars, Coase's works constituting a source of inspiration for this current.

Liberal policies and Keynesian ripostes

In the 1960s and 1970s, analyses based on rational individual behaviour became widespread, the existence was reasserted of a simple relationship between the increase in money supply and the increase of prices, the existence of a natural rate of unemployment was put forward and the strategic role of supply was underlined. These analyses converge to criticize interventionism and advocate reducing the state's role. If the Keynesian revolution consisted in creating economic policies to reduce unemployment, insisting on the strategic role of effective demand, which implies uncertainty and expectations, it is difficult not to see in these new schools the expression of a powerful liberal counter-offensive.

This counter-offensive evidently does not unfold solely in the theoretical field. It translates into a thorough inflexion of economic policies in the industrialized countries in the 1970s, and this whatever the political colour of the governments. Two names symbolize this transformation, those of Margaret Thatcher, who took over the reins of government in Great Britain in 1979, and Ronald Reagan, who became President of the United States in 1981. The expressions Thatcherism, Reaganism and even 'Reaganomics' are sometimes used to characterize the new economic policies and, in particular, their monetarist association. But, as always, the relationship between theory and politics is neither univocal nor simple. It is to the pressure of events as much as to the inspiration of theories – in part conceived a posteriori to rationalize the policies – that the political powers respond. And, at least in the context of democratic systems, governments cannot carry out a 180-degree turn in economic policies without risking breaking the social consensus and considerably disturbing the economic machine.

Nevertheless, it remains true that, virtually everywhere in the world in the 1970s and 1980s, very important changes emerged in relation to postwar policies. In 1977, Friedman published a book entitled *From Galbraith to Economic Freedom*, stemming from conferences held in Great Britain. At one of these conferences, he offered Great Britain, as a means of solving its economic problems, a shock therapy inspired in part by the one applied in Chile. It is indeed a shock therapy, leaning on monetarism, and allowing, among other things, an extensive scheme of privatization and deregulation, as well as the questioning of the rights of unions, which Mrs Thatcher's government started in 1979.

The first budget of the Reagan administration, which also attacked union power, made significant cuts in social spending. It was said that this programme, of which the Economic Recovery Tax Act of 1981 constituted one measure, consisted of taking from the poor to give to the rich. In his first Economic Report, in 1982,[27] the President of the United States declared, of this legislation, described as historic: 'Rather than using the tax system to redistribute existing income, we have significantly restructured it to encourage people to work, save, and invest more' (in Tobin and Weidenbaum 1988, p. 325). Criticizing the lax monetary policy of his predecessors and the continual growth in government economic intervention, which were deemed responsible for the difficulties of the American economy, President Reagan asserted that the government's task must be limited to the construction of 'a sound, stable, long-term framework in which the private sector is the key engine to growth, employment, and rising living standards' (ibid., p. 328), which implies 'a careful combination of reducing incentive-stifling taxes, slowing the growth of Federal spending and regulations, and a gradually slowing expansion of the money supply' (ibid.). More globally, 'my first and foremost objective has been to improve the performance of the economy by reducing the role of the Federal Government in all its many dimensions' (ibid., p. 322), which implies in particular 'eschewing the stop-and-go economic policies of the past which, with their short-term focus, only added to our long-run economic ills' (ibid., p. 323). It is useful to read again 'A Monetary and Fiscal Framework for Economic Stability', published by Friedman in 1948, or 'Rules versus Authorities in Monetary Policy' published by Simons in 1936, to find the sources of inspiration of the writers of Ronald Reagan's discourse.

Of course, this political turning point has given rise to the critiques of post-Keynesians, institutionalists, radicals, Marxists and other heterodoxies. It was also harshly criticized by the neoclassical Keynesians, who had codified the orthodoxy of the preceding decades, in particular by those who were associated, either closely or at a distance, with the 'new economics' of the Kennedy era. Thus, on several occasions, Hahn, Modigliani, Samuelson, Solow and Tobin, among others, criticized, sometimes very severely, monetarism,[28] in particular in its political context. On the theoretical level, the debate was more muffled. Tobin admitted, for example, the idea of the progressive shift towards the north-east of the expectations-augmented Phillips curve, without accepting the hypothesis of the natural rate of unemployment (Tobin 1975). In his presidential address to the American Economic Association, Modigliani declared for his part that 'there are in reality no serious analytical disagreements between leading monetarists and leading nonmonetarists' (Modigliani 1977, p. 1). He added that, if Friedman had already been able to declare himself a Keynesian, then it was possible to consider Modigliani a monetarist, in particular on the basis of his 1944 and 1963 articles, as moreover Keynes could have defined himself. Patinkin, whom some see as a major creator of the neoclassical synthesis and others as a theoretician of monetarism, considers for his part that Friedman, in his monetary theory, simply gave an elegant and sophisticated formulation to Keynes's monetary theory (Patinkin 1969). To this Friedman retorted that the resemblances between his theory and that of Keynes are due to the fact that *The General Theory* retains several elements of the quantity theory of money, of which Keynes was a convinced partisan for most of his career: 'Indeed I may say, as have so many others since there is no way of contradicting it, that if Keynes were alive today he would no doubt be at the forefront of the counter-revolution' (Friedman 1970, p. 8). Some even believed they detected in Keynes's writings the theory of the natural rate of unemployment.[29] Here a certain theoretical confusion may be noticed, which is certainly due to the fact that monetarists as well as Keynesians of the synthesis refer to the same microeconomic foundation.

But the political divergence is very clear. Modigliani thus described it, in his discourse, already quoted, entitled 'The Monetarist Controversy or, Should We Forsake Stabilization Policies?':

> In reality the distinguishing feature of the monetarist school and the real issues of disagreement with nonmonetarists is not monetarism, but rather the role that should probably be assigned to stabilization policies. Nonmonetarists accept what I regard to be the fundamental practical message of *The General Theory*: that a private enterprise economy using an intangible money *needs* to be stabilized, *can* be stabilized, and therefore *should* be stabilized by appropriate monetary and fiscal policies. Monetarists by contrast take the view that there is no serious need to stabilize the economy; that even if there were a need, it could not be done, for stabilization policies would be more likely to increase than to decrease instability; and, at least some monetarists would, I believe, go so far as to hold that, even in the unlikely event that stabilization policies could on balance prove beneficial, the government should not be trusted with the necessary power. (Modigliani 1977, p. 1)

In Modigliani's opinion, the monetarists' attack against Keynesianism is not directed against the Keynesian theoretical structure as such, but revolves around the question of knowing whether this framework implies the need for stabilization policies. Concerning the necessity of state intervention, his position is very clear: 'We must, therefore, categorically reject the monetarist appeal to turn back the clock forty years by discarding the basic message of *The General Theory*. We should instead concentrate our efforts in an endeavour to make stabilization policies more effective in the future than they have been in the past' (ibid., p. 18).

One of the principal creators of the neoclassical synthesis, John Hicks, has never sought to compromise with the monetarist approach. It is by using the *IS–LM* diagram that monetarists, neoclassical Keynesians and new macroeconomists were successfully able to compare their respective positions as regards the mechanisms at play in the economy. From one to the other, only the shape and position of the curves varied. Hicks, as we have already emphasized, preferred to keep his distance in relation to this scheme of analysis, of which he was the initiator.[30] But at the moment of monetarism's rise, one could hardly consider him as still being a member of the neoclassical synthesis camp. Another attack against monetarism came from a totally different quarter, and takes a very different approach. These are economists who share the monetarists' political vision, and are even more radical in their questioning of state economic intervention. But they criticize both the monetarists and the Keynesians, which they sometimes place in the same camp, for a lack of theoretical rigour, and, in particular, for the absence of clear microeconomic foundations for their macroeconomic constructions. These are the new classical macroeconomists to whom we now turn.

Notes

1. *Keynes's 'General Theory': A Retrospective View*, London, Macmillan, 1950.
2. Among them, one may include Armen Alchian, Maurice Allais, Gary Becker, James Buchanan, Harold Demsetz, Walter Eucken, Milton Friedman, Frank H. Knight, Fritz Machlup, Ludwig von Mises, Richard Posner, Lionel Robbins and George Stigler.

3. Besides Friedman, one can mention, among others, Gary Becker, James Buchanan, Ronald Coase, H. Gregg Lewis, Robert Lucas, Loyd Mints, Richard Posner, Theodore Schultz, George Stigler and Allen Wallis. Hayek was also professor of moral and social sciences at the University of Chicago between 1950 and 1961.
4. On the Chicago School, see H. L. Miller, 'On the "Chicago School of Economics"', *Journal of Political Economy*, vol. 70, 1962, 64–9; Patinkin 1969, 1981; Reder 1982; Stigler 1988 (ed.). However, Viner, often considered one of the fathers of this school, denied being a member of what he called a putative school. On this subject, see the correspondence with Patinkin reprinted in Patinkin 1981, 265–71.
5. In the context of a series of conferences held by American recipients of the Nobel Memorial Prize in Economics, Friedman jokingly declared – but jokes are never innocent – that one had maximal chances of receiving this prize if one was American, male and had taught or studied at the University of Chicago (1986, pp. 77–8)!
6. On monetarism, one may consult, in a very abundant literature: Chrystal 1990, *et al.* (an anthology of major articles of this current of thought, in two volumes), Hoover 1984, Laidler 1981, Mayer 1978 and 1990, Steele 1989, Stein 1976. On the evolution of contemporary macroeconomics, and the debates between the competing schools, see, among others, Barro and Fischer 1976, Dore 1993, Dow 1985, and Johnson 1962.
7. 'The Role of Money and Monetary Policy', *Federal Reserve Bank of St Louis Review*, vol. 50, 1968, 8–24.
8. 'The "Monetarist Revolution" in Monetary Theory', *Weltwirtschaftliches Archiv*, vol. 105, 1970, 1–30.
9. *La Response de Maistre Iean Bodin advocat en la cour au paradoxe de monsieur de Malestroit, touchant l'encherissement de toutes choses, & le moyen d'y remédier*, Paris, Chez Martin Lejeune, 1568 [reprint, Paris, Armand Colin, 1932]. Jean Bodin was a jurist and philosopher. Malestroit had written a report on the increase of prices in France, attributing it principally to the debasement of currency. Bodin, to the contrary, deemed that the gold and silver influx from the New World was by far the principal cause of the prices increase. Bodin's theory had already been enunciated by, among others, Martin de Azpicuelta (*Commentarius de usuris*, Rome, 1556) and Copernicus, the astronomer (*Monete Cudende Ratio*, 1526).
10. *Political Discourses*, 1752.
11. For their part, Baumol (1952 *QJE*) and Tobin (1947 *RES*, 1956 *RES*) had developed an analysis of the demand for money inspired by Keynes, but based on the agents' optimizing behaviour.
12. C. Warburton had already looked into this question and had drawn conclusions which can be characterized as monetarist. See 'The Misplaced Emphasis in Contemporary Business-Cycle-Fluctuation Theory', *Journal of Business*, October 1946.
13. *Determinants and Effects of Changes in the Stock of Money*, New York, National Bureau of Economic Research, 1965.
14. See, among others, Mayer 1965 and Modigliani 1965. In 1957, Friedman had launched, with Becker, a preliminary offensive which had provoked a number of reactions ('A Statistical Illusion in Judging Keynesian Models', *Journal of Political Economy*, vol. 65, 64–75).
15. 'Rules versus Authorities in Monetary Policy', *Journal of Political Economy*, vol. 44, 1936, 1–30.
16. See in particular the 'Carnegie-Rochester Conference Series on Public Policy' series, published twice a year under the direction of these two authors (Amsterdam, North-Holland); see also their critique of Friedman, 'Friedman's Monetary Theory', *Journal of Political Economy*, vol. 80, 1972, 837–51, and *Money and the Economy: Issues in Monetary Analysis*, Cambridge, England, Cambridge University Press, 1993.
17. *Essays on Money and Inflation*, Manchester University Press, University of Chicago Press, 1975; *Monetarist Perspectives*, Cambridge, Massachusetts, Harvard University Press, 1982; *Taking Money Seriously and Other Essays*, Cambridge, Massachusetts, MIT Press, 1990; *The Golden Age of the Quantity Theory*, Princeton University Press, 1991.
18. On supply-side economics, see Hailstones 1982, Lucas 1990, Raboy 1982 and Rousseas 1982.

19. Another modern theory about the effect of government debt and deficit, the Ricardian equivalence theorem, named by Buchanan, following an article by Barro (1974), states that these effects are simply non-existent. According to this theorem, the agents' rationality implies that an increase in the budget deficit, financed by a bond issue, will cause a decrease in private spending and an increase in saving, considering that the agents, 'intertemporally rational', anticipate that they themselves, or their descendants, some day will have to pay off the increased public debt through higher taxes. For a review of the literature on this, see John J. Seater, 'Ricardian Equivalence', *Journal of Economic Literature*, vol. 31, 1993, 142–90.
20. New York, Basic Books, 1981.
21. *The Machinery of Freedom: Guide to a Radical Capitalism*, New Rochelle, New York, Arlington House, 1973. Similar positions are defended in France by Henri Lepage (*Demain le libéralisme,* Paris, Hachette, 1980), who attributes them to what he calls the 'new economists'. See also Robert Nozick, *Anarchy, State and Utopia*, Oxford, Basil Blackwell; New York, Basic Books, 1974.
22. See Chapters 6 and 9.
23. Well before him, the mercantilists had affirmed that the population constitutes the real source of the wealth of the nation. Say's theory of productive services, the source of Walras's production theory, which is itself at the basis of modern microeconomic theory, implicitly contains a theory of human capital. And Stalin, in a 4 May 1935 speech at the Red Army Academy, had praised human beings as the most precious capital!
24. This conception of Becker (1965), according to which the principal activity of an individual consists in allocating one's time among diverse activities, was applied, derisively, to the brushing of one's teeth (A.S. Blinder, 'The Economics of Brushing Teeth', *Journal of Political Economy*, vol. 82, 1974, 887–91).
25. See also I. Ehrlich, 'The Deterrent Effect of Criminal Law Enforcement', *Journal of Legal Studies*, vol. 1, 1972, 259–76; G. Radnitzky and P. Bernholz (eds), *Economic Imperialism: The Economic Approach Applied Outside the Field of Economics*, New York, Paragon House, 1987.
26. On this subject see D. Friedman, 'Law and Economics', *New Palgrave* 1987, vol. 3, 144–7; C. J. Goetz, *Cases and Materials on Law and Economics*, St Paul, Minnesota, West; Posner 1973, 1981 and 1987; Tullock 1971.
27. This report and that of the Council of Economic Advisers, as well as President Kennedy's first report, were edited jointly by Tobin and Weidenbaum, under the title of *Two Revolutions in Economic Policy* (1988). See above, Chapter 3, where excerpts from Kennedy's report may be found.
28. See for example Hahn 1971 and 1982, Modigliani 1977, Samuelson 1980, Solow 1980 *AER*, Tobin 1981 and 1987.
29. See for example Hutchison 1977 *Keynes*; A. Meltzer, *Keynes's Monetary Theory: A Different Interpretation*, Cambridge, England, Cambridge University Press, 1988; Phelps 1970.
30. See above, Chapter 5.

8 New macroeconomics

Having begun in the 1960s, the calling into question of Keynesianism took place in the 1970s and 1980s. Part of this criticism involves the inadequacy of its microeconomic foundations. The critique was formulated by authors of very diverse theoretical horizons, among whom were several still regarding themselves as Keynes's disciples. It was also led by those who were very critical of Keynesian theory. Robert Lucas, at first a Keynesian and then principal theoretician of the new classical macroeconomics, assumed leadership of the offensive. Traditional macroeconomics, as much Friedmanian as Keynesian – even though Lucas showed Friedman deference[1] – was left behind as the reconstruction of economic analysis, on the basis of the extension of the rationality postulate to include the acquisition of information and expectations, was witnessed.

It was also on the basis of the rationality postulate (coming within a non-Walrasian perspective) that the disequilibrium theorists, inspired by Patinkin, Clower and Leijonhufvud, attempted to give Keynesian macroeconomics more sturdy microeconomic foundations. Finally, in the 1980s, in opposition to the new classical macroeconomics, there developed a 'new Keynesian economics', which borrowed some elements of the theories of disequilibrium.

New classical macroeconomics[2]

The new classical macroeconomics was born in the 1970s, following works by, principally, Lucas, Leonard Rapping,[3] Thomas Sargent and John Wallace. It rapidly became the dominant current, at least in North American departments of economics. Some enthusiastic partisans did not hesitate to call it a revolution in a discipline indeed accustomed to intellectual upheaval. Others characterized the taking of the leadership by these new theorists as a palace revolution in the monetarist camp, despite the fact that several economists of this school of thought considered themselves as much estranged from monetarism as from Keynesianism.

The designation of 'new classical macroeconomics' constituted an explicit reference to the classical macroeconomic theory which was the object of Keynes's critique. Lucas thus affirmed that it was necessary to come back to the research programme of business cycle theoreticians of the first decades of the century, principal among whom were Mitchell and Hayek.[4] The adjective 'new' indicates that it is not merely a pure and simple retreat. Elements from Keynesianism were retained and the founders of the new classical macroeconomics did not regard themselves as abandoning monetarism: on the contrary, Lucas's explicit ambition was to give sturdier theoretical foundations to the economic policy propositions put forward by Henry Simons, Friedman and the monetarists. It was also a matter of rationalizing the theory of the natural rate of unemployment. Results were to be achieved by giving macroeconomics the microeconomic foundations it lacked. These foundations were to be located in the Walrasian theory of general equilibrium. For Lucas and his disciples, it is necessary, in order to construct a rigorous macroeconomic theory, to begin with the hypothesis that all markets, including the labour market, are always in equilibrium, flexible prices there playing the role anticipated in the Walrasian theory. Thus this is sometimes called equilibrium business cycle theory.

To the traditional neoclassical hypotheses, the new classical macroeconomics added the optimal treatment by agents of the information that they have at their disposal, imperfect information whose acquisition is costly; whereas, in the Walrasian model of general equilibrium, the information is perfect. Two sources must be distinguished here: on the one hand, the theory of information advanced by Stigler in 1961, in accordance with which the acquisition of information is a process to which one must apply the same rules of analysis in terms of optimization as to other economic activities; on the other hand, the rational expectations hypothesis enunciated by Muth the same year.[5] This hypothesis has such an importance in the new approach that it was also called the theory of rational expectations. Indeed, for many, it constitutes its most fundamental core.

Taking expectations into account is evidently not an innovation. The question of the treatment of time and expectations is as old as economic thinking. By explicitly introducing expectations to describe the process of price formation in his doctoral thesis, Myrdal (1927) heralded contemporary thinking on this subject.[6] On this basis, Myrdal (as much as Ohlin, Lindahl and Lundberg) attempted to construct a dynamic macroeconomic analysis, taking expectations into consideration.[7] Of course, expectations play a capital role in Keynes's *General Theory*. They are linked to uncertainty about the future and cannot receive a treatment of the probabilistic type. There is not, among the actors of the Keynesian system, a rational calculation of the expected benefits of actions and choices. In the postwar period, theorists who criticized Keynes for the so-called exogenous nature of expectations in his system attempted to provide an endogenous explanation of expectations formation by agents. Metzler's 1941 article on inventory cycles plays a pioneer role in this respect. In 1956, in the collective book on the quantity theory of money, edited by Friedman, Cagan introduced the hypothesis of adaptive expectations into a study of the money demand function.[8] According to their hypothesis, individuals form their expectations on the basis of the difference between their past expectations and the values actually realized. Thus, for example, the expected rate of inflation is determined by the difference between expected and realized levels of inflation in the past. Such is the hypothesis at the basis of the theory of the natural rate of unemployment. And the variant of the Phillips curve integrating this approach is called the expectations-augmented Phillips curve.

For the new classical macroeconomists, this hypothesis is unsatisfactory because it contradicts rational behavior. It implies that agents only learn through their past mistakes and do not use the new information they may have at their disposal. The rational anticipations hypothesis is meant to correct this weakness. Here is how Muth formulates it:

> I should like to suggest that expectations, since they are informed predictions of future events, are essentially the same as the predictions of the relevant economic theory. At the risk of confusing this purely descriptive hypothesis with a pronouncement as to what firms ought to do, we call such expectations 'rational'. ...
>
> Expectations of firms (or, more generally, the subjective probability distribution of outcomes) tend to be distributed, for the same information set, about the prediction of the theory (or the 'objective' probability distributions of outcomes). (Muth, 'Rational Expectations and the Theory of Price Movements', *Econometrica*, vol. 29, 1961, p. 316)

When it comes down to it, this hypothesis 'is an application of the concept of economic man' (Fischer 1980, p. 13). Its lack of realism was, of course, criticized. Muth already had an answer in his article, analogous to Friedman's methodological arguments (1953): the hypothesis's lack of realism matters little, as long as it permits one to deduce results which can be empirically tested. Constructing the model 'as if' the agents had a perfect knowledge of the economy is thus acceptable. On the whole, the subjective expectations of the agents coincide with the real values of the variables; the uncertainty in face of the future disappears. We are really very far from Keynes's vision. While the latter criticized the classical theory for postulating too much rationality on the part of agents, Muth blamed the economic models for not assuming enough rationality.

The new classical macroeconomics took root in reflections of Friedman (1968 *AER*) and Phelps (1967) on the Phillips curve and the natural rate of unemployment. It applies to macroeconomic analysis the rational expectations hypothesis which Muth had formulated in a microeconomic study, assuming that the agents gather and rationally use information, and that they have the same knowledge of the economy's structure and functioning as they have of the economic theory: 'private agents understand the dynamic environment in which they operate approximately as well as do governments policymakers' (Sargent 1986, p. 102). They modify their behaviour when the rules of the game are changed, with the principal ones being parameters of economic policy. Therefore they cannot be easily fooled. They integrate into their expectations of inflation the expected actions of the monetary authorities. Only unanticipated changes of the stock of money can make the effective inflation rate diverge from the expected rate. From then on, not only is the long-run Phillips curve vertical, so also is the short-run curve. Contrary to what Samuelson and Solow[9] had earlier advanced, there is no trade-off between inflation and unemployment in the short as much as the long run. For classical monetarism, that of Hume as much as that of Friedman, a variation of the stock of money – a nominal shock – may have an effect in the short term on the economy's real aggregates. But for new classical macroeconomics, the economy reacts in the short run to a nominal shock by immediately finding its natural rate of unemployment again, except in the case of an unexpected shock, a surprise on the part of the monetary authorities.

This analysis leads the new classical macroeconomics to a very critical stance towards traditional econometrics, and towards what Lucas calls the 'theory of economic policy' (1976, p. 20). The traditional econometric models, monetarist as much as Keynesian, imply that the agents' behaviour is invariant to changes in the rules of the game and in economic policies. This was why they failed to predict the effects on production, employment and prices of the huge budget deficits and increases in the stock of money observed in the 1970s. Lucas concludes the article in which he calls into question traditional econometrics, and which is at the origin of the expression 'Lucas critique', with this assertion: 'given that the structure of an econometric model consists of optimal decision rules of economic agents, and that optimal decision rules vary systematically with changes in the structure of series relevant to the decision maker, it follows that any change in policy will systematically alter the structure of econometric models' (Lucas, 1976, p. 41).

Any policy of demand stimulation which is expected and systematic can have no effect on production and employment. This is the 'neutrality' or 'policy ineffectiveness theorem' as formulated by Sargent and Wallace (1975) and Barro (1976). As the political decision makers react to the state of the economy, agents guess what they will do and adjust their behaviour accordingly. Deviations in the effective rate of production from the natural rate result from random shocks and not from systematic policies. In accordance with this perspective, cyclical fluctuations are provoked by shocks which are amplified by diverse transmission mechanisms in a world characterized by the rational behaviour of agents and subject to general equilibrium. These shocks, these surprises, induce among agents erroneous perceptions of the price variations, which lead them to take wrong decisions on production. In particular, the supply of labour strongly reacts to small temporary fluctuations in real incomes, in accordance with what is called the intertemporal substitution hypothesis. The fluctuations in employment are provoked by the choice the worker makes between leisure and work. In this perspective, there is no involuntary unemployment: 'involuntary unemployment is not a fact or a phenomenon which it is the task of theorists to explain. It is, on the contrary, a theoretical construct which Keynes introduced in the hope that it would be helpful in discovering a correct explanation for a genuine phenomenon: large-scale fluctuations in measured, total unemployment' (Lucas 1978, p. 354). Lucas and his colleagues consider, of course, that their theoretical construction is superior to that of Keynes in accounting for employment fluctuations, a theory according to which the unemployed person chooses his state as part of a process of optimization.

For the new classical macroeconomics, the shocks which trigger the cyclical process in a universe otherwise in stable equilibrium are of a monetary nature. Diverse critiques of these models were brought forward, not only by resolute adversaries of this approach, but even by those who share some of its postulates. This was how the equilibrium real business cycle approach developed through the impetus given by F.E. Kydland and E.C. Prescott,[10] J.B. Long and C.I. Plosser[11] and R.G. King and Plosser.[12] Gradually, during the 1980s, this vision asserted itself within the new classical macroeconomics, some regarding it as an extension of works by Lucas, Sargent and Wallace, others on the contrary as a rupture of importance.

The theory of real cycles considers that fluctuations are generated by real shocks, for example at the level of productivity, in economies where markets are continuously in equilibrium. For example, in Kydland and Prescott's model, the necessary 'time to build' new investment goods is considered as a technological characteristic which determines the number of periods necessary to produce durable production and consumption goods. These time periods are invariant and are not affected by political factors. It is the construction time which thus contributes to generating the production fluctuations, the employment fluctuations being explained by the hypothesis of intertemporal substitution. Thus it is real shocks, affecting the technology and the workers's productivity, which start the cyclical processes. In Long and Plosser's model, the real shocks spread in view of the agents' desire to smooth their consumption in the long run. For King and Plosser, the correlations between the monetary variations and the real activity, emphasized in the monetarist analyses, are in reality the common results of the influence of other real factors, such as changes in preferences, technology or resources.[13]

The analyses of the partisans of the new classical macroeconomics are therefore quite diversified. Thus Sargent disputed the fact that one could speak of a rational expectations school in the sense of 'a collection of economists with an agreed-upon model of the economy and view about optimal monetary and fiscal policy' (Sargent 1986, p. 101). Nonetheless, one encounters a common attitude with regard to economic policy, distinguished by an absolute scepticism towards the efficiency of state intervention: it only takes stable, clear rules of the game, well known by all. Sargent thus compared the economy to an American football game. Lucas enunciated these rules in a 1980 article, saying that he was only amending what Friedman had already written in 1948 about the monetary and fiscal framework for economic stability. The first rule consists of setting a stable annual rate of growth of the stock of money; the second, rates for spending and governmental transfers which do not vary in real terms over the cycle; the third, permanent tax rates whose objective in the long run is to equilibrate the budget. To these three rules, already suggested by Friedman, Lucas adds: 'A clearly announced policy that wage and price agreements privately arrived at will not trigger governmental reactions of any kind' (Lucas 1980, p. 200). These rules are thus minimal rules. In a certain way, the best economic policy, in the perspective of the new classical economists, is the absence of economic policy.

On the basis of their analyses, the economists of this school of thought are very critical regarding the economic programme developed by United States President Reagan's advisers and its implementation. Their critique is directed towards the lack of consistency and, therefore, the lack of credibility of the suggested measures. To a strict monetarist policy of a cut in the money stock a policy of tax reduction is added, and this is not compensated by the prospect of a decline in spending. Indeed, in the United States, the reduction in social spending was accompanied by a rise in spending on research and on space and military activities, which served overall to increase rather than decrease the budget deficit. From then on, agents anticipated a monetization of the increased government debt. In accordance with the new classical macroeconomic propositions, it would have been necessary to announce clearly both a cut in the stock of money and a tax reduction indicating how the budget deficit was to be made up.[14]

The disequilibrium theories[15]

In the context of the neoclassical synthesis, as was formulated in the textbooks of the 1950s and 1960s, the Keynesian model is conceived as an equilibrium system, save for the labour market characterized by wage rigidity which prevents the emergence of full employment. Such was the analysis which Modigliani proposed in 1944, and which is found in the work of several other authors. Patinkin, however, is an exception. According to him, 'the involuntary unemployment of the *General Theory* need *not* have its origin in wage rigidities' (Patinkin 1956, p. 340). He suggested that *The General Theory* must be interpreted as a dynamic analysis, in which there are insufficient forces to bring the system to equilibrium. It is indeed a question of rigidities, but they are not of the same nature as those postulated in the static neoclassical Keynesian model, where one can demonstrate that the real balance effect is sufficient to ensure full employment. In a dynamic system, consumers and investors do not react fast enough to the movements in prices and to the modification of the real value of their liquid assets; the rigidities in their spending habits prevent equilibrium. This is why Patinkin prefers to call Keynes's theory one of underemployment disequilibrium rather than a theory of underemployment equilibrium.

In an article which gave rise to much discussion, published first in German in 1963 and in English in 1965, Clower developed these ideas, even though he was critical of Patinkin's theses and those of Hicks (who was also, at the same moment, laying the foundations of an approach in terms of disequilibrium (Hicks 1965), rather distant from the ideas of the neoclassical synthesis initiated in his 1937 article). Tackling the said synthesis or 'Keynesian counter-revolution' head-to-head, Clower considered Hicks and Patinkin as its two main inspirers. For Clower, Keynesian macroeconomics is incompatible with the Walrasian microeconomics with which attempts had been made to integrate it. Underemployment equilibrium cannot be conceived as resulting from a lack of rationality on the part of the agents, in particular of money illusion on the part of the workers.

For Clower, there are implicit microeconomic foundations in *The General Theory*, different from the traditional Walrasian hypothesis but which, like the latter, imply rationality of the agents. In the Walrasian model, prices vary instantly so as to clear all markets. Individuals may buy or sell everything they want at the given prices. Clower called these demands and supplies 'notional'. In Keynes's model, there are constraints on the quantities of goods that an individual may buy or sell. For example, in the case of an excess supply of labour, the demand (which is then called effective) of an individual who cannot sell all the labour that he would like is less than the notional demand at the given prices. The demand for the goods is then a function, not of the prices, but of the quantity of labour that an individual can sell. One therefore replaces a system in which the instantaneous variations of prices ensure the equilibrium on the markets with a system in which the quantities adjust rapidly while prices remain fixed or move slowly. In *Capital and Growth*, published in the same year as the English version of Clower's text, Hicks developed the concepts of 'flexprice' and 'fixprice'. He considered, as he did in his work of the 1930s, drawing inspiration from the Swedish theorists, an economy of successive periods of time. The flexprice method, also called temporary equilibrium, supposes that prices adjust within each period in such a way that current transactions equalize supplies and demands. The fixprice method considers that prices are given exogenously at the beginning of each period and remain unchanged during the period so that demand and supply can remain in disequilibrium. Here Hicks suggests that this is a matter of two extreme cases and that the reality is to be found somewhere in between these extremes.

In 1968, Leijonhufvud published a book in which he distinguished Keynesian economics from Keynes's economics, and set himself to heal what he considered the micro–macro schizophrenia, without abandoning the hypothesis of the rationality of agents.[16] For Leijonhufvud, as for Patinkin, the debate on *The General Theory* 'proceeded for a long time in the framework of comparative statics, which obscured the essentially dynamic disequilibrium nature of Keynes's theory' (Leijonhufvud 1968, p. 537). Like Clower, he emphasized that it is necessary to come back to an analysis of a Marshallian type, in which quantities adjust more easily and more rapidly than prices. Leijonhufvud introduced problems of transactions structure, circulation of information and liquidity constraints in order to explain the Keynesian disequilibria. His vision has some kinship with the islands parable presented by Phelps in his introduction to *Microeconomic Foundations of Inflation and Unemployment Theory* (1970). For Leijonhufvud, unemployment and depressions are caused, in great part, by the market system giving the wrong signals to agents.

Constructing a synthesis of the models of Clower and Patinkin, integrating Hicks's contribution, Barro and Grossman (1971) gave to this type of analysis the name 'disequilibrium theory'. However, the analyses of Clower and Leijonhufvud, like that of Barro and Grossman, do not explain the rigidity of prices in their models. A group of economists, largely French, developed the theory of disequilibrium. One of their aims is to give an endogenous explanation of price rigidity. It is not a question of explaining unemployment as the result of prices being set in an exogenous way, but to account simultaneously for endogenous unemployment and prices rigidity. Among the main theorists of this current of thought one may mention J.-P. Bénassy,[17] J.H. Drèze,[18] J. M. Grandmont and G. Laroque,[19] and Y. Younès.[20] Malinvaud also made important contributions to the theory of disequilibrium. It is to him that we owe the distinction between Keynesian unemployment, characterized by an insufficiency of effective demand, and classic unemployment, characterized by real wages being too high (Malinvaud 1977). Negishi, for his part, developed analyses of price formation in the context of monopolistic competition.[21] A sceptical theorist of general equilibrium, Hahn (1975) contributed to the theory of disequilibrium, developing in particular some of the intuitions of Drèze and Negishi.

The new Keynesian economics[22]

The 1980s witnessed the development of a current of thought called the 'new Keynesian economics'. This new wave was born in a reaction to the rejection of the Keynesian approach by the new classical macroeconomics and continued a similar project to that of the theory of disequilibrium, while dissociating itself from the latter. Here again, it was a question of giving Keynesian macroeconomic theory more rigorous microeconomic foundations.

The new Keynesian economics attempted to explain the rigidity of prices and wages, postulated by the neoclassical Keynesians, and to show how these rigidities yield the characteristics called 'Keynesian' of the contemporary economies, premier among which is the persistence of high unemployment rates. In particular, it is a question of seeing how 'small nominal rigidities' can generate important real effects at the macroeconomic level.[23] These frictions in the price flexibility may stem from the rational, or 'near-rational', behaviour of firms, taking into account the costs of price adjustment, or 'menu costs'. Thus there are, as in a restaurant, costs associated with the printing of the new menu, which necessarily accompany any change of price, costs which are sometimes higher than the advantage linked to the price adjustment. The individual firm, therefore, may gain by choosing not to modify its price, despite the fact that the impact of similar individual decisions on the entire economy may be very significant. These phenomena are accentuated when one takes into account the monopolistic nature of contemporary economies.[24] For M. Weitzman,[25] the existence of involuntary unemployment is essentially explained by the monopolistic structure of contemporary economies. (An empirical study conducted by Dennis W. Carlton shows that the rigidity of prices is far more the norm than the exception when one examines the behaviour of large American firms.[26]) The new Keynesians also introduce what they call coordination failures among agents to explain underemployment, that is difficulties linked to problems in the flow of information, which have the consequence of magnifying the effects of any random shock to the economy.[27]

The study of labour market characteristics plays an important role, as much in new Keynesian economics as in the theories of disequilibrium. On this point, some developments are common to these approaches and to currents such as institutionalism and radical economics on the one hand, and new classical macroeconomics on the other. Works of an institutionalist nature on the duality of the labour market,[28] and certain analyses of the radical economists,[29] join with those devoted to implicit contracts and to efficiency wages.[30] According to this latter vision, a higher real wage exerts an upward influence on productivity. Moreover, it may be in firms' interests to pay a higher than equilibrium wage in order to slow down staff turnover, attract more skilled workers and increase discipline within the firm (Stiglitz 1984 with Shapiro). The theory of implicit contracts attempts, for its part, to discover norms and implicit agreements in the labour relations within the firm, often very rigid and long established but not codified in collective agreements.

The staggering of contracts constitutes another source of rigidity and amplification of disequilibria.[31] Here it is as much a question of staggering in the decisions of product price variation as of work contracts. Theoreticians close to new classical macroeconomics emphasized this fact, indicating that it weakens Sargent and Wallace's policy ineffectiveness postulate. Because of the staggering of the contracts, even an expected monetary shock may have a real effect on the economy.[32] In Taylor's model, the interaction between wage contracts and expectations propagates the shock wave beyond the typical contract duration, considering that the contracts are overlapping. Indeed, the effects are all the greater since prices are set by a margin above costs.[33]

By supplying Keynesian macroeconomics with the microeconomic foundations it lacks, several followers of new Keynesian economics claim to go beyond the controversy between Keynesianism and monetarism – to such a point that a new Keynesian may quench his thirst at the two springs, as witnessed in the introduction to a recent collection of major articles of this current of thought:

> An economist can be a monetarist by believing that fluctuations in the money supply are the primary source of fluctuations in aggregate demand and a new Keynesian by believing that microeconomic imperfections lead to macroeconomic price rigidities. Indeed, since monetarists believe that fluctuations in the money supply have real effects but often leave price rigidities unexplained, much of new Keynesian economics could also be called new monetarist economics. (Mankiw and Romer 1991, p. 3)

Thus a new Keynesian may share the hesitations of both monetarists and the new classical economists regarding state intervention. Nonetheless, most of the work carried out by the authors of this current shows that the normal functioning of monetary economies, including the assumption of the perfect rationality of their agents, does not lead to the equilibrium and stability postulated in classical and monetarist models. Consequently, most consider that state intervention may improve the situation. The question of deciding whether it must do so is determined by the political choices of each.

We thus find a picture similar to that painted by Modigliani in his presidential address to the American Economic Association (1977), which we quoted at the end of the previous chapter. In it, he emphasized the convergence between monetarists and Keynesians at the analytical level, indicating that divergence was found at the political level, in particular concerning the necessity and desirability of stabilization policies. In the same way, several convergences have been noted between the authors we have just dealt with.[34]

The book co-authored by Phelps, and published in 1970, devoted to research on the microeconomic foundations of macroeconomics is one illustration of this. Not only does it constitute a transition between monetarism and new classical macroeconomics, but it also presents analyses falling within the theory of disequilibrium and others which announce the new Keynesian economics.

These convergences stem from a common project, which was to give macroeconomics, whatever its colour, rigorous microeconomic foundations while escaping, once and for all, from the micro–macro dichotomy which characterized economic thought of the postwar period. But, more deeply, there is also a convergence on the basic hypothesis according to which economic analysis must be based on the postulate of the agents' rationality, this rationality being exercised in the face of both quantity and price constraints. One is very far, of course, from interpretations of Keynes's work which emphasize the irreducible uncertainty affecting decisions in historical time. One is also far from the analyses which could be called holistic, those of the Kalecki or Weintraub type, in which it is rather a question of giving macroeconomic foundations to microeconomics.

These convergences also stem, in great part, from the formal similarities between those approaches which use the same language. A theoretician of the disequilibrium school justified as follows the very elaborate mathematical sophistication of this current's writings, linking it to assumption of rationality:

> Explanation of macroeconomic phenomena will be complete only when such explanations are consistent with microeconomic choice theoretic behavior and can be phrased in the language of general equilibrium theory. This implies the need for a mathematically rigorous formal statement of framework and results, even when well known. The view, therefore, that all the recent work in non-Walrasian theory states obvious points in highly mathematical and sometimes abstruse ways is, at best, misdirected. (Drazen 1980, p. 293)

What is written above on the theory of disequilibrium applies *mutatis mutandis* to the other schools. The most recent evolution of contemporary macroeconomics comes within an intellectual universe transformed by a wave of formalization and mathematicization, the roots of which we presented in Chapter 4. Certainly, its impact on the nature of economic thought and debate has not been sufficiently measured. The mathematical form leads to a *rapprochement* between the different processes, the differences often depending on the choice of a particular hypothesis, which sometimes gives rise to a certain eclecticism.[35] It tends to be accompanied by an impoverishment of thinking, and translates into discussions among *cognoscenti,* less and less with the complexity of contemporary economic, social and political reality.

Notes

1. Lucas has also been professor at the University of Chicago since 1974.
2. For general presentations and critical assessments of the new classical macroeconomics, see Begg 1982, Kantor 1979, Pesaran 1987, Sheffrin 1983 and Shiller 1978. Fischer 1980 and Lucas and Sargent 1981 constitute useful collections of articles. Klamer 1983 presents interviews with the main protagonists of the debate between Keynesianism, monetarism and new classical macroeconomics.
3. Having contributed to the bases of the new classical macroeconomics with Lucas (see their two joint texts of 1969), Rapping made a radical change of direction, being won over to the post-Keynesian and institutionalist currents (see his interview in Klamer 1983, 218–34). His career was cut short by his premature death in 1991.
4. Some thus described the new classical macroeconomics as a variant of the neo-Austrian school. See, for example, Hoover 1988 and Laidler 1981.
5. 'Rational Expectations and the Theory of Price Movements', *Econometrica*, vol. 29, 1961, 315–35. The same year, E.S. Mills had, independently, developed a similar analysis ('The Use of Adaptive Expectations in Stability Analysis: Comment', *Quarterly Journal of Economics*, vol. 75, 1961, 330–35; 'Reply', 335–8).
6. On this subject, see G. Dostaler, 'An Assessment of Gunnar Myrdal's Early Work in Economics', *Journal of the History of Economic Thought,* vol. 12, 1990, 196–221.
7. See on this subject K. Velupillai, 'Some Swedish Stepping Stones to Modern Macroeconomics', *Eastern Economic Journal,* vol. 14, 1988, 87–98, for whom the Swedish School is a precursor of the new classical macroeconomics.
8. Cagan's work is inspired by a study by L.M. Koyck, *Distributed Lags and Investment Analysis*, Amsterdam, North-Holland, 1954.
9. See above, Chapter 5.
10. 'Time to Build and Aggregate Fluctuations', *Econometrica*, vol. 50, 1982, 1345–70; see also Prescott, 'Theory Ahead of Business Cycle Measurement', *Federal Reserve Bank of Minneapolis Quarterly Review*, vol. 10, 1986, 1–22; Kydland and Prescott, 'Business Cycles: Real Facts and a Monetary Myth', *Federal Reserve Bank of Minneapolis Quarterly Review*, vol. 14, no. 2, 1990, 3–18.
11. 'Real Business Cycles', *Journal of Political Economy*, vol. 91, 1983, 39–69.
12. 'Money, Credit and Prices in a Real Business Cycle', *American Economic Review*, vol. 24, 1984, 363–80; see also Plosser, 'Understanding Business Cycles', *Journal of Economic Perspectives*, vol. 3, n° 3, 1989, 51–77.
13. On the theory of real cycles, see K. Brunner and A. Meltzer (eds), *Real Business Cycles, Real Exchange Rates and Actual Policies*, Amsterdam, North-Holland, 1986; B.T. McCallum, 'Real Business Cycle Models', in Barro 1989, 16–50; Stockman, 'Real Business Cycle Theory: A Guide, an Evaluation, and New Directions', *Federal Reserve Bank of Philadelphia Review*, vol. 24, 1987, 24–47.
14. See for example Sargent 1986, p. 36.
15. On the disequilibrium theories, one may consult, among others, J.-P. Bénassy, 'Disequilibrium Analysis'; *New Palgrave*, vol. 2, 858–63 and 'Rationed Equilibria', ibid., vol. 4, 88–92; Drazen 1980; Grandmont 1977; Hénin and Michel 1982.
16. For Coddington, Leijonhufvud's book, with Clower's article, whose analyses he extends, marks the emergence of a Keynesian 'neo-reductionism' which would henceforth constitute, with the hydraulic Keynesianism of the neoclassical synthesis and the post-Keynesian fundamentalism, one of the three main interpretations of Keynes's work (see Coddington 1976, 1983).
17. 'Neo-keynesian Disequilibrium Theory in a Monetary Economy', *Review of Economic Studies*, vol. 42, 1975, 502–23; *The Economics of Market Disequilibrium*, New York, Academic Press, 1982; *Macroeconomics: An Introduction to the Non-Walrasian Approach*, New York, Academic Press, 1986.
18. 'Existence of an Equilibrium Under Price Rigidity and Quantity Rationing', *International Economic Review*, vol. 16, 1975, 301–20.
19. 'On Keynesian Temporary Equilibria', *Review of Economic Studies*, vol. 43, 1976, 53–67.

20. 'On the Role of Money in the Process of Exchange and the Existence of a Non-Walrasian Equilibrium', *Review of Economic Studies*, vol. 42, 1975, 489–501.
21. 'Involuntary Unemployment and Market Imperfection', *Economic Studies Quarterly*, vol. 25, 1974, 32–41; 'Existence of an Underemployment Equilibrium', in G. Schwödiauer (ed.), *Equilibrium and Disequilibrium in Economic Theory*, Boston, D. Reidel, 1978, 497–510; *Microeconomic Foundations of Keynesian Macroeconomics*, Amsterdam, North-Holland, 1979.
22. On the new Keynesian economics, see Arena and Torre 1992, Gordon 1990, Greenwald and Stiglitz 1987, Hargreaves-Heap 1991 and Mankiw and Romer 1991. David Colander was one of the first to use the expression 'new Keynesian economics' (in *Macroeconomic Theory and Policy*, Chicago, Scott Foresman, 1986).
23. See in particular G.A. Akerlof and J.L. Yellen, 'A Near-Rational Model of the Business Cycle, with Wage and Price Inertia', *Quarterly Journal of Economics*, vol. 100, suppl., 1985, 828–38; A.S. Caplin and D.F. Spulber, 'Menu Costs and the Neutrality of Money', *Quarterly Journal of Economics*, vol. 102, 1987, 703–25; N.G. Mankiw, 'Small Menu Costs and Large Business Cycles: A Macroeconomic Model of Monopoly', *Quarterly Journal of Economics*, vol. 100, 1985, 529–39; M. Parkin, 'The Output–Inflation Trade-off When Prices Are Costly to Change', *Journal of Political Economy*, vol. 94, 1986, 200–24.
24. On the relations between imperfect competition and unemployment see, among others: O.J. Blanchard and N. Kiyotaki, 'Monopolistic Competition and the Effects of Aggregate Demand', *American Economic Review*, vol. 77, 1987, 647–66; R.E. Hall, 'Market Structure and Macroeconomic Fluctuations', *Brookings Papers on Economic Activity*, 1986, no. 2, 285–322; O. Hart, 'A Model of Imperfect Competition with Keynesian Features', *Quarterly Journal of Economics*, vol. 97, 1982, 109–38; R. Startz, 'Monopolistic Competition as a Foundation for Keynesian Macroeconomic Models', *Quarterly Journal of Economics*, vol. 104, 1989, 737–52.
25. 'Increasing Returns and the Foundations of Unemployment Theory', *Economic Journal*, vol. 92, 1982, 787–804.
26. 'The Rigidity of Prices', *American Economic Review*, vol. 76, 1986, 637–58.
27. L. Ball and D. Romer, 'Sticky Prices as Coordination Failure', *American Economic Review*, vol. 81, 1991, 539–52; R. Cooper and A. John, 'Coordinating Coordination Failures in Keynesian Models', *Quarterly Journal of Economics*, vol. 103, 1988, 441–63.
28. For example, M. Piore, *Unemployment and Inflation: Institutionalist and Structuralist View*, White Plains, New York, M.E. Sharpe, 1979.
29. See Bowles 1983, with Gordon and Weisskopf.
30. Akerlof and Yellen 1986; C. Azariadis, 'Implicit Contracts and Underemployment Equilibria', *Journal of Political Economy*, vol. 83, 1975, 1183–202; L. Katz, 'Efficiency Wage Theories: A Partial Evaluation', *NBER Macroeconomics Annual*, 1986, 235–76; A.B. Krueger and L.H. Summers, 'Efficiency Wages and the Interindustry Wage Structure', *Econometrica*, vol. 56, 1988, 259–93; Rosen 1985; Stiglitz 1983 with Azariadis. See also, on implicit contracts, the special issue of the *Quarterly Journal of Economics*, vol. 98, supplement.
31. L. Ball and S.G. Cecchetti, 'Imperfect Information and Staggered Price Setting', *American Economic Review*, vol. 78, 1988, 999–1008; G. Fethke and A. Policano, 'Will Wage Setters Ever Stagger Decisions?', *Quarterly Journal of Economics*, vol. 101, 1986, 867–77; J.B. Taylor, 'Staggered Wage Setting in a Macro Model', *American Economic Review*, vol. 69, 1979, 108–13; id., 'Aggregate Dynamics and Staggered Contracts', *Journal of Political Economy*, vol. 88, 1980, 1–23.
32. S. Fischer, 'Long-Term Contracts, Rational Expectations and the Optimal Money Supply Rule', *Journal of Political Economy*, vol. 85, 1977, 191–206; Phelps 1977 with Taylor.
33. See M. Bils, 'The Cyclical Behavior of Marginal Cost and Price', *American Economic Review*, vol. 77, 1987, 838–55.
34. Moreover, several among them belong to more than one school. For example, Barro and Grossman are simultaneously tied to the new classical macroeconomics and to the disequilibrium theory. Here is an example of remarks one can often read, as written by new Keynesians: 'Our results illustrate the complementarity of new classical and new

Keynesian macroeconomic models' (L. Ball and S.G. Cecchetti, 'Imperfect Information and Staggered Price Setting', *American Economic Review*, vol. 78, 1988, p. 1000). For his part, Malinvaud (1991) put forward the deep unity of macroeconomics, while Hicks, whom all the currents of macroeconomics use as their authority, called his last article, published posthumously, 'The Unification of Macro-Economics' (1990). But the Hicksian vision is rather far from that of the new currents of macroeconomics.

35. For example, Phelps describes in the following manner the evolution of the orthodox theory of unemployment since 1970: 'The theory of unemployment considered as orthodox in the Western World, this is to say that which is presented in manuals is, roughly, Keynesian. It inherits, in particular, from Keynes, Hicks, Tobin, Patinkin, the natural rate and also a theoretical apparatus which either comes within the new microeconomics without rational expectations, or from the Keynesian apparatus compatible with rational expectations in which the inertia in nominal wages or prices generates the unemployment rate. Others develop the idea that hysteresis is at the basis of the relation between the natural rate of unemployment and path of growth.

Monetarists use the same theory, with different accents, and in a way, the neoclassical theory is a particular case, though more elaborate' ('Théorie keynésienne et théorie structuraliste du chômage: analyse des vingt dernières années', *Revue française d'économie*, vol. 5, no. 1, 1990, pp. 3–4).

9 On Babel and three figures of present-day economic thought

Since the end of the 1960s, the processes of internationalization and globalization have thoroughly transformed national economies, restricted their room to manoeuvre and the capacities of governments to act, and emphasized the limits of the welfare state. The collapse of the communist regimes seems to mark the victory of the market system. With the failure of development policies in many countries, massive unemployment, the new rise in poverty and the assault on the environment, the world is suffering at the end of this century from illnesses that economists do not know how to cure. This does not prevent economics from appearing as the most firmly structured of all social sciences, efficient through the multiplicity of its applications to limited domains,[1] both domineering and expansionist. Distracted by continuous doubts about its own enterprise and the pursuit of ever-renewed ambition, the Babel which constitutes the city of present-day economists may be characterized by three mythological figures: Penelope, Sisyphus and Icarus.

Babel: the economists in their new world

One hundred and fifty years ago, an economist could have read all the books of political economy or those related to this field; 60 years ago, he could have obtained a direct knowledge of all the main works; 30 years ago, he could follow the main current developments. Nowadays, an economist must be open-minded and obstinate to be informed about the main debates concerning even just his own narrow field (or fields) of interest. In two centuries, economics (at the outset a small land in the world of human knowledge, with each of its mountains, valleys and paths known by all) has now become a world in unremitting expansion (with new continents and archipelagos appearing and landscapes being continuously reshaped).

In the aftermath of the Second World War, economics was already quite diverse, because of the plurality of objectives and approaches, the diversity of conceptions of the relation between theory and reality, and the multiplicity of schools. Since then, the domain covered by economics has continuously been extended, the fields of applied economics multiplied,[2] the number of schools and their factions increased: a multitude of discourses coexist, confront and influence each other. Moreover, economic discourse is developed and circulated on more and more diverse levels, with very wide differentiation in the degrees of generality, theoretical development and formalization, in the central or marginal nature of the objects being treated, in the proximity of these objects to observable reality, and in the nature and quality of the empirical information.[3] From the book or theoretical article which leaves a lasting mark to the publication which has no impact, from the empirical study which nurtures further analyses and thinking for a long time, to the occasional descriptive study, to the numerous purely academic exercises, the range of economic works is enormous.

In total, present-day economics is characterized by a double dynamic, as revealed by the multiplication of the number of journals: the swelling of the stock of published work[4] and its 'parcelling out'. This has transformed the world of economists into a kind of tower of Babel, where few are those who listen to others and where only a small part of the discourses delivered are actually heard;[5] all the more so since economic knowledge continues to be generated not only in the two languages which have asserted themselves since the war – English and mathematics[6] – but also in a broad variety of national idioms. Whilst economists of non-anglophone cultures follow what is produced in English, increasing numbers of English-speaking economists systematically ignore what is published in tongues other than their own.

In this context, economists tend to constitute a multitude of microcosms, each founded on a common approach or a common field of work and on reciprocal acknowledgement, and anchored in an academic department or a research centre, with its working papers and often its own journal with limited circulation. In a reverse direction, some great associations, international or national (in particular the American Economic Association, with its journals[7]), some important journals and some publishing houses, work at circulating and making available this continually evolving knowledge. Thus economics is undergoing perpetual renewal in its expansionary movement. But, because of the opaqueness of knowledge, of the time dimension, delays in circulation and assimilation, waiting periods and time-lags, this permanent reorganization takes place in a way which can be defined as deformed and discordant: thus texts written in the 1930s, discovered again by economists of a new generation in the 1960s, become inevitable references in the 1970s and 1980s. And of course no one can say which among those published recently will constitute the reference texts around 2020.

All of this is to say that we do not pretend, in this final chapter, to give a rundown of present-day economic knowledge. We will merely attempt, among the present profusion, to discern some significant principal themes in the current movements of economic thought.

Penelope: from theoretical rigour to world complexity, weaving the impossible cloth

While one could think in the 1960s that the blows dealt by Keynes and the Keynesians had got the better of the classical citadel, a new fortress was reconstituted after the war: at once disparate and unified under the banner of general equilibrium theory, and the neoclassical reading grid, equipped with powerful analytical and mathematical weapons and instruments. For a large part, its strength stems from its simplifying postulates, which generate both its lack of realism and its universal appeal.

A specialist in the theory of general equilibrium, and working at enlarging its fields of applicability, Hahn thus explained why he accepts being described as a 'neoclassical':

> There are three elements in my thinking which may justify it:
> (1) I am a reductionist in that I attempt to locate explanations in the actions of individual agents.
> (2) In theorizing about the agent I look for some axioms of rationality.
> (3) I hold that some notion of equilibrium is required and that the study of equilibrium states is useful. (Hahn 1984, pp. 1–2)

And indeed, the decisions of rational individual agents, the market, the equilibrium, the optimum are major constitutive elements of the new orthodoxy; however, in each of these domains, the critiques at once weaken orthodoxy but also help to strengthen it and provoke further questioning. Such was the case for the market. The orthodox or neoclassical vision of the market is that of a mechanical entity, in which uncoordinated individual actors intervene, none exercising a particular influence, with information circulating between them leading to adjustment towards equilibrium.

The simplifying lack of realism of this vision has been criticized for a century by successive generations and all families of heterodoxy. It has also been criticized, for some decades, by the Austrian School,[8] which has not prevented numerous authors from associating this school with the neoclassical stream, probably because the Austrian School is characterized by a radical liberalism, which distinguishes it from other heterodoxies. Hayek's critique had a special impact, mainly because, as a theoretician of classical liberalism of the first rank, he specifically ascribed to the market an essential role, as much in society in general as in the economy. However, Hayek very early rejected the Walrasian conception of a market in which the agents would be perfectly well informed.[9] He developed instead a vision of market competition as a process of learning and coordination of information which is simultaneously multiple, incomplete and, in particular, spread among millions of individuals. The market thus perceived is one of a 'spontaneous order', stemming from the evolution of humanity over several millennia, and not a rational creation of which a mathematical representation may be given. Von Mises developed an analogous view,[10] emphasizing the uncertainty under which entrepreneurs take their decisions. These ideas were developed within the framework of the modern Austrian School, in particular by Israel Kirzner,[11] who developed the concept of the market as a process, whilst Ludwig Lachmann[12] questioned the equilibrating features of the market. And all emphasized the gulf between their conceptualization and that underlying general equilibrium theory.[13] But attempts were also made, in circles closer to the neoclassical orthodoxy, to give greater realism to the mainstream vision of the market. Thus, the field of research, begun in the 1960s, notably by Stigler (1961),[14] on search, use and cost of information, was extended to cover imperfections in the transmission of information, and market equilibria under incomplete information.[15] The economics of information and the economics of uncertainty were thus opened as new fields of specialization.[16] Meanwhile, the theory of games gave a strong impetus to the analysis of the market, agents' strategies and behaviour, different forms of competition, as well as types of market.[17] In this enlarged framework, the standard market model is not invalidated, but its field of application is thereafter better defined. Finally, with the analysis of contestable markets, Baumol, Panzar and Willig (1982) undoubtedly pushed the theory towards the explanation of observable reality.

There was a similar picture as far as rationality was concerned. The orthodox conception is that of a rationality both reductionist – that of an agent reduced to one dimension who seeks to maximize benefits and minimize costs – and general, applicable to all situations, and to any decision: the rationality H. Simon calls substantive. On this point, where numerous critiques had already been made, it was Simon, a polymath, a pioneer in the analysis of complexity and winner of the Nobel Memorial Prize in economics, who made decisive inroads. In 1943, in his doctoral thesis (published in 1947), he introduced the analysis in terms of 'limited rationality', an approach later developed (1957, 1969, 1982 *Models*) in terms of 'bounded rationality', that of an agent who exercises his ability to choose, not simply with the sole concern of maximization or optimization, but in the complexity of the situation, taking account of imperfections in information and the cost of its improvement, and of the multiplicity of constraints, criteria, benefits and difficulties. This rationality is inseparable from the decision process itself, unique to each agent, and in particular to each organization, and within which he may be led to revise his objectives.

These analyses are at the heart of one of the behavioural economics schools, the Carnegie School,[18] whose method – founded on the concrete analysis of the behaviour of firms and organizations – was illustrated by Simon (1958 with March), Cyert and March,[19] followed by the works of March[20] at Stanford

University and by Nelson[21] at Yale University. This work evidently contributed to the revival of the analyses of firms, adding colour to the traditional black box of neoclassical theory. But, in this field, it was the article published by Coase in 1937, widely quoted, which opened new perspectives. Coase sought 'to show the importance for the working of the economic system of what may be termed the institutional structure of production' (Coase 1992, p. 713). In his 1937 article he attempted to explain, while remaining within the framework of neoclassical analysis, the firm's specificity in relation to the market and, therefore, the nature of the firm in a market economy. He did it by developing the thesis according to which the firm is a structure which permits elimination of the costs ensuing from the functioning of the market, costs of information search and contract negotiation, in brief, 'transaction costs'. Unrecognized or misunderstood for a long time,[22] this approach was used again by Coase in his 1960 article, 'The Problem of Social Cost'; in the 1970s, it was increasingly taken into account and gave rise to an abundant literature, in which one may find, for example, contributions by Steven S. Cheung,[23] Harold Demsetz (1967, 1968, 1972) and Oliver Williamson (1975, 1985).

Starting from hypotheses radically different from those of Simon and Coase – not only a situation of uncertainty, but with unmotivated and not necessarily rational agents – Alchian (1950, 1977), taking into account the logic of natural selection, reached similar conclusions. With Demsetz (1972), he put forward the efficiency of 'team production' in explaining the firm. Marschak, in the last part of a long career which first saw him give new impetus to econometrics,[24] also became interested in this question (1972), as well as in the economics of organizations, of decisions and of information (1974). Meanwhile, the explanation of the firm size in terms of economies of scale ended with an enlarged explanation and was enriched by the analysis of the multi-product cost function.[25]

These different breakthroughs had three types of effect: they opened breaches in the fortress of orthodoxy, but, in doing so, they gave rise to works which strengthen it; and they provoked, in different fields of research and in several theoretical currents, a thorough revival of the analyses of the institutions, organizations, firms, markets and relations between organizations and markets. The study of organizations which, in the neoclassical approach, fell within the competence, not of economic theory but of history, has thus been reintegrated – and not only for Marxists and institutionalists – into the field of economic analysis.[26] The simplistic image of the maximizing firm is more and more widely rejected; its analysis, as that of other institutions, is enlightened by game theory, in particular by the theory of repeated games. In this view, the market is no longer the universal – outside history, as it were – mode of adjustment of agents' plans. It is thus necessary to recognize the institutional foundations of its emergence and functioning; this analysis is developed in the institutionalist approach[27] as well as in that of organizational economics. It is also necessary to understand how the division operates between what is relevant to the firm and what is relevant to the market, and how the substitution between one and the other operates.[28]

These works translated into a strong revival of behavioural economics and of its different schools,[29] of the institutionalism's new avatars – new institutional economics[30] and neo-institutional economics[31] – and of industrial economics. This revival translated into different types of *rapprochements* or linkages. Thus Williamson, who is abundantly quoted, and sometimes claimed by the three currents mentioned above, wrote his thesis at Carnegie-Mellon University, and has a form of analysis which bears the hallmarks of both the behavioural and neoclassical approaches. On the other hand, one can note the convergence between post-Keynesian works and the behavioural approach, seen as a new approach to industrial economics.[32] Authors such as Akerlof and Stiglitz were indeed described as 'neoclassical heterodoxes'. Institutionalists sought to generalize neoclassical economics,[33] whilst others inquired about the possibility of a synthesis between neoclassical and behavioural economics.[34] At the heart of this dynamic are K. Arrow's works, which are very often quoted in the abundant literature we have just mentioned, as much for his thinking on the *Limits of Organization* (1974) as for his work on the individual and social choices.[35]

In the opposite direction, we are witnessing a return to the notion of the market to deal with phenomena internal to the firm, and also to take account of 'all social relations ... thus considered as implicit "markets"', the concept of market being then enlarged to encompass the 'systematization of any kind of negotiations between individuals'.[36] Through the theory of contracts,[37] some tend to reduce 'all that is institutional or organizational' to contracts between individuals, being similar to the relations between buyers and sellers in the neoclassical theory: 'the organization, a simple collection of contracts, loses all identity; it disappears as a collective entity, being reduced to interindividual'[38] and can finally be interpreted again in terms of substantive rationality.

It is difficult not to be reminded here of Penelope. While some of the economists work at making the concepts and theoretical tools better able to take account of the reality of the markets and the firms, others apply the most reductionist analyses to the firm, to the organization and beyond the field of economics. In terms of the process of economic knowledge, is this not a case of a few steps forward and many steps back?

Sisyphus: perpetually reconstructing the heterodoxy

In face of the vitality of what we have called 'the new fortress', yesterday's heterodoxies may appear weakened. Thus institutionalism, rather than developing its own coherence, arranges, as we noted, its melodies in counterpoint to the dominant neoclassical theme, constituting a wellspring of revival for different currents of thought. The post-Keynesian current is very much alive, with its own channels of circulation and university departments and research centres where it is influential. Its publications are numerous and diversified. But, at the same time, one may well wonder if it exists as a unique current. For example, often opposed, and sometimes in fierce conflict, are Sraffa's disciples and those who believe the Keynesian and neo-Ricardian approaches to be incompatible.[39]

As for Marxism, it undeniably experienced a revival in the decade following 1968.[40] But in this period it underwent a process of fragmentation into the different academic disciplines (anthropology, sociology and economics in particular) and many authors were associated with political movements (orthodox Communist, Trotskyite, Maoist, Third-worldist). In economics, textbooks of Marxian economics multiplied.[41] The tide of mathematicization gave rise to formalized rewritings of Marx,[42] not solely due to economists claiming Marxism as their authority. Samuelson, among others, after describing Marx as a minor and autodidact post-Ricardian, subsequently regarded him as a significant mathematical economist,[43] whilst Morishima describes him as the co-founder with Walras of modern mathematical economics (Morishima 1973). There was an intense debate, nourished by the contributions of the Sraffian and neo-Ricardian schools, on the significance of Marx's work, and in particular on the secular problem of the transformation of values into prices of production.[44] While several authors of the post-Keynesian and neo-Ricardian currents, for example K. Bharadwaj (1989) and Steedman,[45] and some Marxist economists such as Dobb (1973) and Meek,[46] consider that Sraffa's work extends that of Marx, others believe that it betrays Marx.[47] In this respect, the border between Marxism and post-Keynesian theory, as moreover that between these two and institutionalism, is often blurred and unstable, even more so given that each of these currents of thought is crossed by multiple undercurrents. Meanwhile, besides numerous analyses devoted to global capitalism, imperialism and crisis, one notes S. de Brunhoff's works on money and the state.[48]

The stagflation which hit capitalist economies from the beginning of the 1970s stirred up the flame of liberalism and weakened Keynesianism. For a time it stimulated Marxism, finally destabilizing it in its turn, with the backward surge of social-democratic and socialist ideals in capitalist countries. The collapse of the regimes of the Soviet type dealt another serious blow. Historical events can hardly kill a theoretical current, an approach which itself attempts to take account of such changes, but it is certain that they give, in the eyes of several, an air of obsolescence to certain works. As with Keynesianism, Marxism has, as they say, gone out of fashion.

It is principally through the working of an economics close to the facts and to history that the new waves of heterodoxy are characterized. Beyond economic history[49] and quantitative history,[50] it is a question of attempts at the analysis of economic reality seized in its historical dimension, in brief, of what one may call historical economics.[51] Political economy took root in history. It was historical economics. From Turgot and Smith to Mill and Marx, from the German Historical School, Marshall and Schumpeter to Keynes, Hayek and Perroux, the economists who have marked economic thought took account of the historical dimension. This nod towards history is, moreover, common to all of the heterodoxies. For the quasi-totality of post-Keynesians, institutionalists, radicals and Marxists, a part of the work at least has a historical dimension; and this is also the case for the very diversified whole of the economists who have worked on development, on the future of capitalism and its crises, on national economies and on international and global economies.

More often than not, the way economics and history are articulated remains implicit. Jean Lhomme seeks to clarify the issue: for him, it is 'the historical facts which provide the raw material for economic theory',[52] hence the importance of the work which has to be done on their representativity, homogeneity, cohesion and their continuity in time; besides, the economist must resort to history in order to test the concepts, with, as a criterion, the 'correspondence to reality'.[53] More ambitious is the project of Pierre Dockès and Bernard Rosier 'to practise economics while giving greater emphasis to the analysis of change in historical time, thus to set the unfolding of economic phenomena in a dynamic of irreversibility, of irreducible innovation, but also in the midst of the social and of conflictual games, to uncover the diversity of durations and rythms'.[54] Their ambition as economists is to construct something like the familiar Russian dolls, with a range of theories from the most specific to the most general.

This attempt to express the two dimensions, theoretical and historical, widely adopts the approach underlying a large part of Schumpeter's work, whether it be of his analysis of the entrepreneur, of innovation and its role in economic movements, or his thinking on the long-run evolution of capitalism and socialism. It is closely akin to that of authors such as Perroux, taking into account dominant economy, dominant firm and dominant industry, and of his successors such as M. Byé, with the great interterritorial unit,[55] and J. Weiller with the rational preference for structures.[56] It is also congruent with the works of some institutionalists.[57] In this large domain of historical economics, a systematic attempt at theoretical development was led by the régulation school.[58] It draws its inspiration from different sources: Marxism and post-Keynesianism with a strong Kaleckian influence, the historical school, Schumpeter and the tradition of French academic political economy linked to the study of society and of institutions, the whole being worked again into a new dough which different post-1968 yeasts help to rise. The first works dealt with accumulation in the United States,[59] the construction of a macro-economic model of the French economy of a post-Keynesian inspiration,[60] and inflation in France.[61]

In the words of Boyer,[62] 'Approaches in terms of regulation pay close attention to the precise forms that fundamental social relations take in a given society during a particular historical phase'; in particular, they pay attention to the 'commodity relation' and to the 'labor–capital relation', analysing their 'institutional forms' (p. 13). On the basis of a macroeconomics of post-Keynesian influence, they analyse 'regimes of accumulation' conceived as 'the set of regularities that ensure the general and relatively coherent progress of capital accumulation' (p. 35), as much as the 'modes of regulation' (p. 43). This approach permitted the undertaking, in a coordinated and coherent way, of analyses focused on the dynamics of past and present capitalism, distinguishing in a systematic way the different types of crises, emphasizing the distinction between extensive and intensive regimes of accumulation, and bringing Fordism into the light in the explanation of both postwar growth and the crisis of the 1970s–1980s.[63] It led to new works, in particular on money[64] and labour organization.[65]

In the domain of historical economics one may also find authors who have worked on the global capitalist system[66] and on multinational firms.[67] Their work is in some way parallel to that of the régulation school, since the latter take the national economy as its point of departure. However, they were also led to take capitalism's international dimension into consideration and they put forward the notion of the international regime;[68] here some similarities may be noticed, either with the English approach in term of hegemony,[69] or with those approaches aimed at linking national and global dimensions of capitalism.[70] In this same sphere of influence of historical economics, one can find American radicals such as S. Bowles, D.M. Gordon, T. Weisskopf, R. Edwards and E. Reich. Between their works and those of the régulation school strong convergence may be found: for example, the notion of social structure of accumulation[71] largely covers that of regime of accumulation; a close kinship also exists in the ways that these two schools analyse the 'wage relation' (*rapport salarial*) and the capital–labour compromise, as well as the crisis of the 1970s.[72] Another convergence may be noticed with M. Piore, who, in collaboration with C. Sabel, tackled the analysis of post-Fordism by defining flexible specialization,[73] a theme adopted by the French theoreticians of the régulation school. Finally, one can evoke here some advocates of the modern English approach in terms of 'corporatism',[74] an approach which takes into account the characteristics of the political system and the modes of representation of the interests of each country, the strategies of the principal actors (the state, the employers, the unions) and the nature and role of social relations.

Despite the fact that their works are largely inspired by the debates (mentioned in the previous section) on the market, the firm, rationality and organization, the advocates of 'economics of conventions' (*économie des conventions*)[75] seem more and more to occupy the domain of historical economics. Indeed, if they put at the heart of their analysis the two major forms of coordination which market and firm constitute, they establish that neither can function 'without a common framework, without a constitutive convention',[76] which can itself only be understood if situated in the history of societies. The analysis of conventions may therefore permit the linking of fields, too often separated, as are economics, sociology and history, the establishment of links between theoretical thinking and the analysis of reality, and the constitution of a turning point between individualism and holism and between microeconomics and macroeconomics. Here again, one notices strong convergences with institutionalists and with the régulation school.[77]

With their effort perpetually aimed at giving back historical, sociological and political dimensions to economics, numerous are those who, like Sisyphus, work at a historical economics always to be reconstructed, and who, if not attractive for their formal coherence and purity, must be so for their ability to explain the transformations and evolution of national and global economies.

Icarus: the broken flight of economic thought

For many of its founders, political economy was pluridimensional thought, and this in two ways. First, it was simultaneously a theory of the market and of productive processes, of the individual actor and of society, of rational choice and of historical change. And at the same time it was also an attempt at the comprehension of observable processes, an effort at conceptualization and formalization, a guide for the Prince's decisions and the consideration of ends. A discipline of triple dimensions – human, social and historical – it was a 'moral and political science'. Has this tradition, born with Petty, Turgot, Smith, Malthus and Ricardo, died with Keynes, Frisch, Myrdal, Perroux, Tinbergen and Hayek? Such a possibility is to be feared.

It is not that, among living and thinking economists, all have given up the ghost in the development of a multidimensional approach, but, with the enormous written output of works in economics in recent decades, analysis, theory, research – and with them thought – have exploded in many fields: the market, the firm, public choice, the consumer, the national economy, labour, employment, welfare, international economics, the multinational firms, the processes of globalization, capitalism, technology, innovation, information and uncountable others; with, for each of them, sub-areas of specialization, the whole being enclosed by the structure of schools and theoretical traditions and languages. The debutant economist as much as the seasoned author, having worked hard to win recognition in one or two areas, will justifiably hesitate before embarking on the task of constructing an all-encompassing theoretical approach.

Furthermore, the last 40 years have been marked by a remarkable proliferation of formal, theoretical works on markets, equilibria, choices and strategies, with the study of contemporary economic reality hereafter a second-class activity, attached only tenuously to the former. Advice to governments has declined; and several generations of computers will pass before one is able rigorously to relate the theory of general equilibrium to concrete choices of economic policies, if this is ever possible. As for the ethical dimension, certain economists have tried to reintroduce it, whether to expand the analysis, for example to take account of the notion of fairness and 'superfairness' (Baumol 1986 with Fischer), to offer comment on the way the world is developing (Hirschman 1984; Sen 1985, 1987 *On Ethics*), to criticize the lack of realism of orthodox theory (Bartoli[78]), or again as a point of departure for those who deny the ungovernability of the world (Tinbergen 1990, Gruson 1992).

Witnessing this double explosion in economic knowledge should lead to accepting pluralism and to advocating it. But that should also lead to reflection on the need for thought. Already in the sixteenth century, François Rabelais wrote that '*science sans conscience n'est que ruine de l'âme*'.[79] What can one say today, of formalization without thought? Two recent reports, completed on the initiative of the American Economic Association, show the impasse to which the excessive emphasis on mathematics and formalization in the teaching of economics in the United States has led.[80] Whether through bad luck or as deliberate provocation, the note by Lawrence Summers, an economist at the World Bank, revealed by the English press, is, in its own way, indicative of the incongruities which have been generated by analysis which privileges rational calculation. The author offers a rational justification for the displacement of pollution and waste from the North to the South, where wages are lower, in terms of the relationship between the cost of a pollution dangerous to health and the profits absorbed by the growth of morbidity and mortality.[81]

Is it the current state of the discipline, is it the nature of the problems? Economic thought today appears sickly, even if there remain, here and there, some flames among the embers. Once the last anarcho-capitalist pamphlets and the abundant range of Marxist explanations of the last crisis have been placed on the book shelves, what will have become of systems thinking? For certain authors, today very much in fashion, we have simply reached 'the end of history'.[82] Even the encyclical *Centesimus Annus* of Pope John Paul II barely elicited a response from the economists; it must be said that in the midst of a strong liberal current, he denounced the limits of liberalism and argued a role for the welfare state.[83]

While the nations of the Third World have experienced very different rates of development, doubt prevails: in the North as in the South, voices express doubt about development as a universal objective.[84] In this area, also, certainties disappear rapidly: from confidence in socialism to the hypothesis of rational agents and to liberalism; from the project based on the construction of a national economy to the strategies of diversification at the heart of international markets; from a dominant role for the state to the slogan 'less state'.[85] The principal efforts towards global reflection have been collective and stimulated by politicians: the Brandt Report, which was concerned with the deepening gap between the North and the South;[86] the Brundtland Report, which underlined the impoverishment of the poorest, and, while unable to yield solutions, succeeded in offering a slogan: sustainable development,[87] that is to say that which is capable of preserving the environment and the chances of future generations. For the environment has become, for all scientific disciplines, one of the most important objects of study at the century's end. Inspired economists had already understood it (Boulding 1966 'The Economics', Georgescu-Roegen 1971, 1978, 1979 *Domains*, 1980, 1982, Commoner,[88] Passet[89]). Others had already applied their techniques to the environment quite early on:[90] in particular, input–output analysis (Leontief 1970) and the analysis of externalities (Baumol 1975 with W.E. Oates; 1979 with Oates and Batey Blackman). But do these techniques allow anything beyond the illumination of certain well-defined problems? Is the emergence of global thought not necessary to cast light on the new task, with which, in all its complexity, humanity is confronted?[91]

An exploded discipline, today's economic science develops through a multitude of works, devoted for the most part to limited subjects, broached by means of reductionist approaches. The time for synthesis and for reconstruction seems even further away than ever. A number of economists chose their discipline in the hope of contributing to solving the great problems of their time: unemployment in the 1920s and 1930s, underdevelopment in the post-war period, and today inequality, poverty, hunger and the assault on the environment. But each of these problems constitutes a global social fact.[92] It is not by reducing all to its constituent fragments, to individual choices and to the calculus of maximization, it is not even by constructing a set of local theories of them, that one will gain knowledge of these problems. One must take account of the global social fact, which leads one to overstep narrow economic analysis, as has been done by Myrdal, Perroux, Tinbergen, Boulding and Hirschman; and Sen for hunger, Hayek for the market, Simon for organizations, Kornai for the state system. To find useful enlightenment for the central problems of economics, it is towards the non-economists that one must turn: to Polanyi for the process of social structural change linked to the spread of the market economy, Rawls for inequality and justice, Habermas for the future of our societies, Prigogine for complexity.

Many economists question deeply the methods and very bases of economic inquiry. We have not been able to note here the important work on economic methodology which dates no doubt from the inception of the discipline of economics, but which has seen, in the last 20 years, a resurgence of growth, stimulated by such works as Blaug (1980 *The Methodology*), Boland,[93] Caldwell,[94] Hausman,[95] Hutchison (1978, 1981, 1992), Kolm,[96] Latouche,[97] Mayer (1993), Pheby[98] and many others.[99] The foundation of journals such as *Economics and Philosophy* and of *Journal of Economic Methodology* (linked to the *International Network for Economic Method*), is indicative of this new resurgence. Klamer, McCloskey and others have emphasized the importance, in economics as in other domains of inquiry, of the nature of discourse, of rhetoric and the art of persuasion.[100] P. Mirowski (1989) unleashed a lively debate by giving a new interpretation of the relationship between physics and economics.[101] Based on an approach generated by the study of turbulence in meteorology, the theory of chaos,[102] some seek to rejuvenate the study of cyclical fluctuations without confining themselves to the deterministic structure based on classical physics.[103]

Concerning the training of economic theorists, R.H. Nelson underlines the need to increase their knowledge of such fields as history, law, political science and institutions, with, finally, a return to the tradition of political economy.[104] As early as 1978, T.W. Hutchison wrote: 'Instead of waiting for Newton, or a new Keynes, it may be more promising to seek to restore the historical, institutional and psychological components of the subject, so masterfully incorporated in *The Wealth of Nations*' (Hutchison 1978, p. 320).

In this perspective one can view economic history, already evoked above, and also 'socioeconomics', which, along with sociologist Amitai Etzioni[105] and various social science specialists, the economists Boulding, Hirschman, Leibenstein, Sen, Simon and Thurow have chosen as a banner beneath which to assemble those who wish to see economics escape the straitjacket that is inhibiting it.[106] More broadly, one must not forget, at the same time, those who argue for the reconstruction of political economy,[107] an enlarged political economy,[108] taking into account the ethical dimension, conceived as a moral and political science,[109] in short a multidimensional economics.[110] Thus new seeds have been sown. But when can we hope for the harvest?

Have some economists sought to draw too close to the sun of global knowledge? Today, as we face the great problems of our time, economic thought's broken wing has left the economist unarmed, with his knowledge fragmented, his analyses perfunctory, and helpless before the enormous void separating a theoretical edifice lacking coherence and a world in need of responses and solutions.

Notes

1. See Baumol and Faulhaber 1988.
2. On this subject see Hutchison 1978, pp. 319–20.
3. In sum, a clear predilection emerges from the academic publications for formalized theory: for the period 1982–6, the articles presenting mathematical models without any data represented 52 per cent of the articles published by the *Economic Journal* and 42 per cent of those published in the *American Economic Review*, and a number of economic journals only publish articles of this nature. The corresponding proportion was 18 per cent in political sciences, 12 per cent in physics, 1 per cent in sociology and 0 per cent in chemistry (see T. Morgan, 'Theory versus Empiricism in Academic Economics', *Journal of Economic Perspectives*, vol. 2, no. 4, 1988, p. 163).
4. S.-C. Kolm reckoned the written corpus of economics to be 'several hundred thousand pages, growing at the annual rate of several ten or so thousands pages per year with a very strict definition of the domain (and about ten times more for the whole of economic literature)' (*Philosophie de l'économie*, Paris, Seuil, 1986, p. 30). Stigler estimated the annual production in English of about 6000 economists, properly defined, to be 800 books and 6000 articles, and he evaluated the increase in the stock of writings to be 5 per cent per year, that is to say a doubling every 14 years: this stock, therefore, would be in 1992 16 times what it was in 1936, the year the *General Theory* was published: ('The Literature of Economics: The Case of the Kinked Oligopoly Demand Curve', *Economic Inquiry*, vol. 16, 1978, 185–204).
5. 'It is a literature that no one person could possibly read – the limits imposed by sanity are stricter than those imposed by time. Indeed it is a literature that perhaps is read by a number of economists only moderately larger than the number of writers' (Stigler, op. cit., p. 185).
6. The number of pages published annually in the main journals of mathematical economics (some of which were created during this period, such as the *International Economic Review*, the *Journal of Economic Theory* and the *Journal of Mathematical Economics*) went from 400 to 700 in the 1930s and 1940s to a magnitude of 4000 to 5000 in the 1970s and 1980s (see Debreu 1986).
7. *American Economic Review*, *Journal of Economic Literature* and *Journal of Economic Perspectives*.
8. The appellation 'Austrian' follows from the origins of this current of thought in the works by Carl Menger and his Viennese disciples. But it is in the United States that, nowadays, one finds the greatest number of 'Austrians' or rather of 'neo-Austrians', gathered in the Ludwig von Mises Institute, led by, among others, Murray Rothbard. The institute publishes the *Review of Austrian Economics* and the *Austrian Economic Newsletter*, and organizes a summer school. On the Austrian School, see Dolan 1976, Grassl and Smith 1986, Kirzner 1982, Littlechild 1990, and O'Sullivan 1990.
9. See, for example, Hayek 1937 *Economica*. See above, Chapter 2.
10. *Human Action. A Treatise on Economics*, London, William Hodge; New Haven, Yale University Press, 1949.
11. *Competition and Entrepreneurship*, University of Chicago Press, 1973; *Perception, Opportunity and Profit*, University of Chicago Press, 1979; *Discovery and the Capitalist Process*, University of Chicago Press, 1985.
12. *The Market as an Economic Process*, Oxford, Basil Blackwell, 1986.
13. See also G. O'Driscoll and M.J. Rizzo, *The Economics of Time and Ignorance*, Oxford, Basil Blackwell, 1985; M.N. Rothbard, *Man, Economy, and State: A Treatise on Economic Principle*, Princeton, Van Nostrand, 1962.

14. See above, Chapter 7.
15. See for example P.A. Diamond, 'A Model of Price Adjustment', *Journal of Economic Theory*, vol. 3, 1971, 156–68; F.M. Fisher, 'Stability and Competitive Equilibrium in Two Models of Search and Individual Price Adjustment', *Journal of Economic Theory*, vol. 6, 1973, 446–70; Stiglitz 1976 with S.J. Grossman, 1981 with A. Weiss.
16. See the symposium on the economics of information, *Review of Economic Studies*, vol. 44, 1977, 389–601.
17. A. d'Autume, 'Théorie des jeux et marché', *Cahiers d'économie politique*, no. 20–21, 1992, 155–65; K. Avinash Dixit and Barry J. Nalebuff, *Thinking Strategically: The Competitive Edge in Business, Politics and Everyday Life*, New York: W.W. Norton, 1991.
18. Earl 1988, pp. 3–4.
19. *A Behavioural Theory of the Firm*, Englewood Cliffs, New Jersey, Prentice-Hall, 1963.
20. J.G. March and J.P. Olsen, *Ambiguity and Choice in Organizations*, Bergen, Universitets Forlaget, 1976.
21. R.R. Nelson and S.G. Winter, *An Evolutionary Theory of Economic Change*, Cambridge, Massachusetts, Harvard University Press, 1982.
22. On this point, see Coase 1972.
23. *The Theory of Share Tenancy*, University of Chicago Press, 1969; 'The Contractual Nature of the Firm', *Journal of Law and Economics*, vol. 26, 1982, 1–22.
24. See above, Chapter 4.
25. See, for example, Baumol 1982 with Panzar and Willig.
26. See C. Ménard, *Les Organisations*, Paris, La Découverte, 1990, pp. 16 ff.
27. Among others, Alchian 1977, Williamson 1985.
28. From Coase 1937 to Simon 1991, in the context of a symposium of the *Journal of Economic Perspectives*, introduced by Stiglitz, on the theme 'Organizations and Economics', to Williamson 1975.
29. See Earl 1988, pp. 3 ff.
30. This descriptive term was suggested by Williamson in 1975. It constitutes, more than a school, a programme of research on rationality and institutions (see R.N. Langlois, 'Rationality, Institutions and Explanation', in Langlois 1986, pp. 252–3).
31. See Eggertsson 1990, pp. 6 ff. If the renewal of institutionalism is undeniable, it is not obvious that this distinction is very operative, even less so since, as noted by Eggertsson (p. 10, n. 12), Coase and Williamson use the term 'new institutional economics' to designate two distinct paradigms. For Langlois (1986, pp. 252–3), new institutional economics is principally defined as a research programme.
32. See for example N. Kay, 'Post-Keynesian Economics and New Approaches to Industrial Economics', in Pheby 1989, 191–208; B. Haines and J.R. Shackleton, 'The New Industrial Economics', in Shackleton 1990, 178–204; Shepherd 1990; Engl. transl., *Economics of Order and Disorder: The Market as Organizer and Curator*, Oxford, Clarendon Press, 1992.
33. Eggertsson 1990, chap. 1. For his part, J. Lesourne displays the ambition of contributing to an even bigger synthesis, since his *Économie de l'ordre et du désordre* (Paris, Économica, 1991) is presented as the foundation stone of a construction which draws inspiration from several currents of scientific thought: the general theory of systems, the evolutionist current, the behavioural approach, the institutional approach and the economic theory itself (pp. 10–13).
34. Thus Earl 1988 who calls into question the pseudo-behaviouralists (pp. 9–12).
35. See, for example, in his bibliography, 1983, 1984, 1985, 1986.
36. M. Lagueux, 'Le libéralisme économique comme programme de recherche et comme idéologie', *Cahiers d'économie politique*, no. 16–17, 1989, p. 142.
37. Thus Alchian and Demsetz 1972, p. 778.
38. Y. Giordano, 'Décision et organisations: quelles rationalités?', *Économies et sociétés*, vol. 25, 1991, no. 4, série SG no. 17, p. 172.
39. See above, Chapter 6, where the reader will find many references to the contemporary post-Keynesian literature.

40. See Howard and King 1992, H. Gintis, 'The Re-emergence of Marxian Economics in America', in B. Ollman and E. Vernoff (eds), *The Left Academy: Marxist Scholarship on American Campuses*, vol. 1, New York, McGraw-Hill, 1982. See also the texts gathered in King 1990; G. Caravale (ed.), *Marx and Economic Analysis*, Aldershot, Hants, Edward Elgar, 1990; S.W. Helburn and D.F. Bramhall (eds), *Marx, Schumpeter and Keynes: A Centenary Celebration of Dissent*, Armonk, New York, M.E. Sharpe.
41. See, for example: J.F. Becker, *Marxian Political Economy: An Outline*, Cambridge, England, Cambridge University Press, 1977; G. Catephores, *An Introduction to Marxist Economics*, New York, New York University Press, 1988; L. Gill, *L'Économie capitaliste: une analyse marxiste*, 2 vols, Montréal, Presses socialistes internationales, 1976 and 1979; J. Gouverneur, *Manuel de théorie économique marxiste*, Bruxelles, De Boeck-Wesmael, 1987; M.C. Howard and J.E. King, *The Political Economy of Marx*, Harlow, Longman, 1975; P. Salama and J. Valier, *Une introduction à l'économie politique*, Paris, François Maspero, 1973.
42. In particular Brody 1970; J.E. Roemer, *Analytical Foundations of Marxian Economic Theory*, Cambridge, England, Cambridge University Press, 1981.
43. See in particular 'Wages and Interest: A Modern Dissection of Marxian Economic Models', *American Economic Review*, vol. 47, 1957, 884–912; 'Understanding the Marxian Notion of Exploitation: A Summary of the So-Called Transformation Problem Between Marxian Values and Competitive Prices', *Journal of Economic Literature*, vol. 9, 1971, 399–431; 'Marx as a Mathematical Economist: Steady-State and Exponential Growth Equilibrium', in G. Horwich and P.A. Samuelson (eds), *Trade, Stability, and Macroeconomics: Essays in Honor of Lloyd A. Metzler*, New York and London, Academic Press, 1974, 269–307.
44. See on this subject G. Dostaler, 'Marx's Theory of Value and the Transformation Problem: Some Lessons from a Debate', *Studies in Political Economy*, no. 9, Autumn 1982, 77–101; G. Dumenil, 'Beyond the Transformation Riddle: A Labor Theory of Value', *Science and Society*, vol. 47, 1983–4, 427–50; A. Lipietz, 'The So-Called "Transformation Problem" Revisited', *Journal of Economic Theory*, vol. 26, 1982, 59–88; J.S. Szumski, 'The Transformation Problem Solved?', *Cambridge Journal of Economics*, vol. 13, 1989, 431–52. See the texts gathered in G. Dostaler (ed., with the collaboration of M. Lagueux) *Un Echiquier centenaire: théorie de la valeur et formation des prix*, Paris/Montréal, La Découverte/Presses de l'Université du Québec; and in I. Steedman *et al.*, *The Value Controversy*, London, New Left Books and Verso, 1981.
45. *Marx After Sraffa*, London, New Left Books, 1977.
46. See his preface to the second edition (1973) of *Studies in the Labour Theory of Value*, London, Lawrence & Wishart (1st edn, 1956).
47. See, for example, Amin 1977; C. Benetti, C. Berthomieu and J. Cartelier, *Economie classique, économie vulgaire: Essais critiques*, Grenoble, Presses universitaires de Grenoble; Mandel 1984; B. Rowthorn 'Neo-classicism, Neo-Ricardianism and Marxism', *New Left Review*, no. 86, 1974, 63–87.
48. On these subjects, we should mention, besides S. Amin's numerous works (see titles in the dictionary), the following: A. Brewer, *Marxist Theories of Imperialism, A Critical Survey*, London, Routledge & Kegan Paul, 1980; A. Emmanuel, *Unequal Exchange: A Study of the Imperialism of Trade*, New York, Monthly Review Press, 1972; M. Itoh, *Value and Crisis*, London, Pluto and New York, Monthly Review Press, 1980; H. Magdoff, *Imperialism: From the Colonial Age to the Present*, New York, Monthly Review Press, 1978; P. Mattick, *Marx and Keynes: The Limits of the Mixed Economy*, London, Merlin, 1971; J.J. O'Connor, *The Fiscal Crisis of the State*, New York, St Martin's Press, 1973; R. Owen and B. Sutcliffe (eds), *Studies in the Theory of Imperialism*, London, Longman, 1972; H. Radice, *International Firm and Modern Imperialism*, Harmondsworth, Penguin, 1975.
49. First illustrated by historians from Sombart to F. Braudel, I. Wallerstein and J. Bouvier – but also by specialists of other disciplines, such as the demographer Alfred Sauvy or Karl Polanyi, whom it is difficult to rank in a specific discipline – and to which tens of contemporary economists brought, under diverse forms, their contributions. See Hicks

1969; A.J. Field (ed.), *The Future of Economic History*, Boston, Kluwer-Nijhoff, 1986; W.N. Parker (ed.), *Economic History and the Modern Economist*, Oxford, Basil Blackwell, 1986.

50. Of course, one first thinks of S. Kuznets and, in France, of J. Marczewski.
51. 'Economie et histoire, nouvelles approches', issue edited by P. Dockès and B. Rosier, *Revue économique*, vol. 42, 1991, 145–441; R. Boyer, 'Economie et histoire: vers de nouvelles alliances', *Annales ESC*, 44ème année, 1989, 1397–426; R. Boyer, B. Chavance and O. Godard, *Les figures de l'irréversibilité en économie*, Paris, Ecole des Hautes Etudes en Sciences Sociales, 1991.
52. *Economie et histoire*, Geneva, Droz, 1967, p. 16. See M. Beaud, 'Economie, théorie, histoire: Essai de clarification', *Revue économique*, vol. 42, 1991, 155–72.
53. Ibid., p. 30.
54. Introduction to the special issue 'Economie et histoire: Nouvelles approches' and 'Histoire "raisonnée" et économie historique', *Revue économique*, vol. 42, 1991, p. 150. See also, by the same authors, *Rythmes économiques, crise et changement social. Une perspective historique*, Paris, La Découverte, 1983; *L'Histoire ambiguë: Croissance et développement en question*, Paris, Presses Universitaires de France, 1988.
55. 'La Grande Unité Interterritoriale dans l'industrie extractive', *Cahiers de l'I.S.E.A.*, série F, no. 2, September 1955, 5–97.
56. 'Les préférences nationales de structures et la notion de déséquilibre structurel', *Revue d'économie politique*, vol. 59, 1949, 414–34; *L'Economie internationale depuis 1950*, Paris, Presses Universitaires de France, 1965.
57. R.R. Nelson and S.G. Winter, *An Evolutionary Theory of Economic Change*, Cambridge, Massachusetts, Harvard University Press, 1982.
58. R. Boyer, *La Théorie de la régulation: une analyse critique*, Paris, La Découverte, 1986; Engl. transl., *The Regulation School: A Critical Introduction*, New York, Columbia University Press, 1990; id., 'Les Théories de la régulation: Paris, Barcelone, New-York', *Revue de synthèse* (CNRS, 4° section), no. 2, avril–juin 1989, 277–91. See also: *Le Colloque de Barcelone, Economies et sociétés*, vol. 23, no. 11 (R 4), 1989 and vol. 24, no. 12 (R5), 1990. Bob Jessop ('Regulation Theories in Retrospect and Prospect', *Economies et sociétés*, vol. 23, no. 11 (R 4), 1989, pp. 8 ff.) distinguishes seven schools of regulation: three are issues of Marxian economics (economists from the French Communist Party, with their analysis of state monopoly capital; the Grenoble School; and the Amsterdam School); and three others (in Germany, the Scandinavian countries and the United States) can be situated in relation to the Parisian school, which, with M. Aglietta, H. Bertrand, R. Boyer, A. Lipietz, J. Mistral and others made the founding effort, which we will consider here.
59. M. Aglietta, *Régulation et crises du capitalisme: L'Expérience des Etats-Unis*, Paris, Calmann-Lévy, 1976; Engl. transl., *A Theory of Capitalist Regulation*, London, New Left Books, 1979.
60. J. Mazier, *La Macroéconomie appliquée*, Paris, Presses Universitaires de France, 1978.
61. Works completed in the context of the Centre de Recherches Prospectives d'Economie Mathématique Appliquée à la Planification (CEPREMAP).
62. See R. Boyer, *The Regulation School*, 1989, op. cit. See also R. Boyer and J. Mistral, *Accumulation, inflation, crises*, Paris, Presses Universitaires de France, 1978; R. Boyer (ed.), *Capitalismes fin de siècle*, Paris, Presses Universitaires de France, 1986; id. (ed.), *La Flexibilité du travail en Europe*, Paris, La Découverte, 1986.
63. For a critique of this approach, see, for example, J. Cartelier and M. de Vroey, 'L'approche de la régulation. Un nouveau paradigme?', *Economies et sociétés*, vol. 23, no. 11 (R 4), 1989, 63–87.
64. M. Aglietta and A. Orléan, *La Violence de la monnaie*, Paris, Presses Universitaires de France, 1982.
65. B. Coriat, *L'Atelier et le chronomètre*, Paris, Bourgois, 1979; *L'Atelier et le robot*, Paris, Bourgois, 1990.
66. In particular I. Wallerstein, *Historical Capitalism*, London, Verso, 1983; S. Amin 1970, 1976 *L'Impérialisme*.

67. In particular Vernon 1971, 1985 and C.-A. Michalet, *Le Capitalisme mondial*, Paris, Presses Universitaires de France, 1976 (new edn, 1985).
68. A. Lipietz considers that it may exist 'as a global system of accumulation' (*Mirages et miracles*, Paris, La Découverte, 1985, p. 101; Engl. transl. *Mirages and Miracles*, London, Verso, 1987). J. Mistral links the analysis of strategic areas and of international regimes of accumulation ('Régime international et trajectoires nationales', in R. Boyer (ed.), *Capitalismes fin de siècle*, 1986, pp. 172 ff.). M. Aglietta studies the 'international monetary regime which establishes itself around a key currency' (*La Fin des devises-clés*, Paris, La Découverte, 1986, pp. 44 ff.).
69. R. Gilpin, *The Political Economy of International Relations*, Princeton University Press, 1987; J. Kolko, *Restructuring the World Economy*, New York, Pantheon Books, 1988; S. Strange, *States and Markets*, London, Pinter, 1988.
70. J. O. Anderson, 'Capital and Nation-State: A Theoretical Perspective', *Development and Peace*, vol. 2, 1981, 238–54; M. Beaud, *Histoire du capitalisme*, Paris, Seuil, 1981; Engl. transl., *A History of Capitalism*, New York, Monthly Review Press, 1983, id., *Le système national/mondial hiérarchisé*, Paris, La Découverte, 1987.
71. Bowles 1983.
72. Bowles, Gordon and Weisskopf 1983; R. Edwards, D.M. Gordon and E. Reich, *Segmented Work, Divided Workers*, Cambridge, England, Cambridge University Press, 1982.
73. *The Second Industrial Divide*, New York, Basic Books, 1984.
74. P.C. Schmitter and G. Lehmbruch (eds), *Trends Toward Corporatist Intermediation*, Beverley Hills, California, Sage, 1979; S.D. Berger (ed.), *Organising Interest in Western Europe*, Cambridge, England, Cambridge University Press, 1981; P.J. Katzenstein, *Corporatism and Change*, Ithaca, New York, Cornell University Press, 1984. See also F.L. Pryor, 'Corporatism as an Economic System: A Review Article', *Journal of Comparative Economics*, vol. 12, 1988, 317–44.
75. J.-P. Dupuy, F. Eymard-Duvernay, O. Favereau, A. Orléan, R. Salais, L. Thévenot (eds), 'L'économie des conventions', special issue of the *Revue économique*, vol. 40, 1989, 141–400.
76. *Revue économique*, vol. 40, 1989, p. 142.
77. See, among others R. Boyer and A. Orléan, 'Les transformations des conventions salariales entre théorie et histoire', *Revue économique*, vol. 42, 1991, p. 269. See also Boyer, *The Regulation School*, op. cit., pp. xix–xxii.
78. *Economie et création collective*, Paris, Economica, 1977; *L'Economie multidimensionnelle*, Paris, Economica, 1991.
79. 'Science without conscience spells but destruction of the spirit' (*The Complete Works of Rabelais*, New York, Modern Library, 1944, p. 194).
80. A.O. Krueger *et al.* 'Report of the Commission on Graduate Education in Economics', and W. Lee Hansen, 'The Education and Training of Economics Doctorates', *Journal of Economic Literature*, vol. 29, 1991, 1035–53 and 1054–87.
81. See *The Economist*, 8 February 1992, the *Financial Times*, 10 February 1992, *Courrier international*, 20 February 1992.
82. F. Fukuyama, *The End of History and the Last Man*, New York, Free Press, 1992.
83. See *Le Centenaire de Rerum Novarum*, edited by Hugues Puel, Paris, Cerf, 1991.
84. S. Latouche, *Faut-il refuser le développement?*, Paris, Presses Universitaires de France, 1986.
85. See G. Grellet, 'Un survol critique de quelques orthodoxies contemporaines', *Revue Tiers-Monde*, vol. 33, 1992, 31–66.
86. Willy Brandt (ed.), *North–South: A Programme for Survival*, Report of the Independent Commission on International Development Issues, Cambridge, Massachusetts, MIT Press, 1980.
87. World Commission on Environment and Development, *Our Common Future*, New York, Oxford University Press, 1987. Ignacy Sachs had proposed in 1972 the concept of eco-development.
88. *The Closing Circle: Nature, Man and Technology*, New York, Alfred A. Knopf, 1971.
89. *L'Economique et le vivant*, Paris, Payot, 1979.

90. R. and N. Dorfman (eds), *Economics of the Environment*, New York, W.W. Norton, 1972; A.C. Fisher and F.M. Peterson, 'The Environment in Economics: A Survey', *Journal of Economic Literature*, vol. 14, 1976, 1–33; M.L. Cropper and W.E. Oates, 'Environmental Economics: A Survey', *Journal of Economic Literature*, vol. 30, 1992, 675–740; D. Pearce, 'Green Economics', *Environmental Values*, vol. 1, no. 1, 1992, 3–13; W.E. Oates (ed.), *The Economics of the Environment*, Aldershot, Hants, Edward Elgar, 1992.
91. Can one see a contribution in this sense in the *Declaration for Universal Environmental Rights* circulated by the CSE (Center for Science and Environment) of New Delhi, headed by Anil Agarwal?
92. A *'fait social total'*. Read, among others, Marcel Mauss and Fernand Braudel.
93. *The Foundations of Economic Method*, London, Allen & Unwin, 1982.
94. *Beyond Positivism: Economic Methodology in the Twentieth Century*, London, Allen & Unwin, 1982.
95. *Capital, Profits and Prices: An Essay in the Philosophy of Economics*, New York, Columbia University Press, 1981; *The Inexact and Separate Science of Economics*, Cambridge, England, Cambridge University Press, 1992; *Essays on Philosophy and Economic Methodology*, Cambridge, England, Cambridge University Press, 1992.
96. *Philosophie de l'économie*, Paris, Seuil, 1985.
97. *Epistémologie et économie*, Paris, Anthropos, 1973; *Le Procès de la science sociale*, Paris, Anthropos, 1984.
98. *Methodology and Economics: A Critical Introduction*, London, Macmillan, 1988.
99. See also the texts gathered in N. de Marchi and M. Blaug (eds), *Appraising Economic Theories: Studies in the Methodology of Scientific Research Programmes*, Aldershot, Hants, Edward Elgar, 1991; B.J. Caldwell (ed.), *Appraisal and Criticism in Economics: A Book of Readings*, Boston, Allen & Unwin, 1984; id., (ed.), *The Philosophy and Methodology of Economics*, 3 vols, Aldershot, Hants, Edward Elgar, 1993; A.W. Coats (ed.), *Methodological Controversy in Economics: Historical Essays in Honor of T.W. Hutchison*, Greenwich, Conn. and London, JAI Press, 1983; J. Creedy (ed.), *Foundations of Economic Thought*, Oxford, Basil Blackwell, 1990; F. Hahn and M. Hollis (eds), *Philosophy and Economic Theory*, Oxford and New York, Oxford University Press, 1979; W.J. Samuels (ed.), *Research in the History of Economic Thought and Methodology*, Greenwich, Conn. and London, JAI Press, annual series published since 1983. See also A. Mingat, P. Salmon and A. Wolfelsperger, *Méthodologie économique*, Paris, Presses Universitaires de France, 1985; B. Walliser and C. Prou, *La science économique*, Paris, Seuil, 1988.
100. See, for example, A. Klamer, D.N. McCloskey and R.M. Solow (eds), *The Consequences of Economic Rhetoric*, Cambridge, England, Cambridge University Press, 1988; J.S. Nelson, A. Megill and D. N. McCloskey (eds), *The Rhetoric of the Human Sciences: Language and Argument in Scholarship and Public Affairs*, Madison and London, University of Wisconsin Press, 1987.
101. See also, on the mathematicization of economics, Ingrao and Israel 1987; E.R. Weintraub 1991.
102. J. Gleick, *Chaos*, New York: Viking, 1987; I. Prigogine and I. Stengers, *Entre le temps et l'éternité*, Paris, Fayard, 1988; M. Mitchell Waldrop, *Complexity: The Emerging Science at the Edge of Order and Chaos*, New York, Simon and Schuster, 1992
103. J. Benhabib (ed.), *Cycles and Chaos in Economic Equilibrium*, Princeton University Press, 1992; Goodwin 1990; H.W. Lorenz, *Nonlinear Dynamical Economics and Chaotic Motions*, New York, Springer-Verlag, 1989.
104. 'The Economics Profession and the Making of Public Policy', *Journal of Economic Literature*, vol. 25, 1987, p. 86.
105. 'Toward Deontological Social Sciences', *Philosophy of the Social Sciences*, vol. 19, 1989, 145–56; *The Moral Dimension: Toward a New Economics*, New York, Free Press, 1988. On the inanity of separating the economic and the social, see Marcel Mauss, 'Essai sur le don' [1923–4], in *Sociologie et anthropologie*, Paris, Presses Universitaires de France, 1960, 143–279; and, on the need for a historical social science, I. Wallerstein, 'A

Theory of Economic History in Place of Economic Theory?', *Revue économique*, vol. 42, 1991, 173–80.

106. R. Swedberg, 'The New "Battle of Methods"', *Challenge*, January–February 1990, 33–8.
107. L. Baeck, 'Political Economy as a Science', *Tijdschrift voor Economie en Management*, vol. 33, no. 1, 1988, p. 38.
108. Hirschman 1986 *Vers une économie*.
109. Hirschman 1984, p. 109.
110. Bartoli 1991, op. cit. note 78. See also the works by authors such as Boulding and Sen.

PART II

DICTIONARY OF MAJOR CONTEMPORARY ECONOMISTS

ADELMAN Irma (born 1930)

Irma Adelman was born in Cernowitz, Romania. From 1939, she studied in Palestine, where her family settled. In 1949, she entered the University of California at Berkeley, where she obtained her PhD in 1955. After teaching in temporary posts at Berkeley (1955–8), Oakland (1958–9) and Stanford (1960–62), she held the position of associate professor in Johns Hopkins University, Baltimore (1962–6) and then the position of professor at Northwestern University, Evanson (1966–72). After a year at the World Bank (1971–2), she taught at the University of Maryland (1972–9) and since 1979 at the University of California at Berkeley.

Main publications

1959. With F.L. Adelman, 'The Dynamic Properties of the Klein-Goldberger Model', *Econometrica*, vol. 27, 596–625.
1961. *Theories of Economic Growth and Development*, Stanford University Press.
1967. With C. Morris, *Society, Politics, and Economic Development: A Quantitative Approach*, Baltimore, Johns Hopkins.
1969. *Practical Approaches to Development Planning: Korea's Second Five-Year Plan*, Baltimore, Johns Hopkins.
1973. With C. Morris, *Economic Growth and Social Equity in Developing Countries*, Stanford University Press.
1978. With S. Robinson, *Income Distribution Policy in Developing Countries: A Case Study of Korea*, Stanford University Press and Oxford University Press.
1978. *Redistribution Before Growth: A Strategy for Developing Countries*, The Hague, Martinus Nijhof.
1988. With C. Morris, *Comparative Patterns of Economic Development, 1850–1914*, Baltimore, Johns Hopkins University Press.
1988. 'Confessions of an Incurable Romantic', *Quarterly Review, Banca Nazionale del Lavoro*, no. 166, 243–62; in Kregel 1989, 129–48 and, under the title 'My Life Philosophy', *American Economist*, 1990, vol. 34, no. 2, 3–13.

Irma Adelman's first publications dealt with econometric models (1959) and development theories (1961). With Cynthia Morris, she devised a quantitative analysis of multiple factors in development (1967), which she later applied to the industrialization process in the second half of the nineteenth century (1988).

Also with Cynthia Morris (1973) she studied the relationship between growth and income disparities; this question, with which the World Bank was concerned at the time, became the core of Irma Adelman's studies. She developed such analysis by applying a model developed with Sherman Robinson (1978) first to Korea, a country in which she worked as a consultant between 1964 and 1973. In her view, redistribution, agrarian reform and basic education are necessary prerequisites of any development policy (1978 *Redistribution*); however this thesis did not prevail in the 1980s.

Main references

ADELMAN 1988 'Confessions'.
BLAUG 1985, 1–2.

ALCHIAN Armen Albert (born 1914)

Born in Fresno, California, Armen Alchian began his collegial studies there and completed them at Stanford University (BA in 1936, PhD in 1943). A teaching assistant in economics at Stanford (1937–40) and an instructor and statistician in the US Air Force (1942–6), Alchian has spent his entire career at the University of California where he has been an assistant professor (1946–52), an associate professor (1952–8) and a professor (1958–84), becoming emeritus in 1985. He has worked as an economist for the Rand Corporation (1946–64) and as a consultant to business firms.

Main publications

1950. 'Uncertainty, Evolution and Economic Theory', *Journal of Political Economy*, vol. 58, 211–21.
1964. With W.R. Allen, *University Economics*, Belmont, California, Wadsworth; abridged edn 1969, *Exchange and Production*, Belmont, California, Wadsworth.
1969. 'Information Costs, Pricing and Resource Unemployment', *Western Economic Journal*, vol. 7, 109–28.
1972. With H. Demsetz, 'Production, Information Costs and Economic Organization', *American Economic Review*, vol. 62, 777–95.
1977. *Economic Forces at Work: Collected Papers of Armen Alchian*, Indianapolis, Liberty Press.

Having carried out several studies for the US Air Force, publishing numerous articles in statistics and co-authoring a dictionary of mathematics, Armen Alchian conducted studies on the behaviour of business firms, the effects of inflation, on the distribution of wealth and income (the latter notably with R. Kessel), the economics of education, research and science (in particular for the Rand Corporation).

Known to American students for the textbook he wrote with W.R. Allen, he put forward the thesis in an article published in 1950, that, though all firms do not seek to maximize their profits, only those that do manage to survive, this being sufficient to vindicate the hypothesis of the maximizing firm. He has also developed an analysis of property rights related to the analyses of market prices, competition and transaction costs. He has emphasized the need to take into account the costs of information, notably as an explanatory factor in the study of unemployment. Alchian's 18 main articles form the basis of his 1977 book.

Main references

BLAUG 1985, 3–5. *New Palgrave* 1987, vol. 1, 76.

ALLAIS Maurice (born 1911)

Maurice Allais was born in Paris, where he studied at the Ecole polytechnique (1931–3) and the Ecole nationale supérieure des mines (1934–6). He earned his doctor of engineering degree at the Science Faculty of the University of Paris in 1949. In 1944, he was appointed professor of economics at the Ecole des mines de Paris. In 1946, he became director of the Ecole's Centre for Economic Analysis as well as research director at the Centre National de la Recherche Scientifique (CNRS). He has held many other positions in teaching and public administration, and in 1988 became the second French economist to receive the Nobel Memorial Prize in Economics.

Main publications

1943. *A la Recherche d'une discipline économique, Première partie: L'Economie pure*, Paris, Ateliers Industria; 2nd edn 1952, *Traité d'économie pure*, 5 vols, Paris, Imprimerie nationale, 1952.
1945. *Economie pure et rendement social*, Paris, Sirey.
1945. *Prolégomènes à la reconstruction économique du monde*, Paris, Sirey.
1946. *Abondance ou misère*, Paris, Médicis.
1947. *Economie et intérêt*, 2 vols, Paris, Imprimerie nationale.
1953. 'Fondements d'une théorie positive des choix comportant un risque et critique des postulats et axiomes de l'Ecole américaine', in *Econométrie, Collection des Colloques internationaux du Centre national de la recherche scientifique*, Paris, vol. 40, 127–40.
1954. *Les Fondements comptables de la macroéconomique: Les Équations comptables entre quantités globales et leurs applications*, Paris, Presses Universitaires de France.
1959. *L'Europe unie: route de la prospérité*, Paris, Calmann-Lévy.
1960. *Les Aspects essentiels de la politique de l'énergie*, Paris, Imprimerie nationale.
1965. *Reformulation de la théorie quantitative de la monnaie*, Paris, SEDEIS.
1967. *Les Fondements du calcul économique*, 3 vol., Paris, Ecole nationale supérieure des mines.
1971. *La Libéralisation des relations économiques internationales: Accords commerciaux ou intégration économique*, Paris, Gauthier-Villars.
1976. *L'Impôt sur le capital et la réforme monétaire*, Paris, Hermann.
1978. *La Théorie générale des surplus*, 2 vols, Paris, Institut des sciences mathématiques et économiques; 2nd edn 1989, Presses Universitaires de Grenoble.
1979 (ed., with O. Hagen). *Expected Utility Hypotheses and the Allais Paradox: Contemporary Discussions and Rational Decisions under Uncertainty with Allais' Rejoinder*, Dordrecht, Reidel.
1988. 'Les Lignes directrices de mon oeuvre', in *Les Prix Nobel 1988*, Stockholm, Fondation Nobel; in *L'Actualité économique*, vol. 65, 1989, 323–45.
1989. *Autoportraits: Une Vie, une oeuvre*, Paris, Montchrestien.
1989. *Les Conditions monétaires d'une économie de marché: De la réflexion sur le passé à la préparation de l'avenir*, Paris, Montchrestien.
1989. 'My Life Philosophy', *American Economist*, vol. 33, no. 2, 3–17; under the title 'The Passion for Research', in Szenberg 1992, 17–41.
1989. *Scientific Papers on Risk and Utility Theory. Theory, Experience and Applications*, Dordrecht, Kluwer.

1990. *Pour l'indexation*, Paris, Clément Juglar.
1990. *Pour la réforme de la fiscalité*, Paris, Clément Juglar.

Like many French economists, Allais was trained as an engineer. In the early 1940s, while he was employed in the Nantes mines and quarries service, he read Walras, Fisher and Pareto and wrote a work of over one thousand pages (1943), for which the Nobel Memorial Prize in Economics was awarded to him. Convinced that the economic world admits of the same regularities as the physical world (he has also made important contributions to theoretical physics), Allais therefore gave himself the task of reconstructing modern economics on a more rigorous and more realistic basis. He independently arrived at conclusions comparable to those of Hicks and Samuelson, whose work he was unfamiliar with at the time, and his conclusions were in some ways more general than theirs.

One of the main contributions of Allais' first book is its demonstration of what he terms equivalence theorems, 'the equivalence of situations of general economic equilibrium and situations of maximum efficiency' (1989 *AE*, in Szenberg 1992, p. 23). Allais is a critical follower of Walras, whose lack of realism he criticizes. In the 1960s, he extended this criticism to the developments of Walrasian theory proposed by thinkers such as Debreu and Samuelson, whom he holds to value mathematical virtuosity at the expense of realism, like many other contemporary economists. He suggests that the general model of market equilibrium based on the hypothetical existence of unique prices be replaced with a model of market economies grounded in the concept of surplus; economic dynamism is thus held to be characterized by the search for, realization and distribution of surplus, a theme already present in his 1943 work (1978).

The Royal Swedish Academy of Sciences also mentioned *Economie et intérêt* (1947) in its press release. Here Allais demonstrated what was to become, in the writings of Swan and Phelps, the golden rule of growth, according to which an interest rate equal to the growth rate allows for maximum consumption. This work, like his 1943 book, contains many other findings that postwar neoclassical economics was to take up, in the United Kingdom and, even more so, in the United States. In addition to his studies on market equilibrium, capital theory and intertemporal processes, Allais has also contributed to money and credit theory, reformulating the quantitative theory of money (1965). He has also been interested in the study of choice and rational decision making, framing for the first time (1953) what has since been known as Allais' paradox. This contradicts the traditional model of rational choice, notably its transitivity.

Allais is, moreover, the author of many monographs in applied economics and he has described himself as an advocate of an interweaving of the various social sciences in the hope of discovering better solutions, so as to arrive at economic efficiency and social welfare. Politically, he is in the tradition of liberals such as Tocqueville, Walras and Keynes. However, many of his positions reveal his affinities with Friedman and Hayek, with whom he has associated in the Mont Pèlerin Society.

Main references

'The Nobel Memorial Prize in Economics 1988'. Press release, articles by J.H. Drèze and J.-M. Grandmont, and bibliography (extracted from Boiteux, Montbrial and Munier 1986), *Scandinavian Journal of Economics*, 1989, vol. 91, 1–46.

ALLAIS 1988, 1989 'My Life Philosophy', 1989 *Autoportraits*.
BOITEUX M., MONTBRIAL T. de and MUNIER B. 1986 (eds). *Marchés, capital et incertitude: Essais en l'honneur de Maurice Allais*, Paris, Economica; Engl. transl. 1989, *Markets and Risk: Essays in Honour of Maurice Allais*, Dordrecht, Kluwer.
MUNIER Bertrand 1989. 'Portée et signification de l'oeuvre de Maurice Allais, Prix Nobel d'économie, 1988', *Revue d'économie politique*, vol. 99, 1–27.
MUNIER Bertrand 1991. 'Nobel Laureate: The Many Other Allais Paradoxes', *Journal of Economic Perspectives*, vol. 5, no. 2, 179–99.

New Palgrave 1987, vol. 1, 78–82.

AMIN Samir (born 1931)

Born in Cairo, Samir Amin attended the Lycée français, and then studied political economy in Paris, earning his PhD in 1957. He worked as an economist on the 1957–60 Egyptian Economic Plan and as a planning consultant in Mali (1960–63). From 1964 to 1970 he taught at the Universities of Dakar, Poitiers and Paris 8-Vincennes, and in 1966 he passed the French *agrégation* of economics. From 1970 to 1980 he directed the United Nations African Institute of Economic Development and Planning in Dakar and subsequently the African Office of the Third World Forum, an international non-governmental agency.

Main publications

1964. [Under the pseudonym of Hassan Riad], *L'Egypte nassérienne*, Paris, Éditions de Minuit.
1965. *Trois expériences africaines de développement: le Mali, la Guinée et le Ghana*, Paris, Presses Universitaires de France.
1966. *L'Economie du Maghreb*, 2 vols, Paris, Editions de Minuit.
1967. *Le Développement du capitalisme en Côte d'Ivoire*, Paris, Editions de Minuit.
1969. *Le Monde des affaires sénégalais*, Paris, Editions de Minuit.
1970. *L'Accumulation à l'échelle mondiale: Critique de la théorie du sous-développement*, Dakar, Ifan and Paris, Anthropos; Engl. transl. 1974, *Accumulation on a World Scale*, 2 vols, New York, Monthly Review Press.
1971. *L'Afrique de l'Ouest bloquée, 1880–1970*, Paris, Editions de Minuit; Engl. transl. 1973, *Neocolonialism in West Africa*, Harmondsworth, Penguin.
1973. *Le Développement inégal: Essai sur les formations sociales du capitalisme périphérique*,

Paris, Editions de Minuit; Engl. transl. 1976, *Unequal Development: An Essay on the Social Formations of Peripheral Capitalism*, New York, Monthly Review Press.
1973. *L'Échange inégal et la loi de la valeur: la fin d'un débat*, Paris, Anthropos.
1975. *Et al.*, *La Crise de l'impérialisme*, Paris, Editions de Minuit.
1976. *L'Impérialisme et le développement inégal*, Paris, Éditions de Minuit; Engl. transl. 1977, *Imperialism and Unequal Development*, New York, Monthly Review Press.
1976. *La Nation arabe: Nationalisme et luttes de classes*, Paris, Editions de Minuit; Engl. transl. 1978, *The Arab Nation*, London, Zed.
1977. *La Loi de la valeur et le matérialisme historique*, Paris, Editions de Minuit; Engl. transl. 1978, *The Law of Value and Historical Materialism*, New York, Monthly Review Press.
1979. *Classe et nation dans l'histoire et la crise contemporaine*, Paris, Editions de Minuit; Engl. transl. 1980, *Class and Nation, Historically and in the Current Crisis*, New York, Monthly Review Press.
1980. *L'Économie arabe contemporaine*, Paris, Editions de Minuit; Engl. transl. 1982, *The Arab Economy Today*, London, Zed.
1981. *L'Avenir du maoïsme*, Paris, Editions de Minuit; Engl. transl. 1983, *The Future of Maoism*, New York, Monthly Review Press.
1982 With G. Arrighi, A.G. Frank and I. Wallerstein, *Dynamics of Global Crisis*, New York, Monthly Review Press.
1985. *La Déconnexion: Pour sortir du système mondial*, Paris, La Découverte; Engl. transl. 1990, *Delinking*, London, Zed.
1988. *L'Eurocentrisme: Critiques d'une idéologie*, Paris, Anthropos; Engl. transl. 1989, *Eurocentrism*, London, Zed; New York, Monthly Review Press.
1989. *La Faillite du développement en Afrique et dans le Tiers-Monde: Une analyse politique*, Paris, L'Harmattan; Engl. transl. 1990, *Maldevelopment in Africa and in the Third World*, London, Zed.
1991. *L'Empire du chaos. La nouvelle mondialisation capitaliste*, Paris, L'Harmattan.

After publishing several works on his native Egypt, on the Maghreb and on other African countries, Amin published (1970) a development of his dissertation, *Accumulation on a World Scale.* In this Amin criticized dualist and step-by-step explanations of underdevelopment, as well as orthodox analyses of international relations, developing his arguments within the framework of historical materialism with reference to studies of the means of production and social groups, while at the same time breaking with doctrinaire Marxism. The break is evident in his treatment of the logic of global capitalism which he holds to be more significant than class relations on a national level. This logic involves the relations between a dominant 'centre' and a 'periphery' required to adapt to it, such that the unequal exchange between the two fuels the worldwide accumulation of capital.

These themes, recurrent in the works of Amin, are the source of his contributions to the theoretical debate between Marxists (1973, 1977) as well as to the analysis of the economic crisis of the 1970s (1975, 1982), and to his study of the failure of economic development. His work has led him to develop his concepts of the tributary and state-controlled modes of production and to go beyond the field of economics to deal with the idea of the nation, to analyse ideological and cultural questions and to criticize 'eurocentrism' (1976 *L'Impérialisme*, 1979, 1988).

Motivated at the same time by his profound socialist convictions, by his concern about the possibility of aggravating Third World divisions, and by his analysis of the anti-imperialist nature of contemporary revolutions, he has emphasized 'national and popular construction' and 'delinking' (1985). Amin continues to search for those forces of recomposition capable of allowing for new horizons other than the state into which we have fallen, in his view: worldwide chaos under the American Empire (1991).

Main references

FOSTER-CARTER Aidan, 'The Empirical Samir Amin: A Notice and Appreciation', in Amin [1980] 1982, 1–40.

ARESTIS and SAWYER 1992, 1–7.

ARROW Kenneth (born 1921)

Kenneth Arrow was born in New York. During the Great Depression his father, an immigrant and successful businessman, lost everything, and the family lived in poverty for ten years. He earned his first degree in mathematics from the City College of New York in 1940. He continued his studies at Columbia, earning an MA in mathematics in 1941 and a PhD in economics in 1951; his studies had been interrupted by four years of military service (1942–6). From 1947 to 1949 he was associated with the Cowles Commission in Chicago, and he has been a consultant to the Rand Corporation since 1948. An assistant professor at the University of Chicago in 1948–9, he went on in 1949 to a position at Stanford University where he was named professor in 1953. From 1968 to 1979 he was professor at Harvard University. Since 1979 he has been at Stanford University. In 1962, Arrow was a member of the Council of Economic Advisers of American President J.F. Kennedy. He was awarded the John Bates Clark Medal by the American Economic Association, of which he was president in 1973, and the Nobel Memorial Prize in Economics in 1972, along with John Hicks. He was president of the Econometric Society (1956) and of the International Economic Association (1983–6).

Main publications

1951. 'An Extension of the Basic Theorems of Classical Welfare Economics', in J. Neyman (ed.), *Proceedings of the Second Berkeley Symposium of Mathematical Statistics and Probability*, Berkeley, University of California Press, 507–32.

1951. *Social Choice and Individual Values*, New York, John Wiley & Sons, 2nd edn, 1963.

1953. 'Le rôle des valeurs boursières pour la répartition la meilleure des risques', *Économétrie* [Colloques internationaux du Centre national de la recherche scientifique, Paris], vol. 11, 41–7.

1954. With Gérard Debreu, 'Existence of an Equilibrium for a Competitive Economy', *Econometrica*, vol. 22, 265–90.

1958. With L. Hurwicz and H. Uzawa, *Studies in Linear and Non-Linear Programming*, Stanford University Press; London, Oxford University Press.
1958. With S. Karlin and H. Scarf, *Studies in the Mathematical Theory of Inventory and Production*, Stanford University Press; London, Oxford University Press.
1959. With M. Hoffenberg, *A Time Series Analysis of Interindustry Demands*, Amsterdam, North-Holland.
1962. 'The Economic Implications of Learning by Doing', *Review of Economic Studies*, vol. 29, 155–73.
1965. *Aspects of the Theory of Risk-Bearing*, Helsinki, Yrjö Jahnssonin säätiö.
1970. With M. Kurz, *Public Investment, the Rate of Return and Optimal Fiscal Policy*, Baltimore and London, Johns Hopkins.
1971. *Essays in the Theory of Risk-Bearing*, Chicago, Markham; Amsterdam, North-Holland.
1971. With F.H. Hahn, *General Competitive Analysis*, San Francisco, Holden-Day; Edinburgh, Oliver & Boyd; Amsterdam, North-Holland.
1974. *The Limits of Organization*, New York, W.W. Norton.
1977. With L. Hurwicz, *Studies in Resource Allocation Processes*, Cambridge, England and New York, Cambridge University Press.
1983. *Collected Papers of Kenneth J. Arrow*, vol. 1, *Social Choice and Justice*; vol. 2, *General Equilibrium*, Cambridge, Massachusetts, Harvard University Press.
1984. *Collected Papers of Kenneth J. Arrow*, vol. 3, *Individual Choice under Certainty and Uncertainty*; vol. 4, *The Economics of Information*, Cambridge, Massachusetts, Harvard University Press.
1985. *Collected Papers of Kenneth J. Arrow*, vol. 5, *Production and Capital*; vol. 6, *Applied Economics*, Cambridge, Massachusetts and London, Harvard University Press.
1986. 'My Evolution as an Economist', in Breit and Spencer 1986, 43–57.
1986. With H. Raynaud, *Social Choice and Multicriterion Decision-Making*, Cambridge, Massachusetts and London MIT Press.
1987. 'Arrow's Theorem', in *New Palgrave*, vol. 1, 124–6.
1992. 'I Know a Hawk from a Handsaw', in Szenberg 1992, 42–50.

Kenneth Arrow won the Nobel Memorial Prize for his 'pioneering contributions to general economic equilibrium theory and welfare theory' ('The Nobel', p. 486). However, his first contribution, developed from his doctoral thesis and on the subject of social choice (1951, see also 1983, vol. 1), is without doubt his most famous. Here, Arrow rediscovered and generalized the voting paradox, highlighted by Condorcet in 1785. This holds that it is in effect possible that A receives a majority over B, and B over C, but that C receives a majority over A. The transitivity that characterizes an individual's rational choice cannot be aggregated so as to obtain as a result a process of transitive social choices. The 'impossibility theorem', also known as 'Arrow's theorem', holds that there are no mechanisms, in both economics and politics, that allow for a passage from rational individual choice to rational social choice. This theoretical statement has stimulated a most abundant literature, leading Arrow to correct it (1987); however, it has never been convincingly falsified.

The 1954 article he wrote with Gérard Debreu (although it was the result of independent research) is undoubtedly one of the most important contributions to contemporary microeconomics. Using the techniques of modern mathematics, Arrow and Debreu demonstrated the existence of a general equilibrium based on a limited number of hypotheses concerning the rationality of firms and consumers. In so doing, they completed the Walras system, to which many of their predecessors had already attempted to give firmer foundations than had Walras, who was content simply to count the number of equations and unknowns in order to affirm the existence of general equilibrium. Other economists have independently developed analogous models, but it is the Arrow–Debreu version that has established itself in contemporary economic theory.

Arrow has also demonstrated that any state of general equilibrium is Pareto-optimal and, conversely, that all Pareto-optimal states are states of general equilibrium (1951 'An Extension'). He is also one of the first of those who have tried to integrate uncertainty into the theory of general equilibrium (1953). In addition to these contributions, effected at the start of his career and subsequently developed, Arrow has intervened in many other fields, such as methodology, production theory, growth theory and economic policy.

Arrow is one of the prime contributors to the mathematicization of contemporary economic theory. However, he has also frequently insisted that mathematics is a tool that cannot take the place of economic reasoning, himself underlining the abstract and limited character that many have critically attributed to the general equilibrium theory. He has also drawn attention to the importance of history, and of the variability of economic and institutional conditions between eras and countries.

Main references

'The Nobel Memorial Prize in Economics 1972'. Official Announcement and article by C.C. von Weizsäcker, *Swedish Journal of Economics*, 1972, vol. 74, 486–502.

ARROW 1986, 1992.

DUFFIE Darrell and SONNENSCHEIN Hugo 1989. 'Arrow and General Equilibrium Theory', *Journal of Economic Literature*, vol. 27, 565–98.

FEIWEL George R. 1986 (ed.). *Essays in Honour of Kenneth J. Arrow*, London, Macmillan.

FEIWEL George R. 1987 (ed.). *Arrow and the Foundations of the Theory of Economic Policy*, London, Macmillan.

FEIWEL George R. 1987 (ed.). *Arrow and the Ascent of Modern Economic Theory*, London, Macmillan.

GEANAKOPLOS John 1987. 'Arrow–Debreu Model of General Equilibrium', *New Palgrave*, vol. 1, 116–24.

BLAUG 1985, 6–9.

ASIMAKOPULOS Athanasios (1930–1990)

Born in Montreal, Athanasios Asimakopulos studied at McGill University (1947–53), then at Cambridge, in England (1953–6) where he obtained a PhD in 1959. After a stay as assistant professor at the Royal Military College (1957–9), he spent the rest of his career at McGill University, where he was successively assistant professor (1959–63), associate professor (1963–6) and full professor (from 1966). His career was cut short by his premature death.

Main publications

1965. With J.C. Weldon, 'A Synoptic View of Some Simple Models of Growth', *Canadian Journal of Economics and Political Science*, vol. 31, 52–79.

1969. 'A Robinsonian Growth Model in One-Sector Notation', *Australian Economic Papers*, vol. 8, 41–58.

1971. 'The Determination of Investment in Keynes's Model', *Canadian Journal of Economics*, vol. 4, 382–8.

1975. 'A Kaleckian Theory of Income Distribution', *Canadian Journal of Economics*, vol. 8, 313–33.

1978. *An Introduction to Economic Theory: Microeconomics*, Toronto, Oxford University Press.

1982. 'Keynes' Theory of Effective Demand Revisited', *Australian Economic Papers*, vol. 21, 18–36.

1983. 'Kalecki and Keynes on Finance, Investment and Saving', *Cambridge Journal of Economics*, vol. 7, 221–34.

1986. 'Finance, Saving and Investment', *Journal of Post Keynesian Economics*, vol. 9, 79–90.

1987. 'La Signification théorique de la *Théorie générale* de Keynes', in *La 'Théorie générale' et le keynésianisme*, edited by G. Boismenu and G. Dostaler, Montreal, ACFAS, 38–54.

1988. *Investment, Employment and Income Distribution*, Oxford, Polity Press; Boulder, Colorado, Westview Press.

1988 (ed.). *Theories of Income Distribution*, Boston, Kluwer.

1990 (ed., with R. Cairns and C. Green). *Economic Theory, Welfare and the State. Essays in Honour of John C. Weldon*, London, Macmillan; Montreal and Kingston, McGill-Queen's University Press.

1991. *Keynes's General Theory and Accumulation*, Cambridge, England, Cambridge University Press.

Following a doctoral thesis dealing with the links between technical change and the terms of trade, A. Asimakopulos became interested in, among other subjects, the theory of growth (1965). Developing, from the middle of the 1960s, an increasingly critical attitude towards the neoclassical approach, Asimakopulos drew closer to the post-Keynesian movement, but he always refused to be linked exclusively with any one school, and maintained a critical attitude towards all streams of thought, as witnessed by the controversy generated by his questioning of some aspects of the post-Keynesian analysis of the link between saving and investment (1983, 1986). Close to Joan Robinson, to the clarification of whose theses he contributed much (1969), he nevertheless became critical of some of her views in her later works. He blamed her, as he did Harrod, another author on whom he wrote a good deal, for extending the Keynesian theory in a long-run equilibrium context incompatible with Keynes's vision. He himself drew increasingly close to the theses of Kalecki, to whom he also devoted several articles (1975, 1983).

The clarification of Keynes's work constitutes one of Asimakopulos' major contributions. Beginning with a critique of the Keynesian vision of investment (1971), it resulted in a posthumous work (1991) in which he tries to develop what he calls a 'General Theory', distinct from *The General Theory*, nonetheless inspired by the latter. Indeed, Asimakopulos detects in Keynes's book important contradictions, which stem from a tension between a vision in terms of timeless equilibrium, which needs to be rejected, and a causal analysis which makes room for time and uncertainty.

Asimakopulos also made contributions to microeconomic theory (1978), as well as to the study of taxation and pension schemes.

Main references

HARCOURT G.C. 1991. 'Athanasios (Tom) Asimakopulos, 1930–1990: A Memoir', *Journal of Post Keynesian Economics*, vol. 14, 39–48.

HARCOURT G.C., RONCAGLIA A. and ROWLEY R. 1994 (eds). *Income and Employment in Theory and Practice: Essays in Memory of Athanasios Asimakopulos,* London, Macmillan.

BAIN Joe Staten (1912–1991)

Joe S. Bain was born in Spokane, Washington State. He earned a BA at California University in Los Angeles (1935), an MA (1939) and a PhD (1940) at Harvard University, where he studied under Schumpeter. He started teaching in 1939 at California University at Berkeley, where he was named professor in 1945. He retired in1976 as a professor emeritus.

Main publications

1942. 'Market Classifications in Modern Price Theory', *Quarterly Journal of Economics*, vol. 56, 560–74.

1944, 1945, 1947. *The Economics of the Pacific Coast Petroleum Industry*, 3 vols, Berkeley, University of California Press.

1948. *Pricing, Distribution, and Employment: Economics of an Enterprise System*, New York, Henry Holt; revised and enlarged edn of first part, 1952, *Price Theory*, New York, John Wiley & Sons.

1956. *Barriers to New Competition: Their Character and Consequences in Manufacturing Industries*, Cambridge, Massachusetts, Harvard University Press; London, Oxford University Press.

1959. *Industrial Organization*, New York, John Wiley & Sons; 2nd edn 1968.

1966. *International Differences in Industrial Structure: Eight Nations in the 1950s*, New Haven, Connecticut and London, Yale University Press.

1966. With R.E. Caves and J. Margolis, *Northern California's Water Industry: The Comparative Efficiency of Public Enterprise in Developing a Scarce Natural Resource*, Baltimore, Johns Hopkins.

1970 (ed.). *Essays on Economic Development*, Berkeley, Institute of Business and Economic Research.

1972. *Essays on Price Theory and Industrial Organization*, Boston, Little, Brown.

1973. *Environmental Decay: Economic Causes and Remedies*, Boston, Little, Brown.

1986. 'Structure versus Conduct as Indicators of Market Performance: The Chicago School Attempts Revisited', *Antitrust Law and Economic Review*, vol. 18, no. 2, 19–50.

1987. With T. David Qualls, *Industrial Organization: A Treatise*, 2 vols, Greenwich, Connecticut, J.A.I. Press.

Joe Bain is one of the main architects of industrial economics and has contributed to this discipline an important and widely read manual (1959; the 1987 *Treatise* has replaced it). His main articles on these topics have been gathered in a book published in 1972. While supporting the main axioms of the neoclassical theory, he nonetheless thinks that the traditional analyses of price determination lack realism by not considering the actual characteristics of industrial organization in contemporary economies. Mainly interested in empirical research, Bain devoted much time, in his early career, to the study of the petroleum industry on the Pacific Coast (1944–7), but at the same time, this study sought the 'development of a method of economic analysis more adequate for dealing with the observed character of price and market behavior' (1944, p. viii). A more appropriate price theory has to take into account the relations between the market and its environment, as well as the structures of markets. Furthermore, this research should lead to public intervention proposals.

The textbook he devoted to price theory (1948) is therefore quite different from usual textbooks in that it insists on the importance of price determination in monopolistic or oligopolistic markets. But his book on barriers to entry is his most original and best known contribution (1956). It aims at describing the effects, on the profitability of enterprises among other things, of an important and neglected aspect of market structure: the 'condition of entry', the easiness or uneasiness with which a new competitor enters the industry. He suggests new ways of measuring economies of scale.

While using a more literary than mathematic style of presentation, and not laying claim to a new theory, Bain labelled his own approach as behavioural. He also took an interest in economic development (1970) and pollution problems (1973).

Main references

BLAUG 1985, 10–11. *New Palgrave* 1987, vol. 1, 175–6.

BALASSA Bela (born 1928)

Born in Budapest, B. Balassa graduated in 1948 from the law faculty of the University of Budapest, and the Hungarian Academy of Foreign Trade, obtaining his doctorate in 1951, his thesis being on statistical sampling. After two years of mandatory work in Hungary, he held an important position in a state construction firm; he was required to leave his native country with the Soviet invasion of 1956. He returned to his studies at Yale University (MA, 1958 and PhD, 1959) where he became assistant and later associate professor between 1959 and 1967. Since 1967, he has been a professor of political economy at Johns Hopkins University and a consultant to the World Bank.

Main publications

1959. *The Hungarian Experience in Economic Planning*, New Haven, Connecticut, Yale University Press.

1961. *The Theory of Economic Integration*, Homewood, Illinois, Richard D. Irwin; London, Allen & Irwin.

1964. *Trade Prospects for Developing Countries*, Homewood, Illinois, Richard D. Irwin.

1967. *Trade Liberalization among Industrial Countries: Objectives and Alternatives*, New York, McGraw-Hill.

1971. *The Structure of Protection in Developing Countries*, Baltimore, Johns Hopkins.

1977. *Policy Reform in Developing Countries*, Oxford, Pergamon Press.

1981. *The Newly Industrializing Countries in the World Economy*, New York, Pergamon Press.

1982. *Development Strategies in Semi-Industrial Economies*, Baltimore, Johns Hopkins.

1985. *Change and Challenge in the World Economy*, London, Macmillan.

1987. With John Williamson, *Adjusting to Success: Balance-of-Payments Policy in the East Asian NICs*, Washington, DC, Institute for International Economics.

1989. *Comparative Advantage, Trade Policy and Economic Development*, Hemel Hempstead, Harvester Wheatsheaf.

1989. 'My Life Philosophy', *American Economist*, vol. 33, no. 1, 16–23.
1989. *New Directions in the World Economy*, New York University Press; London, Macmillan.

In Hungary, Balassa's first writings were on the construction industry and on the economic thought of Marx and John Stuart Mill. In the West, he wrote first on the efficiency criteria of economic systems and on national economic planning in Hungary (1959). He then chose to specialize in international economics, publishing works on economic integration (1961), the gains from international trade and more specifically on purchasing power parity, the effective protection rate, intra- (rather than inter) industrial specialization and horizontal (rather than vertical) specialization. From an early point in his career he has defended free trade positions, even for developing countries (1964, 1967, 1971, 1977), against economists such as Myrdal, Prebisch and Singer.

Whether he is examining underdeveloped countries, 'newly industrialized countries' like China, Hungary and other Eastern European countries, or Western European countries like Portugal and France, he highlights consistently and steadily the costs of protectionism and of all economic policies which involve distorting the market; and he advocates liberalization of exchange, export-oriented economy, privatization and, more generally, reduction of public intervention and planification, as is evident in his books published in 1985 and 1989, works which bring together Balassa's main contributions on these questions.

Main references

BALASSA 1989 *AE*.

BLAUG *Who's Who*, 1986, 43–4.

BARAN Paul Alexander (1910–1964)

Born in Nikolaev, Russia, Paul Baran, with his parents, left his native land for Germany after the October revolution and returned with them in 1925 to Moscow, where he began his university studies. He enrolled at the University of Berlin in 1928 (earning his doctorate in 1932) and worked as a researcher at the Institute for Social Research at the University of Frankfurt. He left Germany in the early 1930s, first for France, then for Warsaw, where he worked for one of his uncle's companies. In 1938, he went to London, and, the following year, to the United States.

He was accepted as a graduate student at Harvard University, worked for several government agencies during the Second World War and then in the research department of the Federal Reserve Bank of New York. He was appointed professor at Stanford in 1951. He died of a heart attack at the age of 54.

Main publications

1957. *The Political Economy of Growth*, New York and London, Monthly Review Press.
1966. With Paul M. Sweezy, *Monopoly Capital: An Essay on the American Economic and Social Order*, New York, Monthly Review Press.
1970. *The Longer View: Essays Toward a Critique of Political Economy*, edited by John O'Neill, New York and London, Monthly Review Press.

Paul Baran was never a prolific author, yet he played a major role in the renewal of Marxist analysis both in the United States and in the Western world as a whole. In particular, he facilitated the emergence of radical theories of development, notably of those theories centred on the analysis of dependence. On this question, *The Political Economy of Growth* constitutes an essential contribution. The work must be appreciated from both the theoretical and practical angles. Theoretically, it brought out Baran's central concept of 'potential economic surplus', a key idea in his analysis of monopoly capitalism; this concept is homologous to Marx's concept of surplus value in the analysis of competitive capitalism. In the developed, capitalist countries, the tendency is towards the rise of potential surplus and the increasing difficulty of absorbing it (in spite of the exacerbation of consumption, arms expenditures, and so on) and this has consequently led to economic stagnation. Only a socialist transformation of these countries would allow for a rational use of this surplus, which would benefit the underdeveloped countries as well.

In effect, Baran has articulated the influential view that backward countries are stuck between feudalism and capitalism in its imperialist form: their potential economic surplus is not directed towards a fruitful capital accumulation; it is either used by the ruling classes for unproductive expenditures (the self-enrichment or excessive consumption of these classes, the maintenance of the bureaucratic structure, military expenditures) or it is frequently seized by foreign capital. Thus only a revolutionary break seems a possible means of embarking on a better future.

Finally, for Baran, 'the capitalist system, once a mighty engine of economic development, has turned into a no less formidable hurdle to human advancement' (1957, p. 249). Most of these themes are also developed, and some treated in greater depth, in the book Baran published with Sweezy in 1966 (see Sweezy and Huberman, below).

Main references

FOSTER J.B. 1986. *The Theory of Monopoly Capitalism*, New York, Monthly Review Press.
SWEEZY Paul M. and HUBERMAN Leo (eds) 1965. *Paul Baran: A Collective Portrait*, New York, Monthly Review Press.

ARESTIS and SAWYER 1992, 22–9. *New Palgrave* 1987, vol. 1, 188–9.

BARRERE Alain (1910–1995)

Alain Barrère completed his advanced studies at the Faculty of Law at Toulouse, taking a doctorate in law (mention in economics) in 1938. A prisoner of war from June 1940 to May 1945, he was named professor of law at Toulouse in 1946, and professor at the Faculty of Law and Economics of Paris University in 1957. From 1964, he was research director at the Ecole Pratique des Hautes Etudes (now Ecole des Hautes Etudes en Sciences Sociales). Dean of the Faculty of Law and Economics from 1967 to 1970, he has been professor emeritus at the University of Paris 1 since 1980.

Main publications

1946. *Les Crises de reconversion et la politique économique d'après-guerre*, Paris, Marcel Rivière.
1952. *Théorie économique et impulsion keynésienne*, Paris, Dalloz.
1955. 'L'analyse des rapports entre le capital et la production', *Revue économique*, vol. 6, 332–408.
1958. *Politique financière*, Paris, Dalloz.
1965. *Economie et institutions financières*, Paris, Dalloz.
1974. *Histoire de la pensée économique et analyse contemporaine*, 2 vols, Paris, Montchresien.
1976. *Le Développement divergent: Essai sur la richesse et pauvreté des nations*, Paris, Economica.
1976. With D. Breton *et al.*, *Controverses sur le système keynésien*, Paris, Economica.
1979. *Déséquilibres économiques et contre-révolution keynésienne. Keynes: seconde lecture*, Paris, Economica.
1981. *La Crise n'est pas ce que l'on croit*, Paris, Economica.
1985 (ed.). *Keynes aujourd'hui: Théories et politiques*, Paris, Economica; Engl. transl., vol. 1, *The Foundations of Keynesian Analysis*, 1988; vol. 2, *Money, Credit and Prices in Keynesian Perspective*, 1989; vol. 3, *Keynesian Economic Policies*, 1990, London, Macmillan; New York, St Martin's Press.
1985. 'Price System and Money-Wage System', *Journal of Post Keynesian Economics*, vol. 8, 315–35.
1988. 'La Généralisation de la théorie de la monnaie en économie monétaire de production', *Économie appliquée*, vol. 41, 181–224.
1990. *Macroéconomie keynésienne: Le Projet économique de John Maynard Keynes*, Paris, Dunod.

Alain Barrère is the author of important contributions in several areas of economics: macroeconomic theory, growth theory, development, public finance and the history of economic thought. These works are inspired by an original and innovative reading of the work of Keynes undertaken while he was a prisoner during the war. *The General Theory* appears to him to be a point of departure, renewing the bases of economic analysis, rather than a point of arrival or a completed system. At the moment when the neoclassical synthesis imposed itself and before the development of the post-Keynesian problematics, Barrère was already taking care to emphasize Keynes's break with the orthodox view, stressing the importance of expectations, of non-probabilistic uncertainty and of money, and the need to extend the Keynesian analysis in a long run and dynamic setting (1952). Such is the research programme he has pursued since that date (1976 *Controverses*, 1979, 1990). In this, he has developed a Keynesian theory conceived as a monetary economy of production. It was in this light that Barrère offered an original analysis of the current crisis faced by capitalist economies, conceived as an organic crisis stemming from the disturbance of the systems of production and distribution (1981).

In his research programme, Barrère has attached much importance to history – history of facts as well as that of theories. He considers that economic theories conflict primarily in their bases and by their implicit conceptions of man and society, the Keynesian approach seeing economics as a moral and positive science. Influenced by authors such as Lundberg, Pigou, Harrod, Perroux, Kalecki and Joan Robinson, he has developed a critique of the neoclassical synthesis, and also of the disequilibrium theories (1979), Barrère is, in several respects, close to the post-Keynesian school of thought.

BARRO Robert J. (born 1944)

Robert J. Barro was born in New York. He took a BS in physics at the California Institute of Technology in 1965 and a PhD in economics from Harvard in 1970. He was assistant professor (1968–72), then associate professor (1972–3) at Brown University, associate professor (1973–5) at the University of Chicago, professor at the University of Rochester (1975–82), at the University of Chicago (1982–4), again at Rochester (1984–7), and since 1987 he has been at Harvard University. Since 1978 he has been a researcher at the National Bureau of Economic Research. He was editor of the *Journal of Political Economy* (1973–5, 1983–5).

Main publications

1971. With Hershel I. Grossman, 'A General Disequilibrium Model of Income and Employment', *American Economic Review*, vol. 61, 82–93.

1974. 'Are Government Bonds Net Wealth?', *Journal of Political Economy*, vol. 82, 1095–1117.

1976. 'Rational Expectations and the Role of Monetary Policy', *Journal of Monetary Economics*, vol. 2, 1–32.

1976. With Hershel I. Grossman, *Money, Employment and Inflation*, Cambridge, England, Cambridge University Press.

1981. *Money, Expectations, and Business Cycles: Essays in Macroeconomics*, New York, Academic Press.

1984. *Macroeconomics*, New York, John Wiley & Sons.

1989 (ed.). *Modern Business Cycle Theory*, Cambridge, Massachusetts, Harvard University Press and Basil Blackwell.

1990. *Macroeconomic Policy*, Cambridge, Massachusetts, Harvard University Press.

Robert Barro followed a course typical of several partisans of the new classical macroeconomics, gradually retreating from a Keynesian analysis in which, from the beginning, he criticized a lack of rigour in its microeconomic bases. Extending the analyses advanced by Patinkin, Clower and Leijonhufvud, while attempting to synthesize them, Barro and his colleague Hershel Grossman, from Brown University, thus developed what they were the first to call disequilibrium theory (1971, 1976).

In his subsequent work, rather than developing disequilibrium theory, Barro devoted himself to elaborating what he calls the 'market-clearing approach' to macroeconomic analysis, synonymous with new classical macroeconomics, relegating, for example, Keynesian theory to the second-last chapter of his macroeconomics textbook (1984; see also the introduction to 1989). Barro has also been very interested in economic policy. His article on government debt issue (1974) gave rise to a lively debate. In this article he developed what Buchanan subsequently called the Ricardian equivalence theorem about the relation between taxes and debt (Buchanan 1976 below), according to which 'the economy's path of real interest rates, investment, consumption, and so on is invariant with shifts between taxes and budget deficits or with changes in the initial stock of public debt' (1989, p. 204). The rationality of agents and the existence of intergenerational transfers imply that a reduction in taxes financed by a budget deficit gives rise to an increase in private saving which cancels the reduction in public saving. An increase in public debt, and more generally so-called expansionary fiscal policies, do not have, according to Barro, the stimulative effect on aggregate demand predicted by the traditional Keynesian approach. As such, the Ricardian equivalence theorem fits in with the views of the new classical macroeconomics on policy ineffectiveness (1976 *JME*).

Main reference

BUCHANAN James M. 1976. 'Barro on the Ricardian Equivalence Theorem', *Journal of Political Economy*, vol. 84, 337–42.

BAUMOL William J. (born 1922)

Born in New York, Baumol began his university studies there (BSS, 1942) and then worked as an economist in the United States Department of Agriculture (1942–3 and 1946). He was an assistant lecturer at the London School of Economics (1947–9) and obtained his doctorate at the University of London in 1949. He spent the rest of his career at Princeton University, as a professor from 1954. He also became a professor at New York University in 1971. Being also a wood sculptor, he gave courses on this art at Princeton. A consultant to government and private enterprise, he has served (among other positions) as president of the Association of Environmental and Resource Economists (1979) and of the American Economic Association (1981).

Main publications

1951. With R. Turvey, *Economic Dynamics: An Introduction*, New York, Macmillan.
1952. 'The Transaction Demand for Cash: An Inventory Theoretic Approach', *Quarterly Journal of Economics*, vol. 66, 545–56.
1952. *Welfare Economics and the Theory of the State*, London, Longmans Green.
1959. *Business Behavior, Value and Growth*, New York, Macmillan.
1961. *Economic Theory and Operations Analysis*, Englewood Cliffs, New Jersey, Prentice-Hall.
1966. With W.G. Bowen, *Performing Arts: The Economic Dilemma*, New York, Twentieth Century Fund.
1973. With M. Marcus, *Economics of Academic Libraries*, Washington, American Council on Education.
1975. With W.E. Oates, *The Theory of Environmental Policy*, Englewood Cliffs, New Jersey, Prentice-Hall.
1976. *Selected Economic Writings of William J. Baumol*, edited by E.E. Balley, New York University Press.
1979. With A.S. Blinder, *Economics: Principles and Policy*, New York, Harcourt Brace Jovanovich.
1979. With W.E. Oates and S.A. Batey Blackman, *Economics, Environmental Policy and the Quality of Life*, Englewood Cliffs, New Jersey, Prentice-Hall.
1982. With J.C Panzar and R.D. Willig, *Contestable Markets and the Theory of Industry Structure*, New York, Harcourt Brace Jovanovich.
1983. 'On the Career of a Microeconomist', *Quarterly Review, Banca Nazionale del Lavoro*, no. 147, 311–35; in Kregel 1989, 209–34.
1986. *Microtheory: Applications and Origins*, Cambridge, MIT Press.
1986. With D. Fischer, *Superfairness: Application and Theory*, Cambridge, MIT Press.
1988. With G.R. Faulhaber, 'Economists as Innovators: Practical Products of Theoretical Research', *Journal of Economic Literature*, vol. 26, 577–600.
1989. With S.A. Batey Blackman and E.N. Wolff, *Productivity and American Leadership: The Long View*, Cambridge, Massachusetts, MIT Press.
1992. With S.A. Batey Blackman, *Perfect Markets and Easy Virtue: Business Ethics and the Invisible Hand*, Cambridge, Massachusetts, Blackwell.
1992. 'On my Attitudes: Sociopolitical and Methodological', in Szenberg 1992, 51–9.
1993. *Entrepreneurship, Management, and the Structure of Payoffs*, Cambridge, Massachusetts, MIT Press.

William Baumol's work is marked by a tension between the author's taste for rigorous theoretical analysis, mainly in microeconomics, and his interest in certain practical fields and problems. His first works were concerned with welfare economics (his thesis, published in 1952), growth theory and economic policy (1951, 1959). They also dealt with operations research, linear programming and activity analysis, which he applied to firm's choices, marketing and transport (1961). He subsequently worked on optimality, and the behaviour of the firm, offering a rigorous analysis of the firm as seeking to maximize its sales rather than its profits. He has also worked on public choice and, in a very practical manner, on the urban crisis, the economics of entertainment (especially the theatre, see 1966), university libraries (1973), scientific periodicals and more recently, health care.

Moreover, having worked on externalities, he was among the first systematically to examine environmental economics and the economics of the conservation of resources, especially energy (1975, 1979 with W. Oates). His work on markets, monopolistic competition and oligopoly, effected concurrently with his research on industrial structures and multiproduct firms, led him to suggest that they be analysed in terms of 'contestable markets' in which monopolies and oligopolies must take into account the potential entry of new competitors (1982). In the 1980s, he deepened reflections on 'equity and efficiency' and on the taking into account of distribution in works on optimality. Going beyond the approach to this question via the concept of 'fairness', he set forth the concept of 'superfairness', in which distribution is such that 'each class of participants prefers its own share to the share received by another group' and 'no participant envies the other' (1986, p.15).

Baumol is also interested in the thought of great nineteenth-century and contemporary economists. Recently, he has analysed the long-run evolutions in US productivity and their effects on employment (1989).

Main references

BAUMOL 1983, 1992 'On my Attitudes…'.
BAILEY Elizabeth E. and WILLIG Robert D. 1992. 'William J. Baumol', in Samuels (ed.), 30–57.

BLAUG 1985, 12–14.

BECKER Gary S. (born 1930)

Gary Stanley Becker was born in Pottsville, Pennsylvania. He earned his MA (1953) and his PhD (1955) at the University of Chicago, where he started teaching in 1954. He has been a professor at Columbia University (1957–69) and, since 1969, at the University of Chicago. He is also a member of the Domestic Advisory Board of the Hoover Institution at Stanford University. Becker was awarded the 1967 John Bates Clark Medal and served as president of the American Economic Association in 1987. He was named vice-president of the Mont Pèlerin Society in 1989. In 1992, he was awarded the Nobel Memorial Prize in Economics.

Main publications

1957. *The Economics of Discrimination*, University of Chicago Press.
1957. With M. Friedman, 'A Statistical Illusion in Judging Keynesian Models', *Journal of Political Economy*, vol. 65, 64–75.

1962. 'Investment in Human Capital: A Theoretical Analysis', *Journal of Political Economy*, vol. 70, 9–49.
1964. *Human Capital: A Theoretical and Empirical Analysis with Special Reference to Education*, New York, Columbia University Press; new expanded edn 1993, University of Chicago Press.
1965. 'A Theory of the Allocation of Time', *Economic Journal*, vol. 75, 493–508.
1967. *Human Capital and the Personal Distribution of Income: An Analytical Approach*, Ann Arbor, Institute of Public Administration.
1968. 'Crime and Punishment: An Economic Approach', *Journal of Political Economy*, vol. 76, 196–217.
1971. *Economic Theory*, New York, Alfred A. Knopf.
1973. 'A Theory of Marriage: Part I', *Journal of Political Economy*, vol. 81, 813–46; Part II, vol. 82, 1974, S11–S26
1974. 'A Theory of Social Interactions', *Journal of Political Economy*, vol. 82, 1063–93.
1974 (ed. with William M. Landes). *Essays in the Economics of Crime and Punishment*, New York, Columbia University Press.
1975. With Gilbert Ghez, *The Allocation of Time and Goods Over the Life Cycle*, New York, Columbia University Press.
1976. *The Economic Approach to Human Behavior*, University of Chicago Press.
1981. *A Treatise on the Family*, Cambridge, Massachusetts, Harvard University Press.
1983. 'A Theory of Competition among Pressure Groups for Political Influence', *Quarterly Journal of Economics*, vol. 98, 371–400.
1988. 'Family Economics and Macro Behavior', *American Economic Review*, vol. 86, 1–13.
1988. With Kevin M. Murphy, 'A Theory of Rational Addiction', *Journal of Political Economy*, vol. 96, 675–700.
1989. With R.J. Barro, 'Fertility Choice in a Model of Economic Growth', *Econometrica*, vol. 57, 481–501.

Associated with the Chicago School, whose liberal values he shares, Becker pursued early on (1964, 1967) the path opened by Jacob Mincer and Theodore Schultz to the theory of human capital which consists of applying to investment in human capital the same rules of analysis as are applied to traditional investment. Accordingly, the reason why an individual is held to spend money so as to improve his or her education, health, or whatever other element of their life situation, is the hope of gaining more in the future; thus one invests in oneself. The rational individual makes his decisions by comparing the flow of future benefits with the costs of investment.

Becker has considerably extended the applications of the neoclassical framework which is at the basis of the theory of human capital. One might view his overall work as the implementation of a research programme that has as its goal the explanation of human behaviour as a whole through the use of the basic principles of neoclassical analysis, which are founded on the hypothesis that individuals are rational agents. Whether it be a question of becoming addicted to the use of drugs, of stealing, killing, marrying, having children, of being unfaithful to one's spouse or getting a divorce, the individual brings about his or her choice by rationally comparing costs and benefits, aiming at the maximization of personal satisfaction. For example, in the case of crime, a rational agent compares such activities' benefits with their costs, with particular regard to the probability of being captured and the severity of the resulting punishment. Only a few psychopaths do not conform to the rule. Becker holds that the set of decisions taken within the family unit, such as the division of housework, can also be analysed in this way (1981). Even love itself cannot avoid this: 'At an abstract level, love and other emotional attachments, such as sexual activity or frequent close contact with a particular person, can be considered particular nonmarketable household commodities, and nothing much need be added to the analysis, in Part I, of the demand for commodities' (1976, p. 233). Needless to say, such an approach fuels the accusations of imperialism levelled against a type of economics that claims to be an appropriate substitute for other social sciences, and even for psychology.

Main references

SHACKLETON J.R. 1981. 'Gary S. Becker: The Economist as Empire-Builder', in Shackleton and Locksley 1981, 12–32.

BLAUG 1985, 15–17.

BERGSON Abram (born 1914)

Born in Baltimore, Maryland, A. Bergson first studied at Johns Hopkins (AB, 1940) and subsequently at Harvard (AM, 1935 and PhD, 1940). He was an assistant professor at the University of Texas from 1940 to 1942, and worked at the Office of Strategic Services in Washington between 1940 and 1945. Bergson taught at Columbia, where he was a professor, from 1946 to 1956, and went on to teach at Harvard where he became professor emeritus in 1981. From 1964 to 1980, he was director of the Russian Research Center at Harvard. He was a consultant to the Rand Corporation from 1948 to 1988, as well as to various other federal government agencies.

Main publications

1936. 'Real Income, Expenditure Proportionality and Frisch's New Methods', *Review of Economic Studies*, vol. 4, 33–52.

1938. 'A Reformation of Certain Aspects of Welfare Economics', *Quarterly Journal of Economics*, vol. 52, 310–34.

1944. *The Structure of Soviet Wages: A Study in Socialist Economics*, Cambridge, Massachusetts, Harvard University Press.

1953. *Soviet National Income and Product in 1937*, New York, Columbia University Press.

1954. With Hans Jeymann, Jr., *Soviet National Income and Product, 1940–1948*, New York, Columbia University Press.

1961. *The Real National Income of Soviet Russia since 1928*, Cambridge, Massachusetts, Harvard University Press.

1964. *The Economics of Soviet Planning*, New Haven, Connecticut, Yale University Press.

1966. *Essays in Normative Economics*, Cambridge, Massachusetts, Harvard University Press.

1967. 'Market Socialism Revisited', *Journal of Political Economy*, vol. 75, 655–73.

1968. *Planning and Productivity under Soviet Socialism*, New York, Columbia University Press.
1978. *Productivity and the Social System: The USSR and the West*, Cambridge, Massachusetts, Harvard University Press.
1982. *Welfare, Planning and Employment: Selected Essays in Economic Theory*, Cambridge, Massachusetts, MIT Press.
1987. 'Recollections and Reflections of a Comparativist', *American Economist*, vol. 31, no. 1, 3–8; in Szenberg 1992, 60–68.
1989. *Planning and Performance in Socialist Economies: The USSR and Eastern Europe*, Boston, Massachusetts, Unwin Hyman.

In 1938, Bergson entered the debate on welfare theory by proposing an individual function for social welfare and subsequently contributed to the discussion of a number of other issues, notably the alleged loss of welfare due to monopolization. His articles on the last issue were collected in his works of 1966 and 1982.

However, the essential part of Bergson's contributions is to be found in his work on the Soviet economy. His dissertation (published in 1944), was the result of his key work in compiling and discussing raw data on wages in the Soviet Union. His subsequent work aimed at establishing the most accurate numerical data possible for the Soviet economy by drawing on official Soviet information, among other available sources, and by seeking to develop them in time series comparable to the statistics of Western economies. This involved both overcoming methodological problems (such as the valuation of products) and treating enormous quantities of data (1953, 1954, 1961); the results obtained soon became reference data. Above all else, Bergson has been an analyst of the economic institutions of the USSR and Eastern Europe, as well as of their malfunctions and reforms (1964, 1968, 1989) and he has carried out comparative studies on the efficiency and results of the socialist and capitalist economies (1982).

Main references

BERGSON 1987.
ROSEFIELDE S. 1981 (ed.). *Economic Welfare and the Economics of Soviet Socialism: Essays in Honor of Abram Bergson*, Cambridge, England, Cambridge University Press. [With a bibliography for 1936–80.]

BLAUG 1985, 18–20. *New Palgrave* 1987, vol. 1, 229–30.

BETTELHEIM Charles (born 1913)

Born in Paris, Charles Bettelheim pursued his studies there in law and philosophy (licence, 1935, DES, 1936–7 and doctorate in 1939). A lecturer at the law faculty of the University of Caen in 1939–40, he went on after the war to direct a research centre in the French Labour Ministry and to teach at the Ecole nationale d'administration (1945–9). In 1948 he was appointed research director at the Ecole pratique des hautes études (later the Ecole des hautes études en sciences sociales), where he directed the Centre d'étude des modes d'industrialisation (CEMI). He went on many missions to India between 1953 and 1956, as well as to Egypt, Guinea, Mali, Algeria and Cuba. He retired in 1983.

Main publications

1939. *La Planification soviétique*, Paris, Marcel Rivière.

1946. *L'Économie allemande sous le nazisme: Un aspect de la décadence du capitalisme*, Paris, Marcel Rivière.

1946. *Problèmes théoriques et pratiques de la planification*, Paris, Presses Universitaires de France; Engl. transl. 1959, *Studies in the Theory of Planning*, Bombay and London, Asia Publishing House.

1947. *Bilan de l'économie française*, Paris, Presses Universitaires de France.

1948. *Esquisse d'un tableau économique de l'Europe*, Paris, Domat.

1950. *L'Économie soviétique* (vol. 4 of *Traité d'économie politique* edited by Gaëtan Pirou), Paris, Sirey.

1957. *Some Basic Planning Problems*, London, Asia Publishing House.

1962. *L'Inde indépendante*, Paris, Armand Colin; Engl. transl. 1968, *India Independent*, London, Macgibbon & Kee.

1964. *Planification et croissance accélérée*, Paris, François Maspero.

1965. With Jacques Charrière and Hélène Marchisio, *La Construction du socialisme en Chine*, Paris, François Maspero.

1968. *La Transition vers l'économie socialiste*, Paris, François Maspero; Engl. transl. 1975, *The Transition to Socialist Economy*, Hassocks, Harvester Press.

1969. 'Préface' and 'Remarques théoriques', in Arghiri Emmanuel, *L'Échange inégal*, Paris, François Maspero, 9–21 and 297–341.

1970. *Calcul économique et formes de propriétés*, Paris, François Maspero; Engl. transl. 1976, *Economic Calculation and Forms of Property*, London, Routledge.

1970. With Paul M. Sweezy, *Lettres sur quelques problèmes actuels du socialisme*, Paris, François Maspero.

1973. *Révolution culturelle et organisation industrielle en Chine*, Paris, François Maspero; Engl. transl. 1976, *Cultural Revolution and Industrial Organization in China*, New York, Monthly Review Press.

1974–82. *Les Luttes de classes en URSS*: 1974, *1ère période 1917–1923*; 1977, *2ème période 1923–1930*; 1982, *3ème période 1930–1941*, vol. 1, *Les Dominés*; 1983, vol. 2 *Les Dominants*, Paris, François Maspero/Seuil; Engl. trans. 1976, 1978, *Class Struggles in the USSR, 1917–1923*; *1923–1930*, New York, Monthly Review Press.

1978. *Questions sur la Chine après la mort de Mao Tsé-toung*, Paris, François Maspero.

After a stay in Moscow in 1936, while he was a member of the French Communist Party, Bettelheim wrote his dissertation (1939) on Soviet planning. He devoted a number of other descriptive works to the economy of Nazi Germany as well as to postwar France and Europe (1946 *L'Économie*, 1947, 1948), published many studies on employment during the 1950s and worked on numerous theoretical and practical questions of planning, notably for countries seeking a socialist path of development (1946 *Les Problèmes*, 1957, 1959, 1964). Bettelheim published an important work on India (1962) and participated in the theoretical Marxist debate; in particular he criticized those who put forward the analysis of the alleged exploitation between countries, while neglecting the class relations within each country (1969).

Yet the main aspects of Bettelheim's reflections and work treat the USSR with China as counterpoint (1965, 1973), socialism and transition, and finally the nature of the historical processes at work since 1917. His first works, which are largely descriptive, are marked by the twin concerns of not attacking that society which a large section of the labour movement viewed as the materialization of socialist hopes and, at the same time, of not ignoring its weaknesses and failings (1939, 1950). Then, inspired by Mao Tse-tung, his theoretical analysis toughens: he criticized the idea that one may, by developing production forces, eliminate capitalist social relations; he distinguished between property and possession – state property being capable of becoming the foundation of a new bourgeoisie; he analysed state capitalism and the persistence of wage and monetary relations in a transition economy (1964, 1968, 1970 *Calcul*). Finally, his reflection broadened into an impressive study of the USSR from 1917 to 1941. His verdict was that the 1917 revolution was not a socialist, but rather a capitalist one: setting up in its initial phase a form of state capitalism, it led, from 1929 onwards, to the development of an extreme form of capitalism. As the idea of socialism played a role in this, with the October revolution began the 'great illusion' of the twentieth century (1974, 1977, 1982).

Main references

BLAUG *Who's Who* 1986, 79–80. *New Palgrave*, 1987, vol. 1, 234–5.

BHARADWAJ Krishna R. (1935–1992)

Krishna Bharadwaj was born at Karwar, on the western coast of India. She started her college education in Bombay in 1951, and began studying economics in 1952. Her doctoral dissertation was submitted to the University of Bombay in 1960. Bharadwaj then travelled to Cambridge, Massachusetts, where she joined the Center for International Studies at the MIT. In India in 1962, Bharadwaj became a lecturer at the University of Bombay. She was visiting fellow of Clare Hall and Trinity College in Cambridge, England, in 1967, where she met Sraffa, with whom she remained in close association until his death in 1983. Bharadwaj was senior research officer in the department of applied economics in Cambridge in 1968–9. In 1971, she joined the Jawaharlal Nehru University in Delhi, where she chaired the new Centre for Economic Studies and Planning.

Main publications

1962. 'Structural Linkages in the Indian Economy', *The Economic Weekly*, vol. 14, 1339–42.
1963. 'Value Through Exogenous Distribution', *The Economic Weekly*, vol. 15, 1450–54.
1974. *Production Conditions in Indian Agriculture: A Study Based on Farm Management Studies*, Cambridge, England, Cambridge University Press.
1978. *Classical Political Economy and the Rise to Dominance of Supply and Demand Theories*, Orient Longmans; 2nd revised edn 1986, Calcutta, University Press India.
1980. *On Some Issues of Method in the Analysis of Social Change*, Prasaranga, University of Mysore.
1985. 'A View on Commercialisation in Indian Agriculture and the Development of Capitalism', *Journal of Peasant Studies*, vol. 12, no. 4, 7–25.
1988. 'The Analytics of Agriculture–Industry Relation', in K.J. Arrow (ed.), *The Balance between Industry and Agriculture in Economic Development*, London, Macmillan, vol. 1, 198–217.
1989. *Themes in Value and Distribution: Classical Theory Reappraised*, London, Unwin Hyman.
1989 (ed., with Sudipta Kaviraj). *Perspectives on Capitalism: Marx, Keynes, Schumpeter and Weber*, New Delhi, Sage.
1989 (ed., with Bertram Schefold). *Essays on Piero Sraffa*, London, Unwin Hyman.

Krishna Bharadwaj's early work dealt with development theory. Critical of mainstream neoclassical theory, she was inspired by Leontief's interdependent production model, and Hirschman's concept of key sectors for the analysis of development strategy to study the problems of India's development (1962). Dealing with the relation between industry and agriculture, Bharadwaj criticized the arguments, based on the Lewis model, which advocated priority to industrialization at the expense of agriculture.

Bharadwaj's discovery of Sraffa's *Production of Commodities by Means of Commodities* was a determining event in her career, as was her meeting with Joan Robinson during her stay in Cambridge, Massachusetts, where she became acquainted with the Cambridge capital controversy. Bharadwaj wrote an influential review of Sraffa's book (1963), and became one of his most important disciples and interpreters. Deepening Sraffa's critique of neoclassical economic theory, Bharadwaj considers the transition from classical to neoclassical theory as a shift from an approach based on the concept of surplus to an approach based on demand and supply equilibrium, which she labelled DSE theories (1978). Writing on many aspects of classical theory, she sought to disclose the main common elements of the theoretical structure of the classical authors, renewed by Sraffa, to compare them to those of the DSE theories, and to criticize the attempts to assimilate DSE and surplus theories (see her papers collected in 1989 *Themes*).

Bharadwaj remained interested, until the premature end of her career, in the question of development, and particularly in the problems faced by her country. Convinced that classical analysis constitutes an alternative paradigm, superior to the neoclassical orthodoxy, more adapted to study history and social changes, she tried to extend the surplus approach to the problems of accumulation and development. It is in this context that she forged the concept of interlinked markets (1974, 1985).

Main reference

ARESTIS and SAWYER 1992, 36-45.

BLAUG Mark (born 1927)

Mark Blaug was born in The Hague, Holland, becoming a British citizen in 1982. He obtained an MA (1952) and a PhD (1955) from Columbia University, New York. He taught at Queen's College of New York (1951–2), at Yale University (1954–62), at the London School of Economics (1964–78) and at the Education Institute of London University (1963–84), where he is professor emeritus. Since 1984 he has been consultant professor at the University of Buckingham. He has also acted as consultant for several organizations, including UNESCO and the World Bank.

Main publications

1958. *Ricardian Economics: A Historical Study*, New Haven, Connecticut, Yale University Press.

1962. *Economic Theory in Retrospect*, Homewood, Illinois, Richard D. Irwin; London, Heinemann, 1964.

1965. 'The Rate of Return on Investment in Education in Great Britain', *The Manchester School*, vol. 33, 205–51.

1967. *Economics of Education: A Selected Annotated Bibliography*, London, Pergamon Press.

1968–69 (ed.). *Economics of Education: Selected Readings*, 2 vols, Harmondsworth, Penguin Books.

1970. *An Introduction to the Economics of Education*, London, Allen Lane.

1974. *The Cambridge Revolution: Success or Failure? A Critical Analysis of Cambridge Theories of Value and Distribution*, London, Institute of Economic Affairs.

1976 (ed.). *The Economics of the Arts*, London, Martin Robertson; New York, Praeger.

1976. 'The Empirical Status of Human Capital Theory: A Slightly Jaundiced Survey', *Journal of Economic Literature*, vol. 24, 827–55.

1980. *A Methodological Appraisal of Marxian Economics*, Amsterdam, North-Holland.

1980. *The Methodology of Economics: Or How Economists Explain*, Cambridge, England, Cambridge University Press; 2nd edn 1992.

1983 (ed., with Paul Sturges). *Who's Who in Economics: A Biographical Dictionary of Major Economists, 1700–1981*, Brighton, Harvester Press; Cambridge, Massachusetts, MIT Press; 2nd edn 1986, *Who's Who in Economics: A Biographical Dictionary of Major Economists, 1700–1986*.

1985. *Great Economists Since Keynes: An Introduction to the Lives & Works of One Hundred Modern Economists*, Brighton, Wheatsheaf; New York, Barnes & Noble.

1986. *Economic History and the History of Economics*, Brighton, Harvester Press; New York University Press.

1986. *Great Economists Before Keynes: An Introduction to the Lives & Works of One Hundred Great Economists of the Past*, Brighton, Wheatsheaf; Atlantic Highlands, New Jersey, Humanities Press International.

1987. *The Economics of Education and the Education of an Economist*, New York University Press.

1988. *Economics through the Looking Glass: The Distorted Perspective of Economics. The New Palgrave Dictionary*, London, Institute of Economic Affairs.
1990. *Economic Theories: True or False?*, Aldershot, Hants, Edward Elgar.
1990. *John Maynard Keynes: Life, Ideas, Legacy*, London, Macmillan; New York, St Martin's Press.
1991 (ed.). *The History of Economic Thought*, Aldershot, Hants, Edward Elgar.
1991 (ed., with Neil de Marchi). *Appraising Economic Theories: Studies in the Methodology of Scientific Research Programmes*, Aldershot, Hants, Edward Elgar.

Mark Blaug is known, above all, as a historian of economic thought. His textbook (1962), which has gone through several editions, is certainly the most widely used and most ambitious such text since Schumpeter's posthumous *History of Economic Analysis*. It attests considerable erudition and deep knowledge of the whole of economic literature. The title of the book indicates the intention. It is indeed a question, for Blaug, of studying in the light of past works, 'the logical coherence and explanatory value of what has come to be known as orthodox economic theory ... My purpose is to teach contemporary economic theory' (1962, p. ix). Besides his numerous articles in the field of the history of thought, and his monographs on Ricardo (1958) and on Marxist economics (1980), it is to Blaug we owe the monumental edition of *Who's Who?* of the economists since 1700 (1983) and two books including presentations of a hundred economists before (1986) and after Keynes (1985). Blaug is the general editor of three important series published by Edward Elgar: *Schools of Thought in Economics*, *The International Library of Critical Writings in Economics* and *Pioneers in Economics*.

Blaug has also done a lot to revive interest in the methodology of economics, here again, especially, with the publication of a very successful book (1980 *A Methodological*). Sympathetic towards Popper's falsificationist theses, Blaug here uses Lakatos's concept of a scientific research programme to evaluate diverse currents and debates in contemporary economic thought. Critical of the heterodoxies, such as the post-Keynesian approach, he is so also of several neoclassical theses, which he criticizes for 'the reluctance to produce the theories that yield unambiguously refutable implications, followed by a general unwillingness to confront those implications with the facts' (p. 254). Blaug has never been afraid of provoking controversy, as witnessed, for example, by his assessment of the Cambridge controversy or his critical review of the *New Palgrave* which he accuses of a post-Keynesian bias (1988).

Blaug has made numerous contributions to economic history (texts gathered in 1986), to the economics of art (1976), and above all to economics of education (1965, 1967, 1968–70, 1970, 1987). At first an advocate of the application of the theory of human capital to this field of study, as suggested by Schultz and Denison, Blaug gradually became more and more sceptical regarding this approach (1976 'The Empirical Status'). He became very interested in education issues in the Third World, where he has lived and worked on several occasions.

Main reference

SHAW G.K. 1991 (ed.). *Economics, Culture and Education: Essays in Honour of Mark Blaug*, Aldershot, Hants, Edward Elgar.

BOITEUX Marcel (born 1922)

Born in Niort (France), Marcel Boiteux began his university studies at the Ecole Normale Supérieure (section sciences). Having left occupied France in 1943, he participated in the Italian and French campaigns (1944). Boiteux resumed his studies after the Liberation. Recipient of a diploma from the Ecole Normale Supérieure and of 'agrégation' in mathematics in 1946, he graduated from the Institut d'Etudes Politiques of Paris in 1947. Boiteux joined the Centre National de la Recherche Scientifique (CNRS, 1947–49), and then pursued all his career at Electricité de France (EDF), where he served as an engineer (1949–57), a director (1958–66), a general director (1967–78), and finally as chairman of the board of directors (1979–87). He was also professor of economics at l'Ecole Supérieure d'Electricité (1957–62), at l'Ecole Nationale des Ponts et Chaussées (1963–67), president of the Econometric Society (1959) and president of the World Council of Energy (1986–89).

Main publications

1949. 'La Tarification des demandes en pointe: Application de la théorie de la vente au coût marginal', *Revue générale de l'électricité*, vol. 58, 321–40; Engl. transl. 1960, 'Peak-Load Pricing', *Journal of Business of the University of Chicago*, vol. 33, 157–79.

1951. 'Le "Revenu distribuable" et les pertes économiques', *Econometrica*, vol. 19, 112–33.

1951. 'La Tarification en coût marginal et les demandes aléatoires', *Cahiers du Séminaire d'économétrie*, no. 1, 56–69.

1956. 'Sur la gestion des monopoles publics astreints à l'équilibre budgétaire', *Econometrica*, vol. 24, 22–40.

1956. 'Comment calculer l'amortissement?', *Revue d'économie politique*, vol. 66, 43–74.

1957. 'L'Amortissement peut-il jouer un rôle dans le calcul économique?', *Revue de la recherche opérationnelle*, vol. 1, 232–50; Engl. transl. 1960, 'The Role of Amortization in Investment Programming', *International Economic Papers*, no. 10, 147–62.

1964. 'Marginal Cost Pricing of Electricity', in J.R. Nelson (ed.), *Marginal Cost in Practice*, Englewood Cliffs, New Jersey, Prentice-Hall.

1969. 'Note sur le taux d'actualisation', *Revue d'économie politique*, vol. 79, 117–28.

1986 (ed., with T. de Montbrial and B. Munier). *Marchés, capital et incertitude: Essais en l'honneur de Maurice Allais*, Paris, Économica; Engl. transl. 1989, *Markets and Risk: Essays in Honour of Maurice Allais*, Dordrecht, Kluwer.

Marcel Boiteux is a typical representative of the French tradition of economist-engineers, which includes authors such as Maurice Allais (in whose honour he co-edited the 1986 book), Pierre Massé, Edmond Malinvaud and

Jacques Lesourne. Having fully adopted the mathematicization of economics, his work as an economist-engineer was rooted in the concrete problems of Electricité de France, a public company with a monopoly in the production and distribution of electricity in France (1964). It developed in two directions, one, initiated by G. Dessus, director of EDF after the war, on the fixing of price scales, and the other, initiated by P. Massé, on the choice of investments.

Boiteux applied economic calculation to the fixing of price scales best adapted to a situation of public monopoly, where increasing returns for a given productive capacity coexist with the obligation to meet peak demands (hourly, weekly and yearly) (1949, 1951 *CSE*). This led him to consider problems of maximization under constraint and second best optima (1951 *Econometrica*) and to put forward a solution in terms of Pareto maximization applied to a general model made up of links between quantities and links between prices (1956 *Econometrica*). On this basis, price differences should be applied to the supply of electricity considered as a diversified product in relation to the time and location of its consumption. These prices have been referred to as 'efficient prices' or 'Ramsey–Boiteux prices'; as for the problem of demand peaks, prices should take into account a typology of periods according to levels of demand and the price-elasticity of demand in each period.

He also applied economic calculation and operations research to inventory problems, taking into account both the durability and the cost structure of equipment, the monetary stability or instability and the uncertainty of the future (1956 *REP*, 1957). This led him to consider interest rate and rates of actualization (1969).

Main reference

BLAUG *Who's Who* 1986, 101.

BOULDING Kenneth Ewart (1910–1993)

Kenneth Ewart Boulding was born in Liverpool, England, to a methodist family. He studied at Oxford (1928–32) and subsequently at the University of Chicago (1932–4). Boulding began his teaching career at the University of Edinburgh (Scotland) in 1934 and went on to teach at Colgate University in New York State (1937–41). In 1941, he accepted a position with the League of Nations at Princeton, leaving it in 1942 so as to freely express his pacifist principles. He then went on to teach at Fisk University in Nashville (1942–3), Iowa State College (1943–6, 1947–9), and McGill University (1946–7). In 1948 Boulding became an American citizen. He was professor of economics at the University of Michigan (1949–68) and subsequently at the University of Colorado at Boulder (1968–80), where he became professor emeritus upon his retirement. In 1949, Boulding was awarded the John Bates Clark Medal of the American Economic Association, of which he was president in 1968.

Main publications

1941. *Economic Analysis*, New York, Harper.

1945. *The Economics of Peace*, Englewood Cliffs, New Jersey, Prentice-Hall.

1950. *A Reconstruction of Economics*, New York, Wiley.

1952 (ed., with G. Stigler). *Readings in Price Theory*, Homewood, Illinois, Richard D. Irwin.

1953. *The Organizational Revolution: A Study in the Ethics of Economic Organization*, New York, Harper.

1956. *The Image: Knowledge in Life and Society*, Ann Arbor, University of Michigan Press.

1958. *Principles of Economic Policy*, Englewood Cliffs, New Jersey, Prentice-Hall.

1958. *The Skills of the Economist*, Cleveland, Ohio, Howard Allen.

1960 (ed., with W.A. Spivey). *Linear Programming and the Theory of the Firm*, New York, Macmillan.

1962. *Conflict and Defense; A General Theory*, New York, Harper & Row.

1964. *The Meaning of the Twentieth Century: The Great Transition*, New York, Harper & Row.

1966. 'The Economics of the Coming Spaceship Earth', in Henry Jarrett (ed.), *Environmental Quality in a Growing Economy*, Baltimore, Johns Hopkins, 3–14.

1966. *The Impact of the Social Sciences*, New Brunswick, New Jersey, Rutgers University Press.

1968. *Beyond Economics: Essays on Society, Religion, and Ethics*, Ann Arbor, University of Michigan Press.

1970. *A Primer on Social Dynamics: History as Dialectics and Development*, New York, Free Press.

1970. *Economics as a Science*, New York, McGraw-Hill.

1971–85. *Collected Papers*, 6 vols, edited by F.R. Glahe and L. Singell, Boulder, Colorado, Associated University Press. [Vol. 1 and vol. 2, 1971; vol. 3, 1973; vol. 4, 1974; vol. 5, 1975; vol. 6, 1985.]

1972 (ed., with M. Pfaff). *Redistribution to the Rich and the Poor: The Grants Economics of Income Distribution*, Belmont, California, Wadsworth.

1973. *The Economy of Love and Fear: A Preface to Grants Economics*, Belmont, California, Wadsworth.

1978. *Ecodynamics: A New Theory of Societal Evolution*, Beverly Hills, California, Sage; revised paperback edn, 1981.

1978. *Stable Peace*, Austin, University of Texas Press.

1981. *A Preface to Grants Economics: The Economy of Love and Fear*, New York, Praeger.

1981. *Evolutionary Economics*, Beverly Hills, California, Sage.

1985. *Human Betterment*, Beverly Hills, California, Sage.

1985. 'My Life Philosophy', *American Economist*, vol. 29, 5–14; under the title 'From Chemistry to Economics and Beyond', in Szenberg 1992, 69–83.

1985. *The World as a Total System*, Beverly Hills, California, Sage.

1989. 'A Bibliographical Autobiography', *Quarterly Review, Banca Nazionale del Lavoro*, no. 171, 363–93.

1989. *Three Faces of Power*, Beverly Hills, California, Sage.

1991. *Towards a New Economics: Critical Essays on Ecology, Distribution and Other Themes*, Aldershot, Hants, Edward Elgar.

With over one thousand articles and 40 books and a broad range of modes of expression ranging from poetry to mathematics, a corpus covering many fields in economics as well as in religion, ethics, philosophy, ecology and various social sciences, Boulding's work is difficult to categorize. From 1931 to 1945, his works can be divided into two categories: those of a religious nature, stemming from his membership of the Society of Friends (Quakers), and those in the field of economics, primarily on capital, investment, the firm and economic surplus. His 1941 manual was enriched by Keynes's *General Theory* analyses in its second edition (1948).

From 1945, Boulding has included his commitment to peace and disarmament (1945, 1962, 1978 *Stable*) as well as his moral and religious convictions (1968) in his economic work, all the while publishing numerous articles and books (1952, 1960 *Three Faces*) relative to the inquiries and debates of professional economists. He has done all of this while striving to renew the discipline of economics, notably by stressing stock analysis and by taking into account not only exchange but also constraint and love (1950, 1953, 1989); he has developed especially the economics of non-compensatory transfer ('Grants Economy', 1972, 1973, 1981 *A Preface*). He has elaborated a vision of the evolution of human society in which the growth of knowledge plays a key role (1964, 1970 *A Primer*, 1978 *Ecodynamics*). He has worked, with specialists from other disciplines, on systems theory, and has sought to enrich the field of economics with contributions from other disciplines, from biology to the social sciences (1956, 1966 *The Impact*, 1970 *Economics* 1985 *The World*). A precursor of ecological economics, he has stressed since 1956 the limits of global resources and, since 1966, has illustrated the fact that the earth is a closed system through the image of 'spaceship earth'.

Boulding participated in the creation of the Society for General System Research in 1955, serving as its president from 1955 to 1959, and in 1957 in the launching of *The Journal of Conflict Resolution.* In 1968, he founded the Association for the Study of the Grants Economy, serving as its president from 1970 to 1989. Although Boulding has enjoyed the respect of all members of his discipline, his work has not been well received on the part of many and has often been misunderstood.

Main references

BOULDING 1985 *AE*, 1989 'A Bibliographical Autobiography'.

KERMAN Cynthia E. 1974. *Creative Tension: The Life and Thought of Kenneth Boulding*, Ann Arbor, University of Michigan Press.

PFAFF Martin and HORVATH Janos 1976 (eds). *Frontiers in Social Thought: Essays in Honor of Kenneth E. Boulding*, Amsterdam, North-Holland.

WRIGHT Robert 1988. *Three Scientists and Their Gods: Looking for Meaning in an Age of Information*, New York, Times Books/Random House, 213–95.

ARESTIS and SAWYER 1992, 45–54. BLAUG 1985, 21–3. *New Palgrave* 1987, vol. 1, 265–6. SILK 1976, 189–239. SPIEGEL and SAMUELS 1984, 461–71.

BOWLES Samuel (born 1939)

Samuel Bowles was born in New Haven, Connecticut. He earned his PhD from Harvard University in 1965 and taught there from 1965 to 1974. Since 1974 he has been a professor at Amherst University in Massachusetts.

Main publications

1969. *Planning Educational Systems for Economic Growth*, Cambridge, Massachusetts, Harvard University Press.

1970. With D. Kendrick, *Notes and Problems in Microeconomic Theory*, Chicago, Markham; 2nd edn 1980, with P. Dixon, Amsterdam, North-Holland.

1972. 'Schooling and Inequality from Generation to Generation', *Journal of Political Economy*, vol. 80, supplement, S219–51.

1976. With H. Gintis, *Schooling in Capitalist America: Educational Reform and the Contradictions of Economic Life*, New York, Basic Books.

1983. With D. Gordon and T. Weisskopf, *Beyond the Waste Land: A Democratic Alternative to Economic Decline*, New York, Doubleday; revised edn, London, Verso/New Left Books, 1986.

1983. With D. Gordon and T. Weisskopf, 'Hearts and Minds: A Social Model of U.S. Productivity Growth', *Brookings Papers on Economic Activity*, no. 2, 381–441.

1985. 'The Production Process in a Competitive Economy: Walrasian, Neo-Hobbesian and Marxian Models', *American Economic Review*, vol. 75, 16–36.

1985. With R.C. Edwards, *Understanding Capitalism: Competition, Command, and Change in the U.S. Economy*, New York, Harper & Row.

1986. With H. Gintis, *Democracy and Capitalism: Property, Community, and the Contradictions of Modern Social Thought*, New York, Basic Books.

1988. With R. Boyer, 'Labor Discipline and Aggregate Demand: A Macroeconomic Model', *American Economic Review*, vol. 78, *Papers and Proceedings*, 395–400.

1990 (ed., with R.C. Edwards). *Radical Political Economy*, 2 vols, Aldershot, Hants, Edward Elgar.

1991. With T. Weisskopf and D. Gordon, *After the Waste Land: A Democratic Economics for the Year 2000*, Armonk, New York, M.E. Sharpe.

Samuel Bowles is one of the most renowned of the radical political economists. His early works, however, were within the theoretical framework of neoclassical economics (1969, 1970). A specialist in the economics of education, Bowles has presented an analysis of the evolution of class structure in capitalism and the educational system (in a 1972 article and, more especially, in a 1976 book he wrote with his collaborator, Herbert Gintis). In this work, Bowles and Gintis set forth the 'correspondence principle', according to which the school system tends to adopt the inegalitarian, hierarchical and alienating structure that characterizes society as a whole.

Apart from education, Bowles has shown interest in macroeconomics, the economics of labour and of development, and in ecological issues. More recently, he has sought to give a new microeconomic foundation to the analysis of contemporary capitalism (1985 *AER*), notably by developing the concept of 'contested exchange'. In many works of a more political character, Bowles and his colleagues have proposed a programme of democratic transformation that is clearly different from both Marxian socialism and the prevailing liberal approach (1983 *Beyond*, 1985 *Understanding*, 1986, 1991).

Main references

ARESTIS and SAWYER 1992, 54–9. BLAUG 1985, 24–5.

BRODY Andras (born 1924)

Andras Brody was born in Budapest, Hungary. He earned an MA in 1952 and a PhD in 1960 from Karl Marx University in Budapest. Since 1956, he has worked at the Institute of Economics of Hungary. He has been professor at the University of Zambia (1970–72, 1974–7).

Main publications

1966. 'A Simplified Growth Model', *Quarterly Journal of Economics*, vol. 80, 137–46.
1970. *Proportions, Prices and Planning: A Mathematical Restatement of the Labor Theory of Value*, Budapest, Akadémiai Kiadó; Amsterdam and London, North-Holland.
1970 (ed., with Anne P. Carter). *Applications of Input–Output Analysis: Published in Honor of Wassily Leontief*, Amsterdam, North-Holland.
1970 (ed., with Anne P. Carter). *Contributions to Input–Output Analysis: Published in Honor of Wassily Leontief*, Amsterdam, North-Holland.
1972. With Anne P. Carter, *Input–Output Techniques*, Amsterdam, North-Holland.
1985. *Slowdown: Global Economic Maladies*, Beverly Hill, California, Sage.
1989. 'Observations Concerning the Growth Cycle', in K. Velupillai (ed.), *Nonlinear and Multisectoral Macrodynamics*, London, Macmillan.
1992. 'On Measuring Growth', *Structural Change and Economic Dynamics*, vol. 3, no. 1, 93–102.
1993. With W. Leontief, 'Money-Flow Computations', *Economic Systems Research*, vol. 5, 225–33.

Trained primarily as a mathematician, Andras Brody is among those East European economists who, following the example of Oskar Lange, hold that mathematical discourse renders the synthesis of many seemingly contradictory tendencies in contemporary economic thought entirely possible. Thus it permits 'to translate Marx's original approach into mathematical terms and to indicate the path leading from it to modern quantitative economic reasoning' (1970 *Proportions*, p. 9). In Brody's view, in the work of both Marx and Walras, and earlier in the thought of Quesnay, are to be found the intellectual origins of models such as those used by Leontief and von Neumann and developed in his own work. Such models are especially characterized by what he terms 'duality'. This mathematical principle is applicable to many fields, such as physics and biology, and refers to the relation between the solutions to a system of equations and those of an adjunct or transposed system. Applied to economics, it implies that the activities of production can be analysed from two perspectives: either as technical processes creating objects, or as a process assigning value to these objects.

A specialist in growth theory, Brody has also made important contributions to interindustrial analysis, notably in the works he has published with the American economist Anne Carter (1970, 1972).

Main reference

LEONTIEF Wassily 1970. 'Preface', in BRODY, *Proportions*, 7–8.

BRONFENBRENNER Martin (born 1914)

Martin Bronfenbrenner was born in Pittsburgh. He obtained a BA at Washington University, Saint Louis, in 1934, and a PhD at Chicago University in 1939. He also gained a Japanese language certificate at Colorado University in 1944. He became associate professor, then full professor at Wisconsin University (1947–57), professor at Michigan State University (1957–58), at the University of Minnesota (1958–62), at Carnegie-Mellon (1962–71) and at Duke (1971–84), where he taught Japanese history. From 1984 to 1990, he was professor of international economics at the Aoyoma Gakuin University in Tokyo and afterwards returned to Duke.

Main publications

1945. 'Some Fundamentals of Liquidity Theory', *Quarterly Journal of Economics*, vol. 59, 405–26.
1961. *Academic Encounter*, New York, Free Press.
1963. With F.D. Holzman, 'Survey of Inflation Theory', *American Economic Review*, vol. 53, 593–661.
1965. '*Das Kapital* for the Modern Man', *Science and Society*, vol. 29, 419–38.
1969 (ed.). *Is the Business Cycle Obsolete?*, New York, John Wiley & Sons.
1970. 'Radical economics in America: A 1970 Survey', *Journal of Economic Literature*, vol. 18, 747–66.
1971. *Income Distribution Theory*, Chicago, Aldine Atherton.
1976. *Tomioko Stories*, New York, Exposition Press.
1979. *Macroeconomic Alternatives*, Arlington Heights, Illinois, AHM.
1984. With W. Sichel and M.D. Gardner, *Economics*, Boston, Houghton Mifflin; third edition 1990, under the title *Macroeconomics*.

In the introduction to his textbook on distribution theories, Bronfenbrenner declares that he is 'unwilling to discard neoclassical economics, either marginalism or the production function, either at the micro-economic or the macro-economic level' (1971, p. xi), yet, among all those who claim to draw upon this theory, he is one of the most open to other streams of thought, particularly Marxism. He has devoted many texts to Marx's economics, being among the first to try to reformulate it in terms of Walrasian general equilibrium. In one of these, he defines himself as 'an imperfectly inconsistent eclectic, with non-Marxian elements dominating his private brand of eclecticism' (1965, p. 434).

In his work on distribution theory, of which he writes that certain passages resemble 'Mozart essaying rock and roll' (1971, p. xi), Bronfenbrenner fairly makes way for all views other than those of the neoclassical orthodoxy. He does likewise in his book on macroeconomics (1979), going through all the approaches, Keynesian, classical, Marxian and monetarist in the most objective way, until the reader is able to choose with full knowledge of the different views. This attitude also prevails in the introductory textbook he wrote with collaborators (1984). An economist with a neat, sometimes humorous, style of writing, literary more than mathematical, Bronfenbrenner has also shown interest in the history of economic thought, monetary theory, political economy and development. He also wrote a great deal on the economy of Japan, where he often stayed.

Main reference

New Palgrave, vol. 1, p. 279.

BRUNHOFF Suzanne de (born 1929)

Born in Strasbourg, Suzanne de Brunhoff studied philosophy at the Sorbonne (MA, 1950) and taught philosophy at the secondary school level (1954–6). She studied sociology (licence, 1959) and joined the Centre National de la Recherche Scientifique (CNRS) in 1960, presenting her doctoral thesis in sociology in 1964 and her doctorat d'État in economics in 1978. In 1979, she was appointed research director at the CNRS. She taught at the University of Paris 7-Jussieu (1971–6) and has been teaching at the University of Paris 10-Nanterre since 1977.

Main publications

1965. *Capitalisme financier public*, Paris, SEDES.
1967. *La Monnaie chez Marx*, Paris, Éditions sociales; Engl. transl. 1976, *Marx on Money*, New York, Urizen Books.
1971. *L'Offre de monnaie (critique d'un concept)*, Paris, François Maspero.
1973. With P. Bruini, *La Politique monétaire: Un Essai d'interprétation marxiste*, Paris, Presses Universitaires de France.
1973. 'Marx as a-Ricardian', *Economy and Society*, vol. 2, 421–30.
1976. *État et capital: Recherches sur la politique économique*, Grenoble, François Maspero and Presses Universitaires de Grenoble; Engl. transl. 1978, *The State, Capital and Economic Policy*, London, Pluto Press.
1979. *Les Rapports d'argent*, Grenoble, François Maspero and Presses Universitaires de Grenoble.
1982. 'Questioning Monetarism', *Cambridge Journal of Economics*, vol. 6, 285–94.
1986. *L'Heure du marché: Critique du libéralisme*, Paris, Presses Universitaires de France.
1987. 'Fictitious Capital', *New Palgrave*, vol. 2, 317–18.

1989. 'The Keynesian Critique of Laissez-Faire', in *Keynesian Economic Policy*, edited by A. Barrère, London, Macmillan, 140–52.

While Marxist theory and radical economists in general emphasize the real aspects of economies, de Brunhoff has been a pioneer in this current of thought: she highlighted the important role of money and of monetary phenomena in the theories of Marx (1967, 1979) and developed a Marxian theory of money, linked to the analyses of commodity, credit and accumulation (1971, 1973 *La politique*, 1979). In this manner she has contributed to the renewal of Marxist thought on inflation, national monetary policy and international phenomena.

This has led her to deepen her analysis of the capitalist state, studying how it intervenes in two key areas: the management of the labour force and of money (1976). Observing the continuing economic crisis as well as the resurgence of liberal thought, de Brunhoff has analysed the effective content of liberal policies which, in her view, can be reduced to simple 'police action' on wages and money. State intervention, far from receding, has actually changed form; and the 'truth' of liberalism 'is the very opposite of its proclaimed political discourse' (1986, p.154).

BUCHANAN James McGill (born 1919)

James M. Buchanan was born in Murfreesboro, Tennessee. He obtained an MA from the University of Tennessee in 1941 and a doctorate in 1948 from the University of Chicago. He was associate professor, and subsequently professor at the University of Tennessee (1948–51) and professor at Florida State University (1951–6). After a research year in Italy (1955–6), he taught at the Universities of Virginia (1956–8) and California (1968–9), at Virginia State University (1969–83) and at George Mason University (from 1983). In 1963, Buchanan founded the Public Choice Society and subsequently the journal *Public Choice* with G. Tullock. He directed the Center for the Study of Public Choice at Virginia State University from 1969 to 1983 and at George Mason University from 1983 to 1988. Buchanan was president of the Mont Pèlerin Society from 1984 to 1986. In 1986, he received the Nobel Memorial Prize in Economics.

Main publications

1949. 'The Pure Theory of Public Finance: A Suggested Approach', *Journal of Political Economy*, vol. 57, 496–505.

1954. 'Social Choice, Democracy and Free Markets', *Journal of Political Economy*, vol. 62, 114–23.

1954. 'Individual Choice in Voting and the Market', *Journal of Political Economy*, vol. 62, 334–43.

1958. *Public Principles of Public Debt: A Defense and Restatement*, Homewood, Illinois, Richard D. Irwin.

1960. *Fiscal Theory and Political Economy: Selected Essays*, Chapel Hill, University of North Carolina Press.

1962. With Gordon Tullock, *The Calculus of Consent: Logical Foundations of Constitutional Democracy*, Ann Arbor, University of Michigan Press.

1966. *Public finance in Democratic Process: Fiscal Institutions and Individual Choice*, Chapel Hill, University of North Carolina Press.

1968. *The Demand and Supply of Public Goods*, Chicago, Rand McNally.

1969. *Cost and Choice: An Inquiry in Economic Theory*, Chicago, Markham.

1975. *The Limits of Liberty: Between Anarchy and Leviathan*, University of Chicago Press.

1977. With Richard E. Wagner, *Democracy in Deficit: The Political Legacy of Lord Keynes*, New York, Academic Press.

1977. *Freedom in Constitutional Contract*, Austin, Texas, A & M University Press.

1980. With H. Geoffrey Brennan, *The Power to Tax: Analytical Foundations of a Fiscal Constitution*, Cambridge, England, Cambridge University Press.

1985. *Liberty, Market and State: Political Economy in the 1980s*, Brighton, Wheatsheaf, New York University Press.

1985. With H. Geoffrey Brennan, *The Reason of Rules: Constitutional Political Economy*, Cambridge, England, Cambridge University Press.

1986. 'Better than Ploughing', *Quarterly Review, Banca Nazionale del Lavoro*, no. 159, 359–75; in Kregel 1989, 279–95.

1987. *Economics: Between Predictive Science and Moral Philosophy*, edited by Robert D. Tollison and Viktor J. Vanberg, Austin, Texas, A & M University Press.

1989. *Explorations into Constitutional Economics*, edited by Robert D. Tollison and Viktor J. Vanberg, Austin, Texas, A & M University Press.

1990. 'Born-Again Economist', in Breit and Spencer 1990, 163–80.

1991. *Constitutional Economics*, Oxford, Basil Blackwell.

1992. *Better than Plowing and Other Personal Essays*, University of Chicago Press.

1992. 'From the Inside Looking Out', in Szenberg 1992, 98–106.

1993. *Property as a Guarantor of Liberty*, Aldershot, Hants, Edward Elgar.

From his earliest articles on public finance, taxation and social choice, Buchanan has referred to Wicksell. He translated one of his papers for a book edited by Musgrave in 1958, and he borrowed from him the concept of fiscal exchange. His research year in Italy (1955–6) allowed him to become familiar with the Italian school of public finance and its analyses of public debt.

Buchanan attributes (1986) his conversion from young socialist to adherent of the market economy to the influence of Frank Knight. His overall work is based on the systematic application of methodological individualism to the study of public finance, public economy and collective choices. In effect, he holds that there is no reason for individuals to behave differently in the private and social spheres of life: just as the consumer compares the price of goods with the satisfaction that he expects from them, the citizen relates the taxes he pays to the public services from which he benefits. This allows for the application of microeconomics to public finance as well as to the realm of political science. In this way, Buchanan rejects the traditional argument that government is an agent having the role of defining and enforcing the general interest and focuses his analysis on the individual choices of citizen-electors.

This viewpoint led Buchanan to emphasize, early in his writings (in articles written in 1954, and his 1962 book), the importance of choice in rules of the game and, later, to develop a positive theory of the institutional structure and constitutional framework in which rights and obligations are exercised (1980, 1985 *The Reason*). He has thus studied the mechanism of the division between the private sphere and the market on the one hand, and the public sphere and elections on the other.

Buchanan has also developed a cost analysis of the means of public decision making, taking into account two types of costs: decision costs and external costs which decision makers (minority or majority) deflect to others. Hence, if the decision is made by a small minority, its own costs are minimal, while the external costs, which are deflected, are maximal; but when the decision is made by a large majority, the converse holds. During the 1970s, Buchanan was inclined to take into account the supply of public goods and, hence, the strategies of politicians and bureaucracies.

Main references

'The Nobel Memorial Prize in Economics 1986'. Press release, article by Anthony B. Atkinson and bibliography, *Swedish Journal of Economics*, 1987, vol. 89, 1–17.

BUCHANAN 1986, 1990, 1992 *Better*, 1992 'From the Inside'.
REISMAN David 1989. *The Political Economy of James Buchanan*, London, Macmillan.
ROMER Thomas 1988. 'On James Buchanan's Contributions to Public Economics', *Journal of Economic Perspectives*, vol. 2, no. 4, 165–79.
SANDMO Agnar 1990. 'Buchanan on Political Economy: A Review Article', *Journal of Economic Literature*, vol. 28, 50–65.

BLAUG 1985, 26–8. SHACKLETON and LOCKSLEY 1981, 33–54. SPIEGEL and SAMUELS 1984, 557–69.

BURNS Arthur Frank (1904–1987)

Arthur Frank Burns was born in Stanislau, Austria. In 1914, his family emigrated to the United States and he studied at Columbia University, earning his PhD there in 1934. He was associate professor (1930–33), assistant professor (1933–43) and professor (1943–58) at Rutgers University and then professor at Columbia. However, he devoted much of his career to the National Bureau of Economic Research, which he entered in 1930. He succeeded Wesley Clair Mitchell as director of research in 1945. From 1953 to 1956 he was president of the Council of Economic Advisers of President Eisenhower. He was named president of the NBER in 1957, a position he held until 1967, when he was elected honorary president of the board of directors of the NBER. In 1959, he was president of the American Economic Association. Burns was also an adviser to President Nixon from 1969 to 1970 and chairman of the Federal Reserve System from 1970 to 1978. He held many other public posts, notably as US ambassador to West Germany from 1981 to 1985.

Main publications

1930. *Stock Market Cycle Research*, New York, Twentieth Century Fund.

1934. *Production Trends in the United States since 1870*, New York, National Bureau of Economic Research.

1938. With W.C. Mitchell, *Statistical Indicators of Cyclical Revivals*, New York, National Bureau of Economic Research.

1946. With W.C. Mitchell, *Measuring Business Cycles*, New York, National Bureau of Economic Research.

1947. 'Keynesian Economics Once Again', *Review of Economic Statistics*, vol. 29, 252–68.

1952 (ed.). *Wesley Clair Mitchell: The Economic Scientist*, New York, National Bureau of Economic Research.

1954. *The Frontiers of Economic Knowledge: Essays by Arthur F. Burns*, Princeton University Press; London, Oxford University Press.

1957. *Prosperity without Inflation*, New York, Fordham University Press.

1960. 'Progress Towards Economic Stability', *American Economic Review*, vol. 50, 1–19.

1966. *The Management of Prosperity*, New York, Columbia University Press.

1967. With P.A. Samuelson, *Full Employment, Guideposts and Economic Stability*, Washington, DC, American Enterprise Institute for Public Policy Research.

1968. With J.K. Javits and C.J. Hitch, *The Defense Sector and the American Economy*, New York University Press; University of London Press.

1969. *The Business Cycle in a Changing World*, New York, National Bureau of Economic Research.

1978. *Reflections of an Economic Policy Maker. Speeches and Congressional Statement: 1969–1978*, Washington, DC, American Enterprise Institute for Public Policy Research.

A pupil, friend and collaborator of Wesley Clair Mitchell, Burns is also his intellectual inheritor and successor. Mitchell coined the term 'business cycle' in 1913 in order to account for the cyclical fluctuations of economic activity. In 1920, he founded the National Bureau of Economic Research, one of whose tasks is to gather data on economic activities. Mitchell, identified with the institutionalist school, believed in the virtues of induction and empirical observation. He was wary of abstract theoretical deductions. Burns shared this vision of economics and, in the 1930s, the two of them undertook a working partnership whose most important product is the book they published together in 1946, with Burns being its principal author. That same year, in the annual report of the NBER, Burns criticized the Keynesians for deducing political statements from debatable theoretical grounds. The Keynesian analysis, in its exclusive use of aggregates, suggests an excessively abstract and simplistic image of cyclical fluctuations, to whose theoretical analysis Burns devoted a significant part of his research career: 'Since Keynes works with an artificially simplified business cycle, it is not surprising that his explanation collides with the facts of experience' (1954, p. 18; see also 1947). The work of Burns and Mitchell has itself been strongly criticized, notably by the econometricians of the Cowles Commission, who describe it as 'measurement without theory', to quote the title of an article by Tjalling Koopmans (Koopmans 1947).

From the 1950s, Burns was increasingly absorbed in the administrative and political tasks that made him one of the most influential of the postwar economists. Yet he continued his scholarly work, drawing more and more attention to problems linked to inflation, as provoked by government intervention in the economy, whose efficiency he doubted (1957, 1960, 1966, 1967, 1969). From 1970 to 1978, while chairman of the Federal Reserve System, he presided over the transition from Keynesian to monetarist policies. However, Burns was no more a monetarist than a Keynesian; his public actions were characterized by pragmatism, and his scholarly work by empiricism.

Main references

In Memoriam: Arthur F. Burns, 1904–1987, Washington, DC, Board of Governors of the Federal Reserve System.

BLAUG 1985, 29–30. *New Palgrave* 1987 vol. 1, 300–301. SILLS 1979, 81–6. SOBEL 1980, 37–64.

CHENERY Hollis B. (born 1918)

Hollis Chenery was born in Richmond, Virginia. Holding diplomas in mathematics and engineering, he afterwards earned an MA in economics at the University of Virginia (1947) and a PhD at Harvard (1950). He advanced between 1952 and 1961 from assistant professor to full professor at Stanford University. He then became Assistant Administrator for Program at the Agency for International Development (1961–5), professor at Harvard (1965–70), vice-president, Development Policy at the World Bank (1970–82) and again professor at Harvard, where he was named professor emeritus in 1988. He has been economic adviser and consultant for many governments.

Main publications

1949. With R. Mikesell, *Arabian Oil: America's Stake in the Middle East*, Chapell Hill, University of North Carolina Press.
1959. With Paul G. Clark, *Interindustry Economics*, New York, John Wiley & Sons.
1960. 'Patterns of Industrial Growth', *American Economic Review*, vol. 50, 624–54.
1961. With K. Arrow, B.S. Minhas and R.M. Solow, 'Capital–Labor Substitution and Economic Efficiency', *Review of Economic and Statistics*, vol. 43, 225–50.
1971 (ed.). *Studies in Development Planning*, Cambridge, Massachusetts, Harvard University Press.
1974. *Et al.*, *Redistribution with Growth*, London, Oxford University Press.
1975. With M. Syrquin, *Patterns of Development, 1950–1970*, London, Oxford University Press.
1979. *Et al.*, *Structural Change and Development Policy*, New York, Oxford University Press.
1986. *Et al.*, *Industrialization and Growth: A Comparative Study*, New York, Oxford University Press.
1988–9 (ed., with T.N. Srinivasan). *Handbook of Development Economics*, 2 vols, Amsterdam, North-Holland.

Most of Chenery's main contributions remain within the framework of development economics. The nature of this discipline, the fact that he carried out his career alternately in university circles and in governmental organisms and the numerous empirical studies he dedicated to developed or less developed countries, have probably contributed to forming a vision which, while partly subscribing to the neoclassical theory, distinguishes itself in many respects, among others by its mistrust of abstract principles claiming universal validity. Revealing in this sense is, among other things, the variety of points of view exposed in the important handbook on development he edited with T.N. Srinivasan (1988–9), or again in a book published in his honour where viewpoints range from Marxism to neoclassical theory (Syrquin *et al.* 1984).

Chenery sees economic development as 'a set of interrelated changes in the structure of an economy that are required for its continued growth' (1979, p. xvi). This definition explains the strategy of research he engaged in from the beginning of his career. Here it is the term 'interrelated' which is important: industrialization plays a key role in development and is closely linked to investment, foreign aid and government policies; but one must be attentive to the complex interrelations between all sectors of an economy, which are sustained by these factors. This implies a quantitative approach. Moreover, this approach must rely on Walrasian general equilibrium, but concretely expressed through Leontief's input–output model, which Chenery calls inter-industry economics and to which he has devoted a work co-authored with Paul Clark (1959). Linear programming must be combined with this analysis. In this way only is it possible to analyse structural changes associated with economic growth.

Convinced that planning has a major role to play in development, Chenery deems it necessary that it be given a more rational foundation. He also considers that problems of growth and distribution cannot be dissociated, as is the case in traditional approaches. The fact that growth in less developed countries often results, at least in the initial stages, in emphasizing the income gaps and increasing poverty for important sectors of these populations is a major problem of our times. It calls for new and more sophisticated strategies of development which consider the specific situation of the various social groups as well as the various sectors of the economy (1974).

Main references

SYRQUIN Moshe, TAYLOR Lance and WESTPHAL Larry E. 1984 (eds). *Economic Structure and Performance: Essays in Honor of Hollis B. Chenery*, Orlando, Florida, Academic Press.

BLAUG 1985, 31–2.

CLARK Colin Grant (1905–1989)

Born in London, Colin Clark was appointed lecturer in statistics at Cambridge (1931–7) after graduating in chemistry at Oxford (1924). He was invited in 1937 to the University of Melbourne. He remained in Australia until 1952, serving as a government adviser and director of the Queensland Bureau of Industry. He taught as a visiting professor at the University of Chicago and, from 1953 to 1968, was director of the Institute of Agricultural Economics at Oxford University. He then returned to Australia, continuing his research at Monash University (1969–77) and becoming a research consultant in economics at Queensland University.

Main publications

1932. *The National Income, 1924–1931*, London, Macmillan.

1937. *National Income and Outlay*, London, Macmillan.

1938. 'Determination of the Multiplier from National Income Statistics', *Economic Journal*, vol. 48, 435–48.

1938. With J.G. Crawford, *The National Income of Australia*, Sydney, Angus & Robertson.

1939. *A Critique of Russian Statistics*, London, Macmillan.
1940. *The Conditions of Economic Progress*, London, Macmillan; New York, St Martin's.
1942. *The Economics of 1960*, London, Macmillan.
1949. 'A System of Equations Explaining the United States Trade Cycle, 1921–41', *Econometrica*, vol.17, 93–124.
1949–52. *Review of Economic Progress*, 4 vols, Brisbane, Government Printer.
1951. 'World Resources and World Population', *Economia Internazionale*, vol. 4, 15–40.
1954. *Welfare and Taxation*, New York, Oxford University Press.
1961. *Growthmanship: A Study in the Methodology of Investment*, London, Institute of Economic Affairs.
1964. With M.R. Haswell, *Economics of Subsistence Agriculture*, London, Macmillan; New York, St Martin's.
1967. *Population Growth and Land Use*, London, Macmillan; New York, St Martin's.
1970. *Starvation or Plenty*, London, Secker & Warburg; New York, Taplinger.
1976. 'Economic Development in Communist China', *Journal of Political Economy*, vol. 84, 239–64.
1981. With J. Carruthers, *The Economics of Irrigation*, Liverpool University Press.
1982. *Regional and Urban Location*, St Lucia, University of Queensland Press.
1984. 'Development Economics: The Early Years', in Meier and Seers (eds), 59–77.

Devoted to empirical observation and the classification of facts, Colin Clark was a pioneer in the estimation of national income, national expenditure and their components, and contributed to the refinement of the concept of gross national product (GNP) (1937, 1938 with Crawford, and 1939). He was also one of the first economists to set up statistical series for labour productivity and capital formation, as well as evaluations of the national income multiplier (1938 *EJ*).

In his major work (1940), Clark sought to identify the sources of growth and, more generally, to explain economic progress on the basis of the gathering and analysis of statistics from many countries. From his evaluations of national purchasing powers and his related estimates in 'international units', he made possible international comparisons and highlighted the significance of the gap between rich and poor nations. Yet, above all else, he pointed out the structuring of human activities, dividing them into primary, industrial and service categories; and he put forth the thesis that, in the course of economic development, there is a progression of the second group of activities relative to the first one, and of the third group relative to the others. In this way he demonstrated the importance of productivity reserves in agriculture. This 1940 book gave rise to much debate and conceptual discussion; Clark took this into account in its subsequent editions and, in fact, edited a journal on these questions over a period of three years (1949–52).

Conversely, his 1942 work on what the 1960 economy would be like showed a posteriori, through his mistakes, the difficulty of confirming medium-term predictions. Clark, who was converted to catholicism before the Second World War, became an influential member of the Pope's Commission on Population (1964–6) and defended, in many of his publications, the thesis that available resources should allow for the dietary needs stemming from population growth, holding that this growth is accompanied by growth in product per capita (1951, 1967, 1970). He also wrote on the limits of the welfare state (1954), on agricultural economics, notably in developing countries (1964 with Haswell and 1981 with Carruthers) and on economic development in China (1976).

Main references

CLARK 1984.
WOLFF Jacques 1982. *Les Grandes oeuvres économiques*, Paris, Cujas, vol. 4, 253–70.

New Palgrave 1987, vol. 1, 428. SILLS 1979, 121–4.

CLOWER Robert Wayne (born 1926)

Robert Wayne Clower was born in Pullman, Washington. In 1949, he earned an MA in economics from Washington State University and in 1952, another MA, from Oxford University, which awarded him a PhD in 1978. He was assistant professor at Washington State University (1952), professor at Northwestern University (1963), professor (1971) and professor emeritus (1987) at the University of California at Los Angeles and, from 1986, professor at the University of South Carolina.

Main publications

1947. With J.F. Due, *Intermediate Economic Analysis: Resource Allocation, Factor Pricing, and Welfare*, Homewood, Illinois, Richard D. Irwin; 6th edn, *Microeconomics*, 1972.
1957. With D. W. Bushaw, *Introduction to Mathematical Economics*, Homewood, Illinois, Richard D. Irwin.
1963. 'Die Keynesianische Gegenrevolution: eine theoretische Kritik', *Schweizerische Zeitschrift*, 8–31; Engl. transl. 1965, 'The Keynesian Counterrevolution: A Theoretical Appraisal', in F.H. Hahn and F.P. Brechling (eds), *Theory of Interest Rates*, London, Macmillan,103–25.
1965. With J. Harris, *Puerto Rico Shipping and the U.S. Maritime Laws*, Evanston, Illinois, Transportation Center, Northwestern University.
1966. With G. Dalton, A. Walters and M. Harwitz, *Growth Without Development: An Economic Survey of Liberia*, Evanston, Illinois, Northwestern University Press.
1967. 'A Reconsideration of the Microfoundations of Monetary Theory', *Western Economic Journal*, vol. 6, 1–8.
1969 (ed.). *Monetary Theory: Selected Readings*, Harmondsworth, Penguin Books.
1975. With A. Leijonhufvud, 'The Coordination of Economic Activities: A Keynesian Perspective', *American Economic Review*, vol. 65, *Papers and Proceedings*, 182–8.
1984. *Money and Markets: Essays by Robert W. Clower*, edited by D.A. Walker, Cambridge, England, Cambridge University Press.
1988. With Phil Graves and Robert Sexton. *Intermediate Microeconomics*, San Diego, Harcourt Brace Jovanovich.

Robert W. Clower is the author of widely used textbooks on microeconomics and mathematical economics (1947, 1957, 1988). He has also written on problems of development (1966). However, Clower is best known for his contributions to macroeconomics and monetary theory (his main papers edited by Walker in 1984; see also 1969). His article describing what he terms the 'Keynesian counterrevolution', first published in German in 1963 and then in English in 1965, has had a great influence. Some consider him the father of a new current in economics, 'disequilibrium theory', but Clower does not recognize himself as its founder (1984, pp. 270–71).

In Clower's view, the Keynesian revolution was undermined by its integration into a neo-Walrasian model that is incompatible with the foundations of Keynes's theory. He holds that *The General Theory* has implicit microeconomic foundations that are non-Walrasian. They are in fact characterized by behaviour that must be analysed in terms of disequilibrium. In particular, it is necessary to distinguish between planned or 'notional' demand and realized or 'effective' demand in what Clower terms a dual decision process, as well as to distinguish between flow and stock. In this analysis, money must also be integrated, as it is the active structural component of contemporary economies. More recently, Clower has devoted much of his research to the integration of monetary theory and disequilibrium theory and, more generally, to what he terms the 'general process analysis'. He criticizes the Keynesianism of the neoclassical synthesis, monetarism, as well as the new classical macroeconomics, for not taking into account the processes by which agents carry out their transactions in markets. These markets are multifarious and dispersed, and information circulates between them in a manner that is far from instantaneous, perfect and free. Only a full analysis of these processes on a Marshallian rather than on a Walrasian basis can enable us to understand both the dynamics and the instability of contemporary economies.

Main references

WALKER Donald A. 1984. 'Preface' and 'Introduction' in Clower 1984, ix–xi and 1–18.

BLAUG 1985, 33–5.

COASE Ronald (born 1910)

Ronald Coase was born in Middlesex, England. He earned a BComm degree from the London School of Economics in 1932, and a PhD in economics from the same institution in 1951. He taught at the Dundee School of Economics and Commerce (1932–4), at Liverpool University (1934–5), the London School of Economics (1935–51), the University of Buffalo (1951–8), the University of Virginia (1958–64) and, from 1964, at the University of Chicago, where he has been professor emeritus since 1982. He was editor of the

Journal of Law and Economics from 1964 to 1982. In 1991, he was awarded the Nobel Memorial Prize in Economics.

Main publications

1937. 'The Nature of the Firm', *Economica*, vol. 4, 386–405.
1946. 'The Marginal Cost Controversy', *Economica*, vol. 13, 169–82.
1950. *British Broadcasting: A Study in Monopoly*, London, Longmans Green; Cambridge, Massachusetts, Harvard University Press.
1959. 'The Federal Communications Commission', *Journal of Law and Economics*, vol. 2, 1–40.
1960. 'The Problem of Social Cost', *Journal of Law and Economics*, vol. 3, 1–44.
1972. 'Industrial Organization: A Proposal for Research', in V.R. Fuchs (ed.), *Policy Issues and Research Opportunities in Industrial Organization*, Cambridge, Massachusetts, National Bureau of Economic Research, 59–73.
1974. 'The Lighthouse in Economics', *Journal of Law and Economics*, vol. 17, 357–76.
1988. *The Firm, the Market, and the Law*, University of Chicago Press.
1992. 'The Institutional Structure of Production' [1991 Alfred Nobel Memorial Prize Lecture in Economic Sciences], *American Economic Review*, vol. 82, 713–19.
1994. *Essays on Economics and Economists*, University of Chicago Press.

Ronald Coase holds a very particular place in contemporary economic thought. On the one hand, some of his articles (1937, 1960) are among the most frequently cited. On the other hand, as he explains in the introduction to a re-edition of his main articles (1988), his perspective has been misunderstood and has lacked influence. A disciple of Adam Smith and Alfred Marshall, Coase is a believer in the virtues of the market, and has been associated with both the Virginia and the Chicago Schools (and hence with theoretical tendencies considered conservative), while at the same time systematically criticizing all forms of dogmatism. Notably, he has been critical of the manner in which political propositions have been held to be derived from what he terms 'blackboard economics'.

In Coase's view, economists have a tendency to construct theories in a manner so as to base themselves on realities that they have never actually studied. His article 'The Lighthouse in Economics' (1974) is an illuminating example of this. Using the example of a minutely documented study of the lighthouse industry in England since the sixteenth century, Coase shows that the foremost economists, from Mill to Samuelson, were misled in thinking that they had shed light on their arguments by using a wholly inadequate example; they had never actually bothered to study the workings involved, merely contenting themselves with generally accepted ideas. Coase criticizes mainstream economics for dealing with entities such as the firm, the market and consumer satisfaction without questioning their nature. Throughout his career he has used as a starting-point in the elaboration of his theories in-depth studies on the workings of various industries. Handling language and logic rather than symbols and equations, with great dexterity, Coase writes:

'In my youth it was said that what was too silly to be said may be sung. In modern economics it may be put into mathematics' (1988, p. 185).

His first important contribution (1937) raises the problem of the existence of firms, whose internal organization is completely different from the price system with which economists are exclusively preoccupied. Here Coase developed the concept later termed 'transaction costs'. Such costs are not the result of production, but of the functioning of markets, such as the search for information and contract negotiation. The firm is a structure that allows for the elimination of these costs. The optimal size of the firm can be determined through the comparison of these costs to those that result from its internal organization.

In his 1960 article, Coase focuses on legal procedures brought about so as to correct externalities, such as the inconveniences for a neighbourhood caused by factories' chimney smoke. In the view of Pigou and his disciples, the fact of these external effects justifies government intervention so as to equalize the private and social costs of the activity called into question. Generalizing from the workings of resource exchange to the exchange of property rights, Coase demonstrates that, if property rights are initially clearly demarcated for all the resources in question, and if they can be freely exchanged, a negotiating process between the parties involved will ensue in which the results will be independent of the legal stipulations foreseen to correct the external effects. In the absence of transaction costs, these will be the optimal results, reducing the consequences of externalities to a minimum. According to 'Coase's theorem', private and social costs are equal in the absence of transaction costs. When there are in fact transaction costs, the legal rules have an effect on the allocation of resources, but it cannot be determined in advance which stipulations would be the most efficient. Rather, cases should be studied and dealt with on a case-by-case basis. Coase's work contributed to the development of a new specialization known in the USA as 'law and economics'.

Main references

'The Nobel Memorial Prize in Economics 1991'. Press release, articles by K. Brunner and by Y. Barzel and L.A. Kochin, and bibliography, *Scandinavian Journal of Economics*, 1992, vol. 94, 1–36.

COOTER Robert D. 1982. 'The Cost of Coase', *Journal of Legal Studies*, vol. 11, 1–34.

COOTER Robert D. 1987. 'Coase Theorem', *New Palgrave*, vol. 1, 457–60.

MEDEMA Steven G. 1995 (ed.). *The Legacy of Ronald Coase in Economic Analysis*, Aldershot, Hants, Edward Elgar.

SAMUELS Warren J. 1974. 'The Coase Theorem and the Study of Law and Economics', *Natural Resources Journal*, vol. 14, 1–33.

SPITZER M. 1982. 'The Coase Theorem: Some Experimental Tests', *Journal of Law and Economics*, vol. 25, 73–98.

WILLIAMSON Oliver E. and WINTER Sidney G. (eds) 1991. *The Nature of the Firm: Origins, Evolution, and Development*, New York and Oxford, Oxford University Press. [Includes Coase 1937 and three papers by Coase on that article.]

BLAUG 1985, 36–8. SILLS 1979, 125–7. SPIEGEL and SAMUELS 1984, 571–8.

CODDINGTON Alan (1941–1982)

Alan Coddington was born in Doncaster, Yorkshire (England). He earned a PhD from York University in 1966. That year, he began teaching at Queen Mary College, London, where he was appointed professor in 1980. His most promising career was cut short by his suicide.

Main publications

1968. *Theories of the Bargaining Process*, London, George Allen & Unwin.
1975. 'The Rationale of General Equilibrium Theory', *Economic Inquiry*, vol. 13, 539–58.
1976. 'Keynesian Economics: The Search for First Principles', *Journal of Economic Literature*, vol. 14, 1258–73.
1979. 'Hick's Contribution to Keynesian Economics', *Journal of Economic Literature*, vol. 17, 970–88.
1979. 'Friedman's Contribution to Methodological Controversy', *British Review of Economic Issues*, vol. 2, 1–13.
1982. 'Deficient Foresight: A Troublesome Theme in Keynesian Economics', *American Economic Review*, vol. 72, 480–87.
1983. *Keynesian Economics: The Search for First Principles*, London, George Allen & Unwin.

Coddington's doctoral thesis gave rise to an important and original work on bargaining processes, prefaced by Shackle (1968). However, it is mainly through his contributions to economic methodology and the study of the evolution of macroeconomics that Coddington left his mark. He is the originator of the classification of interpretations of Keynes's theory as 'hydraulic' (Samuelson and the neoclassical synthesis), 'fundamentalist' (Shackle, Robinson and the post-Keynesians) or 'reductionist' (Clower, Leijonhufvud, Malinvaud and disequilibrium theory). Coddington concluded, in his posthumous work that: 'the thrust of these comments will be that the various approaches are, in their contribution to understanding, largely complementary' (1983, p. 112).

Main references

HICKS John 1979. 'On Coddington's Interpretation: A Reply', *Journal of Economic Literature*, vol. 17, 989–95.
SHACKLE G.L.S. 1983. 'The Romantic Mountain and the Classic Lake: Alan Coddington's *Keynesian Economics*', *Journal of Post Keynesian Economics*, vol. 6, 241–57.

New Palgrave 1987, vol. 1, 464.

DAVIDSON Paul (born 1930)

Paul Davidson was born in New York. After beginning his university studies in biochemistry at the University of Pennsylvania (1950–52), he earned an MA from the City University of New York (1955) and a PhD from the University of Pennsylvania (1959). Davidson was first an assistant professor at Rutgers University from 1958 to 1960, assistant and then associate professor at the University of Pennsylvania, professor at Rutgers (1966–86) and, since 1986, has been professor at the University of Tennessee. Since its foundation in 1978, he has edited the *Journal of Post Keynesian Economics*.

Main publications

1960. *Theories of Aggregate Income Distribution*, New Brunswick, New Jersey, Rutgers University Press.

1964. With Eugene Smolensky, *Aggregate Supply and Demand Analysis*, New York, Harper & Row.

1965. 'Keynes's Finance Motive', *Oxford Economic Papers*, vol. 17, 47–65.

1968. 'Money, Portfolio Balance, Capital Accumulation, and Economic Growth', *Econometrica*, vol. 36, 291–321.

1972. *Money and the Real World*, London, Macmillan; New York, John Wiley & Sons, 1973.

1977. 'Post-Keynesian Monetary Theory and Inflation', in S. Weintraub (ed.), *Modern Economic Thought*, Philadelphia, University of Pennsylvania Press, 275–94.

1982. *International Money and the Real World*, London, Macmillan; New York, John Wiley & Sons.

1988. With Greg Davidson, *Economics for a Civilized Society*, London, Macmillan; New York, W.W. Norton.

1989 (ed., with Jan Kregel). *Macroeconomic Problems and Policies of Income Distribution: Functional, Personal, International*, Aldershot, Hants, Edward Elgar.

1990. *The Collected Writings of Paul Davidson*, vol. 1, *Money and Employment*; vol. 2, *Inflation, Open Economies and Resources*, edited by Louise Davidson, London, Macmillan.

1991. *Controversies in Post-Keynesian Economics*, Aldershot, Hants, Edward Elgar.

1991 (ed., with Jan Kregel). *Economic Problems of the 1990's: Europe, the Developing Countries and the United States*, Aldershot, Hants, Edward Elgar.

1994. *Post Keynesian Macroeconomic Theory: A Foundation for Successful Economic Policies for the Twenty-First Century*, Aldershot, Hants, Edward Elgar.

In his doctoral thesis, written under Sidney Weintraub's direction (1960), as well as in a microeconomics textbook written with E. Smolensky (1964), Davidson began a vigorous critique of the neoclassical synthesis, a project continued throughout his career. In addition to this, he has played an important role in the building of a post-Keynesian current in economics, in part through his founding of the *Journal of Post Keynesian Economics*. Like other theoretical currents, it is far from homogeneous, and Davidson is particularly critical of the Cambridge post-Keynesians, criticizing them, along with the neoclassical theorists, for not taking into account the role of money in economics. The integrating of the monetary and real aspects of economic analysis is one of Davidson's key research interests. He has attempted to interpret

Keynes's perspective as a monetary theory of production and to reconcile the analysis of inflation, distribution and money. In his first important article on this theme, he pointed out that, for Keynes, the financial motive of the demand for money plays a crucial role in the linking of the monetary and real sectors, and that the obscuring of this motive by most of Keynes's interpreters is at the root of a misinterpretation of *The General Theory* (1965). His 1972 book represents his most ambitious work, as well as his primary contribution to the integration of money and the theory of effective demand.

Davidson extended his reflections with a study of international financial relations between open economies (1982). In this work he suggested proposals for the reform of the international monetary system, suggesting a return to Keynes's original project, updated so as to take current conditions into account. Davidson, who worked for some time for an oil company, has also contributed to the economics of energy and natural resources. He has always been interested in economic planning, recommending, along with his post-Keynesian colleagues, active state intervention in order to stimulate effective demand, along with a revenue policy aimed at fighting inflation.

Main references

BRONFENBRENNER Martin 1980. 'Davidson on Keynes on Money', *Journal of Post Keynesian Economics*, vol. 2, 308–13.

ARESTIS and SAWYER 1992, 109–15.

DEBREU Gérard (born 1921)

Gérard Debreu was born in Calais, France. He became an American citizen in 1975. He studied mathematics and history at Paris's Ecole Normale Supérieure (1941–4). Agrégé de l'Université in mathematics in 1946, he became research associate of the Centre National de la Recherche Scientifique (CNRS, 1946–8). From 1948 to 1950 he spent time in the United States, Sweden and Norway as a Rockefeller fellow. He was a research associate of the Cowles Commission for research in economics at the University of Chicago from 1950 to 1955, and then at Yale University, where he was appointed associate professor (1955–61). In 1956, he received a doctorate from the Université de Paris. Since 1962 he has been a professor of economics and of mathematics (since 1975) at the University of California at Berkeley. In 1971, he was president of the Econometric Society and of the American Economic Association in 1990. He was awarded the Nobel Memorial Prize in Economics in 1983.

Main publications

1951. 'The Coefficient of Resource Utilization', *Econometrica*, vol. 19, 273–92.
1952. 'A Social Equilibrium Existence Theorem', *Proceedings of the National Academy of Sciences*, vol. 38, 886–93.
1954. With Kenneth J. Arrow, 'Existence of an Equilibrium for a Competitive Economy', *Econometrica*, vol. 22, 265–90.
1956. 'Market Equilibrium', *Proceedings of the National Academy of Sciences*, vol. 42, 876–8.
1959. *Theory of Value: An Axiomatic Analysis of Economic Equilibrium*, New York, John Wiley & Sons.
1960. 'Une économie de l'incertain', *Économie appliquée*, vol. 13, 111–16.
1962. 'New Concepts and Techniques for Equilibrium Analysis', *International Economic Review*, vol. 3, 257–73.
1963. With H. Scarf, 'A Limit Theorem on the Core of an Economy', *International Economic Review*, vol. 4, 235–46.
1964. 'Continuity Properties of Paretian Utility', *International Economic Review*, vol. 5, 285–93.
1969. 'Neighboring Economic Agents', *La Décision* [Paris, colloques internationaux du Centre National de la Recherche Scientifique], no. 171, 85–90.
1970. 'Economies with a Finite Set of Equilibria', *Econometrica*, vol. 38, 387–92.
1972. 'Smooth Preferences', *Econometrica*, vol. 40, 603–15.
1974. 'Excess Demand Functions', *Journal of Mathematical Economics*, vol. 1, 15–21.
1982. 'Existence of a Competitive Equilibrium', in K.J. Arrow and M.D. Intriligator (eds), *Handbook of Mathematical Economics*, vol. 2, 697–743.
1983. *Mathematical Economics: Twenty Papers of Gerard Debreu*, Cambridge, England, Cambridge University Press.
1984. 'Economic Theory in the Mathematical Mode', in *Les Prix Nobel 1983*, Stockholm, Almquist and Wiksell, 231–46; *American Economic Review*, vol. 74, 267–78.
1986. 'Theoretic Models: Mathematical Form and Economic Content', *Econometrica*, vol. 54, 1259–70.
1987. 'Mathematical Economics', *New Palgrave*, vol. 3, 399–404.
1987. 'Existence of General Equilibrium', *New Palgrave*, vol. 2, 216–19.
1991. 'The Mathematization of Economic Theory', *American Economic Review*, vol. 81,1–7.
1991. 'Random Walk and Life Philosophy', *The American Economist*, vol. 35, no. 2, 3–7; in Szenberg 1992, 107–14.

As evaluated by the quantity of his publications, Debreu's work is far from being the most imposing among contemporary economists, many of whom are obsessed with the 'publish or perish' requirement. A small book of 107 pages (1959) and 20 articles anthologized in another work (1983) contain the gist of his contributions. However, they represent some of the most influential works in contemporary economic theory, and Debreu is without any doubt one of the most frequently cited economists of our time. His name is especially associated with two aspects of recent developments in economic thought: mathematical economics and the theory of general equilibrium.

Debreu has himself described very clearly, in his few non-mathematical texts (1984, 1986, 1987 'Mathematical', 1991 *AER*), the important transformations that mathematizing work has brought about since 1944. Originally trained as a mathematician and a professor of mathematics, he introduced in the early 1950s mathematical techniques never before used in economics, with the exception of certain works of John von Neumann, whose enormous influence on contemporary developments in mathematical economics Debreu recognizes. Among the originators of these techniques, termed fixed point theorem, convexity and minimax, are Brouwer, Kakutani and Nash. Set theory and topology replace differential calculus and linear algebra.

With the help of these instruments, Debreu gave general equilibrium theory its definitive form (1954 with Arrow, 1956; see also 1987 'Existence' for an account which is more accessible to the general reader). Walras had opened the way in 1874, while attempting a rigorous answer to the question posed by Adam Smith a century earlier: how can an order emerge through the interaction of agents motivated solely by self-interest; in other words, how does the invisible hand work? Walras never succeeded in demonstrating the existence of a general equilibrium. In the 1930s, Wald presented an initial demonstration of it, but Arrow and Debreu (and at the same time, although in a different manner, L.W. McKenzie) gave it a rigorous and definitive proof. In *Theory of Value*, first presented as his doctoral thesis in 1956, Debreu offers what he terms 'an axiomatic analysis of economic equilibrium': 'An axiomatized theory first selects its primitive concepts and represents each one of them by a mathematical object. ... Next, assumptions on the objects representing the primitive concepts are specified, and consequences are mathematically derived from them. The economic interpretation of the theorems so obtained is the last step of the analysis. According to this schema, an axiomatized theory has a mathematical form that is completely separated from its economic content' (1987 'Mathematical', p. 401). In his book, Debreu thus rigorously defines commodity, price, consumer and producer. He presents specific hypotheses concerning the links between these various elements (much of the subsequent work done on general equilibrium theory, including Debreu's own, has consisted in relaxing some of these hypotheses). From them he has deduced the existence of a price system and then shown that this system corresponds to an optimum, and that every optimum is associated with an equilibrium price system. As early as 1952, he offered a proof of the equivalence between competitive equilibrium and Pareto optimality.

In Debreu's view, axiomatic analysis alone allows for rigour, simplicity and generality, qualities which characterize his works. It also permits us to delimit better the applications of economic theory, and to avoid reading into it what it cannot affirm. Debreu himself is the first to acknowledge his approach's limitations. Thus he has clearly highlighted the impossibility of demonstrating the uniqueness and the stability of general equilibrium, except under certain very restrictive hypotheses that are far removed from actual circumstances (1974). It would therefore be risky to conclude from, for example, the equivalence between optimum conditions and general equilibrium that a market economy is superior to other models. In fact, Debreu has himself pointed out that supporters of active government intervention could also support their views with this analysis by bringing out its lack of realism (1987 'Mathematical', p. 402).

Main references

'The Nobel Memorial Prize in Economics 1983'. Official announcement, article by Hal R. Varian and bibliography, *Scandinavian Journal of Economics* 1984, vol. 86, 1–16.

DEBREU 1991 *AE*.

GEANAKOPLOS John 1987. 'Arrow–Debreu Model of General Equilibrium', *New Palgrave*, vol. 1, 116–24.

HILDEBRAND Werner 1983. 'Introduction', in Debreu 1983, 1–29.

BLAUG 1985, 39–40.

DEMSETZ Harold (born 1930)

Harold Demsetz was born in Chicago. He earned an MA in administration (1954), then a PhD in economics (1959), from Northwestern University, in Evanston, Illinois. He taught at the University of Michigan, in Ann Arbor (1958–60), at the University of California in Los Angeles (1960-63) and at the University of Chicago (1963–71), where he gained the rank of professor. Since1971, he has been professor at the University of California in Los Angeles. He chaired the membership committee of the Mont Pèlerin Society from 1981 to 1986. He was a member of president-elect Ronald Reagan's Transport Regulation Task Force.

Main publications

1967. 'Toward a Theory of Property Rights', *American Economic Review*, vol. 57, *Papers and Proceedings*, 347–59.

1968. 'The Cost of Transacting', *Quarterly Journal of Economics*, vol. 82, 33–53.

1972. 'Wealth Distribution and the Ownership of Rights', *Journal of Legal Studies*, vol. 1, 13–28.

1972. With A.A. Alchian, 'Production, Information Costs, and Economic Organization', *American Economic Review*, vol. 62, 777–95.

1982. *Economic, Legal, and Political Dimensions of Competition*, Amsterdam, North-Holland.

1988–9. *The Organization of Economic Activity*, vol. 1, *Ownership, Control, and the Firm*; vol. 2, *Efficiency, Competition, and Policy*, Oxford, Basil Blackwell.

Harold Demsetz extended the concept of property rights, put forward by Coase (Coase 1960), to the analysis of all market processes. This concept is based on that of transaction cost which can be found initially in another well-known article by Coase (1937). Transaction costs are themselves closely linked to the costs of acquiring information which is necessarily imperfect. It is in the field of labour market analysis that this new problematics has been most popular. Here, Demsetz is, with Alchian (1972), one of the initiators of the theory of implicit contracts.

More generally, Demsetz, one of the founders of the North American Law and Economics Society, is interested in the links between the political, legal and economic dimensions of modern societies (1982). He is convinced that the principle of individual interest and that of the rationality of agents must be at the basis of all such analysis. Hence, for Demsetz, the new formal political science is based on the fact that 'competition subjects politicians and political parties to the filter of the polling place, much as competition subjects managers to the filter of the market place' (1982, p. 68).

Demsetz has also turned his attention to, among other things, antimonopolistic legislation, publicity, regulation and pollution control. His major articles and many of his unpublished texts have been gathered in two volumes (1988–9).

Main reference

BLAUG 1985, 41–2.

DENISON Edward F. (1915–1992)

Edward F. Denison was born in Omaha, Nebraska, in the United States. He studied at Brown University, where he was awarded a MA in1938 and a PhD in 1941. He was in the employ of the Office of Business Economics of the US Department of Commerce from 1941 to 1956 and was named its assistant director in 1949. From 1956 to 1962 he was associate director of the Committee for Economic Development. He has also been associate director for national economic accounts of the Bureau of Economic Analysis of the Department of Commerce (1979 to 1982). In 1962, he became a senior fellow of the Brookings Institution, which named him emeritus fellow in 1978.

Main publications

1962. *The Sources of Economic Growth in the United States and the Alternatives before Us*, New York, Committee for Economic Development.

1967. *Why Growth Rates Differ: Postwar Experience in Nine Western Countries*, Washington, DC, Brookings Institution.

1974. *Accounting for United States Economic Growth, 1929–1969*, Washington, DC, Brookings Institution.

1976. With William K. Chung, *How Japan's Economy Grew So Fast: The Sources of Postwar Expansion*, Washington, DC, Brookings Institution.

1979. *Accounting for Slower Economic Growth: The United States in the 1970s*, Washington, DC, Brookings Institution.

1985. *Trends in American Economic Growth, 1929–1982*, Washington, DC, Brookings Institution.

1989. *Estimates of Productivity Change by Industry: An Evaluation and an Alternative*, Washington, DC, Brookings Institution.

Edward Denison is a pioneer in the field of sources of growth analysis, also called growth accounting. He has devoted all of his writings to this subject, continually proposing new ways of measuring economic data. Denison has also contributed to the progress of national accounting by working for the United States government. Among the sources of growth he more specifically indentifies 'the number, composition, and skills of workers engaged in production, the capital and land with which they work, the existing state of knowledge on producing at low cost, the size of markets served, and the efficiency with which resources are allocated among uses' (1974, p.1). This is not of course a restrictive list.

In his first book (1962), centred on the United States, Denison concluded that around half of growth may be explained by growth of the inputs, the other half resulting from growth of the outputs per unit of input. He indicates that growth of the capital stock plays a relatively small role. Moreover, he stresses that, among what he calls residual factors of growth, progress in knowledge and education play a major role. He does not substantially modify these conclusions in his subsequent works. Denison then applied this analysis to eight European countries (1967), attempting to explain how the rates as well as the types of growth differ between these countries. He also applied his method of analysis to Japan, trying to penetrate the mystery of its fast growth (1976). But he was always particularly interested in the United States, and more specifically from the moment that postwar growth started to decelerate, a process which became, as Denison puts it, 'more disturbing and also more puzzling' from 1974 onwards, when there was a decline in the constant-dollar national income per person employed (1979, p. 1). From 1974 on, the gap between actual production and what Denison calls the potential production became more pronounced. The situation ten years later was, according to him, even more worrying (1985) and the government's responses to the situation seem to him both insufficient and ill-directed.

Main reference

BLAUG 1985, 43–5.

DOBB Maurice Herbert (1900–1976)

Maurice Dobb was born in London, where he began his university studies in history. From 1919 to 1922, he studied history and economics at Cambridge, where he was a member of Keynes's political economy club. He attended the London School of Economics, where he earned a PhD in 1924, and began teaching at Cambridge that same year, remaining there until his retirement in 1967. In 1959, he was appointed reader there, at the same time as Nicholas Kaldor and Joan Robinson.

Main publications

1925. *Capitalist Enterprise and Social Progress*, London, Routledge & Kegan Paul.
1928. *Russian Economic Development since the Revolution*, London, Routledge & Kegan Paul.
1928. *Wages*, Cambridge, England, Cambridge University Press.
1937. *Political Economy and Capitalism: Some Essays in Economic Tradition*, London, Routledge & Kegan Paul.
1946. *Studies in the Development of Capitalism*, London, Routledge & Kegan Paul; US edn 1947, New York, International Publishers.
1948. *Soviet Economic Development since 1917*, London, Routledge & Kegan Paul; New York, International Publishers.
1951. *Some Aspects of Economic Development: Three Lectures*, Delhi, Ranjit Publishers.
1951–73 Collaboration with P. Sraffa (ed.). *The Works and Correspondence of David Ricardo*, 11 vols, Cambridge, England, Cambridge University Press.
1955. *On Economic Theory and Socialism: Collected Papers*, London, Routledge & Kegan Paul.
1960. *An Essay on Economic Growth and Planning*, London, Routledge & Kegan Paul; New York, Monthly Review Press.
1963. *Economic Growth and Underdeveloped Countries*, London, Lawrence & Wishart.
1967. *Papers on Capitalism, Development and Planning*, London, Routledge & Kegan Paul; New York, International Publishers.
1969. *Welfare Economics and the Economics of Socialism: Towards a Commonsense Critique*, Cambridge, England, Cambridge University Press.
1970. *Socialist Planning: Some Problems*, London, Lawrence & Wishart.
1973. *Theories of Value and Distribution since Adam Smith: Ideology and Economic Theory*, Cambridge, England, Cambridge University Press.
1976 (ed., with Paul M. Sweezy). *The Transition from Feudalism to Capitalism*, London, New Left Books.
1978. 'Random Biographical Notes', *Cambridge Journal of Economics*, vol. 2, 115–20.

Dobb holds a very special place in the panorama of contemporary economic thought. He was an active member of the British Communist Party from 1922 until his death. Apart from his academic work, he edited many popularized works and newspaper articles. He lived at various times in the Soviet Union, learning Russian and continuously defending Soviet policy even while criticizing Stalinist dogmatism.

For many years, Dobb was a rarity: one of the very few, if not the only, academic economist in the English-speaking world to profess Marxism and communism. In spite of, and perhaps in part because of this, Dobb has always been held in great esteem, even by those who were at the opposite pole from him politically and ideologically. One notes, for example, the list of economists who agreed to contribute to his *Festschrift,* given him on the occasion of his retirement from Cambridge (Feinstein 1967). From the beginning of his career, he enjoyed the high esteem of Keynes and his Cambridge colleagues. In addition to his affable temperament, frequently unnerving to his potential adversaries, his profound grasp of orthodox economic theory, lack of theoretical dogmatism and his numerous scholarly contributions earned him prestige in an academic milieu long hostile to Marxism.

Before Joan Robinson and Paul Sweezy, Dobb introduced a refined, non-dogmatic Marxist perspective to English-speaking academia, underlining

Marxism's historic continuity with the classical tradition, notably Ricardian thought (1937). In a synthesis of the history of economic thought in the light of Sraffa's work (1973), he reiterated this theme. However, it would be unfair to speak of a one-way influence from Sraffa to Dobb, knowing as we do that Dobb actively contributed to Sraffa's edition of the complete works of Ricardo, including the famous introduction to the *Principles* in the first volume. In fact, Dobb claimed that he wrote this introduction (1978, p. 119). Were this the case, Dobb is just as much the initiator of the neo-Ricardian trend as Sraffa; in fact he was criticized by orthodox Marxists on this account.

Dobb is also the author of major contributions to economic history. His study of the transition from feudalism to capitalism (1946) is perhaps his most famous work. His theses provoked a sharp polemic (see the texts in Dobb and Sweezy 1976), as did his analysis of the economic development of the Soviet Union (1948), the first major work on the subject to appear in English. Taking part in the debate about market socialism, Dobb remained, *contra* Lange and Lerner, an advocate of central planning (see articles in 1955, 1967). However, his position moderated somewhat towards the end of his career, as witnessed especially by his analysis of welfare (1969). From the 1950s, Dobb also took an interest in growth theory and in the problems of Third World development, teaching in many underdeveloped countries (1951, 1960, 1963).

Main References

Cambridge Journal of Economics 1978, 'Maurice Dobb Memorial Issue', vol. 2, no. 2.

DOBB 1978.

FEINSTEIN C.H. 1967 (ed.). *Socialism, Capitalism and Economic Growth. Essays Presented to Maurice Dobb*, Cambridge, England, Cambridge University Press. [With a bibliography of Dobb's work up to 1967.]

MEEK Ronald 1978. 'Obituary of Maurice Herbert Dobb', *Proceedings of the British Academy 1977*, vol. 53, 333–44.

ARESTIS and SAWYER 1992, 128–34. BLAUG 1985, 49–50. *New Palgrave* 1987, vol. 1, 913. SILLS 1979, 142–4. SPIEGEL and SAMUELS 1984, vol. 2, 595–621.

DOMAR Evsey David (born 1914)

Evsey David Domar (born Domashevitsky) was born in Lodz, Russia (now Poland). He lived in Harbin, Manchuria, before settling in the United States in 1936. He earned an MA in mathematics from the University of Michigan (1941) and an MA (1943) and PhD (1947) in economics from Harvard, where he studied under Alvin Hansen. From 1943 to 1946, he worked as an economist for the board of governors of the Federal Reserve System. He was assistant professor at the Carnegie Institute of Technology (1946–7), at the

University of Chicago (1947–8), where he was an associate in the Cowles Commission, and first associate (1948–55) then full professor (1955–8) at the Johns Hopkins University. He was a professor at the Massachusetts Institute of Technology from 1958 until his retirement in 1984, when he became professor emeritus. In 1970, he was president of the Association for Comparative Economics.

Main publications

1944. 'The "Burden of the Debt" and the National Income', *American Economic Review*, vol. 34, 798–827.
1946. 'Capital Expansion, Rate of Growth, and Employment', *Econometrica*, vol. 14, 137–47.
1947. 'Expansion and Employment', *American Economic Review*, vol. 37, 34–55.
1948. 'The Problem of Capital Accumulation', *American Economic Review*, vol. 38, 777–94.
1953. 'Depreciation, Replacement and Growth', *Economic Journal*, vol. 63, 1–32.
1957. *Essays in the Theory of Economic Growth*, New York, Oxford University Press.
1961. 'On the Measurement of Technological Change', *Economic Journal*, vol. 71, 709–29.
1966. 'The Soviet Collective Farm as a Producer Cooperative', *American Economic Review*, vol. 56, 734–57.
1970. 'The Causes of Slavery or Serfdom: A Hypothesis', *Journal of Economic History*, vol. 30, 18–32.
1974. 'On the Optimal Compensation of a Socialist Manager', *Quarterly Journal of Economics*, vol. 88, 1–18.
1989. *Capitalism, Socialism, and Serfdom: Essays by Evsey Domar*, Cambridge, England, Cambridge University Press.
1992. 'How I Tried to Become an Economist', in Szenberg 1992, 115–27.

Domar is part of the circle of economists whose names have been used to designate well known theoretical constructions. The 'Harrod–Domar growth model' is the starting-point of the abundant literature on growth that appeared during the 1950s and 1960s. In fact, Domar published in 1946 (seven years after Harrod) the results of his independent research, which were in some respects different from Harrod's (see also 1947, 1948). He explicitly identifies with a tradition going back to Marx and extending to underconsumption theories, in which a link is established between employment and capital accumulation. Domar criticizes Keynes and his disciples for only taking into account one aspect of investment: its effect on income, given by the multiplier. But, he holds, investment also increases the productive capacities of the economy. Investment is thus seen to be at once a remedy for unemployment and the source of greater problems in the future. In order to maintain full employment, income must grow at an annual rate, shown by Domar to be necessarily equal to the product of the marginal propensity to save and the average productivity of investment. Obviously, nothing guarantees that this can be realized in modern capitalist economies.

Domar was the first to underline the limits of abstract models of growth. A complete growth theory 'requires a mass of empirical work. It also requires the ability to synthesize data and ideas from all social sciences, and most of all it requires that breadth of vision and imagination and that degree of understanding which is called "wisdom". In short, it is a job for sages' (1957, p. 12). Domar himself has engaged in more extended, multidisciplinary research projects (1970, 1989). He has also written on the functioning of the Soviet economy, a subject that has always interested him (1966, 1974). He discovered the theoretical progenitor of the 'Harrod–Domar model' in the writings of Fel'dmann during the 1920s (1957, pp. 223–62).

Main references

ASIMAKOPULOS A. 1986. 'Harrod and Domar on Dynamic Economics', *Quarterly Review, Banca Nazionale del Lavoro*, no. 158, 275–98.

DOMAR 1992.

FRISCH Ragnar 1961. 'A Reconsideration of Domar's Theory of Economic Growth', *Econometrica*, vol. 29, 406–13.

HAMBERG Daniel 1977. 'Early Growth Theory: The Harrod–Domar Models', in S. Weintraub (ed.), *Modern Economic Thought*, Philadelphia, University of Pennsylvania Press, 333–46.

BLAUG 1985, 49–50. *New Palgrave* 1987, vol. 1, 913.

DOWNS Anthony (born 1930)

Born in Evanston, Illinois, A. Downs studied at Carleton College (Northfield, Minnesota) and subsequently at Stanford (MA, 1953, PhD, 1956). From 1959 to 1977 he was a member, then chairman of Real Estate Research Corporation, a consulting firm advising decision makers on housing policies, real estate investment and urban affairs. He has been senior fellow at the Brookings Institution in Washington since 1977.

Main publications

1957. *An Economic Theory of Democracy*, New York, Harper & Brothers.

1967. *Inside Bureaucracy*, Boston, Little, Brown.

1970. *Urban Problems and Prospects*, Chicago, Markham.

1973. *Federal Housing Subsidies: How are they Working?*, Lexington, Massachusetts, D.C. Heath.

1973. *Opening up the Suburbs: An Urban Strategy for America*, New Haven, Connecticut, Yale University Press.

1983. *Rental Housing in the 1980s*, Washington, DC, Brookings Institution.

1985. *The Revolution in Real Estate Finance*, Washington, DC, Brookings Institution.

Since 1950, in conjunction with his professional activities, Anthony Downs has published many articles on the different issues concerning real estate (management, market, public policy). He has also published on the state of cities (city centres and suburbs), urban policy, housing, racism in the cities, the rent paid by poor and modest-income families and the financing of construction (1970, 1973, 1983, 1985).

It was his first book (1957) that earned him the recognition of the Anglo-American economic profession. In effect, he was one of the first to use the conventional tools of economics – the analysis of maximizing rational agents – beyond the field of economics, to analyse the behaviour of politicians and of the electorate in a democracy. Subsequently, working for the Rand Corporation, he applied this analysis to administration policies (1967).

Main reference

BLAUG 1985, 56–7.

DUESENBERRY James Stemble (born 1918)

James Duesenberry studied at the University of Michigan (BA in 1939, MA in 1941, PhD in 1948). A researcher with the Social Science Research Council from 1941, he was an instructor at the Massachusetts Institute of Technology in 1946, and from that year began his teaching career at Harvard University, where he has remained ever since, having been appointed professor in 1957. He was a member of the President's Council of Economic Advisers from 1966 to 1968.

Main publications

1948. 'Income–Consumption Relations and Their Implications', in L. Metzler (ed.), *Income, Employment and Public Policy: Essays in Honor of Alvin H. Hansen*, New York, W.W. Norton, 54–81.

1949. *Income, Saving and the Theory of Consumer Behavior*, Cambridge, Massachusetts, Harvard University Press.

1958. *Business Cycles and Economic Growth*, New York, McGraw-Hill.

1964. *Money and Credit: Impact and Control*, Englewood Cliffs, New Jersey, Prentice-Hall.

1965 (ed., with G. Fromm, L. Klein and E. Kuh). *The Brookings Quarterly Econometric Model of the United States*, Chicago, Rand McNally; Amsterdam, North-Holland.

1969 (ed., with G. Fromm, L. Klein and E. Kuh). *The Brookings Model: Some Further Results*, Chicago, Rand McNally.

1981. With T. Mayer and R.T. Aliber, *Money, Banking and the Economy*, New York, W.W. Norton.

In his doctoral thesis, published in 1949, Duesenberry sought to test statistically the Keynesian consumption function with household samples and time series. Lacking satisfactory results from this latter category, he got better ones by introducing a supplementary variable, the preceding period's highest income (1948, 1949), thus paving the way for life cycle theories (see Modigliani) and permanent income theories (see Friedman).

During the heyday of growth theory, he struggled to elaborate an integrated analysis of cycles and growth, inspired by Keynesian as well as the classical tradition (1958). He then invested, notably with L. Klein, in the building of the Brookings quarterly econometric model of the United States (1965, 1969). He also published a short introductory work on money and on monetary policy (1964) and a textbook on the financial system and national and international monetary issues (1981).

Main reference

BLAUG *Who's Who* 1986, 231.

EATWELL John (born 1945)

John Eatwell was born in Great Britain, where he began his university studies at Cambridge. He continued at Harvard (1967–9) where he obtained an MA (1969), then a PhD (1975). He has taught since 1970 at Cambridge, where he is a fellow of Trinity College and, since 1977, a University lecturer at the Faculty of Economics and Politics. He has also been, since 1982, professor at the New School for Social Research, New York. From 1985 to 1992 he was economic adviser to the leader of the British Labour Party, Neil Kinnock. He was named a member of the House of Lords in 1992.

Main publications

1973. 'Mr Sraffa's Standard Commodity and the Rate of Exploitation' [in Polish] *Ekonomiska*, no. 4; Engl. version 1975, *Quarterly Journal of Economics*, vol. 89, 543–55.

1973. With Joan Robinson, *An Introduction to Modern Economics*, Maidenhead, Berkshire, McGraw-Hill.

1977. 'The Irrelevance of Returns to Scale in Sraffa's System', *Journal of Economic Literature*, vol. 15, 61–8.

1982. *Whatever Happened to Britain? The Economics of a Decline*, London, Gerald Duckworth.

1983. 'The Long-Period Theory of Unemployment', *Cambridge Journal of Economics*, vol. 7, 269–85.

1983 (ed., with Murray Milgate). *Keynes's Economics and the Theory of Value and Distribution*, New York, Oxford University Press.

1987 (ed., with Murray Milgate and Peter Newman). *The New Palgrave: A Dictionary of Economics*, 4 vols, London, Macmillan; New York, Stockton Press.

John Eatwell first became known as co-author, with Joan Robinson, of an original economics textbook, which broke with the neoclassical orthodoxy, fitting in with the post-Keynesian school (1973). In this book and in several articles, Eatwell emerged as an obstinate critic, as much of monetarism and new classical macroeconomics as of the neoclassical synthesis and of the disequilibrium theory which, he considers, betray the true contribution of Keynes. In place of these theoretical constructions, he offers an analysis based on a synthesis of Keynesian and Sraffian approaches. To succeed, though, it is necessary to renounce seeing Keynes's theory as located in a short run context, even if it is as such that the latter presented his analysis: 'it is the long-period implications of his analysis, as a theory of employment, which represent the significant contribution' (1983, *Keynes's*, p. 97). Only in this manner is it possible to avoid the pitfall of reducing Keynesian to neoclassical theory, and to reconcile it with a theory of value and distribution inspired by Ricardo, Marx and Sraffa, which, however, lacks a theory of employment.

Eatwell is one of the founders of the *Cambridge Journal of Economics* (1977) and of *Contributions to Political Economy* (1982). But one of his most ambitious enterprises has probably been the edition, with his colleagues Murray Milgate of Harvard and Peter Newman of Johns Hopkins, of a new version of the dictionary of political economy, first completed by R.H. Inglis Palgrave, in three volumes, between 1894 and 1899. It is a 3500-page book in four volumes and 2000 entries, whose objective is to cover the whole of contemporary economic theory (1987).

Eatwell also became interested in the problems of economic policy, both in Great Britain and in other Western countries. Critical of Thatcherism, he became the apostle of long-term growth policies based on industrial investment (1982).

Main reference

ARESTIS and SAWYER 1992, 135–40.

EICHNER Alfred S. (1937–1988)

Alfred Eichner was born in Washington, DC, and obtained his PhD in 1966 from Columbia University. He started teaching as professor of human resources at Columbia in 1961, before being named professor of economics at the State University of New York at Purchase in 1971. In 1980, he was named professor at Rutgers University. There he set up and directed the Center for Economic and Anthropogenic Research.

Main publications

1964. With Eli Ginsberg, *The Troublesome Presence: The American Democracy and the Negro*, New York, Free Press.

1969. *The Emergence of Oligopoly: Sugar Refining as a Case Study,* Baltimore, Johns Hopkins.

1973. 'A Theory of the Determination of the Mark-up Under Oligopoly', *Economic Journal,* vol. 83, 1184–1200.

1975. With Jan Kregel, 'An Essay on Post-Keynesian Theory: A New Paradigm in Economics', *Journal of Economic Literature,* vol.13, 1293–1314.

1976. *The Megacorp and Oligopoly: Micro Foundations of Macro Dynamics*, Cambridge, England, Cambridge University Press.

1978 (ed.). *A Guide to Post-Keynesian Economics,* White Plains, New York, M.E. Sharpe.

1979. 'A Post-Keynesian Short-Period Model', *Journal of Post Keynesian Economics,* vol. 1, 38–63.

1979. With Charles Brecker, *Controlling Social Expenditures: The Search for Output Measure*, New York, Allenheld Osmun.

1982. 'La théorie post-keynésienne et la recherche empirique', *L'Actualité économique*, vol. 58, 223–47.

1983 (ed.). *Why Economics is not yet a Science,* Armonk, New York, M.E. Sharpe.

1985. *Towards a New Economics: Essays in Post-Keynesian and Institutionalist Economics,* Armonk, New York, M.E. Sharpe.

1987. *The Macrodynamics of Advanced Market Economies,* Armonk, New York, M.E. Sharpe.

1988. 'The Reagan Record: A Post Keynesian View', *Journal of Post Keynesian Economics,* vol. 10, 541–56.

Alfred S. Eichner made important contributions to the study of oligopoly, and particularly to the study of price determination by oligopolistic firms, which he termed the 'megacorps' (1976). Following the example of Kalecki and Weintraub, among others, he considers that firms with market power fix prices by establishing a mark-up on costs. Eichner sought to complete this analysis by explaining how the mark-up rate is established in this process (1973). Apart from both what Kalecki called the degree of monopoly and the rate of capacity utilization, Eichner considered it necessary to take account of firms' self-financing needs, linked to their investment projects. A link is thus established between growth and price determination. Given that oligopolies dominate modern economies, Eichner's opinion was that his theory provides new microeconomic foundations for Keynesian macrodynamics. It also supplies an explanation of contemporary inflation, as resulting from the interaction of the pricing policies of the 'megacorporations' and wage-push by the large unions. It is on this basis that Eichner suggests, in order to control inflation, incomes policies, which must be the outcome of a social contract between employers' organizations and unions, and should apply to all types of incomes and not wages alone.

Eichner pursued an ambitious programme during his career. It consisted of replacing the dominant neoclassical paradigm, which revealed itself incapable of accounting for the actual behaviour of modern economies (1983), with a new paradigm, which he labelled 'post-Keynesian' in an article with Jan Kregel (1975). For Eichner, this replacement is now entering into a third, decisive phase (1982, p. 224), which will be a phase of empirical validation of the new theory, after the phases of criticism and construction. This theory incorporates elements of Marxism, Keynesianism and institutionalism, and utilizes the contributions of Leontief and Sraffa, among others. It tries to account for both cyclical fluctuations and long-run trends. Eichner set out this theory in a collective work (1979), a number of articles (1979, 1982, 1985) and, above all, a textbook of close to one thousand pages (1987). Eichner tried to integrate into a coherent whole the theory of effective demand, production theory, theory of growth and of distribution, and theories of prices, money and credit, relying on a systemic analysis which he directly opposed to the atomistic vision of orthodox theory.

Main references

ARESTIS Philip 1989. 'Pricing, Distribution, Investment and Growth: The Economics of A.S. Eichner', *Review of Political Economy*, vol. 1, 7–22.

GROVES Miles, LEE Frederic and MILBERG William 1989. 'The Power of Ideas and the Impact of one Man: Alfred Eichner 1937–1988', *Journal of Post Keynesian Economics*, vol. 11, 491–6.

MILBERG William 1991 (ed.). *The Megacorp and Macrodynamics: Essays in Memory of Alfred Eichner*, Armonk, New York, M.E. Sharpe.

ARESTIS and SAWYER 1992, 140–47.

EISNER Robert (born 1922)

Robert Eisner was born in New York. He gained an MA at Columbia University in 1942, and a PhD from Johns Hopkins in 1951. He also studied in Paris in 1945–6. He worked as an economist and a statistician for various American government agencies between 1941 and 1947. He taught at the University of Illinois, in Urbana, from 1950 to 1952, and afterwards was successively assistant (1952–4), associate (1954–60) and full professor (from 1960) at Northwestern University. He was senior research associate at the National Bureau of Economic Research between 1969 and 1978. He was president of the American Economic Association in 1988.

Main publications

1956. *Determinants of Capital Expenditures: An Interview Study*, University of Illinois.

1962. 'Investment Plans and Realisations', *American Economic Review*, vol. 52, 190–203.

1963. With Robert H. Strotz, 'The Determinants of Business Investment', in D.B. Suits *et al.*, *Impacts of Monetary Policy*, Englewood Cliffs, New Jersey, Prentice-Hall, 60–337.

1965. 'Realization of Investment Anticipations', in Duesenberry *et al.* (eds) , 95–128.

1966. *Some Factors in Growth Reconsidered*, Athens, Center of Planning and Economic Research.

1967. 'A Permanent Income Theory for Investment: Some Empirical Explanations', *American Economic Review*, vol. 57, 363–90.

1978. *Factors in Business Investment*, Cambridge, Massachusetts, Ballinger for the National Bureau of Economic Research.

1986. *How Real is the Federal Deficit?*, New York, Free Press; London, Collier Macmillan.

1988. 'Extended Accounts for National Income and Product', *Journal of Economic Literature*, vol. 26, 1611–84.

1989. *The Total Incomes System of Accounts*, University of Chicago Press.

1989. 'Budget Deficits: Rhetoric and Reality', *Journal of Economic Perspectives*, vol. 3, no. 2, 73–93.

Robert Eisner has devoted much of his research to the analysis of investment's determination. Interviews held in the early 1950s, within the scope of a project supervised by F. Modigliani, convinced him that 'an economist can no more rely on businessmen's perceptions and rationalizations to explain the determinants of investment than a physician can rely on patients' introspections alone to explain illness' (1978, p. xxi). What is decisive is the detailed quantitative study of the activities of firms in relation to their plans and expectations. For 20 years, Eisner gathered and analysed, with the help of his assistants, data which allowed him to improve the knowledge of the behaviour of firms and refine the aggregate investment function by considering a more diversified range of explicative variables. This research gave rise to a series of important articles (1962, 1965, 1967) and a book which sums up its main results (1978).

Eisner is also led by his concern for accurate measurement in other fields of research, namely the more recent ones on national accounts (1988, 1989

The Total Incomes) as well as on deficit and public debt (1986, 1989 *JEP*). In the latter, he resolutely takes the opposite view to the neo-liberal theories nourished by the resurgence of the 'Treasury View', fought by Keynes, metamorphosed in modern times into the crowding-out effect. Eisner stresses that one must never forget that all debt has an asset as a counterpart and that the budget deficit can contribute in stimulating consumption and investment, as Keynes has already shown. Hence the rise of the US deficit has enabled, in recent years, to avoid cumulative deflation that could have been catastrophic for the world economy. Moreover, Eisner thinks that proof has not been given that deficits, the importance of which is exaggerated, foster inflation. Besides his books and scientific papers, Eisner has written many newspaper and popular magazine articles, and given many statements before congressional committees and commissions.

FELDSTEIN Martin (born 1939)

Martin Feldstein was born in New York. In 1967, he gained a PhD at Oxford, where he taught from 1965 to 1967, being appointed professor at Harvard in 1967. Since 1977 he has been president of the National Bureau of Economic Research. He was chairman of the Council of Economic Advisers to President Reagan from 1982 to 1984.

Main publications

1967. *Economic Analysis for Health Service Efficiency*, Amsterdam, North-Holland.
1977 (ed., with Robert P. Inman). *The Economics of Public Services*, London, Macmillan.
1979. *Health Care Economics*, New York, John Wiley.
1980 (ed.). *The American Economy in Transition*, University of Chicago Press.
1983. *Inflation, Tax Rules, and Capital Formation*, University of Chicago Press.
1983. *Capital Taxation*, Cambridge, Massachusetts, Harvard University Press.
1983 (ed.). *Behavioral Simulation Methods in Tax Policy Analysis*, University of Chicago Press.
1985–7 (ed., with Alan J. Auerbach). *Handbook of Public Economics*, 2 vols, Amsterdam, North-Holland.
1987 (ed.). *The Effects of Taxation on Capital Accumulation*, University of Chicago Press.
1987 (ed.). *Taxes and Capital Formation*, University of Chicago Press.
1988 (ed.). *The United States in the World Economy*, University of Chicago Press.
1992. 'The Council of Economic Advisers and Economic Advising in the United States', *Economic Journal*, vol. 102, 1223–34.

In Feldstein's view, the public sector was neglected for far too long by economic theory. Since the end of the Second World War, 'the public sector has grown rapidly and spread into a wide range of previously private activities' (1977, p. xi). Feldstein has devoted a large part of his research to the study of various aspects of the public sector. His work has led to numerous publications, earning him the 1977 John Bates Clark Medal of the American Economic Association. He has been especially interested in the economics of medical and hospital care, in social security, charitable donations and inheritances. Yet he has undoubtedly contributed most, in terms of both number of publications and influence, in the area of taxation (many of these works have been collected in two anthologies of his articles; see 1983). Aside from the public sector economy, Feldstein is equally interested in macroeconomics and in growth theory. He is convinced of the existence of close and complex links between fiscal policy, the working of economies and the behaviour of agents. These links can only be ascertained through empirical studies, he holds.

Feldstein's influence has been due as much to his work as editor as to his own publications. As president of the National Bureau of Economic Research since 1977, he has been responsible for the many publications of this famous institution founded by Wesley Clair Mitchell in 1920. In commemoration of its sixtieth anniversary, he edited a work on the transformations of the US economy (1980). Underlining the slowing of growth and the rising inflation that have taken place since the 1960s, he expressed his conviction in this work 'that government policies do deserve substantial blame for the adverse experience of the past decade' (1980, p. 3). Since he considers governments to be shortsighted in their decision-making processes, Feldstein is among the advocates of a reduction in state intervention. As chief economic adviser to President Reagan from 1982 to 1984, he is one of the few economists who have been able to exercise influence through their direct access to political power (1992).

Main reference

BLAUG 1985, 58–9.

FELLNER William John (1905–1983)

Born in Budapest, William Fellner earned a diploma in chemical engineering in Zurich in 1927 and a doctorate in Berlin in 1929. After working in his family business in Hungary, he became assistant and then associate professor at the University of California at Berkeley (1939–52) and went on to become a professor at Yale University (1952–73). President of the American Economic Association in 1969, he was a member of the President's Council of Economic Advisers from 1973 to 1975. He died in the United States.

Main publications

1946. *Monetary Policies and Full Employment*, Berkeley, University of California Press.
1949. *Competition Among the Few*, New York, Alfred A. Knopf.
1955. *Trends and Cycles in Economic Activity*, New York, Holt, Rinehart and Winston.
1960. *Emergence and Content of Modern Economic Analysis*, New York, McGraw-Hill.
1965. *Probability and Profit*, Homewood, Illinois, Richard D. Irwin.
1976. *Towards a Reconstruction of Macroeconomics: Problems of Theory and Policy*, Washington, DC, American Enterprise Institute.
1976. 'Lessons from the Failure of Demand-Management Policies: A Look at the Theoretical Foundations', *Journal of Economic Literature* , vol. 14, 34–53.

Fellner worked in the areas of Keynesian theory, monopoly and oligopoly competition, price formation, uncertainty and expectation, monetary problems and growth in its relation to induced innovations and cycles. He had a continuing interest in economic policy, as witnessed by his 1946 and 1976 works. Fellner was never identified with a specific school or system, and he deplored false divisions. On the eve of the Second World War, as a circumspect Keynesian, he feared the prospect of lost efficiency and inflation resulting from activist policies of full employment; he recommended, rather, mixed policies which would allow for small fluctuations. Moreover, when he observed the failure of demand management policies in the 1970s, he was also circumspect with regard to monetarist arguments, not excluding the possibility that some types of unemployment might be fought through an expansionist policy, and he highlighted the responsibility of those in authority to create a climate of confidence favouring stable expectations.

Main references

BALASSA Bela and NELSON Richard 1977 (eds). *Economic Progress, Private Values, and Public Policy: Essays in Honor of William Fellner*, Amsterdam, North-Holland.

BLAUG *Who's Who* 1986, 263. *New Palgrave*, 1987, vol. 2, 301.

FOGEL Robert William (born 1926)

Born in New York, Robert Fogel earned his BA from Cornell University in 1948. He subsequently gained an MA from Columbia in 1960 and a PhD from Johns Hopkins in 1963. From 1960 to 1964, he was an assistant professor and later (1964–5) an associate professor at the University of Rochester, and then professor of economic history at the University of Chicago (1965–75). For part of this time he was also a professor at the University of Rochester (1968–75). He was later appointed professor at Harvard (1975–81) and, from 1981, once again professor at the University of Chicago, where he directed the Walgreen Foundation and the Center for Population Economics. He was awarded the Nobel Memorial Prize in Economics in 1993, along with Douglass North.

Main publications

1960. *The Union Pacific Railroad: A Case in Premature Enterprise*, Baltimore, Johns Hopkins.

1964. *Railroads and American Economic Growth: Essays in Econometric History*, Baltimore, Johns Hopkins.

1971 (ed., with S.L. Engerman *et al.*). *The Reinterpretation of American Economic History*, New York, Harper & Row.

1974. With S.L. Engerman, *Time on the Cross: The Economics of American Negro Slavery*, Boston, Little, Brown & Co.

1983. With G.R. Elton, *Which Road to the Past? Two Views of History*, New Haven, Connecticut, Yale University Press.

1989. *Without Consent or Contract: The Rise and Fall of American Slavery*, New York, W.W. Norton.

1991. With S.L. Engerman *et al.*, *Without Consent or Contract: The Rise and Fall of American Slavery, Evidence and Methods* (1 vol.); *Technical Papers* (2 vols), New York, W.W. Norton.

After his first book, on the history of a railroad company, Fogel published an essay in econometric history in 1964 that dealt with the role of railroads in the economic growth of the United States. This book is generally considered to represent the beginning of the new quantitative economic history, also known as cliometrics, a method that stresses the systematic econometric processing of quantitative data, whether general, semi-general or highly precise (having the family as its object). Fogel's position is that two paths of historic research now coexist: traditional history and 'scientific' or cliometric history. He nonetheless tempers the word 'scientific' with quotation marks and reassures traditional historians that: 'Cliometry has not made narrative history obsolete' (1983, p. 69). With his research team, Fogel has applied his method to many objects of study, in particular to American slavery, which he initially analysed economically so as to establish its profitability (1974), recently devoting new research to it (1989, 1991).

Main reference

BLAUG 1985, 60–61.

FRANK André Gunder (born 1929)

A.G. Frank was born in Berlin and left Germany for Switzerland with his family in 1933. They then moved to the USA, where he studied economics, earning a BA from Swarthmore College in 1950, and his MA and PhD from the University of Chicago in 1952 and 1957. Between 1954 and 1961, he held many research and teaching positions, first in the United States at the Universities of Chicago, Iowa, Michigan, California at Berkeley and Detroit, among others. Except from 1966 to 1968, which he spent in Montreal, he taught from 1962 to 1973 in Latin America, at the Universities of Brasilia, Rio de Janeiro, Santiago, Mexico and elsewhere, being professor at the University of Chile from 1970 to 1973. Since 1973 he has taught and done research in Europe, at the Starnberg Max Planck Institute (1974 to 1978), the University of East Anglia (1978 to 1985) and, since 1981, at the University of Amsterdam, where he directs the Institute for Socio-Economic Studies of Developing Regions (ISMOG).

Main publications

1967. *Capitalism and Underdevelopment in Latin America: Historical Studies of Chile and Brazil*, New York, Monthly Review Press.

1969. *Latin America: Underdevelopment or Revolution: Essays on the Development of Underdevelopment and the Immediate Enemy*, New York, Monthly Review Press.

1972. *Lumpenbourgeoisie, Lumpendevelopment: Dependency, Class and Politics in Latin America*, New York, Monthly Review Press.

1978. *World Accumulation, 1492–1789*, New York, Monthly Review Press.

1981. *Reflections on the World Economic Crisis*, New York, Monthly Review Press.

1989. With Marta Fuentes, 'Ten Theses on Social Movements', *World Development*, vol. 17, 179–92.

1990. 'A Theoretical Introduction to Five Thousand Years of World System History', *Review*, vol. 13, 155–248.

A.G. Frank was one of the most radical critics of the dominant theories of development of the 1960s, namely dualism, Rostow's stages of growth analysis and sociological explanations. He conducted studies on Brazil and Chile (1967) using the terms 'centres' and 'peripheries' to express hierarchical relations; he highlighted the notions of 'development of underdevelopment','capitalist underdevelopment' and 'lumpendevelopment' (1969, 1972): since the capitalist system is worldwide, development (of capitalist centres) and underdevelopment (of the peripheries) are two indissociable sides of the same phenomenon, that is global capitalist development, leaving only revolution as an alternative.

André G. Frank has also worked on the world system, its history (1978), and its current crisis interpreted in terms of long movements *à la* Kondratiev (1981). He has recently engaged a research on very long period development (1990).

Main reference

ARESTIS and SAWYER 1992, 154–63.

FRIEDMAN Milton (born 1912)

Born in Brooklyn, Milton Friedman is the son of Romanian immigrants. He studied at the University of Chicago and at Columbia University where he earned his PhD in 1946. In 1937, he became a member of the National Bureau of Economic Research (NBER) with which he remained associated until 1981. Friedman obtained a teaching position at the University of Chicago in 1946 which he held until 1977. He has been a member of the Mont Pèlerin Society since its foundation by a group of liberal intellectuals brought together by Friedrich Hayek in 1947, and served as its president from 1970 to 1972. Friedman contributed a regular column on economics in *Newsweek* magazine from 1966 to 1984. In 1964, he was an economic adviser to Republican presidential candidate Barry Goldwater and performed the same function for candidates Richard Nixon in 1968 and Ronald Reagan in 1980. He was a member of the Economic Policy Advisory Board, having been selected in 1981 by then President Reagan. Friedman was elected president of the American Economic Association in 1967 and received the Nobel Memorial Prize in Economics in 1976. Since 1977 he has been a senior fellow at the Hoover Institution of Stanford University in California.

Main publications

1945. With Simon Kuznets, *Income from Independent Professional Practice*, New York, National Bureau of Economic Research.

1948. 'A Monetary and Fiscal Framework for Economic Stability', *American Economic Review*, vol. 38, 245–64.
1951. 'Les Effets d'une politique de plein emploi sur la stabilité économique: Une Analyse formelle', *Économie appliquée*, vol. 4, 441–56; revised English version, 'The Effects of a Full-Employment Policy on Economic Stability: a Formal Analysis', in Friedman 1953, 117–32.
1953. *Essays in Positive Economics*, University of Chicago Press.
1956 (ed.). *Studies in the Quantity Theory of Money*, University of Chicago Press; London, Cambridge University Press.
1957. *A Theory of the Consumption Function*, Princeton University Press; London, Oxford University Press.
1960. *A Program for Monetary Stability*, New York, Fordham University Press.
1962. *Capitalism and Freedom*, University of Chicago Press.
1962. *Price Theory*, Chicago, Aldine.
1963. With D. Meiselman, 'The Relative Stability of Monetary Velocity and the Investment Multiplier in the United States, 1897–1958', in E. Cary Brown *et al.*, *Stabilization Policies*, Englewood Cliffs, New Jersey, Prentice-Hall, 165–268.
1963. With A.J. Schwartz, *A Monetary History of the United States, 1867–1960*, Princeton University Press for the National Bureau of Economic Research.
1968. *Dollars and Deficits: Inflation, Monetary Policy and the Balance of Payments*, Englewood Cliffs, New Jersey, Prentice-Hall.
1968. 'The Role of Monetary Policy', *American Economic Review*, vol. 58, 1–17.
1969. *The Optimum Quantity of Money and Other Essays*, Chicago, Aldine.
1969. With W.W. Heller, *Monetary vs Fiscal Policy: A Dialogue*, New York, W.W. Norton.
1970. *The Counter-Revolution in Monetary Theory*, London, Institute of Economic Affairs.
1970. With A.J. Schwartz, *Monetary Statistics of the United States: Estimates, Sources, Methods*, New York, Columbia University Press for the National Bureau of Economic Research.
1971. *A Theoretical Framework for Monetary Analysis*, New York, National Bureau of Economic Research.
1972. *An Economist's Protest: Columns in Political Economy*, Glen Ridge, New Jersey, Thomas Horton & Daughters; 2nd edn 1975, *There's no such Thing as a Free Lunch*, Lassalle, Illinois, Open Court; 3rd edn 1983, *Bright Promises, Dismal Performance: An Economist's Protest*, New York, Harcourt Brace Jovanovich.
1977. *From Galbraith to Economic Freedom*, London, Institute of Economic Affairs.
1977. 'Nobel Lecture: Inflation and Unemployment', *Journal of Political Economy*, vol. 85, 451–72.
1980. With Rose Friedman, *Free to Choose: A Personal Statement*, New York, Harcourt Brace Jovanovich.
1982. With A.J. Schwartz, *Monetary Trends in the United States and the United Kingdom: Their Relation to Income, Prices, and Interest Rates, 1867–1975*, University of Chicago Press.
1984. With Rose Friedman, *Tyranny of Status Quo*, San Diego, Harcourt Brace Jovanovich.
1986. 'My Evolution as an Economist', in Breit and Spencer 1986, 77–92.
1987. *The Essence of Friedman*, edited by K.R. Leube, Stanford, Hoover Institution Press.
1991. *Monetarist Economics*, Oxford, Basil Blackwell.
1992. *Money Mischief: Episodes in Monetary History*, New York, Harcourt Brace Jovanovich.

Since the late 1950s Milton Friedman has established himself as the leading opponent of Keynesian interventionism, the most dynamic advocate of thoroughgoing liberalism and the principal instigator of new economic policies implemented since the 1970s. His name is associated with monetarism. Friedman vigorously defends his political vision, enjoying the controversy he provokes. In his exposition of political philosophy (1962 *Capitalism*), he asserts that market mechanisms are enough to regulate most of the economic and social problems of our time. Thus he holds that the power of the state should be reduced to the minimum and decentralized, since the foundation of political freedom is free enterprise. Friedman advocates replacing all social welfare programmes with a negative income tax. He witnessed the triumph of his views in the 1970s. In order to disseminate them, he has used the entire media, including newspapers and popular magazines, as well as radio and television. Friedman has assumed the task of popularizing his own ideas, which has undoubtedly helped him to become the most widely known contemporary economist.

However, Friedman is primarily a theorist and it is as such that his ideas have established themselves, in spite of the fact that his fellow economists initially disparaged them. The Swedish Royal Academy of Sciences awarded him the Nobel Prize 'for his achievements in the fields of consumption analysis, monetary history and theory, and for this demonstration of the complexity of stabilization policy' (*SJE* 1977, p. 54). His many contributions attest an unshakeable faith in the market mechanism in the resolution of problems of production and resource allocation. Price theory was one of the main subjects that he taught at the University of Chicago and it inspired a textbook (1962 *Price*) which contains some of the contributions he has made and considers to be among his most important achievements.

Friedman's work is based on methodological positions made public in 1953 and which immediately inspired a continuing debate. In his approach, Friedman defends the view that holds economics to be as much an empirical science as the natural sciences. He maintains that it develops statements, primarily of a predictive nature, which should be subject to falsification by empirical testing. It is his view that the correspondence of the initial hypotheses used in this process to reality is not in and of itself important; rather, a theory should be rejected because of the refutation of its deducted predictions by empirical testing, and not because of a lack of correspondence in the sense indicated above. Thus, for Friedman, criticisms of neoclassical price theory which are based upon the allegation that its hypotheses are not 'realistic' are irrelevant.

This approach is implemented in a study of the consumption function (1957), a factor of central importance in Keynesian theory. In this work, considered by many to be his main scholarly contribution, Friedman sets forth the permanent income hypothesis (which he had already touched upon in 1945), which affirms that the greater part of consumption is not linked to current income, as held by Keynes, but rather to its principal part, termed 'permanent income'. From this he concludes that modern economies are more stable than Keynesians have thought.

Friedman is chiefly known for this reinstatement of the quantity theory of money (1956, 1969 *The Optimum*). Of his principal thesis, which holds that all variations in the money supply are followed by corresponding variations in prices, production and incomes, Friedman asserts that this constitutes a law which has been observed for centuries and which has the same regularity as the laws of the natural sciences. He holds inflation to be a strictly monetary pheonomenon. Over a 25 year period Friedman carried out a lengthy study for the NBER with Anna J. Schwartz on the monetary history of the United States (1963, 1970, 1982; in this last book, the analysis is extended to the United Kingdom). The results demonstrated to his advantage the empirical validity of his version of the quantity theory of money (1971). In particular, Friedman and Schwartz showed that cyclical fluctuations are, if not provoked, at least aggravated by erratic monetary policies. Thus the Federal Reserve System is in the final analysis to be held responsible for the severity of the Great Depression (1963 with A.J. Schwartz). It is because of this that Friedman advocates his famous monetary rule: decree, in the constitution if possible, that the money supply must vary at a constant long-term growth rate, which is to be equal to the growth rate of national product. In a study carried out with David Meiselmen (1963) for the NBER, Friedman claims to have refuted the corresponding Keynesian analysis definitively by showing that, in the long run, the relationship between the quantity of money and income is far more stable than that between autonomous expenditures and income, a link termed 'the multiplier'. Yet Friedman thinks that a simplistic version of the quantity theory is usually opposed to an equally simplistic version of Keynes's theory and that his own theory (1971) encompasses the above two theories as particular cases. Briefly put, the counter-revolution which Friedman claims to have started at the end ot the 1950s retained certain elements of the Keynesian revolution (1970 *The Counter-Revolution*).

In Friedman's view, economic policies have no real effects on the economy in the long run. In his famous presidential address before the American Economic Association, Friedman put forward the concept of a natural rate of unemployment (1968 *AER*). He holds that, at any given moment in an economy, there is a natural rate of unemployment determined by a number of real forces, such as the structure of the labour market, the imperfections of the market-place and unemployment insurance. Any effort to lower the unemployment rate to a point below the natural rate would, if unemployment were maintained at such a low level, trigger a steadily increasing rate of inflation. This hypothesis rests on the taking into account of an expectation of rising prices on the part of economic agents, implying that the Phillips curve is vertical in the long term rather than indicative of a negative relationship between the rates of unemployment and inflation. Friedman asserts that one might even observe a positive Phillips curve (1977 *JPE*) in that the inflation and unemployment rates would from that point increase together, stimulating each other. This novel phenomemon could be accounted for by political considerations factored into the models used.

Initially decried as reactionary, if not clearly erroneous, Friedman's positions have gradually imposed themselves. Friedman shares with Keynes the ability to provoke controversy and the power to emerge from it victoriously, as well as the ability to impose a new orthodoxy. Much like those of Keynes, his views are contested emphatically, even by his own disciples.

Main references

'The Nobel Prize in Economics 1976'. Official announcement, article by Niels Thygesen and bibliography, *Swedish Journal of Economics*, 1977, vol. 79, 54–97.

BUTLER E. 1985. *Milton Friedman: A Guide to his Economics*, Aldershot, Hants, Gower; New York, Universe Books.

FRAZER W. 1988. *Power and Ideas: Milton Friedman and the Big U-Turn*, Gainesville, Florida, Gulf/Atlantic.

GORDON Robert J. 1974 (ed.). *Milton Friedman's Monetary Framework: A Debate with his Critics*, University of Chicago Press.

HIRSCH Abraham and DE MARCHI Neil 1990. *Milton Friedman: Economics in Theory and Practice*, Ann Arbor, University of Michigan Press.

LAVOIE Marc and SECCARECCIA Mario 1993 (eds). *Milton Friedman et son oeuvre*, Montreal, Presses de l'Université de Montréal.

SELDEN Richard T. 1975 (ed.). *Capitalism and Freedom*, Charlottesville, University of Virginia Press.

WOOD John Cunningham and WOODS Ronald N. 1990 (eds). *Milton Friedman. Critical Assessments*, 4 vols, London, Routledge.

BLAUG 1985, 62–3. BREIT and RANSOM 1971, 223–56. *New Palgrave* 1987, vol. 2, 422–7. SHACKLETON and LOCKSLEY 1981, 53–71. SILK 1976, 45–93. SOBEL 1980, 144–74.

FRISCH Ragnar Anton Kittil (1895–1973)

Ragnar Frisch was born in Oslo and was apprenticed as a goldsmith, his father's trade, while pursuing his studies in economics at Oslo University where he graduated in 1919. He continued his studies in France (1921–3) and in Great Britain (1923), being awarded a doctorate in mathematical statistics at Oslo University in 1926. After stays in the United States, France and Italy (1927–8), he taught for two years at Oslo University and was subsequently invited to Yale University. So as to bring him home to Norway, a chair in economics was created in 1931 at Oslo University, a position which he held until his retirement in 1965. From its creation in 1932 until 1965 he directed the Institute for Social Economy of Oslo University.

Frisch was an adviser to the Norwegian Labour Party during the 1930s and the immediate postwar period; he carried out numerous missions to the governments of India (1954–5) and Egypt (1957–64). Having received many governments of India (1954–5) and Egypt (1957–64). Having received many other distinctions, he received in 1969 the newly created Nobel Memorial Prize in Economics, jointly with Jan Tinbergen.

Main publications

1926. 'Sur un problème d'économie pure', *Norsk Matematisk Forenings Skrifter*, no. 16, 1–40; repr. 1957, *Metroeconomica*, vol. 9, 79–111.
1929. 'Statikk og dynamikk i den okonomiske teorie' [Statics and dynamics in economic theory], *Nationalokonomisk Tidsskrift*, vol. 67, 321–79.
1932. *New Methods of Measuring Marginal Utility*, Tübingen, Mohr.
1933. 'Propagation Problems and Impulse Problems in Dynamic Economics', in *Economic Essays in Honor of Gustav Cassel*, London, George Allen & Unwin, 171–205.
1934. 'Circulation Planning', *Econometrica*, vol. 2, 258–336 and 422–35.
1936. 'On the Notion of Equilibrium and Disequilibrium', *Review of Economic Studies*, vol. 3, 100–105.
1947. *Noen trekk av konjunkturlæren* [Elements of business cycle theory], Oslo, H. Aschehoug & Co.
1950. 'Alfred Marshall's Theory of Value', *Quarterly Journal of Economics*, vol. 64, 495–524.
1950. 'L'emploi des modèles pour l'élaboration d'une politique économique rationnelle', *Revue d'économie politique*, vol. 60, 474–99 and 601–35.
1952. 'Wicksell', in H.W. Spiegel (ed.), *The Development of Economic Thought: Great Economists in Perspective*, New York, John Wiley, 652–99.
1954. 'La théorie de l'avantage collectif et les régions de Pareto', *Économie appliquée*, vol. 7, 211–80.
1956. 'Macroeconomics and Linear Programming', in 'Twenty-Five Economic Essays in Honour of Erik Lindahl', *Ekonomisk Tidskrift*, vol. 58, 38–67.
1959. 'A Complete Scheme for Computing all Direct and Cross-Demand Elasticities in a Model with Many Sectors', *Econometrica*, vol. 27, 177–96.
1960. *Maxima et minima: Théorie et applications économiques*, Paris, Dunod; Engl. transl. 1966, *Maximas and Minimas*, Dordrecht, D. Reidel.
1960. *Planning for India: Selected Explorations in Methodology*, New York, Asia Publishing House.
1962. *Innledning til produksjonsteorien*, Oslo, Universitets Forlaget; Engl. transl. 1965, *Theory of Production*, Dordrecht, D. Reidel; Chicago, Rand McNally.
1970. 'Econometrics in the World of Today', in W.A. Eltis, M.F. Scott and J.N. Wolfe (eds), *Induction Growth and Trade: Essays in Honour of Sir Roy Harrod*, Oxford, Clarendon Press, 152–66.
1976. *Economic Planning Studies: A Collection of Essays*, Dordrecht, D. Reidel.

Most of Frisch's work is in Norwegian; of his approximately 400 scientific papers, perhaps a mere quarter have been published in English, either directly or by translation. His work covers a large field, beginning in the 1920s, with work in mathematics and mathematical statistics published in Norway and in France and moving into economics through a rigorous mathematical treatment of consumer theory (1926, 1932). It embodies publications that have proved to be of pioneer value in numerous fields: the methodological elaboration of the concepts of macroeconomics, of statics and dynamics (1929) and of equilibrium and disequilibrium (1936), the construction of the first macrodynamic model explaining cycles (1933), an outline of the input–output approach and, two years before Keynes's *General Theory*, an analysis of the processes of production and circulation in an economy undergoing a depression due to an insufficiency of demand (1934).

From 1930 on, Frisch worked on putting foward and developing econometrics, which he conceived of as the unification of economic theory, mathematics and statistics. He was one of the founders (1930) of the Econometric Society. He was editor of *Econometrica*, the society's journal, from its creation in 1933 until 1955, the year in which he became chairman of its editorial board. In this journal's first issue, he wrote: 'The policy of *Econometrica* will be as heartily to denounce futile playing with mathematical symbols in economics as to encourage their constructive use' (*Econometrica*, vol. 1, 1933, p. 3). His work deals mainly with linear models, the analysis of multiple data systems and the estimate of parameters in dealing with correlated explanatory variables. In the 1950s and 1960s, he explored different methods of linear programming: the logarithmic potential method, the multiplex method and the nonplex method.

All the while pursuing his efforts to reveal the laws of economic dynamics and cycles (1947), he systematized the study of production, notably analysing the temporal structures of production processes (1962). He had an important influence on the elaboration of national accounting in the Scandinavian countries and worked at constructing tools and models which would serve to implement economic policy and rational planning, constantly keeping in mind the practical questions of economic development and of development planning (1950 *REP*, 1960 *Planning* and articles reprinted in 1976).

Pushing rigour to the point of perfection so that frequently he had either to refrain from publishing or at least to delay the publication of many of his works, Frisch was highly conscious of the scholar's social responsibility. In his view, econometrics must, in order not to engage in futile games, stay in touch with practical realities (1970) and the economist should not allow himself to be discouraged by the fact that the problems that form the object of his work are infinitely more complex than those studied by the physicist.

Main references

'The First Nobel Prize in Economics'. Official announcement, and article by L. Johansen, and bibliography, *Swedish Journal of Economics*, 1969, vol. 71, 300–324; article repr. in SPIEGEL and SAMUELS 1984, 299–317.

ANDVIG Jens C. 1985. *Ragnar Frisch and the Great Depression: A Study in the Interwar History of Macroeconomics Theory and Policy*, Oslo, Norwegian Institute of International Affairs.

ARROW Kenneth J. 1960. 'The Work of Ragnar Frisch, Econometrician', *Econometrica*, vol. 28, 175–92.

BLAUG Mark 1992 (ed.). *Pioneers in Economics*, section 4, *Twentieth Century Economics*, vol. 41, Aldershot, Hants, Edward Elgar.

European Economic Review, 1974, vol. 5, 3–66, with contributions by Jan Tinbergen, Paul Samuelson and Leif Johansen.

EVARDSEN Kare 1970. 'A Survey of Ragnar Frisch's Contribution to the Science of Economics', *De Economist*, vol. 118, 174–96.

BLAUG 1985, 66–7. *New Palgrave* 1987, vol. 2, 428–30. SILLS 1979, 211–15.

FURTADO Celso (born 1920)

Celso Furtado was born in Pombal, in the state of Paraiba, Brazil; he studied in Rio de Janeiro and entered Brazilian public service in 1943, subsequently earning his doctorate in Paris in 1948. He directed the Development Division of the United Nations Commission on Latin America (1950–57), the Brazilian National Development Bank (1958–9) and the Development Agency of North-East Brazil (1959–63) before becoming the Minister of Planning (1963–64). Deprived of his political rights following the military coup d'état in 1964, he taught at American universities, was a professor at the University of Paris (1965–79) and went on to become research director at the Ecole des Hautes Etudes en Sciences Sociales. In 1985–6, he was the Brazilian ambassador to the European Economic Community, and from 1986 to 1988 he was Brazil's Minister of Culture.

Main publications

1952. 'Formação de capital e desenvolvimento econômico', *Revista Brasileira de Economia*, vol. 6, no. 3; Engl. transl. 1954, 'Capital Formation and Economic Development', *International Economic Papers*, no. 4, 124–44.

1959. *Formação econômica do Brasil*, Rio de Janeiro, Fundo de Cultura; Engl. transl. 1963, *The Economic Growth of Brazil*, Berkeley, University of California Press.

1961. *Desenvolvimento e subdesenvolvimento*, Rio de Janeiro, Fundo de Cultura; Engl. transl. 1964, *Development and underdevelopment*, Berkeley, University of California Press.

1964. *Dialética do desenvolvimento: diagnostico de la crisis del Brezil*, Rio de Janeiro, Fundo de Cultura; Engl. transl. 1965, *Diagnosis of the Brazilian Crisis*, Berkeley, University of California Press.

1967. *Subdesenvolvimento e estagnação na América latina*, Rio de Janeiro, Civilização Brasileira; and 1968, *Um Projeto para o Brasil*, Rio de Janeiro, Fundo de Cultura; Engl. transl. 1970, *Obstacles to Development in Latin America*, Garden City, New York, Anchor Books.

1967. *Teoria e politica do desenvolvimento econômico* [Theory and policy of economic development], São Paulo, Companhia editorial national.

1969. *Formação econômica da América Latina*, Rio de Janeiro, Lia Editora; Engl. transl. 1970, *Economic Development of Latin America*, Cambridge, England, Cambridge University Press.

1972. *Analise do 'modelo' brasileiro* [Analysis of the Brazilian 'model'], Rio de Janeiro, Paz e Terra.

1973. 'Aventures d'un économiste brésilien', *Revue internationale des sciences sociales*, vol. 25, 28–39.

1974. *O Mito do desenvolvimento econômico* [The myth of economic development], Rio de Janeiro, Paz e Terra.

1978. *Criatividade e dependência na civilização industrial*, Rio de Janeiro, Paz e Terra; Engl. transl. 1983, *Accumulation and Development: The Logic of Industrial Civilization*, Oxford, Martin Robertson.

1980. *Pequena introdução ao desenvolvimento. Enfoque interdisciplinar* [Brief introduction to development: an interdisciplinary approach], São Paulo, Companhia editorial national.

1981. *O Brasil pós-'milagre'* [Brazil after the 'miracle'], Rio de Janeiro, Paz e Terra.
1985. *A Fantasia organizada* [The organized fantasy], Rio de Janeiro, Paz e Terra.
1987. *Transformãçao e crise na economia mundial* [Transformation and crisis in the world economy], Rio de Janeiro, Paz e Terra.
1989. *A Fantasia desfeita* [The fantasy defeated], Rio de Janeiro, Paz e Terra.
1991. *Os ares do mundo* [The world's appearances], Rio de Janeiro, Paz e Terra.
1992. *A construção interrompida [The interrupted construction*], Rio de Janeiro, Paz e Terra.

Furtado has written primarily on growth, underdevelopment and development policies in Brazil and, more generally, in Latin America. In his first works, he analysed the historical process of the formation and transformation of Brazil's economy and brought out, without excessive systemization, the dislocation of industrializing economies as well as their dependence on foreign forces, notably with reference to exchange (1959, 1961, 1964). Then, retaining his descriptive methodology, he took up a moderate analysis in terms of dependence, highlighting what he holds to be the fact that development and underdevelopment are two aspects of the same process, and deepened the analysis of Brazil's (as well as other Latin American countries') relations with their polar centre, the United States, all the while paying due attention to the internal factors (political, social, cultural) contributing to the slowing down or total interruption of accumulation (books of 1967, 1972 and 1974).

In his recent works, Furtado has placed a greater emphasis on both the 'transnationalization' and the globalization of economy, notably with reference to debt, as well as the social and cultural aspects of development, noting that development theory has tended to 'fuse with the explanation of the behaviour of the productive system which is to emerge with industrial society'; in order to 'conceive of development as a global process', he constructed 'a conceptual framework which can allow for the understanding of society in its many dimensions' (1980, pp. 8–9 of the French translation, *Brève introduction au développement: Une Approche interdisciplinaire*, Paris, Publisud, 1989).

Main references

FURTADO 1973.

BLAUG *Who's Who* 1986, 295–6.

GALBRAITH John Kenneth (born 1908)

John Kenneth Galbraith was born in Canada, in a rural, predominantly Scottish Ontario community. Having begun his studies in agronomy, he studied agricultural economics at the University of California at Berkeley, earning his doctorate there in 1934. From then on, his career developed in the United States. Appointed instructor in agricultural economics at Harvard in 1936, he also taught at Princeton, later becoming deputy administrator of the Price Section of the Office of Price Administration (1941–3). After 1943, he was assigned several public missions, notably related to the economies of occupied countries. In 1948, he returned to Harvard, becoming professor of economics in 1949; he retired in 1975 with the title professor emeritus.

Galbraith has written many books and articles, given many conferences and written in diverse periodicals ranging from the *New York Times* to *Playboy.* He was a personal adviser to President Kennedy, ambassador to India (1961–3), president of Americans for Democratic Action (1967–9), president of the American Economic Association (1972) and president of the American Academy and Institute of Arts and Letters (1984–7).

Main publications

1938. With Henry S. Dennison, *Modern Competition and Business Policy*, New York, Oxford University Press.

1952. *A Theory of Price Control*, Cambridge, Massachusetts, Harvard University Press.

1952. *American Capitalism: The Concept of Countervailing Power*, Boston, Houghton Mifflin.

1955. *Economics and the Art of Controversy*, New Brunswick, New Jersey, Rutgers University Press.

1955. *The Great Crash, 1929*, Boston, Houghton Mifflin.

1958. *The Affluent Society*, Boston, Houghton Mifflin.

1960. *The Liberal Hour*, Boston, Houghton Mifflin.

1962. *Economic Development in Perspective*, Cambridge, Massachusetts, Harvard University Press.

1967. *How to Get out of Vietnam*, New York, New American Library.

1967. *The New Industrial State*, Boston, Houghton Mifflin.

1969. *Ambassador's Journal*, Boston, Houghton Mifflin.

1971. *A Contemporary Guide to Economics, Peace and Laughter*, edited by Andrea D. Williams, Boston, Houghton Mifflin.

1973. *Economics and the Public Purpose*, Boston, Houghton Mifflin.

1975. *Money, Whence it Came, Where it Went*, Boston, Houghton Mifflin.

1977. *The Age of Uncertainty*, Boston, Houghton Mifflin.

1979. *Annals of an Abiding Liberal*, Boston, Houghton Mifflin.

1979. *The Nature of Mass Poverty*, Cambridge, Massachusetts, Harvard University Press.

1981. *A Life in our Times: Memoirs*, Boston, Houghton Mifflin.

1983. *The Anatomy of Power*, Boston, Houghton Mifflin.

1983. *The Voice of the Poor*, Cambridge, Massachusetts, Harvard University Press.

1987. *Economics in Perspective. A Critical History*, Boston, Houghton Mifflin; British edition, *A History of Economics: the Past as the Present*, London, Hamish Hamilton.

1988. With S.M. Menshikov, *Capitalism, Communism and Coexistence*, Boston, Houghton Mifflin.

1990. *A Short History of Financial Euphoria*, Knoxville, Tennessee, Whittle Communications.

1990. *A Tenured Professor*, Boston, Houghton Mifflin.
1992. *The Culture of Contentment*, Boston, Houghton Mifflin.

Along with the rest of his generation, J.K. Galbraith was deeply affected by the crash of 1929, to which he devoted a 1955 work, by the New Deal, and by interventionist and Keynesian ideas. His first work (1938), co-authored with a liberal industrialist, highlighted market imperfections and the economy's rigidities, offering a sketch of a regulation programme for industry. After the Second World War, he argued once again for state intervention and price control (1952 *A Theory)*. He has written on American policy (1960, 1967 *How to Get*, 1977, 1979 *Annals*), development (1962, 1983 *The Voice)*, poverty (1979 *The Nature*), economics (1955, 1971, 1975, 1987) and a number of other subjects having little to do with economics.

Four major books distinguish his work. *American Capitalism* (1952) depicts the American economy as dominated by the major corporations, with a high level of concentration. Rather than express concern about this fact, Galbraith accepts the system as it is, pointing out its efficiency; in his view, a new equilibrium has resulted from the development of 'countervailing powers' (unions, major commercial chains) counterbalancing the power of the major firms.

In *The Affluent Society* (1958), his vision is less optimistic; although it is certainly the case that the system proves efficient in producing more and more consumer goods, the consumers are increasingly subject to advertising pressures that render the very notion of consumer sovereignty devoid of meaning. Moreover, private affluence stands in direct contrast to public squalor; roads, schools, public housing, museums and the police are neglected and the very framework of life and the environment is degraded. Growth is not a panacea; rather, it is necessary to reaffirm the value of public action, which must have greater means at its disposal (although this might very well involve a reduction in military expenditures). He also advocates improving the quality of education so as to render citizen-consumers better able to choose.

In *The New Industrial State* (1967), Galbraith once again underlines the role of big business which must, so as to strengthen itself and guarantee the research that allows for technological innovation, obtain state support, control the market (notably through advertising) and, in its own way, plan ahead. Power is no longer in the hands of the entrepreneur, but in the 'technostructure': salaried managers and technicians who have the knowledge required by those of the system. Anxious to safeguard its autonomy, the technostructure seeks to satisfy its shareholders and to maintain growth, growth being the best guarantee of its survival and also the goal of the military leadership. Yet this growth leaves the main problems of society untouched, and at times aggravates them. In this work, Galbraith also makes an appeal for a renewal of public policy and a new burst of dynamism from the professional and intellectual elites.

In *Economics and the Public Purpose* (1973), Galbraith continues his attempt to construct an overall vision of contemporary affairs. He distinguishes two sectors in the economy, the planning system and the market system, the first consisting of large firms and the second of small businesses dependent upon the market. In this analysis he takes into account the question of the state and transnationalization. In keeping with his earlier analyses, he shows that this state of affairs creates distortions, instability and inflation; he advocates major reforms aimed at freeing the state from the power of private enterprise, at creating a better balance between the market sector and the planning sector, at ensuring a better national and international coordination of planning and at reconciling the interests of the citizenry and of consumers with a genuine respect for the environment.

Thus, in a period of increasing formalization in economics, Galbraith effected a major contribution to the analysis of the institutions and tendencies of American capitalism; and, at a time of rising liberalism, he advanced views approaching those of European democratic socialism.

Main references

FRIEDMAN Milton 1977. *From Galbraith to Economic Freedom*, London, Institute of Economic Affairs.
GALBRAITH 1969, 1981.
GAMBS John S. 1975. *John Kenneth Galbraith*, Boston, Twayne.
HESSION C.H. 1972. *John Kenneth Galbraith and his Critics*, New York, New American Library.
Journal of Economic Issues 1989, vol. 23, 357–416: 'The Economic Legacy of John Kenneth Galbraith'.
MUNRO C. Lynn 1977. *The Galbraithian Vision: The Cultural Criticism of John Kenneth Galbraith*, Washington, DC, University Press of America.
REISMAN David 1980. *Galbraith and Market Capitalism*, London, Macmillan; New York University Press.
SHARPE M.E. 1973. *John Kenneth Galbraith and the Lower Economics*, London, Macmillan.

ARESTIS and SAWYER 1992, 164–70. BLAUG 1985, 68–70. BREIT and RANSOM 1971, 159–88. *New Palgrave* 1987, vol. 2, 455. SHACKLETON and LOCKSLEY 1981, 72–86. SILK 1976, 95–148. SILLS 1979, 223–6. SOBEL 1980, 66–92. SPIEGEL and SAMUELS 1984, 657–85.

GAREGNANI Pierangelo (born 1930)

Pierangelo Garegnani was born in Milan. He first studied at the University of Pavia and then at Cambridge, England, where he obtained his PhD in 1958. He started teaching at the University of Sassari in 1962. He was named professor there in 1963, before successively moving to the universities of

Pavia (1966), Florence (1970) and Rome (1974). Piero Sraffa named him literary executor of his work.

Main publications

1960. *Il capitale nelle teorie della distribuzione*, Milano, Giuffré.
1966. 'Switching of Techniques', *Quarterly Journal of Economics*, vol. 80, 554–67.
1970. 'Heterogeneous Capital, the Production Function and the Theory of Distribution', *Review of Economic Studies*, vol. 37, 407–36.
1976. 'On a Change in the Notion of Equilibrium in Recent Work on Value and Distribution', in M. Brown, K. Sato and P. Zarembka (eds), *Essays in Modern Capital Theory*, Amsterdam, North-Holland, 25–45.
1978–9. 'Notes on Consumption, Investment and Effective Demand', *Cambridge Journal of Economics*, vol. 2, 335–53 and vol. 3, 63–82.
1981. *Marx e gli economisti classici* [Marx and the Classical economists], Torino, Einaudi.
1985. 'Capital et demande effective', in A. Barrère (ed.), *Keynes aujourd'hui: théories et politiques*, Paris, Économica, 195–222.
1985. 'La théorie classique de la répartition et le problème dit de la "transformation" chez Marx', in G. Dostaler (ed.), *Un Echiquier centenaire: Théorie de la valeur et formation des prix*, Paris, La Découverte; Québec, Presses de l'Université du Québec, 157–81.
1987. 'Surplus Approach to Value and Distribution', *New Palgrave*, vol. 4, 560–74.

The renaissance of Ricardian thought, with the neo-Ricardian school, is generally associated with the name of Piero Sraffa. His compatriot Pierangelo Garegnani also played an important role in this process. His book, *Capital in the Theory of Distribution* (1960), stemming from his doctoral dissertation, appeared in Italian in the same year as Sraffa's *Production of Commodities by Means of Commodities*. The two books arrived, by different means, at similar conclusions. Both contain a fundamental critique of the marginalist theory of distribution, and as such they constitute the point of departure for the controversy between the two Cambridges, in which Garegnani was one of the most active players (1966, 1970).

Garegnani distinguishes two approaches to the problem of distribution in the history of economic thought. To the surplus approach, developed by the physiocrats, Smith, Ricardo and Marx, is opposed the modern approach based on the marginal productivity of factors of production. He considers that the two approaches encounter the same difficulty: the necessity of measuring capital in terms which are independent of variations in distribution and which are, at the same time, in a definable relation to the value of capital. However, while this problem is unsolvable in the marginalist framework, it may be resolved in the surplus approach. Indeed, one can show how the profit rate is determined, in a non-circular manner, beginning either from Sraffa's model or from the one suggested by Garegnani in his book.

Garegnani has tried to achieve a synthesis of the classical–Marxian approach to value and distribution, modified by Sraffa, and the Keynesian theory of effective demand. He argues that the latter can be given an interpretation in terms of long-run equilibrium which allows 'the liberation of the novel part of Keynes theory from the weight of the traditional part which, in the meantime, had caused the former to be practically forgotten' (in Barrère 1985, p. 198). This interpretation gave rise to lively debates between neo-Ricardians and post-Keynesians.

Main references

ROBINSON Joan 1979. 'Garegnani on Effective Demand', *Cambridge Journal of Economics*, vol. 3, 179–80.

ARESTIS and SAWYER 1992, 170–79.

GEORGESCU-ROEGEN Nicholas (born 1906)

Nicholas Georgescu-Roegen was born to a modest family in Constanza, Romania. He studied mathematics at the University of Bucharest, obtained his doctorate in statistics from the Sorbonne (Paris) in 1930 and subsequently worked in London with Karl Pearson. He was a professor at the University of Bucharest from 1932 to 1946 and spent two years in Harvard University's economics department (1934–6), while J. Schumpeter was teaching there. He was also the assistant director of the Central Statistical Institute in Bucharest from 1932 to 1938, director of the Board of Trade from 1939 to 1944, and secretary-general of the Romanian Armistice Commission in 1944–5. He emigrated to the United States in 1948 and was employed as lecturer and associate researcher by Harvard University (1948–9), subsequently being appointed professor of economics at Vanderbilt University (Nashville, Tennessee) in 1949, retiring with the status of professor emeritus in 1976.

Main publications

1933. *Metoda Statistica*, Bucarest, Biblioteca Institutului Central de Statistica.
1936. 'The Pure Theory of Consumer's Behavior', *Quarterly Journal of Economics*, vol. 50, 545–93.
1951. 'The Aggregate Linear Production Function and its Applications to von Neumann's Economic Model', in T. Koopmans (ed.), *Activity Analysis of Production and Allocation*, New York, John Wiley & Sons; London, Chapman & Hall, 98–115.
1960. 'Economic Theory and Agrarian Economics', *Oxford Economic Papers*, vol. 12, 1–40.
1966. *Analytical Economics: Issues and Problems*, Cambridge, Massachusetts, Harvard University Press.
1971. *The Entropy Law and the Economic Process*, Cambridge, Massachusetts, Harvard University Press.
1976. *Energy and Economic Myths: Institutional and Analytical Economic Essays*, Oxford, Pergamon Press.
1978. 'De la science économique à la bioéconomie', *Revue d'économie politique*, vol. 88, 337–82.
1979. *Demain la décroissance: Entropie, écologie, économie*, Lausanne, Pierre-Marcel Favre.
1979. 'Methods in Economic Science', *Journal of Economic Issues*, vol. 13, 317–28.
1980. *Entropy and Economic Myths*, Ottawa, Science Council of Canada.

1982. 'La dégradation entropique et la destinée prométhéenne de la technologie humaine', *Économie appliquée*, vol. 35, 1–26.
1983. 'Hermann Heinrich Gossen: His Life and Work in Historical Perspective', introduction to H.H. Gossen, *The Laws of Human Relations and the Rules of Human Actions Derived Therefrom*, Cambridge, Massachusetts, MIT Press, xi–cxiv.
1988, 'An Emigrant From a Developing Country: Autobiographical Notes I', *Quarterly Review, Banca Nazionale del Lavoro*, no. 164, 3–32; in Kregel 1989, 99–127.
1992. 'Nicholas Georgescu-Roegen about Himself', in Szenberg 1992, 128-59.

Georgescu-Roegen came from mathematics to statistics, and then to economics and epistemology; his research encompasses all of the fields of the natural and social sciences. His first publications on Pareto, on the pure theory of consumer behaviour (1936) as well as his work on the production function and Leontief's system (1951) earned him his place among economists in spite of the troublesome questions he raised. However, Georgescu-Roegen soon proved to be a dissenting economist. Having known all too well the problems of peasant economies, he denied that the marginal analysis of prices was valid for such economies (1960). He highlighted the fact that the Arrow–Debreu general equilibrium model implies that each individual disposes of an income sufficient for him or her to live on. He also challenged the neoclassical dogma according to which the price mechanism alone is capable of ensuring the rational allocation of resources from generation to generation (1971); he criticized the growth paradigm, without taking up the stationary state thesis (1976, 1979 *Methods)*.

Georgescu-Roegen also criticized 'arithmomorphism', a procedure that involves reducing the subject-matter of economics to that which can be measured, proposing rather to complete analysis by dialectics (1966, 1971). He has increasingly emphasized the need to take into account the use of non-renewable energy sources and their degradation, and waste in the analysis of the production process. In this, his economic analysis forms the link between the 'metabolism' of biology and the 'entropy' of thermodynamics (1971, 1976, 1979 *Demain*, 1980, 1982). Concerned with rendering economics more humane (see the manifesto signed 'Dai Dong' published in 1974 in *AER*, vol. 64, *Papers and Proceedings*, pp. 449–50), he worked on establishing a new approach to the discipline, 'bioeconomics' (1976, 1978). Isolated in the economic profession, Georgescu-Roegen is increasingly viewed as a precursor, especially in environmentalist circles.

Main references

DRAGAN J.C. and DEMETRESCU M.C. 1986. *Entropy and Bioeconomics: The New Paradigm of Nicholas Georgescu-Roegen*, Milan, Nagard Editrice.
GEORGESCU-ROEGEN 1988, 1992.
GRINEVALD Jacques 1980. 'La perspective bioéconomique de Nicholas Georgescu-Roegen', *Cahiers du Germes* (Paris), no. 4, 27–44.
GRINEVALD Jacques 1980. 'Le sens bioéconomique du développement humain: L'Affaire

Nicholas Georgescu-Roegen', *Revue européenne des sciences sociales (Cahiers Vilfredo Pareto)*, vol. 18, no. 51, 59–75.
MIROWSKI Philip 1988. 'Nicholas Georgescu-Roegen', *Journal of Economic Issues*, vol. 22, 820–28.
MIROWSKI Philip 1992. 'Nicholas Georgescu-Roegen', in Samuels (ed.), 86–105.
TANG A.M., WESTFIELD F.M. and WORLEY J.S. 1976 (eds). *Evolution, Welfare and Time in Economics: Essays in Honor of Nicholas Georgescu-Roegen*, Lexington, Massachusetts, Lexington Books,
ZAMAGNI Stefano 1979. *Georgescu-Roegen: I fondamenti della teoria del consumatore*, Milan, Etas Libri.

ARESTIS and SAWYER 1992, 179–87. BLAUG 1985, 71–2. *New Palgrave*, 1987, vol. 2, 515–16.

GOODWIN Richard Murphey (1913–1996)

Richard M. Goodwin was born in Newcastle, Indiana, in the United States. His father and grandfather were both financially ruined in the Great Depression. He studied at Harvard University (1930–34), then at Oxford (1934–7), before returning to Harvard, where he obtained a PhD in 1941. At Harvard University, he first taught in economics (1939–41), then in physics (1941–5), before being named assistant professor in economics in 1945. He left Harvard in 1949 and went, on a Rockefeller grant, to the department of applied economics at Cambridge, where he worked with Richard Stone. He obtained a position at Cambridge, first as an instructor, then as a reader, and taught there between 1952 and 1980. In 1980, he was appointed professor at the University of Sienna, which named him professor emeritus. He worked on the preparation of the second quinquennial plan in India, where he frequently stays. Primarily an economist, Richard Goodwin has also painted throughout his life and a catalogue of his work is under preparation.

Main publications

1948. 'Secular and Cyclical Aspects of the Multiplier and the Accelerator', in Lloyd A. Metzler (ed.), *Income, Employment and Public Policy. Essays in Honor of Alvin Hansen* , New York, W.W. Norton, 108–32.

1951. 'The Non-Linear Accelerator and the Persistence of Business Cycles', *Econometrica*, vol. 19, 1–17.

1953. 'The Problem of Trend and Cycle', *Yorkshire Bulletin of Economic and Social Research*, vol. 5, 89–97.

1955. 'A Model of Cyclical Growth', in E. Lundberg (ed.), *The Business Cycle in the Post-War World*, London, Macmillan, 203–21.

1967. 'A Growth Cycle', in C.H. Feinstein (ed.), *Capitalism and Economic Growth*, Cambridge, England, Cambridge University Press, 54–8; revised and enlarged version in E.K. Hunt and J.G. Schwartz (eds), *A Critique of Economic Theory*, Harmondsworth, Penguin Books, 1972, 442–9.

1970. *Elementary Economics from the Higher Standpoint*, Cambridge, England, Cambridge University Press.

1982. *Essays in Economic Dynamics*, London, Macmillan.

1983. *Essays in Linear Economic Structures*, London, Macmillan.
1984 (ed., with M. Kurger and A. Vercelli). *Nonlinear Models of Fluctuating Growth*, Berlin, Springer.
1985. 'A Personal Perspective on Mathematic Economics', *Quarterly Review, Banca Nazionale del Lavoro*, no. 152, 3–13; in Kregel 1988, 157–67.
1987. With L. Punzo, *The Dynamics of a Capitalist Economy*, Oxford, Polity Press.
1989. *Essays in Nonlinear Economic Dynamics*, Frankfurt am Main, P. Lang.
1990. *Chaotic Economic Dynamics*, Oxford and New York, Clarendon Press.

Defining himself 'as a lifelong, though wayward, Marxist' (1983, p. vii), but also as Keynesian, Richard M. Goodwin was a student and collaborator of Schumpeter. In fact, he contributed to the posthumous edition of his *History of Economic Analysis*. The original analysis of the functioning of capitalism, developed by Goodwin in a series of articles, of which the main ones were gathered in 1982, 1983 and 1989, draws on these three authors. It uses new and sophisticated mathematical techniques, though Goodwin declared himself a 'Sunday mathematician' ([1985] in Kregel 1988, p. 158). The main objective pursued by Goodwin was, following the examples of Marx and Schumpeter, to take account in the same model of the cyclical fluctuations and the growth process, the latter stemming from 'the dynamic interaction of profits, wages and unemployment' ([1967] in Hunt and Schwartz 1972, p. 442). In particular, he attempted to show that cyclical fluctuations are purely endogenous and that external shocks are not necessary to provoke and sustain them. In order to explain them, following Harrod, Kalecki, Samuelson and Hicks, Goodwin constructed models based on the combination of the multiplier and the accelerator (1948). But, convinced of the sterility of the linear models used by these authors, he borrowed from the French engineer Le Corbeiller his theory of oscillations, elaborated in the 1930s, to construct a non-linear model of growth, equipped with a flexible accelerator (1951).

Goodwin considers that it is towards biology more than towards physics that we need to turn to find techniques likely to help us understand an object as complex as the economy. Thus he was inspired by a model developed by Volterra, with the aim of studying the fish population in the Adriatic Sea, in constructing his non-linear dynamic model, based on the struggle for the distribution of the national production between employers and employees. More recently, he turned towards the chaos theory to enrich his analysis of the dynamics of capitalist economies (1990).

Main references

HARCOURT G.C. 1985. 'A Twentieth-Century Eclectic: Richard Goodwin', *Journal of Post Keynesian Economics*, vol. 7, 410–21.
GOODWIN 1985.
VELUPILLAI Kumaraswamy 1989 (ed.). *Nonlinear and Multisectoral Macrodynamics. Essays in Honour of R. Goodwin*, London, Macmillan.

ARESTIS and SAWYER 1992, 201–10.

GRUSON Claude (born 1910)

Claude Gruson was born in Paris. After graduating from the Ecole polytechnique and having completed the Corps des Mines, he chose a career in public administration. An inspector of finance in 1936, he subsequently worked closely with the Minister of Finance (1939) and the general secretary of industrial production (September 1940–April 1941). After several years in a sanatorium (1941–6), he carried out many functions in his capacity as inspector of finance. Gruson was delegated by the Treasury of the Ministry of Finance to establish the Service des Etudes Economiques et Financières (SEEF), which he directed from 1952 to 1961. From 1961 to 1967 he was general director of the Institut National de la Statistique et des Etudes Economiques (INSEE). He later left public service and held various positions in banking and finance. From 1968 to 1989 he was the president of the Bureau d'Informations et de Prévisions Economiques (BIPE), which he founded with François Bloch-Lainé.

Main publications

1948. 'La Préférence pour la liquidité', *Economie appliquée*, vol. 1, 301–56.
1949. *Esquisse d'une théorie générale de l'équilibre économique. Réflexions sur la théorie générale de Lord Keynes*, Paris, Presses Universitaires de France.
1950. 'Note sur les conditions d'établissement d'une comptabilité nationale et d'un budget économique national', *Statistiques et études financières*, vol. 2, 517–38.
1957. *La Prévision économique aux Etats-Unis, Cahiers de l'ISEA*, série K, no. 2.
1959. With Jean Bénard and Simon Nora, *Les méthodes actuelles soviétiques de planification*, *Cahiers de l'ISEA,* série G, no. 7.
1968. *Origine et espoirs de la planification française*, Paris, Dunod.
1971. *Renaissance du Plan*, Paris, Seuil.
1976. *Programmer l'espérance*, Paris, Stock.
1992. With Paul Ladrière, *Éthique et gouvernabilité*, Paris, Presses Universitaires de France.

Claude Gruson is one of those prominent civil service economists, such as F. Bloch-Lainé, R. Marjolin, S. Nora, P. Uri, P. Delouvrier and G. Ardant, who played a major role in France after the Second World War. Having read Keynes's *General Theory* during the war, he was among the first to present and to debate Keynes's arguments in France (1948, 1949). Like many young civil servants in France at the time, Gruson was able to establish links between macroeconomic theory, the organization of economic data and national economic policy.

Gruson therefore played a significant role in developing a system of national accounts in France (1950): with J. Dumontier, A. Piatier and P. Uri, he was a member of a committee of experts established in 1950 to develop the basis for a system of national accounts. The SEEF, which he directed, was responsible, from 1951 to 1954, for completing the technical work. During the same period, from 1952 to 1967, Gruson led the 'Groupe équilibre' which worked for French planning on the main macroeconomic equilibria. Inspired by Keynesianism, Gruson's work is part of the legacy of French contributions to the development of national economic accounting, applied macroeconomics, economic policy and planning (1968).

Gruson's interest in prediction and planning, his contribution and strong belief in planning in France and his commitment to the Plan (1968, 1971, 1976) are rooted in an ethic and a sense of responsibility for the future enriched by a deep religious faith and a calvinist conception of history. His ethical philosophy provides Gruson with a 'perspective of a just and fraternal world' (1992, p. 11) in the face of the economic decline and growing despair which has marked the world since 1971 (1976, 1992).

Main reference

FOURQUET François 1980. *Les Comptes de la puissance*, Paris, Recherches.

HAAVELMO Trygve (born 1911)

Trygve Haavelmo was born in Skedsmo, Norway. He obtained a university degree at Oslo in 1933 and became research assistant at the Institute of Economics, created by Ragnar Frisch. During the Second World War, he stayed in the United States, obtaining a PhD from Harvard University in 1946. With Jacob Marschak, he began in 1941, in New York, an econometric seminar. Closely linked to the Cowles Commission from the moment Marschak assumed its leadership, Haavelmo obtained a tenured position there in 1946. He returned to Norway in 1947 and was appointed professor at the University of Oslo in 1948. He retired in 1979. President of the Econometric Society in 1957, he won the Nobel Memorial Prize in Economics in 1989.

Main publications

1938. 'The Method of Supplementary Confluent Relations, Illustrated by a Study of Stock Prices', *Econometrica*, vol. 6, 203–18.
1943. 'Statistical Testing of Business-Cycle Theories', *Review of Economic Statistics*, vol. 25, 13–18.
1943. 'The Statistical Implications of a System of Simultaneous Equations', *Econometrica*, vol. 11, 1–12.
1944. 'The Probability Approach in Econometrics', *Econometrica*, vol. 12, supplement; new edn 1994, *The Probability... And Other Essays*, West Caldwell, New Jersey, Augustus M. Kelley.
1945. 'Multiplier Effects of a Balanced Budget', *Econometrica*, vol. 13, 311–18.
1947. With M.A. Girshick, 'Statistical Analysis of the Demand for Food: Examples of Simultaneous Estimation of Structural Equations', *Econometrica*, vol. 15, 79–110.
1954. *A Study in the Theory of Economic Evolution*, Amsterdam, North-Holland.
1958. 'The Role of the Econometrician in the Advancement of Economic Theory', *Econometrica*, vol. 26, 351–7.
1960. *A Study in the Theory of Investment*, University of Chicago Press.
1970. 'Some Observations on Welfare and Economic Growth', in W.A. Eltis, M.F. Scott and J.N. Wolfe (eds), *Induction, Growth and Trade: Essays in Honour of Sir Roy Harrod*, Oxford, Clarendon Press, 65–75.
1982. 'On the Dynamics of Global Economic Inequality', in *Economic Essays in Honour of Jorgen H. Gelting*, supplement to *Nationaløkonomisk Tidsskrift* (Copenhagen).
1990. 'Econometrics and the Welfare State', in *Les Prix Nobel 1989*, Stockholm, Fondation Nobel, 283–9.

Rarely has a mimeographed dissertation had, before its publication, such an impact on economic research as that of Haavelmo (1944). First issued in 1941, from that moment it started to influence those who, in subsequent years, were to rethink econonometrics at the Cowles Commission under Marschak. Haavelmo acknowledges Frisch's influence at the beginning of his work (1944, p. v), but it is certain that, as far as his essential contribution is concerned, Haavelmo took a very different view from that of Frisch. As he did, moreover, to that of Keynes in his debate with Tinbergen, in which he himself intervened (1943 *RES*). Almost all economists, in fact, including those who used statistical methods, were, until then, reluctant to employ the probabilistic method in economics. Haavelmo, on the contrary, believed it to be the only way 'to supply a theoretical foundation for the analysis of interrelations between economic variables' (1944, p. iii). This is because 'of the very nature of economic behavior, its dependence upon an enormous number of factors' (1943 *Econometrica*, p. 1). The variables which are dealt with in economics are stochastic variables. One cannot know the future, one cannot perform experiments, and one cannot expect the data observed, even if they could be perfectly measured, to match the predictions of the theory, which, anyway, is only a construction for interpreting reality. This is true, according to Haavelmo, of all empirical sciences. Only methods founded on probability permit one to test these theories empirically. These are the methods applied to, among others, the simultaneous systems of equations (1943 *Econometrica*) that Haavelmo developed in his work of the 1940s, and which were to have such an impact that some spoke of a probability theory revolution in econometrics to describe Haavelmo's contribution. Klein and Koopmans, among others, were inspired by his work.

Aware of the limits of econometrics, as well as of the flaws of the orthodox economic theory, Haavelmo drew attention, in his presidential address to the Econometric Society (1958), to the dangers of developing a technical expertise devoid of both coherent theoretical foundations and fruitful links with reality. He became interested, from the 1950s, in more concrete questions, such as that of economic development and the income disparities it provokes (1954, 1982). In his 1954 book, he constructed a growth model, prefiguring those of Solow and Swan, but he also looked into demographic growth, migration and education issues. In his book on investment (1960), Haavelmo, who also took an interest in the history of economic thought, studied the debates on the theory of capital, looking back to Böhm-Bawerk and Wicksell. He questioned the existence, postulated by the neoclassical theory, of an investment demand function founded on the assumption of profit maximization by entrepreneurs.

Haavelmo also gave his name to a theorem which concerns the multiplier effect of a balanced budget. It had already been enunciated by others (see Matthiessen 1966), but it was Haavelmo who was first to give it a rigorous formulation and a proof. The theorem shows that, in a situation of underemployment, an increase in governmental expenditures, even if accompanied by an equal increase in revenues collected, for example in the form of taxes, has a stimulative effect on national income. A balanced budget, therefore, is not neutral. Haavelmo demonstrated that the multiplier of such a balanced budget is equal to one.

Main references

'The Nobel Memorial Prize in Economics 1989'. Press release, article by Marc Nerlove and bibliography, *Scandinavian Journal of Economics* 1990, vol. 92, 11–30.

MATTHIESSEN Lars 1966. 'A Note on the Haavelmo Theorem', *Swedish Journal of Economics*, vol. 68, 261–80.
MOENE Karl Ove and RØDSETH Asbjørn 1991. 'Nobel Laureate: Trygve Haavelmo', *Journal of Economic Perspectives*, vol. 5, no. 3, 175–92.
SPANOS Aris 1989. 'On Rereading Haavelmo: A Retrospective View of Econometric Modeling', *Econometric Theory*, vol. 5, 405–29.

New Palgrave 1987, vol. 2, 580.

HABERLER Gottfried (1900–1995)

Gottfried Haberler was born in Vienna. He gained doctorates in law (1923) and political science (1925) at the University of Vienna, where he studied under Friedrich von Wieser and Ludwig von Mises. He visited universities and research centres in the United States and Britain in 1927 on a Rockefeller fellowship, and was appointed *privatdozent* at the the University of Vienna in 1928. He was visiting lecturer at Harvard in 1931–32, and expert in the Financial and Economic Intelligence Service of the Secretariat of the League of Nations in Geneva from 1934 to 1936. After emigrating to the United States in 1936, he was professor at Harvard University from that year until he retired in 1971. Since 1971, he has been a resident scholar at the American Enterprise Institute of Public Policy Research. President of the International Economic Association in 1950–51, he became honorary president in 1953. He was president of the American Economic Association in 1963 and was editor of the *Quarterly Journal of Economics* from 1965 to 1970.

Main publications

1927. *Der Sinn der Indexahlen* [The meaning of index numbers], Tübingen, J.C.B. Mohr.
1929. 'The Theory of Comparative Cost Once More', *Quarterly Journal of Economics*, vol. 43, 376–81.
1930. 'Die Theorie der komparativen Kosten und ihre Auswertung für die Begründung des Freihandels' [The theory of comparative cost and its utilization in the defence of free trade], *Weltwirtschaftliches Archiv*, vol. 32, 350–70.
1933. *Die internationale Handel: Theorie der weltwirtschaftlichen Zusammenhänge sowie Darstellung und Analyse der Aussenhandelspolitik*, Berlin, Julius Springer; revised Engl. transl. 1936, *The Theory of International Trade with its Applications to Commercial Policy*, London, William Hodge & Co.
1937. *Prosperity and Depression: A Theoretical Analysis of Cyclical Movements*, Geneva, League of Nations.
1942. *Consumer Instalment Credit and Economic Fluctuations*, New York, National Bureau of Economic Research.
1946. 'The Place of the *General Theory of Employment, Interest and Money* in the History of Economic Thought', *Review of Economic Statistics*, vol. 28, 187–94.
1949. 'The Market for Foreign Exchange and the Stability of Payments: A Theoretical Analysis', *Kyklos*, vol. 3, 193–218.
1950. 'Some Problems in the Pure Theory of International Trade', *Economic Journal*, vol. 61, 223–40.
1951 (ed.). *Readings in Business Cycle Theory*, Homewood, Illinois, Richard D. Irwin.

1952. 'The Pigou Effect Once More', *Journal of Political Economy*, vol. 60, 240–46.
1966. *Inflation, Its Causes and Cures*, revised and enlarged edition, *With a New Look at Inflation in 1966*, Washington, DC, American Enterprise Institute.
1968. *U.S. Balance-of-Payments Policy and International Monetary Reform: A Critical Analysis*, Washington, DC, American Enterprise Institute.
1972. With Michael Parkin and Henry Smith, *Inflation and the Unions*, London, Institute of Economic Affairs.
1974. *Economic Growth and Stability*, Los Angeles, Nash.
1976. *The World Economy, Money and the Great Depresssion 1919–1939*, Washington, DC, American Enterprise Institute.
1981. *The Great Depression of the 1930s: Can It Happen Again?*, Washington, DC, American Enterprise Institute.
1985. *Selected Essays of Gottfried Haberler*, edited by A.Y.C. Koo, Cambridge, Massachusetts, MIT Press. [With a bibliography.]
1988. *International Trade and Economic Development*, San Francisco, California, International Center for Economic Growth.
1993. *The Liberal Economic Order*, 2 vols, edited by A.Y.C. Koo, Aldershot, Hants, Edward Elgar.

Following a first book stemming from his doctoral thesis, in which he proposed a new method of measuring price and cost of living indexes (1927), Haberler turned towards what was to be his main field of intervention, the theory of international trade, giving it its modern formulation by translating the Ricardian theory of comparative cost in terms of general equilibrium (1929, 1930, 1933). It was he who opened up the way to the works of Ohlin, Samuelson and others. He was the first to apply the concept of opportunity cost to international trade. An untiring advocate of free trade, Haberler never stopped criticizing all the arguments put forward to justify all forms of protectionism, in less developed as well as in developed countries. He was indeed convinced that international trade free from all constraints has constituted since the last century and still constitutes the main factor of development (1988). He deplored the fact that, since the end of the Second World War, constraints upon free trade have multiplied. He attacked the theses of the neo-Marxists and non Marxists, such as Myrdal, who put forward the lack of harmony between rich and poor, developed and less developed countries. Haberler has always been very interested in international monetary questions (see, for example, 1949, 1968), favouring since the 1950s the establishment of flexible exchange rates.

Haberler undertook, for the League of Nations, research on trade cycle theory, which resulted in his most famous book (1937), revised many times up to 1964. Haberler presented in it a precise taxonomy of all trade cycle theory and proposed a detailed analysis of them. He then put forward an explanation of the nature and causes of fluctuations, borrowing from all of these theories. He thought that the divergences between them were, indeed, exaggerated, that rather they are often complementary and apply to problems which are different at different phases of the cycle. He could not take into account Keynes's theory in the first edition of his book, but this was to become in subsequent editions, as well as in many other writings (see, for example 1946), a steady object of interest. While acknowledging Keynes's genius, Haberler thinks, along with others, that his theory is neither really new nor particularly revolutionary. He considers that the hypothesis of wages' rigidity is indispensable to an underemployment equilibrium model. Moreover, he had already introduced in his 1937 book, hence before Pigou, the idea of the real-balance effect, named 'the Pigou effect' by Patinkin in 1948 (see also 1952). Haberler thinks that Keynes was mistaken in attributing the 1930 crisis to the endogenous and inherent instability of capitalism, to a combination of a tendency to excess saving and insufficient investment. He thinks, on the contrary, along with the monetarists – even though he does not share all their views – that errors in monetary policy were responsible for it.

In more recent years, particularly in the context of many of his American Enterprise Institute's papers, Haberler constantly criticized the policy proposals put forward by Keynes's disciples, which he furthermore distinguishes from those Keynes stood up for at the end of his life. An advocate of free trade at the international level, he is also for unfettered liberalism at the national level, convinced that contemporary economic problems will be solved 'by breaking down barriers to the movement of factors of production, (especially in the labor market?), making wages more flexible, curbing the power of labor unions' (1988, p. 15; see also 1966, 1972, 1981). Hence he proved to be in favour of the policies associated with Ronald Reagan's and Margaret Thatcher's governments, as they were, according to him, likely to lead to an economic revival.

Main references

BALDWIN Robert E. *et al.* 1965. *Trade, Growth, and the Balance of Payments: Essays in Honor of Gottfried Haberler*, Chicago, Rand McNally; Amsterdam, North-Holland.

KOO, A.Y.C. Introduction to Haberler 1993, ix–xxi.

Quarterly Journal of Economics, 1982, vol. 97, 'Gottfried Haberler: Contributions Upon Entering his Ninth Decade'; introduction by Malcolm Gillis and articles by Robert E. Baldwin, Lawrence H. Officer and Thomas D. Willett, 139–69.

BLAUG 1985, 75–6. *New Palgrave* 1987, vol. 2, 581–2.

HAHN Frank Horace (born 1925)

Frank Hahn was born in Berlin and settled with his family in England in the 1930s. He studied at the London School of Economics, obtaining his PhD in 1950 (his thesis was published in 1972). He was first a lecturer, then reader in mathematical economics at the University of Birmingham (1948–60), later to become a lecturer at Cambridge (1960–65), professor of economics at the

London School of Economics (1965–70) and, since 1970, at Cambridge where he is fellow of Churchill College. Hahn was managing editor of the *Review of Economic Studies* (1963–7), president of the Econometric Society (1968) and of the Royal Economic Society (1986).

Main publications

1952. 'The General Equilibrium Theory of Money: A Comment', *Review of Economic Studies*, vol. 19, 179–85.
1955. 'The Rate of Interest and General Equilibrium Analysis', *Economic Journal*, vol. 65, 52–61.
1960. 'The Stability of Growth Equilibrium', *Quarterly Journal of Economics*, vol. 74, 206–26; and 1962, 'Reply', vol. 76, 502.
1962. 'On the Stability of a Pure Exchange Equilibrium', *International Economic Review*, vol. 3, 206–14.
1962. With T. Negishi, 'A Theorem on Non-Tâtonnement Stability', *Econometrica*, vol. 30, 463–9.
1964. With R.C.O. Matthews, 'The Theory of Economic Growth: A Survey', *Economic Journal*, vol. 74, 779–902.
1965. 'On Some Problems of Proving the Existence of an Equilibrium in a Monetary Economy', in F.H. Hahn and F.P.R. Brechling (eds), *The Theory of Interest Rates*, London, Macmillan, 126–35.
1971. 'Professor Friedman's Views on Money', *Economica*, vol. 38, 61–80.
1971 (ed.). *Readings in the Theory of Growth*, London, Macmillan.
1971. With Kenneth J. Arrow, *General Competitive Analysis*, San Francisco, Holden-Day; Edinburgh, Oliver & Boyd; Amsterdam, North-Holland.
1972. *The Share of Wages in the National Income: An Enquiry into the Theory of Distribution*, London, Weidenfeld & Nicolson.
1973. 'The Winter of Our Discontent', *Economica*, vol. 40, 322–30.
1975. 'On the Role of Money in the Process of Exchange and the Existence of a Non-Walrasian Equilibrium', *Review of Economic Studies*, vol. 42, 489–501.
1979 (ed., with Martin Hollis). *Philosophy and Economic Theory*, New York, Oxford University Press.
1981. *Three Lectures in Monetary Theory*, Stanford University, Institute for Mathematical Studies in the Social Sciences.
1982. *Money and Inflation*, Oxford, Basil Blackwell.
1984. *Equilibrium and Macroeconomics*, Oxford, Basil Blackwell.
1985. *Money, Growth and Stability*, Oxford, Basil Blackwell.
1987. 'Information, Dynamics and Equilibrium', *Scottish Journal of Political Economy*, vol. 34, 321–34.
1988 (ed.). *The Economics of Missing Markets, Information, and Games*, New York, Oxford University Press.
1989 (ed., with Ben Friedman). *Handbook of Monetary Economics*, Amsterdam, North-Holland.
1990. 'On Inflation', *Oxford Review of Economic Policy*, vol. 6, no. 4, 15–25.
1992. 'Autobiographical Notes with Reflections', in Szenberg 1992, 160–66.

In addition to contributing to the development of a more accessible version of general equilibrium theory (1971 with Arrow), Frank Hahn has expanded its range of application. Following his early work on the share of wages in national income and on business cycles, he devoted most of his abilities as a mathematical economist to deepening the theory of general equilibrium and expanding it to other fields. On the one hand, he worked in line with Arrow and Debreu (1954) on the problems of general market equilibrium, notably on the question of its stability (1962 *IER*, 1962 *Econometrica*, 1971 with Arrow). On the other hand, using these analytical works, he also tackled important fields that are beyond the framework in which the existence of general equilibrium has been proved: namely money (1952, 1981, 1985, 1989 ed.), interest rate (1955, 1965) and growth (1960, 1964, 1971 ed., 1985). So, starting from the fundamental works, he is seeking to contribute to a rigorous re-elaboration of economic theory.

Hahn criticized Patinkin's efforts to elaborate a theory of money (1952) and went on to reveal several stumbling-blocks in the way of his attempt to integrate money into general equilibrium (1965). On the grounds of intellectual rigour, he criticized the monetarist theses of Friedman, including his references to neoclassical economics, his lack of precision and his tendency to slip from the empirical to the theoretical (1971 *Economica*). Hahn's criticisms of new classical macroeconomists were based on the lightness of their contribution to the nexus of economic theory and of their scientific backing of liberal policies: 'And when one turns to the best of the new orthodox and finds that they exclude the possibility of someone willing to work at the current wage but not finding a job, by assumption and not by argument, then a little stridency may be just what is needed' (1982, p. x). He argues that general equilibrium theory by no means gives any foundation for the thesis that a high unemployment economy can only be the object of policies related to money supply. Hahn has also applied his critical verve to his post-Keynesian and neo-Ricardian colleagues (1973), and has even focused it on his own thinking, to the point of questioning the usefulness of work on general equilibrium.

Specifically, Hahn holds that there remains an immense gap between the theoretical fields, in which scientific rigour is applicable, and practical economics, in which the economist still has little to say as a scholar. He considers Keynes's insights, even if he 'left many gaping holes in his theory', 'several orders more profound and realistic than those of his recent critics' (1982, p. xi.). However, he questions the status of macroeconomics (1984) which, although necessary, notably for economic policy, currently remains without theoretical grounding and requires reconstruction. This reconstruction can only be based on a dynamic theory of general equilibrium that would integrate time, money and growth, a goal that seems remote at this point.

Main references

DASGUPTA Partha *et al.* 1993 (eds). *Economic Analysis of Markets and Games: Essays in Honor of Frank Hahn*, Cambridge, Massachusetts, MIT Press.
HAHN 1992.

BLAUG 1985, 77–8. LOASBY 1989, 119–39.

HANSEN Alvin Harvey (1887–1975)

Alvin H. Hansen was born in Viborg, a rural community in South Dakota. He studied first at Sioux Falls, then at Yankton College, where he graduated in 1910. He taught in high school, then entered the University of Wisconsin in 1914, earning his PhD in 1918 (his thesis was published in 1921). He took up an appointment at the University of Minnesota, spending a year abroad in 1928 on a Guggenheim fellowship. In 1933–4, he was research director of the Committee of Inquiry on International Economic Relations. In 1937, he was appointed professor of political economy at Harvard. He was a member of the President's Advisory Council on Social Security (1937–8), president of the American Economic Association in 1939, president of the US–Canadian Joint Economic Commission (1941–3) and economic advisor to the Federal Reserve Board. Upon his retirement, in 1957, he settled in Belmont, Massachusetts, moving to Virginia in 1972.

Main publications

1921. *Cycles of Prosperity and Depression in the United States, Great Britain and Germany: A Study of Monthly Data 1902–1908*, Madison, University of Wisconsin Press.
1927. *Business-Cycle Theory: Its Development and Present Status*, Boston, Ginn.
1928. With F.B. Garver, *Principles of Economics*, Boston, Ginn.
1932. *Economic Stabilization in an Unbalanced World*, New York, Harcourt Brace; repr. 1971, Clifton, New Jersey, Augustus M. Kelley.
1933. With H. Tout, 'Annual Survey of Business Cycle Theory: Investment and Saving in Business Cycle Theory', *Econometrica*, vol.1, 119–47.
1936. 'Mr Keynes on Underemployment Equilibrium', *Journal of Political Economy*, vol. 44, 667–86.
1938. *Full Recovery or Stagnation?*, New York, W.W. Norton.
1939. 'Economic Progress and Declining Population Growth', *American Economic Review*, vol. 29, 1–15.
1941. *Fiscal Policy and Business Cycles*, New York, W.W. Norton.
1944. With H.S. Perloff, *State and Local Finance in the National Economy*, New York, W.W. Norton.
1947. *Economic Policy and Full Employment*, New York, McGraw-Hill.
1949. *Monetary Theory and Fiscal Policy*, New York, McGraw-Hill.
1951. *Business Cycles and National Income*, New York, W.W. Norton; augm. edn, 1964.
1953. *A Guide to Keynes*, New York, McGraw-Hill.
1953 (ed., with R.V. Clemence). *Readings in Business Cycles and National Income*, London, George Allen & Unwin.
1957. *The American Economy*, New York, McGraw-Hill.
1960. *Economic Issues of the 1960s*, New York, McGraw-Hill.
1965. *The Dollar and the International Monetary System*, New York, McGraw-Hill.
1966. 'Keynes After Thirty Years (with Special Reference to the United States)', *Weltwirtschaftliches Archiv*, vol. 97, 213–31.

Considered by many to be the 'American Keynes', Alvin H. Hansen made a wide range of contributions as an analyst of business cycles, a propagator of Keynesian ideas in the United States and a leading author of the neoclassical synthesis. He was also the prime exponent of stagnationism, according to which capitalism contains within itself a deep tendency towards stagnation.

Like many of his contemporaries, Hansen worked on business cycles; starting from his first empirical study in 1921, he highlighted the importance of monetary factors. In his study of theories he brought out the phenomenon's complexity, notably the interaction of short-run and long-run movements and their cause (1927). In all of this, his position was scarcely interventionist: budget deficits and great public works that some American economists were beginning to advocate struck him as inherently detrimental, notably towards savings, capital markets and private investment (1932, 1933).

However, the long duration and seriousness of the Depression led him to advocate public intervention, notably through investment. In his public finance seminars at Harvard, he presented and discussed the analyses of Keynes, and it is to him that many of his students, including J.K. Galbraith, P.A. Samuelson and J. Tobin owe their introduction to Keynesian ideas. He himself adopted most of Keynes's tools and concepts, notably his macroeconomic approach, the idea that an underemployment equilibrium could persist, and the taking into account of uncertainty and anticipations. He concomitantly developed his own analysis of the tendency towards stagnation as linked to low population growth, as well as the tendency of the capital coefficient to decrease and thus to slow the growth of investment (1938, 1939, 1941, 1957).

After the Second World War, Hansen's work drew on Keynes's works as well as the debates and interpretations which stemmed from them. The Keynesianism he helped spread became increasingly that of the neoclassical synthesis: a synthesis which allows a central place for the *IS–LM* model, and leaves no space for some of the main aspects of Keynes's contributions (1947, 1949, 1953). As for economic policy, he held it to be not only indispensable for the re-establishment of full employment, but also necessary because of the new characteristics of modern capitalism (1947, 1957).

All in all, though he rejected or neglected some of the main aspects of Keynes's thought, Hansen played an essential role in the spreading of postwar Keynesianism, presenting himself as a resolute advocate of interventionist policies.

Main references

METZLER Lloyd A. 1948 (ed.). *Income Employment and Public Policies: Essays in Honor of Alvin Hansen*, New York, W.W. Norton.

Quarterly Journal of Economics, 1976, vol. 90, 1–37 (with articles by R.A. Musgrave, J.H. Williams, G. Haberler, W.S. Salant, P.A. Samuelson and J. Tobin).

BLAUG 1985, 79–81. BREIT and RANSOM 1971, 85–110. *New Palgrave* 1987, vol. 2, 591–2. SILLS 1968, vol. 6, 319–23.

HARCOURT Geoffrey Colin (born 1931)

G.C. Harcourt was born in Melbourne, Australia. He studied at the University of Melbourne (1950–55), then at the University of Cambridge (1955–8), where he gained a PhD in 1960, and a Litt D (Doctor of Letters) in 1988. In 1958, he started teaching at the University of Adelaide, where he was appointed to a professorship in 1967, then named professor emeritus in 1988. Between 1963 and 1966 he was a university lecturer in economics and politics at the university of Cambridge and a fellow of Trinity Hall. In 1982, he returned to a University lectureship in economics and politics, together with a fellowship at Jesus College, Cambridge, and was elected to an *ad hominem* readership in the history of economic theory in 1990. He was president of the Economic Society of Australia and New Zealand between 1974 and 1977. G.C. Harcourt was an anti-war campaigner for over five years when Australia was involved in the Vietnam war.

Main publications

1965. 'A Two-Sector Model of the Distribution of Income and the Level of Employment in the Short Run', *Economic Record*, vol. 41, 103–17.
1965. 'The Accountant in a Golden Age', *Oxford Economic Papers*, vol. 17, 66–80.
1967. With P.H. Karmel and R.H. Wallace, *Economic Activity*, Cambridge, England, Cambridge University Press.
1969 (ed. with R.H. Parker). *Readings in the Concept and Measurement of Income*, Cambridge, England, Cambridge University Press; 2nd edn, with R.H. Parker and G. Whittington, Oxford, Philip Allan, 1986.
1969. 'Some Cambridge Controversies in the Theory of Capital', *Journal of Economic Literature*, vol. 7, 369–405.
1971 (ed., with N.F. Laing). *Capital and Growth: Selected Readings*, Harmondsworth, Penguin Books.
1972. *Some Cambridge Controversies in the Theory of Capital,* Cambridge, England, Cambridge University Press.
1975. 'The Cambridge Controversies: The Afterglow', in *Contemporary Issues in Economics*, edited by M. Parkin and A.R. Nobay, Manchester University Press, 305–34.
1976. With Peter Kenyon, 'Pricing and the Investment Decision', *Kyklos*, vol. 29, 449–77.
1977 (ed.). *The Microeconomic Foundations of Macroeconomics*, London, Macmillan.
1982. *The Social Science Imperialists: Selected Essays*, edited by Prue Kerr, London, Routledge & Kegan Paul.
1985. *Keynes and his Contemporaries. The Sixth and Centennial Keynes Seminar Held at the University of Kent at Canterbury, 1983*, London, Macmillan; New York, St Martin's Press.
1986. *Controversies in Political Economy: Selected Essays of G.C. Harcourt*, edited by O.F. Hamouda, Brighton, Wheatsheaf.
1986 (ed., with Jon Cohen). *International Monetary Problems and Supply-Side Economics: Essays in Honour of Lorie Tarshis*, London, Macmillan.
1987. 'Post-Keynesian Economics', *New Palgrave*, vol.3, 924–8.
1992. *On Political Economists and Modern Political Economy: Selected Essays of G.C. Harcourt*, edited by Claudio Sardoni, London and New York, Routledge.
1993. *Post-Keynesian Essays in Biography. Portraits of Twentieth Century Political Economists*, London, Macmillan.
1993 (ed., with Mauro Baranzini). *The Dynamics of the Wealth of Nations. Growth, Distribution and Structural Changes. Essays in Honour of Luigi Pasinetti*, Basingstoke, Macmillan.

A Cambridge person by adoption, close to Joan Robinson and Piero Sraffa, Geoff Harcourt is one of the most efficient spokespersons of the post-Keynesian tradition whose characteristics and various undercurrents he has himself defined precisely (1987). In a subject characterized by discourses that are often boring and pompous and, indeed, even obscure, Harcourt stands out with his humour and lively and clear style, in his written as in his oral contributions. He managed to give life to the controversy, at first sight very abstract, which in the 1950s and 1960s divided theoreticians from Cambridge, England and those from Cambridge, Massachussetts, concerning growth and capital theory. His descriptions (1969 *JEL*, 1972, 1975) have become standard references. He succeeded in explaining with clarity the 'double-switching' and 'capital-reversing debate' ('associated essentially with the possibility that the same method of production may be the most profitable of a number of methods of production at more than one rate of profits even though other methods are more profitable at rates in between', 1972, p. 124) and the disastrous consequences for the neoclassical theory of distribution and its significance on the ideological as well as on the political level.

Harcourt's contributions, however, are not limited to the history of a debate in which he has been an active participant. He has contributed many works on growth theory, distribution, tax theory, price determination and investment decisions. Author of many academic biographies (collected together in the 1993 *Post-Keynesian Essays*), he has been particularly involved, since his return to Cambridge in 1982, in a study of the Cambridge disciples of Keynes.

Harcourt has also often contributed to debates on political economy, particularly concerning the situation in his country, where he has always been politically active, among other places, within the Australian Labor Party. Firmly critical of both monetarism and traditional Keynesian management, he has sought to outline a 'middle way' between liberal capitalism and a state-controlled economy, advocating a mixed economy which emphasizes reduction of income disparities and full employment, through the means of social dialogue.

Main references

DIXON Robert 1988. 'Geoff Harcourt's Selected Essays: A Review Article', *Economic Analysis and Policy*, vol. 18, 245–53.

JENSEN H.E. 1988–9. 'The Civilized Economies of Geoffrey C. Harcourt – A Review Article', *Journal of Post Keynesian Economics*, vol. 11, 305–12.

ARESTIS and SAWYER 1992, 232–41.

HARROD Roy Forbes (1900–1978)

Roy Harrod was born in Norfolk, England. He entered Oxford in 1919 and studied classical literature, ancient history and philosophy. He graduated in 1922, earning a further degree in modern history in 1923. After being appointed lecturer in economics at Christ Church College, Oxford, he spent time at Cambridge, studying this same subject under Keynes, whose friend and collaborator he was to become. Harrod's whole career was spent at Oxford. In 1945, he succeeded Keynes as editor of the *Economic Journal*, a position he held until 1966. He was a Liberal Party candidate in the 1945 general elections and a member of the party's shadow cabinet. From 1957 to 1963, Harrod was an advisor to conservative prime minister Harold Macmillan. He was knighted in 1959 and served as president of the Royal Economic Society from 1962 to 1964. He retired from Oxford in 1967, but continued nonetheless to teach in many North American universities.

Main publications

1930. 'Notes on Supply', *Economic Journal*, vol. 40, 232–41.
1933. *International Economics*, Cambridge, England, Cambridge University Press.
1936. *The Trade Cycle: An Essay*, Oxford, Clarendon Press.
1937. 'Mr. Keynes and Traditional Theory', *Econometrica*, vol. 5, 74–86.
1939. 'An Essay in Dynamic Theory', *Economic Journal*, vol. 49, 14–33.
1944 (anonymous). *A Liberal Plan for Peace*, London, Gollancz.
1946. *A Page of British Folly*, London, Macmillan.
1947. *Are These Hardships Necessary?*, London, Rupert Hart-Davis.
1948. *Towards a Dynamic Economics: Some Recent Developments of Economic Theory and their Application to Policy*, London, Macmillan.
1951. *And So It Goes: Further Thoughts on Present Mismanagement*, London, Rupert Hart-Davis.
1951. *The Life of John Maynard Keynes*, London, Macmillan.
1952. *Economic Essays*, London, Macmillan.
1952. *The Pound Sterling*, Princeton University Press.
1953. *The Dollar*, London, Macmillan.
1956. *Foundations of Inductive Logic*, London, Macmillan.
1958. *Policy against Inflation*, London, Macmillan.
1958. *The Pound Sterling, 1951–1958*, Princeton University Press.
1959. *The Prof: A Personal Memoir of Lord Cherwell*, London, Macmillan.
1961. *Topical Comments: Essays in Dynamic Economics Applied*, London, Macmillan.
1963. *The British Economy*, New York, McGraw-Hill.
1965. *Reforming the World's Money*, London, Macmillan.
1967. *Towards a New Economic Policy*, Manchester University Press.
1969. *Money*, London, Macmillan.
1970. *Sociology, Morals and Mystery*, London, Macmillan.
1973. *Economic Dynamics*, London, Macmillan.

Harrod was originally destined for a career in philosophy. He was dissuaded from following this course by one of his professors, but retained a lifelong interest in this field, publishing many philosophical articles as well as a book on logic (1956) in which he criticized David Hume's scepticism, a work which he considered to be his most important scholarly contribution. However, it was as an economist that Harrod became famous. His extensive output touched upon many fields, from highly abstract theory to contributions to Great Britain's political and economic debates. Thus Harrod is the author of many newspaper articles and official documents as well as economic studies for a brokerage firm. He wrote extensively about international monetary problems, defending the views advanced by Keynes and the British delegation at Bretton Woods (1952 *The Pound*, 1958 *The Pound*, 1965). Above all else, Harrod is known as the creator of the modern theory of growth, developing its main elements before the Second World War.

As early as his first article, written in 1928 and published in 1930, Harrod introduced an important innovation, the marginal revenue curve, to be subsequently popularized by Joan Robinson and Edward Chamberlin in the development of the theory of monopolistic competition. He later developed the concept of foreign trade multiplier (1933). His correspondence with Keynes indicates the extent to which Harrod played an important role in the development of *The General Theory*, whose proofs Keynes had sent him. From the beginning of the postwar period to his death, Harrod remained a consistent defender of Keynesianism (1958 *Policy*, 1963, 1967). At the time of Keynes's death, it was to Harrod that Keynes's brother turned in seeking a biographer (1951).

However, Harrod should not be classified as an unswerving disciple of Keynes. In fact he criticized Keynes's analyses as static. Shortly after the publication of *The General Theory*, Harrod wrote *The Trade Cycle* (1936). He declared himself a Keynesian in this work with reference to the relations between investment, saving and the determination of national income via the multiplier. Yet he added that it is necessary to take into account the effects of growth on investment in order to understand the cyclical fluctuations of economic activities. He thus termed 'relation' the concept better known as the 'accelerator'.

Between 1936 and 1939, Harrod elaborated his famous growth model in order to dynamize the analysis of *The General Theory*. In effect, he held that the mere fact of attaining full employment through demand management, or through war, is in no sense a guarantee of stable growth and, even less, of the future maintenance of full employment. Moreover, the fundamental characteristics of modern capitalist economies tend towards unstable growth. This, the main message of his 1939 article, was initially overlooked because of the war, but when it was reformulated in 1948 it made a major impact. Meanwhile, Evsey Domar had developed (independently of Harrod) a model which in some ways is analagous; one of the common points between the two, highlighted by Solow, is the use made of the form $GC=s$, an equation that came to characterize a model popularized in postwar textbooks as 'the Harrod–Domar model'.

This model is based on a very simple relation between the growth rate of national income, G, the society's propensity to save, s, considered by Harrod to be relatively stable, and the relation between the increase of capital and that of production, C, termed by Harrod the capital coefficient. As derived from the Keynesian equality between investment and savings, the relation takes the form $GC=s$. This is a truism, invariably confirmed *ex post*. Harrod also identified a second growth rate, Gw, termed 'warranted'. If this rate is realized, entrepreneurs are satisfied with the results thereby obtained and are furthermore stimulated to continue their investment activities on an identical scale. Harrod designates the capital coefficient they seek C_r, corresponding to this growth rate, resulting in the equation: $G_wC_r=s$.

The last equation is not a truism, but a condition of equilibrium and stable growth. There exists a specific relation between the growth rate, the capital coefficient and the saving rate, ensuring stable growth. Granted the propensity to save, s, the greater G is, the weaker will be C. G, the effective growth rate of the economy, is the result of a multitude of decisions made both by individuals and entrepreneurs, and it is only as the result of unusual coincidence that the value of G corresponds to that of the warranted growth rate, G_w. If G is greater than G_w, C is lesser than C_r. The effective capital coefficient is less than the desired capital coefficient. This encourages entrepreneurs to increase investment and hence G will tend to be higher. Conversely, if G is less than G_w, entrepreneurs tend to reduce the growth of capital stock. Briefly, as soon as a distance from stable growth is brought about, forces that make it yet further remote come into play; this is known as 'knife-edge equilibrium'. One might also term it 'Harrod's unstable growth principle'.

The situation becomes yet more complicated with the introduction of a third growth rate, the natural rate, G_n, the maximum rate allowed by population increase and technical progress. Harrod effectively demonstrates that, if G_w is greater than G_n, the economy is in a state of chronic depression. If, however, G_w is less than G_n, the economy is in a state of permanent overheating. All of this has important consequences for economic policy. The divergence between G_w and G_n explains chronic unemployment, and the tendency of G to distance itself from G_w accounts for the problem of business cycles. The standard situation in developed capitalist countries is characterized by warranted rates that are excessively high compared to natural rates, held Harrod. Thus it is necessary to elaborate policies which will allow for the manipulation of warranted rates so as to equalize them with natural rates. Specifically, a reduction of the saving rate is thus seen to be desirable, and public works projects cannot suffice to resolve the problems of chronic unemployment.

Harrod's model stimulated a vast literature, with some contributors seeking to demonstrate that the instability postulated by Harrod stems from hypotheses that are relatively restricted with reference to technology. Harrod himself repeatedly intervened in these discussions, underlining in his last contribution (1973) that the deviations with reference to the equilibrium growth path must be very large for the principle of instability to apply.

Main references

ELTIS Walter A., SCOTT Maurice F. and WOLFE James N. 1970 (eds). *Induction, Growth and Trade: Essays in Honour of Sir Roy Harrod*, Oxford, Clarendon Press. [Contains a bibliography, 361–76.]

PHELPS BROWN Henry 1980. 'Sir Roy Harrod: a Biographical Memoir', *Economic Journal*, vol. 90, 1–33.

YOUNG Warren 1989. *Harrod and his Trade Cycle Group. The Origins and Development of the Growth Research Programme*, London, Macmillan.

BLAUG 1985, 82–4. *New Palgrave* 1987, vol. 2, 595–602. SILLS 1979, 271–4. SPIEGEL and SAMUELS 1984, 85–92.

HAYEK Friedrich August (1899–1992)

Friedrich August von Hayek was born in Vienna, and earned a doctorate in law from the University of Vienna in 1921 and a doctorate in political science from the same university in 1923. In 1927, he founded, along with Ludwig von Mises, the Austrian Institute for Business Cycle Research, directing it until 1931. He began teaching at the University of Vienna in 1929. In 1931, he emigrated to England, where he taught at the London School of Economics until 1950. In 1947, he founded the Mont Pèlerin Society, an association of intellectuals devoted to the study and defence of liberalism. From 1950 to 1961 Hayek was professor of social and moral sciences at the University of Chicago. In 1962, he was appointed to the chair of political economy at the University of Freiburg (West Germany), becoming professor emeritus in 1977. Between 1969 and 1977, he was at Salzburg University, in Austria, before returning to Freiburg to spend his last years. In 1974, he was awarded the Nobel Memorial Prize in Economics, along with Gunnar Myrdal.

Main publications

1929. *Geldtheorie und Konjunkturtheorie*, Vienna, Hölder-Pichler-Tempsky; Engl. transl. 1933, *Monetary Theory and the Trade Cycle*, London, Jonathan Cape.

1931. *Prices and Production*, London, George Routledge & Sons.

1935 (ed.). *Collectivist Economic Planning: Critical Studies on the Possibilities of Socialism*, London, George Routledge & Sons.

1937. 'Economics and Knowledge', *Economica*, vol. 4, 33–54.

1937. *Monetary Nationalism and International Stability*, London, Longmans, Green.

1939. *Profits, Interest and Investment: And Other Essays on The Theory of Industrial Fluctuations*, London, Routledge & Kegan Paul.

1941. *The Pure Theory of Capital*, London, Routledge & Kegan Paul; University of Chicago Press.
1944. *The Road to Serfdom*, London, George Routledge; University of Chicago Press.
1948. *Individualism and Economic Order*, London, Routledge & Kegan Paul; University of Chicago Press.
1951. *John Stuart Mill and Harriet Taylor: Their Friendship and Subsequent Marriage*, London, Routledge & Kegan Paul; University of Chicago Press.
1952. *The Counter-Revolution of Science: Studies on the Abuse of Reason*, Glencoe, Illinois, Free Press.
1952. *The Sensory Order: An Inquiry into the Foundations of Theoretical Psychology*, London, Routledge & Kegan Paul; University of Chicago Press.
1960. *The Constitution of Liberty*, London, Routledge & Kegan Paul; University of Chicago Press.
1967. *Studies in Philosophy, Politics and Economics*, London, Routledge & Kegan Paul; University of Chicago Press.
1973. *Law, Legislation and Liberty: A New Statement of the Liberal Principles of Justice and Political Economy*, vol. 1, *Rules and Order*, London, Routledge & Kegan Paul; University of Chicago Press.
1976. *Denationalisation of Money: An Analysis of the Theory and Practice of Concurrent Currencies*, London, Institute of Economic Affairs.
1976. *Law, Legislation and Liberty*, vol. 2, *The Mirage of Social Justice*, London, Routledge & Kegan Paul; University of Chicago Press.
1978. *New Studies in Philosophy, Politics, Economics and the History of Ideas*, London, Routledge & Kegan Paul; University of Chicago Press.
1979. *Law, Legislation and Liberty*, vol. 3, *The Political Order of a Free People*, London, Routledge & Kegan Paul; University of Chicago Press.
1984. *Money, Capital and Fluctuations: Early Essays*, translated and edited by Roy McCloughry, London, Routledge & Kegan Paul; University of Chicago Press.
1984. *The Essence of Hayek*, edited by C. Nishiyama and K. Leube, Stanford, Hoover Institution Press.
1988. *The Collected Works of F.A. Hayek*, vol. 1, *The Fatal Conceit: The Errors of Socialism*, edited by W.W. Bartley III, London, Routledge; University of Chicago Press.
1991. *Economic Freedom*, Oxford, Basil Blackwell.
1991. *The Collected Works of F.A. Hayek*, vol. 3, *The Trend of Economic Thinking: Essays on Political Economists and Economic History*, edited by W.W. Bartley III and S. Kresge, London, Routledge; University of Chicago Press.
1992. *The Collected Works of F.A. Hayek*, vol. 4, *The Fortune of Liberalism: Essays on Austrian Economics and the Ideal of Freedom*, edited by P.G. Klein, London, Routledge; University of Chicago Press.

Hayek first gained fame with his trade cycle theory, elaborated during the 1920s and 1930s (1929, 1931, 1939; 1984 *Money* brings together English translations of some of Hayek's first articles), a perspective presented for some years as the main alternative to the views that Keynes was beginning to put forth. The success of Keynes's *General Theory* eclipsed Hayek's vision; his last work in the field of pure economic theory was published in 1941. However, during the last 20 years or so, a spectacular turnabout has taken place; among others, some theoreticians of the new classical macroeconomics claim to be pursuing the research programme laid out by Hayek since the late 1920s.

Hayek's economic theory draws from two sources: Wicksell's theory and that of the founders of the Austrian school, notably Böhm-Bawerk. This last thinker held that investment should be viewed as a roundabout production process whose duration varies in accordance with a community's eagerness to consume, as revealed by the saving rate. In a state of equilibrium, the time structure of production chosen by entrepreneurs corresponds to the willingness of consumers to save. This equilibrium can be offset by the presence of money in the form of credits which are introduced into the economy. Such an action would produce a disequilibrium of the price structure, notably a lowering of interest rates to a point below their natural level, in accordance with the vision elaborated by Wicksell. This lowering of rates leads to a rise in investment, beyond its equilibrium level as determined by saving, and the resulting overinvestment is funded by what Hayek terms forced saving. Such is the root cause of the reversal that occurs sooner or later when the artificial source of forced saving runs out. Then the economy must surely undergo a period of unemployment and readjustments in order to restore the equilibrium disturbed by careless monetary policies.

This perspective is diametrically opposed to that of Keynes, who held that the lack of investment is the root cause of unemployment. Needless to say, the two scholars were equally opposed on the subject of which policies to implement: stimulation of investment, through increasing the money supply, among other means, for Keynes, and austerity and monetary discipline for Hayek. Hayek attributed the long postwar inflation as well as the recession and increase in unemployment within capitalist economies since the 1970s to the Keynesian policies he struggled so arduously against without respite. He compared Keynes's 'medicine' to a drug that produced a euphoria that lasted longer than he expected, but whose effects have been all the more deleterious.

The critique of Keynesianism is but one element of Hayek's political struggle, and the theory described above was merely one of his weapons. Beginning in the mid-1930s, Hayek started a crusade against socialism and what he termed planism and collectivist rationalism (1935, 1944, 1952 *The Counter-Revolution*), followed through in his 1988 work, subtitled *The Errors of Socialism*. This struggle was based on the concept of spontaneous order and on the notion of the division of knowledge, two key ideas of Hayek's perspective. Although he considered the second of the two to be his own contribution and the more original, Hayek traced the first to the great Scottish social philosophers of the eighteenth century, notably Ferguson, Hume and Smith.

There thus exists between natural orders, which the natural sciences seek to explain, and artificial orders, constructed by human beings in accordance with predetermined plans, a third type of order characterized by being the product of human action without being the result of a human design: spontaneous orders. These include, for example, the market, money, language and morality; no one has ever consciously constructed them. The error of constructivist rationalists, from Descartes and Rousseau to their modern disciples, the socialists, social-democrats and even liberals in the American sense of the term, is to hold that spontaneous orders are actually artificial and can thus be destroyed and reconstituted. This error is supported by 'scientism', which is based on the illusion that it is possible to understand society by viewing it as a natural organism. It is thus clear that socialism rests upon an intellectual mistake. Moreover, this mistake, shared by the greatest scientists of our time, constitutes a threat to civilization.

Hayek, by drawing an analogy to the Smithian concept of the division of labour, introduced the concept of the division of knowledge. According to this principle, all societies are characterized by the fact that knowledge, which is by nature as practical as it is theoretical, is fragmented and dispersed between millions of individuals. The fundamental problem of society is thus the following: how can an order emerge from such a diffusion and dispersal? The answer to this question is clear: the market, an order brought about in the development of human societies, much like language, allows for it. No single brain, as powerful as it might be, can attain this order and, hence, planning is clearly impossible. The will to impose it can only lead to 'the road to serfdom'; to totalitarianism, in effect. Such is the ultimate fate of all types of interventionism.

Having undergone a long purgatory, Hayek established himself as the prime contemporary theoretician of liberalism, to which he has sought to give a new foundation in law, politics, and ideology as much as in pure economics. He proposed a general project for the organization of modern society (1960, 1973, 1976 *Law*, 1979) in which the state, which is to have the essential role of setting legal boundaries to the market and ensuring individual liberty through its monopoly on coercion, must itself be circumscribed by the rule of law. However, in Hayek's last work, there is a clear sense of pessimism concerning the future of civilization.

Main references

'The Nobel Memorial Prize in Economics 1974'. Official annoucement and article by F. Machlup, *Swedish Journal of Economics*, 1974, vol. 76, 469 and 498–531.

BARRY Norman P. 1979. *Hayek's Social and Economic Philosophy,* London, Macmillan.

BLAUG Mark 1992 (ed.). *Pioneers in Economics*, section 4, *Twentieth Century Economics*, Aldershot, Hants, Edward Elgar, vol. 41.

BUTLER Eamonn 1985. *Hayek: His Contribution to the Political and Economic Thought of Our Time*, New York, Universe Books; London, Temple Smith.

COLONNA Marina, HAGEMANN Harald and HAMOUDA Omar (eds) 1994. *The Economics of Hayek*, 2 vol., Aldershot, Hants, Edward Elgar.

CROWLEY Brian L. 1987. *The Self, the Individual, and the Community: Liberalism and Political Thought of F.A. Hayek and Sidney and Beatrice Webb*, Oxford, Clarendon Press.

DOSTALER Gilles and ÉTHIER Diane 1988 (eds). *Friedrich Hayek: Philosophie, économie et politique*, Montréal, ACFAS; Paris, Economica, 1989.
GRAY John 1984. *Hayek on Liberty*, Oxford, Basil Blackwell; 2nd edn 1986.
KUKATHAN Chandras 1989. *Hayek and Modern Liberalism*, Oxford, Clarendon Press.
MACHLUP Fritz 1976 (ed.). *Essays on Hayek*, New York University Press.
NEMO Philippe 1988. *La Société de droit selon F.A. Hayek*, Paris, Presses Universitaires de France.
O'DRISCOLL Gerald P., Jr. 1977. *Economics as a Coordination Problem: The Contributions of Friedrich A. Hayek*, Kansas City, Sheed Andrews & McMeel.
STEELE G.R. 1993. *The Economics of Friedrich Hayek*, New York, St Martin's Press.
TOMLINSON Jim 1990. *Hayek and the Market*, London, Pluto Press.
WOOD John Cunningham and WOODS Ronald N. 1991 (eds). *Friedrich A. Hayek: Critical Assessments*, 4 vols, London, Routledge.

BLAUG 1985, 87–90. *New Palgrave* 1987, vol. 2, 609–14. O'BRIEN and PRESLEY 1981, 234–61. SILLS 1979, 274–82. SPIEGEL and SAMUELS, 251–84.

HEILBRONER Robert Louis (born 1919)

Robert Heilbroner was born in New York and studied at Harvard, earning his BA in 1940. He then worked in management and the business world, and went on to obtain a PhD in 1963 at the New School for Social Research. Since 1968 he has been a professor of economics at the Graduate Faculty of the New School for Social Research.

Main publications

1953. *The Worldly Philosophers*, New York, Simon & Schuster.
1962. *The Making of Economic Society*, Englewood Cliffs, New Jersey, Prentice-Hall.
1966. *The Limits of American Capitalism*, New York, Harper & Row.
1970. *Between Capitalism and Socialism*, New York, Random House.
1980. *Marxism: For and Against*, New York, W.W. Norton.
1981. With Lester Thurow, *Five Economic Challenges*, Englewood Cliffs, New Jersey, Prentice-Hall.
1985. *The Nature and Logic of Capitalism*, New York, W.W. Norton.
1986. With Laurence Malone, *The Essential Adam Smith*, New York, W.W. Norton.
1988. *Behind the Veil of Economics: Essays in the Worldly Philosophy*, New York, W.W. Norton.
1989. With P.L. Bernstein, *The Debt and the Deficit*, New York, W.W. Norton.
1990. 'Analysis and Vision in the History of Modern Economics', *Journal of Economic Literature*, vol. 28, 1097–1114.

After publishing a very successful book on the great economists from Smith to Keynes (1953), Heilbroner wrote a book on the economic history of capitalism (1962) and various textbooks which he updated in successive editions, some of them with the collaboration of James K. Galbraith and Lester Thurow.

Having started from what he has termed a 'naive Keynesianism', he worked, from a Galbraithian and then a more radical perspective, on the limits of and prospects for American capitalism (1966, 1981, 1989). Enriching his analyses with the thoughts of Marx and Schumpeter, as well as various institutional, historic and radical influences, Heilbroner has pleaded for an open consideration of Marxism (1980); and in an accessible and moderate mode, he has taken up once again the task of exposing the nature of capitalism and the analysis of both its decline and the roots of its crisis (1985, 1988).

Main references

BLACKWELL Ron, CHATHA Jaspal and NELL Edward J. 1993 (eds). *Economics as Worldly Philosophy: Essays in Political and Historical Economics in Honour of Robert Heilbroner*, New York, St Martin's Press.

ARESTIS and SAWYER 1992, 241–8. BLAUG *Who's Who* 1986, 386.

HELLER Walter Wolfgang (1915–1987)

Born in Buffalo (New York), Walter Heller began his studies at Oberlin College (BA, 1935) and continued them at the university of Wisconsin (MA, 1938, PhD, 1941). Starting in 1942, he worked for the Treasury Department and, from 1946 on, took up a position at the University of Minnesota, where he spent his entire teaching career. In 1947–8 he was a finance advisor to the American military government in Germany. In 1951, Heller took part in a mission to the West German government concerning these same issues. From 1961 to 1964 he was chairman of the Council of Economic Advisers to presidents John F. Kennedy and Lyndon B. Johnson. In 1960, he was appointed director of the National Bureau of Economic Research and served as its chairman from 1971 to 1974. He was president of the American Economic Asociation in 1974.

Main publications

1959. With Clara Penniman, *State Income Tax Administration*, Madison, University of Wisconsin Press.

1966. *New Dimensions of Political Economy*, Cambridge, Massachusetts, Harvard University Press.

1969. With Milton Friedman, *Monetary vs Fiscal Policy. A Dialogue*, New York, W.W. Norton.

1975. 'What's Right with Economics?', *American Economic Review*, vol. 65, 1–26.

1976. *The Economy: Old Myths and New Realities*, New York, W.W. Norton.

Heller began his career as a specialist on fiscal questions, notably at local and state levels. His wartime and postwar activities strengthened and expanded his competence in the fields of taxation and public finance. He left his true mark as chairman of the Council of Economic Advisers of Presidents Kennedy and Johnson. Having been deeply affected, along with his entire generation, by the Great Depression and the New Deal, he was convinced that government has a responsibility towards employment and growth (1966, 1969). Heller was at home with the body of economic literature developed since Keynes, and hoped to place it at the service of economic policies favouring a return to full employment and social policies aimed at fighting poverty. Pragmatic and level-headed by disposition, he advocated a clear articulation of monetary and fiscal policies. In order to revive demand, he persuaded decision makers to reduce taxes, in opposition to Galbraith, who advocated enlarging the role of government and, consequently, of public expenditure.

In Heller's view, 'economics has come of age in the 1960s'; the fact that two presidents were willing to use, for the first time, the full range of modern economic tools underlies the unbroken U.S. expansion since early 1961 (1966, p. 1). Seeing in these advances the 'completion of the Keynesian Revolution' (ibid., p. 2), he personifies the postwar interventionist economist, at once confident in the progress of economics as a science and convinced that economists had finally mastered the main keys to prosperity.

Main references

BLAUG and STURGES 1983, 164. *New Palgrave* 1987, vol. 2, 637. SOBEL 1980, 118–43.

HICKS John Richard (1904–1989)

John Hicks was born in Warwick, England. After studies at Oxford University (1922–6), he taught at the London School of Economics from 1926 to 1935, and at Manchester University from 1935 to 1946, before moving to Oxford in 1946. He was knighted in 1964 and retired in 1965, but continued to publish prolifically until the end of his life. In 1972, he was awarded the Nobel Memorial Prize in Economics, sharing the award with Kenneth Arrow. The award was made in recognition of 'their pioneering contributions to general economic equilibrium theory and welfare theory'.

Main publications

1932. *The Theory of Wages*, London, Macmillan; 2nd edn 1963.
1934. With R.G.D. Allen, 'A Reconsideration of the Theory of Value', *Economica*, vol. 1, 52–76 and 196–219.
1935. 'A Suggestion for Simplifying the Theory of Money', *Economica*, vol. 2, 1–19.
1936. 'Mr. Keynes' Theory of Employment', *Economic Journal*, vol. 46, 238–53.
1937. 'Mr. Keynes and the "Classics": A Suggested Interpretation', *Econometrica*, vol. 5, 147–59.
1939. *Value and Capital: An Inquiry Into Some Fundamental Principles of Economic Theory*, Oxford, Clarendon Press; 2nd edn, 1946.
1942. *The Social Framework: An Introduction to Economics*, Oxford, Clarendon Press.
1945. 'La théorie de Keynes après neuf ans', *Revue d'économie politique*, vol. 55, 1–11.
1950. *A Contribution to the Theory of the Trade Cycle*, Oxford, Clarendon Press.
1956. *A Revision of Demand Theory*, Oxford, Clarendon Press.

1959. *Essays in World Economics*, Oxford, Clarendon Press.
1965. *Capital and Growth*, New York and Oxford, Oxford University Press.
1967. *Critical Essays in Monetary Theory*, Oxford, Clarendon Press.
1969. *A Theory of Economic History*, Oxford, Clarendon Press.
1973. *Capital and Time : A Neo-Austrian Theory*, Oxford, Clarendon Press.
1973. 'The Mainspring of Economic Growth', *Swedish Journal of Economics*, vol. 75, 336–48.
1974. *The Crisis in Keynesian Economics*, Oxford, Basil Blackwell; New York, Basic Books.
1975. 'Revival of Political Economy: The Old and the New', *Economic Record*, vol. 51, 365–7.
1976. 'Some Questions of Time in Economics', in A. Tang, F.M. Westfield and J.S. Worley (eds), *Evolution, Welfare and Time in Economics. Essays in Honor of Nicholas Georgescu-Roegen*, Lexington, Massachusetts, Lexington Books, 135–51.
1977. *Economic Perspectives: Further Essays on Money and Growth*, Oxford, Clarendon Press.
1979. *Causality in Economics*, Oxford, Basil Blackwell; New York, Basic Books.
1979. 'The Formation of an Economist', *Quarterly Review, Banca Nazionale del Lavoro*, no. 130, 195–204; in Kregel 1988, 1–10.
1980–1. 'IS-LM – An Explanation', *Journal of Post Keynesian Economics*, vol. 3, 139–54.
1981. *Wealth and Welfare, Collected Essays on Economic Theory*, vol. 1, Oxford, Basil Blackwell; Cambridge, Massachusetts, Cambridge University Press.
1982. *Money, Interest and Wages, Collected Essays on Economic Theory*, vol. 2, Oxford, Basil Blackwell; Cambridge, Massachusetts, Cambridge University Press.
1983. *Classics and Moderns, Collected Essays on Economic Theory*, vol. 3, Oxford, Basil Blackwell; Cambridge, Massachusetts, Cambridge University Press [with a bibliography of Hicks's works, 376–86].
1984. *The Economics of John Hicks*, edited by Dieter Helm, Oxford, Basil Blackwell.
1985. *Methods of Dynamic Economics*, Oxford, Clarendon Press [new edn of the first part of Hicks 1965].
1989. *A Market Theory of Money*, Oxford, Clarendon Press.
1990. 'The Unification of Macro-Economics', *Economic Journal*, vol. 100, 528–38.
1991. *The Status of Economics*, Oxford, Basil Blackwell.

John Hicks is one of the most influential economists of the twentieth century. His many contributions have for the most part been incorporated in his colleagues' writings, notably in their textbooks, and remain part of contemporary economic theory, even though their origin in Hicks's work is at times unnoticed. Hicks's work touches upon all of the fields of economics. He has made major contributions to both what are generally known as micro- and macroeconomics, which he preferred to term 'value theory' and 'monetary theory', respectively. He also attempted to integrate these two fields, as he was convinced of the essential unity of economic theory.

Early in his career, while at the London School of Economics, Hicks's views were close to those of Robbins and Hayek. He described in 'The Hayek Story' (in Hicks, 1967) how in the early 1930s he, along with many other young economists, hesitated to choose between the explanations of economic fluctuations and depressions suggested by Hayek and those suggested by Keynes. His first book (1932) is an orthodox treatment of the neoclassical arguments concerning the labour market. Two years later, Hicks, along with mathematician R.G.D. Allen, suggested a reformulation of value theory that is now found in all microeconomics textbooks (1934). He had then set out to accomplish a most ambitious project: to reformulate and modernize the general equilibrium theory elaborated by Walras and Pareto, to integrate money into the theory, and to extend it dynamically. The results of this effort appear in *Value and Capital* (1939). This book is undoubtedly Hicks's best known and most influential work, since most of the instruments of analysis proposed therein have been gradually integrated into contemporary economic theory. Until that time, the English version of marginalist theory proposed by Jevons and Marshall was dominant in the English-speaking world. Hicks then introduced the Walrasian approach of general equilibrium, which rapidly established itself in modern microeconomics.

Hicks had already begun to move closer to Keynes's views even before the publication of *The General Theory*. Some of his works, such as 'A Suggestion for Simplifying the Theory of Money' (1935), might even be considered as precursors of Keynes's analysis. At that time, Hicks, who was familiar with Wicksell, also assessed the significance of the work of Myrdal and the Stockholm School. He drew inspiration from them in the dynamic analysis found in *Value and Capital*, notably in his taking expectations into account.

Much like the Swedes, Hicks was somewhat sceptical before the total novelty claimed by Keynes in his book. In one of his most famous articles, 'Mr. Keynes and the Classics' (1937), he situated Keynes's system along with the classical system in a more general framework. Keynes, on the contrary, considered the classical model as a particular case of his own general model, of some use once full employment is achieved. The article's three equations to illustrate the models and, more especially, its graphic illustrations, showing how the interest rate and income level are established at the intersection point of curves *IS* and *LL* (which became *LM*), were to provide the framework for the main interpretation of Keynes's theory during the folowing decades. They are also found in all textbooks of macroeconomics from that period. The *IS–LM* model, taken up and developed by Hansen, Lerner and others, became the nexus of the so-called 'neoclassical synthesis'. In spite of his success, Hicks was nonetheless moved to warn against a non-critical application of his model, underlining that it by no means expresses the full meaning of Keynes's work: 'I must say that that diagram [*IS–LM*] is now much less popular with me than I think it still is with many other people. It reduces the *General Theory* to equilibrium economics; it is not really *in* time' (1976, p. 141). In fact, he actually offered a form of self-criticism in the *Journal of Post Keynesian Economics* (1980–1), a journal that incessantly criticized neoclassical Keynesianism, symbolized by the *IS–LM* model. Throughout his life, Hicks questioned the meaning of Keynes's work and of the Keynesian revolution, and also acted as a sharp critic of monetarism, whose roots he showed to be the theses of the Currency school of the nineteenth century.

In a field increasingly characterized by specialization, if not fragmentation, Hicks did not fear taking on very diverse problems. Apart from his writings on general equilibrium and Keynesian theory, he published important monographs on welfare theory (anthologized in the first volume of his *Collected Essays*, 1981), trade cycle (1950), growth (1965, 1977), capital theory (1973 *Capital*), international economics (1959) and intellectual history (1983), not counting his many contributions in applied economics and economic policy. Towards the end of his career, he suggested a general theory of economic history (1969) and an analysis of causality in economics (1979 *Causality*), among his other contributions. Hicks is effectively one of the last great generalists in economics. He is, moreover, an author who is extremely difficult to classify as belonging to a particular school of thought. Influenced by many theoretical currents, Hicks never ceased to question himself during his long career, and himself exercised considerable influence on many schools. The theoreticians of the neoclassical synthesis school, as well as the post-Keynesians, and both the disequilibrium school and the new classical macroeconomics, all draw inspiration from, and are indebted to him. It is noteworthy that his last article, written at the age of 85 and published posthumously, is entitled 'The Unification of Macro-Economics' (1990). He once wrote that there are two Hicks, an uncle and a nephew. The uncle is a neoclassical theorist whose nephew is by no means proud of his work (1975).

Main references

'The Nobel Memorial Prize in Economics 1972'. Official Announcement and article by William J. Baumol, *Swedish Journal of Economics*, 1972, vol. 74, 486–527.

BAUMOL William J. 1990. 'Sir John Versus the Hicksians, or Theorist Malgré Lui?', *Journal of Economic Literature*, vol. 28, 1708–15.

COLLARD David A. 1984 (ed.). *Economic Theory and Hicksian Themes*, Oxford, Clarendon Press.

GOODHART Charles A.E. and COURAKIS Anthony 1990 (eds). *The Monetary Economics of John Hicks*, London, Macmillan.

HAHN Frank 1990. 'John Hicks the Theorist', *Economic Journal*, vol. 100, 539–49.

HAMOUDA Omar 1993. *John R. Hicks: The Economist's Economist*, Oxford, Basil Blackwell.

McKENZIE Lionel and ZAMAGNI Stefano 1990 (eds). *Value and Capital: Fifty Years Later*, London, Macmillan.

WOLFE James N. 1968 (ed.). *Value, Capital, and Growth: Papers in Honour of Sir John Hicks*, Edinburgh University Press.

WOOD John Cunningham and WOODS Ronald N. 1989 (eds). *Sir John Hicks: Critical Assessments*, 4 vols, London, Routledge.

BLAUG 1985, 91–3. GREENAWAY and PRESLEY 1989, 97–119. KREGEL, 1988, 1–10. KUPER and KUPER 1985, 355–6. *New Palgrave* 1987, vol. 2, 641–6. SHACKLETON and LOCKSLEY 1981. SILLS 1979, 300–302. SPIEGEL and SAMUELS 1984, 78–98.

HIRSCHMAN Albert Otto (born 1915)

Albert Hirschman was born in Berlin and began his studies there (1932–3). He left Hitler's Germany to continue his education at the Paris Ecole des Hautes Études Commerciales and the Institute of Statistics at the Sorbonne (1933–5), at the London School of Economics, and finally at the University of Trieste, where he obtained his doctorate in economics (1938). He worked for a year in Paris, and fought with the French army (1939–1940). He then left for the United States and was awarded a research grant from the University of California at Berkeley (1941–3). He served in the ranks of the American army, worked at the Federal Reserve Board in Washington (1946–52) and went on to serve as an economic advisor (1952–4) and consultant (1954–6) in Bogotà, Colombia. Hirschman was a visiting professor at Yale University from 1956 to 1958, a professor of international economic relations at Columbia from 1958 to 1964 and a professor of political economy at Harvard from 1964 to 1974. He then went to the Institute for Advanced Study at Princeton as professor of social science, from 1974, and has been professor emeritus since 1985.

Main publications

1945. *National Power and the Structure of Foreign Trade*, Berkeley, University of California Press.

1958. *The Strategy of Economic Development*, New Haven, Connecticut, Yale University Press.

1963. *Journeys Toward Progress: Studies of Economic Policy-Making in Latin America*, New York, Twentieth Century Fund.

1967. *Development Projects Observed*, Washington, DC, Brookings Institution.

1970. *Exit, Voice, and Loyalty: Responses to Decline in Firms, Organizations, and States*, Cambridge, Massachusetts, Harvard University Press.

1971. *A Bias for Hope: Essays on Development and Latin America*, New Haven, Connecticut, Yale University Press.

1977. *The Passions and the Interests: Political Arguments for Capitalism Before Its Triumph*, Princeton University Press.

1981. *Essays in Trespassing: Economics to Politics and Beyond*, Cambridge, England, Cambridge University Press.

1982. *Shifting Involvements: Private Interest and Public Action*, Princeton University Press.

1984. *L'Economie comme science morale et politique*, Paris, Gallimard – Seuil.

1986. *Vers une économie politique élargie*, Paris, Editions de Minuit.

1986. *Rival Views of Market Society and Other Essays*, New York, Viking-Penguin.

1991. *The Rhetoric of Reaction: Perversity, Futility, Jeopardy*, Cambridge, Massachusetts, Harvard University Press.

Albert Hirschman entered the debate on development in 1958, going against the stream. Whereas many sought a path to balanced development, he underlined the fact that growth is necessarily a source of disequilibrium and tension. To those who made reference to the existence of a unique economic rationality, he submitted, agreeing with Schultz on this matter, that there are 'hidden rationalities'. Against those holding that industrialization tends to be harmonious, he emphasized, like Perroux, that main sectors are able to give impetus to others, through upward and downward links with them. He developed these themes with reference to concrete analyses (1963, 1967, 1971).

But Hirschman's thought cannot be confined either within the development field or within the agreed upon boundaries of economics. In dealing with contemporary changes (1970) he continued his search for hidden rationalities. In addition to interests, on which economists focus their attention, he added love, generosity, giving, loyalty and ethics; in addition to the capacity or lack thereof to participate – the market's prime alternatives are to buy, or not, and to sell, or not – Hirschman highlights the capacity to use voice in contesting and suggesting. Reflecting his interest in the ideological roots of capitalism (1977) and of the permanent character of the discourse set forth by those opposed to reform (1991), he has dipped into political science and sociology, intellectual history and philosophy. Does all of this represent a desire to move beyond the beaten path, to contribute to an expanded political economy? Or, quite simply, are his the methods of a non-conformist who, as noted by François Furet (1984 'Introduction', p.6), seeks 'that which is not economic within economics, while at the same time, acting on or resulting from economics' – an attitude which risks disconcerting a lot of economists?

Main references

WILBER Charles K. and JAMESON Kenneth P. 1992. 'Albert O. Hirschman', in SAMUELS (ed.), 106–28.

ARESTIS and SAWYER 1992, 256–62. BLAUG 1985, 94–6. MEIER and SEERS 1984, 87–111. *New Palgrave*, 1987, vol. 2, 658–9.

HUTCHISON Terence Wilmot (born 1912)

Terence Hutchison was born in Bournemouth (Hampshire, England). He studied at Cambridge University from 1931 to 1934, obtaining a Master's from the same university in 1937. He lived in Bonn until 1938, at which point he began teaching English and social sciences at the Teachers' Training College in Baghdad. He taught at Hull University in 1946 and then joined the London School of Economics, before being named professor at the University of Birmingham in 1956. He retired in 1978.

Main publications

1935. 'A Note on Tautologies and the Nature of Economic Theory', *Review of Economic Studies*, vol. 2, 159–61.
1938. *The Significance and Basic Postulates of Economic Theory*, London, Macmillan.
1953. *A Review of Economic Doctrines, 1870–1929*, Oxford, Clarendon Press.

1964. *Positive Economics and Policy Objectives*, London, George Allen & Unwin.
1966. *Markets and the Franchise: A Review of the Relationships Between Economic and Political Choice*, London, Institute of Economic Affairs.
1968. *Economics and Economic Policy in Britain, 1946–1966: Some Aspects of their Interrelations*, London, George Allen & Unwin.
1977. *Keynes versus the 'Keynesians'...? An Essay in the Thinking of J.M. Keynes and the Accuracy of its Interpretation by his Followers*, London, Institute of Economic Affairs.
1977. *Knowledge and Ignorance in Economics*, Oxford, Basil Blackwell; University of Chicago Press.
1978. *On Revolutions and Progress in Economic Knowledge*, Cambridge, England, Cambridge University Press.
1980. *The Limitations of General Theories in Macroeconomics*, Washington, DC, American Enterprise Institute.
1981. *The Politics and Philosophy of Economics: Marxians, Keynesians and Austrians*, Oxford, Basil Blackwell.
1988. *Before Adam Smith: The Emergence of Political Economy, 1662–1776*, Oxford, Basil Blackwell.
1992. *Changing Aims in Economics*, Oxford, Basil Blackwell.

With regard to Terence Hutchison, Haberler in 1980 wrote that he is 'the foremost living historian of economic thought' (Preface to Hutchison 1980); Coats has said: 'If the economics profession can be said to have a conscience, then Hutchison is unquestionably one of its most persuasive and insistent voices – a voice that cannot easily be ignored' (Coats 1983, *Methodological*, p. xi); and Stigler has estimated that, in over 40 years, Hutchison had always been 'unfailingly honest, deeply and widely read, and frequently completely dissatisfied with the literature of which he is so completely a master' (Stigler 1965 below, p. 596). Such commentary illustrates the importance of an influential *oeuvre*, which extends over half a century.

Terence Hutchison is certainly one of the most erudite economists of our age. Author of a classic work on the evolution of economic thought during what became known as the marginalist revolution (1953), he has also written extensively on both the classical and on the contemporary periods, and a recent book is a monumental and thorough work on economic thought before Smith (1988). Hutchison believes that the evolution of economic thought has been marked by certain periods of deep change, which may be called revolutions, associated with the names of Smith, Jevons, Keynes and perhaps Ricardo (1978). Not simply the result of an internal dynamic, these changes also reflect broader historical change (1966). In several of his works, Hutchison dismantles many pre-existing conceptions, and roundly criticizes the way in which economists rewrite the history of their discipline in order to defend their own particular position. Keynes's followers were among his later targets in this regard (1977 *Keynes*).

A historian of thought, Hutchison is also a specialist of methodology. His first book (1938) became a classic and gave rise to a debate which has not yet ended. Influenced by logical positivism, and espousing a methodology containing elements of naturalism and empiricism, Hutchison was the first to introduce into economics Popper's demarcation criteria for distinguishing science from pseudo-science, or empirical propositions from definitions and tautologies. A believer in the distinction between the positive and the normative (1964) and a critic of all forms of dogmatism, Hutchison has often accused his peers of abuse in basing political conclusions on debatable theoretical foundations (1968). He recently criticized the excessive formalization of modern economics (1992).

Main references

COATS A.W. 1983 (ed.). *Methodological Controversy in Economics: Historical Essays in Honor of T. W. Hutchison*, Greenwich, Connecticut and London, JAI Press. [With a bibliography of T.W. Hutchison, 265–9.]

COATS A.W. 1983. 'T.W. Hutchison as a Historian of Economics', in Warren J. Samuels, (ed.), *Research in the History of Economic Thought and Methodology*, vol. 1, *The Craft of the Historian of Economic Thought*, Greenwich, Connecticut and London, JAI Press, 187–207.

STIGLER George J. 1965. 'The History of Economics Through Professor Hutchison's Spectacles', *Minerva*, vol. 16, 596–9.

New Palgrave 1987, vol. 2, 703.

ISARD Walter (born 1919)

Walter Isard was born in Drexel Hill, Pennsylvania. He earned an MA (1941) and a PhD (1943) at Harvard University. He taught at the American University (1948–9), at Harvard (1949–53) and at the Massachusetts Institute of Technology (1953–6). He was then named professor of economics, regional science and peace science at the University of Pennsylvania and chairman of the department of regional science that he founded in 1956. He occupied this position until 1979, when he was appointed professor at Cornell University. He founded the Regional Science Association (1954) and the Peace Science Society (1963). Since 1960, he has been editor of the *Journal of Regional Science*, and sits on the editorial boards of many journals devoted to peace as well as to regional science.

Main publications

1949. 'The General Theory of Location and Space Economy', *Quarterly Journal of Economics*, vol. 63, 476–506.

1956. *Location and Space-Economy: A General Theory Relating to Industrial Location, Market Areas, Land Use, Trade, and Urban Structure*, Cambridge, Massachusetts, Technology Press of Massachusetts Institute of Technology; New York, John Wiley & Sons; London, Chapman & Hall.

1960. *Et al., Methods of Regional Analysis: An Introduction to Regional Science*, Cambridge, Massachusetts, MIT Press.

1969. With T.E. Smith *et al., General Theory: Social, Political, Economic, and Regional, with Particular Reference to Decision-Making Analysis*, Cambridge, Massachusetts, Cambridge University Press.

1975. *Introduction to Regional Science*, Englewood Cliffs, New Jersey, Prentice-Hall.

1979. With P. Liossatos, *Spatial Dynamics and Optimal Space-Time Development*, New York, North-Holland.

1982. With C. Smith, *Conflict Management Analysis and Practical Conflict Management Procedures*, Cambridge, Massachusetts, Ballinger Press.

1988. *Arms Races, Arms Control, and Conflict Analysis: Contributions from Peace Science and Peace Economics*, New York, Cambridge University Press.

1990. *Selected Papers of Walter Isard*, edited by Christine Smith, 2 vols, New York University Press.

1992. *Understanding Conflict and the Science of Peace*, Oxford, Basil Blackwell.

Walter Isard is the founder of a new discipline called regional science. He has gradually elaborated it, along with many collaborators, through four ambitious books (1956, 1960, 1969, 1979) and has set down its basic principles in a manual (1975). Isard clearly defined his research programme from the start of his career (1949), blaming all social sciences, but economic science in particular, for not only their unsatisfactory treatment of time but also their even more anaemic approach to problems related to space and localization. The first book of what he calls his 'quadrilogy' aims at reviving the analysis of which von Thünen, among others, had been a pioneer in Germany in the early nineteenth century, and which has gradually been abandoned. It is not, however, Isard's aim to limit himself to what is called regional economics and spatial location. Hence this new regional science he intends to build can only be multidisciplinary, involving sociology, geography, political science, anthropology and psychology as well as economics. It is necessary 'to develop a general theory on the social, political, and economic structure and function of regions, synthetizing strong elements of the fields already mentioned, and hopefully at the same time deepening relevant theory in each field' (1969, p. viii). Isard emphasizes that his theoretical approach is necessarily eclectic because it must borrow from many techniques with different levels of abstraction. The importance of this new exploratory field explains the length of the main theoretical book of this 'quadrilogy' (1969): more than a thousand pages.

Isard is a particularly prolific author and has published a number of research reports as well as over 200 scientific articles, the main ones having been recently gathered in two volumes (1990). Besides regional science, he is also interested in many topics, such as the arms race, military conflicts and, more generally, peace science, of which he is also one of the main architects (1982, 1988).

Main reference

BLAUG 1985, 99–100.

JOHNSON Harry Gordon (1923–1977)

Harry Johnson was born in Toronto, Canada. He studied at the Universities of Toronto (BA in 1943, MA in 1947), Cambridge, England (BA in 1946, MA in 1951) and Harvard (MA in 1948, PhD in 1958). He began his teaching career at the University of St Francis Xavier, in the Canadian province of Nova Scotia. He taught at the University of Cambridge (England) from 1949 to 1956, then at the University of Manchester from 1956 to 1959. In 1959, he was named professor at the University of Chicago. From 1966 to 1974 he divided his time between the University of Chicago and the London School of Economics, where he was also a professor. He died in Geneva where he was teaching at the Graduate School of International Studies. A president of the Canadian Association of Economic and Political Sciences (1965–6), Harry Johnson was editor of the *Journal of Political Economy* (1960–66, 1969–77), of *Economica* (1969–70) and of the *Journal of International Economics* (1969–76).

Main publications

1952. *The Overloaded Economy: The Economic Problems of Great Britain*, University of Toronto Press.
1958. *International Trade and Economic Growth: Studies in Pure Theory*, London, George Allen & Unwin.
1962. *Canada in a Changing World Economy*, University of Toronto Press.
1962. 'Monetary Theory and Policy', *American Economic Review*, vol. 52, 335–84.
1962. *Money, Trade and Economic Growth: Survey Lectures in Economics*, London, George Allen & Unwin; Cambridge, Massachusetts, Harvard University Press.
1963. *The Canadian Quandary: Economic Problems and Policies*, Toronto, McGraw-Hill.
1965. *The World Economy at the Crossroads: A Survey of Current Problems of Money, Trade and Economic Development*, Oxford, Clarendon Press.
1967. *Essays in Monetary Economics*, London, George Allen & Unwin.
1968. *Comparative Cost and Commercial Policy Theory for a Developing World Economy*, Stockholm, Almqvist & Wiksell.
1968. With Paul Wonnacott and Hirofumi Shibata, *Harmonization of National Economic Policies under Free Trade*, University of Toronto Press.
1971. *Aspects of the Theory of Tariffs*, London, George Allen & Unwin; Chicago, Aldine-Atherton.
1971. *Macroeconomics and Monetary Theory*, London, Gray-Mills.
1971. 'The Keynesian Revolution and the Monetarist Counter-Revolution', *American Economic Review*, vol. 61, *Papers and Proceedings*, 1–14.
1971. *The Two-Sector Model of General Equilibrium*, London, George Allen & Unwin.
1972. *Further Essays in Monetary Economics*, London, George Allen & Unwin.
1972. *Inflation and the Monetarist Controversy*, Amsterdam, North-Holland.
1973. *The Theory of Income Distribution*, London, Gray-Mills.
1974. With Melvyn B. Kraus, *General Equilibrium Analysis: A Microeconomic Text*, London, George Allen & Unwin.
1975. *On Economics and Society*, University of Chicago Press.
1976. *Technology and Economic Interdependence*, London, Macmillan.
1976 (ed., with J.A. Frenkel). *The Monetary Approach to the Balance of Payments*, London, George Allen & Unwin.
1978. *Selected Essays in Monetary Economics*, London, George Allen & Unwin.

1978 (ed., with J.A. Frenkel). *The Economics of Exchange Rates*, Reading, Massachusetts, Addison-Wesley.
1978. With Elizabeth S. Johnson, *The Shadow of Keynes: Understanding Keynes, Cambridge and Keynesian Economics*, Oxford, Basil Blackwell; University of Chicago Press.

Harry Johnson engaged in intense activity during his brief career, which was cut short by his premature death. Defining himself as a 'cosmopolitan economist', simultaneously teaching in several universities throughout the world, a tireless lecturer, an organizer of colloquia and conferences, editor and member of editorial boards of numerous journals, economic adviser to public organizations, Johnson exerted considerable influence on what he called the 'economic profession'. His intellectual output is impressive, as much for the diversity of questions studied as for its quantity. Johnson himself estimated that he was the economist who had published the greatest number of scientific articles. With the 524 compiled by Vicky Longawa (in *JPE* memorial issue, see below, 1984, 659–711), he certainly was not wrong. Johnson, who considered that an economist must make the science progress by relying on the work of others, made numerous syntheses of the leading postwar theoretical contributions. The clarity of his style, his pedagogical talent and his efforts to use accessible techniques of presentation ensured that several of his articles, in numerous fields, appeared in students' reading lists and in numerous anthologies.

Johnson's contribution, however, is not limited to the synthesis of the thinking of others. He made original contributions to several fields of economic theory. It is in that of international economics that they are the most numerous and influential. In its current form, the neoclassical theory of international trade is, in large part, the work of Johnson. In the field of international finances, it is necessary to mention in particular the development of the monetary approach to the balance of payments, which revives the tradition initiated by Hume and abandoned by Keynes and his disciples. Always concerned with linking theory and economic policy, Johnson was during his career a tireless advocate of free trade.

Johnson also intervened in the fields of macroeconomics, the theory of growth, income distribution and development economics. He considered that all aspects of economic theory were closely linked, and often criticized as too elaborate the specialization in the current training of economists. He also believed that the economic must always, in the last instance, be linked to the political. He often intervened on questions of economic policy, as much in Great Britain, the United States and his own country as in the fields of global economics and development.

First influenced by Keynes's radical disciples at Cambridge, Johnson came closer to the positions of the monetarist economists, without, for all that, adhering to this school of thought. The author of articles which became main references on the debate between monetarism and Keynesianism (1962 *AER*, 1971 *AER*), he estimated that there was, between Keynes's thinking and that of his opponents, in particular Friedman, not so great a division as one has been led to believe.

Main references

BLAUG Mark 1992 (ed.). *Harry Johnson (1923–1977), Pioneers in Economics*, vol. 42, Aldershot, Hants, Edward Elgar.

Canadian Journal of Economics 1978, vol. 11, supplement.

Journal of Political Economy 1984, vol. 92, 565–711.

REUBER Grant and SCOTT Anthony 1977. 'Harry Gordon Johnson', *Canadian Journal of Economics*, vol. 10, 670–77.

TOBIN James 1978. 'Harry Gordon Johnson 1923–1977', *Proceedings of the British Academy*, vol. 64, 443–58.

BLAUG 1985, 101–3. GREENAWAY and PRESLEY 1989, 170–210. *New Palgrave* 1987, vol. 2, 1022–6. SILLS 1979, 351–8.

JORGENSON Dale Weldeau (born 1933)

Dale Jorgenson was born in Bozeman, Montana. He studied at Harvard, earning an AM in 1957 and a PhD in 1959. He started teaching in 1959 at the University of California, Berkeley, where he was appointed professor in 1963. Since 1969 he has been a professor at Harvard. In 1971, he was awarded the John Bates Clark Medal of the American Economic Association, and he was president of the Econometric Society in 1987.

Main publications

1963. 'Capital Theory and Investment Behavior', *American Economic Review*, vol. 53, 247–59.

1966. 'Testing Alternative Theories of the Development of a Dual Economy', in I. Adelman, and E. Thorbecke (eds), *The Theory and Design of Economic Development*, Baltimore, Johns Hopkins, 45–60.

1967. With J.J. McCall and R. Radner, *Optimal Replacement Policy*, Chicago, Rand McNally; Amsterdam, North-Holland.

1967. With Zvi Griliches, 'The Explanation of Productivity Change', *Review of Economic Studies*, vol. 34, 249–84.

1967. With J.A. Stephenson, 'Investment Behavior in U.S. Manufacturing, 1947–60', *Econometrica*, vol. 35, 169–220.

1968. With C. Siebert, 'Optimal Capital Accumulation and Corporate Investment Behavior', *Journal of Political Economy*, vol. 76, 1123–51.

1971. 'Econometric Studies of Investment Behavior: A Survey', *Journal of Economic Literature*, vol. 9, 1111–47.

1973. With L.R. Christensen and L.J. Lau, 'Transcendental Logarithmic Production Frontiers', *Review of Economics and Statistics*, vol. 55, 28–45.

1986. 'Econometric Methods for Modeling Producer Behavior', in Zvi Griliches and Michael D. Intriligator, (eds), *Handbook of Econometrics*, Amsterdam, North-Holland, vol. 3, 1841–1915.

1987. With Frank M. Gollop and Barbara M. Fraumeni, *Productivity and U.S. Economic Growth*, Cambridge, Massachusetts, Harvard University Press.

1990. 'Aggregate Consumer Behavior and the Measurement of Social Welfare', *Econometrica*, vol. 58, 1007–40.
1990. 'Productivity and Economic Growth', in Ernst R. Berndt, and Jack E. Triplett (eds), *Fifty Years of Economic Measurement,* University of Chicago Press, 19–118.
1991. With K.-Y. Yun, *Tax Reform and the Cost of Capital,* Oxford, Clarendon Press; New York, Oxford University Press.
1993. With Peter J. Wilcoxen, 'Energy, the Environment, and Economic Growth', in Alan V. Kneese and James L. Sweeny (eds), *Handbook of Natural Resource and Energy Economics,* Amsterdam, North-Holland, vol. 3, 1267–1349.

Dale Jorgenson is primarily known for his contributions to investment and capital theory. He has rejected both Keynes's analysis in terms of the marginal efficiency of capital and studies such as those of Haavelmo and Simon, which imply that the neoclassical framework is unable adequately to account for investment decisions. He has sought, rather, to account for such decisions through a formulation based on the hypothesis that firms maximize their current value. In his analysis, capital is treated as a factor of production whose cost, taking into account the taxation of capital income, is a key factor in the investment function (1963, 1971, 1991). A specialist in econometrics, Jorgenson developed sophisticated techniques in the study of consumption and production behaviour (1986, 1990 *Econometrica*), thus giving the analysis involved an econometric formulation in terms of general equilibrium.

His studies of productivity and its measurement, development and relation to economic growth have undoubtedly formed the basis of highly fruitful, but most controversial, empirical studies (1967 *RES*, 1987, 1990 in Berndt and Triplett). For Jorgenson and his associates, production growth results primarily from the increase in capital and labour inputs, rather than from technological change. Technological progress should be considered embodied to a great extent in new investments rather than as an autonomous factor, contrary to Solow's approach (Solow 1957). Jorgenson considers that 'the most fruitful approach to research in economic measurement is one that combines national accounting, econometrics, and economic theory' (1990 in Berndt and Triplett, p. 89). He has shown interest in many other questions, notably the problems of energy and environmental policy, where he tries to show 'that intertemporal general equilibrium modeling provides a very worthwhile addition to methodologies for modeling the economic impact of energy and environmental policies' (1993, p. 1342). He is also interested in development and in particular the duality hypothesis concerning underdeveloped economies, which he has attempted to explain in neoclassical terms (1966).

Main reference

BLAUG 1985, 104–5.

KALDOR Nicholas (1908–1986)

Nicholas Kaldor was born in Budapest, Hungary. He was educated in Berlin and London, graduating from the London School of Economics in 1930, where he taught from 1932 to 1947. He was then recruited by Gunnar Myrdal as the first director of the research and planning division of the United Nations Economic Commission for Europe. He became a fellow of King's College, Cambridge in 1949, and a professor of economics in 1966. He retired in 1975. Kaldor was a financial adviser to many Third World countries. He was also a financial advisor to the British Chancellor of the Exchequer under two Labour governments, from 1964 to 1968 and from 1974 to 1976. He was elevated to the peerage in 1974.

Main publications

1938. 'Stability and Full Employment', *Economic Journal*, vol. 48, 642–57.

1940. 'A Model of the Trade Cycle', *Economic Journal*, vol. 50, 78–92.

1948. *A Statistical Analysis of Advertising Expenditures and of the Revenue of the Press*, Cambridge, England, Cambridge University Press.

1955. *An Expenditure Tax*, London, George Allen & Unwin.

1956. 'Alternative Theories of Distribution', *Review of Economic Studies*, vol. 23, 83–100.

1957. 'A Model of Economic Growth', *Economic Journal*, vol. 67, 591–624.

1960. *Essays on Economic Stability and Growth* (*Collected Economic Essays*, vol. 2), London, Gerald Duckworth.

1960. *Essays on Value and Distribution* (*Collected Economic Essays*, vol. 1), London, Gerald Duckworth.

1961. 'Capital Accumulation and Economic Growth', in F.A. Lutz and D.C. Hague (eds), *The Theory of Capital*, London, Macmillan, 177–222.

1964. *Essays on Economic Policy I* (*Collected Economic Essays*, vol. 3), London, Gerald Duckworth.

1964. *Essays on Economic Policy II* (*Collected Economic Essays*, vol. 4), London, Gerald Duckworth.

1966. *Causes of the Slow Rate of Economic Growth in the United Kingdom: An Inaugural Lecture*, Cambridge, England, Cambridge University Press.

1967. *Strategic Factors in Economic Development*, Ithaca, New York, ILR Press.

1971 (ed.). *Conflicts in Policy Objective*, Oxford, Basil Blackwell.

1978. *Further Essays on Applied Economics* (*Collected Economic Essays*, vol. 6), London, Gerald Duckworth; New York, Holmes & Meier.

1978. *Further Essays on Economic Theory* (*Collected Economic Essays*, vol. 5), London, Gerald Duckworth .

1980. *Reports on Taxation I* (*Collected Economic Essays*, vol. 7), London, Gerald Duckworth .

1980. *Reports on Taxation II* (*Collected Economic Essays*, vol. 8), London, Gerald Duckworth .

1982. *The Scourge of Monetarism*, Oxford and New York, Oxford University Press.

1983. *Limitations of the 'General Theory'*, Oxford, Oxford University Press.

1983. *The Economic Consequences of Mrs Thatcher*, London, Gerald Duckworth.

1984. *Economics without Equilibrium*, New York, M.E. Sharpe.

1986. 'Recollections of an Economist', *Quarterly Review, Banca Nazionale del Lavoro*, no. 156, 3–26; in Kregel 1988, 11–35.

1987. *Économie et instabilité*, edited by R. Boyer *et al.*, Paris, Économica.

1989. *The Essential Kaldor*, edited by F. Targetti and A.P. Thirlwall, London, Gerald Duckworth.

1989. *Further Essays on Economic Theory and Policy* (*Collected Economic Essays*, vol. 9), London, Gerald Duckworth; New York, Holmes & Meier.

1991. *Causes of Growth and Stagnation in the World Economy*, Cambridge, England, Cambridge University Press.

At the start of his career, at the London School of Economics, Kaldor made a number of contributions to neoclassical theory. The appearance of *The General Theory* marked a turning point in his career; he then took on the task of developing various aspects of the work, notably the construction of a trade cycle theory (1940), with the purpose of isolating the factors that allow for the taking into account of investment instability. He became, along with Joan Robinson, one of the main initiators of what is termed post-Keynesianism, characterized by a 'non neoclassical' interpretation of Keynes's work and, in particular, its extension to the study of cycles, growth and distribution. Kaldor contrasts a synthesis of the theory of effective demand and a theory of distribution inspired by Kalecki, based on class struggle between capitalists and workers, with the neoclassical synthesis. In one of his most influent articles (1956), Kaldor demonstrates that capitalists' investment and consumption expenditures determine national income and profit levels. He developed a model, sometimes known as the Cambridge equation, in which the rate of profit in the economy is determined by the growth rate and by the propensity to save of capitalists. The parallel development of neoclassical models of growth in Cambridge, Massachussetts, notably by Robert Solow, gave rise to the 'war of the two Cambridges' in the 1960s.

Kaldor's contributions to growth and distribution theory are but one aspect of his fertile scholarly production. His main articles were published in nine volumes between 1960 and 1980 (*Collected Economic Essays*). He has made important contributions to many fields of economic theory, writing on value and distribution, money, capital, development, technological progress, welfare economics and international trade. A reformer and implacable adversary of monetarism (1982), he is a critical disciple of Keynes (1983 *Limitations*), whose interests are as concerned with policy as with theory (two books of 1964, 1971, 1983 *The Economic*). In particular, he has produced many valuable works on fiscal policy (1955, two books of 1980).

Main references

Cambridge Journal of Economics, Memorial issue, March 1989, vol. 13, no. 1, 1–272; reprinted as *Kaldor's Political Economy*, edited by T. Lawson, J. Gabriel Palma and J. Sender, London, Academic Press; San Diego, California, Harcourt Brace Jovanovich.

HARCOURT, G.C. 1988. 'Nicholas Kaldor, 12 May 1908–30 September 1986', *Economica*, vol. 55, 159–70.

KALDOR 1986.

NELL Edward J. and SEMMLER Willi (eds) 1991. *Nicholas Kaldor and Mainstream Economics: Confrontation or Convergence?*, London, Macmillan; New York, St Martin's Press.

PASINETTI Luigi L. 1986. 'Nicholas Kaldor: An Appreciation', *Cambridge Journal of Economics*, vol. 10, 301–3.

TARGETTI Ferdinando 1988. *Nicholas Kaldor: Economia e politica di un capitalismo in*

mutamento, Bologne, il Mulino; Engl. transl. 1992, *Nicholas Kaldor: The Economics and Politics of Capitalism as a Dynamic System*, New York, Oxford University Press.
THIRLWALL A.P. *et al.* 1983. 'Symposium: Kaldor's Growth Laws', *Journal of Post Keynesian Economics*, vol. 5, 341–429.
THIRLWALL A.P. 1987. *Nicholas Kaldor, Economist and Adviser*, Brighton, Wheatsheaf.
TURNER Marjorie S. 1993. *Nicholas Kaldor and the Real World*, Armonk, New York, M.E. Sharpe.

ARESTIS and SAWYER 1992, 293–302. BLAUG 1985, 106–8. GREENAWAY and PRESLEY 1989, 68–95. *New Palgrave* 1987, vol. 3, 3–8. SILLS 1979, 366–9.

KALECKI Michal (1899–1970)

Michal Kalecki was born in the Polish city of Lodz, at a time when it was under Russian occupation. For financial reasons, he was forced to abandon his studies in civil engineering at the Warsaw and Gdansk Polytechnics. In 1929, he was appointed to a position at the Institute of Research on Business Cycles and Prices, in Warsaw, where he began his work as an economist. In 1936, a Rockefeller fellowship gave him the opportunity to visit Sweden, where he met such economists as Lindahl, Myrdal and Ohlin, and the United Kingdom, where he met Kahn, Sraffa and Joan Robinson, among others. In 1937, Kalecki resigned from the Institute where he worked in Warsaw, following the politically motivated firing of two of his colleagues within the context of an antisemitic campaign. He then settled in England. From 1940 to 1945, he was employed by the Oxford University Institute of Statistics. He worked one year in Montreal for the International Labour Office and in 1946 became deputy director of a section of the economics department of the United Nations secretariat in New York. He resigned in protest against the political discrimination linked to the rise of McCarthyism and returned to Poland in 1955. He was appointed professor in 1956 and held various public positions, notably that of chairman of the Commission on Perspective Planning. In 1961, he began his affiliation with the Central School of Planning and Statistics. Kalecki resigned all of his official positions in 1968, following the Polish government's antisemitic and anti-revisionist campaign that year. Many of his friends, students and colleagues were also victims at that time. He continued his own research until the end of his life.

Main publications

1933. *Proba teorii koniunktury* [Essays on business cycle theory], Warsaw, Instytut Badania Koniunkture Gospodarczych i Cen; partial Engl. transl., 'Outline of a Theory of the Business Cycle', in Kalecki 1966 and 1971.
1935. 'A Macrodynamic Theory of Business Cycles', *Econometrica*, vol. 3, 327–44.
1935. 'Essai d'une théorie du mouvement cyclique des affaires', *Revue d'économie politique*, vol. 49, 285–305.
1939. *Essays in the Theory of Economic Fluctuations*, London, George Allen & Unwin.

1943. *Studies in Economic Dynamics*, London, George Allen & Unwin.
1954. *Theory of Economic Dynamics: An Essay on Cyclical and Long-Run Changes in Capitalist Economy*, London, George Allen & Unwin.
1966. *Studies in the Theory of Business Cycles 1933–1939*, Oxford, Basil Blackwell.
1971. *Selected Essays on the Dynamics of the Capitalist Economy, 1933–1970*, Cambridge, England, Cambridge University Press.
1972. *Selected Essays on the Economic Growth of the Socialist and the Mixed Economy*, Cambridge, England, Cambridge University Press.
1972. *The Last Phase in the Transformation of Capitalism*, New York, Monthly Review Press.
1976. *Essays on Developing Economies*, Brighton, Harvester Press.
1976–86. *Dziela*, 6 vols, edited by J. Osiatynski, Warsaw, Panstwowe Wydawnictwo Ekonomiczne; Engl. transl. 1990–, *Collected Works of Michal Kalecki*, Oxford University Press; Oxford, Clarendon Press.
1976. *Selected Essays on Economic Planning*, edited by Jan Toporowski, Cambridge, England, Cambridge University Press.

In 1933, the Warsaw Institute of Research on Business Cycles and Prices published a 55-page book (in Polish) (entitled Essays on business cycle theory). This work alone would have sufficed to establish Kalecki's reputation. He here formulated concisely the theory of effective demand of which Keynes is generally considered the author. Moreover, it contains analyses of distribution and of business cycles. Kalecki's attitude upon reading the *General Theory* during his stay in Stockholm is a good indication of his character. He confessed to Joan Robinson that the book disconcerted him, as he had been getting ready to write an analogous work of his own (Robinson 1973 *Collected*, p. 87). He had also been able to detect the fact that Myrdal and his colleagues were on the same track. He spent time in Cambridge, meeting Keynes, with whom his relations were never very close owing partly to personality differences. Kalecki never once made public the fact that he had published his work before Keynes, speaking of it only to Keynes's disciples, and never to the economist himself. Only in the preface to one of his posthumous works do we read: 'The first part includes three papers published in 1933, 1934 and 1935 in Polish before Keynes' *General Theory* appeared, and containing, I believe, its essentials' (1971, p. vii). Kalecki and Keynes arrived at similar conclusions by quite different means. Whereas Keynes developed his theory from orthodox, essentially Marshallian theory, Kalecki initiated himself into economic thought via his reading of Marx, Tugan-Baranovski and Rosa Luxemburg.

In the autumn of 1933, Kalecki presented his model to the new Econometric Society. Ragnar Frisch and Jan Tinbergen well realized the importance of his contribution. In 1935, English and French articles containing his arguments were published, but were scarcely noticed. Their mathematical formulation and Kalecki's dense style made them most difficult to read. In the following years, and indeed for the rest of his life, Kalecki developed his theory of the dynamics of capitalist economies, integrating analyses of price formation, distribution, growth and investment into the theory of effective demand, something not done by Keynes. In so doing, he played a crucial role in the birth of the post-Keynesian stream of thought, and was an important influence on thinkers such as Kaldor, Joan Robinson and Pasinetti.

Kalecki based his analysis of prices on the consideration of monopolies and oligopolies. In his view, the prices of most manufactured goods are determined by the addition to average variable costs, mainly wages and raw materials, of a mark-up linked to what he termed the 'degree of monopoly'. His analysis of distribution takes into account the existence of two classes in the economy: workers and capitalists. Investment and consumption expenditures of capitalists determine national income and its distribution between wages and profits. This is illustrated by Kaldor's aphorism, coined so as to characterize Kalecki's distribution theory: 'capitalists earn what they spend, and workers spend what they earn' (Kaldor [1956] 1960 *Essays* I, p. 230).

Kalecki criticised Keynes for offering a static account of the multiplier, and for the inadequacy of his analysis of investment decision. In his 1933 text, he suggested an analysis of cyclical fluctuations based on the temporal distinction between the orders, the production and the deliveries of investment goods. He continuously sought satisfactory solutions in the theory of investment decison, holding that this is the true 'Achilles' heel' of economic theory. Also he never gave up trying to combine analyses of cyclical fluctuations with those of growth, his last message being that it is impossible to construct a closed model of growth; such an attempt would invariably lie outside the boundaries of economic theory.

Kalecki was a theoretician of the dynamics of modern capitalist economies and of underdeveloped and socialist economies as well. After his return to Poland in 1955, he conducted research on growth in socialist economies and on planning (1972 *Selected Essays*, 1986), pointing out many errors in traditional central planning, notably its stress on investment without taking into account its effects on popular consumption. His plan for the Polish economy was not to be implemented. Kalecki also wrote extensively, especially during the last decade of his life, on the problems faced by Third World countries, some of whose governments he advised (1976). On these issues he also warned against the mechanical application of instant recipes drawn from traditional economic models, holding that only effective interaction between economic and political factors is capable of resolving development problems; here, too, his advice went unheeded.

Kalecki ended his career on a pessimistic note. An advocate of full employment and a more equitable distribution of wealth, much like Keynes, he nonetheless disagreed with Keynes's view that capitalist economies are able to realize these goals. Kalecki held to democratic, decentralized socialism and viewed the Soviet bloc as increasingly remote from this model, rather becoming increasingly bogged down in irresolvable economic problems and political repression. He advocated a new international economic order, yet witnessed the widening of the gap between rich and poor countries.

Main references

BLAUG Mark 1992 (ed.). *Michal Kalecki (1899–1970)*, Aldershot, Hants, Edward Elgar.

FEIWEL George R. 1975. *The Intellectual Capital of Michal Kalecki*, Knoxville, University of Tennessee Press.

KRIESLER Peter 1987. *Kalecki's Microanalysis: The Development of Kalecki's Analysis of Pricing and Distribution*, New York, Cambridge University Press.

NUTI Domenico M. 1986. *Michal Kalecki's Contributions to the Theory and Practice of Socialist Planning*, Florence, European University Institute.

OSIATYNSKI Jerzy 1988. *Michal Kalecki on Socialist Economy*, London, Macmillan; New York, St Martin's Press.

Oxford Bulletin of Economics and Statistics, vol. 39, 1977, special issue on Kalecki.

Problems of Economic Dynamics and Planning: Essays in Honour of Michal Kalecki, Warsaw, Polish Scientific Publisher, 1964.

SAWYER Malcolm C. 1982. *Macro-economics in Question: Orthodoxies and the Kaleckian Alternative*, Brighton, Wheatsheaf.

SAWYER Malcolm C. 1985. *The Economics of Michal Kalecki*, Armonk, New York, M.E. Sharpe.

SEBASTIANI, Mario 1989 (ed.). *Kalecki's Relevance Today*, London, Macmillan.

ARESTIS and SAWYER 1992, 302–10. BLAUG 1985, 109–11. *New Palgrave* 1987, vol. 3, 8–14. SHACKLETON and LOCKSLEY, 1981, 141–59. SILLS 1979, 369–72.

KANTOROVICH Leonid Vitalievich (1912–1986)

Leonid Kantorovich was born in Saint Petersburg (Leningrad from 1924 until recently), Russia, and thanks to his exceptional mathematical ability entered the University of Leningrad at age 14. He thus earned his degree in mathematics in 1930, teaching that same subject at an engineering school and at the University of Leningrad from 1934, and earned his doctorate in it in 1935. Kantorovich was head of the department of mathematics at the Leningrad Academy of Sciences (1948–60) and was appointed a corresponding member of the Soviet Academy of Sciences (in mathematics) in 1958.

Because he was not a member of the Communist Party, he could not be the director of the department of mathematical methods of the Siberian branch of the Soviet Academy of Sciences (at Novosibirsk). However, he had founded it and was effectively its head from 1960 to 1971. In 1964, Kantorovich was made a full member of the Soviet Academy of Sciences and, from 1971, he directed the Gosplan's National Economic Management Institute in Moscow. From 1976 he directed the Soviet Academy of Science's Systems Analysis Institute. Winner of the 1949 Stalin Prize in mathematics, he received the 1965 Lenin Prize for his work in economics, along with V.S. Nemchinov and V.V. Novozhilov. In 1975, he was awarded the Nobel Memorial Prize in Economics, along with T.C. Koopmans.

Main publications

1939. *Matematicheskie metody organizatsii i planirovaniia proizvodstva*, Leningrad University Press; Engl. transl. 1960, 'Mathematical Methods of Organising and Planning Production', *Management Science*, vol. 6, 363–422; 2nd version, with some minor corrections, 1959, in V.S. Nemchinov (ed.), 251–309; Engl. transl. 1964, 'Mathematical Methods of Production Planning and Organization', in A. Nove (ed.), *The Use of Mathematics in Economics*, Edinburgh and London, Oliver & Boyd, 225–80.

1959. 'Dal'neishee razvitie matematicheskikh metodov i perspektivy ikh primenenia v planirovanii i ekonomike', in V.S. Nemchinov (ed.), vol. 1, 310–53; Engl. transl. 1964, 'Further Development of Mathematical Methods and Prospects of Their Application in Economic Planning', in A. Nove (ed.), *The Use of Mathematics in Economics*, Edinburgh and London, Oliver & Boyd, 281–321.

1959. *Ekonomicheskii raschet nailuchshego ispol'zovaniia resursov*, Moscow, State Publishing House; Engl transl. 1963, *The Best Use of Economic Resources*, Oxford, Pergamon Press.

1959. With G.P. Akilov, *Funktsionnal'nyi analiz v normirovannykh prostranstvakh*, Moscow, Nauka; 2nd edn 1982; Engl transl. 1982, *Functional Analysis*, Oxford, Pergamon Press.

1968. With A.V. Gorstko, *Matematicheskoe optimal'noe progammivoranie v ekonomike* [Mathematical optimal programming of an economy], Moscow, Nauka.

1972. With A.V. Gorstko, *Optimal'nye resheniia v ekonomike* [Optimal solutions in an economy], Moscow, Nauka.

1976. 'Economic Problems of Scientific and Technical Progress', *Scandinavian Journal of Economics*, vol. 78, 521–41.

1976. *Essays in Optimal Planning*, edited by Leon Smolinski, White Plains, New York, International Arts and Sciences Press.

1987. 'Moi put'v nauke' [My path in science], *Uspechi matematicheskich nauk*, vol. 42, 183–213.

1989. 'Mathematics in Economics: Achievements, Difficulties, Perspectives – Nobel Memorial Lecture, December 11, 1975', *American Economic Review*, vol. 79, 18–22.

1989. *Problemy effektivnogo ispol'zovaniia i razvitiia transporta* [Problems of efficient utilization and development of transports], Moscow, Nauka.

Kantorovich was primarily a mathematician; his dissertation is on the functional analysis of partially ordered function spaces which, in honour of his name, have been named K-spaces. There are those in his country who would like him to be recognized as the inventor of linear programming. In the light of what we know about his work on optimization, he certainly was among the first to plunge into this field, but it was von Neumann who formulated the duality theorem and G. Dantzig who invented the simplex algorithm (Gardner 1990).

It must be borne in mind that his work and his publications were effected within the highly oppressive conditions of the former USSR, with the sending of scientists such as Kondratiev and Fel'dmann to the Gulags, the ordeal of the Second World War and the evacuation of Leningrad in 1943, as well as the daily oppression of the police state. As a mathematician, he was asked in 1937 to limit the amount of wood lost in a plywood factory as the result of cutting. In doing so, he made it a point of honour to elaborate a scientific method: this was the object of his 1939 study, which for a long time remained confidential. Yet when he wrote to Gosplan, suggesting a reform in the price system as applied to planning, he was told that such a reform would be unnecessary. Moreover, when he applied his method to a firm specializing in the building of railway wagons, there was a 50 per cent drop in wasted steel: but that reduced steel factory supplies and placed him at risk of being accused of industrial sabotage. He avoided this fate thanks to the support of the military authorities: they used his work for the building of tanks, the setting up of minefields and for their nuclear programme. However, the full story of this matter is unknown. Kantorovich remained suspect in the eyes of official economists for engaging in 'bourgeois economics' (because of his use of higher mathematics, the relationship between prices and scarcity, optimization) until the early 1970s.

Kantorovich's key contribution to economics is his theory of the optimal allocation of resources, for which he won the Nobel Prize (1959 *Economicheskii*, 1968, 1972, 1976 *Essays*). He developed a method that, starting from given heterogeneous resources and diversified goals with unknown prices, is based on the iterative calculation of resolving multipliers. These resolving multipliers were called 'objectively determined evaluations' in the Marxist jargon of that period; they are in fact fictitious prices that (like Lagrange's resolving multipliers) allow for the attainment of an optimal solution. Kantorovich and his Novosibirsk team applied this method to many areas: problems in transportation, localization, investment choice, intertemporal choice and depreciation (1976 *Essays*, 1989 *Problems*). More generally, he firmly established that there can be no optimal planning without a correct price system.

In the last phase of his working life, Kantorovich worked on the question of technological progress (1976 *SJE*).

Main references

'The Nobel Memorial Prize in Economics 1975'. Official announcement, article by Leif Johansen and bibliography, *Swedish Journal of Economics*, 1976, vol. 78, 59–80; article repr. in Spiegel and Samuels 1984, 373–94.

Bibliographies in M. Ellman 1973. *Planning Problems in the USSR*, Cambridge University Press,197–9, and in Kantorovich 1976 *Essays*, xxviii–xxxii .

GARDNER Roy 1990. 'L.V. Kantorovich: The Price Implication of Optimal Planning', *Journal of Economic Literature*, vol. 28, 638–48.

KANTOROVICH 1987.

BLAUG *Who's Who* 1986, 451–2. *New Palgrave*, 1987, vol. 3, 14–15.

KATONA George (1901–1981)

Born in Budapest, George Katona began his studies there in 1918 and continued them at Göttingen, where he earned a doctorate in psychology in 1921. He continued his research at the University of Frankfurt, worked in a bank in that city, and subsequently for an economic publication. In 1933, Katona emigrated to the United States, becoming an American citizen in 1939. He worked with the Cowles Commission in Chicago and, subsequently, at the Department of Agriculture's Division of Program Surveys. In 1946, he established the Survey Research Center at the University of Michigan at Ann Arbor, where he taught psychology and economics until his retirement in 1972.

Main publications

1940. *Organizing and Memorizing: Studies in the Psychology of Learning and Teaching*, New York, Columbia University Press.
1951. *Psychological Analysis of Economic Behavior*, New York, McGraw-Hill.
1960. *The Powerful Consumer: Psychological Studies of the American Economy*, New York, McGraw-Hill.
1964. *The Mass Consumption Society*, New York, McGraw-Hill.
1968. *Consumer Response to Income Increase*, Washington, DC, Brookings Institution.
1975. *Psychological Economics*, New York, Elsevier.
1980. *Essays on Behavioral Economics*, Ann Arbor, University of Michigan Press.

A psychologist interested in economics, Katona published a newspaper article in Germany after the First World War on the theme of hyperinflation as a type of contagious hysteria. Until the Second World War, he worked primarily in the area of experimental psychology, notably the psychology of teaching (1940).

In the early 1940s, he was called upon to examine the reactions to price controls of firms' managers, distributors, tradesmen and households. Shortly before the Second Word War, having just effected a preliminary study of the holding of liquid assets, Katona and the Survey Research Center established a series of periodic surveys on planned and realized consumption and savings. He developed an indicator of the opinion (attitudes and expectations) of consumers, studying the relations between attitudes and behaviour and analysing how they react to economic events. His studies were the subject of annual publications and led him to underline the existence of multiple motives and to develop the idea of 'bounded rationality', themes one also finds in the work of H. Simon. He was, moreover, interested in the formation of social learning and in the role of collective behaviour in the economy.

Main references

STRUMPEL B., MORGAN N.J. and ZAHN E. 1972 (eds). *Human Behavior In Economic Affairs: Essays in Honor of George Katona*, San Francisco, Jossey Bass. [With a bibliography of Katona's works, 587–90.]

New Palgrave 1987, vol. 3, 14–15. SPIEGEL and SAMUELS 1984, 495–522.

KINDLEBERGER Charles Poor (born 1910)

Charles Kindleberger was born in New York and studied at the University of Pennsylvania (BA, 1932) and at Columbia University (MA, 1934, PhD, 1937). He was a research economist at the Federal Reserve Bank of New York (1936–9), at the Bank for International Settlements at Basle (Switzerland, 1939–40) and at the Board of Governors of the Federal Reserve System in Washington (1940–42). During the Second World War, he worked at the Office of Strategic Services in Washington (1942–3), then in London (1943–4) and served as an officer with the American army in Europe (1944–5).

Kindleberger went on to work for the Department of State as chief of division in the section dealing with German and Austrian affairs (1945–7) and as an advisor on the European recovery programme (1947–8). He then taught at the Massachusetts Institute of Technology, successively as associate professor (1948–51), professor (1951–76) and professor emeritus (from 1976). He was president of the American Economic Association in 1985.

Main publications

1937. *International Short-Term Capital Movements*, New York, Columbia University Press; repr. 1965, Clifton, New Jersey, Augustus M. Kelley.

1950. *The Dollar Shortage*, Cambridge, Massachusetts, MIT Press.

1953. *International Economics*, Homewood, Illinois, Richard D. Irwin; 6th edn 1978, with Peter Lindert.

1956. *The Terms of Trade: A European Case Study*, Cambridge, Massachusetts, MIT Press.

1958. *Economic Development*, New York, McGraw-Hill.

1962. *Foreign Trade and the National Economy*, New Haven, Connecticut, Yale University Press.

1964. *Economic Growth in France and Britain: 1851–1950*, Cambridge, Massachusetts, Harvard University Press.

1966. *Europe and the Dollar*, Cambridge, Massachusetts, MIT Press.

1967. *Economic Growth in France and Europe*, Cambridge, Massachusetts, Harvard University Press.

1967. *Europe's Postwar Growth: The Role of Labor Supply*, Cambridge, Massachusetts, Harvard University Press.

1969. *American Business Abroad*, New Haven, Connecticut, Yale University Press.

1970. *Power and Money: The Economics of International Politics and the Politics of International Economics*, New York, Basic Books.

1973. *The World in Depression: 1929–1939*, London, Allen Lane; 2nd rev. edn 1986, Berkeley, University of California Press.

1978. *Economic Response: Comparative Studies in Trade, Finance, and Growth*, Cambridge, Massachusetts, Harvard University Press.

1978. *Manias, Panics, and Crashes: A History of Financial Crises*, New York, Basic Books.
1980. 'The Life of an Economist', *Quarterly Review, Banca Nazionale del Lavoro*, no. 134, 231–45; in Kregel 1989, 149–62.
1981. *International Money: A Collection of Essays*, London, George Allen & Unwin.
1983. With D.B. Audretsch, *The Multinational Corporations in the 1980s*, Cambridge, Massachusetts, MIT Press.
1984. *A Financial History of Western Europe*, London, George Allen & Unwin.
1984. *Multinational Excursions*, Cambridge, Massachusetts, MIT Press.
1985. *Keynesianism vs Monetarism and Other Essays in Financial History*, London, George Allen & Unwin.
1987. *International Capital Movements*, Cambridge, England, Cambridge University Press.
1987. *Marshall Plan Days*, London, George Allen & Unwin.
1988. *The International Economic Order: Essays on Financial Crisis and International Public Goods*, Cambridge, Massachusetts, MIT Press.
1989. *Economic Laws and Economic History*, Cambridge, England, Cambridge University Press.
1989. *The German Economy, 1945–47: Charles P. Kindleberger's Letters from the Field*, Westport, Connecticut, Meckler.
1990. *Historical Economics: Art or Science?*, Berkeley, University of California Press.
1991. *Life of an Economist: An Autobiography*, Oxford, Blackwell.
1992. *Mariners and Markets*, London, Harvester/Wheatsheaf.
1992. 'My Working Philosophy', in Szenberg 1992,167–79.

Kindleberger is one of the few American economists to have avoided the wave of mathematization in the field, and to have conceived of economics as literary and historical. His first publications in the 1930s and 1940s reflect a continuing interest in international economics and monetary questions such as capital movements, international investment, exchange rates, fluctuation in the demand for foreign goods and the foreign trade multiplier. His activities during the war and immediate postwar period sharpened his interest in the European economies. These two fields were the subject of many of his articles and were collected in several books (1966, 1978 *Economic Response*, 1981, 1984 *Multinational Excursions*, 1987 *Marshall Plan*, 1988).

In addition to his textbook on international economics (1953), a work that was republished in several new editions, Kindleberger has addressed himself to major international problems: the Bretton Woods agreements and the dollar shortage (1950), the problems posed by flexible exchange rates and the dollar's instability, the difficulties of the pound sterling, the questions regarding international payments, liquidities and the international monetary system. Other topics he has examined include European integration, international fluctuations, tariff policies, multinational firms and the trading of new products. Kindleberger has also worked in the area of economic, financial and monetary history, mostly European (1964, his 1967 books, 1973, 1978 *Manias*) and has resituated the debate between Keynesians and monetarists with reference to controversies in past centuries (1984 *A Financial History*, 1985).

The idea of a hierarchical international system and the essential role played by a hegemonic power in it – whether in the role of a last resort lender within the international monetary system or as a maker of necessary decisions when the operating rules are no longer sufficient – are salient in his works. The seriousness of the 1930s depression is largely explicable in terms of the absence of a power that could have assumed these responsibilities (1973) and, conversely, the responsibilities taken on by the United States during the postwar period explain much of that period's prosperity, along with the fact that Europe had access to the unlimited reserve of labour coming from countries with high emigration (1967 *Europe*). For Kindleberger, whether through hegemonic power or accords between great powers, it is essential for international prosperity that the international public goods – peace, as well as monetary and financial stability – be guaranteed.

Main references

BHAGWATI J.N. *et al.* 1971 (eds). *Trade, Balance of Payments and Growth – Papers in International Economics in Honor of Charles P. Kindleberger*, Amsterdam, North-Holland. [With a bibliography of Kindleberger's works, 1934–70, 524–9.]
KINDLEBERGER 1980, 1991, 1992 'My Working'.

BLAUG 1985, 112–13. *New Palgrave* 1987, vol. 3, 51–2.

KLEIN Lawrence Robert (born 1920)

Born in Omaha, Nebraska, Lawrence Klein studied at the University of California at Berkeley (BA in 1942) and obtained his PhD in 1944 at the Massachusetts Institute of Technology, where he was research assistant to Paul Samuelson. He first worked as research associate at the Cowles Commission, at the University of Chicago (1944–7), then at the National Bureau of Economic Research (NBER) (1948–51) and at the Survey Research Center at the University of Michigan (1949–54), where he taught from 1950.

Reacting against the activities of the McCarthy Committee, he left for Great Britain, where he was a senior research officer and then reader at the Oxford University Institute of Statistics (1954–8). He was a professor at the University of Pennsylvania from 1958. In 1959 he received the John Bates Clark Medal of the American Economics Association, becoming president of that association in 1977, having already been elected president of the Econometric Society in 1960. He has had many responsibilities in areas of research, in particular as director at the National Bureau of Economic Research since 1989. For his work on econometric modelling he received the Nobel Memorial Prize in Economics in 1980.

Main publications

1947. *The Keynesian Revolution*, New York, Macmillan.

1947. 'The Use of Econometric Models as a Guide to Economic Policy', *Econometrica*, vol. 15, 111–51.
1947. 'Theories of Effective Demand and Employment', *Journal of Political Economy*, vol. 55, 108–31.
1950. *Economic Fluctuations in the United States: 1921–1941*, New York, John Wiley.
1953. *A Textbook of Econometrics*, Evanston, Row Peterson and Co.
1955. With A.S. Goldberger, *An Econometric Model of the United States: 1929–1951*, New York, John Wiley.
1961. With R.J. Ball *et al.*, *An Econometric Model of the United Kingdom*, Oxford, Basil Blackwell.
1962. *An Introduction to Econometrics*, Englewood Cliffs, New Jersey, Prentice-Hall.
1965 (ed., with J. Duesenberry, G. Fromm and E. Kuh). *The Brookings Quarterly Econometric Model of the United States*, Chicago, Rand McNally.
1967. With M.K. Evans, *The Wharton Econometric Forecasting Model*, Philadelphia, Wharton School of Finance and Commerce.
1969 (ed., with J. Duesenberry, G. Fromm and E. Kuh). *The Brookings Model: Some Further Results*, Chicago, Rand McNally.
1969. With M.K. Evans and M. Hartley, *Econometric Gaming: A Kit for Computer Analysis of Macroeconomic Models*, New York, Macmillan.
1969–71 (ed.). *Essays in Industrial Econometrics*, 3 vols, Philadelphia, Wharton School of Finance and Commerce.
1975 (ed., with G. Fromm). *The Brookings Model: Perspective and Recent Developments*, New York, John Wiley.
1976 (ed., with Edwin Burmeister). *Econometric Model Performance*, Philadelphia, University of Pennsylvania Press.
1978. 'The Supply Side', *American Economic Review*, vol. 68, 1–7.
1980. With R.M. Young, *An Introduction to Econometric Forecasting and Forecasting Models*, Lexington, Massachusetts, Lexington Books.
1981. *Econometric Models as Guides for Decision Making*, New York, Free Press.
1983. *Lectures in Econometrics*, Amsterdam, North-Holland.
1983. *The Economics of Supply and Demand*, Oxford, Basil Blackwell.
1985. *Economic Theory and Econometrics*, edited by Jaime Marquez, Oxford, Basil Blackwell.
1986. 'My Evolution as an Economist', in Breit and Spencer 1986, 21–42.
1989 (ed., with Jaime Marquez). *Economics in Theory and Practice: An Eclectic Approach*, Dordrecht, Kluwer.
1991 (ed.). *Comparative Performance of US Econometric Models*, New York, Oxford University Press.
1991. With Ronald G. Bodkin and Kanta Marwah, *A History of Macroeconometric Model-Building*, Aldershot, Hants, Edward Elgar.
1992. 'My Professional Life Philosophy', in Szenberg 1992, 180–89.

Klein's earliest works, completed while working with Samuelson, were concerned with the mathematical formalization of economic theory. As part of the team of economists working at the Cowles Commission, he found a stimulating intellectual atmosphere and participated in research and heady discussions on economic theory as well as formalization and applied economics. His 1944 doctoral thesis was published with revisions in 1947; introducing for the first time the expression 'Keynesian revolution', he there presented the structure of Keynesian theory, offering both a formalized version – and thus clarification and simplification – and an account of the current debates and disputes – thus helping to enrich the theory itself. The publication in 1947 of both this work and an article on the use of econometric models as guides to economic policy, illustrates and symbolizes Klein's triple interest in economic theory, econometric modelling and their application to economic policy, three areas which are deeply linked in his work and constitute the focus of his entire scholarly career.

It was thus on the base provided by Keynesian theory that Klein worked on the development and formalization of economics, with a view to establishing the links between macro- and microeconomic approaches, deepening the analysis of investment and saving, and integrating the study of money markets and the rate of interest. During his career he distanced himself somewhat from certain Keynesian influences, notably the central position accorded to effective demand, so as to better analyse and take account of the workings of the supply side (1978, 1983 *The Economics*). He was ultimately one of the principal architects who used Keynesian theory to construct modern macroeconomics, a body of theory in which, incidentally, references to Keynes have become increasingly indistinct.

In parallel manner, Klein pursued his work in econometrics, deepening the analysis of various problems (accounting for lags in the effect of explanatory variables, multicollinearity) and publishing textbooks and other works in this area (1953, 1962, 1980, 1983 *Lectures*). But the major part of Klein's research effort has been taken up by applied econometrics with the design, construction and elaboration of econometric models. He completed pioneer work in building, with A.S. Goldberger, in 1951–3, the first econometric model of the United States (1955) and then did the same for the United Kingdom (1961). From 1961 to 1972, he played a central role in the establishment, with Duesenberry, of the ambitious Brookings–Social Science Research Council model (1965, 1969, 1975); at the same time, he directed the more modest, but ultimately more operational, project of the Wharton School (1967); beginning in 1968, he ran project LINK, which connected the national econometric models of Eastern and Western countries. Using his intuition that the combination of the Keynesian macroeconomic and Leontief input–output approaches would likely be fruitful, Klein sought to integrate into these models the principal and most recent contributions in theoretical research and applied econometrics and, moreover, to take greater account of monetary factors, particularly in the Wharton School model. He also sought to develop econometric models for developing countries.

Thus Klein's contributions essentially centre upon creating and increasing the use of econometric models, work carried out with an eye to both theoretical research (1980) and economic policy (1947 *Econometrica*, 1981); and in his evaluation of these models he has sought to take into account both technical and historical factors (1976, 1991 ed., 1991). Appearing at the confluence of the two great revolutions of the 1940s and 1950s, the Keynesian revolution and the revolution of mathematical formalization, Klein chose, and expressly adhered to, the path of applied econometrics, thereby playing a major role in the creation of modern macroeconomics.

Main references

'The Nobel Memorial Prize in Economics 1980'. Official announcement, article by R.J. Ball and bibliography, *Swedish Journal of Economics*, 1981, vol. 83, 79–103. Article reprinted in Spiegel and Samuels 1984, 333–49.

ADAMS F. Gerard and HICKMAN Bert G. 1983 (eds). *Global Econometrics: Essays in Honor of Lawrence F. Klein*, Cambridge, Massachusetts, MIT Press.
KLEIN 1986, 1992.

BLAUG 1985, 114–15.

KOOPMANS Tjalling Charles (1910–1985)

Born in Graveland, Holland, Tjalling Koopmans studied mathematics and theoretical physics at Utrecht (MA in 1933) and obtained in 1936 a doctorate in mathematical statistics at the University of Leiden. After working at the Rotterdam School of Economics, then at the United Nations in Geneva, he emigrated to the United States in 1940; he worked at Princeton University, at New York University, at the Penn Mutual Life Company and finally at the Combined Shipping Adjustment Board in Washington. He was research associate (1944–8), then research director (1948–67) of the Cowles Commission, first at the University of Chicago, then from 1955 at Yale University; he was professor of economics in Chicago from 1948 to 1955, then at Yale, from 1955 until his retirement in 1981.

He was president of the Econometric Society in 1950 and of the American Economic Association in 1978 and he received the Nobel Memorial Prize in Economics, jointly with Kantorovich, in 1975. He died in New Haven, United States.

Main publications

1937. *Linear Regression Analysis of Economic Time Series*, Haarlem, De Erven, F. Bohn.
1939. *Tanker Freight Rates and Tankship Building*, Haarlem, De Erven, F. Bohn.
1941. 'The Logic of Econometric Business-Cycle Research', *Journal of Political Economy*, vol. 49, 157–81.
1945. 'Statistical Estimation of Simultaneous Economic Relations', *Journal of the American Statistical Association*, vol. 40, 448–66.
1947. 'Measurement without Theory', *Review of Economic Statistics*, vol. 29, 161–72; 'Reply', vol. 31, 1949, 86–91.
1949. 'Identification Problems in Economic Model Construction', *Econometrica*, vol. 17, 125–44.
1950 (ed.). *Statistical Inference in Dynamic Economic Models*, New York, John Wiley & Sons; London, Chapman & Hall.
1951 (ed.). *Activity Analysis of Production and Allocation*, New York, John Wiley & Sons; London, Chapman & Hall.

1951. 'Analysis of Production as an Efficient Combination of "Activities"', in Koopmans 1951 (ed.), 33–97.
1951. With S. Reiter, 'A Model of Transportation', in Koopmans 1951 (ed.), 222–59.
1953. 'La Notion d'utilité dans le cas de décisions concernant le bien-être futur', *Cahiers du séminaire d'économétrie*, 7–10.
1953 (ed., with William C. Hood). *Studies in Econometric Method*, New York, John Wiley & Sons.
1957. *Three Essays on the State of Economic Science*, New York, McGraw-Hill.
1964. 'Economic Growth at a Maximal Rate', *Quarterly Journal of Economics*, vol. 78, 355–94.
1970. *Scientific Papers of Tjalling C. Koopmans*, Berlin, Springer.
1973. 'Economics among the Sciences', *American Economic Review*, vol. 69, 1–13.
1985. *Scientific Papers of Tjalling C. Koopmans*, vol. 2, Cambridge, Massachusetts, MIT Press.

After publishing two articles in physics in 1933 and 1934, T. Koopmans completed in 1936 a thesis on econometric methodology, dealing with issues in linear regression when the variables are subject to errors in measurement (1937). He carried on this work in the methodology of econometrics, exploring a probabilist analysis for the study of the relations between variables subject to such errors or to chance and, through his work on the resolution of simultaneous equations systems, contributed to the identification of systems and the evaluation of parameters (1945, 1950).

On the other hand, his studies of maritime transport (1939) led him to work during the war on the optimal allocation of convoys on sea routes (1942 study, unpublished until 1970) and, at the same time as Kantorovich, to become one of the pioneers of linear programming, a field in which he cooperated fruitfully with G.B. Dantzig (1951 ed.). His works on activity analysis simultaneously owe much to his training as a physicist and to his applied economic experience; on the one hand, he was concerned to study production activity independently from that of its ends; on the other hand, he studied the resources–production relation, not from the point of view of the traditional production function, but from that of the production choices under constraints; he then analysed their efficiency and optimality in relation to the price system (1951 'Analysis', 1957). Beyond that, Koopmans tackled the issue of the optimal allocation of resources in time and the maximization of the growth rate (1953 *CSE*, 1964). And it is for his contributions to the theory of optimal allocation of resources that he received, jointly with Kantorovich, the Nobel Memorial Prize.

A mathematician–economist, Koopmans had a very demanding conception of scientific work: Malinvaud (1972) emphasizes that he abstained from considering fields to which he estimated he had no scientific contribution to offer, and that he published his results even when his research seemed not to have succeeded. A theoretician, he was also an organizer and a promoter. He played a key role in the Cowles Commission, where he succeeded Marschak as director, in both the conception and the dissemination of the new econometric approach linked to the names of Tinbergen and Haavelmo. He answered (1941) Keynes's critique of Tinbergen. But, above all, he attacked the fortress of the National Bureau of Economic Research, severely criticizing Burns and Mitchell's book (1946), describing it as 'measurement without theory' (1947). This article gave rise to a lively debate, traces of which are still to be found. More fundamentally, distinguishing economics as practical art from economics as science, Koopmans deepened the questions of the relations between choices of methods and instruments of analysis, between the taking into consideration of facts and theoretical reasoning, between economic science and other sciences, and between ethical position and scientific process (1957, 1973, 1985).

Main references

'The Nobel Memorial Prize in Economics 1975'. Official announcement, articles by Lars Werin and Karl G. Jugenfelt, and bibliography, *Swedish Journal of Economics*, 1976, vol. 78, 59–60 and 81–102. Articles reprinted in Spiegel and Samuels 1984, 351–71.

MALINVAUD Edmond 1972. 'The Scientific Papers of Tjalling C. Koopmans: A Review Article', *Journal of Economic Literature*, vol. 10, 798–802.
SCARF H.E. 1985. Foreword to Koopmans 1985, xi–xii.
VINING Rutledge 1949. 'Koopmans on the Choice of Variables to be Studied and of Methods of Measurement', *Review of Economics and Statistics*, vol. 31, 77–86; 'A Rejoinder', 91–4.

BLAUG 1985, 119–21. *New Palgrave* 1987, vol. 3, 62–7.

KORNAI János (born 1928)

Born in 1928 in Budapest, János Kornai first studied history and philosophy. He obtained a 'Candidate of economic science' degree (CSc equivalent of an American PhD) from the Hungarian Academy of Sciences in 1956. After a term as a research fellow at the Institute of Economics of the Hungarian Academy of Sciences (1955–8), he was then head of department at the Institute of Textile Industry, in Budapest (1958–63), and head of department at the Computing Centre of the Hungarian Academy of Sciences (1963–7). Since 1967 he has been head of department of the Institute of Economics of the Hungarian Academy of Sciences. In 1986, he was named professor of economics at Harvard University. He was vice-chairman of the United Nations Development Planning Committee (1972–7) and president of the Econometric Society (1978) and of the European Economic Association (1987).

Main publications

1957. *A gazdasági vezetés tulzott központositása*, Budapest, Közgazdasagi és Jogi Könyvkiado; revised Engl. transl. 1959, *Overcentralization in Economic Administration: A Critical Analysis Based on Experience in Hungarian Light Industry*, London, Oxford University Press.
1962. With Tamas Lipták, 'Kétszintü tervezés' [Two-Level Planning], *MTA Matematikai Kutato Intézetének Közleményei*, vol. 7, 577–621.

1965. *A gazdasági szerkezet matematikai tervezése*, Budapest, Közgazdasagi és Jogi Könyvkiado; Engl. transl. 1967, *Mathematical Planning of Structural Decisions*, Amsterdam, North-Holland; 2nd enlarged edn, 1975.
1965. With Tamas Lipták, 'Two-Level Planning', *Econometrica*, vol. 33, 141–69.
1971. *Anti-Equilibrium*, Budapest, Közgazdasagi és Jogi Könyvkiadó; Engl. transl. 1971, *Anti-Equilibrium*, Amsterdam, North-Holland.
1972. *Eröltetett vagy harmonikus növekedés*, Budapest, Akadémiai Kiadó; Engl. transl. 1972, *Rush Versus Harmonic Growth*, Amsterdam, North-Holland.
1980. *A hiány*, Budapest, Közgazdasagi és Jogi Könyvkiado; Engl. transl. 1980, *Economics of Shortage*, 2 vols, Amsterdam, North-Holland.
1981 (ed., with Bela Martos). *Szabályozás árjelzések nélkül*, Budapest, Akadémiai Kiadó; Engl. transl. 1981, *Non-price control*, Amsterdam, North-Holland.
1982. *Növekedés, hiány és hatékonysag*, Budapest, Közgazdasagi és Jogi Könyvkiado; Engl. transl. 1982, *Growth, Shortage and Efficiency*, Oxford, Basil Blackwell; Berkeley, University of California Press.
1983. *Ellentmondások és dilemmák*, Budapest, Magvetö; Engl. transl. 1985, *Contradictions and Dilemmas*, Budapest, Corvina and 1986, Cambridge, Massachusetts, MIT Press.
1986. 'The Hungarian Reform Process: Visions, Hopes and Reality', *Journal of Economic Literature*, vol. 24, 1687–1737.
1986. 'The Soft Budget Constraint', *Kyklos*, vol. 39, 3–30.
1986 (ed., with Xavier Richet). *La Voie hongroise: Analyses et expérimentations économiques*, Paris, Calmann-Lévy.
1989. *Indulatos röpirat a gazdasági atmenet ügyeben* [A passionate pamphlet in the cause of Hungarian economic transition], Budapest, HVG Kiado; Engl. transl. 1990, *The Road to a Free Economy. Shifting from a Socialist System: The Example of Hungary*, New York, W.W. Norton.
1989. *Régi és uj ellentmondások és dilemmák*, Budapest, Magvetö; Engl. transl. 1990, *Vision and Reality, Market and State: Contradictions and Dilemmas Revisited*, New York, Routledge; London, Harvester Wheatsheaf.
1992. *The Socialist System: The Political Economy of Communism*, Princeton University Press and Oxford University Press.

The first of Kornai's works, published in Hungary or in other Eastern countries from the second half of the 1950s, are devoted to Hungarian and other Eastern European economic issues and to questions of planning: choice and efficiency of investment, profitability, productivity, use of quantitative techniques such as operation research and linear programming. Very early, he emphasized the drawbacks of extremely centralized planning (1957) and sketched out the model of two-tier planning – then of several tiers – in which truly interactive procedures between the centre and other authorities would be established (1962, 1965 *Econometrica*); beyond this, he has taken part, through both his theoretical work and his broader thinking, in the different steps of the reform and transformation of his country's economic system (1965, 1972, 1983, 1986 *JEL*, 1986 ed.).

At the same time, he has asserted himself as a theoretician, in the East and the West alike, with his critique of the theory of general equilibrium and his efforts to lay the foundations of a theory of economic systems (1971). In the 1970s, he elaborated the concept of 'hiany' (shortage), which – with the incorporation of the budget constraint, hard or flexible (1986 *Kyk*, 1986 ed.) – he turned into one of the keys to the analysis of the economies described at that time as socialist: the need for investment, linked to the logic of firm organization, leads to situations where production is always constrained by a shortage (of energy, material, pieces, and so on) and the efforts of each enterprise to guard against this evil lead to its aggravation – it inexorably extends to all fields of economic and social life, even to the extent of modelling the behaviour of consumers, who are both subject to this logic and contribute to reproducing it (1980, 1982). This analysis, which the author is keen to distinguish from those of the disequilibrium school, may contribute to shedding light on some aspects of Western economies.

Following the deep transformations at the end of the 1980s and the beginning of the 1990s, Kornai analysed the relations between forms of property (private or public) and the modes of coordination (market and plan) and took note of the existence of strong relations, first between private ownership and market, and second between public property and plan: hence the difficulties encountered in constructing an economy based on both public ownership and the market. Considering the prospect of a transition towards a free society and a free economy, he sketched out (1989 *Indulatos*) the methods and stages of what could be a controlled transition, without illusion and well aware of the enormity of the forces which oppose the setting into place of the ideas he put forward. He pleaded for 'stabilization surgery' which, at one stroke, would make it posible to halt inflation, restore budget equilibrium, recover the control of aggregate demand, establish rational prices and introduce convertibility at a uniform exchange rate, conditions, according to Kornai, for the approach to a market economy.

Main references

CSIKOS-NAGY Béla 1992. 'Janos Kornai', in Samuels ed., 129–55.

BLAUG 1985, 122–3.

KREGEL Jan Allen (born 1944)

Jan Kregel was born in Dallas, Texas. He was research student at the University of Cambridge, England, between 1968 and 1970 and received a PhD from Rutgers University (New Brunswick, New Jersey) in 1970. After teaching at the University of Bristol (1969–72), he was a lecturer and senior lecturer at the University of Southampton (1973–9), a professor at Rutgers University (1977–81), at the Rijkuniversiteit Groningen (Holland, 1980–85) and at the Johns Hopkins University School of Advanced International Studies at Bologna (1985–90). Since 1990, he has been professor of political economy at the Università degli Studi di Bologna.

Main publications

1971. *Rate of Profit, Distribution and Growth: Two Views*, London, Macmillan.
1972. *The Theory of Economic Growth*, London, Macmillan.
1973. *The Reconstruction of Political Economy: An Introduction to Post-Keynesian Economics*, London, Macmillan.
1975. With A.S. Eichner, 'An Essay on Post-Keynesian Theory: A New Paradigm in Economics', *Journal of Economic Literature*, vol. 13, 1293–1314.
1976. 'Economic Methodology in the Face of Uncertainty: The Modelling Methods of Keynes and the Post-Keynesians', *Economic Journal*, vol. 86, 209–25.
1976. *Theory of Capital*, London, Macmillan.
1983 (ed.). *Distribution, Effective Demand and International Economic Relations*, London, Macmillan.
1985. 'Hamlet without the Prince: Cambridge Macroeconomics without Money', *American Economic Review*, vol. 75, *Papers and Proceedings*,133–9.
1988. 'The Multiplier and Liquidity Preference: Two Sides of the Theory of Effective Demand', in A. Barrère (ed.), *The Foundations of Keynesian Analysis*, London, Macmillan, 231–50.
1988 (ed., with E. Matzner and A. Roncaglia). *Barriers to Full Employment*, London, Macmillan; New York University Press.
1989 (ed.). *Inflation and Income Distribution in Capitalist Crisis: Essays in Memory of Sidney Weintraub*, London, Macmillan.
1989 (ed., with Paul Davidson). *Macroeconomic Problems and Policies of Income Distribution: Functional, Personal, International*, Aldershot, Hants, Edward Elgar.
1991 (ed., with Paul Davidson). *Economic Problems of the 1990's: Europe, the Developing Countries and the United States*, Aldershot, Hants, Edward Elgar.

Since the beginning of the 1970s, Jan Kregel has been one of the most active spokesmen of the post-Keynesian school of thought. In the 1980s, he was one of the organizers of the Trieste International School of Advanced Economic Theory which, each summer, brought together for two weeks several of the main theoreticians of this school. He edited several books which drew together important texts of this current of thought. It was he who, with Alfred Eichner (1975), defined this approach as a new paradigm, likely to replace the neoclassical paradigm. But, before this date, he had already presented its elements: first, in two books devoted to the theory of growth (1971, 1972), in which, to the static neoclassical theory, he opposed a classical vision, renewed by the post-Keynesian current, which tries to integrate growth analysis, the theory of value, profit and distribution; second, in what can be considered one of the first texts presenting the post-Keynesian theory as a 'reconstruction of political economy' (1973).

There is, for Kregel, an incompatibility, at the methodological level, between Keynes's approach and that of the neoclassical synthesis, as well as modern approaches in terms of disequilibrium or non-Walrasian equilibrium. To the contrary, he sees it as possible and desirable to integrate the Keynesian theory of effective demand in a monetary economy with the classical vision, renewed by authors such as von Neumann, Kalecki and Sraffa. The post-Keynesian theory thus stresses, following the example of classical theory, the 'social relations, the distribution of income and the analysis of an economy that changes and grows over time' (1973, p. xv). For this reconstruction, Kregel drew his inspiration from, among others, Joan Robinson, and from her attempt at 'generalizing the *General Theory*'. He interpreted Keynes's model as that of a 'shifting equilibrium', integrating uncertainty and anticipations (1976 *EJ*), and tried to reconcile it with that of Sraffa.

Main references

HARCOURT G.C. 1973. 'The Rate of Profits in Equilibrium Growth Models: A Review Article', *Journal of Political Economy*, vol. 81, 1261–77.

BLAUG *Who's Who* 1986, 477–8.

KUZNETS Simon Smith (1901–1985)

Born in Russia, Simon Kuznets emigrated to the United States in 1922; following studies in economics at Columbia University, where he obtained a doctorate in 1926, he entered, with the help of W.C. Mitchell, the National Bureau of Economic Research (NBER), of which he was a member until 1961. He taught at the University of Pennsylvania from 1930 to 1954. From 1942 to 1944 he was associate director of the Bureau of Planning and Statistics of the US War Production Board; beginning in the 1950s, he organized the works of the Committe on Economic Growth of the Social Science Research Council (SSRC); he taught at Johns Hopkins (1954–60) and Harvard (1960–71). His post-retirement work has focused principally on issues concerning population. Kuznets was president of the American Statistical Association (1949), the American Economic Association (1954) and, from 1953 to 1963, of the Falk Programme for Economic Research in Israel. He won the Nobel Memorial Prize in Economics in 1971. He died in Cambridge, Massachusetts.

Main publications

1930. *Secular Movements in Production and Prices: Their Nature and their Bearing upon Cyclical Fluctuations*, Boston, Houghton Mifflin; reprint 1967, New York, Augustus M. Kelley.

1933. *Seasonal Variations in Industry and Trade*, New York, National Bureau of Economic Research.

1934. *National Income, 1929–1932*, New York, National Bureau of Economic Research.

1938. *Commodity Flow and Capital Formation*, New York, National Bureau of Economic Research; reprint 1975, New York, Arno Press.

1941. *National Income and Capital Formation, 1919–1935*, New York, National Bureau of Economic Research.

1941. With E. Jenks and L. Epstein, *National Income and its Composition, 1919–1938*, New York, National Bureau of Economic Research.

1946. *National Income: A Summary of Findings*, New York, National Bureau of Economic Research.

1946. With E. Jenks and L. Epstein, *National Product since 1869*, New York, National Bureau of Economic Research.
1953. With the collaboration of E. Jenks, *Shares of Upper Income Groups in Income and Savings*, New York, National Bureau of Economic Research.
1957 (ed., with D.S. Thomas). *Population Redistribution and Economic Growth: United States, 1870–1950*, Philadelphia, American Philosophical Society.
1959. *Six Lectures on Economic Growth*, Glencoe, Illinois, Free Press.
1961. With the collaboration of E. Jenks, *Capital in the American Economy: Its Formation and Financing*, Princeton University Press.
1964. *Postwar Economic Growth: Four Lectures*, Cambridge, Massachusetts, Harvard University Press.
1965. *Economic Growth and Structure: Selected Essays*, New York, W.W. Norton.
1966. *Modern Economic Growth: Rate, Structure and Spread*, New Haven, Connecticut, Yale University Press.
1968. *Toward a Theory of Economic Growth: With Reflections on the Economic Growth of Modern Nations*, New York, W.W. Norton.
1971. *Economic Growth of Nations: Total Output and Production Structure*, Cambridge, Massachusetts, Harvard University Press.
1972. *Quantitative Economic Research: Trends and Problems*, New York, National Bureau of Economic Research.
1973. *Population, Capital and Growth : Selected Essays*, New York, W.W. Norton.
1979. *Growth, Population and Income Distribution: Selected Essays*, New York, W.W. Norton.

Kuznets's doctoral thesis and early work were devoted to the study of time series: fluctuations, cycles and long waves. In the course of his research he identified a cycle of 15 to 20 years (1930), the existence and nature of which were the subject of debate and which entered the literature under the title 'Kuznets cycle' or 'Kuznets swings' (*New Palgrave* 1987, vol. 3, 71–2). This led him, well before the establishment of national income accounts, to work on the conception, definition and measurement of gross national product, national income and their elements, consumption, saving and investment (1934, 1938 and the two books of 1941). In this context, he identified a certain long-run stability of the rate of saving in the United States (around 12 per cent), which seemed to contradict the views of Keynes.

His postwar work was largely devoted to what he called 'modern growth' (1966, 1973), to its determinants (scientific and technical progress and the innovations it engenders) and its characteristics (growth per capita, productivity increase, technical change, structural transformations); these researches combine the concern for rigorous work on long statistical time series, characteristic of the NBER tradition, and the incorporation of the contributions of other social sciences and the historical dimension, in an approach which is situated on the border between German historicism and American institutionalism. These studies allowed him to pursue the analysis of the conditions and determinants of modern economic growth: the relations between cycles and growth (1946 *National Income*), the role of capital formation and saving (1961), the relation between structural change and productivity improvement and demographic growth, variation in real national income and income per capita (1965, 1971, 1973) and the impact of income distribution (1966, 1979).

Kuznets himself described his method as going 'from measurement to estimation to classification to explanation to speculation' (quoted in 'The Nobel' 1971, p. 460). The Official Announcement of the Royal Academy of Sciences emphasized that 'more than any other scientist he has illuminated with facts – and explained through analysis – the economic growth from the middle of last century' (ibid., p. 443).

Main references

'The Nobel Memorial Prize in Economics 1971'. Official announcement and article by E. Lundberg, *Swedish Journal of Economics*, vol. 73, 1971, 443–61. Article reprinted in Spiegel and Samuels 1984, 523–42.

FLOERSHEIM Rachel 1961. 'Bibliography of the Works of Simon Kuznets', *Economic Development and Cultural Change*, vol. 9, 550–60.

BLAUG 1985, 124–6. *New Palgrave* 1987, vol. 3, 69–71. SILLS 1979, 393–7.

LAFFER Arthur (born 1941)

Arthur Laffer taught at the University of Chicago before becoming professor at the University of Southern California at Los Angeles. He is also director of a consulting firm in Boston. He served as chief economist in the Nixon Office of Management and Budget.

Main publications

1975 (ed., with D.I. Meiselman). *The Phenomenon of Worldwide Inflation*, Washington, American Enterprise Institute.

1979. With J.P. Seymour, *The Economics of the Tax Revolt*, New York, Harcourt Brace Jovanovich.

1983. With Victor A. Canto and Douglas H. Joines, *Foundations of Supply-Side Economics: Theory and Evidence*, New York, Academic Press.

Arthur Laffer is one of the major representatives of the supply-side school, which he defined as being 'little more than a new label for standard neoclassical economics' (1983, p. xv). A theoretician of the anti-tax revolt which began in California in the 1970s, when Ronald Reagan was governor, he gave his name to a curve which illustrates the relation between the state total tax revenue and the rate of taxation. Starting from zero, an increase of the taxation rate would gradually raise fiscal revenues. But Laffer estimates that decreasing returns also apply in this field. There thus exists an optimal taxation rate above which total tax revenues will decrease if taxation rates continue to rise. From this moment, the tax system's disincentive effects on both saving and the supply of factors of production provoke a decline in output. In particular, entrepreneurs and high-income earners will devote more energy to finding tax shelters than to increasing production. For Laffer and his disciples, it is a tax system which is too heavy and too unequal which explains the main difficulties of modern economies, the slowing down of growth. A lowering of taxation rates and a decrease in income tax progressivity are thus necessary for stimulating supply and boosting production.

Main references

BUCHANAN James M. and LEE Dwight R. 1982. 'Where Are We on the Laffer Curve? Some Political Considerations', in *Supply-Side Economics in the 1980's*, Westport, Connecticut, Quorum Books, 183–95.

THÉRET B. 1988. 'La courbe de Laffer dix ans après: un essai de bilan critique', *Revue économique*, vol. 39, 753–808.

LANGE Oskar Ryszard (1904–1965)

Born near Lodz, Poland, Oskar Lange studied in Poznan, then in Cracow; graduating in 1928, he went the following year to the London School of Economics. He taught at the University of Cracow, and in 1936 at the University of Michigan, settling in the United States the following year. Between 1938 and 1945, he taught at the University of Chicago, where he became professor in 1943, taking American citizenship in the same year. He participated in the setting up of a new regime for Poland after the war, reassumed Polish nationality in 1945, was ambassador of the Polish People's Republic in Washington (1945–6), then Polish delegate to the United Nations Security Council (1946–9). He returned to Poland in 1949; here the official functions conferred on him were largely honorary. He went on assignments with the governments of India, Ceylon, the United Arab Republic and Iraq. He was the rector of the Central School for Planning and Statistics in Warsaw (1952–5), then professor at the University of Warsaw (1955–65). He died in a London hospital.

Main publications

1935. 'Marxian Economics and Modern Economic Theory', *Review of Economic Studies*, vol 2, 189–201.

1936–7. 'On the Economic Theory of Socialism', *Review of Economic Studies*, vol. 4, 53–71 and 123–44.

1938. 'The Rate of Interest and the Optimum Propensity to Consume', *Economica*, vol. 5, 12–32.

1943. 'Gospodarcze podstawy demokracji w Polsce' [Economic foundations of democracy in Poland], in *Ku gospodarce planowej* [Towards a centrally planned economy], London.

1945. *Price Flexibility and Employment*, Bloomington, Principia Press of Trinity University.

1953. *Zagadnienia ekonomii politycznej w swietle pracy J. Stalina 'Ekonomiczne problemy socjalizmu w ZSRR'* [Problems of political economy in the light of J. Stalin's work, 'Economic problems of socialism in the USSR'], Warsaw, Panstwowe Wydawnictwo Naukowe.

1957. *Dlaczego kapitalizm nie potrafi rozwiazac problemu krajów gospodarczo zacofanych* [Why capitalism is unable to solve the problems of backward countries], Warsaw, Panstwowe Wydawnictwo Naukowe.

1958. *Wstep do ekonometrii*, Warsaw, Panstwowe Wydawnictwo Naukowe; Engl. transl. 1962, *Introduction to Econometrics*, Oxford, Pergamon Press.

1959–66. *Ekonomia polityczna*, 2 vols, Warsaw, Panstwowe Wydawnictwo Naukowe; Engl. transl. 1963–71, *Political Economy*, 2 vols, Oxford, Pergamon Press.

1961. *Pisma ekonomiczne i spoleczne: 1930–1960*, Warsaw, Panstwowe Wydawnictwo Naukowe; Engl. transl. 1970, *Papers in Economics and Sociology*, Oxford, Pergamon Press.

1961. *Teoria reprodukcji y Akumulacji*, Warsaw, Panstwowe Wydawnictwo Naukowe; Engl. transl. 1969, *Theory of Reproduction and Accumulation*, Oxford, Pergamon Press.

1963. *Economic Development, Planning and International Cooperation*, New York, Monthly Review Press.

1963. *Essays on Economic Planning*, Bombay, Asia Publishing House.

1964. *Optymalne decysje: Zasady programowania*, Warsaw, Panstwowe Wydawnictwo Naukowe; Engl. transl. 1971, *Optimal Decisions, Principles of Programming*, Oxford, Pergamon Press.

1965. *Wholes and Parts: A General Theory of System Behaviour*, Oxford, Pergamon Press.

1965. *Wstep do cybernetyki ekonomiczne*, Warsaw, Panstwowe Wydawnictwo Naukowe; Engl. transl. 1970, *Introduction to Economic Cybernetics*, Oxford, Pergamon Press.

1973–7. *Dziela* [Works], 5 vols, Warsaw, Panstwowe Wydawnictwo Ekonomiczne.
1994. *Economic Theory and Market Socialism: Selected Essays of Oskar Lange*, edited by Tadeusz Kowalix, Aldershot, Hants, Edward Elgar.

At the end of the 1920s and the beginning of the 1930s, O. Lange's first works were about the analysis of business cycles. A socialist, he presented, in the early1930s, his vision of socialist economy: socialization of the big firms and the banks, centralization of credit, power lying with both workers and market. An econometrician, concerned to base his analysis on what, in his opinion, constitutes the heart of economic science, the theory of general equilibrium, but also a socialist and a Marxist, rejecting the labour theory of value but attached to historical materialism, Lange very early assumed this plurality (1935) which it was his ambition to present in a synthesis, never to be accomplished.

In the 1930s, he worked, in the framework of the dominant economic theory, on welfare, interest rates, prices, money and Keynesian theory – which he did not view as a revolution; works which would lead him to stress the importance of price flexibility (1945). Against von Mises, he tried to demonstrate, starting from the theory of general equilibrium, the theoretical feasibility of socialism securing an optimum, as well as perfect competition, thanks to the possibilities of economic calculation (1936–7); the discussions he had with Lerner then induced him to clarify his conception of socialism, combined with and aided by the market. And from 1943, concerned by the reforms to be instituted in Poland, he recommended limiting socialization to key industries, allowing a substantial private sector to function, and being vigilant of the dangers resulting from the power of the state bureaucracy. Aware of the faults of both central planning and of capitalism, and having published books marked by the official socialism of the time (1953, 1957, 1959), his conception became more and more that of a mixed economy, enlightened and guided by planning.

Constituting the materials of an unfinished synthesis, his econometrics and cybernetic economics lectures (1958, 1961 *Teoria*, 1965 *Wstep*) were as much concerned with the treatment of time series, the analysis of market mechanisms, the Keynesian multiplier and the input–output analysis as they were with Marx's schemes of reproduction.

Main references

Bibliography 1925–61, in LANGE 1961 *Pisma*.
KOWALIK Tadeusz 1970. 'Oskara Langego Wczesne modele socjalismu' [O. Lange's early models of socialism], *Ekonomista*, vol. 5, 965–1000.
KOWALIK Tadeusz 1974. 'Zur klassischem Modell des Sozialismus' [On the classical model of socialism], in *Sozialismus Geschichte und Wirtschaft: Festschrift für Eduard Marz*, Vienna, Europaverlag.

New Palgrave 1987, vol. 3, 123–9 and 129–31. SILLS 1978, vol. 8, 581–4.

LEIBENSTEIN Harvey (1922–1993)

Harvey Leibenstein was born in Russia and his family emigrated to Montreal when he was very young. After beginning his university studies at Sir George Williams University, he gained an MA from Northwestern in 1946 and a PhD from Princeton University in 1951. He was first assistant professor (1951–60) then professor (1960–67) at the University of California at Berkeley. In 1967, he was appointed professor at Harvard. A severe car accident ended his career in 1987. In 1989, he was named professor emeritus.

Main publications

1950. 'Bandwagon, Snob, and Veblen Effects in the Theory of Consumers' Demand', *Quarterly Journal of Economics*, vol. 54, 183–207.
1954. *A Theory of Economic–Demographic Development*, Princeton University Press.
1957. *Economic Backwardness and Economic Growth: Studies in the Theory of Economic Development*, New York, John Wiley & Sons.
1960. *Economic Theory and Organizational Analysis*, New York, Harper.
1966. 'Allocative Efficiency vs. X-Efficiency', *American Economic Review*, vol. 56, 392–415.
1974. 'An Interpretation of the Economic Theory of Fertility: Promising Path or Blind Alley?', *Journal of Economic Literature*, vol. 12, 457–9.
1976. *Beyond Economic Man: A New Foundation for Microeconomics*, Cambridge, Massachusetts and London, Harvard University Press.
1978. *General X-Efficiency Theory and Economic Development*, New York, Oxford University Press.
1979. 'A Branch of Economics is Missing: Micro-Micro Theory', *Journal of Economic Literature*, vol. 17, 477–502.
1980. *Inflation, Income Distribution and X-Efficiency Theory*, London, Croom Helm; New York, Barnes & Noble.
1985. 'On Relaxing the Maximization Postulate', *Journal of Behavioral Economics*, vol. 14, 5–20.
1987. *Inside the Firm: The Inefficiencies of Hierarchy*, Cambridge, Massachusetts, Harvard University Press.
1987. 'X-Efficiency Theory', *New Palgrave*, vol. 4, 934–5.
1989. 'Organizational Economics and Institutions as Missing Elements in Economic Development Analysis', *World Development*, vol. 17, 1361–73.
1989. *The Collected Essays of Harvey Leibenstein*, edited by Kenneth J. Button, vol. 1, *Population, Development and Welfare*; vol. 2, *X-Efficiency and Micro-Macro Theory*, Aldershot, Hants, Edward Elgar.

Leibenstein's first works were on development, a subject that has interested him throughout his career. His reflections on the problems of underdeveloped countries as well as his personal experiences with various firms led him to become increasingly dissatisfied with traditional microeconomic theory as an instrument for analysing concrete economic problems (1976, p. viii). In particular, Leibenstein is convinced that neoclassical hypotheses on maximization and optimization are unsuitable in these matters. His first article is a reflection on the limits of demand theory in the light of Veblen's arguments, among other sources (1950).

Leibenstein has sought to formulate an alternative microeconomic analysis, using his concept of X-efficiency. In his famous 1966 article, he explained that the allocation of productive factors and the state of technology are not entirely adequate explanations of a firm's productivity. Something more, that might be termed effort, not in the strictly physical sense, but in a larger, partially psychological sense, is implied here. Usually, there is a noticeable gap between a firm's optimal activity, as predicted by economic theory, and its effective activity, due in part to the absence of an assumed competitive pressure. X-efficiency is an attempt to take this missing factor into account. Thus, 'X-inefficiency', rather than the inefficient allocation of resources, causes many actual economic problems. In order to take into account the behaviour of individuals who, rather than firms, constitute the basic decision-making unit, Leibenstein uses the concept of selective rationality, related to Simon's notion of bounded rationality. Indeed, Leibenstein and Simon can be considered as two of the most important developers of a new current of thought, behavioural economics, of which one source can ultimately be traced back to Coase's work on the nature of the firm.

Leibenstein, who held his first post in 1949 at the United Nations' Population Division, has also been interested in demography, notably in the question of fertility. He is highly critical of the arguments of the Chicago school of economists, and of Becker in particular, who have attempted to account for decisions to procreate via traditional neoclassical analysis.

Main references

PERLMAN Mark 1992. 'Harvey Leibenstein', in Samuels (ed.), 184–201.

WEIERMAIR Klaus and PERLMAN Mark 1990 (eds). *Studies in Economic Rationality: X-Efficiency, Examined and Extolled. Essays Written in the Tradition of and to Honor Harvey Leibenstein*, Ann Arbor, Michigan University Press.

BLAUG 1985, 129–30.

LEIJONHUFVUD Axel (born 1933)

Axel Leijonhufvud was born in Stockholm. He began his studies at the University of Lund. In 1961, he earned an MA from the University of Pittsburgh; he gained a PhD from Northwestern in 1967. Since 1964 he has taught at the University of California at Los Angeles, where he was appointed professor in 1971.

Main publications

1967. 'Keynes and the Keynesians: A Suggested Interpretation', *American Economic Review*, vol. 57, *Papers and Proceedings*, 401–10.

1968. *On Keynesian Economics and the Economics of Keynes: A Study in Monetary Theory,* New York, Oxford University Press.
1969. *Keynes and the Classics: Two Lectures on Keynes' Contribution to Economic Theory,* London, Institute of Economic Affairs.
1973. 'Effective Demand Failures', *Swedish Journal of Economics,* vol. 75, 27–48.
1975. With Robert W. Clower, 'The Coordination of Economic Activities: A Keynesian Perspective', *American Economic Review,* vol. 65, *Papers and Proceedings,* 182–8.
1981. *Information and Coordination: Essays in Macroeconomic Theory,* New York, Oxford University Press.
1989. 'Information Costs and the Division of Labour', *International Social Science Journal,* May.

Leijonhufvud is among those economists whose reputations were firmly established early in their careers after the publication of their first book, based on their doctoral dissertation (1968). The 1967 article and 1969 publication sum up its main arguments. In it, Leijonhufvud distinguishes between the Keynesianism of the neoclassical synthesis, termed Keynesian economics, and Keynes's economic theory: 'let "Keynesian economics" be synonymous with the "majority school" macroeconomics which has evolved out of the debates triggered by Keynes's *General Theory.* ... This standard model appears to me a singularly inadequate vehicle for the interpretation of Keynes's ideas' (1967, p. 401). There is no doubt that this notion did not possess the total newness claimed for it by Leijonhufvud and his more enthusiastic readers. For some time, authors such as Joan Robinson, Sidney Weintraub and many others had stressed the gap between Keynes's own thought and that of his neoclassical interpreters. Like these interpreters of Keynes, Leijonhufvud rejects the suggestion that the underemployment equilibrium stems from wage stickiness.

The actual originality of his thesis consists in his attempt to resolve what he terms the micro–macro schizophrenia, without giving up the hypothesis of agent rationality. However, Leijonhufvud rejects Walras's auctioneer mechanism, denying that demand and supply equilibrium can be brought about by price movements. This is especially due to the various obstacles to the perfect and instantaneous flow of information. Clower had also advanced this idea (Clower 1963). Because of this, Clower and Leijonhufvud are often considered the originators of disequilibrium theory, which aims at building a new, non-Walrasian, economic foundation for Keynesian macroeconomics.

Leijonhufvud developed his arguments in numerous subsequent works and contributed to other topics of macroeconomics and growth theory (see in particular the articles collected in 1981). He is the originator of the concept of a 'corridor' to characterize the deviation from a balanced growth path, within which the mechanism of cumulative disequilibrium suggested in Harrod's 'knife-edge equilibrium' model does not come into play.

Main references

LITTLEBOY Bruce 1990. *On Interpreting Keynes. A Study in Reconciliation*, London and New York, Routledge.

BLAUG 1985, 131–2.

LEONTIEF Wassily W. (born 1906)

Born in Saint Petersburg, which in 1924 was to become Leningrad and so remain for several decades, Wassily Leontief went to the university of this town at age 15 and graduated in 1925; he then went to Germany, worked at the Institute für Weltwirtschaft of the University of Kiel and obtained his doctorate from the University of Berlin in 1928. He spent a year in China and then, in 1931, went to the United States. After some months at the National Bureau of Economic Research, he went to Harvard University, where he was named professor in 1946; he was in charge of the Harvard Economic Research Project from 1946 to 1972. President of the American Economic Association in 1970, he received the Nobel Memorial Prize in Economics in 1973. In 1975, he was appointed professor at New York University, where he became director of the Institute for Economic Analysis.

Main publications

1936. 'Quantitative Input and Output Relations in the Economic System of the United States', *Review of Economics and Statistics*, vol. 18, 105–25.

1941. *The Structure of the American Economy, 1919–1929*, Cambridge, Massachusetts, Harvard University Press; 2nd augm. edn 1951, *The Structure of the American Economy, 1919–1939* New York, Oxford University Press.

1953. 'Domestic Production and Foreign Trade: The American Capital Position Re-examined', *Proceedings of the American Philosophical Society*, vol. 97, 332–49.

1953. *Et al.*, *Studies in the Structure of the American Economy*, New York, Oxford University Press.

1966. *Essays in Economics: Theories and Theorizing*, New York, Oxford University Press.

1966. *Input–Output Economics*, New York, Oxford University Press; 2nd augm. edn, 1986.

1970. 'Environmental Repercussions and the Economic Structure – An Input–Output Approach', *Review of Economics and Statistics*, vol. 52, 262–71.

1971. 'Theoretical Assumptions and Nonobserved Facts', *American Economic Review*, vol. 61, 1–7.

1973. 'Structure of the World Economy: Outline of a Simple Input–Output Formulation', in *Les Prix Nobel 1973*, Stockholm, Nobel Foundation; *Swedish Journal of Economics*, vol. 76, 1974, 387–401.

1976 (ed., with Herbert Stein). *The Economic System in an Age of Discontinuity: Long-Range Planning or Market Reliance?*, New York University Press.

1977. *Essays in Economics*, vol. 2, *Theories, Facts, and Policies*, White Plains, New York, International Arts and Sciences; Oxford, Basil Blackwell.

1977. With Anne P. Carter and Peter Petri, *The Future of the World Economy*, New York, Oxford University Press.

1983. With Faye Duchin, *Military Spending: Facts and Figures, Worldwide Implications and Future Outlook*, New York, Oxford University Press.

1986. *Wassily Leontief: Textes et itinéraires*, edited by Bernard Rosier, Paris, La Découverte [bibliography].

1986. With Faye Duchin, *The Future Impact of Automation on Workers*, New York, Oxford University Press.

Some early articles – on the Russian economy, the statistical analysis of supply and demand, the analysis of foreign trade, interest and the marginal productivity of capital – published in *Weltwirtschaftliches Archiv* and the *Quarterly Journal of Economics*, revealed Leontief as being capable of combining theoretical thinking, statistical work and mastery of mathematical tools. During the course of his life, he has devoted these talents to the development of a particular process: input–output analysis, for the development of which he received the Nobel Memorial Prize. This system had its roots in a youthful intuition, which suggested that the Walrasian system of general equilibrium might be studied in concrete terms by analysing the technical coefficients of the relations between the different branches of industry. He developed it through very demanding theoretical and statistical work – in particular considering the means of computation of the time – which aimed at constructing the matrix of relations between 44 sectors, therefore evaluating the input–output flows between each sector and every other, calculating the coefficients (around 2000) and then the inverse matrix (1936, 1941 and articles published in the *Review of Economic Statistics* and *Econometrica*).

From this basic structure, and thanks to increased computing capabilities, Leontief was able, with the Bureau of Labor Statistics, and then at the Harvard Economic Research Project, to increase the number of the sectors studied, to complete the inter-industry matrix by taking into account purchases and sales to households, businesses and the rest of the world, to examine the interactions between sectors, to study the variations in time of the technical coefficients, to calculate production and employment multipliers and to take into account the interregional dimension (2nd edn of 1941, 1953 *Studies*). Applying his analysis to the study of US foreign trade, he showed that US exports were more labour-intensive and less capital-intensive than imports (1953 *PAPS*): this is the 'Leontief's paradox', which was the subject of much debate (*New Palgrave*, 1987, vol. 3, 166–7).

Untiringly, Leontief enlarged the applications of input–output analysis to fields as diverse as foreign trade, analysing the effects of disarmament, development, environmental and pollution issues, employment and automation, and technical change (1983, 1986 *The Future* and numerous articles reproduced in part in 1977 *Essays*), using it also as a planning instrument, especially for indicative planning, of which he became the advocate (1976). This analysis having been taken up in most countries and developed in connection with national accounts, Leontief made it the basis of a renewed analysis of the global economy (1973, 1977 *The Future*).

Throughout his work, Leontief has thus put into practice the conception of economics formulated in his presidential address to the American Economic Association (1971), the concern to link theoretical development and mathematical modelling with the attempt to know reality and, therefore, with the examination of statistics and raw data this implies.

Main references

'The Nobel Memorial Prize in Economics 1973'. Official Announcement and article by R. Dorfman, *Swedish Journal of Economics*, 1973, vol. 75, 428–49. Article reprinted in Spiegel and Samuels 1984, 407–21.

CARTER Anne P. and BRODY Andras 1970 (eds). *Applications of Input–Output Analysis: Published in Honor of Wassily Leontief*, Amsterdam, North-Holland.

CARTER Anne P. and BRODY Andras 1970 (eds). *Contributions to Input–Output Analysis: Published in Honor of Wassily Leontief*, Amsterdam, North-Holland.

GEORGESCU-ROEGEN Nicholas 1950. 'Leontief's System in the Light of Recent Results', *Review of Economics and Statistics*, vol. 32, 214–22.

BLAUG 1985, 133–6. *New Palgrave* 1987, vol. 3, 164–6. SHACKLETON and LOCKSLEY 1981, 160–82. SILK 1976, 151–90. SILLS 1979, 435–8.

LERNER Abba Ptachya (1903–82)

Born in Bessarabia, A. Lerner moved to London with his family while very young. After holding several jobs, he went, in 1929, to the London School of Economics, where, a convinced socialist, he was taught by Lionel Robbins; he obtained a doctorate in economics from the University of London in 1932. He spent some months at the University of Cambridge in 1935, and was assistant lecturer at the London School of Economics (1935–7). But it was essentially in the United States that he made his career as a teacher: in the universities of Columbia, Virginia and Kansas City (1940–42), at the New School for Social Research (1942–7), at Roosevelt University (1947–59), Michigan State University (1959–65), the University of California at Berkeley (1965–71), Queen's College in New York (1971–8) and at the State University of Florida (1978–80).

Main publications

1932. 'The Diagrammatic Representation of Cost Conditions in International Trade', *Economica*, vol. 12, 346–56.

1933–4. 'The Concept of Monopoly and the Measurement of Monopoly Power', *Review of Economic Studies*, vol. 1, 157–75.

1934. 'The Diagrammatic Representation of Demand Conditions in International Trade', *Economica*, n.s., vol. 1, 317–34.

1934–5. 'Economic Theory and Socialist Economy', *Review of Economic Studies*, vol. 2, 51–61.

1936. 'Mr Keynes' *General Theory of Employment, Interest and Money*', *International Labour Review*, vol. 34, 435–54.

1938. 'Alternative Formulations of the Theory of Interest', *Economic Journal*, vol. 48, 211–30.
1939. 'Ex-Ante Analysis and Wage Theory', *Economica*, vol. 6, 436–49.
1940. 'Some Swedish Stepping Stones in Economic Theory', *Canadian Journal of Economics and Political Science*, vol. 6, 574–91.
1944. *The Economics of Control: Principles of Welfare Economics*, London, Macmillan.
1951. *The Economics of Employment*, New York, McGraw-Hill.
1953. *Essays in Economic Analysis*, London, Macmillan.
1967. 'Employment Theory and Employment Policy', *American Economic Review*, vol. 57, *Papers and Proceedings*, 1–18.
1972. *Flation: Not Inflation of Prices, not Deflation of Jobs*, Chicago, Quadrangle Books.
1980. With D.C. Colander, *MAP, A Market Anti-inflation Plan*, New York, Harcourt Brace Jovanovich.
1983. *Selected Economic Writings of Abba P. Lerner*, edited by D.C. Colander, New York, Columbia University Press. [With a bibliography.]

In the 1930s, Lerner published several articles on monopoly power (1933–4) and, with the use of geometric techniques, on the pure theory of international trade (1932 and 1934). He also took part in the debate on socialism (1934–5), defending, like Lange, the possibility of market socialism tending towards an optimum given a system of prices based on marginal costs.

Socialist convictions and Keynesian affinities, respect for the market as an instrument of distribution, concern for full employment and awareness of the necessity of economic policy: all these factors characterize Lerner's work. Thus the 1944 book (partly based on his 1932 thesis) was intended, as its title suggests, to constitute a practical guide to economic policy; however, it was mostly read, in accordance with its subtitle, as a new presentation of the principles of economic welfare; but the idea according to which an egalitarian income distribution may ensure welfare maximization was hardly likely to convince the neoclassical economists. Likewise, the critique of the notion of sound public finances and the advancement of the idea of 'functional finance', which must be appreciated with respect to their effects on income, employment and prices, were not appreciated by those in favour of laissez-faire and were criticized by Friedman (1947).

Lerner considered it desirable to find that combination of monetary and fiscal policies which ensures both full employment and the stability of prices. He was one of the first, among proponents of active economic policy, to fear the effect of full employment on prices (1951). Distinguishing two levels of full employment – the first one high, which, thanks to the absence of rigidities, can be reached without inflation, the other one low, as a result of the inflationary factors created by institutional rigidities and monopoly powers – he first advocated a wage policy based on the fixing of objectives and on collective bargaining. Then, taking into account several types of inflation (1972) – one stemming from the excess of demand, a second due to the excessive claims by agents and a third resulting from the expectation of inflation – he advocated actions adapted to each case. Finally, he arrived (1980) at a 'Market Anti-inflation Plan' (MAP), which is based on the public authority's granting rights to raise prices, which themselves would become the object of transactions between enterprises.

An original thinker, Lerner enjoyed, like Calder, building mobiles, and left some of them at the universities where he taught.

Main references

FRIEDMAN Milton 1947. 'Lerner on the Economics of Control', *Journal of Political Economy*, vol. 55, 405–16.

SAMUELSON Paul A. 1964. 'A.P. Lerner at Sixty', *Review of Economic Studies*, vol. 31, 169–78.

SCITOVSKY T. 1984. 'Lerner's Contribution to Economics', *Journal of Economic Literature*, vol. 22, 1547–71.

SOBEL Irvin 1979. 'Abba Lerner on Employment and Inflation: A Post-Keynesian Perspective', in J.H. Gapinski and C.E. Rockwood (eds), *Essays in Post-Keynesian Inflation*, Cambridge, Massachusetts, Ballinger, 265–85.

BLAUG 1985, 137–9. BREIT and RANSOM 1971, 139–58. *New Palgrave* 1987, vol. 3, 167–9. SILLS 1979, 438–42. SPIEGEL and SAMUELS 1984, 185–200.

LEWIS William Arthur (1915–91)

W. Arthur Lewis was born in St Lucia (West Indies). He started working at 14. In 1932, he received a scholarship to study at the London School of Economics, where he obtained his PhD in 1940. He was lecturer at the University of London (1938–48), professor at the University of Manchester (1948–58), vice-chancellor of the University of West Indies (1959–63) and professor at Princeton University (1963–83). Parallel to his academic career, he worked in the British colonial administration (1943–52); he was adviser to the Prime Minister of Ghana (1957–8), deputy managing director of the United Nations Special Fund (1959–60), special adviser to the prime minister of the West Indies (1961–2); he was director of the Central Bank of Jamaica (1961–2), and president of the Caribbean Development Bank (1970–73). He was president of the American Economic Association in 1983. In 1979, W.A. Lewis shared the Nobel Memorial Prize in Economics with Theodore W. Schultz.

Main publications

1939. *Labour in the West Indies*, London, Fabian Society.

1945. *Monopoly in British Industry*, London, Fabian Society.

1949. *Economic survey, 1919–1939*, London, George Allen & Unwin.

1949. *Overhead Costs*, London, George Allen & Unwin.

1950. *The Principles of Economic Planning*, London, George Allen & Unwin.

1954. 'Economic Development with Unlimited Supplies of Labour', *Manchester School of Economic and Social Studies*, vol. 22, 139–91.

1955. *The Theory of Economic Growth*, London, George Allen & Unwin.

1966. *Development Planning: The Essentials of Economic Policy*, London, George Allen & Unwin.

1967. *Reflections on the Economic Growth of Nigeria*, Paris, OECD.
1969. *Some Aspects of Economic Development*, Accra, Ghana Publishing Corporation.
1978. *Growth and Fluctuations: 1870–1913*, London, George Allen & Unwin.
1978. *The Evolution of the International Economic Order*, Princeton University Press.
1980. *Selected Economic Writings of W. Arthur Lewis*, edited by M. Gersovitz, New York, Columbia University Press.
1984. 'The Economics of Development in the 1950s', in Meier and Seers (eds), 121–37.
1985. *Racial Conflict and Economic Development*, Cambridge, Massachusetts, Harvard University Press.
1986. 'My Evolution as an Economist', in Breit and Spencer 1986, 1–20.

W.A. Lewis's first works were about costs and tariffs (articles gathered in 1949 *Overhead*); besides his country of origin, he studied in numerous Third World countries, particularly in the Caribbean and West Africa; he worked on planning and the political economy of developing countries (1955, 1966), also writing on development (1955, 1985) and on economic history (1949 *Economic*, 1978), in both cases with a method which goes far beyond pure economic analysis.

For Lewis, the world economy is organized around a 'core', constituted by developed economies. For the first half of the twentieth century, he distinguished two 'peripheries': one the temperate zone, with populations principally of European origin, the other the tropical zone and characterized by 'unlimited supplies of labour'. This notion is at the basis of his 1954 article, certain theses in which were the object of much discussion: the dual character of the model (modern–traditional); its use of two analyses – classical and neoclassical – of the reward of labour; and its explanation of the terms of trade. In this article, Lewis analyses a 'dual economy' composed of a modern sector and a traditional sector. The first includes manufacturing and mining activities, and commercial agriculture: it is oriented towards profit, devoted to the financing of investment. The second sector includes farming agriculture and urban informal activities and is oriented towards subsistence: as a result of rural underemployment, urban unemployment and demographic growth, it is the source of an 'unlimited labour supply'.

Reviving the classical tradition of the first half of the nineteenth century, while adopting a model of growth close to that of Cambridge, Lewis shows that the combination of a massive supply of cheap labour and a capitalist sector reinvesting its profits can, in the long run, ensure high profit and growth rates – which England had known between 1780 and 1840 and which newly industrialized countries would experience in the 1960s and 1970s. In the same article, Lewis explains the terms of trade between developed countries and poor countries by the relation between their respective rates of productivity in food production, the high agricultural productivity of the North and the low productivity of the South thus explaining the unfavourable character of the latter's terms of trade.

Main references

'The Nobel Memorial Prize in Economics 1982'. Official Announcement and article by R. Findlay, *Swedish Journal of Economics*, 1982, vol. 80, 59–79. Article reprinted in Spiegel and Samuels 1984, 123–39.

GERSOVITZ M. *et al.* 1982 (eds). *The Theory and Experience of Economic Development: Essays in Honour of W. Arthur Lewis*, London, George Allen & Unwin.
LEWIS 1984, 1986.

BLAUG 1985, 140–42. KUPER and KUPER 1985, 459–60. *New Palgrave* 1987, vol. 3, 170–71.

LIPSEY Richard G. (born 1928)

Richard Lipsey was born in Victoria, British Columbia (Canada). He earned an MA from the University of Toronto (1953) and a PhD from the London School of Economics (1957), where he taught from 1955 to 1963. He was then professor at the University of Essex (1964–1970), and at Queen's University in Kingston (Ontario) from 1970 to 1986. Since 1989, he has been professor at Simon Fraser University in British Columbia. He was editor of the *Review of Economic Studies* (1962–4) and president of the Canadian Economics Association (1980–81). From 1983 to 1989, he was senior adviser for the C.D. Howe Institute.

Main publications

1956. With K. Lancaster, 'The General Theory of Second Best', *Review of Economic Studies*, vol. 24, 11–32.
1957. 'The Theory of Customs Unions: Trade Diversion and Welfare', *Economica*, vol. 24, 40–6.
1960. 'The Relation between Unemployment and the Rate of Change of Money Wage Rates in the United Kingdom, 1861–1957: A Further Analysis', *Economica*, vol. 27, 1–31.
1963. *An Introduction to Positive Economics*, London, Weidenfeld & Nicolson.
1966. With Peter O. Steiner [and Douglas D. Purvis for the 5th edn (1985)], *Economics: An Introductory Analysis*, New York, Harper & Row.
1967. With G.C. Archibald, *An Introduction to a Mathematical Treatment of Economics*, London, Weidenfeld & Nicolson.
1970. *The Theory of Customs Union: A General Equilibrium Analysis*, London, Weidenfeld & Nicolson.
1976. With G.C. Archibald, *An Introduction to Mathematical Economics: Methods and Application*, New York, Harper & Row.
1981. 'The Understanding and Control of Inflation: Is there a Crisis in Macro-economics?', *Canadian Journal of Economics*, vol. 14, 545–76.
1988. With C. Harbury, *First Principles of Economics*, London, Weidenfeld & Nicolson.
Forthcoming. *The Collected Essays of Richard G. Lipsey*, vol. 1, *Macroeconomics and Monetary Economics*; vol. 2, *Microeconomics*; vol. 3, *Political Economy*, Aldershot, Hants, Edward Elgar.

Richard Lipsey wrote his PhD dissertation on the theory of customs unions. A revised version of it was published in 1970, and it represents an important contribution to this field, in which Lipsey's compatriot Harry Johnson has also done renowned work. Yet it was a 1956 article that was to represent one of Lipsey's most famous contributions. In it, he set forth the general theory of second best, which invalidates certain results of welfare theory. For example, Lipsey demonstrates that if, given a specific economic situation, exogenous constraints (such as a tax, a tariff or the existence of monopolies) prevent the attainment of Pareto-optimality, any attempt to bring such a situation closer could just as easily diminish as increase general welfare: 'The general theorem for the second best optimum states that if there is introduced into a general equilibrium system a constraint which prevents the attainment of one of the Paretian conditions, the other Paretian conditions, although still attainable, are, in general, no longer desirable' (1956, p.11). There is no way of classifying alternative situations on a welfare scale. Therefore, for example, it is by no means obvious that the whole world would gain were a particular country to effect a unilateral lowering of customs duties.

Lipsey co-wrote an article that played an important role in the popularization of the Phillips curve, whose foundations he sought to examine, while at the same time correcting some of Phillips's errors (1960). The challenge of monetarism and new classical macroeconomics led Lipsey to reaffirm his confidence in Keynesian macroeconomics in his address as president of the Canadian Economics Association (1981). Lipsey is also the author of many textbooks, published in numerous editions and translations (1963, 1966, 1967, 1976). As indicated by the very title of the first of these works, one of the most widely used textbooks of the past few decades, Lipsey defends a positivist methodology inspired by Popper: only those statements that can be falsified by empirical tests are valid and scientific.

Main reference

BLAUG 1985, 143–5.

LITTLE Ian M. David (born 1918)

Ian Little was born in Rugby, England. He earned a PhD at Oxford University in1949. From 1952 to 1976 he taught at Nuffield College, in Oxford. He was named professor at Oxford University in 1972. He worked for the British Treasury (1953–5), for the OECD (1965–7), and he has been a member of the United Nations Committee on Development Planning (1972–5). In 1976, he became economic adviser for the World Bank in Washington. He retired in 1978.

Main publications

1950. *A Critique of Welfare Economics*, Oxford, Clarendon Press.
1953. *The Price of Fuel*, Oxford, Clarendon Press.
1957. With P.N. Rosenstein-Rodan, *Nuclear Power and Italy's Energy Position*, Washington, DC, National Planning Association.
1960. With R.W. Evely, *Concentration in British Industry: An Empirical Study of the Structure of Industrial Production, 1935–51*, Cambridge, England, Cambridge University Press.
1964. *Aid to Africa: An Appraisal of U.K. Policy for Aid to Africa South of the Sahara*, Oxford, Pergamon Press.
1965. With J.M. Clifford, *International Aid: A Discussion of the Flow of Public Resources from Rich to Poor Countries*, London, George Allen & Unwin.
1966. With A.C. Rayner, *Higgledy Piggledy Growth Again: An Investigation of the Predictability of Company Earnings and Dividends in the U.K., 1951–1961*, Oxford, Basil Blackwell.
1968. With J.A. Mirrlees, *Manual of Industrial Project Analysis in Developing Countries*, vol. 2, *Social Cost–Benefit Analysis*, Paris, OECD.
1970. With T. Scitovsky and M.F. Scott, *Industry and Trade in Some Developing Countries: A Comparative Study*, London, Oxford University Press.
1974. With J.A. Mirrlees, *Project Appraisal and Planning for Developing Countries*, London, Heinemann Educational Books.
1976 (ed., with M.F. Scott). *Using Shadow Prices*, London, Heinemann Educational Books.
1982. *Economic Development: Theory, Policy and International Relations*, New York, Basic Books.
1987. With D. Mazumpar and J.M. Page, *Small Manufacturing Enterprises: A Comparative Study of India and Other Economies*, New York, Oxford University Press.

As is the case with a few other economists, it was a first book (1950), and still his best-known, published early in his career, that made Ian Little famous. In this he attacked some of the essential aspects of welfare economics, founded by Pigou and developed by Bergson, Hicks, Kaldor and Lerner, among others. Long before McCloskey, he underscored the importance of persuasive rhetoric in economic discourse, sustained as it is, for example, by terms like 'welfare' or 'optimum'. He questioned the thesis according to which perfect competition may be qualified as an optimal solution, and stressed that it is erroneous to separate matters of efficiency and matters of equity.

Starting off with the 1960s, Little concentrated his research on the issue of development. Here also, he has made significant and controversial contributions, applying as he did so some of the principles developed in his 1950 book, particularly that of the necessity of conciliating the criteria of efficiency and those of equity while evaluating development strategies. Along with Scitovsky and Scott, he conducted a vast research on the problems of industrial development of seven countries, which resulted in six case studies and a synthesis (1970). Noticing that the import substitution policy comes up against increasing difficulties, Little and his collaborators propose new industrialization strategies, associated with social and political transformations in these countries, and a reorganization of world markets favouring less developed countries. In two books written with Mirrlees (1968, 1974; see also 1976 with Scott), widely used in less developed countries, Little proposed concrete measures of evaluation of the costs and benefits of projects, public and private, considering exchange rates as well as equity criteria.

Main reference

BLAUG 1985, 146–7.

LUCAS Robert E., Jr. (born 1937)

Robert E. Lucas was born in Yakima, Washington. He earned a BA in history (1959) and a PhD in economics (1964) at the University of Chicago. He was assistant professor at the Carnegie Institute of Technology (1963–7), then associate professor (1967–70) and full professor (1970–74) at Carnegie-Mellon University. Since 1974, he has been a professor at the University of Chicago, and he is currently co-editor of the *Journal of Political Economy.*

Main publications

1969. With Leonard A. Rapping, 'Price Expectations and the Phillips Curve', *American Economic Review*, vol. 59, 342–50.
1969. With Leonard A. Rapping, 'Real Wages, Employment, and Inflation', *Journal of Political Economy*, vol. 77, 721–54.
1972. 'Expectations and the Neutrality of Money', *Journal of Economic Theory*, vol. 4, 103–24.
1973. 'Some International Evidence on Output-Inflation Tradeoffs', *American Economic Review*, vol. 63, 326–34.
1975. 'An Equilibrium Model of the Business Cycle', *Journal of Political Economy*, vol. 83, 1113–44.
1976. 'Econometric Policy Evaluation: A Critique', in K. Brunner and A.H. Meltzer (eds), *The Phillips Curve and the Labor Market*, Amsterdam, North-Holland, 19–46.
1977. 'Understanding Business Cycles', in K. Brunner and A.H. Meltzer (eds), *Stabilization of the Domestic and International Economy*, Amsterdam, North-Holland, 7–29.
1978. 'Unemployment Policy', *American Economic Review*, vol. 68, *Papers and Proceedings*, 353–7.
1980. 'Rules, Discretion, and the Role of the Economic Advisor', in S. Fischer (ed.), *Rational Expectations and Economic Policy*, Chicago, National Bureau of Economic Research, 199–210.
1981. *Studies in Business-Cycle Theory*, Cambridge, Massachusetts, MIT Press.
1981 (ed., with T.S. Sargent). *Rational Expectations and Econometric Practice: A Book of Readings*, 2 vols, Minneapolis, University of Minnesota Press.
1983. 'Interview', in Klamer 29–57.
1987. *Models of Business-Cycle*, Oxford, Basil Blackwell.
1989. With N.L. Stokey and Edward C. Prescott, *Recursive Methods in Economic Dynamics*, Cambridge, Massachusetts, Harvard University Press.
1990. 'Supply-Side Economics: An Analytical Review', *Oxford Economic Papers*, vol. 42, 293–316.

Robert Lucas is the most renowned of the theoreticians of the new classical macroeconomics, and the first to apply John Muth's 1961 hypothesis of rational expectations to the study of the cyclical fluctuations of economic activity. From 1970 to 1980, Lucas, along with other young American economists, developed a new approach that sought to replace a weakened Keynesian theory by giving to the monetarist alternative theoretically strengthened bases. Thus Lucas holds that his theory of business cycle seeks to 'make more explicit the implicit model policy proposals of Henry Simons, Milton Friedman, and other critics of activist aggregative policy' ([1977] 1981 *Studies*, p. 234). He is convinced that the effectiveness of any government intervention aimed at countering the effects of cyclical fluctuations is limited, and that economic policy should be restricted to the implementation of stable and foreseeable rules, in both the fiscal and monetary spheres (1980). These proposals were made by Simons in the 1930s and by Friedman in the 1940s, but they had little effect in a milieu then dominated by Keynesianism.

According to Lucas, the theory of the natural rate of unemployment, as formulated by Friedman and Phelps, represents a basic change of perspective from the neoclassical synthesis based on Keynes's *General Theory*. This theory affirms that there exists an equilibrium level of employment in the economy that in the long run cannot be modified by any economic policy. Therefore there is no trade-off between inflation and unemployment, as suggested by the Phillips curve. Lucas and Rapping arrived at the same conclusion as Friedman and Phelps independently, and at about the same time, to the effect that there is no involuntary unemployment, starting from an analysis involving an economy in a continuous state of equilibrium. Actions undertaken so as to reduce unemployment can only attain their goal temporarily, while increasing inflation.

From that point on, Lucas, who initially described himself as a Keynesian, set himself the research programme of accounting for this situation theoretically. In order to accomplish this, he thought it necessary to rehabilitate pre-Keynesian analyses of business cycles, giving rise to the expression 'new classical macroeconomics'. In particular Lucas holds that it is important to revive Hayek's research programme, proposed during the late 1920s, which involves an integration of the theory of cycles and Walras's general equilibrium theory (1981 *Studies*, pp. 215–17). This implies giving macroeconomics real microeconomic foundations, to be found within the traditional neoclassical approach. For example, the study of the labour market should be based on the postulate that workers behave rationally when they choose between work and leisure time.

The foundation of Lucas's theory of business cycles is to be found in its combination of neoclassical hypotheses on market clearing and the hypothesis of the optimal use by economic agents of available information in the formation of their expectations (1975). On this basis he sought to demonstrate that the instability of contemporary economies is unconnected to market failures, but is rather linked to erratic government interventions. Such interventions can only have a real effect on the economy if they are unexpected, taking the agents involved by surprise. In the long run, government policies that aim at stimulating demand are inefficient. Rather, market forces should normally suffice to generate stable economic growth, in which unemployment remains at its natural level.

Main references

BLINDER Alan S. 1987. 'Keynes, Lucas and Scientific Progress', *American Economic Review*, vol. 77, *Papers and Proceedings*, 130–36.

VERCELLI Allessandro 1991. *Methodological Foundations of Economics: Keynes and Lucas*, Cambridge, England, Cambridge University Press.

BLAUG 1985, 148–50.

LUNDBERG Erik Filip (1907–1987)

Born in Stockholm, E. Lundberg studied there and obtained his PhD in economics in 1937. He was director of the Government Economic Research Institute from 1937 to 1955, held different official positions and, from 1955, was adviser to one of the largest Swedish banks. At the same time, he was professor of economics at the University of Stockholm (1946–65), then at the Stockholm School of Economics (1965–70). He was president of the Royal Swedish Academy of Sciences (1973–6) and chairman of the Nobel Prize Committee for Economics (1975–80).

Main publications

1937. *Studies in the Theory of Economic Expansion*, London, P.S. King & Sons; New York, Kelley & Millman, 1955.

1953. *Konjunkturer och ekonomisk politik*, Stockholm, SNS; Engl. transl. 1957, *Business Cycles and Economic Policy*, London, George Allen & Unwin; Cambridge, Massachusetts, Harvard University Press.

1955 (ed.). *The Business Cycle in the Post-War World*, London, Macmillan.

1961. *Produktivitet och räntabilitet* [Productivity and profitability], Stockholm, SNS.

1968. *Instability and Economic Growth*, New Haven, Connecticut, Yale University Press.

1969. 'On Incomes Policy in Sweden', in *On Incomes Policy*, Papers and Proceedings from a Conference in Honour of E. Lundberg, Stockholm, Studieforbundet Naringsliv och Samhalle, 11–20.

1970. *Ekonomisk politik i förvandling*, Stockholm, P.A. Norstedts.

1985. 'The Rise and Fall of the Swedish Model', *Journal of Economic Literature*, vol. 23, 1–36.

Erik Lundberg belongs to what is sometimes called the second generation of the Stockholm School, after that of the founders, Lindahl, Myrdal and Ohlin. He was the author of the first important book, stemming from this current, published in English (1937), the first English translation of a book by Lindahl, as well as one by Myrdal appearing two years later. It was also in 1937 that, for the first time, Ohlin identified a Stockholm School, underlining the fact that, in many respects, it had anticipated the Keynesian revolution. In his book, evolving from his doctoral thesis, Lundberg presented, on the basis of the combination of the accelerator and the multiplier, an explanation of growth instability; he also presented a cycle model linked to the variations in stock resulting from unexpected sales increases; and especially he used 'sequence analysis', in which all the data of a sequence are functionally linked to those of the preceding one. In so doing, he was providing a dynamic context and a microeconomic basis for a macroeconomics close to that of Keynes, but inspired rather by the works of Lindahl, Myrdal, Ohlin and, of course, Wicksell. For Schumpeter, not only was Lundberg's work conceived before the latter read *The General Theory*, but 'we might well speak of superiority, especially (but not only) because Lundberg tackled from the first the problem of sequence which had to be done for Keynes by followers' (Schumpeter 1954, p. 1174).

Lundberg devoted a large part of his thinking and of his works to economic policy, to the relations between ends and means, to the evaluation of different types of policy (monetary, fiscal and others) and to incorporating the international dimension. Opposed to the maintenance of regulations and detailed controls in time of peace, he criticized the excessively interventionist nature of Swedish governments. Concerned with contributing to the definition of a policy which would ensure economic stability, he analysed the effects of taxes on the increase of purchasing power in times of rises in nominal wages, and therefore its incidence on cost-push inflation; he also studied the inflationist (or deflationist) tendencies resulting from excess demand or supply, whether on the goods market or on the labour market (1953). In the same spirit, he analysed productivity changes, studying in particular the durability of labour productivity growth in the absence of new investment – the 'Horndal effect' (1961) – and conducted comparative studies on economic policy and growth in different countries (1968). Taking into account the growing complexity of economies, he tried to contribute to defining, for Sweden, a less burdensome, better adapted, economic policy (1969).

In one of his last texts, he explained the decline, in the 1970s and 1980s, of what was called the Swedish model (1985). He attributed it to the bad functioning of the system of price and wage determination, to the vulnerability of the Swedish economy to international shocks, but above all to fundamentally political causes, notably the breakdown of consensus. However, he found hope in the fact that it was only the temporary interruption of a tendency, the fundamental objectives of the welfare state being maintained in a country 'which stands out and probably will continue to stand out as an exception (together with a few other countries) in a world of high unemployment' (1985, p. 34).

Main references

BARRE Raymond 1954. 'Erik Lundberg et l'analyse des fluctuations économiques', in *Fluctuations économiques*, Paris, Domat-Montchrestien, vol. 2, 123–43.

BAUMOL William J. 1990. 'Erik Lundberg, 1907–1987', *Scandinavian Journal of Economics*, vol. 92, 1–9.

UHR Carl G. 1990. 'Erik Lundberg and Dynamic Economics: A Review Article', *Journal of the History of Economic Thought*, vol. 12, 222–35.

New Palgrave 1987, vol. 3, 252.

MACHLUP Fritz (1902–1983)

Fritz Machlup was born near Vienna. He earned his doctorate at the University of Vienna in 1923, under the direction of Ludwig von Mises. From 1922 to 1932 he directed a cardboard-manufacturing company while pursuing his studies in economics and participating in von Mises' seminars. Because of his Jewish background, he could not find a teaching position in Austria, and he went to the United States in 1933 as a Rockefeller fellow. Machlup found a position at the University of Buffalo, where he taught until 1947. He went on to become a professor at Johns Hopkins University (1947–60), at Princeton (1960–71) and, finally, at New York University in 1971. He was president of the American Economic Association in 1966 and of the International Economic Association from 1971 to 1974.

Main publications

1925. *Die Goldkernwährung* [The gold-exchange standard], Halberstadt, Meyer.

1927. *Die neuen Währungen in Europa* [The new monetary systems in Europe], Stuttgart, Enke.

1931. *Börsenkredit, Industriekredit und Kapitalbildung*, Vienna, Springer; revised Engl. transl. 1940, *The Stock Market, Credit and Capital Formation*, London, Hodge.

1934. *Führer durch die Krisenpolitik* [A guide to crises policies], Vienna, Springer.

1943. *International Trade and the National Income Multiplier*, Philadelphia, Blakiston.

1946. 'Marginal Analysis and Empirical Research', *American Economic Review*, vol. 36, 519–54.

1949. *The Basing-Point System: An Economic Analysis of a Controversial Pricing Practice*, Philadelphia, Blakiston.

1952. *The Economics of Sellers' Competition: Model Analysis of Sellers' Conduct*, Baltimore, Johns Hopkins.

1952. *The Political Economy of Monopoly: Business, Labor and Government Policies*, Baltimore, Johns Hopkins.

1955. 'The Problem of Verification in Economics', *Southern Economic Journal*, vol. 22, 1–21.

1962. *The Production and Distribution of Knowledge in the United States*, Princeton University Press.

1963. *Essays on Economic Semantics*, edited by M. Miller, Englewood Cliffs, New Jersey, Prentice-Hall; paperbound edn 1967, *Essays in Economic Semantics*, New York, W.W. Norton; 2nd edn 1991, *Economic Semantics*, New Brunswick, New Jersey and London, Transaction.

1964. *International Payments, Debts, and Gold: Collected Essays*, New York, Charles Scribner's Sons.

1965. *Involuntary Foreign Lending*, Stockholm, Almqvist & Wiksell.

1967. 'Theories of the Firm: Marginalist, Behavioral, Managerial', *American Economic Review*, vol. 57, 1–33.

1968. *Remaking the International Monetary System: The Rio Agreement and Beyond*, Baltimore, Johns Hopkins.

1970. *Education and Economic Growth*, Lincoln, University of Nebraska Press.

1972. *The Alignment of Foreign Exchange Rates*, New York, Praeger.

1976. *Selected Economic Writings of Fritz Machlup*, edited by George Bitros, New York University Press.

1977. *A History of Thought on Economic Integration*, London, Macmillan.

1978. *Methodology of Economics and Other Social Sciences*, New York, Academic Press.

1980. 'My Early Work on International Monetary Problems', *Quarterly Review, Banca Nazionale del Lavoro*, no. 133, 113–46; in Kregel 1989, 17–72.

1980–84. *Knowledge: Its Creation, Distribution, and Economic Significance*, vol. 1, *Knowledge and Knowledge Production*, 1980; vol. 2, *The Branches of Learning*, 1982; vol. 3, *The Economics of Information and Human Capital*, 1984, Princeton University Press.

Fritz Machlup published his first book, developed from his doctoral thesis and devoted to the gold standard, in 1925. When he died at the age of 80, he had recently completed the third volume of a planned eight-volume series on 'knowledge, its creation, distribution and economic significance'. Within a working period of approximately 60 years, Machlup produced a most abundant and varied corpus. He was one of the few economists to have actually had the practical experience of working as an entrepreneur. A man of broad culture, he had a lifelong interest in philosophy, and participated actively in the intense debates that took place in Vienna in the early 1930s, all in all occupying a unique place in the realm of twentieth-century economic thought.

For a long time Machlup, along with Terence Hutchison, with whom he had a vibrant debate (1955), was also one of the few economists to be interested in the methodology of economics. He never failed to flush out implicit hypotheses and value judgements as well as the linguistic and conceptual ambiguities that are so abundant in the work of economists. This trait inspired the title of the anthology of some of his most important articles, published on the occasion of his sixtieth birthday: *Essays on Economic Semantics*. He wrote in the preface to the French edition: 'The aim was to dispel semantic and conceptual fogs in sectors where visibility was reduced and traffic heavy' (Paris, Calmann-Lévy, 1971, pp. 7–8).

Microeconomics, the theory of the firm and industrial organization are among the fields in which Machlup made significant contributions. In his contribution to the debate on marginalism that raged in the pages of the *American Economic Review* during the 1940s (Lester 1947), he developed the line of defence perfected by Friedman in 1953 and subsequently elaborated it on his own: 'We should understand that the construction of a pattern for the analytical description is not the same thing as the actual process in everyday life' (1946, p. 547). Thus, for Machlup, the goal of neoclassical theory is not the giving of a realist description of the firm. Rather, it attempts to predict the reaction of certain variables (prices, quantities) to the modification of other, external variables. Hence the neoclassical firm is a purely fictitious heuristic device, a mental construct, in effect; other approaches are required in the examination of the empirical firm (1967).

Machlup published most of his articles in the field in which he began his career, international economics, and especially on the international monetary system. He was a respected expert on this issue and actively participated in many international conferences on it during the 1960s and 1970s, and also edited numerous publications dealing with the question. A long-time advocate of flexible exchange rates, he made a number of proposals for the transformation of the international monetary system. Yet it was in the field that he named 'the industry of knowledge' that Machlup's contributions were the most novel. His giant project of bringing up to date his 1962 book was cut short by his death. This work, on the production and distribution of knowledge, had already stimulated much interest and some surprise when it first appeared, in its affirmation that the production of knowledge represents 29 per cent of gross national product (1980, p. xxvi). Evidently, this fundamental research went beyond the framework of economics, and Machlup conducted it with the aid of numerous scholars from many fields.

Main references

DREYER J.S. 1978 (ed.). *Breadth and Depth in Economics. Fritz Machlup: The Man and His Ideas*, Lexington, Massachusetts, Heath.

HUTCHISON Terence W. 1956. 'Professor Machlup on Verification in Economics', *Southern Economic Journal*, vol. 22, 476–83.

LESTER Richard A. 1947. 'Marginalism, Minimum wages, and Labor Markets', *American Economic Review*, vol. 37, 135–48.

BLAUG 1985, 151–3. *New Palgrave* 1987, vol. 3, 267–8. KREGEL 1989, 17–72. SILLS 1979, 486–91.

MALINVAUD Edmond (born 1923)

Edmond Malinvaud was born in Limoges; after his studies at the local secondary school, he received training at the Lycée du Parc at Lyon, then at l'Ecole Polytechnique, from which he entered l'Ecole d'Application de l'Institut National de la Statistique et des Etudes Economiques (INSEE). There he was part, along with Gérard Debreu and Marcel Boiteux, of a small group working with Maurice Allais. A grant from the Rockefeller Foundation allowed him to spend 1950–51 at the University of Chicago, as a guest of the Cowles Commission.

An administrator, then general inspector of INSEE (1946–87), he taught at l'Ecole Nationale de la Statistique et de l'Administration Economique (ENSAE), of which he was director in 1962–6 and 1971–2. Having been the director of the Forecasting Department at the Ministry of Economy and Finance (1972–4), he became general director of INSEE (1974–87). Since 1957, he has been research director at l'Ecole des Hautes Etudes en Sciences Sociales (EHESS) and, since 1987, professor at the Collège de France.

Malinvaud has been president of the Econometric Society (1963), the International Economic Association (1974–7), the International Institute of Statistics (1980–81), the French Association of Economic Sciences (1986–7) and the European Economic Association (1988).

Main publications

1953. 'Capital Accumulation and Efficient Allocation of Resources', *Econometrica*, vol. 21, 233–68.
1954. 'Aggregation Problems in Input–Output Models', in T. Barna (ed.), *The Structural Interdependence of the Economy*, New York, John Wiley, 188–202.
1956. 'L'agrégation dans les modèles économiques', *Cahiers du séminaire d'économétrie*, CNRS, no. 4, 69–146.
1957. *Initiation à la comptabilité nationale*, Paris, Imprimerie Nationale.
1964. *Méthodes statistiques de l'économétrie*, Paris, Dunod; Engl. transl. 1966, *Statistical Methods of Economics*, Amsterdam, North-Holland.
1969. *Leçons de théorie microéconomique*, Paris, Dunod; Engl. transl. 1972, *Lectures on Microeconomic Theory*, Amsterdam, North-Holland.
1972. With J.-J. Carré and P. Dubois, *La Croissance française: un essai d'analyse économique causale de l'après-guerre*, Paris, Seuil.
1977. *The Theory of Unemployment Reconsidered*, Oxford, Basil Blackwell.
1980. *Profitability and Unemployment*, Cambridge, England, Cambridge University Press; Paris, Maison des Sciences de l'Homme.
1981–2. *Théorie macroéconomique*, 2 vols, Paris, Dunod.
1983. *Essais sur la théorie du chômage*, Paris, Calmann-Lévy.
1984. *Mass Unemployment*, Oxford, Basil Blackwell.
1986. 'Reflecting on the Theory of Capital and Growth', *Oxford Economic Papers*, vol. 38, 367–85.
1987. 'The Challenge of Macroeconomic Understanding', *Quarterly Review, Banca Nazionale del Lavoro*, no. 162, 219–38; in Kregel 1989, 297–316.
1987. 'The ET Interview: Professor Edmond Malinvaud', *Econometric Theory*, vol. 3, 273–95.
1990. 'Propos de circonstances sur les orientations de la discipline économique', *Annales – Economies, sociétés, civilisations*, no. 1, 115–21.
1991. *Voies de la recherche macroéconomique*, Paris, Odile Jacob.
1993. *Equilibre général dans les économies de marché: L'Apport de recherches récentes*, Paris, Economica.

Edmond Malinvaud very early entered the world of English-speaking economists, thanks to his stay at the University of Chicago and to articles such as the one published in 1953, in which he offered a unified approach to capital theory. However, all his career unfolded in France. An econometrician, he began a long list of publications with two articles on the aggregation problem (1954, 1956); he was joint editor of *Econometrica* from 1954 to 1964 and in 1964 published a fundamental book on statistical methods in econometrics. He published in 1957 an introductory book on national accounts which he helped set up in France, and in 1972, a work based on extensive statistical sources, on French postwar economic growth. His microeconomic teachings form the material of a textbook (1969) which has since become a classic; those in macroeconomics were published in 1981–2.

The theory of general equilibrium with fixed prices and rationing allowed him to formulate a new macroeconomic analysis of unemployment, in which two forms of unemployment, Keynesian and classical, are distinguished (1977). When supplies by sellers of both goods and labour are rationed, 'there is unemployment and firms do not produce more because of lack of effective demand: this is the Keynesian case. When labour is not fully employed but firms sell all their supply, we may speak of classical unemployment' (pp. 31–2). In this situation the consumers are rationed in the market for labour and the market for goods. Finally, when buyers' demand for goods and employers' demand for labour are rationed, there is 'repressed inflation'.

Malinvaud enriched this analysis by taking into account the relations between investment, profitability and the level of real wages (1980). Beyond this, he proposed to apply this approach to growth (1986). Malinvaud thus became the most eminent spokesperson of the disequilibrium school which, despite its American roots (Clower, Leijonhufvud), has grown principally in France.

Utterly convinced of the necessity of combining theoretical deepening and the double effort of observation and induction, Malinvaud stands back from the disciplinary quarrels and changes in fashion; in his eyes, if recent debates and works may 'suggest certain reorientations ... these do not throw into question the general process adopted by macroeconomics for the last forty years' (1991, p. 9).

Main references

Essais en l'honneur de Edmond Malinvaud, Paris, Économica. [With a biography and a bibliography.]

KAHN Richard F. 1977. 'Malinvaud on Keynes: A Review of Edmond Malinvaud, *The Theory of Unemployment Reconsidered*', *Cambridge Journal of Economics*, vol. 1, 375–88.

MALINVAUD 1987 *QR*, 1987 *ET*.

MOLINS-YSAL Georges 1983–4. 'Malinvaud et la théorie macroéconomique', in 2 parts, *L'Actualité économique*, vol. 59, 89–107 and vol. 60, 95–105.

BLAUG 1985, 154–5.

MANDEL Ernest (1923–1995)

Ernest Mandel was born in Belgium, where he began to study at the Free University of Brussels. He then carried on his studies at the Ecole Pratique des Hautes Etudes, in Paris, and ended them at the Free University of Berlin, where he earned a PhD. Having worked as a journalist and been in the employ of the Belgian Trade Union Federation, he was then named professor at the Vrije University in Brussels in 1972, and was director of its Institute of Political Studies until he retired in 1988. He was, throughout his career, a militant and a leader of the Fourth International. For this reason, he was denied access to France and the United States.

Main publications

1962. *Traité d'économie marxiste*, 2 vols, Paris, Julliard; Engl. transl. 1968, *Marxist Economic Theory*, London, Merlin Press.

1967. *La formation de la pensée économique de Karl Marx, de 1843 jusqu'à la rédaction du*

'Capital': Étude génétique, Paris, François Maspero; Engl. transl. 1971, *Formation of the Economic Thought of Marx*, London, New Left Books.
1972. *Der Spätkapitalismus*, Frankfurt am Main, Suhrkamp Verlag; Engl. transl. 1975, *Late Capitalism*, London, New Left Books/Verso.
1977. *Ende der Krise oder Krise ohne Ende?*, Berlin, Wagenbuch Verlag; Engl. transl. 1978, *The Second Slump: A Marxist Analysis of Recession in the Seventies*, London, New Left Books.
1980. *Long Waves of Capitalist Development: The Marxist Interpretation*, Cambridge, England, Cambridge University Press.
1982. *La crise 1974–1982: Les faits, leur interprétation marxiste*, Paris, Flammarion.
1984 (ed., with A. Freeman). *Ricardo, Marx, Sraffa*, London, Verso.
1988. *Où va l'URSS de Gorbatchev?*, Paris, La Brèche-PEC; Engl. transl. 1988, *Beyond Perestroïka*, London, Verso.
1990. *The Marxist Theory of Bureaucracy*, London, Verso.

Ernest Mandel is one of the best known Marxist economists. His textbook (1962), translated into many languages, was rapidly viewed as a classic. Mandel wanted to shake the dust off Marxism – understood as a synthesis of economic history and economy theory – with regard to the dogmatic interpretation, based on scholastic exegesis of sacred texts, which can be found, for example, in the textbooks published in the USSR. Hence Mandel tried to understand the Soviet reality, of which he was most critical, in the light of Marx's theory; he viewed the USSR and the East European countries as workers' states suffering from bureaucratic degeneracy. He also proposed an interpretation of the evolution of Marx's economic thought that breaks with the traditional vision (1967) underlining, for example, the importance of the concept of alienation.

He probably made his most original contribution by attempting to reactualize the long waves theory, reminding us that its origin can be found in Marxists' writings, particularly Trotsky's. Mandel is opposed to purely endogenous explanations of the long waves mechanism. This is why he prefers the expression 'long waves' to that of 'long cyles', the latter implying a mechanical regularity which he rejects. He considered that these waves follow from 'long-term movements in the rate of profit determining, in the last analysis, quicker and slower long-term paces in capital accumulation (of economic growth and of expansion in the world market)' (1980, pp. vii–viii).

Mandel considered that a third phase has begun in the long-term evolution of capitalism, a phase qualified as neo-capitalism, capitalism in decline, or else late capitalism (*Spätkapitalismus*), which follows the competitive phase and the imperialist phase, which Lenin wrongly thought to be the last phase of capitalism's evolution. He examined its characteristics in a book which can be considered as the continuation of his 1962 *Traité* (1972); he uses in it his conception of the long waves. The long post war period of growth must necessarily end through a new 'long wave' of increased tensions and social and economic crises, with a much lower average growth rate of the international capitalist economy. Mandel considered that events proved him right (1977, 1982).

In favour of a radical transformation of contemporary societies and a militant of the International founded by Leon Trotsky, Mandel is the author of numerous books of a more political flavour.

Main reference

ARESTIS and SAWYER 1992, 336–41.

MARSCHAK Jacob (1898–1977)

Jacob Marschak was born in Kiev, Russia and studied mechanical engineering at the Kiev Institute of Technology. A member of the Menshevik party at the time of the Russian revolution, he became actively involved in its struggle against the Bolsheviks. In 1919, he left Russia, first studying for six months at the University of Berlin, then at the University of Heidelberg, where he earned his doctorate in economics in 1922. After holding several positions as a research associate and economic journalist, he was appointed Privatdozent at Heidelberg University in 1930. In 1933, he left Germany for England, teaching at Oxford until 1939, while concurrently directing the Oxford Institute of Statistics (after 1935). In 1940, he settled in the United States, teaching at the New School for Social Research (1940–42), the University of Chicago (1943–55), Yale (1955–60) and the University of California at Los Angeles (1960–77). He was director of the Cowles Commission from 1943 to 1948. Shortly before his death in Los Angeles, he was elected president of the American Economic Association for the year 1978.

Main publications

1923. 'Wirtschaftsrechnung und Gemeinwirtschaft' [Economic calculation and community economy], *Archiv für Sozialwissenschaft*, vol. 51, 488–500.
1931. *Elastizität der Nachfrage* [The elasticity of demand], Tübingen, J.C.B. Mohr.
1938. 'Money and the Theory of Assets', *Econometrica*, vol. 6, 311–25.
1942. 'Identity and Stability in Economics: A Survey', *Econometrica*, vol. 12, 61–74.
1944. With W.H. Andrews, 'Random Simultaneous Equations and the Theory of Production', *Econometrica*, vol. 12, 143–205.
1949. 'Role of Liquidity under Complete and Incomplete Information', *American Economic Review*, vol. 39, 182–95.
1950. 'Statistical Inference in Economics: An Introduction', in T.C. Koopmans (ed.), *Statistical Inference in Dynamic Economic Models*, New York, John Wiley, 1–50.
1951. *Income, Employment, and the Price Level*, New York, Augustus M. Kelley.
1954. 'Towards an Economic Theory of Organization and Information', in R.M. Thrall, C.H. Coombs and R.L. Davis (eds), *Decision Process*, New York, John Wiley, 187–220.
1964. 'Actual versus Consistent Decision Behavior', *Behavioral Science*, vol. 9, 103–10.
1969. 'On Econometric Tools', *Synthese*, vol. 20, 483–8.
1971. 'Economics of Information Systems', in M. Intriligator (ed.), *Frontiers of Quantitative Economics*, Amsterdam, North-Holland, 32–107.

1972. With Roy Radner, *Economic Theory of Teams*, New Haven, Connecticut, Yale University Press.

1974. *Economic Information, Decision, and Prediction: Selected Essays*, vol. 1, *Economics of Decision* [bibliography of Marschak's works, xvii–xviii]; vol. 2, *Economics of Information and Organization*; vol. 3, *Money and Other Assets; Economic Measurements; Contributions to the Logic of Economics*, Dordrecht, D. Reidel.

Jacob Marschak devoted his first publication to the examination of the debate, initiated by von Mises, on the possibility of a rationally planned socialist society (1923). In it, he defended the idea that the market system is likely to be more efficient in a socialist economy than in a capitalist economic structure dominated by monopolies. Until the very end of his long career, Marschak remained interested in the economics of organizations, decisions and information. His main publications were anthologized in 1974. On the frontier between these fields and game theory, he founded what is termed the economic theory of teams, which has made an important contribution towards understanding the process of social interaction in contemporary societies.

However, Marschak especially distinguished himself in the birth of modern econometrics. In his own work, as well as in his activities as an organizer, research director and driving force in scholarship, he was one of the main architects of what some have termed the econometric revolution of the 1940s. It is enough to point out here that, while he directed the Cowles Commission, he brought into his entourage Kenneth Arrow, Gérard Debreu, Trygve Haavelmo, Lawrence Klein, Tjalling Koopmans and many other future renowned economists.

If there is one concept that has played a key role in Marschak's research, it is probably uncertainty. This is reflected in his first works on demand and money, as well as in his subsequent and more multidisciplinary research in the area of the behavioural sciences. The processing of uncertainty within the framework of probabilistic analysis underlies the methodological unity of the sciences that he upheld. He wrote: 'Econometrics shares its logical foundations with psychometrics and biometrics and, for that matter, with meteorology and even with experimental physics. ... The methodological agreement between social and natural sciences was enhanced when, in the latter, statistical propositions replaced some deterministic ones' (1969, pp. 483–5).

Main references

McGUIRE C.B. and RADNER Roy 1970 (eds). *Decision and Organization: A Volume in Honor of Jacob Marschak*, Amsterdam, North-Holland; 2nd edn 1986, Minneapolis, University of Minnesota Press. [Contains a bibliography of Marschak.]

BLAUG 1985, 156–8. *New Palgrave* 1987, vol. 3, 348–59. SILLS 1979, 500–507. SPIEGEL and SAMUELS 1984, vol. 2, 443–60.

MAYER Thomas (born 1927)

Thomas Mayer was born in Vienna. He settled with his father in England in September 1938, after Hitler's invasion of Austria, while his mother went to the United States, where they all moved in 1944. Mayer earned an MA (1949) and a PhD (1953) at Columbia. After holding several positions in the public service, he began teaching in 1953 at the University of West Virginia. He went on to become an assistant professor at Notre Dame University (1954–6), assistant and then associate professor at Michigan State University (1956–61) and was finally appointed professor at the University of California at Davis. He was also visiting associate professor at the University of California, Berkeley, in 1961–2.

Main publications

1958. 'The Inflexibility of Monetary Policy', *Review of Economics and Statistics*, vol. 40, 358–74.

1959. 'The Empirical Significance of the Real Balance Effects', *Quarterly Journal of Economics*, vol. 73, 275–91.

1960. 'The Distribution of Ability and Earnings', *Review of Economics and Statistics*, May, vol. 42, 189–95.

1965. With M. de Prano, 'Tests of the Relative Importance of Autonomous Expenditure and Money', *American Economic Review*, vol. 55, 729–52.

1967. 'The Lag in the Effect of Monetary Policy: Some Criticisms', *Western Economic Journal*, vol. 5, 324–42.

1968. *Monetary Policy in the United States*, New York, Random House; abridged paperback version, *Elements of Monetary Policy*, New York, Random House, 1968.

1972. *Permanent Income, Wealth, and Consumption: A Critique of the Permanent Income Theory, the Life-Cycle Hypothesis, and Related Theories*, Berkeley, University of California Press.

1975. 'Selecting Economic Hypotheses by Goodness of Fit', *Economic Journal*, vol. 85, 877–83.

1978. *Et al.*, *The Structure of Monetarism*, New York, W.W. Norton.

1980. 'David Hume and Monetarism', *Quarterly Journal of Economics*, vol. 95, 89–101.

1980. 'Economics as a Hard Science: Realistic Goal or Wishful Thinking?', *Economic Inquiry*, vol. 18, 165–78.

1981. With James S. Duesenberry and Robert T. Aliber, *Money, Banking, and the Economy*, New York, W.W. Norton.

1982. 'Federal Reserve Policy in the 1973–75 Recession: A Case Study of Fed Behaviour in a Quandary', in Paul Wachtel (ed.), *Crises in the Economic and Financial Structure*, Lexington, D.C. Heath, 41–84.

1984. 'The Government Budget Constraint and Standard Macrotheory', *Journal of Monetary Economics*, vol. 13, 371–79.

1985. With M. Chatterji, 'Political Shocks and Investment: Some Evidence from the 1930s', *Journal of Economic History*, vol. 45, 913–24.

1990. *Monetarism and Macroeconomic Policy*, Aldershot, Hants, Edward Elgar.

1990 (ed.). *The Political Economy of American Monetary Policy*, Cambridge, England, Cambridge University Press.

1993. *Truth versus Precision in Economics*, Aldershot, Hants, Edward Elgar.

Mayer was initially a Keynesian and then (from the 1950s) developed into what he terms a 'moderate monetarist'. Inspired by his parents, he was a social-democrat early in his career, but gradually moved towards liberal, then increasingly conservative, views. He attributes this to his pessimism concerning the possibility of correcting economic problems through government intervention (1990 *Monetarism*, p.12).

Besides his contributions to monetary theory, notably on the question of the effect of lags on the consequences of economic policy (1967), and his critical evaluation of various theories of consumption (1972), Mayer is the author of one of the clearest descriptions of what has been termed (since 1968) monetarism and its divergence from Keynesianism (1978; see also his 1980 article characterizing Hume as a precursor of monetarism). He described monetarism in 12 points, of which the first three, constituting its theoretical core, are as follows: '1) The quantity theory of money, in the sense of the predominance of the impact of monetary factors on nominal income; 2) The monetarist model of the transmission process; 3) Belief in the inherent stability of the private sector' (1978, p. 2). However, monetarists need not accept all of the 12 points, and it is also the case that Keynesians might agree with some of them. Mayer views the polarization between the two schools as deplorable, and as stemming in part from the fact that 'the Keynesians have a predisposition to reject all monetarist propositions on the basis of their "guilt by association" with other monetarist propositions, while monetarists have the opposite tendency' (1978, p.1). In more recent assessments of this issue, Mayer attributed the decline of monetarism to the integration of some of its ideas by Keynesianism, yet he also attributed it in part to the methodology associated with the new classical macroeconomics, which emphasizes deriving results from the maximization hypothesis, of which he is highly critical (1990 *Monetarism*, pp. 61–90). Working more recently on the methodoloy of economics, Mayer criticized the formalism of contemporary economic theory and pleaded for a trade-off between rigour and relevance (1993).

McCLOSKEY Donald Nansen (born 1942)

Donald McCloskey was born in Ann Arbor, Michigan (United States). He earned his BA (1964), MA (1967) and PhD (1970) from Harvard. He was assistant (1968–73) and then associate professor (1973–80) of economics at the University of Chicago. He was also associate professor of history at the University of Chicago (1979–80). Since 1980, he has been a professor of economics and history at the University of Iowa. In 1984, he founded the International Cliometric Society with Samuel Williamson.

Main publications

1973. *Economic Maturity and Entrepreneurial Decline: British Iron and Steel, 1870–1913*, Cambridge, Massachusetts, Harvard University Press.
1981. *Enterprise and Trade in Victorian Britain: Essays in Historical Economics*, London, George Allen & Unwin.
1981 (ed., with Roderick Floud). *The Economic History of Britain since 1700*, 2 vols, Cambridge, England, Cambridge University Press; 2nd edn 1994.
1982. *The Applied Theory of Price*, London, Collier-Macmillan; 2nd edn 1985.
1983. 'The Rhetoric of Economics', *Journal of Economic Literature*, vol. 21, 482–517.
1985. *The Rhetoric of Economics*, Madison, University of Wisconsin Press; Brighton, Wheatsheaf.
1987. *Econometric History*, London, Macmillan.
1987 (ed., with John S. Nelson and Allan Megill). *The Rhetoric of the Human Sciences: Language and Argument in Scholarship and Public Affairs*, Madison, University of Wisconsin Press.
1990. *If You're so Smart: The Narrative of Economic Expertise*, University of Chicago Press.
1993. *Knowledge and Persuasion in Economics*, Cambridge, England, Cambridge University Press.

Donald McCloskey first made himself known through his work in economic history and, in particular, his research on Great Britain (1973, 1981). Along with Robert Fogel and many others, he is one of the architects of the 'new economic and social history'. This field is based on the use of quantitative models and statistics, and is also known as 'cliometrics'. Nonetheless, McCloskey is highly critical of the scientific pretensions of contemporary economic theory, which he terms 'modernism' and 'scientism'. This modernist tendency, found in all fields of science, is linked philosophically to positivism and logical empiricism. He holds, moreover, that it has been institutionalized as an effective methodological police force, notably with its assertion of the existence of a demarcation criterion between science and non-science.

In a 1983 article and 1985 book (see also 1990 and 1993), which provoked much intense debate, McCloskey asserted that economics, as well as all other sciences, is first and foremost a conversation, in effect a language which uses the same processes as any other. Regardless of the degree of mathematical sophistication of his or her arguments, the economist seeks above all else to convince and persuade peers as well as the general public. This involves using the many techniques of rhetoric known and used by others, including poets and preachers, since classical antiquity; that is, reasoning via analogy, metaphors, appeals to authority, allegory, tales and ad hoc arguments. From this perspective, the aesthetic and literary aspects of economic texts (as well as of all scientific writings) are just as important, if not more so, than their frequently uncertain fidelity to methodological prescriptions such as the requirement of testing empirical results. This is true with reference to their influence as well. According to McCloskey, the continuousness of many fundamental debates in economics shows clearly that alleged empirical facts can never resolve the disagreement.

Main reference

BLAUG 1985, 159–60.

MEADE James Edward (1907–1995)

Born in Swanage, Dorset, in England, James Meade studied classics and economics at Oxford (BA in 1930). Appointed in 1930 by Hertford College, Oxford, to a lectureship in economics which he held until 1937, he was sent to Cambridge for a year to improve his professional training, which gave him the opportunity to work with Kahn and to participate in the meetings of the 'Circus' with Keynes's followers.

He worked as an economist at the League of Nations (1937–40), was a member (1940–45) then director (1945–7) of the Economic Section of the British Cabinet Office, professor of commerce at the London School of Economics (1947–57) and professor of economics at Cambridge University (1957–68). He retired five years before the statutory age to devote himself to the writing of his *Principles*. He was chairman of an Economic Survey Mission to Mauritius (1961) and of a Committee of the Institute of Fiscal Studies (1975–8). He was president of the Royal Economic Association (1964–6) and received in 1977, with Bertil Ohlin, the Nobel Memorial Prize in Economics.

Main publications

1936. *An Introduction to Economic Analysis and Policy*, London, Oxford University Press; 2nd edn 1939.
1937. 'A Simplified Model of Mr. Keynes' System', *Review of Economic Studies*, vol. 4, 98–107.
1938. *Consumers' Credit and Unemployment*, London, Oxford University Press.
1940. *The Economic Basis of a Durable Peace*, London, Oxford University Press.
1944. With Richard Stone, *National Income and Expenditure*, London, Oxford University Press.
1948. *Planning and the Price Mechanism: The Liberal–Socialist Solution*, London, George Allen & Unwin.
1951–5. *The Theory of International Economic Policy*, vol. 1, 1951, *The Balance of Payments*; vol. 2, 1955, *Trade and Welfare*, London, Oxford University Press.
1952. *A Geometry of International Trade*, London, George Allen & Unwin.
1955. *The Theory of Customs Unions*, Amsterdam, North-Holland.
1961. *A Neo-Classical Theory of Economic Growth*, London, George Allen & Unwin.
1964. *Efficiency, Equality and the Ownership of Property*, London, George Allen & Unwin.
1965–76. *Principles of Political Economy*, vol. 1, 1965, *The Stationary Economy*; vol. 2, 1968, *The Growing Economy*; vol. 3, 1971, *The Controlled Economy*; vol. 4, 1976, *The Just Economy*, London, George Allen & Unwin.
1974. *The Inheritance of Inequalities*, London, Oxford University Press.
1975. *The Intelligent Radical's Guide to Economic Policy*, London, George Allen & Unwin.
1978. *Et al.*, *The Structure and Reform of Direct Taxation*, London, George Allen & Unwin.
1982–3. *Stagflation*, vol. 1, 1982, *Wage Fixing*; vol. 2, 1983 with D. Vines and J. Maciejowsky, *Demand Management*, London, George Allen & Unwin.

1985. *Alternative Forms of Business Organisation and Workers' Remuneration*, London, George Allen & Unwin.
1986. *Different Forms of Share Economy*, London, Public Policy Centre.
1988–9. *Collected Papers*, vols 1, 2 and 3, 1988; vol. 4, 1989, London, Unwin Hyman.
1989. *Et al., Macroeconomic Policy: Inflation, Wealth and the Exchange Rate*, London, Unwin Hyman.

Faced with the problems of the day, the young Meade decided to study economics, and it was in the diversity of the English classical tradition, the Fabians' socialist ideals, the efforts made around Keynes to renew economic analysis and policy, that his thinking took root. He was among the first to include in a textbook (1936), with the essential of classical teaching, elements on imperfect competition and included a first presentation of the main Keynesian functions. A supporter of Keynesian policies (1938, 1940), he presented with Stone (1944) the principles and framework of national accounts which they had developed in the course of the Second World War. Later, he devoted several years to the writing of the treatise which was to render intelligible to *l'honnête homme* the best of economic theory (1965–76).

His 1951–5 book, emphasized in the granting of the Nobel Prize, was motivated by the ambition to offer a broad understanding of the problems, and was linked directly to the two dimensions to which Meade devoted the bulk of his work: international economics and economic policy. Concerned with defining the conditions for achieving the double objective of internal and external equilibrium, he linked pursuit of full employment and welfare with equilibrium of the balance of payments. Taking into account both the price effects (in the classical tradition) and income effects (in the new Keynesian vein), he advocated the implementation of two types of instruments, some centred on the exchange rate and others on effective demand.

Having great confidence in the market as the first means of resource allocation, he considered it the government's responsibility to ensure effective competition, to control the effect of externalities and to limit inequalities in the distribution of income and wealth (1964, 1974, 1965–76 vol. 4). He advocated the 'lib–lab policy' – with 'lab' for labour – an economic policy mixing classicism and radicalism, liberalism and the taking into consideration of the world of labour (1948, 1975). And when the new situation of coexistence of unemployment and inflation developed, he advocated a policy combining management of demand, action on wage setting, and reform of the international financial institutions (1982–3, 1985).

In the field of international economics, Meade developed the analysis of the relations between international trade, protectionism and welfare (1951–5 vol. 2, 1952) (in particular resorting to the concept of 'second best'), he deepened the question of European integration and of the customs unions

(1955 *The Theory*) and contributed – as adviser to the government at the end of the war, then as academic economist – to the conception and construction of an international system, in particular an international monetary order, and to keeping it as efficient and fair as possible.

Perpetually preoccupied with the issue of fairness, always concerned with finding, in the theory, the tools for understanding reality and defining economic policy, Meade was considered by Solow as a great utilitarian in the line of Mill, Sidgwick, Marshall and Pigou (Solow 1987 *EJ*, p. 986).

Main references

'The Nobel Memorial Prize in Economics 1977'. Official announcement, article by Harry Johnson and bibliography, *Swedish Journal of Economics*, 1978, vol. 80, 62–85; article reprinted in Spiegel and Samuels 1984, 19–36.

HOWSON Susan and MOGGRIDGE D.E. 1990 (eds). *The Wartime Diaries of Lionel Robbins and James Meade 1943–45*, London, Macmillan.

SOLOW Robert 1987. 'James Meade at Eighty', *Economic Journal*, vol. 97, 986–8.

BLAUG 1985, 161–3. GREENAWAY and PRESLEY 1989, 121–43. *New Palgrave* 1987, vol. 3, 410–7. SILLS 1979, 528–32.

METZLER Lloyd Appleton (1913–1980)

Born in Lost Springs, Kansas, L.A. Metzler began his studies at Kansas University and continued them at Harvard, where he obtained his PhD in 1942. From 1943 to 1946 he worked for different government agencies, in particular the Office of Strategic Services, and for the Federal Reserve System. In 1946–7 he taught at Yale University, and then, from 1947 until he died, at the University of Chicago. Health problems forced him to reduce his activities from the beginning of the 1950s.

Main publications

1941. 'The Nature and Stability of Inventory Cycles', *Review of Economics and Statistics*, vol. 23, 113–29.

1942. 'The Transfer Problem Reconsidered', *Journal of Political Economy*, vol. 50, 397–414.

1942. 'Underemployment Equilibrium in International Trade', *Econometrica*, vol. 10, 97–112.

1945. 'Stability of Multiple Markets: The Hicks Conditions', *Econometrica*, vol. 13, 277–92.

1947. 'Factors Governing the Length of Inventory Cycles', *Review of Economics and Statistics*, vol. 29, 1–15.

1947. With R. Triffin and G. Haberler, *International Monetary Policies*, Washington, DC, Board of Governors of the Federal Reserve System.

1949. 'Tariffs, International Demand, and Domestic Prices', *Journal of Political Economy*, vol. 57, 345–51.

1949. 'Tariffs, the Terms of Trade, and The Distribution of National Income', *Journal of Political Economy*, vol. 57, 1–29.

1949 (ed., with Howard Sylvester Ellis). *Readings in The Theory of International Trade*, Homewood, Illinois, Richard D. Irwin.

1951. 'A Multiple Country Theory of Income Transfers', *Journal of Political Economy*, vol. 59, 329–54.
1951. 'Wealth, Saving, and the Rate of Interest', *Journal of Political Economy*, vol. 59, 93–116.
1973. *Collected Papers*, with a foreword by Alice Bourneuf, Evsey Domar, Paul Samuelson and Richard Caves, Cambridge, Massachusetts, Harvard University Press.

In large part, L. Metzler's works came within the framework of efforts to develop new theoretical analyses, on the basis of the Keynesian system, concerning the analysis of cyclical fluctuations, with its attempt to provide an endogenous explanation of expectations formation (1941) and concerning international economics, with its thesis on the 'interregional income generation', presented in 1942. This thesis was not published as a book, but gave rise to the publication of several articles: one, in 1942, examined the proprieties of the stability of a two-country world whose economies display the Keynesian conditions; another, in the same year, studied the capital transfer problem in the context of a two-country Keynesian model.

Besides the examination – through the matrix which henceforth bears his name, of the stability conditions of multiple markets (1945), Metzler devoted a great part of his work to international economic and monetary theory: on the effects of international transfers on income, spending and the trade balance (1942 *JPE*, 1951 *JPE* 329–54), on the theory of trade tariffs and the influence of tariffs on the terms of trade and income distribution (1949 articles) and on exchange rate problems (contribution to the 1947 book).

He was one of the first to revive thinking on monetary theory (1951 *JPE* 93–116); placing himself at the turning point of the classical and Keynesian positions, he did so by taking into account the wealth-saving relationship in analysing the determination of the interest rate, comparing monetary policies in terms of their macroeconomic effects and emphasizing that the effects of money on interest rate depend on the nature of money creation, positions which the monetarists would later oppose.

Main references

HORWICH George and SAMUELSON Paul Anthony 1974 (eds). *Trade, Stability, and Macroeconomics: Essays in Honor of Lloyd A. Metzler*, New York, Academic Press.
NIEHANS Jürg 1978. 'Metzler, Wealth and Macroeconomics: A Review', *Journal of Economic Literature*, vol. 16, 84–95.

New Palgrave 1987, vol. 3, 458–61.

MINCER Jacob (born 1922)

Jacob Mincer was born in Tomaszow, Poland. He earned a PhD at Columbia in 1957. He taught at the City College of New York (1954–9) and, from 1959, at Columbia, where he was appointed professor in 1962. Mincer has been a research associate at the National Bureau of Economic Research since 1960.

Main publications

1958. 'Investment in Human Capital and Personal Income Distribution', *Journal of Political Economy*, vol. 66, 281–302.
1962. 'On-the-Job Training: Costs, Returns, and Some Implications', *Journal of Political Economy*, vol. 70, 50–80.
1962. 'Labor Force Participation of Married Women', in H.G. Lewis (ed.), *Aspects of Labor Economics*, Princeton University Press, 63–106.
1969 (ed.). *Economic Forecasts and Expectations: Analyses of Forecasting Behavior and Performance*, New York, Columbia University Press.
1970. 'The Distribution of Labor Incomes: A Survey with Special References to the Human Capital Approach', *Journal of Economic Literature*, vol. 8, 1–26.
1974. *Schooling, Experience and Earnings*, New York, Columbia University Press.
1974. With S. Polachek, 'Family Investment in Human Capital: Earnings of Women', *Journal of Political Economy*, vol. 82, Supplement, S76–108.
1976. 'Unemployment Effects of Minimum Wages', *Journal of Political Economy*, vol. 84, Supplement, S87–104.
1978. 'Family Migration Decisions', *Journal of Political Economy*, vol. 86, 749–73.
1985 (ed., with R. Layard). *Trends in Women's Work*, special volume of *Journal of Labor Economics*, vol. 3, S1–396.
1993. *Studies in Human Capital*, Aldershot, Hants, Edward Elgar.
1993. *Studies in Labor Supply*, Aldershot, Hants, Edward Elgar.

Jacob Mincer is, along with Gary Becker and Theodore Schultz, one of the originators of human capital theory. In a 1958 article, he constructed a model linking the distribution of personal income to the individual's investment in education (see also 1970, 1974). However, the educational system is but one means of increasing abilities, what he terms 'human capital'. Hence, in another frequently cited article (1962 *JPE*), Mincer pointed out the existence of various types of apprenticeship at the worksite, which he terms 'on-the-job training'. He has sought to appraise this form of investment and assess its consequences for income differences, concluding that it makes up a very important part of the investment in human capital, which is, moreover, positively linked to formal education.

Also in 1962, Mincer published a monograph in which he attempted to explain the participation rate of married women in the labour market in terms of individual maximization. He is also one of the first scholars to analyse household decisions using the individual rationality of neoclassical economic reasoning. He has pursued this line of thought in many directions, examining decisions related to procreation and family mobility (1974, 1978) among other questions. He has also produced many studies which seek to demonstrate the harmful effects of minimum wage legislation on the unemployment rate: 'The theoretical analysis indicates that minimum wages generate socially wasteful labor mobility between the "covered" and not-covered sectors and between the labour market and the non-market' (1976, p. S87). Two books containing a number of his articles, some previously unpublished, appeared in 1993.

Main reference

BLAUG 1985, 164–5.

MINSKY Hyman P. (1919–1996)

Hyman Minsky was born in Chicago. His father had left Russia after the failure of the 1905 revolution. In 1937, he began studying at the University of Chicago, from which he obtained a BA in mathematics in 1941, all the while studying economic theory. Called up in 1943, he resumed his studies in 1946 at Harvard, from which he obtained a Master's in 1947, then a PhD in 1954. He was successively assistant and associate professor at Brown University (1949–57), associate professor at the University of California at Berkeley (1957–65) and professor at Washington University at Saint Louis (1965–90). Since 1990 he has been professor emeritus of this institution, and distinguished scholar of the Jerome Levy Economics Institute of Bard College, in New York State.

Main publications

1957. 'Monetary Systems and Accelerator Models', *American Economic Review*, vol. 47, 859–83.
1957. 'Central Banking and Money Market Changes', *Quarterly Journal of Economics*, vol. 71, 171–87.
1963. 'Can "It" Happen Again?', in S. Carson (ed.), *Banking and Monetary Studies*, Homewood, Illinois, Richard D. Irwin, 101–11.
1964. 'Financial Crises, Financial Systems and the Performance of the Economy', in *Private Capital Markets*, Commission on Money and Credit Research Study, Englewood Cliffs, New Jersey, Prentice-Hall, 173–380.
1969. 'Private Sector Asset Management and the Effectiveness of Monetary Policy: Theory and Practice', *Journal of Finance*, vol. 24, 223–38.
1975. *John Maynard Keynes*, New York, Columbia University Press.
1977. 'The Financial Instability Hypothesis: An Interpretation of Keynes and an Alternative to "Standard" Theory', *Nebraska Journal of Economics and Business*, vol. 16, 5–16.
1980. 'Money, Financial Markets and the Coherence of a Market Economy', *Journal of Post Keynesian Economics*, vol. 3, 21–31.
1982. *Inflation, Recession and Economic Policy*, Brighton, Wheatsheaf; US edn, *Can 'It' Happen Again? Essays on Instability and Finance*, Armonk, New York, M.E. Sharpe.
1985. 'Beginnings', *Quarterly Review, Banca Nazionale del Lavoro*, no. 154, 211–21; in Kregel 1988, 169–79.
1986. *Stabilizing an Unstable Economy*, New Haven, Connecticut, Yale University Press.
1989 (ed., with Philip Arestis). *Post-Keynesian Monetary Economics*, Aldershot, Hants, Edward Elgar.

Influenced by economists apparently as different as Oskar Lange, Henry C. Simons and Joseph Schumpeter, who were his teachers, Minsky is identified with what is known as the post-Keynesian school. Very critical of the neoclassical synthesis, Minsky attempted to rediscover what he called 'the revolutionary thrust of *The General Theory*' (1975, p. v). The key elements of this new approach, overshadowed by the neoclassical synthesis, are 'decision-making under uncertainty, the cyclical character of the capitalist process, and financial relations of an advanced capitalist economy' (1975, p. ix). It was to this last aspect, in particular, that Minsky made some of his most important contributions (several of which are reproduced in his 1982 book, which gathers together 13 articles published between 1957 and 1980). For him, a realistic analysis of contemporary economies must take account of their complex, sophisticated and changing financial institutions. It is these institutions, set in place after the crisis of the 1930s, which explain the absence of major financial collapses in the 1970s and 1980s. But it is also these which explain what Minsky calls 'financial instability hypothesis' (1977). According to this hypothesis, during the periods of prosperity, the financial structures of the capitalist economies evolve, according to an endogenous process, from robustness to fragility, until the existence of a sufficiently large number of weakened financial institutions is capable of provoking a deflation of debts, which the activity of the central bank transforms into depression.

For Minsky, Keynes's theory is primarily an explanation of fluctuations based on investment, coupled with a financial theory of investment. Money, therefore, plays an essential role here. Contrary to the usual interpretations of *The General Theory*, it must be considered as endogenous, generated by the banking system to answer the financial needs of the firms. Minsky, on several occasions, thus criticized the hypothesis of money neutrality which is found in both the neoclassical synthesis, in particular in Patinkin's analysis, and in Friedman's monetarism.

In spite of the rise of policies based on a blind faith in the market mechanism, productive of instability, Minsky retained the hope that institutional reforms and active state intervention in the economy would be able to 'stabilize instability' (1986, p. 10).

Main references

DIMSKY Gary and POLLIN Robert 1994 (eds). *New Perspectives in Monetary Macroeconomics: Explorations in the Tradition of Hyman P. Minsky*, Ann Arbor, University of Michigan Press.

FAZZARI Steven and PAPADIMITRIOU Dimitri 1992 (eds). *Financial Conditions and Macroeconomic Performance: Essays in Honor of Hyman P. Minsky*, Armonk, New York and London, M.E. Sharpe.

LEONARD Jacques 1985. 'Minsky entre Keynes et Hayek: une autre lecture de la crise', *Economies et sociétés*, vol. 19, no. 8, 117–44.

MINSKY 1985.

WEISE Peter and KRAFT Manfred 1981. 'Minsky's View of Fragility: A Game Theoretic Interpretation', *Journal of Post Keynesian Economics*, vol. 3, 519–27.

ARESTIS and SAWYER 1992, 352–8.

MODIGLIANI Franco (born 1918)

Franco Modigliani was born in Rome, where he obtained a doctorate in law from the University of Rome in 1939. Strongly opposed to the Mussolini regime, he emigrated the same year to the United States and studied economics at the New School for Social Research where he received a doctorate in 1944. He taught at the New Jersey College for Women (1942) and at the New School for Social Research (1943–8), where he was named assistant professor in 1946. Associate professor (1949), then professor (1950–52) at the University of Illinois, he was professor at the Carnegie Institute of Technology (1952–60), at the Northwestern University (1960–62) and, from 1962, at the Massachusetts Institute of Technology, where he rose to emeritus professor in 1988. He was consultant for the Cowles Commission (1949–54) and, among other professional activities, consultant to the secretary to the treasury of the United States (1964–72). He was president of the Econometric Society (1962), of the American Economic Association (1976), of the American Finance Association (1981) and honorary president in 1983 of the International Economic Association. He was awarded the Nobel Memorial Prize in Economics in 1985.

Main publications

1944. 'Liquidity Preference and the Theory of Interest and Money', *Econometrica*, vol. 12, 45–88.

1953. With Hans Neisser, *National Incomes and International Trade*, Urbana, University of Illinois Press.

1954. With Richard Brumberg, 'Utility Analysis and the Consumption Function: An Interpretation of Cross-Section Data', in K.K. Kurihara (ed.), *Post-Keynesian Economics*, New Brunswick, New Jersey, Rutgers University Press, 388–436.

1956. *Problems of Capital Formation: Concepts, Measurements and Controlling Factors*, Princeton University Press.

1958. With Merton H. Miller, 'The Cost of Capital, Corporation Finance and the Theory of Investment', *American Economic Review*, vol. 48, 261–97.

1960. With Charles C. Holt, John F. Muth and Herbert A. Simon, *Planning Production, Inventories and Work Forces*, Englewood Cliffs, New Jersey, Prentice-Hall.

1963. 'The Monetary Mechanism and Its Interaction with Real Phenomena', *Review of Economics and Statistics*, vol. 45, 79–107.

1963. With Albert K. Ando, 'The "Life-Cycle" Hypothesis of Saving: Aggregate Implications and Tests', *American Economic Review*, vol. 53, 55–84.

1965. With Albert K. Ando, 'The Relative Stability of Monetary Velocity and the Investment Multiplier', *American Economic Review*, vol. 55, 693–728.

1975. 'The Life Cycle Hypothesis of Saving Twenty Years Later', in M. Parkin and A.R. Nobay (eds), *Contemporary Issues in Economics*, Manchester University Press, 2–36.

1977. 'The Monetarist Controversy or, Should We Forsake Stabilization Policies?', *American Economic Review*, vol. 67, 1–19.
1980. *The Collected Papers of Franco Modigliani*, vol. 1, *Essays in Macroeconomics*; vol. 2, *The Life Cycle Hypothesis of Saving*; vol. 3, *The Theory of Finance and Other Essays*, edited by Andrew Abel, Cambridge, Massachusetts, MIT Press.
1983. Interview, in Klamer 1983, 114–26.
1985. 'Life Cycle, Individual Thrift, and the Wealth of Nations', in *Les Prix Nobel 1985*, Stockholm, Nobel Foundation; *American Economic Review*, vol. 76, 1986, 297–313.
1986. *The Debate Over Stabilization Policy*, Cambridge, England, Cambridge University Press.
1986. 'My Evolution as an Economist', in Breit and Spencer 1986, 137–62.
1989. *The Collected Papers of Franco Modigliani*, vol. 4, *Monetary and Stabilization Policies*; vol. 5, *Savings, Deficits, Inflation, and Financial Theory*, edited by Simon Johnson, Cambridge, Massachusetts, MIT Press.

Franco Modigliani is one of the main artisans of the neoclassical synthesis. He thus describes the first basic theme of his 'scientific concern' as 'integrating the main building blocks of the *General Theory* with the more traditional and established methodology of economics that rests on the basic postulate of rational maximizing behavior on the part of economic agents' (1980 vol. 1, p. xi). Stemming from his doctoral thesis, his 1944 article is one of his major contributions. In it, beginning from Hicks's *IS–LL* model, Modigliani proceeds to demonstrate that the hypothesis crucial for explaining underemployment equilibrium in the Keynesian system is that of wage rigidity. Only in one case does this hypothesis appear to be superfluous: the 'Keynesian case' where the interest rate reaches the minimum corresponding to the liquidity trap, money demand becoming infinitely elastic. Subsequently, Modigliani improved this initial model (1963 *REStat*; see also the texts gathered in 1980, vol. 1 and 1989, vol. 5) and submitted it to empirical testing, constructing, with Albert Ando, an econometric model for the United States, known as FMP (Federal Reserve–MIT–University of Pennsylvania).

It was for 'his pioneering analyses of saving and financial markets' (*SJE* 1986, p. 305) that Modigliani was awarded the Nobel Memorial Prize. Two major contributions characterize his work in this domain: the life cycle hypothesis to explain saving, and the Modigliani–Miller theorems on the valuation of firms and the cost of capital. The first stemmed from thinking about Keynes's consumption function (1954, 1963 *AER*,1975, 1980 vol. 2). It aimed at explaining saving based on the hypothesis of the rationality of consumers who maximize their utility and allocate their resources in an optimal way over their life horizon. At the beginning of their active life, individuals consume more than they earn, borrowing in order to, on the contrary, spend their savings after retirement. It follows that consumption is not determined by current income.

In their joint work, Modigliani and Miller developed the thesis according to which firms do not maximize their profit rate, but rather their market value

(1958; see also 1980 vol. 3). This value is independent of the way the firm finances its capital, and stems rather from the income flows generated by the assets. Thus a much indebted firm may nevertheless have a higher market value than a more prudent one. Modigliani and Miller's contributions draw closer two fields of study traditionally not connected: pure economic theory and the study of the firms' financial behaviour. A new specialization, which has multiple concrete implications, was thus born: finance economics. For his contributions in this field, Merton Miller received the Nobel Prize in 1990, with Harry Markowitz and William Sharpe.

Modigliani was very active in the controversy between Keynesianism and monetarism (1965, 1977, 1986 *The Debate*). He admitted that some objections formulated by the monetarists against the first Keynesian models were well-founded, and that the gap at the theoretical level between these two approaches was not so large as is generally considered. But he viewed it as very deep politically, and he was convinced that there always remains an important space for very active stabilization policy in modern economies. He is also very critical of new classical macroeconomics.

Main references

'The Nobel Memorial Prize in Economics 1985'. Press release, article by P. Kouri and bibliography, *Swedish Journal of Economics* 1986, vol. 88, 305–53.

DORNBUSCH Rudiger, FISCHER Stanley and BOSSONS John D. 1987 (eds), *Macroeconomics and Finance: Essays in Honor of Franco Modigliani*, Cambridge, Massachusetts, MIT Press.
MODIGLIANI 1986 'My Evolution'.

BLAUG 1985, 169–71. SPIEGEL and SAMUELS 1984, vol. 1, 175–84.

MORGENSTERN Oskar (1902–1977)

Oskar Morgenstern was born in Goerlitz, Silesia, in Germany. He obtained a doctorate from the University of Vienna in 1925. Between 1925 and 1928 he went to several universities, in the United States and in Europe, as holder of a Rockefeller fellowship. In 1929, he started teaching as Privatdozent at the University of Vienna, where he reached the rank of professor in 1935. From 1931 to 1938, he directed the Austrian Institute for Business Cycle Research. In 1938, he left Austria to settle in the United States, where he started teaching at Princeton University. He was named professor in 1944 and taught there until he retired in 1970. Among numerous other activities, he was a consultant to the Rand Corporation, the Atomic Energy Commission and the White House.

Main publications

1928. *Wirtschaftsprognose, eine Untersuchung ihrer Voraussetzungen und Möglichkeiten* [Economic forecasting, research on its hypotheses and possibilities], Vienna, Julius Springer.
1934. *Die Grenzen der Wirtschaftspolitik*, Vienna, Julius Springer; revised Engl. version 1937, *The Limits of Economics*, London, W. Hodge.
1935. 'Vollkommene Voraussicht und wirtschaftliches Gleichgewicht', *Zeitschrift für Nationalökonomie*, vol. 6, 337–57; Engl. transl., 'Perfect Foresight and Economic Equilibrium', in 1976, ed. by A. Schotter, 169–83.
1941. 'Professor Hicks on Value and Capital', *Journal of Political Economy*, vol. 49, 361–93.
1944. With John von Neumann, *Theory of Games and Economic Behavior*, Princeton University Press; 3rd edn 1953.
1948. 'Demand Theory Reconsidered', *Quarterly Journal of Economics*, vol. 62, 165–201.
1950. *On the Accuracy of Economic Observations*, Princeton University Press.
1956. With John G. Kemeny and Gerald L. Thompson, 'A Generalization of the von Neumann Model of an Expanding Economy', *Econometrica*, vol. 24, 115–35.
1959. *The Question of National Defense*, New York, Random House.
1967. With Klaus Peter Heiss, *General Report on the Economics of the Peaceful Uses of Underground Nuclear Explosions*, Princeton, Mathematica.
1970. With Clive W.J. Granger, *Predictability of Stock Market Prices*, Lexington, D.C. Heath.
1972. 'Thirteen Critical Points in Contemporary Economic Theory: An Interpretation', *Journal of Economic Literature*, vol. 10, 1163–89.
1972. With K.P. Heiss, *Economic Analysis of the Space Shuttle System*, 4 vols, Washington, DC, Mathematica.
1973. With K.P. Heiss and Klaus Knorr, *Long Term Projections of Power: Political, Economic, and Military Forecasting*, Cambridge, Massachusetts, Ballinger.
1976. *Selected Economic Writings of Oskar Morgenstern*, edited by Andrew Schotter, New York University Press. [Contains a bibliography, 513–27.]
1976. 'The Collaboration Between Oskar Morgenstern and John von Neumann on the Theory of Games', *Journal of Economic Literature*, vol. 14, 805–16.
1976. With Gerald L. Thompson, *Mathematical Theory of Expanding and Contracting Economies*, Lexington, Massachusetts, D.C. Heath.

Oskar Morgenstern was one of those intellectuals, emanating from Central Europe, whom the rise of Fascism made emigrate to the United States. A man of multiple interests, he was a member of the Vienna circle which brought together some of the most important mathematicians and philosophers of our century. In his first book (1928), stemming from his doctoral thesis, written in 1926 and 1927, he pondered over the problem of the epistemological foundations of prediction in economics. Indeed, he emphasized, at the time Heisenberg had enunciated the uncertainty principle in physics, that the prediction has an effect on what is predicted. He told the story of the well-known pursuit of Sherlock Holmes by Professor Moriarty, showing that the solution to this problem must be thought of in terms of interactive and of strategic decisions. It was the first sketching out of the application of game theory to social behaviour. The same year, the mathematician John von Neumann proved the minimax theorem. Morgenstern reached a new stage in 1935, showing that 'the assumption of perfect foresight leads to paradoxes and is inadmissible for general equilibrium theory, which was thus found critically wanting' (1976 *JEL*, p. 806). Morgenstern met von Neumann in

Princeton in 1939. He began writing an article on which von Neumann offered his collaboration. This was eventually to become a major book, which marked the real birth of game theory as a full discipline (1944) and which would have an influence not only in contemporary economic thought but in several other fields of social sciences, in military research and, more recently, in the field of biology. For Morgenstern, the sophisticated techniques used in the study of interaction, whether conflictual or cooperative, of rational agents, each trying to maximize his profits, in both zero- and non zero-sum situations, are necessary for the explanation of most of the problems to which economic theory is addressed.

Always interested in methodology (1934, 1950, 1976 *Selected*), Morgenstern remained, until the end of his life, very critical of contemporary economic theory, for its lack of realism, its lack of rigour and its primitive mathematical techniques, as shown, for example, by his critique of Hicks (1941), his attack upon the traditional theory of demand (1948), or his 'Thirteen Critical Points in Contemporary Economic Theory' (1972), a kind of theoretical testament which constituted a direct charge against contemporary economics, which, he believed, had not yet absorbed the message contained in his1944 book, and was still very far from having acquired the maturity of the natural sciences. Moreover, the situation is made even more complicated by the fact that the collection of data in the social sciences is more difficult than in the natural sciences, where the objects and even the animals cannot lie (1950).

Morgenstern also became interested in the study of business cycles and their international transmission (1959, 1976 *Selected*). He also attempted to generalize the growth model suggested by von Neumann in 1937 (1956), his last book being devoted to this task (1976). During the last part of his career, Morgenstern worked on questions as diverse as national defence (1959), the peaceful use of atomic energy (1967), stock prices (1970), spaceships (1972 with K.P. Heiss) and long-term military projections (1973).

Main references

MARSCHAK Jacob 1946. 'Von Neumann's and Morgenstern's New Approach to Static Economics', *Journal of Political Economy*, vol. 54, 97–115.

SCHOTTER Andrew 1992. 'Oskar Morgenstern's Contribution to the Development of the Theory of Games', *History of Political Economy*, vol. 24, annual supplement, 95–112.

SHUBIK Martin 1967 (ed.). *Essays in Mathematical Economics: In Honor of Oskar Morgenstern*, Princeton University Press. [Bibliography of Morgenstern, ix–xviii.]

BLAUG 1985, 172–4. *New Palgrave* 1987, vol. 3, 556. SILLS 1979, 541–4. SPIEGEL and SAMUELS 1984, vol. 1, 395–406.

MORISHIMA Michio (born 1923)

Michio Morishima was born in Osaka. He obtained a BA in economics from the University of Kyoto in 1946. He was assistant professor here (1950–51), then associate professor (1951–62) and professor (1963–9) at the University of Osaka. Beginning in 1970, he was professor at the London School of Economics, where he attained the level of emeritus professor in 1988. He was president of the Econometric Society in 1965, and co-editor of the *International Economic Review* (1960–68).

Main publications

1964. *Equilibrium, Stability and Growth: A Multi-Sectoral Analysis,* London, Oxford University Press.
1969. *Theory of Economic Growth,* London, Oxford University Press.
1973. *Marx's Economics: A Dual Theory of Value and Growth,* Cambridge, England, Cambridge University Press.
1976. *The Economic Theory of Modern Society,* Cambridge, England, Cambridge University Press.
1977. *Walras Economics: A Pure Theory of Capital and Money,* Cambridge, England, Cambridge University Press.
1978. With George Catephores, *Value, Exploitation and Growth,* Maidenhead, Berkshire, McGraw-Hill.
1982. *Why Has Japan Succeeded?: Western Technology and The Japanese Ethos,* Cambridge, England, Cambridge University Press.
1984. *The Economics of Industrial Society,* Cambridge, England, Cambridge University Press.
1989. *Ricardo's Economics: A General Theory of Distribution and Growth,* Cambridge, England, Cambridge University Press.
1992. *Capital and Credit: A New Formulation of General Equilibrium Theory,* Cambridge, England and New York, Cambridge University Press.

A mathematical economist and growth theorist, Morishima is evidence of an unusual synthesis between theoretical currents often regarded as irreconcilable. Like several others of his Japanese colleagues, Morishima always took Marx's economic thought very seriously, while considering the theory of general equilibrium as the inevitable framework of any economic analysis worthy of the name. He devoted three books to the mathematical analysis of the works of those he considers to be the 'first-generation of scientific economists' (1989, p. 1): Marx (1973), Walras (1977) and Ricardo (1989). Far from seeing significant divergences between these three authors, he rather considers the two former as disciples of the latter, in whom one can already find the theory of general equilibrium. The three of them are thus for him the co-founders of modern scientific economics, in particular of the dynamic analysis.

It was by using the approaches developed by Leontief and von Neumann that Morishima demonstrated these unusual parallels. Morishima criticized the modern theories of growth for their aggregative nature. In a famous article, von Neumann (1937), on the contrary, suggested a dynamic analysis taking into account the interaction between all the sectors of an economy. It was this model that Morishima developed in numerous works (1964, 1969): 'I graft J. von Neumann on Walras to grow a new kind of the theory of general equilibrium. The von Neumann Revolution thus brought about in dynamic economics might be comparable with the Keynesian Revolution in static economics' (1969, p. v).

Although himself a mathematical economist, Morishima blames modern theoretical economics for having 'become no more than a mathematical skeleton' (1984 p. 9). He himself became interested in, among other things, the link between ethics and economics, in attempting to explain some aspects of Japan's economic history (1982).

Main reference

BLAUG 1985, 175–6.

MUSGRAVE Richard Abel (born 1910)

Born in Königstein, Germany, R. Musgrave studied in Munich and then Heidelberg, where he graduated in 1933; the same year, he left for the United States. He began his studies at the University of Rochester and finished them at Harvard, where he obtained his PhD in 1937. He taught at Harvard, worked for the Federal Reserve System and then was professor of economics at the University of Michigan (1948–58), Johns Hopkins (1958–61), Princeton (1962–5) and finally at Harvard, where he became emeritus in 1981. Since then, his wife having been appointed to the University of California at Santa Cruz, he has taught there as adjunct professor.

Main publications

1944. With E.D. Domar, 'Proportional Income Taxation and Risk Taking', *Quarterly Journal of Economics*, vol. 58, 388–422.
1958 (ed., with Alan T. Peacock). *Classics in The Theory of Public Finance*, London, Macmillan.
1959. *The Theory of Public Finance: A Study in Public Economy*, New York, McGraw-Hill.
1965 (ed.). *Essays in Fiscal Federalism*, Washington, DC, Brookings Institution.
1969. *Fiscal Systems*, New Haven, Connecticut, Yale University Press.
1973. With Peggy B. Musgrave, *Public Finance in Theory and Practice*, New York, McGraw-Hill.
1986. *Public Finance in a Democratic Society, Collected Papers of Richard A. Musgrave*, vol. 1: *Social Goods, Taxation and Fiscal Policy*, vol. 2: *Fiscal Doctrine, Growth and Institutions*, Brighton, Wheatsheaf.
1992. 'Social Science, Ethics, and the Role of the Public Sector', in Szenberg 1992, 190–202.

R. Musgrave has studied numerous aspects of taxation (1944, 1965, 1969, 1986): from the effects on investment of the taxation of capital income to the incidence of different types of taxes; from the analysis of the tax burden on different categories of income to the definition of the conditions of fair taxation; from federal to international tax issues. He has also studied numerous questions dealing with history, theory, practice and the policies of public finance. But, above all, he is the author of a book, now a classic as regards public economics and public finance. This book, published in 1959, is the result of about 20 years' work; it simultaneously presents past analyses and debates and a modern theory of public finance in their economic context.

Ascribing a fundamental place to the private sector, the firm and the market, Musgrave considers that an efficient public sector must constitute an essential complement. Besides the tasks which fall within the state's responsibility, such as maintaining competition, supervising financial institutions and protecting the environment, he observes that the public sector takes on three great functions: the acceptance of financial liability for public goods such as national defence, the redistribution of income to prevent inequality reaching a degree jeopardizing democracy, and the mixing of monetary policy and public finance measures, permitting one to ensure an appropriate level of activity and employment. Thus at the heart of his analyses he puts the three sides of public economics: allocation of public goods, income redistribution and macroeconomic stabilization. This analytical distinction makes it possible to determine from which side an objective may be best reached, to detect the incompatibilities or, on the contrary, the complementarities, in the pursuit of several objectives, to give a complete diagnosis of complex problems of disequilibria or distortions in the public finances and, finally, to clarify the decisions of those responsible for economic and social policy and the state finances.

Essentially, Musgrave's approach is based on a clear separation between knowledge, which finds its roots in the objective analysis of the phenomena, and the choices of society, which imply an ethical vision: the knowledge having both to clarify the choices and to help reach the set objectives.

Main references

MUSGRAVE 'In Retrospect', in Musgrave 1986, vol. 1, vii–xiii; 1992.

BLAUG 1985, 177–8. *New Palgrave* 1987, vol. 3, 577–8.

MYRDAL Karl Gunnar (1898–1987)

Karl Gunnar Myrdal was born in Sweden. In 1927, he obtained his doctorate in economics from the University of Stockholm, under the supervision of Gustav Cassel. In 1932, he became economic adviser to the new social-democratic government of Sweden. He was appointed professor at the University of Stockholm in 1934. Twice member of parliament (1934–6 and 1942–6), he was Swedish ambassador to India from 1939 to 1942, minister for trade and commerce (1945–7) and chairman of the Swedish Planning Commission (1945–8). In 1938, he was invited by the Carnegie Foundation to study the problems of the black community in the United States. Beginning in 1947, he was for ten years executive secretary of the United Nations Economic Commission for Europe, in Geneva. He spent time in India between 1957 and 1966, conducting research on the problems of Asian development. In 1974, he shared the Nobel Memorial Prize in Economics with Friedrich Hayek. His wife, Alva, a sociologist, who also collaborated with him throughout his career, received the Nobel Peace Prize in 1982.

Main publications

1927. *Prisbildningsproblemet och föränderligheten* [The problem of price formation and economic change], Uppsala and Stockholm, Almqvist & Wiksell.

1930. *Vetenskap och politik i nationalekonomien*, Stockholm, P.A. Norstedt & Soners; Engl. transl. 1953, *The Political Element in the Development of Economic Theory*, London, Routledge & Kegan Paul; New Brunswick, New Jersey, Transaction Books, 1990.

1931. 'Om penningteoretisk jämvikt. En studie över den "normala räntan" i Wicksells penninglära', *Ekonomisk Tidskrift*, vol. 33, 191–302; revised German version 1933, 'Der Gleichgewichtsbegriff als Instrument der geldtheoretischen Analyse' in F.A. Hayek (ed.), *Beiträge zur Geldtheorie*, Vienna, Julius Springer, 361–485; revised Engl. version 1939, *Monetary Equilibrium*, London, William Hodge; New York, A.M. Kelley, 1962.

1934. *Finanspolitikens ekonomiska verkningar* [The economic effects of fiscal policy], Stockholm, P.A. Norstedt & Soners.

1934. With Alva Myrdal, *Kris i befolkningsfrågan* [Crisis in the population question], Stockholm, Bonnier.

1940. *Population: A Problem for Democracy*, Cambridge, Massachusetts, Harvard University Press.

1944. *An American Dilemma: The Negro Problem and Modern Democracy*, 2 vols, New York, Harper & Brothers; condensed version edited by A. Rose, 1948.

1956. *An International Economy: Problems and Prospects*, London, Routledge & Kegan Paul; New York, Harper & Brothers.

1957. *Economic Theory and Under-Developed Regions*, London, Gerald Duckworth; US edn, *Rich Lands and Poor: The Road to World Prosperity*, New York, Harper & Row.

1958. *Value in Social Theory: A Selection of Essays on Methodology*, edited by Paul Streeten, London, Routledge & Kegan Paul; New York, Harper & Row.

1960. *Beyond the Welfare State: Economic Planning and its International Implication*, New Haven, Connecticut, Yale University Press.

1963. *Challenge to Affluence*, New York, Pantheon Books.

1968. *Asian Drama: An Inquiry into the Poverty of Nations*, 3 vols, New York, Twentieth Century Fund; condensed version edited by S.S. King 1971, New York, Pantheon Books.

1969. *Objectivity in Social Research*, New York, Pantheon Books.

1970. *The Challenge of World Poverty: A World Anti-Poverty Program in Outline*, New York, Pantheon Books.

1973. *Against the Stream: Critical Essays on Economics*, New York, Pantheon Books.

1973. *Essays and Lectures*, edited by Mutsumi Okada, Kyoto, Keibunsha.

1975. 'The Equality Issue in World Development', in *Les Prix Nobel en 1974*, Stockholm, P.A. Norstedt & Soners, 263–81; *American Economic Review*, 1989, vol. 79, 8–17.

1979. *Essays and Lectures After 1975*, edited by Mutsumi Okada, Kyoto, Keibunsha.

1982. *Hur styrs landet?* [How is the country governed?], Stockholm, Raben& Sjögren.

It was as a theorist, a specialist in monetary theory, that Gunnar Myrdal started his career. In his doctoral thesis, published in 1927, he opened up little-explored terrain by introducing expectations into the analysis of price formation. This book had a profound influence on a colleague of Myrdal's, Erik Lindahl. With Bertil Ohlin, these economists formed the kernel of what has been called the Stockholm School. In *Monetary Equilibrium* (first published as an article in Swedish in 1931) Myrdal applied his method to the analysis of monetary theory and business cycles, proposing an 'immanent critique' of the theories of the Swedish economist Knut Wicksell, who had also inspired, at that time, Hayek and Keynes. In the German version of this text (1933), Myrdal introduces the concepts of *ex ante* and *ex post*, to distinguish between the intended levels of saving and investment and those actually realized. An *ex ante* disequilibrium between these magnitudes, which are equal *ex post*, creates economic fluctuations, inflation and unemployment. Some results of Keynes's *General Theory* are included, in both this work and in the report written by Myrdal for the committee on unemployment set up by the Swedish government (1934 *Finanspolitikens*). Some consider Myrdal, like Kalecki, to be a precursor of the revolution dubbed Keynesian.

From the beginning of his career, Myrdal showed a critical attitude towards the orthodox economic theory held by his seniors. In *The Political Element in the Development of Economic Theory* (1930), he asserts that it is impossible to dissociate the normative and the positive, that value judgements are always present in every scientific undertaking, and that it is the duty of the scientist to make his own clear at the outset. He never stopped repeating this conviction for the whole of his career, which led to his increasing estrangement from orthodox theory. Although initially very critical of institutionalism, at first contact with it in the United States, at the end of the 1920s, Myrdal drew increasingly close to it, finally embracing it at the end of his career.

The major part of Myrdal's work is situated outside the domain of pure economics, even though he widely uses concepts drawn from his early works as an economic theorist. In his voluminous book on the problems of blacks in the United States (1944), Myrdal presented his conception of cumulative causality, inherited from Wicksell: contrary to the teachings of orthodox theory, there exists no force which tends to return to equilibrium once a significant departure from it has been made; on the contrary, a cumulative process accentuates the disequilibria. For black Americans, discrimination aggravates economic inferiority, which in turn increases discrimination. Myrdal insists on the fact that the analysis of this problem, like that of all large social problems, must take account simultaneously of all aspects of reality: economic, social, political, ideological, cultural and psychological. This is the approach adopted by Myrdal in his numerous studies of the problems of inequality, underdevelopment and industrialization (1957), whose point of culmination was his long work on the problems of industrialization in Asia (1968).

In granting Myrdal the Nobel Prize in Economics, the Royal Academy of Sciences of Sweden underlined his 'ability to combine economic analysis with broad sociological perspective' (*SJE* 1974, p. 470). Myrdal defined himself as the inheritor of the ideals of rationality and social justice of the Enlightenment. A critic of liberalism, he was also critical of Marxist socialism. An advocate of social democracy, he concretely shaped its contours in Sweden, as advisor to politicans and as a politican himself. He was also very active at the international level, as an important figure in the United Nations. He unceasingly made the case for a new international economic order, based on equality and cooperation among nations. In the last years of his life, he was nonetheless pessimistic concerning global issues; he then, along with his wife Alva, devoted much of his energy to the problems of peace and disarmament.

Main references

'The Nobel Memorial Prize in Economics 1974'. Official announcement and articles by E. Lundberg and L.G. Reynolds, *Swedish Journal of Economics,* 1974, vol. 76, 469–97.

ASSARSSON-RIZZI Kerstin and BOHRN Harald 1984. *K. Gunnar Myrdal, a Bibliography, 1919–1981,* New York, Garland.

CARLSON Allan C. 1990. *The Swedish Experiment in Family Politics: The Myrdals and the Interwar Population Crisis,* New Brunswick, New Jersey, Transaction.

DOSTALER Gilles 1990. 'An Assessment of Gunnar Myrdal's Early Work in Economics', *Journal of the History of Economic Thought,* vol. 12, 196–221.

DOSTALER Gilles, ÉTHIER Diane and LEPAGE Laurent 1992 (eds). *Gunnar Myrdal et son oeuvre,* Montréal, Presses de l'Université de Montréal; Paris, Economica; Engl. transl. 1992, *Gunnar Myrdal and his Works,* Montreal, Harvest House.

JACKSON Walter A. 1990. *Gunnar Myrdal and America's Conscience: Social Engineering and Racial Liberalism, 1938–87,* Chapel Hill, University of North Carolina Press.

KINDLEBERGER Charles P. 1987. 'Myrdal, Gunnar, 1898–1987', *Scandinavian Journal of Economics,* vol. 89, 393–403.

SHACKLE George L.S. 1945. 'Myrdal's Analysis of Monetary Equilibrium', *Oxford Economic Papers,* no. 7, 47–66.

SOUTHERN David W. 1987. *Gunnar Myrdal and Black–White Relations: The Use and Abuse of An American Dilemma, 1944–1969,* Baton Rouge, Louisiana State University Press.

ARESTIS and SAWYER 1992, 366–73. BLAUG 1985, 179–81. *New Palgrave* 1987, vol. 3, 581–3. SILLS 1979, 571–8. SPIEGEL and SAMUELS 1984, 688–94.

NEMCHINOV Vasili Sergeevich (1894–1964)

Born in Grabovo (Russia), V.S. Nemchinov graduated from the Moscow Commercial Institute in 1917. A specialist in statistics, and in particular of agricultural statistics, he led from 1926 the statistics department of the Timiriazev Agriculture Academy, but only officially became director there after he joined the Communist Party in 1940. He had to leave this position in 1948, having publicly opposed Lyssenko's theses on genetics. However, he was elected to the Academy of Sciences in 1946 and, in 1947, was named professor in the political economy department of the Party's Academy of Social Sciences, a position he was to retain until 1957; from 1953 to 1962 he was a member of the Presidium of the Academy of Sciences. In 1965, he was awarded posthumously, jointly with L. Kantorovich and V.V. Novozhilov, the Lenin Prize, for his work in economics.

Main publications

1959–65 (ed.). *Primenenye matematiki v ekonomicheskikh issledovaniyakh* [Applications of mathematics to economics research], Moscow, Izdatel'stvo sotsial' no-ekonomicheskoi literatury, 3 vols, 1959, 1961, 1965; Engl. transl. of vol. 1 (with A. Nove ed.) 1964, *The Use of Mathematics in Economics*, Edinburgh, Oliver & Boyd.

1962. *Ekonomiko-matematicheskie metody i modeli* [Methods and models of mathematical economics], Moscow, Sotsegiz; in 1967–9, vol. 3, 138–478.

1967–9. *Izbrannye proizvedeniya* [Selected works], Moscow, Nauka, 6 vols.

In the 1920s and 1930s, V.S. Nemchinov worked on agriculture statistics and on the statistical analysis of the peasantry (1967–9 vol. 1); some of the statistical data thus developed were used by Stalin, in particular in his 1928 speech 'On the Grain Front'. In the 1930s and 1940s, Nemchinov published articles and books of mathematical statistics and applied mathematics. In 1952, he published an article on 'Statistics as a Science' and he had to face the advocates of a position, then dominant in the USSR, which rejected as bourgeois the analysis based on statistical and mathematical methods.

After the death of Stalin, he pleaded for the publication of official statistics and for the use of modern quantitative techniques. In 1958, he formed a study group in mathematical economics, which became an institute in 1963. He worked on regional and national input–output tables – which, as he indicated in his 1959 book, were the object of work in the USSR as early as 1923–4 – and on the establishment, for planning purposes, of a large system of 'social evaluations' (1962). He edited various books on statistics and the application of mathematics to economics and planning. He thus played a major role in the revival of mathematical economics in the USSR. In the last years of his life, he was an advocate of economic reform.

Main references

ELLMAN Michael 1973. *Planning Problems in the USSR*, Cambridge, England, Cambridge University Press.

NEMCHINOVA M.B. 1984; Engl. transl. 'The Scientific Work of Vasili Sergeevich Nemchinov (on the 90th Anniversary of his Birth)', *Matekon. Translations of Russian and East European Mathematical Economics*, vol. 21, no. 2, 3–25.

New Palgrave 1987, vol. 3, 624–5.

NEUMANN John von (1903–1957)

Born in Budapest, Jansci von Neumann early showed remarkable abilities in both languages and mathematics. He published his first scientific paper in mathematics at 18 years of age. In 1921, he enrolled in mathematics at the University of Budapest, but studied at the University of Berlin, travelling often to Göttingen to see David Hilbert, then considered the greatest living mathematician. Beginning in 1923, he studied at the Zurich Polytechnic Institute, where he obtained a degree in chemical engineering in 1925. He completed a doctorate in mathematics at Budapest in 1926. He was appointed Privatdozent at the University of Berlin in 1927 and at the University of Hamburg in 1929. Invited to visit Princeton in 1930, he was appointed professor there in 1931 and in 1933 joined the newly-founded Institute for Advanced Study, where Einstein and Gödel were also on the faculty. During the Second World War, von Neumann was actively involved in military consultation in both the United States and Great Britain. In 1943, he became consultant to the Manhattan Project, charged with developing the atomic bomb at Los Alamos. Appointed to the Atomic Energy Commission in 1955, he took leave from the Institute for Advanced Study at Princeton and moved to Washington, DC. He was then discovered to have advanced bone cancer. He continued to work energetically, despite intense pain, until his death at 53 years of age.

Main publications

1928. 'Zur Theorie der Gesellschaftsspiele', vol. 100, 295–320; Engl. transl. 1959, in A. Tucker and H. Kuhn (eds), *Contributions to the Theory of Games*, Princeton University Press, vol. 4, 13–42.

1932. *Mathematical Foundations of Quantum Mechanics*, Princeton University Press, 1955.

1937. 'Über ein ökonomisches Gleichungssystem und eine Verallgemeinerung des Brouwerschen Fixpunktsatzes', in K. Menger (ed.), *Ergebnisse eines Mathematischen Kolloquiums*, Vienna, vol. 8, 73–83; Engl. transl. 1945–6, 'A Model of General Economic Equilibrium', *Review of Economic Studies*, vol. 13, 1–9.

1944. With Oskar Morgenstern, *Theory of Games and Economic Behavior*, Princeton University Press; 3rd edn 1953.

1954. 'A Numerical Method to Determine Optimal Strategy', *Naval Research Logistics Quarterly*, vol. 1, 109–15.

1956. 'The Mathematician', in James R. Newman (ed.), *The World of Mathematics*, New York, Simon & Schuster, vol. 4, 2053–63.
1958. *The Computer and the Brain*, New Haven, Connecticut, Yale University Press.
1963. *Collected Works*, 6 vols, edited by Alfred H. Taub, New York, Pergamon Press.

John von Neumann possessed remarkable scientific gifts. It was above all as a mathematician that he excelled, but his accomplishments overflowed the area of pure mathematics. He provided axiomatic foundations for quantum mechanics, and he was interested in cybernetics, astrophysics and meteorology. He played a key role in the development of the first electronic computer and, at the end of his life, he worked on automata. He was always interested in the social sciences, in economics in particular, as well as in military strategy.

In fact, it is at the frontiers of economics, strategy, politics, psychology and mathematics that one of his most original contributions, the development of game theory, is situated. In a paper published in 1928, inspired by Hilbert's aim of providing all of mathematics with axiomatic foundations, von Neumann proved a theorem applicable to two-person, zero-sum games, such as chess. He proved that, in every such game, there is a best way to play, mathematically determined. This rational strategy assures the player maximal advantage, regardless of the strategy adopted by his opponent. This advantage involves minimizing the maximum loss he can incur. This minimax theorem is a basic foundation in game theory, developed by von Neumann and Morgenstern in their 1944 book, the objective of which was to show that 'the typical problems of economic behavior [are] strictly identical with the mathematical notions of suitable games of strategy' (1944, p. 2). It is concerned with developing a general method of solution in which rational behaviour of the agent depends on the behaviour of other agents, on which he in turn exerts an influence. Such a situation is common in economics, as it is also in the political or military arena.

Another brief paper by von Neumann, presented in 1932 and published in 1937 under the title 'A Model of General Economic Equilibrium', was also very influential, both in the areas of general equilibrium and growth theory and that of the development of linear programming. Here von Neumann examined the growth conditions in a stylized model of classical inspiration and prefiguring those of Leontief and Sraffa. Goods produce goods, by means of well-defined production processes. Wages are fixed at subsistence level and profits are entirely reinvested. By means of sophisticated mathematical devices, employing topology and Brouwer's fixed point theorem, von Neumann showed that there exists an equilibrium growth path, and that prices, entirely determined by technical conditions, are such that the rate of interest equals the rate of growth, which is itself technically determined. Von Neumann underlines, in particular, 'the remarkable duality (symmetry) of the monetary variables (prices y_j, interest factor β) and the technical variables' (intensities of production x_i, coefficient of expansion of the economy α) ([1937] 1945–46, p. 1). Von Neumann's model was developed and generalized by several authors who relaxed its initial assumptions; among them, Morishima spoke of the 'von Neumann revolution' (Morishima 1969).

Though few in number, the contributions of von Neumann to contemporary economic theory were very influential indeed. Further, several of his other contributions as pure mathematician and as architect of the modern computer have had and will continue to have an indirect influence on economics and the other social sciences. For von Neumann, even if the ultimate criterion of success in mathematics is essentially aesthetic, 'much of the best mathematical inspiration comes from experience and ... it is hardly possible to believe in the existence of an absolute, immutable concept of mathematical rigor, dissociated from all human experience' (1956, p. 2059).

Main references

CHAMPERNOWNE D.G. 1945–6. 'A Note on J. von Neumann's Article on "A Model of Economic Equilibrium"', *Review of Economic Studies*, vol. 13, 10–18.

DORE Mohammed, CHAKRAVARTY Sukhamoy and GOODWIN Richard 1989 (eds). *John von Neumann and Modern Economics*, Oxford, Clarendon Press.

GEORGESCU-ROEGEN Nicholas 1951. 'The Aggregate Linear Production Function and Its Applications to von Neumann's Economic Model', in T. Koopmans (ed.), *Activity Analysis of Production and Allocation*, New York, John Wiley & Sons; London, Chapman & Hall, 98–115.

GOLDSTINE Herman 1972. *The Computer from Pascal to von Neumann*, Princeton University Press.

HEIMS Steve J. 1980. *John von Neumann and Norbert Wiener*, Cambridge, Massachusetts, MIT Press.

KEMENY John G., MORGENSTERN Oskar and THOMPSON Gerald L. 1956. 'A Generalization of the von Neumann Model of an Expanding Economy', *Econometrica*, vol. 24, 115–35.

MORGENSTERN Oskar 1958. 'John von Neumann, 1903–1957', *Economic Journal*, vol. 68, 170–74.

VANEK Jaroslav 1968. *Maximal Economic Growth: A Geometric Approach to von Neumann's Growth Theory and the Turnpike Theorem*, Ithaca, New York, Cornell University Press.

New Palgrave 1987, vol. 4, 818–26. SILLS 1968, 385–7.

NORTH Douglass C. (born 1920)

Douglass North was born in Cambridge, Massachusetts. He obtained a BA (1942) and a PhD (1952) from the University of California at Berkeley. He was successively assistant (1951–6), associate (1956–60) and full professor (1960–83) at the University of Washington, in Seattle. Since 1983, he has been professor of law and liberty at the Washington University in Saint Louis, where he is in charge of the Center in Political Economy. He has been co-editor of the *Journal of Economic History* (1960–66) and president of the Economic History Association (1972–73). He was awarded the Nobel Memorial Prize in Economics in 1993, along with Robert Fogel.

Main publications

1961. *The Economic Growth of the United States, 1790–1860*, Englewood Cliffs, New Jersey, Prentice-Hall.
1966. *Growth and Welfare in the American Past: A New Economic History*, Englewood Cliffs, New Jersey, Prentice-Hall.
1968 (ed., with Robert P. Thomas). *A Documentary History of American Economic Growth*, New York, Harper & Row.
1971. With Lance E. Davis, *Institutional Change and American Economic Growth 1607–1860*, Cambridge, England, Cambridge University Press.
1971. With Roger Leroy Miller, *The Economics of Public Issues*, New York, Harper & Row.
1973. With Robert P. Thomas, *The Rise of the Western World: A New Economic History*, Cambridge, England, Cambridge University Press.
1981. *Structure and Change in Economic History*, New York, W.W. Norton.
1990. *Institutions, Institutional Change and Economic Performance*, New York, Cambridge University Press.
1991. 'Institutions', *Journal of Economic Perspectives*, vol. 5, no. 1, 97–112.

Douglass North is one of the main architects of the 'new economic history'. He blames traditional history for restricting itself to a descriptive treatment of economic activities and institutions which does not manage to explain the nature and rhythm of long-term economic evolution. In his first book (1961), he questioned the thesis according to which the economic growth of the United States began mainly after the Civil War, and was propelled by the latter. He maintains on the contrary that this war interrupted a process engaged long before and inherently related to the evolution of the market economy and to the movements of commodity and factor prices.

The new economic history is characterized by the interpretation of quantitative data in the light of the current economic theory, and more particularly the neoclassical theory. But it is not limited to economics. Economic, social, political and ideological histories are closely linked. More specifically, the evolution of institutions plays a major role, and it is a theory of this evolution that North wishes to elaborate, using concepts such as the theory of transactions costs and property rights, and relying on political process theory inspired by the neoclassical approach: 'The central issue of economic history and economic development is to account for the evolution of political and economic institutions that create an economic environment that induces increasing productivity' (1991, p. 98). North's research programme is thus very ambitious. He describes as 'revolutionary' the book in which he applies his analytical approach to the Western history from 900 to 1700 (1973) and in which he elaborates an interpretation that runs counter to many received ideas, particularly those developed in the Marxist tradition (see, for example, Dobb 1946).

Main reference

BLAUG 1985, 182–4.

NOVE Alexander N. (1915–1994)

A. Novakovski was born in Petrograd, formerly Saint Petersburg, which, in 1924, became Leningrad for several decades. His father being a Menshevik, his family emigrated to London in 1923. He studied at the London School of Economics (BSc in 1936), served in the British army (1939–46), then in government (1946–58). In 1958, he was appointed reader in Russian social and economic studies at the University of London and, in 1963, he was named professor of economics at the University of Glasgow, where he set up and directed the Institute of Soviet and East European Studies. He was named professor emeritus in 1982.

Main publications

1961. *The Soviet Economy*, London, George Allen & Unwin.
1964. *Was Stalin Really Necessary?*, London, George Allen & Unwin.
1969. *An Economic History of the USSR*, London, Allen Lane; new edn 1988.
1973. *Efficiency Criteria for Nationalised Industries*, London, George Allen & Unwin.
1975. *Stalinism and After*, London, George Allen & Unwin; new edn, 1988.
1977. *The Soviet Economic System*, London, George Allen & Unwin.
1979. *Political Economy and Soviet Socialism*, London, George Allen & Unwin.
1983. *The Economics of Feasible Socialism*, London, George Allen & Unwin; new edn 1991, *The Economics of Feasible Socialism Revisited.*
1986. *Socialism, Economics and Development*, London, George Allen & Unwin.
1989. *Glasnost in Action; Cultural Renaissance in Russia*, London, Unwin Hyman.
1990. *Studies in Economics and Russia*, London, Macmillan.

After remaining outside the academic world for about 20 years, A. Nove was struck, when he came back to it in 1958, by the surge of mathematical formalism and by the fact that the 'emphasis was much more on equilibrium than on process' ([1983] 1991, p. 390). For a third of a century, he worked, taught and published on the history of the USSR (1969), on Soviet economics and planning (1961, 1977), on socialism in the USSR and in Eastern Europe, and incorporated a vast range of available material: historical, institutional, statistical and factual. He thus became part of the circle of Soviet Union specialists. He was also led to deal with the comparison of economic systems and with public enterprise efficiency criteria, in both the West and the East (1973).

Measuring the gap between socialism, as sketched out in Marx's works, and the reality, as it was built in the USSR, Nove undertook the analysis of the vague impulses, attempts and beginnings of reform, trying to bring out what could be a 'possible socialism' (1983, 1990). In the face of current changes, he came back to the nature of Stalinism and the effects of terror, and analysed the roots and chances of a possible Russian cultural revival (1989).

Main references

ARESTIS and SAWYER 1992, 390–401. BLAUG *Who's Who* 1986, 643. *New Palgrave* 1987, vol. 3, 684–5.

NOVOZHILOV Viktor Valentinovich (1892–1970)

Born in Kharkov (Russia), V.V. Novozhilov graduated from the University of Kiev in 1915; he taught in various institutions in the Ukraine. From 1922, he taught and did research in Leningrad, at the Polytechnique Institute from 1935, and at the head of the Statistics Department of the Engineering–Economics Institute from 1944 to 1952. He was a member of two scientific boards of the Academy of Sciences, one on the use of mathematics in economics and in planning, the other on the scientific bases of planning. With L. Kantorovich and V.S. Nemchinov, for their work in economics, he received the Lenin Prize in 1965. From then until his death, he was the head of the Economic Evaluation Systems Laboratory of the Leningrad branch of the Central Institute for Mathematical Economics (TsEMI).

Main publications

1926. 'Nedostatok tovarov' [The goods shortage], *Vestnik finansov*, no. 2.

1959. 'Izmerenie zatrat i ikh rezul'tatov v sotsialistischeskom khozyaistve', in V.S. Nemchinov (ed.); Engl. transl. 1964, 'Cost–Benefit Comparisons in a Socialist Economy', in V.S. Nemchinov (ed., with A. Nove), 33–190.

1967. *Problemy izmereniia zatrat i resul'tatov pri optimal'nom planirovanii*, Moscow, Ekonomika; Engl. transl. 1970, *Problems of Cost–Benefit Analysis in Optimal Planning*, White Plains, New York, International Arts and Sciences Press.

1972. *Voprosy razvitiia sotsialisticheskoi ekonomiki* [Questions on the development of the socialist economy], Moscow, Nauka.

In the burgeoning of ideas in the 1920s, V.V. Novozhilov, like many other economists of the time, among them Preobrajenski and Kondratiev, attempted to explain the shortages suffered by the Soviet economy (1926); he characterized this situation as one where, contrary to the market economy, where the goods seek buyers, here it is the buyers that search for goods. He developed a macroeconomic model, on the basis of which he established the following law: that shortage progresses at the same rate as that at which the economy grows. All these debates and works were suppressed by the repression at the end of the 1920s.

Having worked in the 1930s on the measurement of the effects of different economic projects and on the choices between different investment variants, Novozhilov devoted his thesis, which he presented in 1941, to these issues, and published in Leningrad several articles on these themes at the end of the 1930s and during the 1940s. From the mid-1950s, he contributed, with Kantorovich and Nemchinov, to the revival of works of mathematical economics. Like Kantorovich, he worked on the problem of production resources optimization: in the face of a demand whose structure is considered as determined (by the authorities), it was a question of finding, while minimizing labour costs (direct and indirect), the optimal combination of current and capital expenditure (1967).

Main references

ELLMAN Michael 1973. *Planning Problems in the USSR*, Cambridge, England, Cambridge University Press.

PETRAKOV N.I. 1972. 'Nauchnaia i pedagigicheskaia deiatel'nost' V.V. Novozhilova' [The scientific and pedagogical work of V.V. Novozhilov], in Novozhilov 1972.

BLAUG *Who's Who* 1986, 643. *New Palgrave* 1987, vol. 3, 685–6.

NURKSE Ragnar (1907–1959)

Ragnar Nurkse was born in Kaeru, near the Estonian village of Viru, of an Estonian father and a mother of Swedish origin. He studied in the universities of Tartu and then of Edinburgh (1928–32) and Vienna (1932–4). From 1934, he worked as an economist at the League of Nations, first in Geneva, then at Princeton. In 1945, he was named professor at Columbia University, New York. He had accepted a position at Princeton and had just given a series of lectures (Wicksell Lectures) in Stockholm, when he was struck down by a heart attack while walking on Mont Pèlerin.

Main publications

1944. *International Currency Experience: Lessons of the Interwar Period*, Princeton, League of Nations.

1953. *Problems of Capital Formation in Underdeveloped Countries*, Oxford, Basil Blackwell; 7th edn 1960.

1961. *Equilibrium and Growth in the World Economy: Economic Essays*, edited by Gottfried Haberler and Robert M. Stern, Cambridge, Massachusetts, Harvard University Press.

1961. *Patterns of Trade and Development*, Oxford, Basil Blackwell.

1967. *Problems of Capital Formation in Underdeveloped Countries and Patterns of Trade and Development*, New York, Oxford University Press. [This book groups together 1953 and 1961 *Patterns*.]

If his first articles (republished, along with other main ones, in the 1961 book *Equilibrium*) are marked by an Austrian influence, R. Nurkse did not avoid that of Keynesian theory. Of the numerous texts he wrote for publication (without signature) for the League of Nations – he was, in particular, responsible for the annual publication *Monetary Review* – one is retained in his bibliography because he is presented in the introduction as its principal author (1944). Besides financial questions, international monetary issues and international trade, Nurkse wrote on balanced growth, on development issues and, in particular, on the problem of capital formation in underdeveloped countries.

Often resorting to the drawing of a parallel between the twentieth and nineteenth centuries, he did not have a taste for clear-cut affirmations. If he was advocating neither protectionism nor dumping policies, he did not exclude the possibility that, in the framework of a policy of support for exports aimed at enhancing internal growth, a country might practise a reasonable degree of devaluation or begin a temporary period of customs protection. Even with the 'vicious circle of poverty' which he had brought to light (1953) and which limited the formation of capital both on the supply side (deficient savings) and on the demand side (narrowness of internal markets), Nurkse did not exclude the possibility that it might some day become a virtuous circle.

Main references

HABERLER G. 'Introduction' to Nurkse 1961 *Equilibrium*, vii–xiii.
LUNDBERG E. 'Introduction' to Nurkse 1961 *Patterns*, 7–8.

New Palgrave 1987, vol. 3, 687–8.

OHLIN Bertil Gotthard (1899–1979)

Bertil Ohlin was born in Klippan, Sweden. He studied at the University of Lund, at the Stockholm School of Economics and Business Administration, at Cambridge and at Harvard, before obtaining a doctorate from the University of Stockholm in 1923. He taught at the University of Copenhagen (1925–9) and at the Stockholm School of Economics and Business Administration (1929–65). He was a member of the Swedish Parliament (1938–70), leader of the Liberal Party (1944–67) and Trade Minister (1944–5). He received, in 1977, jointly with James Meade, the Nobel Memorial Prize in Economics.

Main publications

1927. *Saet produktionen i gang* [Get production going], Stockholm, H. Aschehaug.

1929. 'The Reparation Problem: A Discussion, I. Transfer Difficulties, Real and Imagined', *Economic Journal*, vol. 39, 172–8.

1931. *The Course and Phases of the World Economic Depression: Report Presented to the Assembly of the League of Nations*, Geneva, League of Nations.

1933. *Interregional and International Trade*, Cambridge, Massachusetts, Harvard University Press; revised edn 1967.

1933. 'Till frågan om penningteoriens uppläggning', *Ekonomisk Tidskrift*, vol. 35, 45–81; Engl. transl. 1978, 'On the Formulation of Monetary Theory', *History of Political Economy*, vol. 10, 353–88.

1934. *Penningpolitik, offentliga arbeten, subventioner och tullar som medel mot arbetslöshet* [Monetary policy, public works, subsidies and tariffs as means against unemployment], Stockholm, P.A. Norstedt.

1934. *Utrikeshandel och handelspolitik* [Foreign trade and trade policy], Stockholm; French transl. 1955, *La politique du commerce extérieur*, Paris, Dunod.

1936. 'La politique économique de la Suède pendant la crise', *Revue d'économie politique*, vol. 50, 312–26.

1937. 'Some Notes on the Stockholm Theory of Savings and Investment', in two parts ['… Investments' in part II], *Economic Journal*, vol. 47, 53–69 and 221–40.

1941. *Kapitalmarknad och räntepolitik* [Capital market and interest rate policy], Stockholm, Kooperative förbundets bokförlag.

1949. *The Problem of Employment Stabilization*, New York, Columbia University Press.

1958. 'Problèmes d'harmonisation et de coordination des politiques économiques et sociales', *Revue d'économie politique*, vol. 68, 264–90.

1972–5. *Bertil Ohlin's Memoarer* [Bertil Ohlin's Memoirs], 2 vols, Stockholm, Bonnier.

1977 (ed., with Per Magnus Wijkman and Per Ove Hesselborn). *The International Allocation of Economic Activity*, London, Macmillan.

1978. '1933 and 1977 – Some Expansion Policy Problems in Cases of Unbalanced Domestic and International Economic Relations' [Nobel Lecture], *Scandinavian Journal of Economics*, vol. 80, 360–74.

1981. 'Stockholm and Cambridge: Four Papers on the Monetary and Employment Theory of the 1930s', edited by O. Steiger, *History of Political Economy*, vol. 13, 189–255.

Ohlin first became well known because of his controversy with Keynes over the problem of transfers, in the context of the discussion of the war reparations issue (1929). By giving prominence to the relations between transfers of purchasing power, variations in national income and the balance of payments, Ohlin maintained a position which would later be called Keynesian, contrary to Keynes, who was then holding to the traditional vision of the achievement of balance of payments equilibrium through price variation. But it was his book on international trade (1933), a point of departure of the modern neoclassical theory of international trade, which won him the Nobel Prize. Developing a thesis first enunciated by his teacher, Eli Heckscher, Ohlin explained in it that a country, or a region, exports the goods it produces with factors with which it is abundantly endowed, and that the opposite holds for imports. He drew from this the existence of a tendency towards equalization of factor prices between trading countries. Samuelson and Stolper called this exposition the Hecksher–Ohlin theorem (Samuelson 1941).

Ohlin's contributions to modern macroeconomic theory took much more time to be recognized for their true value, some significant texts having been translated only very recently (1933 *ET*) and others still existing in Swedish only (1934 *Penningpolitik*). It was Ohlin who coined, after the publication of *The General Theory* by Keynes, the expression 'Stockholm School' to describe his contribution and that of his colleagues Lindahl and Myrdal, who, inspired by Wicksell and Cassel, developed theses similar, in many respects, to those of Keynes. The theoretical foundations of Keynesian interventionism, in particular the concepts of the multiplier, of liquidity preference and the role of the variations of aggregate output in equilibrating saving and investment, are thus present in Ohlin's writings (1927, 1931, 1933 *ET* and 1934 *Penningpolitik*). Insisting on the role of expectations and uncertainty, Ohlin opposed Keynes's analysis, in terms of static equilibrium, with the dynamic Swedish sequence analysis. Death prevented his completing a text he was writing on the relations between the Stockholm School and the Keynesian revolution (1981), an issue which has often been the subject of discussion (*HPE* 1978, Landgren 1960, Steiger 1976).

Main references

'The Nobel Memorial Prize in Economics 1977'. Official announcement, article by Richard E. Caves and bibliography (prepared by B. Ohlin), *Scandinavian Journal of Economics*, 1978, vol. 80, 62–3 and 86–99.

BLAUG Mark 1992 (ed.). *Bertil Ohlin (1899–1979)*, Aldershot, Hants, Edward Elgar.

History of Political Economy 1978, 'A Bertil Ohlin Symposium', vol. 10, 353–453: Engl. transl. of Ohlin 1933 'Till' and articles by Hans Brems, Otto Steiger, Don Patinkin and William P. Yohe.

KEYNES John M. 1929. 'The Reparation Problem: A Discussion, II. A Rejoinder', *Economic Journal*, vol. 39, 179–82.

LANDGREN Karl-Gustaf 1960. *Den 'nya ekonomien' i Sverige. J.M. Keynes, E. Wigforss, B. Ohlin och utvecklingen 1927–39* [The 'New Economics' in Sweden: J.M. Keynes, E. Wigforss, B. Ohlin and the development 1927–1939], Stockholm, Almqvist & Wiksell.

SAMUELSON, Paul A. 1981. 'Bertil Ohlin (1899–1979)', *Scandinavian Journal of Economics*, vol. 82, 355–71.

STEIGER Otto 1976. 'Bertil Ohlin and the Origins of the Keynesian Revolution', *History of Political Economy*, vol. 8, 341–66.

STEIGER Otto 1981. 'Bertil Ohlin, 1899–1979', *History of Political Economy*, vol. 13, 179–88.

BLAUG 1985, 185–7. *New Palgrave* 1987, vol. 3, 697–700. SILLS 1979, 603–7.

OKUN Arthur M. (1928–1980)

Arthur Okun was born in Jersey City, New Jersey. He obtained a PhD from Columbia University in 1956, having begun teaching in 1952 at Yale University, where he was appointed professor in 1963. In 1961–2, he worked for President John F. Kennedy's Council of Economic Advisers. In 1964, he became a member of President Johnson's Council, chairing it in 1968–9. In 1969, he joined the Brookings Institution as a senior fellow, and remained there until his sudden death, aged 52. He edited the *Brookings Papers on Economic Activity*.

Main publications

1962. 'Potential Output: Its Measurement and Significance', *Proceedings of the Business and Economic Statistics Section, American Statistical Association*, Washington, American Statistical Association, 98–103.

1965 (ed.). *The Battle Against Unemployment*, New York, W.W. Norton.

1970. With Henry H. Fowler and Milton Gilbert, *Inflation: The Problems It Creates and The Policies It Requires*, New York University Press; University of London Press.

1970. *The Political Economy of Prosperity*, Washington, DC, Brookings Institution.

1975. *Equality and Efficiency: The Big Tradeoff*, Washington, DC, Brookings Institution.

1975. 'Inflation: Its Mechanics and Welfare Costs', *Brookings Papers on Economic Activity*, vol. 2, 351–401.

1978 (ed., with George L. Perry). *Curing Chronic Inflation*, Oxford, Basil Blackwell.

1980. 'Rational-Expectations-with-Misperceptions as a Theory of the Business Cycle', *Journal of Money, Credit and Banking*, vol. 12, 817–25.

1981. *Prices and Quantities: A Macroeconomic Analysis*, Washington, DC, Brookings Institution.

1983. *The Economics of Policy-Making*, edited by J.A. Pechman, Cambridge, Massachusetts, MIT Press.

During his brief career, Arthur Okun won fame as both a macroeconomic theorist and an architect of economic policy. He was always actively involved in the policy arena, in particular within the presidential Council of Economic Advisers, tirelessly looking for the best way to ensure full employment, price stability and social justice. A supporter of the market economy, Okun was nonetheless convinced that the state had an essential role to play. Very critical towards monetarism and the new classical macroeconomics, he considered, however, that orthodox Keynesianism had to be revised, in order to take account of price rigidities and the existence in the economy of long-term contracts both on goods and labour markets, where Smith's invisible hand was replaced by what he called the 'invisible handshake' (1983).

Okun is especially renowned for having brought to light an empirical regularity to which his name was given. Thus 'Okun's Law', enunciated for the first time in 1962, establishes a correlation between the unemployment rate and the potential national income which is lost as a result of the under-employment of the economy's productive capacities. Considering that, for the United States, a 4 per cent unemployment rate corresponds to a full use of the productive capacities, therefore to the fulfilment of the potential gross national product, Okun's Law established that to each 1 per cent increase of the unemployment rate above this rate, there corresponds a 3 per cent decrease of the effective gross national product relative to its potential. The economic cost of unemployment is thus widely underestimated if one considers the rate alone. The difference between the economy's growth rate and inflation rate was also termed 'the Okun Index'.

Main references

PHELPS Edmund S. 1981. 'Okun's Micro–Macro System: A Review Article', *Journal of Economic Literature*, vol. 19, 1065–73.

TOBIN James 1983 (ed.). *Macroeconomics, Prices, and Quantities: Essays in Memory of Arthur M. Okun*, Washington, DC, Brookings Institution.

BLAUG 1985, 188–9. *New Palgrave* 1987, vol. 3, 700–701.

PASINETTI Luigi L. (born 1930)

Luigi Lodovico Pasinetti was born in Zanica (Bergamo), Italy. He studied at the Catholic University of Milan, Harvard and Cambridge (England), obtaining a PhD from the latter in 1962. Appointed a fellow of King's College, he stayed at Cambridge until 1976. Since then, he has been professor at the Catholic University of Milan. He was president of the Italian Society of Economists (Società Italiana degli Economisti) from 1986 to 1989, and president of the Confederation of European Economic Associations (CEEPA) in 1992–3.

Main publications

1960. 'A Mathematical Formulation of the Ricardian System', *Review of Economic Studies*, vol. 27, 78–98.

1962. 'Rate of Profit and Income Distribution in Relation to the Rate of Economic Growth', *Review of Economic Studies*, vol. 29, 267–79.

1966. 'Changes in the Rate of Profit and Switches of Techniques', *Quarterly Journal of Economics*, vol. 80, 503–17.

1969. 'Switches of Technique and the "Rate of Return" in Capital Theory', *Economic Journal*, vol. 79, 508–31.

1973. 'The Notion of Vertical Integration in Economic Analysis', *Metroeconomica*, vol. 25, 1–29.

1974. *Growth and Income Distribution: Essays in Economic Theory*, Cambridge, England, Cambridge University Press.

1975. *Lezioni di teoria della produzione*, Bologna, Il Mulino; Engl. transl. 1977, *Lectures on the Theory of Production*, New York, Columbia University Press; London, Macmillan.

1977 (ed.). *Contributi alla teoria della produzione congiunta*, Bologna, Il Mulino; Engl. transl. 1980, *Essays on the Theory of Joint Production*, New York, Columbia University Press; London, Macmillan.

1981. *Structural Change and Economic Growth: A Theoretical Essay on the Dynamics of the Wealth of Nations*, Cambridge, England, Cambridge University Press.

1986 (ed.). *Mutamenti strutturali del sistema produttivo: Integrazione tra industria e settore terziario*, Bologna, Il Mulino.

1987 (ed., with Peter Lloyd). *Structural Change, Economic Interdependence and World Development*, vol. 3, *Structural Change and Adjustment in the World Economy*, London, Macmillan.

1989 (ed.). *Aspetti controversi della teoria del valore*, Bologna, Il Mulino.

1993. *Structural Economic Dynamics: A Theory of the Economic Consequences of Human Learning*, Cambridge, England, Cambridge University Press.

Luigi Pasinetti is a theorist of the post-Keynesian school. With Pierangelo Garegnani and Joan Robinson, he led the attack of Cambridge, England, against the neoclassical theorists of Cambridge, Massachusetts. This debate dealt, in particular, with the possibility of measuring capital, of basing on that measure an aggregate production function and of deducing, from the marginal productivities of capital and labour, the rate of profit and level of wages. Pasinetti and his colleagues maintained that it is impossible to measure capital in physical terms, and that its measure in terms of price implies a prior knowledge of the profit rate, which must therefore be determined in an exogenous way. The profit rate, therefore, cannot be deducted from the marginal productivity of capital, which invalidates the neoclassical theory of distribution (1966, 1969).

Beyond the critique of orthodox theory, Pasinetti set himself the task of developing the foundations of a new non-marginalist economic theory, on the basis of the classical theory and that of Keynes. With this aim in view, he employed, among other things, sophisticated mathematical techniques (e.g. the notion of vertically integrated sectors, 1973), to give a clear presentation of Ricardian dynamics and the labour theory of value (1960), and Leontief's and Sraffa's models (1975).

A specialist in the theory of growth and of distribution, Pasinetti corrected and generalized Kaldor's model by showing that, even in the presence of saving by workers, the profit rate in the economy depends only on the growth rate and the capitalists' propensity to save (1962): what was described as Pasinetti's theorem, or the new Cambridge equation. Thus Pasinetti formulated rigorously the link, brought to light by the classics, between capital accumulation, profit rate and income distribution. In his later works, he also enlarged his analysis of growth by combining it with the study of the structural change in the economy (1981). It is in order to do so that he developed new techniques of analysis, such as that of vertical integration (1973).

Main references

BARANZINI Mauro and HARCOURT G.C. 1993 (eds). *The Dynamics of the Wealth of Nations. Growth, Distribution and Structural Changes: Essays in Honor of Luigi Pasinetti*, Basingstoke, Macmillan .

MODIGLIANI Franco and SAMUELSON Paul A. 1966. 'The Pasinetti Paradox in Neoclassical and More General Models', *Review of Economic Studies*, vol. 33, 269–301.

ARESTIS and SAWYER 1992, 417–25. BLAUG 1985, 190–92.

PATINKIN Don (1922–1995)

Don Patinkin was born in Chicago. He studied at the University of Chicago, earning an MA in 1945 and a PhD in 1947. A researcher at the Cowles Commission between 1946 and 1948, he was assistant professor at the University of Chicago (1947–8) and associate professor at the University of Illinois (1948–9). He emigrated to Israel in 1949 and there began teaching at the Hebrew University of Jerusalem, where he was appointed associate professor in 1952 and full professor in 1957. He was director of the Maurice Falk Institute for Economic Research in Israel (1956–72). He was also president of the Econometric Society (1974) and president of the Israel Economic Association (1976). He has various other university and public functions in Israel.

Main publications

1948. 'Price Flexibility and Full Employment', *American Economic Review*, vol. 38, 543–64.
1949. 'The Indeterminacy of Absolute Prices in Classical Economic Theory', *Econometrica*, vol. 17, 1–27.
1956. *Money, Interest, and Prices: An Integration of Monetary and Value Theory*, Evanston, Illinois, Row, Peterson; 2nd edn 1965, New York, Harper & Row; abridged edn 1989, with a new introduction, Cambridge, Massachusetts, MIT Press.
1959. 'Keynesian Economics Rehabilitated: A Rejoinder to Professor Hicks', *Economic Journal*, vol. 69, 582–7.
1959. *The Israel Economy: The First Decade*, Jerusalem, Maurice Falk Institute for Economic Research in Israel [in English and Hebrew].
1967. *On the Nature of Monetary Mechanism*, Stockholm, Almqvist & Wiksell.
1969. 'The Chicago Tradition, the Quantity Theory and Friedman', *Journal of Money, Credit and Banking*, vol. 1, 46–70.
1972. *Studies in Monetary Economics*, New York, Harper & Row.
1976. *Keynes' Monetary Thought: A Study of its Development*, Durham, North Carolina, Duke University Press.
1978 (ed., with James Clark Leith). *Keynes, Cambridge and The General Theory: The Process of Criticism and Discussion Connected With the Development of The General Theory*, London, Macmillan; University of Toronto Press.
1981. *Essays On and In the Chicago Tradition*, Durham, North Carolina, Duke University Press.
1982. *Anticipations of the General Theory? And Other Essays on Keynes*, University of Chicago Press; Oxford, Basil Blackwell.
1987. 'Keynes, John Maynard (1883–1946)', *New Palgrave*, vol. 3, 19–41.
1990. 'On Different Interpretations of the *General Theory*', *Journal of Monetary Economics*, vol. 26, 205–43.

Don Patinkin has made contributions, to both macroeconomic theory and the history of economic thought, which have been the subject of much debate and discussion. Based on his doctoral thesis, concerned with the 'consistence of economic models', whose principal results were originally presented in articles (among others, 1948 and 1949), the book published by Patinkin in 1956 sought to integrate real and monetary theory, by giving to macroeconomics rigorous foundations in the microeconomics of general equilibrium.

The point of departure for Patinkin's thinking consists in a critique of what he calls the classical dichotomy, which opposes the real and monetary sectors of the economy and, to the formation of relative prices, that of the general price level. Relative prices are thus determined in the real sector of the economy, by the forces of supply and demand, and the general price level then set by the quantity of money. For Patinkin, this dichotomy is contradictory and unacceptable, permitting the determination of neither absolute prices nor relative prices: 'The only way out of this difficulty is to discard completely the classical dichotomy between the real and monetary sectors, and to recognize that prices are determined in a truly general-equilibrium fashion, by both sectors simultaneously' (1949, p. 2).

The integration of the monetary and real sectors in economic analysis is effected by means of what Patinkin called first of all 'the Pigou effect' (1948) and which he then called 'the real-balance effect' (1956). The term 'real balances' designates the real value of money balances held by individuals. The adjective 'real' signifies the absence of money illusion. A general decrease in prices thus implies an increase in the value of a constant stock of money held by individuals. The equilibrium relation between the stock of money and total wealth being thus modified, the demand for goods and services in the economy will grow, which in turn will stimulate production and employment. Neglected by Keynes, the real balance effect constitutes a means of achieving full employment, in an economy in which wages and prices are flexible. At the same time, in a dynamic perspective, both Pigou and Patinkin realize that the decrease in prices and wages necessary to achieve this result could unleash a situation of uncertainty and a wave of bankruptcies which would prevent ultimately the achievement of the desired objective. In short, the real balance effect is largely of theoretical significance and cannot be used as an instrument of economic policy.

Believing that he has shrunk the gap between Keynes and the classics, on a theoretical level, Patinkin believes nonetheless that the distance in political terms remains undiminished. Furthermore, Patinkin rejects the idea, put forward in the context of the neoclassical synthesis, according to which the persistence of involuntary unemployment stems from wage rigidity or the liquidity trap. Acceptable in the case of a static framework, this idea is not acceptable when in a dynamic framework, which is for him the case of *The General Theory*, the central message of which resides in the theory of effective demand viewed as the equilibrating effect exercised by a decrease in production, thus permitting the persistence of a state of underemployment. Thus several view Patinkin as the father of disequilibrium theory. Others see in his work the essence of the neoclassical synthesis, and others again that of monetarism. He himself considers Friedman's monetary theory to be 'a most elegant and sophisticated statement of modern Keynesian monetary theory – misleadingly entitled "The Quantity Theory of Money – A Restatement"' ([1969] 1981, p. 256).

For the last 20 years, Patinkin has devoted part of his research time to the study of the development of Keynes's monetary theory (1976, 1978, 1982, 1987). In these works, which display considerable erudition, Patinkin shows no fear of advancing interpretations which contradict a number of widely held views, supporting them with careful textual analysis.

Main references

ARCHIBALD G.C. and LIPSEY R.G. 1958. 'Monetary and Value Theory: A Critique of Lange and Patinkin', *Review of Economic Studies*, vol. 26, 1–22.

ASIMAKOPULOS A. 1973. 'Keynes, Patinkin, Historical Time and Equilibrium Analysis', *Canadian Journal of Economics*, vol. 6, 179–88.

BARKAI Haim, FISCHER Stanley and LIVIATAN Nissan 1993 (eds). *Monetary Theory and Thought: Essays in Honor of Don Patinkin*, London, Macmillan.
DAVIDSON Paul 1967. 'A Keynesian View of Patinkin's Theory of Employment', *Economic Journal*, vol. 77, 559–78.
HICKS J.R. 1957. 'A Rehabilitation of "Classical" Economics', *Economic Journal*, vol. 67, 278–89.
MAURER L.J. 1966. 'The Patinkin Controversy: A Review', *Kyklos*, vol. 19, 299–314.

BLAUG 1985, 193–5.

PERROUX François (1903–1987)

Born in Lyon, François Perroux studied there, and began a teaching career which he pursued in Paris, beginning in 1936–7. In 1934, as a Rockefeller fellow, he went to Vienna, where he followed the seminars of von Mises; he also went to Berlin and spent some time in Rome. From 1944, Perroux, in addition to teaching, led a team of researchers in mathematical economics, with F. Divisia and R. Roy, and created the Institut de Sciences Economiques Appliquées (ISEA); he worked on the development of national accounting and travelled to England, making numerous contacts, notably with J. Hicks, J. Robinson and R. Stone. Perroux was professor at the Collège de France from 1955 to 1974. He continued his activities beyond retirement, notably at the old ISEA, which became the Institut de Sciences Mathématiques et Economiques Appliquées (ISMEA).

Main publications

1926. *Le Problème du profit*, Paris, Marcel Giard.
1938. *Capitalisme et communauté de travail*, Paris, Sirey.
1939. *Syndicalisme et capitalisme*, Paris, Librairie générale.
1940. *Autarcie et expansion: empire ou empires*, Paris, Médicis.
1943. *La Valeur*, Paris, Presses Universitaires de France.
1947. *Le Revenu national, son calcul et sa signification*, Paris, Presses Universitaires de France.
1948. *Le Capitalisme*, Paris, Presses Universitaires de France.
1948. *Le Plan Marshall ou l'Europe nécessaire au monde*, Paris, Médicis.
1954. *L'Europe sans rivages*, Paris, Presses Universitaires de France.
1950. 'The Domination Effect and Modern Economic Theory', *Social Research*, vol. 17, 188–206.
1956, 1957. *Théorie générale du progrès économique*, 3 vols, Paris, Cahiers de l'ISEA Série I, fasc. 1, 2 et 3.
1958. *La Coexistence pacifique*, 3 vols, Paris, Presses Universitaires de France.
1960. *Economie et société: contrainte – échange – don*, Paris, Presses Universitaires de France.
1961. *L'Economie du XXe siècle*, Paris, Presses Universitaires de France.
1962. *L'Economie des jeunes nations*, Paris, Presses Universitaires de France.
1963. *Indépendance de l'économie nationale et interdépendance des nations*, Paris, Union Générale d'Edition; new edn 1969, Paris, Aubier-Montaigne.
1964. *Industrie et création collective*, vol. 1, *Saint-Simonisme du XXe siècle et création collective*, Paris, Presses Universitaires de France.

1965. *La Pensée économique de Joseph Schumpeter: Les Dynamiques du capitalisme*, Geneva, Droz.
1965. *Les Techniques quantitatives de la planification*, Paris, Presses Universitaires de France.
1968. *Le Pain et la parole*, Paris, Cerf.
1970. *Industrie et création collective*, vol. 2, *Images de l'homme nouveau et techniques collectives*, Paris, Presses Universitaires de France.
1971. *Indépendance de la nation*, Paris, Union Générale d'Edition.
1972. *Masse et classe*, Tournai, Casterman.
1973. *Pouvoir et économie*, Paris, Bordas.
1975. *Unités actives et mathématiques nouvelles: Révision de la théorie de l'équilibre économique général*, Paris, Dunod.
1980. *Les Entreprises transnationales et le nouvel ordre économique international*, Lyon, Croissance des jeunes nations.
1980. 'Peregrinations of an Economist and the Choice of his Route', *Quarterly Review, Banca Nazionale del Lavoro*, no. 133, 147–62; in Kregel 1989, 1–15.
1981. *Pour une philosophie du nouveau développement*, Paris, Aubier/UNESCO.
1982. *Dialogue des monopoles et des nations: 'Équilibre' ou dynamique des unités actives*, Presses Universitaires de Grenoble.
1983. *A New Concept of Development: Basic Tenets*, London, Croom Helm.
1987. *Economie appliquée*, vol. 15, no. 2 [reprint of 12 papers published by F. Perroux between 1926 and 1980, with a bibliography of the author].
1990–. *Oeuvres complètes* [publication in progress], Presses Universitaires de Grenoble.

This long list, which excludes articles, courses and mimeographed publications, as well as numerous collective works, bears witness to the breadth and depth of the economic work of F. Perroux; many of his works have been translated into various languages, but few in English. And one should also mention the journals he founded: *Cahiers de l'ISEA*, *Economie appliquée*, *Revue Tiers-Monde*, *Mondes en développement*. For Perroux, economics is inseparable from his philosophical and ethical stance: Christian humanism. This inspired his early interest in 'communauté de travail' (1938), his rejection of Marxism and his emphasis on solidarity, the gift economy and an economics for man. Economics cannot be reduced simply to commercial relations between homogeneous agents: power relations (constraint), but also solidarity (the gift) are integral elements (1960). In short, focusing his studies on the economy, Perroux rejects the basic principles of the neoclassical universe.

After the Second World War, Perroux contributed greatly to the presentation and diffusion of Keynes's ideas in France, and to the opening of French thought to authors as dissimilar as J. Schumpeter, E.H. Chamberlin, M. Kalecki, W. Leontief and P. Samuelson. He also played a major role in the establishment of a system of national accounts, the development of French-style planning, the introduction of mathematics and quantitative techniques and, finally, the rejuvenation of economic thought in France.

More fundamentally, he worked on the elaboration of a theory capable of accounting for contemporary realities: beyond the analysis of imperfect competition (Chamberlin), the dynamics of innovation and the entrepreneur

(Schumpeter) and the vision of macroeconomics profoundly changed by Keynes, he sought to construct a new theoretical coherence, assuming the inequality of agents, strategies and power, and organized around the domination effect. He presented at Oxford in 1947, and then in numerous issues of *Economie appliquée* in 1948 (nos 2–3), his 'Esquisse d'une théorie de l'économie dominante' (An outline of a theory of the dominant economy): asymmetry, unintended influence and irreversibility are its main elements, which were intended to make possible the description of a 'dynamics of inequality'. His works of the 1950s (and notably that of 1954) involve large analyses: the dominant firm, dominant industry, dominant national economy, growth poles, propulsion effect (*effet d'entraînement*), as well as profoundly renewed visions of the global economy, spatial economics, growth and development policies.

In many other areas, Perroux stimulated important theoretical innovations, from the incorporation of economic structures, in 1939 (in *Mélanges Witmeur*, Paris, Sirey) to the taking into account the control of structure (*emprise de structure*) (1963 (*Indépendance*), from the founding firm (*firmes motrices)* to the large conglomeration (1975, 1980 *Les Entreprises*, 1982). These analyses largely form the basis for the work done in 1960–70 on development, and in which he emphasizes his affirmation of man as the ultimate concern in economics. His objective thus is to 'develop all man and all men' – that is to say, to feed, house, educate and care for men, in short, to cover the 'costs of man' (1961).

Faced with the coherence of neoclassicism, Perroux opened breaches and shaped approaches; he tried to place man in the centre of economics; but he did not succeed in developing the new economic theory on which he long laboured. In the 1950s and 1960s, the rise of Keynesianism left little room, and in the following period it was liberalism which won out. His influence, which was profound in France, even on those who would deny it or have forgotten it, touched the whole of the Latin world. Perroux tackled the essential questions and opened paths to be followed by new generations of economists.

Main references

BLAUG Mark 1964. 'A Case of Emperor's Clothes: Perroux's Theories of Economic Domination', *Kyklos*, vol. 17.

BOCAGE Ducarmel 1985. *The General Economic Theory of François Perroux*, Lanham, Maryland, University Press of America.

DENOEL François 1990 (ed.). *François Perroux*, Lausanne, L'Age d'Homme.

Hommage à F. Perroux, 1978. Presses Universitaires de Grenoble.

KRISHNAM-KUTTY G. 1964. *Perroux's Theory of Dominant Economy*, Kerala, India, Union Press.

LEROY Marie-Christine 1986. *La Monnaie chez L. Walras, J.M. Keynes, F. Perroux*, Paris, Editions de l'Épargne.

PERROUX 1980 'Peregrinations'.
URI Pierre 1984. 'Uri on Perroux', in Spiegel and Samuel 1984, 543–56.
WEILLER Jean 1989. 'François Perroux, un grand contestataire', *Revue française d'économie*, vol. 4, no. 2, 27–41.

ARESTIS and SAWYER 1992, 425–32. *New Palgrave* 1987, vol. 3, 851–2.

PHELPS Edmund S. (born 1933)

Born in Evanston, Illinois, E. Phelps studied at Amherst College (BA in 1955), then at Yale (MA in 1957, PhD in 1959). He did teaching and research at Yale (1958–9, 1960–2, 1963–6), at the Rand Corporation (1959–60) and at MIT (1962–3), before becoming professor of economics at the University of Pennsylvania (1966–71) and, since 1971, at Columbia University, New York.

Main publications

1962 (ed.). *Private Wants and Public Needs: Issues Surrounding the Size and Scope of Government Expenditure*, New York, W.W. Norton.
1962 (ed.). *The Goal of Economic Growth: Sources, Costs, Benefits*, New York, W.W. Norton.
1965. *Fiscal Neutrality Toward Economic Growth: Analysis of a Taxation Principle*, New York, McGraw-Hill.
1966. *Golden Rules of Economic Growth: Studies of Efficient and Optimal Investment*, New York, W.W. Norton.
1967. 'Phillips Curves, Expectations of Inflation and Optimal Unemployment over Time', *Economica*, vol, 34, 254–81.
1968. 'Money-Wages Dynamics and Labour–Market Equilibrium', *Journal of Political Economy*, vol. 76, 678–711.
1970. *Et al., Microeconomic Foundations of Employment and Inflation Theory*, New York, W.W. Norton; London, Macmillan, 1971.
1972. *Inflation Policy and Unemployment Theory*, New York, W.W. Norton.
1973 (ed.). *Economic Justice*, Harmondsworth, Penguin Books.
1975 (ed.). *Altruism, Morality and Economic Theory*, New York, Basic Books.
1977. With John B. Taylor, 'Stabilizing Powers of Monetary Policy with Rational Expectations', *Journal of Political Economy*, vol. 85, 163–90.
1979–80. *Studies in Macroeconomic Theory*, vol. 1, 1979, *Employment and Inflation*; vol. 2, 1980, *Redistribution and Growth*, New York, Academic Press.
1982. 'Cracks on the Demand Side: A Year of Crisis in Theoretical Macroeconomics', *American Economic Review*, vol. 72, *Papers and Proceedings*, 378–81.
1985. *Political Economy: An Introductory Text*, New York, W.W. Norton.
1988. With Jean-Paul Fitoussi, *The Slump in Europe: Open Theory Reconstructed*, Oxford, Basil Blackwell.
1990 (ed.). *Recent Development in Macroeconomics*, Aldershot, Hants, Edward Elgar.
1990. *Seven Schools of Macroeconomic Thought*, Oxford, Clarendon Press.
1990. 'Théorie keynésienne et théorie structuraliste du chômage: analyse des vingt dernières années', *Revue française d'économie*, vol. 5, 3–28.

E. Phelps wrote his first works while the neoclassical synthesis was still dominant. Concerned both to reconstruct the microeconomic foundations of macroeconomics and to analyse formally the impacts of economic policy and public finances, he approached a wide range of fields, notably growth and investment (1965, 1966), employment and inflation (1967, 1968, 1970, 1972).

He is particularly credited with having, parallel with Friedman, elaborated the concept of the 'natural rate of unemployment' (1967); because of this natural rate, all governmental action aimed at raising the level of employment will be without any lasting effect on employment, but will lead to a marked rise in the rate of inflation. This analysis fits, according to Phelps, into a larger approach based on job search and the cost it involves, and thus its limits for the unemployed.

The book whose publication he directed in 1970 played an important role in the transformation of contemporary macroeconomics, to which Phelps and his colleagues attempted to give rigorous microfoundations, in part with a view to going beyond the controversy between Keynesianism and monetarism. The way was thus open for the new classical macroeconomics and the theory of disequilibrium and the new Keynesian economics. Phelps sought to emphasize what unified, rather than divided, these streams of thought. In the 1970s, he devoted various works to questions concerning money and the rate of interest, and renewed his analysis of public finance, taking into account the perspective of Rawlsian equity between generations, and with links to questions on welfare, altruism and ethics (1973, 1975 and articles reprinted in 1979–80).

In the 1980s Phelps distanced himself from Keynesianism (in the larger sense), while remaining outside other approaches and trying to construct a new complete theory, which he called 'structuralist'. In this approach, in particular with J.P. Fitoussi (1988), he worked on models to explain recessions and booms: one of the associated interpretations, based on a two-country model, is that US expansionary policy, leading to a rise in interest rate, produces deflationary effects in Europe.

Phelps represents the generation of economists coming after that of the neoclassical synthesis: well trained in mathematical techniques and theoretical reasoning, with a certain syncretism, he sails with virtuosity upon the ever-renewed waves of discussion on models and debates between schools.

Main reference

BLAUG 1985, 196–8.

PHELPS BROWN Henry (born 1906)

Born in Calne, Wiltshire (England), H. Phelps Brown studied at Oxford. Apart from an interruption during the Second World War, which he spent in the Royal Artillery, he taught at New College, Oxford, from 1930 to 1947. He was then at the London School of Economics from 1947 to 1968, at which date he retired as professor emeritus. He held various public offices and presided over the Royal Economic Society from 1970 to 1972.

Main publications

1936. *The Framework of the Pricing System*, London, Chapman & Hall.
1951. *A Course in Applied Economics*, London, Sir Isaac Pitman & Sons; new edn 1964, with J. Wiseman.
1959. *The Growth of British Industrial Relations: A Study from the Standpoint of 1906–14*, London, Macmillan.
1962. *The Economics of Labor*, New Haven, Connecticut and London, Yale University Press.
1968. *A Century of Pay: The Course of Pay and Production in France, Germany, Sweden, the United Kingdom and the United States of America, 1860–1960*, London, Macmillan.
1972. 'The Underdevelopment of Economics', *Economic Journal*, vol. 82, 1–10.
1977. *The Inequality of Pay*, New York, Oxford University Press.
1980. 'The Radical Reflections of an Applied Economist', *Quarterly Review, Banca Nazionale del Lavoro*, no. 132, 3–14; in Kregel 1989, 197–207.
1983. *The Origin of Trade Union Power*, New York, Oxford University Press.
1988. *Egalitarianism and the Generation of Inequality*, Oxford, Clarendon Press.

Although his first book was about marginalist theory (1936), H. Phelps Brown dedicated himself principally to the study of the world of labour. After the Second World War, he was the first professor of labour economics at the University of London and he contributed to the creation of a new field of specialization, the economic analysis of labour and wage and the study of industrial relations. Besides his book on labour economics (1962), he published historical studies, combining economic and social perspectives and gathering significant statistical material and rich data, in particular on industrial relations in Great Britain (1959), on wages and their evolution (1968, 1977, 1988) and on the history of the workers' movement and of unions (1983).

Phelps Brown went against the trend when, in 1980, he pleaded for the training of economists to make adequate provision for economic, social and political history, as well as the study of contemporary society.

Main references

PHELPS BROWN 1980.

BLAUG *Who's Who* 1986, 304–5. *New Palgrave* 1987, vol. 3, 855–6.

PHILLIPS A. William (1914–1975)

Alban William Housego Phillips was born in Te Rehunga, near Dannevirke, in New Zealand; he studied in the field of electrical engineering, went to London, where he worked for the Electricity Board, served as an officer during the Second World War and was made prisoner by the Japanese. After the war, he studied at the London School of Economics (BSc in 1949, PhD in 1952) where he taught from 1950, becoming professor in 1958. He left the LSE in 1967 to take up a position at the National University of Australia. Illness forced him to give up teaching in 1969; he went back to New Zealand and died in Auckland.

Main publications

1950. 'Mechanical Models in Economic Dynamics', *Economica*, vol. 17, 283–305.
1954. 'Stabilisation Policy in a Closed Economy', *Economic Journal*, vol. 64, 290–323.
1958. 'The Relation Between Unemployment and the Rate of Change of Money Wage Rates in the United Kingdom, 1861–1957', *Economica*, vol. 25, 283–99.
1961. 'A Simple Model of Employment, Money and Prices in a Growing Economy', *Economica*, vol. 28, 360–70.
1962. 'Employment, Inflation and Growth', *Economica*, vol. 29, 1–16.

At the London School of Economics, W. Phillips rapidly became interested in the new Keynesian macroeconomics; his engineering know-how led him to conceive a hydraulic system of tanks and tubes, making it possible to model physically the relations between stocks and flows, which he made with W.T. Newlyn from Leeds University and to which he devoted his first article (1950). He was then to devote several articles to the problem, which preoccupied him for several years, of the econometric modelling of the various dimensions of stabilization policy (1954, 1961, 1962).

But it was for the article published in 1958 that the name of Phillips is known in the world of economists: beginning with statistics concerning Great Britain, he observed a negative relation between the level of unemployment and the growth rate of the money wage. The article ends with a very cautious conclusion: a rate of unemployment of 5.5 per cent might correspond to a certain stability of the wage rate, but more detailed research was necessary, taking into account, in particular, prices and productivity (1958, p. 299). The following year, at the annual meeting of the American Economic Association, Samuelson and Solow, using this article and a graph concerning the United States, put forward the idea that the curve developed by Phillips expresses the trade-off between inflation and unemployment. Meanwhile, Lipsey was trying to give a rigorous theoretical foundation to the relation put forward by Phillips. It was in this manner that the Phillips curve was born: it served to complete the *IS–LM* diagram in the textbooks, improve the macroeconomic functions in the econometric models and thus complete the tool-kit of the economic policy adviser; in brief, it became an integral part of the macroeconomics, often described as Keynesian, of the 1960s.

In Australia, Phillips devoted himself to the study of the Chinese economy.

Main references
LIPSEY 1960.
SAMUELSON and SOLOW 1960.
SAWYER Malcolm C. 1991. *The Political Economy of the Phillips Curve*, Aldershot, Hants, Edward Elgar.

BLAUG 1985, 199–201. *New Palgrave* 1987, vol. 3, 857–8; and, on the Phillips Curve, 858–61. SILLS 1979, 632–4.

POSNER Richard A. (born 1939)

Born in the United States, Richard Posner gained a BA at Yale University in 1959 and a diploma in law (LLB) at Harvard University in 1962. Associate professor of law at Stanford University (1968–9) and professor at the University of Chicago (1969–81), he has been senior lecturer since 1981 at the University of Chicago Law School. He was research associate at the National Bureau of Economic Research from 1971 to 1981. Parallel to his academic career, he also had a career as a jurist and was named in 1981 circuit judge of the United States Court of Appeals for the Seventh Circuit. He was editor of the *Journal of Legal Studies* from 1972 to 1981. He is a member of the Mont Pèlerin Society.

Main publications
1973. *Economic Analysis of Law*, Boston, Little, Brown.
1976. *Antitrust Law: An Economic Perspective*, University of Chicago Press.
1978. With A.T. Kronman, *The Economics of Contract Law*, Boston, Little, Brown.
1981. *The Economics of Justice*, Cambridge, Massachusetts, Harvard University Press.
1982. *Tort Law: Cases and Economic Analysis*, Boston, Little, Brown.
1985. *The Federal Courts: Crisis and Reform*, Cambridge, Massachusetts, Harvard University Press.
1987. With W.M. Landes, *The Economic Structure of Tort Law*, Cambridge, Massachusetts, Harvard University Press.
1988. *Law and Literature: A Misunderstood Relation*, Cambridge, Massachusetts, Harvard University Press.
1990. *The Problems of Jurisprudence*, Cambridge, Massachusetts, Harvard University Press.
1992. *Sex and Reason*, Cambridge, Massachusetts, Harvard University Press.

Teaching at the University of Chicago, among his numerous activities which led him, for example, to write about a hundred judicial opinions a year, R. Posner shares the theoretical and political vision of the Chicago school of political economy. Defining himself as a libertarian, favourable to minimal government intervention in social and economic affairs, he considers that the laws of market constitute the best mechanism of resource allocation. His research is mainly in the field of the relations between law and economics, some of his manuals having become classics (1973, 1981). Relying on the concept of transaction cost elaborated by Coase, Posner has constructed an analysis of legal activities within the neoclassical framework of rationality, efficiency and comparison between costs and benefits. In his most recent book (1992), he attempts to apply this analysis to sexual issues, considering that the concepts of search costs and benefits are more likely to shed new light on these questions than those of emotion and ethics. Sexologists should be inspired by Smith and Friedman, rather than by Freud. As for all other behaviour, sexual behaviour can be analysed in terms of market forces, the only ones likely to clarify rationally questions such as abortion or the sale of 'parental rights', which may be comparable to property rights. Posner is at present working on an economic analysis of the AIDS epidemic.

Main references

ANDERSON Robert M. 1993. 'EP seeks EP: A Review of *Sex and Reason* by Richard A. Posner', *Journal of Economic Literature*, vol. 31, 191–8.

BLAUG 1985, 202–3.

PREBISCH Raul (1901–1986)

Born in Tucuman (Argentina), Raul Prebisch studied at the University of Buenos Aires, where he graduated in economics in 1923. Assistant, and then full professor of political economy at the University of Buenos Aires (1925–48), he was under-secretary of finance from 1930 to 1932 and after the creation of the Argentine Central Bank was its first director-general from 1935 to 1943. From 1950 to 1962 he was executive secretary of the Economic Commission for Latin America (ECLA). From 1963 to 1969, he was secretary-general of the United Nations Conference on Trade and Development (UNCTAD) and, from 1969 to 1973, director of the Latin American Institute for Economic and Social Planning. He was then adviser to the secretary-general of the United Nations on development problems and, beginning in 1976, edited the journal *ECLA Review*.

Main publications

1947. *Introduccion a Keynes* [Introduction to Keynes], Mexico/Buenos Aires, Fondo de Cultura Economica.

1950. *Economic Survey of Latin America 1949*, New York, United Nations.

1950. *The Economic Development of Latin America and its Principal Problems*, New York, United Nations.

1951. *Theoretical and Practical Problems of Economic Growth*, Santiago, United Nations–ECLA.

1959. 'Commercial Policy in the Underdeveloped Countries', *American Economic Review*, vol. 49, *Papers and Proceedings*, 251–73.

1963. *Towards a Dynamic Development Policy for Latin America*, New York, United Nations.

1964. *Towards a New Trade Policy for Development*, New York, United Nations.

1965. *Transformacion y desarrollo* [Change and development], Mexico, Fondo de Cultura Economica.

1968. 'A New Strategy for Development', *Journal of Economic Studies*, vol. 3, 1–14.
1970. *Transformacion y desarrollo: la gran tarea de America Latina*, Mexico, Fondo de Cultura Economica; Engl. transl. 1971, *Change and Development: Latin America's Great Task*, New York, Praeger.
1976. 'A Critique of Peripheral Capitalism', *ECLA Review*, vol. 1, 9–76.
1980. Introduction to Rodriguez 1980 below.
1981. *Capitalismo periferico: crisis y tranformacion* [Peripheral capitalism: crisis and change], Mexico, Fondo de Cultura Economica.
1984. 'Five Stages in my Thinking on Development', in Meier and Seers, 175–91.

Attached to neoclassical theory at the beginning of his career, R. Prebisch evolved under the successive influences of the depression of the 1930s, of Keynes's ideas, which he helped spread in Latin America, and of the postwar problems of the Third World. In his early career, he published numerous articles in Spanish: between 1920 and 1927, on the economic, monetary, financial and demographic problems of his country; in 1944–5, on financial problems; in 1947, with the appearance of his book on Keynes, on Keynesian theory.

From 1949 to 1962, the writings of Prebisch and those of ECLA, of which he was secretary, are difficult to distinguish; he published the main ideas in numerous contributions to Latin American journals. In 1950, at the same time as H. Singer, he observed the tendency towards deterioration of the terms of trade of Third World countries, the 'Prebisch–Singer' thesis which became the subject of much debate. Explaining this tendency by the nature of the supply of exports and the demand for imports and, therefore, basically, by the structure of production, Prebisch advocated industrialization, primarily by substituting domestic production for imports; he also recommended greater openness on the part of developed countries to Third World exports, and it was during his UNCTAD mandate that agreement was reached on the system of generalized preferences.

A principal author of the dependency school, Prebisch used a form of analysis described as structuralist, since it takes account of the structure of the entity studied as a system. At the global level, he carried out analysis in terms of the centre and periphery. According to this view, the economies of the centre have a structure which is both diversified and homogeneous, whilst those of the periphery are specialized and heterogeneous; underdevelopment therefore cannot be interpreted as a simple time-lag, as suggested, for example, in the analysis of W. Rostow; it results from this duality of structures and the manner in which Third World countries participate in the global system, which generates the double handicap of drains on their income and obstacles to the diffusion of technical progress.

From 1963 to 1969, Prebisch's publications were indistinguishable from those of UNCTAD. Beginning in 1976, he returned to, and deepened his analysis of, the world economic system and development strategies, and particularly – in several articles published in ECLA's journal and the book of 1981 – peripheral capitalism. Prebisch certainly had some influence, having succeeded in spending a large part of his life in international organizations, all the while developing an original theoretical approach.

Main references

Di MARCO Luis Eugenio 1972 (ed.). *International Economics and Development: Essays in Honor of Raul Prebisch*, New York, Academic Press. [With a bibliography of R. Prebisch for the period 1918–1970, 487–99.]

LIRA Maximo 1986. 'La larga marcha de Prebisch hacia la critica del capitalismo periferico y su teoria de la transformacion de la sociedad', *El Trimestre Economico* (Mexico), vol. 53, 451–76; preceded by Victor L. Urquid, 'In memoriam: Raul Prebisch', 441–9.

PREBISCH 1984. With commentaries by Jagdish Bhagwati and Albert Fishlow, 207–22.

RODRIGUEZ O. 1980. *La teoria del subdesarrollo de la CEPAL*, Mexico, Siglo XXI.

ARESTIS and SAWYER 1992, 438-48. *New Palgrave* 1987, vol. 3, 934–6.

ROBINSON Joan Violet (1903–1983)

Joan Violet Maurice was born in Camberley, Surrey, in Great Britain. After studies in London, she was admitted in 1922 to Cambridge's Girton College, graduating in 1925. In 1926, she married Austin Robinson, and they spent two years in India. On their return, Austin obtained a position as assistant professor of economics at Cambridge, where they spent the rest of their time together. Appointed assistant lecturer in 1931, Joan Robinson rose only slowly through the Cambridge ranks. A lecturer in 1937 and reader in 1949, she attained the position of full professor only in 1965, being named to the chair vacated by her husband, who had just retired. She was fellow of Girton and Newnham Colleges. The prestigious King's College, that of Keynes, having finally resolved to accept women into its ranks, elected her an honorary fellow in 1970.

Having retired in 1971, Joan Robinson continued to write, teach and supervise students until the end of her life. An indefatigable traveller, she did not hesitate to live in difficult conditions in order to gain an understanding of the societies in which she found herself. Until the end, she enjoyed ridiculing the theories of orthodox economists often much younger than herself. Her speeches and presentations were heard by numerous students the world over.

Main publications

1933. *The Economics of Imperfect Competition*, London, Macmillan; 2nd edn 1969.
1933. 'The Theory of Money and the Analysis of Output', *Review of Economic Studies*, vol. 1, 22–6.
1937. *Essays in the Theory of Employment*, London, Macmillan.
1937. *Introduction to the Theory of Employment*, London, Macmillan.
1942. *An Essay on Marxian Economics*, London, Macmillan.
1948. 'La Théorie générale de l'emploi', *Economie appliquée*, vol. 1, 185–96.
1951. *Collected Economic Papers*, vol. 1, Oxford, Basil Blackwell.
1952. *The Rate of Interest and Other Essays*, London, Macmillan.
1953. *On Re-reading Marx*, Cambridge, Students' Bookshop.
1953–4. 'The Production Function and the Theory of Capital', *Review of Economic Studies*, vol. 21, 81–106.
1956. *The Accumulation of Capital*, London, Macmillan; New York, St Martin's Press.
1960. *Collected Economic Papers*, vol. 2, Oxford, Basil Blackwell.
1960. *Exercises in Economic Analysis*, London, Macmillan; New York, St Martin's Press.
1962. *Economic Philosophy*, London, C.A. Watts.
1962. *Essays in the Theory of Economic Growth*, London, Macmillan; New York, St Martin's Press.
1965. *Collected Economic Papers*, vol. 3, Oxford, Basil Blackwell.
1966. *Economics: An Awkward Corner*, London, George Allen & Unwin.
1966. *The New Mercantilism: An Inaugural Lecture*, Cambridge, England, Cambridge University Press.
1969. *The Cultural Revolution in China*, London, Penguin Books.
1970. *Freedom and Necessity: An Introduction to the Study of Society*, London, George Allen & Unwin.
1971. *Economic Heresies: Some Old-Fashioned Questions in Economic Theory*, London, Macmillan; New York, Basic Books.

1973 (ed.). *After Keynes*, Oxford, Basil Blackwell.
1973. *Collected Economic Papers*, vol. 4, Oxford, Basil Blackwell.
1973. With John Eatwell, *An Introduction to Modern Economics*, London, McGraw-Hill.
1974. *Reflections on the Theory of International Trade*, Manchester University Press.
1978. *Contributions to Modern Economics*, Oxford, Basil Blackwell.
1979. *Aspects of Development and Underdevelopment*, Cambridge, England, Cambridge University Press.
1979. *Collected Economic Papers*, vol. 5, Oxford, Basil Blackwell.
1979. *Generalization of the General Theory and Other Essays*, London, Macmillan.
1980. *Collected Economic Papers*, 5 vols and general index, Cambridge, Massachusetts, MIT Press.
1980. *Further Contributions to Modern Economics*, Oxford, Basil Blackwell.
1981. *What are the Questions? And other Essays*, Armonk, New York, M.E. Sharpe.

At the beginning of her career, Joan Robinson published one of her best known books, which gave rise to what some called the imperfect competition revolution (1933). Inspired by Sraffa's devastating 1925 criticism of the Marshallian theory of value, Joan Robinson tried to reconstruct the latter taking account of the existence of monopolies. In particular, she introduced the concept of marginal revenue, which Harrod had also independently elaborated. However, Robinson gradually distanced herself from the theses of this book. She prefaced a new edition, in 1969, with an autocritique, showing how she had not sufficiently broken with the neoclassical orthodoxy. She regretted the fact that her book's weakest points had had the most influence, whilst the strong points had passed unnoticed.

At the time her first book was published, Joan Robinson was already carrying her research efforts in another direction. She had become a disciple of Keynes. In the first months of 1931, she was involved, along with Richard Kahn, James Meade, Austin Robinson and Piero Sraffa, in Cambridge's 'Circus', which gathered to discuss Keynes's recently published *Treatise on Money*. In fact, it was the beginnings of *The General Theory* which were taking form. What we now know as the Keynesian revolution must thus be considered a collective effort, in which Joan Robinson played an important role (see 1933 *RES*). It may be gauged by her correspondence with Keynes, whose writings she did not hesitate to criticize, sometimes strongly. Thus in 1948 she wrote, in the first issue of the journal *Economie appliquée*, concerning Keynes's book: 'This work is very important, but it is neither complete, nor definitive. When it first appeared, it constituted a sort of provisional account of ideas then being developed' (1948, p. 185). Robinson participated in this flux of ideas by publishing, in 1937, *Essays in the Theory of Employment*, a collection of papers written in 1935, and *Introduction to the Theory of Employment*.

It was at this point that Kalecki, who had himself elaborated a similar theory, arrived at Cambridge. An important collaboration with Joan Robinson began immediately. It was she who, in the 1950s, emphasized the anteriority of Kalecki's discovery of the theory of effective demand. Indeed, she drew closer and closer to his theses with the passing years. He helped her discover in Marx a basis of the theory of effective demand, and a dynamic view absent from orthodox economics. She then wrote *An Essay on Marxian Economics* (1942), whose object was to present, for the first time, in a sympathizing, accessible manner, Marx's ideas to an audience of orthodox economists. Her virulent critique of certain aspects of Marx's theory, in particular of the labour theory of value, earned her, however, the enmity of orthodox Marxists. Robinson, in fact, always managed to win the opposition of all the orthodoxies. In an 'open letter from a Keynesian to a Marxist' (1953 *On Rereading Marx)*, she described herself as a Keynesian of the Left, adding that it was a position with few adherents.

After the Second World War, Robinson became increasingly interested in the problems linked to growth and capital accumulation. It was in a book published in 1952, *The Rate of Interest and Other Essays*, that she announced her project of 'generalizing the *General Theory*'. In 1953–4, in 'The Production Function and the Theory of Capital', she launched a big attack on neoclassical capital and distribution theory. The article by Robinson may be considered the first shot in the war between the two Cambridges on capital theory, and it drew a quick reaction. In 1956, Robinson published her major work, *The Accumulation of Capital*, which, with her *Essays in the Theory of Economic Growth* (1962), contains her theory of growth. Here she developed a model, inspired by Kalecki, in which the rate of investment chosen by entrepreneurs constitutes the fundamental variable. She demonstrated the determination, on this basis, of the level of consumption, saving and, above all, profits, which react in turn to future investment decisions. Further, she insisted on the need to take account of what she called historical time, expectations, the institutions of contemporary capitalism and the rules of the game.

Joan Robinson was also involved in other areas of research: development (1979 *Aspects*), international trade (1966 *The New Mercantilism*, 1974), the history of economic thought (1971) and economic philosophy (1962 *Economic Philosophy*, 1970). She was, at the end of her life, increasingly hostile towards the conservative and formal turn being taken by economic theory. In a book on Robinson's relations with the American economists, Marjorie S. Turner (1989) deduced from numerous interviews that Joan Robinson had not obtained the Nobel Memorial Prize in Economics because, as a Keynesian leftist from Cambridge and an outspoken woman, she had made too many enemies. But this is, without doubt, also linked to the place of women in economics.

Main references

ASIMAKOPULOS A. 1969. 'A Robinsonian Growth Model in One-Sector Notation', *Australian Economic Papers*, vol. 8, 41–58.

ASIMAKOPULOS A. 1984. 'Joan Robinson and Economic Theory', *Quarterly Review, Banca Nazionale del Lavoro*, no. 151, 381–409.

BLAUG Mark 1992 (ed.). *Pioneers in Economics*, section 4, *Twentieth Century Economics*, vol. 45, Aldershot, Hants, Edward Elgar.

FEIWEL George R. 1989 (ed.) *Joan Robinson and Modern Economic Theory*, London, Macmillan.

FEIWEL George R. 1989 (ed.). *The Economics of Imperfect Competition and Employment. Joan Robinson and Beyond*, London, Macmillan.

GRAM Harvey and WALSH Vivian 1983. 'Joan Robinson's Economics in Retrospect', *Journal of Economic Literature*, vol. 21, 518–50.

GRELLET Gérard 1985. 'Quelques questions hérétiques à l'analyse de Joan Robinson', followed by a bibliography, *Économie appliquée*, vol. 37, 519–39.

HARCOURT, G.C. 1984. 'Harcourt on Robinson', in Spiegel and Samuels, 639–58.

RIMA Ingrid 1991 (ed.). *The Joan Robinson Legacy*, Armonk, New York, M.E. Sharpe.

SKOURAS T. 1981. 'The Economics of Joan Robinson', in Shackleton and Locksley 1981.

TURNER Marjorie S. 1989. *Joan Robinson and the Americans*, Armonk, New York, M.E. Sharpe.

ARESTIS and SAWYER 1992, 454–63. BLAUG 1985, 207–9. LOASBY 1989, 71–85. *New Palgrave* 1987, vol. 4, 211–17. SILLS 1979, 663–71.

ROSTOW Walt Whitman (born 1916)

Born in New York, W.W. Rostow obtained his BA in 1936 at Yale University, his MA in 1938 at Balliol College, Oxford, and his PhD at Yale in 1940. An instructor at Columbia (1940–41), he served in the army (1942–5) and then in the State Department's German–Austrian Economic Division. In 1947, he was assistant to the executive secretary of the Economic Commission for Europe. He taught at Oxford (1946–7) and Cambridge, England (1949–50) and was professor of economic history at the Massachusetts Institute of Technology from 1950 to 1961.

In 1961, during Kennedy's presidency, he was deputy special assistant to the President for national security affairs; he was then counsellor of the Department of State and chairman of the Policy Planning Council, with, furthermore, beginning in 1964, the task of representing the United States, with the rank of ambassador, at the Inter-American Committee of the Alliance for Progress. In 1966, he was again called to the White House by President Johnson as special assistant for national security affairs; he was deeply involved in policy concerning Vietnam and the subsequent war. Since 1969, he has been professor of economics and history at the University of Texas, at Austin.

Main publications

1948. *Essays on the British Economy of the Nineteenth Century*, Oxford, Clarendon Press.
1952. *The Process of Economic Growth*, New York, W.W. Norton.
1952. With Alfred Levin *et al.*, *The Dynamics of Soviet Society*, New York, W.W. Norton.
1953. With Arthur D. Gayer and Anna Jacobson Schwartz, *The Growth and Fluctuation of the British Economy, 1790–1850*, 2 vols, Oxford, Clarendon Press.
1954. With Richard W. Hatch, Frank A. Kierman and Alexander Eckstein, *The Prospects for Communist China*, New York, Technology Press, MIT and John Wiley.
1955. With Richard W. Hatch, *An American Policy in Asia*, New York, Technology Press, MIT and John Wiley.
1960. *The Stages of Economic Growth: A Non-Communist Manifesto*, Cambridge, England, Cambridge University Press.
1960. *The United States in the World Arena: An Essay in Recent History*, New York, Harper & Row.
1971. *Politics and The Stages of Growth*, Cambridge, England, Cambridge University Press.
1972. *The Diffusion of Power: An Essay in Recent History*, New York, Macmillan.
1975. *How It All Began: Origins of the Modern Economy*, New York, McGraw-Hill.
1978. *The World Economy: History and Prospect*, Austin, University of Texas Press; London, Macmillan.
1981. *British Trade Fluctuations, 1868–1896: A Chronicle and a Commentary*, Arno Press.
1984. 'Development: The Political Economy of the Marshallian Long Period', in Meier and Seers, 229–61.
1986. 'My Life Philosophy', *American Economist*, vol. 30, Autumn, 3–13; reprint, 'Reflections on Political Economy: Past, Present, and Future', in Szenberg 1992, 222–35.
1987. 'Reflections on the Drive to Technological Maturity', *Quarterly Review, Banca Nazionale del Lavoro*, no. 161, 115–46; in Kregel 1989, 163–95.
1990. *Theorists of Economic Growth from David Hume to the Present: With a Perspective on the Next Century*, New York, Oxford University Press.

Between the end of the 1930s and the beginning of the 1950s, W. Rostow completed his thesis on the history of the British economy (published in 1981) and published several articles and a few books in economic history, principally on Great Britain (1948, 1953). He also published, in the 1950s, several works on the communist countries (1952 with Levin, 1954, 1955) and then various books dealing with geopolitics and global strategy (1960 *The United States*, 1971, 1972).

But it is for his theses on growth and development that Rostow became a necessary reference in the world of academic economists. On the basis of his analyses intended to explain growth, development and especially 'take off', he underscored the role of an effective institutional structure, the impact of certain sectors and the importance of six basic propensities: developing science, applying it to economic ends, embracing innovations, the pursuit of material gain, consumption and having children (1952 *The Process*). His thesis was simplifed, with the presentation of 'five stages' of growth, characterized mainly by rates of investment, rates of growth and economic structures: traditional society, the phase before take-off, take-off, maturity and mass consumption (1960 *The Stages*). The author presented these stages as a chronological succession which he subsequently dated for the main industrialized countries and which, for others, he projected into the future. This theory, presented by Rostow as capable of countering Marxist analyses, was the subject of much discussion and criticism by those who considered that historical processes and social change cannot be reduced to such a simple linear scheme and by those who deemed it necessary to take account of the dependency relations and the interactions which characterize the modern world.

Main references

LODEWIJKS John 1991. 'Rostow, Developing Economies, and National Security Policy', in C.D. Goodwin (ed.), *Economics and National Security. A History of their Interaction*, Durham, Duke University Press, 285–310.

ROSTOW 1984. With commentaries by Gerald Helleiner and Mohammed F. Azizali, 286–96.

ROSTOW 1986, 1987.

BLAUG 1985, 210–12.

SAMUELSON Paul Anthony (born 1915)

Paul Anthony Samuelson was born in Gary, Indiana. He began his studies at Chicago (BA in 1935), then enrolled at Harvard University (MA in 1936, PhD in 1941). He made his entire career at the Massachussetts Institute of Technology (MIT), in Cambridge, where he was successively assistant professor (1940), associate professor (1944), professor (1947) and professor emeritus in 1986. Among many other activities, Samuelson has been consultant to the National Resources Planning Board (1941–3), staff member of the MIT's Radiation Laboratory (1944–5), professor of international economic relations at the Fletcher School of Law and Diplomacy (1945), consultant to the Rand Corporation (1948–75), economic advisor to the senator, candidate, then president, J.F. Kennedy, consultant to the Council of Economic Advisers (1960–68) and, since 1965, to the Federal Reserve Board; he collaborated regularly with *Newsweek* from 1966 to 1981.

In 1947 he received the John Bates Clark Medal of the American Economic Association, of which he was president in 1961. He was also president of the Econometric Society in 1951 and of the International Economic Association (1965–8), of which he is lifetime honorary president. He was the first American to receive, in 1970, the Nobel Memorial Prize in Economics.

Main publications

1937. 'Some Aspects of the Pure Theory of Capital', *Quarterly Journal of Economics*, vol. 51, 469–96.
1938. 'A Note on the Pure Theory of Consumers' Behaviour', *Economica*, vol. 5, 61–71.
1938. 'The Empirical Implications of Utility Analysis', *Econometrica*, vol. 6, 344–56.
1938. 'Welfare Economics and International Trade', *American Economic Review*, vol. 28, 261–6.
1939. 'A Synthesis of the Principle of Acceleration and the Multiplier', *Journal of Political Economy*, vol. 47, 786–97.
1939. 'Interactions Between the Multiplier Analysis and the Principle of Acceleration', *Review of Economic Statistics*, vol. 21, 75–8.
1939. 'The Gains from International Trade', *Canadian Journal of Economics and Political Science*, vol. 5, 195–205.
1941. With W.F. Stolper, 'Protection and Real Wages', *Review of Economic Studies*, vol. 9, 58–73.
1947. *Foundations of Economic Analysis*, Cambridge, Massachusetts, Harvard University Press.
1948. 'Consumption Theory in Terms of Revealed Preference', *Economica*, vol. 15, 243–53.
1948. *Economics: An Introductory Analysis*, New York, McGraw-Hill (15 editions, the most recent with W. Nordhaus, 1988, New York, McGraw-Hill).
1948. 'International Trade and the Equalisation of Factor Prices', *Economic Journal*, vol. 58, 163–84.
1949. 'International Factor Price Equalisation Once Again', *Economic Journal*, vol. 59, 181–97.
1952. 'Economic Theory and Mathematics: An Appraisal', *American Economic Review*, vol. 52, *Papers and Proceedings*, 56–66.
1954. 'The Pure Theory of Public Expenditure', *Review of Economics and Statistics*, vol. 36, 387–9.

1958. With R. Dorfman and R.M. Solow, *Linear Programming and Economic Analysis*, New York, McGraw-Hill.
1960. With R.M. Solow, 'Analytical Aspects of Anti-Inflation Policy', *American Economic Review*, vol. 50, *Papers and Proceedings*, 177–94.
1962. 'Economists and the History of Ideas' [Presidential address, American Economic Association], *American Economic Review*, vol. 52, 1–18.
1966–86. *The Collected Scientific Papers of Paul A. Samuelson*, Cambridge, Massachusetts, MIT Press, 5 vols: 1966, vols 1 and 2, edited by Joseph E. Stiglitz: 1970, vol. 3, edited by R.C. Merton; 1977, vol. 4, edited by H. Nagatani and K. Crowley; 1986, vol. 5, edited by K. Crowley.
1967. With A.F. Burns, *Full Employment: Guideposts and Economic Stability*, Washington, DC, American Enterprise Institute for Public Policy Research.
1970. 'Maximum Principles in Analytical Economics', in *Les Prix Nobel 1970*, Stockholm, Nobel Foundation; in *Collected Scientific Papers*, vol. 3, 2–17.
1972. 'Economics in a Golden Age: A Personal Memoir', in Gerald Holton (ed.), *The Twentieth Century Sciences: Studies in the Biography of Ideas*, New York, W.W. Norton, 155–70.
1973. *The Samuelson Sampler*, Glen Ridge, New Jersey, Thomas Horton & Daughters.
1980. 'The Economic Responsibility of Government', in *Milton Friedman and Paul Samuelson Discuss the Economic Responsibility of Government*, College Station, Texas, Center for Education and Research in Free Enterprise, A & M University.
1983. 'My Life Philosophy', *American Economist*, Autumn, 5–12; in Szenberg 1992, 236–47.
1986. 'My Evolution as an Economist', in Breit and Spencer 1986, 59–76.

'Samuelson is one of the greatest economic theorists of all time': this description by Kenneth Arrow (1967, p. 735) summarizes the opinion of the whole profession. However, as Stanley Fischer remarks, 'there is no Samuelson school of economics' (*New Palgrave*, vol. 4, p. 235). This paradox describes the singularity of the work of this *enfant terrible* of economics, as he was considered for a long time.

While Keynes rejected it, and Hicks had too large an economic culture to find it satisfying, and Frisch became involved in it to create a new discipline, econometrics, the young Samuelson undertook, in a systematic manner and despite the reticence of his professors, the introduction of mathematical formalization into the core of economic theory. It was thus – noting here only his first contributions – that he renewed, with the theory of revealed preference, consumer theory (1938 *Economica*, 1948 *Economica*); he systematized the combination of the multiplier, which had an important place in Keynes's *General Theory*, and the accelerator, to yield a new tool of analysis of short-run fluctuations (1939 *RES*, 1939 *JPE*); he gave a new account of the gains of trade between two countries (1939 *CJEPS*) and clarified the conditions in which international trade ensures the equalization of factor prices between countries (1948 *EJ*, 1949 *EJ*).

More generally, in his thesis, presented in 1941 and not published until 1947, the use of a unified methodology (maximization under constraints, use of second-order conditions) revealed its effectiveness for the analysis of different fields, such as microeconomics (production, consumer behaviour), macroeconomics, international trade and public finance; it also allows the clarification of the content and the implications of technical analysis: comparative statics and dynamics, general equilibrium and partial equilibrium (cf. Lindbeck 1970, *SJE*, pp. 343–4). The publication in 1948 of *Economics* extended Samuelson's audience to a very large public, and especially students (more than four million copies sold in more than forty translations); in the first edition, this textbook – combining classical, marginalist and Keynesian contributions, microeconomics and macroeconomics – gave a presentation of the analysis of the determinants of national income, the theory of production and prices, and distribution theory.

Beyond this, Samuelson's theoretical work was carried out – renewed sometimes by the use of new mathematical tools (1958) – in both the areas already mentioned and in the analysis of capital (involvement in the Cambridge controversy), welfare theory, general equilibrium, public goods, balanced growth, consumption loan theory and the interpretation of the Phillips curve (1966–86); to such an extent, as Lindbeck remarks (1970, *SJE*, p. 354), that 'a survey of Samuelson's main research areas also becomes a survey of many of the great economic problems of our time'. Suspicious of dogmas and extremes, Samuelson has, as policy adviser, opted for a moderate form of Keynesianism; but he did not succeed in persuading President Kennedy or his successor of the validity of a conviction he had held since 1959, that the dollar was overvalued and that it was necessary to raise the price of gold (*Washington Post*, 17 March 1968).

Thus is seen the paradox personified by Samuelson. A great theorist he certainly was: he was the first systematically to give mathematical form to the main contributions of economic theory – classical and neoclassical, with or without perfect competition, Keynesian – from the end of the 1930s, which allowed for greater rigour, undeniable clarifications and significant advances; and he was one of the last to achieve such standing in such a large number of fields, while having a large knowledge of past economic thought. If he has not given his name to a school, it is simply that he was at the heart of what he called the 'neoclassical synthesis', a large movement during the years 1950–60, which he estimated to have rallied 90 per cent of economists; but formal unification, through the mathematical reformulation of economic theories, and syncretism, particularly striking in *Economics* (1948), do not constitute a synthesis, even if they contributed to making the need for one felt and perhaps to opening the way.

Samuelson finally personifies a double swing: from the old theory of political economy to the new formalized economics and from British disciplinary dominance in the early decades of the century to the new American supremacy.

Main references

'The Nobel Memorial Prize in Economics 1970'. Official Announcement and article by Assar Lindbeck, *Swedish Journal of Economics*, 1970, vol. 72, 341–54. Article reprinted in Spiegel and Samuels 1984, 5–18.

ARROW K.J. 1967. 'Samuelson Collected', *Journal of Political Economy*, vol. 75, 730–37.
BROWN E.C. and SOLOW R.M. 1983 (eds). *Paul Samuelson and Modern Economic Theory*, New York, McGraw-Hill.
FEIWEL G. 1982 (ed.). *Samuelson and Neoclassical Economics*, Boston, Kluwer Nijhoff.
HOLLANDER Samuel 1980. 'On Professor Samuelson's Canonical Classical Model of Political Economy', *Journal of Economic Literature*, vol. 18, 559–74.
SAMUELSON 1972, 1983, 1986.
WONG S. 1978. *The Foundations of Paul Samuelson's Revealed Preference Theory*, London, Routledge & Kegan.
WOOD John Cunningham and WOODS Ronald N. 1989 (eds). *Paul A. Samuelson: Critical Assessments*, 4 vols, London, Routledge.

BLAUG 1985, 213–16. *New Palgrave*, vol. 4, 234–41. BREIT and RANSOM 1971, 111–38. SHACKLETON and LOCKSLEY 1981 219–39. SILK 1976, 3–46. SOBEL 1980, 93–117.

SARGENT Thomas J. (born 1943)

Thomas J. Sargent was born in Pasadena, California. He received a BA from California University at Berkeley in 1964 and a PhD from Harvard University in 1968. After being a research associate at the Carnegie Institute of Technology (1967–8) and then serving in the American army (1968–9), he became associate professor at the University of Pennsylvania (1970–71), and then associate professor (1971–5) and professor (1975–87) at the University of Minnesota. A research associate at the National Bureau of Economic Research (1970–73 and since 1979), he has been senior fellow at the Hoover Institution of Stanford University, California since 1987.

Main publications

1971. 'A Note on the Accelerationist Controversy', *Journal of Money, Credit and Banking*, vol. 3, 721–5.
1972. 'Rational Expectations and the Term Structure of Interest Rates', *Journal of Money, Credit and Banking*, vol. 4, 74–97.
1973. 'Rational Expectations, the Real Rate of Interest, and the Natural Rate of Unemployment', *Brookings Papers on Economic Activity*, 2, 429–72.
1975. With N. Wallace, '"Rational" Expectations, the Optimal Monetary Instrument, and the Optimal Money Supply Rule', *Journal of Political Economy*, vol. 83, 241–57.
1976. 'A Classical Macroeconomic Model for the United States', *Journal of Political Economy*, vol. 84, 207–37.
1979. *Macroeconomic Theory*, New York, Academic Press.
1979. With Robert E. Lucas, Jr., 'After Keynesian Macroeconomics', *Federal Reserve Bank of Minneapolis Quarterly Review*, vol. 3, no. 2, 1–16.
1981 (ed., with Robert E. Lucas, Jr.). *Rational Expectations and Econometric Practice: A Book of Readings*, 2 vols, Minneapolis, University of Minnesota Press.
1983. Interview, in Klamer 1983, 58–80.

1985 (ed.). *Energy, Foresight and Inflation*, Washington, Resources for the Future.
1986. *Rational Expectations and Inflation*, New York, Harper & Row.
1987. *Dynamic Macroeconomic Theory*, Cambridge, Massachusetts, Harvard University Press.
1987. 'Rational Expectations', *New Palgrave*, vol. 3, 76–85.

Thomas Sargent and Robert Lucas are the main theoreticians of the new classical macroeconomics. They jointly edited a book which gathers together the founding articles of this current of thought (1981). But it was independently of one another that they discovered the use which could be made in the field of macroeconomic theory of the rational expectations hypothesis, formulated in the early 1960s by John Muth, an hypothesis based on 'the principle of strategic interdependence, which holds that one person's pattern of behavior depends on the behavior patterns of those forming his environment' (1986, p. x). In particular, agents will change their behaviour when the government modifies its policies. It was on the basis of this idea that Sargent and Wallace developed the thesis according to which only a monetary policy that is not anticipated by agents may have a real effect on the economy (1975). Without rejecting in principle any governmental intervention, Sargent is nonetheless, among the new macroeconomists, one of the most sceptical as regards the efficiency of governmental policies to fight unemployment. Sargent also developed new econometric instruments to make the new approach operational and capable of empirical tests. He is the author of a widely used textbook, which has contributed to the success of the new macroeconomics with new generations of students (1979).

Main reference
BLAUG 1985, 217–18.

SCHULTZ Theodore W. (born 1902)

Theodore W. Schultz was born in a rural community of German origin in South Dakota; he completed his undergraduate studies at the local state college, before continuing his studies at the University of Wisconsin, where he obtained his PhD in agricultural economics in 1930. He then began a career as a teacher at Iowa State College, where he chaired the department of economics and sociology from 1934 to 1943. He was subsequently professor at the University of Chicago, where he was the head of the department of economics (1946–61) and played an active role until he retired in 1974. He was also adviser to the American government, to the United Nations and to non-governmental organizations. Schultz presided over the American Economic Association in 1961; he received its Walker medal in 1972 and shared with W. Arthur Lewis, in 1979, the Nobel Memorial Prize in Economics.

Main publications

1940. 'Capital Rationing, Uncertainty, and Farm Tenancy Reform', *Journal of Political Economy*, vol. 48, 309–24.
1941. 'Economic Effects of Agricultural Programs', *American Economic Review*, vol. 30, 127–54.
1943. *Redirecting Farm Policy*, London, Macmillan.
1945. *Agriculture in an Unstable Economy*, New York, McGraw-Hill.
1945 (ed.). *Food for the World*, University of Chicago Press.
1949. *Production and Welfare of Agriculture*, London, Macmillan.
1950. 'Reflections on Poverty within Agriculture', *Journal of Political Economy*, vol. 43, 1–15.
1953. *The Economic Organization of Agriculture*, New York, McGraw-Hill.
1958. 'The Emerging Economic Scene and its Relation to High School Education', in F.S. Chase and H.A. Anderson (eds), *The High School in a New Era*, University of Chicago Press.
1960. 'Capital Formation by Education', *Journal of Political Economy*, vol. 68, 571–83.
1961. 'Investment in Human Capital', *American Economic Review*, vol. 51, 1–17; 'Reply', 1962, vol. 52, 1035–9.
1962 (ed.). 'Investment in Human Being', *Journal of Political Economy*, vol. 70, supplement.
1963. *The Economic Value of Education*, New York, Columbia University Press.
1964. *Transforming Traditional Agriculture*, New Haven, Connecticut, Yale University Press.
1965. *Economic Crises in World Agriculture*, Ann Arbor, University of Michigan Press.
1965. 'Investing in Poor People: An Economist's View', *American Economic Review*, vol. 45, 510–20.
1968. *Economic Growth and Agriculture*, New York, McGraw-Hill.
1971. *Investment in Human Capital: The Role of Education and of Research*, New York, Free Press.
1972. *Human Resources*, New York, National Bureau of Economic Research.
1972 (ed.). *Investment in Education: The Equity-Efficiency Quandary*, University of Chicago Press.
1975 (ed.). *Economics of the Family: Marriage, Children, and Human Capital*, University of Chicago Press.
1975. 'The Value of the Ability to Deal with Disequilibria', *Journal of Economic Literature*, vol. 13, 827–46.
1978 (ed.). *Distortions of Agricultural Incentives*, Bloomington, Indiana University Press.
1980. *Investing in People: The Economics of Population Quality*, Berkeley, University of California Press.
1990. *Restoring Economic Equilibrium: Human Capital in the Modernizing Economy*, Oxford, Basil Blackwell.
1993. *The Economics of Being Poor*, Oxford, Basil Blackwell.
1993. *Origins of Increasing Returns*, Oxford, Basil Blackwell.

Having studied in agricultural economics, T.W. Schultz worked in the 1930s on the crisis in American agriculture, especially in Iowa, and on governmental measures, and, during the Second World War, on agricultural programmes (1941, 1943); from the end of the war, he tackled the issue of agriculture in developing countries (1945 *Food*). He became a specialist in this field (1949, 1953, 1964, 1965, 1968, 1978) associated with some leading ideas: the rejection of the thesis according to which the marginal productivity of the farmer's labour would be nil; the conviction that the role of prices in orientating the use of resources is essential, and therefore a deep suspicion of anything that can distort them; a confidence in the rationality of farmers, forced to make choices in situations of change and uncertainty.

It was when this process was in full swing that, with his 1958 article, he opened up the field of human capital: facing the questions of the time on the factors explaining growth, he emphasized the importance of the quality of resources, both human and non-human. He then developed this thesis, advancing the themes of investment in human beings (1961, 1962 'Investment', 1971, 1972 *Human*), investment in education, training and information for the people (1960, 1963, 1965, 1972 *Investment* 1980). Schultz's works gave a decisive impulse both to the theory of human capital and to economics of education. He emphasized the role that education and training must play in the development of the farm economy (1964), while expanding his thinking to consider the overall logic of the family (birth, children) (1975 *Economics*). Far from shutting himself up, as many economists did subsequently, in a narrow conception of economics, Schultz opened his thinking to the contributions of the sociologists and anthropologists, and attempted to grasp the relations between the different components of reality.

Main references

'The Nobel Memorial Prize in Economics 1980'. Official announcement and article by M.J. Bowman, *Swedish Journal of Economics*, 1980, vol. 82, 59–61 and 80–107. Article reprinted in Spiegel and Samuels 1984, 103–21.

BLAUG 1985, 219–21. *New Palgrave* 1987, vol. 4, 262–3. SILLS 1979, 707–9.

SCHWARTZ Anna J. (born 1915)

Anna Jacobson was born in New York, receiving an MA (1935) and a PhD (1964) from Columbia University. She began her research career at the US Department of Agriculture and continued it at the Columbia University Social Science Research Council (1936–41) before becoming associated, in 1941, with the National Bureau of Economic Research, of which she was named emeritus researcher in 1985. She taught at various New York academic institutions. She has been staff director of the US Commission on the role of gold in the domestic and international monetary system (1981–2).

Main publications

1947. 'An Attempt at Synthesis in American Banking History', *Journal of Economic History*, vol. 7, 208–16.

1953. With A.D. Gayer and W.W. Rostow, *The Growth and Fluctuation of the British Economy, 1790–1850*, 2 vols, Oxford, Clarendon Press.

1963. With Milton Friedman, *A Monetary History of the United States, 1867–1960*, Princeton University Press for the National Bureau of Economic Research.

1969. With Milton Friedman, 'The Definition of Money: Net Wealth and Neutrality as Criteria', *Journal of Money, Credit and Banking*, vol. 1, 1–14.

1970. With Milton Friedman, *Monetary Statistics of the United States: Estimates, Sources,*

Methods, New York, Columbia University Press for the National Bureau of Economic Research.

1973. 'Secular Price Change in Historical Perspective', *Journal of Money, Credit, and Banking*, vol. 5, 243–69.

1975. 'Monetary Trends in the United States and the United Kingdom, 1878–1970: Selected Findings', *Journal of Economic History*, vol. 35, 138–59.

1982. With Milton Friedman, *Monetary Trends in the United States and the United Kingdom: Their Relation to Income, Prices, and Interest Rates, 1867–1975*, University of Chicago Press.

1983. With M.R. Darby *et al.*, *The International Transmission of Inflation*, University of Chicago Press.

1986. With Milton Friedman, 'Has Government Any Role in Money?', *Journal of Monetary Economics*, vol. 17, 37–62.

1987. *Money in Historical Perspective*, University of Chicago Press.

Anna J. Schwartz made significant contributions to economic history, monetary theory, the study of economic policies and the analysis of the international monetary system (see in particular the articles reproduced in 1987). Besides her knowledge of history and the institutions, in particular monetary and financial, Anna Schwartz is a specialist in the use of statistics and the author of long-term statistical series on the United States and Great Britain. These, among others, are found in three monumental books (1963, 1970, 1982) and the numerous articles which she co-authored with Milton Friedman, in the context of a research project of the National Bureau of Economic Research on business cycles and money. The first result of this work, which extended over nearly 30 years, and which greatly contributed to the rehabilitation of the quantity theory of money, was a publication, written with Elma Oliver, in 1947. Her researches convinced Anna Schwartz that 'the quantity of money has a significant influence on the level of economic activity' (1987, p. 106), that erratic monetary policies bear a heavy share of responsibility for both the gravity of depressions and the worsening of inflation, that a rule of stable increase of the stock of money is the wisest policy to follow and that the state must leave to the market mechanism the task of ensuring growth and the distribution of resources.

Main references

BORDO Michael D. 1989 (ed.). *Money, History, and International Finance: Essays in Honor of Anna J. Schwartz*, University of Chicago Press.

New Palgrave 1987, vol. 4, 267.

SCITOVSKY Tibor (born 1910)

Born in Budapest, T. Scitovsky studied in that city (1928–32), and at Trinity College, Cambridge (1929–31). He worked in a bank in Budapest in 1934–5, but left it to resume his studies at the London School of Economics (MSc in

1938). He emigrated to the United States in 1939, served in the American army (1943–6) and worked at the US Department of Commerce in 1946. Associate professor, then professor, at Stanford (1946–58), he became professor at Berkeley (1958–66) before working at the OECD in Paris (1966–8). He was then a professor at Yale (1968–70), at Stanford (1970–76 and 1978–81), at the London School of Economics (1976–8) and at the University of California at Santa Cruz (1978–82), where he reached the rank of emeritus professor.

Main publications

1941. 'A Note on Welfare Propositions in Economics', *Review of Economic Studies*, vol. 9, 77–88.
1951. *Welfare and Competition: The Economics of A Fully Employed Economy*, London, George Allen & Unwin.
1958. *Economic Theory and Western European Integration*, London, George Allen & Unwin.
1960. 'Standards for the Performance of Our Economic System', *American Economic Review*, vol. 50, *Papers and Proceedings*, 13–20.
1962. 'On the Principle of Consumer's Sovereignty', *American Economic Review*, vol. 52, *Papers and Proceedings*, 262–8.
1964. *Papers on Welfare and Growth*, Stanford University Press.
1969. *Money and The Balance of Payments*, Chicago, Rand McNally.
1970. With I.M.D. Little and M.F. Scott, *Industry and Trade in Some Developing Countries*, London, Oxford University Press.
1973. 'The Place of Economic Welfare in Human Welfare', *Quarterly Review of Economics and Business*, vol. 13, 7–19.
1974. 'Are Men Rational or Economists Wrong?', in P.A. David and M.W. Reder (eds), *Nations and Households in Economic Growth*, New York, Academic Press, 224–35.
1976. *The Joyless Economy: An Inquiry into Human Satisfaction and Consumer Dissatisfaction*, New York, Oxford University Press.
1978. 'Market, Power, and Inflation', *Economica*, vol. 45, 221–33.
1986. *Human Desire and Economic Satisfaction: Essays on the Frontiers of Economics*, Brighton, Wheatsheaf.
1992. 'My Search for Welfare', in Szenberg 248–60.

T. Scitovsky worked in varied areas and published on a broad range of subjects. For him, *The General Theory* appeared, when it was published, as the book which brought all the answers to a young economist who was fascinated by the gap between equilibrium theory and the reality of mass unemployment (1992, p. 250). And a great part of his work aimed at bringing closer to reality theoretical representations based on excessively unrealistic assumptions.

One of his contributions was to integrate into the analysis of markets the power that better or superior knowledge gives and from which results the existence of asymmetrical relations: he did this in his 1951 book, by introducing the notions of price-maker and price-taker and by bringing out, on this basis, four main types of relations likely to establish themselves between buyers and sellers. This led him to differentiate the power structures characterizing the goods markets and the labour markets, and to find in them the sources of the inflationist spiral of prices and wages (1978).

Scitovsky also dealt with numerous subjects concerning international economics: the question of tariffs and economic integration (1958), the balance of payments and the international monetary system (1969), the relations between industrialization, customs protection and the policy of import substitution (1970). Having been interested very early in the field of welfare economics (1941), he made, in article after article, by successive refinement, a certain number of contributions to this domain, sifting through his own critical filter a number of the assertions which constitute orthodox economics, reflecting upon, *inter alia,* the efficiency criteria of the market economy and the price of economic progress (1960, 1962, 1964).

He confronted economic welfare with human welfare (1973) and made inroads by countering the economists' conception of rationality (1974) with the actual rationality of man, as one may observe it and as psychologists analyse it: this led him to question the sources of human satisfaction and the relations between economy, joy and happiness, and to develop a critical perspective both on the way in which economics deals with consumption and on the consumer society, as it evolved in the United States with the 'American way of life' (1976, 1986).

Main references

BOSKIN Michael J. 1979 (ed.). *Economics and Human Welfare: Essays in Honor of Tibor Scitovsky*, New York, Academic Press.
EARL Peter 1992. 'Tibor Scitowsky', in Samuels ed., 265–93.
SCITOVSKY 1992.

BLAUG 1985, 222–3. *New Palgrave* 1987, vol. 4, 268–9.

SEN Amartya Kunar (born 1933)

Born in Santiniketan (Bengal), into a Hindu family, Amartya Sen studied in Calcutta (BA, 1953), then Cambridge, where he obtained his PhD in 1959. He was professor at Jadavpur University in Calcutta (1956–8), fellow of Trinity College, Cambridge (1957–63); then professor of economics at the University of Delhi (1963–71), at the London School of Economics (1971–7), at Oxford (1977–88) and finally at Harvard. He has been president of the Econometric Society (1984), of the International Economic Association (1986–9), of the Indian Economic Association (1989) and of the American Economic Association (1994).

Main publications

1960. *Choice of Techniques: An Aspect of the Theory of Planned Economic Development,* Oxford, Basil Blackwell.
1970 (ed.). *Growth Economics: Selected Readings*, Harmondsworth, Penguin Books.

1970. *Collective Choice and Social Welfare*, San Francisco, Holden Day.
1970. 'The Impossibility of a Paretian Liberal', *Journal of Political Economy*, vol. 78, 152–7.
1972. With P. Dasgupta and S.A. Marglin, *Guidelines for Project Evaluation*, New York, United Nations.
1973. *On Economic Inequality*, Oxford, Clarendon Press.
1975. *Employment, Technology and Development*, Oxford, Clarendon Press.
1980. *Levels of Poverty*, Washington, DC, World Bank.
1981. *Poverty and Famines: An Essay on Entitlement and Deprivation*, Oxford, Clarendon Press.
1982. *Choice, Welfare and Measurement*, Oxford, Basil Blackwell.
1984. *Resources, Values and Development*, Oxford, Basil Blackwell.
1985. *Commodities and Capabilities*, Amsterdam, North-Holland.
1987. *On Ethics and Economics*, Oxford, Basil Blackwell.
1987. *The Standard of Living*, Cambridge University Press.
1989. With Jean Drèze, *Hunger and Public Action*, Oxford, Clarendon Press.

Through nearly 200 books, articles and other contributions, Amartya Sen has presented his analysis of development and the choice of appropriate technology (1960, 1972, 1975), criticized the rationality assumption (1970 *JPE*), probed deeply into the theory of social welfare, taking into account the relations between social objectives and interdependent choices of individuals (1970 *Collective*, 1982), considered the measurement of inequality, of the standard of living and of poverty (1973, 1975, 1980, 1987 *The Standard*) and explained the great famines, not as the outcome of an absolute lack of food, but of the unequal attribution of rights to this food, linked to the unequal distribution of purchasing power (1981). Furthermore, by his thinking on the conceptions of individual freedom – with its double definition (positive and negative) and its foundation in the social – which leads to the notion of 'capability', or real opportunity for life choices, by the emphasis he put on the necessity to grasp economy embedded in society and by the prominent place he accorded to ethics (1985, 1987 *On Ethics*), he accentuated his criticism of any narrow economic approach.

Main references

CANTO-SPERBER Monique 1991. 'Choix de vie et liberté. Sur l'oeuvre d'Amartya Sen', *Esprit*, March–April, 26–38.
KLAMER Arjo 1989. 'A Conversation with Amartya Sen', *Journal of Economic Perspectives*, vol. 3, no. 1, 135–50.
McPHERSON Michael 1992. 'Amartya Sen', in Samuels ed., 294–309.

ARESTIS and SAWYER 1992, 498–505. BLAUG 1985, 224–5.

SHACKLE George Lennox Sharman (1903–1992)

George Shackle was born in Cambridge, England. Having worked in a bank, then in a tobacco company, and having taught in a school for nine years, he enrolled in 1935 at the London School of Economics, where he earned a doctorate in 1937. He then began to work at the Oxford Institute of Statistics. From 1939 to 1945 he was a member of the wartime statistical research committee assembled by Winston Churchill (S. Branch) and was then a member of the Economic Section of the Cabinet Office from 1945 to 1950. A reader at the University of Leeds in 1950–51, he was named professor at the University of Liverpool in 1951, where he remained until his retirement in 1969.

Main publications

1933. 'Some Notes on Monetary Theories of the Trade Cycle', *Review of Economic Studies*, vol. 1, 27–38.
1938. *Expectations, Investment, and Income*, London, Oxford University Press; 2nd edn 1968, Oxford, Clarendon Press.
1949. *Expectations in Economics*, Cambridge, England, Cambridge University Press.
1952. *Mathematics at the Fireside*, Cambridge, England, Cambridge University Press.
1953. *What Makes an Economist*, Liverpool University Press.
1955. *Uncertainty in Economics and other Reflections*, Cambridge, England, Cambridge University Press.
1958. *Time in Economics*, Amsterdam, North-Holland.
1959. *Economics for Pleasure*, Cambridge, England, Cambridge University Press.
1961. *Decision, Order and Time in Human Affairs*, Cambridge, England, Cambridge University Press.
1965. *A Scheme of Economic Theory*, Cambridge, England, Cambridge University Press.
1966. *The Nature of Economic Thought: Selected Papers 1955–1964*, Cambridge, England, Cambridge University Press.
1967. *The Years of High Theory: Invention and Tradition in Economic Thought 1926–1939*, Cambridge, England, Cambridge University Press.
1970. *Expectation, Enterprise and Profit: The Theory of the Firm*, London, George Allen & Unwin.
1972. *Epistemics & Economics: A Critique of Economic Doctrines*, Cambridge, England, Cambridge University Press.
1974. *Keynesian Kaleïdics: The Evolution of a General Political Economy*, Edinburgh University Press.
1979. *Imagination and the Nature of Choice*, Edinburgh University Press.
1983. 'A Student's Pilgrimage', *Quarterly Review, Banca Nazionale del Lavoro*, no. 145, 107–16; in Kregel 1988, 57–66.
1989. *Business, Time and Thought. Collected Essays 1964–88*, edited by S. Frowen, London, Macmillan.
1990. *Time, Expectations and Uncertainty in Economics. Selected Essays of G.L.S. Shackle*, edited by J. L. Ford, Aldershot, Hants, Edward Elgar.

Throughout his career, George Shackle pursued a solitary path, well away from all the orthodoxies. He is impossible to classify in any particular school of thought. Considered by Coddington (1983) to be the most radical of the 'fundamental Keynesians', he has also been claimed as one of their own by the neo-Austrians (Lachmann 1976). As fascinated by Hayek's *Prices and Production* as by Keynes's *Treatise on Money*, he sought to achieve a synthesis between these two authors (1933). He was then among the first, with Hicks, to recognize the importance of Myrdal's *Monetary Equilibrium*. In his doctoral thesis (1938) he attempted a synthesis between these authors, who, at first glance, seem to be diametrically opposed. But they share a feature which Shackle recognized as casting doubt upon the dominant current based on general equilibrium: that is, the taking into account of historical and psychological time, of expectations, of the limited and incomplete nature of knowledge and of uncertainty. From this moment, and until the end of his life, it was clear to him that '*expectation* was the informing notion and basic theme. For already it was overwhelmingly evident to me that if economics is the endeavour to understand one broad source and aspect of human conduct, it is concerned with *thoughts about time to come*' (1983 in Kregel 1988, p. 65).

What Shackle sought to construct was a general theory of decision making under uncertainty. Rejecting the traditional probabilistic approach, he elaborated, in his early works, what he calls functions of potential surprise, represented by three-dimensional graphs, in an attempt to illustrate the decision-making process. In the description of potential surprise, the expectation of joy or suffering and the imagination play a key role. The future neither exists nor is known, but man has the unique capacity to imagine it and to hope for happiness. For Shackle, reflection on the economy and human affairs in general is not concerned with objects such as the stars or the elementary particles, whose movements can be predicted; it is concerned rather with thoughts, thoughts that are unpredictable and constantly modified by unforeseen events and the changing configuration of relationships between individuals.

In his more recent works, Shackle became more and more sceptical as regards the possibility of modelling anything in the domain of economics, or human action in general, developing a reaction to all economic theory which was characterized by some as nihilistic. Himself using language with dexterity and elegance, Shackle emphasized, well before recent related discussion, the importance of the art of persuasion and of rhetoric in scientific activity. A historian of economic thought, he wrote a work that became a classic in the field, *The Years of High Theory* (1967), which discusses important breakthroughs in economic thought from 1926 to 1939, whose consequences were not recognized by the new orthodoxies.

Main references

BLAUG Mark 1992 (ed.). *Pioneers in Economics*, section 4, *Twentieth Century Economics*, Aldershot, Hants, Edward Elgar, vol. 45.

EARL P.E. and KAY N.M. 1985. 'How Economists can Accept Shackle's Critique of Economic Doctrines without Arguing Themselves out of their Jobs', *Journal of Economic Studies*, vol. 12, 34–48.

FROWEN Stephen F. 1990 (ed.). *Unknowledge and Choice in Economics*, London, Macmillan.

LACHMANN Ludwig M. 1976. 'From Mises to Shackle: An Essay on Austrian Economics and the Kaleidic Society', *Journal of Economic Literature*, vol. 14, 54–62.

PHEBY John 1987. 'A New Perspective on Shackle's Keynesian Fundamentalism', *Journal of Economic Studies*, vol. 14, 24–35.
PHEBY John and BOEHM Stephen 1993 (ed.). *Essays in Honour of G.L.S. Shackle*, London, Routledge.
Review of Political Economy 1993, *G. L. S. Shackle Memorial Issue*, vol. 5, no. 2.
SHACKLE 1983.

ARESTIS and SAWYER 1992, 505–10. BLAUG 1985, 226–7. *New Palgrave* 1987, vol. 4, 315–16. GREENAWAY and PRESLEY 1989, 24–67. LOASBY 1989, 1–14. SPIEGEL and SAMUELS 1984, 579–90.

SIMON Herbert Alexander (born 1916)

Born in Milwaukee, Wisconsin, Herbert Simon studied at the University of Chicago, where he obtained a BA in 1936 and a PhD in 1943. He worked at the International City Managers' Association (1938–9), at the Bureau of Public Administration of the University of California at Berkeley (1939–42) and then was successively assistant professor (1942–5), associate professor (1945–7) and professor (1947–9) of political science at the Illinois Institute of Technology, professor of administration (1949–62) and then of administration and psychology (1962–6) at the Carnegie Institute of Technology and finally, since 1966, professor of computer science and psychology at Carnegie-Mellon University.

H. Simon has had many responsibilities at the universities at which he has taught; he has been consultant for various organizations, public and private, and has been an important figure in the scientific institutions of the United States. As a computer scientist and specialist in artificial intelligence he won the Türing medal; as a psychologist, he was a laureate of the American Psychological Association; and in 1978 he was awarded the Nobel Memorial Prize in Economics.

Main publications

1947. *Administrative Behavior*, New York, Macmillan; 3rd edn 1976.
1949. With D. Hawkins, 'Note: Some Conditions of Macroeconomic Stability', *Econometrica*, vol. 17, 245–8.
1950. With Victor A. Thompson and Donald W. Smithburg, *Public Administration*, New York, Alfred A. Knopf.
1954. *Et al., Centralization vs. Decentralization in Organizing the Controller's Department*, New York, Controllership Foundation.
1957. *Models of Man: Social and Rational. Mathematical Essays on Rational Human Behavior in a Social Setting*, New York, John Wiley.
1958. With James G. March, *Organizations*, New York, John Wiley.
1960. *The New Science of Management Decision*, New York, Harper & Row; rev. edn 1977, Englewood Cliffs, New Jersey, Prentice-Hall.
1960. With C.C. Holt, F. Modigliani and J. Muth, *Planning Production, Inventories and Work Force*, Englewood Cliffs, New Jersey, Prentice-Hall.

1963. With Albert Ando and Franklin M. Fisher, *Essays on the Structure of Social Science Models*, Cambridge, Massachusetts, MIT Press.
1965. *The Shape of Automation for Men and Management*, New York, Harper & Row.
1969. *The Sciences of the Artificial*, Cambridge, Massachusetts, MIT Press.
1972. With Allen Newell, *Human Problem Solving*, Englewood Cliffs, New Jersey, Prentice-Hall.
1977. *Models of Discovery*, Dordrecht, D. Reidel.
1979. *Models of Thought*, New Haven, Connecticut, Yale University Press.
1979. 'Rational Decision Making in Business Organizations' (Nobel Lecture), *American Economic Review*, vol. 69, 493–513.
1982. *Behavioral Economics and Business Organization*, Cambridge, Massachusetts, MIT Press.
1982. *Economic Analysis and Public Policy*, Cambridge, Massachusetts, MIT Press.
1982. *Models of Bounded Rationality*, 2 vols, Cambridge, Massachusetts, MIT Press.
1985. 'My Life Philosophy', *American Economist*, vol. 21, no. 1, 15–20; in Szenberg 1992, 261–9.
1986. 'The Failure of Armchair Economics', *Challenge*, November–December, 18–25.
1991. *Models of My Life*, New York, Basic Books.
1991. 'Organizations and Markets', *Journal of Economic Perspectives*, vol. 5, no. 2, 25–44.
1992. *Et al., Economics, Bounded Rationality and the Cognitive Revolution*, Aldershot, Hants, Edward Elgar.

The announcement of the Royal Swedish Academy of Sciences for the Nobel Memorial Prize in Economics (*SJE* 1979, p. 72) asserted that H. Simon 'is, first and foremost, an economist', adding: 'in the widest sense of the word'. For nothing, neither in his university training, nor in his numerous publications, allows one to conclude that he is merely an economist. His first works of the 1930s and 1940s dealt with the measurement and evaluation of public activity, particularly that of local government; and whilst he published articles in *Econometrica*, in 1948 on technical progress and in 1949, with Hawkins, on a central problem in input–output analysis, he also published, during this period, in journals concerning public administration, political science, operations research, mathematics, statistics, psychology and philosophy.

He made his reputation, in the field of behavioural economics, with his work on organizations, administrations and large firms, and in particular with the concrete analysis of the processes by which decisions are made (1947, 1950, 1954, 1958); the latter work was published with J. March, who, in the same vein, published in 1963, with R. Cyert, *A Behavioural Theory of the Firm*. One of the themes illuminated by Simon is that firms' managers do not seek to 'maximize' any quantity, but rather seek a 'satisfactory' route based on several objectives and constraints, and taking account of the limited information at their disposal. In his doctoral thesis, written in 1943, published in 1947, he had advanced the limited rationality argument; in time, what had been initially a simple theoretical hypothesis increasingly appeared as a good description of human rationality as it is observed (1976 introduction to the 3rd edition of 1947).

Adept in mathematical analysis and concerned with developing its potentialities for the social sciences – which were made correspondingly greater through advances in computing – H. Simon did not, however, choose the path typically taken in economics, which consists of favouring the internal logic of theoretical construction: for him, the validity of an analysis depends on its empirical verification. Is this not also the condition necessary to enable computers increasingly to help public or private managers, control stocks, play chess or, in short, take risky decisions in a context characterized by complexity and an uncertain future? Throughout his work on these themes (1957, 1960 with Holt *et al.*, 1960, 1963, 1965, 1982 *Models*), Simon went deeper into the questions of causal relations and 'causal ordering', of rational behaviour and rationality, of cognitive processes and artificial intelligence, and finally of systems analysis and of complexity (1969, 1977, 1979 *Models*). In particular, he emphasized that decisions are taken in a complex universe, poorly known and uncertain, which implies that, in the solution, account be taken of the costs of information and 'search process'. More generally, he has insisted on the limited nature of rationality and he has been opposed to the unreal 'substantive' rationality ascribed to agents by neoclassical theory; he developed the concept of the 'limited' rationality, which he subsequently named 'bounded' rationality, of actors when making decisions (1979 *AER*, 1982 *Models*).

In relation to the dominant current of contemporary economics, the contributions of Simon are double-edged. In the first instance, they lead to the rejection of all theories depending on simplistic hypotheses of economic agents maximizing an objective function in a certain world, that is to say the greater part of contemporary economics – which he has indeed vigorously criticized (1986). At a second level, they constitute an incitement to renew the analysis of organizations and markets and to enrich the analysis of both the institutionalist tradition and industrial economics, and of numerous authors who regard themselves as neoclassical.

In sum, one can agree with Baumol (*SJE* 1979) that the importance of Simon's contributions to economics is all the more remarkable given that it is not his main research area. For the area of economics alone, his contribution exceeds the analysis of 'decision-making within economic organizations' for which he was chosen by the Nobel committee. Being more interested in process than in equilibrium, and in rational choice than in optima, and emphasizing organizations more than markets (1991 *JEP*), underlying procedural rationality, Simon has, in an age dominated by abstraction and formalization, kept economic thought alive, and put the best knowledge of his era to the service of intellectual inquiry. It is too early to say whether his work will have been merely a comet in the sky of modern economics, or whether it will have succeeded in generating a new current in thought and analysis.

Main references

'The Nobel Memorial Prize in Economics 1978'. Official announcement, articles by William J. Baumol and Albert Ando, and bibliography, *Swedish Journal of Economics*, 1979, vol. 81, 72–114. Articles reprinted in Spiegel and Samuels 1984, 474–82.

DEMAILLY André and LE MOIGNE Jean-Louis (eds, with the collaboration of H.A. Simon) 1986. *Sciences de l'intelligence, sciences de l'artificiel*, Presses Universitaires de Lyon.
MONGIN Philippe 1986. 'Simon, Stigler et les théories de la rationalité limitée', *Information sur les sciences sociales*, vol. 25, 555–606.
SIMON 1985, 1991 *Models*.

BLAUG 1985, 229–31. LOASBY 1989, 140–54.

SINGER Hans Wolfgang (born 1910)

Born in Eberfeld (Rhineland), H.W. Singer first studied in Bonn. He left Germany in 1933, completed his studies in Cambridge (PhD in 1936) and obtained British citizenship. From 1947 to 1969, at the United Nations, he contributed to the development of its Economics Department and participated in a broad range of activities concerning the Third World. In 1969, he was named fellow of the Institute of Development Studies of the University of Sussex where he acquired the rank of emeritus. This period included many consultancies to developing countries and for international organizations.

Main publications

1937. *Men without Work*, Cambridge, England, Cambridge University Press.
1940. *Unemployment and Unemployed*, London, King.
1950. 'Gains and Losses from Trade and Investment in Under-Developed Countries', *American Economic Review*, vol. 40, *Papers and Proceedings*, 473–85.
1964. *International Development, Growth and Change*, New York, McGraw-Hill.
1975. *The Strategy of International Development*, London, Macmillan.
1979. *Rich and Poor Countries*, London, George Allen & Unwin.
1984. 'The Terms of Trade Controversy and the Evolution of Soft Financing: Early Years at the UN', in Meier and Seers, 275–303.
1987. With J. Wood and T. Jennings, *Food Aid, The Challenge and the Opportunity*, Oxford, Clarendon Press.
1993. With Sumit Roy, *Economic Progress and Prospects in the Third World: Lessons of Development Experience Since 1945*, Aldershot, Hants, Edward Elgar.

H.W. Singer's significant contribution lies in the thesis, which he presented in 1950, at the same time as R. Prebisch, of the tendency towards deterioration of the terms of trade of 'underdeveloped' countries, a thesis which was criticized, in particular, by Haberler and Viner and was the subject of much discussion. Since the 1960s, Singer has advocated food aid, working to specify the conditions and procedures for its distribution (1987). He tackled numerous issues concerning the Third World and development, especially appropriate technologies, industrialization and debt.

Main references

SINGER 1984; with a commentary by Bela Balassa, 333–41.

ARESTIS and SAWYER 1992, 526–32.

SOLOW Robert M. (born 1924)

Robert Solow was born in Brooklyn. He obtained a PhD from Harvard University in 1951. Since 1950 he has taught in the department of economics of the Massachusetts Institute of Technology, where he had a long collaboration with his colleague and friend Paul A. Samuelson. In 1961, he received the John Bates Clark Medal of the American Economic Association, of which he was president in 1979. In 1987, he received the Nobel Memorial Prize in Economics.

Main publications

1956. 'A Contribution to the Theory of Economic Growth', *Quarterly Journal of Economics*, vol. 70, 65–94.
1957. 'Technical Change and the Aggregate Production Function', *Review of Economics and Statistics*, vol. 39, 312–20.
1958. With R. Dorfman and P.A. Samuelson, *Linear Programming and Economic Analysis*, New York, McGraw-Hill.
1960. 'Investment and Technical Progress', in K.J. Arrow, S. Karlin and P. Suppes (eds), *Mathematical Methods in the Social Sciences*, Stanford University Press, 89–104.
1960. With Paul A. Samuelson, 'Analytical Aspects of Anti-Inflation Policy', *American Economic Review*, vol. 50, *Papers and Proceedings*, 177–94.
1963. *Capital Theory and the Rate of Return*, Amsterdam, North-Holland.
1964. *The Nature and Sources of Unemployment in the United States*, Stockholm, Almqvist & Wiksell.
1966. With J. Tobin, C.C. von Weizsäcker and M. Yaari, 'Neoclassical Growth with Fixed Factor Proportions', *Review of Economic Studies*, vol. 33, 79–116.
1969. *Price Expectations and the Behaviour of the Price Level*, Manchester University Press.
1970. *Growth Theory: An Exposition*, New York, Oxford University Press.
1973. With A.S. Blinder, 'Does Fiscal Policy Matter?', *Journal of Public Economics*, vol. 2, 319–37.
1974 (ed., with E. Ginzberg). *The Great Society: Lessons for the Future*, New York, Basic Books.
1980. 'On Theories of Unemployment', *American Economic Review*, vol. 70, 1–11.
1980. *The Story of a Social Experiment and Some Reflections*, Dublin, Economic and Social Research Institute.
1983. Interview, in Klamer 1983, 127–48.
1983 (ed., with E.C. Brown). *Paul Samuelson and Modern Economic Theory*, New York, McGraw-Hill.
1988. 'Growth Theory and After' (Nobel lecture), *American Economic Review*, vol. 78, 307–17.
1988 (ed., with A. Klamer and D. McCloskey). *The Consequences of Economic Rhetoric*, Cambridge, England, Cambridge University Press.
1989. With M. Dertouzos and R.K. Lester, *Made in America: Regaining the Productive Edge*, Cambridge, Massachusetts, MIT Press.
1990. 'My Evolution as an Economist', in Breit and Spencer 1990, 181–201.

1990. *The Labor Market as a Social Institution*, Cambridge, Massachusetts and Oxford, Basil Blackwell.
1992. 'Notes on Coping', in Szenberg 1992, 270–74.

Robert Solow received the Nobel Memorial Prize for his contributions to the theory of economic growth. His writings on this subject are numerous, but the best known and most influential is that of 1956, in which he developed a neoclassical model of growth inspired by the works of Harrod and Domar. In it, he demonstrated how, if one introduced into the Harrod–Domar model substitution between the factors of production, capital and labour, it was possible to reach a stable growth path at full employment, thanks to price flexibility. Solow also proved that the growth rate of the output–labour ratio was independent of the propensity to save and depended entirely on the rate of technological progress. In another influential article (1957), he examined the relation between economic growth, the increase of the quantity of factors of production and technological progress. Suggesting new techniques to measure the contribution of factors of production to growth, he showed that, over a long period, it is technological progress which is the principal source of growth, rather than, for example, the increase in the quantity of capital per worker. This progress includes the improvement of labour qualifications, by means of, *inter alia*, education. Solow also showed that this progress is neutral, in the sense that it does not modify the distribution of national revenue between profits and wages. In another important contribution (1960 in Arrow *et al.*), Solow explained that technical progress is incorporated into capital, and that it is necessary to take into account the age structure of capital, by constructing 'vintage models'. These articles are at the origin of an abundant literature on the mechanisms of economic growth, in both developed and underdeveloped economies.

Robert Solow has made contributions in several other fields of economic theory: macroeconomics, labour economics, natural resources and environmental economics, urban economics, employment and stabilization policies. Defining himself as an eclectic Keynesian, on the centre-left of the political field, Solow is a fierce polemicist. He led the fight against Joan Robinson and the post-Keynesian economists in the 'war of the two Cambridges' which raged in the 1960s, and which had to do with the theory of capital and growth, in particular with the existence of aggregate production functions which Solow and his colleagues postulated. In one of his contributions to the theory of capital (1963), Solow attempted to answer the critiques of the post-Keynesians by showing that the measure of physical capital has no importance. The problem is to know how the rate of return on capital is determined, and the latter depends on the nominal value and not on the real value of capital.

Solow also fought with the monetarists and, more recently, with the new classical economists, whom he accuses of making a virtue of mathematical expertise at the expense of the realist study of contemporary economic problems. Himself a skilled mathematician, Solow has nonetheless opposed the claim of several economists that it is possible to construct a social physics equipped with models valid at any time and in any place. He considers economics as a social science, inexact, and in which it is necessary to take into account institutions, social structures and history. Unlike the new classical economists, he also estimates that the state retains an important role to play to ensure full employment, growth stability and technological progress.

Main references

'The Nobel Memorial Prize in Economics 1987'. Press release, articles by E.C. Prescott and R.C.O. Matthews, and bibliography, *Scandinavian Journal of Economics*, 1988, vol. 90, 1–26.

ROBINSON Joan 1964. 'Solow on the Rate of Return', *Economic Journal*, vol. 74, 410–17.
SOLOW 1990 'My Evolution', 1992.

BLAUG 1985, 232–3.

SPENCE Michael A. (born 1943)

Michael Spence was born in Montclair, New Jersey. He gained an MA in mathematics at Oxford University in 1968 and a PhD from Harvard in 1972. An assistant professor at Harvard (1971–3) and associate professor at Stanford University (1973–5), since 1977 he has been a professor at Harvard, and dean of the Faculty of Arts and Sciences of that University since 1984. In 1981, he received the John Bates Clark Medal from the American Economic Association.

Main publications

1974. *Market Signalling: Information Transfer in Hiring and Related Screening Processes*, Cambridge, Massachusetts, Harvard University Press.
1976. 'Product Selection, Fixed Costs, and Monopolistic Competition', *Review of Economic Studies*, vol. 43, 217–35.
1977. 'Entry, Capacity, Investment and Oligopolistic Pricing', *Bell Journal of Economics*, vol. 8, 534–44.
1980. 'Notes on Advertising, Economies of Scale, and Entry Barriers', *Quarterly Journal of Economics*, vol. 95, 493–507.
1980. With Richard E. Caves and Michael E. Porter, *Competition in the Open Economy: A Model Applied to Canada*, Cambridge, Massachusetts, Harvard University Press.
1983. With Samuel Hayes and David Marks, *Competitive Structure in Investment Banking*, Cambridge, Massachusetts, Harvard University Press.
1984. 'Cost Reduction, Competition and Industry Performance', *Econometrica*, vol. 52, 101–21.

M. Spence's reputation is based on a book published very early in his career (1974), based on his PhD thesis, and which constitutes an important contribution in the new field of economics of information. Spence examined, in particular, the way the participants in any market choose each other according to attributes whose characteristics are uncertain. Some of these attributes were qualified as 'market signals'. This type of analysis was used, in particular, to examine the functioning of the labour market and its links to education.

Spence also made contributions to industrial economics and to the research on market structures, studying in particular the relations between the competitive strategies of firms and their performances. He formalized the model, put forward by Chamberlin, of the coexistence of market power and freedom of entry in an industry (1976). He showed how excess capacity may be used as a barrier (1977).

Main reference

BLAUG 1985, 234–5.

SRAFFA Piero (1898–1983)

Piero Sraffa was born in Turin, Italy. He began his studies in 1916 at the Faculty of Law of the University of Turin, interrupted them for military service, and obtained his doctorate in 1920, under the supervision of Luigi Einaudi. In 1919, he met Antonio Gramsci, to whom he would remain close until the death of the latter in 1937. During the 11 years of Gramsci's imprisonment, Sraffa created international awareness on the subject, opened for him an unlimited account in a Milan bookstore and played a key role in the preservation of his *Prison Notebooks*.

Sraffa spent time in 1921 and 1922 at the London School of Economics and was introduced to Keynes. In 1923, he was named lecturer at the University of Perugia. In 1926, he took up a chair in political economy at the University of Cagliari, where, whilst he would only teach until 1927, he retained a position *in abstentia* until the end of his life, donating his salary to the university's library. The accentuation of political repression in Italy, and in particular the persecution of the Jewish community to which he belonged, and the fact that Cambridge University, at Keynes's instigation, offered him a lectureship, led him to move to Great Britain in 1927. He remained there until his death, without, however, giving up his Italian nationality, something which led to his brief imprisonment in 1940 on the Isle of Man, from which he was freed following Keynes's intervention.

Experiencing much difficulty in teaching, he gave up this task in 1930. He was named librarian of the Marshall Library of Economics, a position he held until 1973, and assistant research director, a position created for him to supervise theses. In 1930, he was a member of the 'Circus', a group composed of, among others, Richard Kahn, James Meade and Austin and Joan Robinson, created to discuss Keynes's *Treatise on Money*. In 1939, Sraffa was elected a fellow of Trinity College. He died in Cambridge after a two-year illness.

Main publications

1920. *L'Inflazione monetaria in Italia durante et dopo la guerra*, Milan, Scuola Tipografica Salesiana.

1922. 'Italian Banking To-Day', *The Manchester Guardian Commercial, Reconstruction in Europe*, Supplement no. 11, December 7, 675–6.

1922. 'The Bank Crisis in Italy', *Economic Journal*, vol. 32, 178–97.

1925. 'Sulle relazioni fra costo e quantità prodotta', *Annali di Economia*, vol. 2, 277–328.

1926. 'The Laws of Returns under Competitive Conditions', *Economic Journal*, vol. 36, 535–50.

1927. 'The Methods of Fascism: The Case of Antonio Gramsci', *Manchester Guardian*, 24 October.

1930. 'An Alleged Correction of Ricardo', *Quarterly Journal of Economics*, vol. 44, 539–44.

1932. 'Dr. Hayek on Money and Capital', *Economic Journal*, vol. 42, 42–53; and 'Money and Capital: A Rejoinder', ibid., 249–51.

1938 (ed., with J.M. Keynes). David Hume's, *An Abstract of a Treatise on Human Nature (1740)*, Cambridge, England, Cambridge University Press.

1951. 'Introduction', in *The Works and Correspondance of David Ricardo*, vol. 1, *On the Principles of Political Economy and Taxation*, Cambridge, England, Cambridge University Press, xiii–lxii.

1951–73 (ed., with the collaboration of M.H. Dobb). *The Works and Correspondence of David Ricardo*, 11 vols, Cambridge, England, Cambridge University Press for the Royal Economic Society.

1960. *Production of Commodities by Means of Commodities: Prelude to a Critique of Economic Theory*, Cambridge, England, Cambridge University Press.

1962. 'Production of Commodities: A Comment', *Economic Journal*, vol. 72, 477–9.

1975. *Ecrits d'économie politique*, introduction and translation by Gilbert Faccarello, Paris, Economica.

1986. *Saggi* [Essays], Bologna, Il Mulino.

Very concise, Piero Sraffa's economic work has nonetheless caused much ink to flow. After a doctoral thesis (1920) and two articles in 1922 on the financial situation in Italy, which aroused the anger of the chief of government Benito Mussolini, Sraffa undertook a thorough critique of the neoclassical theory of value. Two articles on this issue (1925, 1926) ensured his scientific fame; the second is certainly one of his most quoted publications to date. In it, Sraffa criticized the logical coherence of the modern theory of value based on the symmetry of the forces determining supply and demand. Underlining the fact that increasing and decreasing returns respond to different logics, he concluded that 'as a simple way of approaching the problem of competitive value, the old and now obsolete theory which makes it dependent on the cost of production alone appears to hold its ground as the best available' (1926, p. 541). But, as modern economies are anyway characterized by the existence of monopolies, Sraffa explained why 'It is necessary, therefore, to abandon the path of free competition and turn in the opposite direction, namely, towards monopoly' (ibid., p. 542). It was in this direction that authors such as Chamberlin, Harrod, Kahn and Joan Robinson would embark, thus initiating what some called the revolution of monopolistic competition.

But Sraffa himself, from the end of the 1920s, chose an entirely different path, writing the first drafts of a book which would finally be published in 1960, based on the classical, and in particular Ricardian, vision of value and distribution. In 1930, he was assigned by the Royal Economic Society the task of editing Ricardo's works. This painstaking job ultimately required more than 20 years and produced, as a result, a masterpiece of scientific publishing. The first volume was released in 1951 and contained an important introduction which put forward a new interpretation of Ricardo's theory of value and profits. In it, Sraffa underlined the fact that 'the problem of value which interested Ricardo was how to find a measure of value which would be invariant to changes in the division of the product' (1951, p. xlviii). This issue, which was not solved to Ricardo's satisfaction, was solved by Sraffa in *Production of Commodities by Means of Commodities* (1960). The latter book, of less than a hundred pages, was subtitled *Prelude to a Critique of Economic Theory*, but Sraffa left to others the task of developing this critique. He explicitly indicated that he was taking up again in this book the 'standpoint, which is that of the old classical economists from Adam Smith to Ricardo ... submerged and forgotten since the advent of the "marginal" method' (1960, p. v). Sraffa showed that, in a capitalist economy, prices and the rate of profit are simultaneously set by the conditions of production alone. The link, necessarily antagonistic, between this profit rate and the level of wages must be determined in a way exogenous to the system, for example by the level of the bank interest rate, as suggested by Sraffa, or by the class struggle, as suggested by some of his followers.

Sraffa's brief and dense book led to a spate of articles and books. It gave birth to what some called the Sraffian revolution or the post-Ricardian current of thought, expressions for which Sraffa declined to accept responsibility. Joan Robinson and other authors of the post-Keynesian current, enthusiastic at first, ended by criticizing Sraffa for confining himself to a model of static, long-run equilibrium incompatible with the spirit of the Keynesian revolution. For others such as Eatwell, Garegnani or Kregel, Sraffa definitively demonstrated the coherence of Ricardo's and Marx's approaches to the theory of value and distribution, thus having a fatal effect on the neoclassical theory. Samuelson (1987, below), on the contrary, concluded that what he calls Sraffian economics, with the contributions of Leontief and von Neumann, to which it is close, confirms rather than denies the validity of the theory of general equilibrium perfected by Arrow and Debreu.

Main references

ARENA Richard 1990 (ed.). *Piero Sraffa trente ans après*, Paris, Presses Universitaires de France.

BHARADWAJ Krishna and SCHEFOLD Bertram 1989 (eds). *Essays on Piero Sraffa*, London, Unwin Hyman.

BLAUG Mark 1992 (ed.). *Piero Sraffa (1898–1983)*, Aldershot, Hants, Edward Elgar.

Cahiers d'économie politique 1976, no. 3 , 'Actes du colloque Sraffa'.

Cambridge Journal of Economics 1988, 'Piero Sraffa Memorial Issue', vol. 12, no. 1.

FACCARELLO G. and LAVERGNE P. de. 1977 (eds). *Une nouvelle approche en économie politique? Essais sur Sraffa*, Paris, Economica.

HODGSON Geoffrey M. 1991. *After Marx and Sraffa: Essays in Political Economy*, New York, St Martin's Press.

POTIER Jean-Pierre 1991. *Piero Sraffa, Unorthodox Economist (1898–1983): A Biographical Essay*, London, Routledge.

RONCAGLIA Alessandro 1975. *Sraffa e la teoria dei prezzi*, Rome, Gius. Laterza & Figli Spa; Engl. transl. 1978, *Sraffa and the Theory of Prices*, Chichester, John Wiley & Sons.

SAMUELSON P.A. 1987. 'Sraffian Economics', *New Palgrave*, vol. 4, 452–60.

STEEDMAN Ian 1977. *Marx After Sraffa*, London, NLB.

STEEDMAN Ian 1989 (ed.). *Sraffian Economics*, 2 vols, Aldershot, Hants, Edward Elgar.

WOODS John E. 1990. *The Production of Commodities: An Introduction to Sraffa*, London, Macmillan.

ARESTIS and SAWYER 1992, 536–45. BLAUG 1985, 236–8. *New Palgrave* 1987, vol. 4, 445–52. SILLS 1979, 736–9. SHACKLETON and LOCKSLEY 1981, 240–56.

STEINDL Josef (1912–1993)

Josef Steindl was born in Vienna, where he studied economics at the Business School, and received his doctorate in 1935. He worked at the Austrian Institute of Economic Research from 1935 to 1938, when he was dismissed as a result of the Nazi takeover and emigrated to England. He was a lecturer at Balliol College, Oxford (1938–41) and then a researcher at the Oxford Institute of Statistics (1941–50), where he was in close contact with Michal Kalecki. Returning to Austria, he worked at the Austrian Institute of Economic Research from 1950 until his retirement in 1978. The University of Vienna awarded him an honorary professorship in 1970. Steindl was visiting professor at Stanford University in 1974–5. In 1987, an international conference on his work was held in Trieste, Italy.

Main publications

1945. *Small and Big Business: Economic Problems of the Size of Firms*, Oxford, Basil Blackwell.

1952. *Maturity and Stagnation in American Capitalism*, Oxford, Basil Blackwell; New York, Monthly Review Press, 1976.

1964. 'On Maturity in Capitalist Economy', in *Problems of Economic Dynamics and Planning: Essays in Honour of Michal Kalecki*, Oxford, Pergamon Press, 423–32.

1965. *Random Processes and the Growth of Firms: A Study of the Pareto Law*, London, Charles Griffin; New York, Hafner.

1979. 'Stagnation Theory and Stagnation Policy', *Cambridge Journal of Economics*, vol. 3, 1–14.

1984. 'Reflections on the Present State of Economics', *Quarterly Review, Banca Nazionale del Lavoro*, no. 148, 3–14; in Kregel 1988, 97–108.
1989. 'From Stagnation in the 1930s to Slow Growth in the 1970s', in Maxine Berg (ed.), *Political Economy in the Twentieth Century*, London, Philip Allan; Savage, Maryland, Barnes & Noble, 97–115.
1990. *Economic Papers, 1941–88*, London, Macmillan; New York, St Martin's Press.

Josef Steindl was raised in the tradition of the Austrian School and remained, until the end of his life, grateful to the leaders of that current of thought, such as Haberler, Hayek and Mises, who helped him and other Austrian economists to find jobs in other countries after the *Anschluss* of 1938. But he soon moved very far from the political as well as theoretical positions of those ultra-liberal economists: under, first, the influence of Keynes's *General Theory*, which he read and discussed as soon as it was published, and which led to a radical reorientation of his work; and second, probably the main influence on his research, that of Michal Kalecki, with whom he worked and discussed endlessly in Oxford between 1940 and 1945; and finally, there was the influence of Marx. While he criticized Marxists for their exegesis of their master's work and their exclusive concentration on value theory, he praised the historical perspective of Marx and his perception of history as an endogenous process.

Until the end of his career, Steindl (whose main papers were collected in 1990) was interested in the theory of the firm, in oligopoly and in concentration. He also wrote, in the last half of his career, on education and technology. The study of the size, profitability, competitiveness and growth of firms, in particular, led to two original books (1945, 1965). Steindl argued for the application of a stochastic approach in economics, 'where even the behaviour of aggregates is hard to approximate by a deterministic model' (1965, p. 5).

It is in the field of business cycle and growth theory that Steindl made his most lasting contributions and wrote his major book (1952; see also 1964, 1979, 1989). When he left Oxford, Kalecki suggested to Steindl that he try to explain why capitalist growth collapsed in the 1930s. Steindl looked for an explanation of the world depression by examining the behaviour of firms, oligopoly and, in particular, their link with excess capacity, rates of profit and the movements of investment. This led him to an original approach. According to this view, the roots of the Great Depression are to be found in long-run and secular processes, and in particular in the movement of industrial concentration and the rise of oligopolies at the end of the nineteenth century. This rise is associated with a growth in the profit margins of oligopolistic firms, but also with the diminishing flexibility of these margins, the emergence and persistence of overcapacity. According to Steindl, the amount of investment is greatly influenced by the degree of utilization. The end result of this process is the weakening of the incentive to invest, a resultant fall in effective demand and a decline in the rate of accumulation. Therefore, according to Steindl, this is an endogenous and cumulative process, not explicable by such exogenous factors as population growth, technical innovations or wars. This represents, in his words, following Hansen, the 'maturity' of capitalism, characterized by the exhaustion of growth potentialities and the tendency to stagnation which were the profound causes of the depression of the 1930s. These phenomena were also aggravated by financial aspects. The tremendous development of capital markets, and the power of finance, at first a lever of growth, finally became an additional factor of stagnation.

When it appeared in 1952, in a context of growth and near full employment, Steindl's book went unnoticed, except by Baran and Sweezy, who measured its importance and used some of its theses in their analysis of monopoly capital. The return of stagnation in the 1970s gave new relevance to Steindl's thesis. Steindl himself endeavoured to develop and revise some of his theses to account for the postwar developments because 'new explanations were required in the new situation, part of which was the change in economic policy of the early 1970s' (1989, p. 101).

Main references

DUTT Amitava Krishna. 1990. *Growth, Distribution, and Uneven Development*, New York, Cambridge University Press.
ROTHSCHILD Kurt W. 1994. 'Josef Steindl: 1912–1993', *Economic Journal*, vol. 104, 131–7.
STEINDL 1984.

ARESTIS and SAWYER 1992, 549–55. *New Palgrave* 1987, vol. 4, 494.

STIGLER George J. (1911–1991)

George Stigler was born in Renton, Washington. He obtained an MBA at Northwestern University (1932) and a PhD at the University of Chicago (1938). He was assistant professor at Iowa State University (1936–8), assistant, associate and full professor at the University of Minnesota (1938–46), professor at Brown University (1946–7), at Columbia University (1947–58) and at the University of Chicago (1958–81), where he became emeritus professor in 1981. He did research at the National Bureau of Economic Research from 1941 to 1976 and was editor of the *Journal of Political Economy* from 1973 until his death. President of the American Economic Association in 1964, he received the Nobel Memorial Prize in Economics in 1982. He held various functions on public bodies, including that of president of the Task Force on Competition and Productivity established by President Nixon in 1969. He was president of the Mount Pèlerin Society in 1977–8.

Main publications

1941. *Production and Distribution Theories*, New York, Macmillan.
1942. *The Theory of Competitive Price*, New York, Macmillan.
1946. *The Theory of Price*, New York, Macmillan.
1947. *Domestic Servants in the United States*, New York, National Bureau of Economic Research.
1947. *Trends in Output and Employment*, New York, National Bureau of Economic Research.
1949. *Five Lectures on Economic Problems*, New York, Longmans, Green Co.
1950. *Employment and Compensation in Education*, New York, National Bureau of Economic Research.
1954. 'The Early History of Empirical Studies of Consumer Behavior', *Journal of Political Economy*, vol. 62, 95–113.
1955. 'The Nature and Role of Originality in Scientific Progress', *Economica*, vol. 22, 293–302.
1956. *Trends in Employment in the Service Industries*, Princeton University Press.
1957. With David Blank, *Supply and Demand for Scientific Personnel*, Princeton University Press.
1961. 'The Economics of Information', *Journal of Political Economy*, vol. 69, 213–25.
1963. *Capital and the Rate of Return in Manufacturing Industries*, Princeton University Press.
1963. *The Intellectual and the Market Place and other Essays*, Glencoe, Illinois, Free Press; London, Collier-Macmillan; rev. augm. edn 1984, Cambridge, Massachusetts, Harvard University Press.
1965. *Essays in the History of Economics*, University of Chicago Press.
1965. 'The Economist and the State', *American Economic Review*, vol. 55, 1–18 [presidential address to the American Economic Association].
1968. *The Organization of Industry*, Homewood, Illinois, Richard D. Irwin.
1970. With James K. Kindahl, *The Behavior of Industrial Prices*, New York, National Bureau of Economic Research.
1975. *The Citizen and the State: Essays on Regulation*, University of Chicago Press.
1982. *The Economist as Preacher and other Essays*, University of Chicago Press; Oxford, Basil Blackwell.
1983. 'The Process and Progress of Economics', in *Les prix Nobel en 1982*, Stockholm, Nobel Foundation; *Journal of Political Economy*, vol. 91, 529–45.
1984. 'Economics: The Imperial Science', *Scandinavian Journal of Economics*, vol. 86, 301–13.
1986. 'My Evolution as an Economist', in Breit and Spencer 1986, 93–112.
1986. *The Essence of Stigler*, edited by Kurt R. Leube and Thomas Gale Moore, Stanford, California, Hoover Institution Press.
1988 (ed.). *Chicago Studies in Political Economy*, University of Chicago Press.
1988. *Memoirs of an Unregulated Economist*, New York, Basic Books.

Stigler's doctoral thesis (1941) was a significant contribution to the history of economic thought, which is for him an essential complement of economic research. In it, he examined the emergence of the neoclassical theory of value and distribution. There can already be found clearly indicated some elements of the approach which Stigler would apply in numerous other publications in this area (see in particular the articles collected in 1965 and 1982). To ensure his fame, it is not enough that an economist should find a new idea (1955). It is necessary that he be able to convince his contemporaries of the importance of this idea. Stigler was also convinced that one cannot establish, between economic history, another field to which he contributed, and the history of economic ideas, any simple and univocal relation of cause and effect. For him, there is an internal logic to the development of theories.

The Nobel Memorial Prize was awarded to him 'for his seminal studies of industrial structures, functioning of markets and causes and effects of public regulation' (*SJE* 1983, p. 61). A follower of the neoclassical theory of prices, to which he devoted widely circulated books (1942, 1946), Stigler was not a pure theorist, concerned with the development and sophistication of abstract models. In the Chicago tradition and in that of the National Bureau of Economic Research, with which he was associated throughout his career, he was always interested in empirical research and in the application of theory to the understanding of reality (1947, 1950, 1956, 1957, 1970). This was how he looked into the structures of markets, the nature and the functioning of enterprises and the determination of prices in situations of monopoly and oligopoly, in which he showed himself to be very critical of the traditional approaches inspired by Chamberlin's works. His numerous works in this field (of which the main ones were gathered together in 1968) are at the departure point of the development of industrial economics, which Stigler himself sees as applied microeconomics rather than as an autonomous branch of economic theory.

The article on the economics of information which he published in 1961 also had an important influence, in particular on the evolution of macroeconomics and labour economics. Stigler developed the thesis according to which the acquiring of information is a costly process, to which one must apply the same rules of analysis in terms of optimization as for other economic activities. The rational agent devotes himself to the research of additional information as long as the marginal revenue of this activity exceeds its marginal cost. Stigler played an important role in the generalization of the neoclassical problematics based on the rationality of the agent to diverse domains of activity, for example to the legal and political processes, generalizations which, moreover, are associated in great part with the University of Chicago. He himself defined economics as an 'imperial science' (1984). His work in the domain of regulation (1975, 1982) was situated in this perspective. In it, he attacked the idea according to which state regulations aim at correcting market imperfections in the interest of the public. He claimed, on the contrary, that these interventions result from the collusion between the interests of pressure groups and the bureaucratic apparatus. For this reason, Stigler was one of the most fervent partisans of deregulation.

Main references

'The Nobel Memorial Prize in Economics 1982'. Official announcement, articles by Jacob Mincer and Richard Schmalensee, and bibliography, *Scandinavian Journal of Economics*, 1983, vol. 85, 61–93.

COASE Ronald H. 1982. 'George J. Stigler: An Appreciation', *Regulation*, vol. 6, 21–4.
RIMA Ingrid H. 1983. 'George J. Stigler as a Historian of Economic Thought', in Warren J. Samuels (ed.), *Research in the History of Economic Thought and Methodology*, vol. 1, *The Craft of the Historian of Economic Thought*, Greenwich, Connecticut and London, JAI Press, 271–89.
STIGLER 1986 'My Evolution', 1988, *Memoirs*.

BLAUG 1985, 239–41. *New Palgrave* 1987, vol. 4, 498–500.

STIGLITZ Joseph E. (born 1943)

Joseph Stiglitz was born in Gary, Indiana, in the United States. He obtained a PhD from the Massachusetts Institute of Technology in 1966. He was assistant professor at MIT (1966–7), associate professor (1968–70), then professor (1970–74) at Yale University, professor at Stanford University (1974–6), at the University of Oxford (1976–9), at Princeton University (1979–88) and, from 1988, again at Stanford. He received the John Bates Clark Medal from the American Economic Association in 1979. He was editor of the *Journal of Economic Perspectives* until 1993 and co-editor of the *American Economic Review* (1968–76), the *Review of Economic Studies* (1968–76) and the *Journal of Economic Theory* (1968–73). He was named member of President Clinton's Council of Economic Advisers in 1994.

Main publications

1966 (ed.). *The Collected Scientific Papers of Paul A. Samuelson*, vols 1 and 2, Cambridge, Massachusetts, MIT Press.
1969 (ed., with Hirofumi Uzawa). *Readings in the Modern Theory of Economic Growth*, Cambridge, Massachusetts, MIT Press.
1976. With S.J. Grossman, 'Information and Competitive Price Systems', *American Economic Review*, vol. 66, *Papers and Proceedings*, 246–53.
1980. With Anthony B. Atkinson, *Lectures on Public Economics*, Maidenhead, Berkshire, McGraw-Hill.
1981. With David M.G. Newbery, *The Theory of Commodity Price Stabilization: A Study in the Economics of Risk*, Oxford, Clarendon Press; New York, Oxford University Press.
1981. With Andrew Weiss, 'Credit Rationing in Markets with Imperfect Information', *American Economic Review*, vol. 71, 393–410.
1983. With Costas Azariadis, 'Implicit Contracts and Fixed-Price Equilibria', *Quarterly Journal of Economics*, vol. 98, supplement, 1–22.
1983. With Peter Neary, 'Toward a Reconstruction of Keynesian Economics: Expectations and Constrained Equilibria', *Quarterly Journal of Economics*, vol. 98, supplement, 199–227.
1984. 'Price Rigidities and Market Structure', *American Economic Review*, vol. 74, 350–56.
1984. With Carl Shapiro, 'Equilibrium Unemployment as a Worker-Discipline Device', *American Economic Review*, vol. 74, 433–44.
1985. 'Information and Economic Analysis: A Perspective', *Economic Journal*, vol. 95, supplement, 21–41.
1986. *Economics of the Public Sector*, New York, W.W. Norton.
1986 (ed., with G. Frank Mathewson). *New Developments in the Analysis of Market Structure*, London, Macmillan; Cambridge, Massachusetts, MIT Press.

1987. 'The Causes and Consequences of the Dependence of Quality on Price', *Journal of Economic Literature*, vol. 25, 1–48.
1987. With B. Greenwald, 'Keynesian, New Keynesian and New Classical Economics', *Oxford Economic Papers*, vol. 37, 119–32.

The editor, while very young, of the first two volumes of Paul Samuelson's *Collected Scientific Papers* (1966), Joseph Stiglitz has published more than 250 articles and book chapters in many domains, from macroeconomics and the theory of growth and capital to agriculture economics, to, among others, insurance, taxation, public finance and the theory of finance, industrial organization and natural resource economics.

However, it is in information economics and the analysis of market imperfections that Stiglitz has made his most significant contributions. In fact, in all of his works, he never ceases to draw attention to the fact that imperfections in both the market and the circulation of information must force a considerable transformation of traditional economic analysis if it is to take account of the concrete phenomena characterizing contemporary economies, such as involuntary unemployment or credit rationing. Critical of both the new classical macroeconomics and the fix-price models of the disequilibrium theorists, Stiglitz is one of the main architects of the new Keynesian economics, which he defined as an attempt to adapt microtheory to macrotheory (1987 *OEP*, p. 120), while the other currents try to adapt macrotheory to an unreal Walrasian microtheory: 'The New Keynesian Economics begins with Keynes' basic insights. But it recognizes the need for a more radical departure from the neoclassical framework, and for a much deeper study of the consequences of imperfections in capital markets, imperfections which can be explained by the costs of information' (ibid., p. 123).

Main reference

BLAUG 1985, 242–3.

STONE John Richard Nicholas (1913–1991)

Born in London, Richard Stone studied at Cambridge University, first law, then economics (BA in 1935, MA in 1938) and had Colin Clark as a teacher. He first worked in the City and, from 1940, at the Central Statistical Office, where, at J.M. Keynes's instigation, he led, with J. Meade, for the British Cabinet, the implementation of the system of national economic accounts. From 1945 to 1955 he was director of the department of applied economics created at Cambridge on Keynes's initiative. From 1955 until he retired in 1980, he was professor of finance and accounting at Cambridge University. He was the president of a United Nations Committee on National Accounts in

1945–6, of the Econometric Society in 1955 and of the Royal Economic Society in 1978–80. Knighted in 1978, Sir Richard received the Nobel Memorial Prize in Economics in 1984.

Main publications

1938. With W.M. Stone, 'The Marginal Propensity to Consume and the Multiplier', *Review of Economic Studies*, vol. 6, 1–24.
1941. With J.E. Meade, 'The Construction of Tables of National Income, Savings and Investment', *Economic Journal*, vol. 51, 216–31.
1944. With J. E. Meade, *National Income and Expenditure*, London, Oxford University Press.
1945. 'The Analysis of Market Demand', *Journal of the Royal Statistical Society*, vol. 108, 1–98.
1947. 'Definition and Measurement of the National Income and Related Totals', appendix to *Measurement of National Income and Construction of Social Accounts*, Geneva. United Nations.
1954. 'Linear Expenditure Systems and Demand Analysis: An Application to the Pattern of British Demand', *Economic Journal*, vol. 64, 511–27.
1954–66. With D.A. Rowe *et al.*, *The Measurement of Consumers' Expenditure and Behaviour in the United Kingdom, 1920–1938*, vol. 1, 1954; vol. 2, 1966, Cambridge, England, Cambridge University Press.
1956. *Quantity and Price Indexes in National Accounts*, Paris, OECD.
1957. With D.A. Rowe, 'The Market Demand for Durable Goods', *Econometrica*, vol. 25, 423–43.
1962. With Alan Brown, *A Computable Model of Economic Growth*, London, Chapman & Hall.
1964. 'Private Saving in Britain, Past, Present and Future', *Manchester School of Economic and Social Studies*, vol. 32, 79–112.
1964. *The Model in its Environment*, London, Chapman & Hall.
1970. *Mathematical Models of the Economy and Other Essays*, London, Chapman & Hall.
1971. *Demographic Accounting and Model Building*, Paris, OECD.
1978 (ed.). *Econometric Contributions to Public Policy*, London, Macmillan.
1978. 'Keynes, Political Arithmetic and Econometrics', *Proceedings of the British Academy*, vol. 64, 55–92.
1985. 'The Accounts of Society', Nobel Memorial Lecture, in *Les Prix Nobel 1984*, Stockholm, Almqvist and Wiksell; in *Journal of Applied Economics*, 1986, vol. 1, 5–28.

After some statistical studies of the economic situation, published, some jointly with his spouse, in the second half of the 1930s, R. Stone focused his works on two main fields: national accounts and consumption analysis.

The development, with Meade (1941, 1944), of the conceptual framework and the laborious work on statistical material permitted the calculation of the first evaluations of production and demand, and the placing of the war budget in its economic context. In this domain, where works were under way in other countries, this progress constituted a decisive impetus for the development of national accounts: Stone largely contributed to this development after the war, as much through his participation in work carried out in the context of the League of Nations, then of the United Nations (1947) and of the Organization for European Economic Cooperation (1956 and OECD, *Standardised System of National Accounting*, Paris, 1952) as through countless conferences, colloquia and seminars. One of his principal objectives was to make appear as income for a category of agents what is expenditure for another; and vice versa. One of his main lines of research, in the 1950s, was to systematize this approach with the help of a social accounting matrix, a double-entry table, of the same structure as Leontief's input–output matrix, but broader (and therefore meant to include it) since it had to make an inventory of all the transactions and payments among all the categories of agents. But already the frameworks within which the national accountants of more and more countries were implementing or improving their accounts were being established.

At the same time, Stone developed the analysis of the consumption demand function: he did this, by product or categories of product, based on the consideration of the determinants of consumption demand and on the econometric treatment of important statistical material (1945, 1954, 1954–66). But – at once an illustration of the depreciation of work on data relative to theoretical development and of the loss of influence of the English School in relation to the new American School – Modigliani's hypotheses on the life cycle and Friedman's on permanent income were to occupy the forefront of the scene. This did not prevent Stone from carrying on with his work on the consumption of durable goods and on savings (1957, 1964 'Private').

Stone also worked on the construction of a large growth model, integrating interindustrial relations, for Great Britain (1962, 1964 *The Model*), on the enlarging of national accounts to encompass demographic and social domains (1971, 1985) and on education economics. However, as the Royal Swedish Academy of Sciences emphasized in 1984, 'it is his initiative and pioneering research in regard to national accounts systems which represent Stone's central contribution in the economic sciences' (*SJE* 1985, p. 3).

Main references

'The Nobel Memorial Prize in Economics 1984'. Press release, article by Leif Johansen and bibliography, *Swedish Journal of Economics*, 1985, vol. 87, 1–43.

New Palgrave 1987, vol. 4, 509–12.

SWEEZY Paul Marlor (born 1910)

Born in New York, Paul Sweezy studied at Harvard, where he obtained a BA in 1931 and a PhD in 1937, having, in between, spent a year at the London School of Economics (1932–3). A lecturer, then assistant professor at Harvard (1934–42), he worked for different agencies of the New Deal; he was posted during the Second World War to the Office of Strategic Services. In 1949, he founded, with Leo Huberman, the *Monthly Review*, of which he was the co-editor, first with Huberman, then, after the death of the latter in 1968, with Harry Magdoff.

Main publications

1938. *Monopoly and Competition in the English Coal Trade, 1550–1850*, Cambridge, Massachusetts, Harvard University Press.
1942. *The Theory of Capitalist Development: Principles of Marxian Political Economy*, New York, Oxford University Press.
1948. *Socialism*, New York, McGraw-Hill.
1953. *The Present As History: Essays and Reviews on Capitalism and Socialism*, New York, Monthly Review Press.
1960. With Leo Huberman, *Cuba: Anatomy of a Revolution*, New York, Monthly Review Press.
1965. With Leo Huberman, *Paul Baran: A Collective Portrait*, New York, Monthly Review Press.
1966. With Paul A. Baran, *Monopoly Capital: An Essay on the American Economic and Social Order*, New York, Monthly Review Press.
1969. With Leo Huberman, *Socialism in Cuba*, New York, Monthly Review Press.
1970. With Charles Bettelheim, *Lettres sur quelques problèmes actuels du socialisme*, Paris, François Maspero; Engl. transl. 1971, *On the Transition to Socialism*, New York, Monthly Review Press.
1972. *Modern Capitalism and Other Essays*, New York, Monthly Review Press.
1972. With Harry Magdoff, *The Dynamics of Modern Capitalism*, New York, Monthly Review Press.
1977. With Harry Magdoff, *The End of Prosperity: The American Economy in the 1970s*, New York, Monthly Review Press.
1981. *Post-Revolutionary Society: Essays*, New York, Monthly Review Press.
1987. With Harry Magdoff, *Stagnation and the Financial Explosion*, New York, Monthly Review Press.
1988. With Harry Magdoff, *The Irreversible Crisis*, New York, Monthly Review Press.

After his involvement in the New Deal, P. Sweezy chose very early the main axes of his thinking and work: the critical analysis of capitalism, activism in favour of socialism, historical analysis and Marxism (1938, 1942, 1948). Such were and are the main themes of the editorial policy of *Monthly Review*, an independent socialist magazine, and of the publishing house constituted around it, to which he devoted the bulk of his life and intellectual activity. Prosecuted in 1953 in the context of the procedures initiated by senator McCarthy, sentenced in a judgement finally repealed in 1957 by the Supreme Court, Sweezy remained a witness, and often an advocate, of the construction of socialism (1960, 1969); he was convinced that a reorganization on the basis of the market mechanisms could only lead back to capitalism (1970), and was led to believe that, after the October socialist revolution, a class society of a new type was set in place at the beginning of the Stalinist era (1981).

He also continued working on the Marxist analysis of capitalism. In this field, his major book was written with Baran and published after the latter died (1966): whereas in competitive capitalism the law identified by Marx was that of the tendency of the rate of profit to decrease, in monopoly capitalism the long-term law is, according to Baran and Sweezy, that of an increase in the surplus. In spite of the efforts to sell, the waste, the military spending, the swelling of the financial sector, this tendency is at the roots of stagnation and crisis. These conclusions went against the then dominant Keynesian certainties.

The 1970s and 1980s provided an opportunity to follow the stages and avatars of this crisis: the end of prosperity, the worsening of recession with, in particular, its financial turbulence, and the vigorous return to liberalism (1977, 1987, 1988).

Main references

LEBOWITZ Michael A. 1990. 'Paul M. Sweezy', in Berg 1990, 131–61.

ARESTIS and SAWYER 1992, 562–70. *New Palgrave* 1987, vol. 4, 580–2.

TARSHIS Lorie (1911–1993)

Lorie Tarshis was born in Toronto, Canada. He obtained a BA in commerce at the University of Toronto in 1932, then continued his studies at Cambridge, England, where he obtained an MA in 1938 and a PhD in 1939. Instructor (1936–9) and assistant professor (1942–6) at Tufts University, Massachusetts, he was in-between Carnegie Fellow at the National Bureau of Economic Research. He was then successively assistant, associate and full professor at Stanford University (1946–71), professor at the University of Toronto (1971–8), director of research at the Ontario Economic Council (1978–80) before returning to teaching at York University in 1980, where he remained until 1990. Stanford University and the University of Toronto both conferred on him the rank of emeritus professor.

Main publications

1938. 'Real Wages in the United States and Great Britain', *Canadian Journal of Economics and Political Science*, vol. 4, 362–76.
1938. With R.V. Gilbert *et al.*, *An Economic Program for American Democracy*, New York, Vanguard Press.
1939. 'Changes in Real and Money Wages', *Economic Journal*, vol. 49, 150–54.
1947. *The Elements of Economics*, Boston, Houghton Mifflin.
1948. 'An Exposition of Keynesian Economics', *American Economic Review*, vol. 38, *Papers and Proceedings*, 261–72.
1951. With T. Scitovsky and E.S. Shaw, *Mobilizing Resources for War: The Economic Alternatives*, New York, McGraw-Hill.
1955. *International Economics*, New York, John Wiley.
1967. *Modern Economics: An Introduction*, Boston, Houghton Mifflin.
1972 (ed., with Fritz Machlup and Walter S. Salant). *International Mobility and Movement of Capital*, New York, Columbia University Press.
1978. 'Keynes as seen by his Students in the 1930s', in D. Patinkin and J. Clark Leith (eds), *Keynes, Cambridge, and the General Theory*, University of Toronto Press; London, Macmillan, 59–64.
1984. *World Economy in Crisis: Unemployment, Inflation and International Debt*, Toronto, James Lorimer.
1987. 'Keynesian Revolution', *New Palgrave*, vol. 3, 47–50.

Lorie Tarshis had the privilege of attending the classes given by John Maynard Keynes between October 1932 and December 1935, during the elaboration of *The General Theory*: 'What Keynes supplied was the excitement of a new beginning as the residue of Classical economics was swept away. He supplied too that measure of impatience the situation called for and the opportunity for all of us to be a part of a great adventure' (1987, p. 50). Although a disciple of Keynes since that time, he cannot be linked to any of the currents claiming the latter as their authority, towards which he, moreover, revealed himself capable of being critical. It is to Tarshis that we owe, in particular, the analysis of the links between the movements of real and money wages which contradicts the affirmation put forward by Keynes of the inverse relation of these two magnitudes (1938 *CJE*, 1939). Keynes modified his position, following the articles cited by Tarshis and another by Dunlop (see Keynes 1939).

Co-author with a group of American economists of the first call to implement Keynesian policies in the United States (1938), Tarshis is also the author of one of the first openly Keynesian textbooks (1947). He was also one of the first to become interested in what is called the microeconomic foundations of Keynesian theory. Convinced, furthermore, that 'the level of prosperity, the stability of prices and the state of international economy are inextricably bound together' (1984, p. 112), Tarshis made several contributions to the study of international economics (1955, 1972).

Main references

COHEN J. and HARCOURT G.C. 1986 (eds). *International Monetary Problems and Supply-Side Economics: Essays in Honour of Lorie Tarshis*, London, Macmillan.

HARCOURT G.C. 1982. 'An Early Post Keynesian: Lorie Tarshis (or: Tarshis on Tarshis by Harcourt)', *Journal of Post Keynesian Economics*, vol. 4, 609–19.

KEYNES John Maynard 1939. 'Relative Movements of Real Wages and Output', *Economic Journal*, vol. 49, 34–51.

ARESTIS and SAWYER 1992, 571–8. *New Palgrave* 1987, vol. 4, 588–9.

TINBERGEN Jan (1903–1994)

Born in The Hague, Jan Tinbergen studied physics at the University of Leiden (1922–6); a member of the Dutch Labour Party Youth Organization, he refused to undertake military service and had to work first in a jail's administration. In 1929, he obtained, at Leiden, a doctorate in physics with a thesis on 'Minimum Problems in Physics and Economics'; he was then recruited to work on business cycles by the Dutch Central Statistical Bureau Office, where he remained (with the exception of two years spent in the League of Nations, 1936–8) until 1945. He taught statistics at the University of Amsterdam from 1931; and from 1933 until 1955 he was a part-time professor at the Netherlands School of Economics in Rotterdam.

In 1945, he was named director of the new Central Planning Bureau in The Hague, a position he would occupy until 1955. After a year in Harvard, he was, until 1973, a full-time professor at the Netherlands School of Economics, which has now become Erasmus University. He was adviser to numerous developing countries, as well as to the Organization for European Cooperation and Development, to the World Bank and to United Nations agencies. From 1966 to 1975 he chaired the United Nations Committee on Development Planning. From 1973 to 1975 he was professor of international cooperation at the University of Leiden.

After many other distinctions, he was the first – jointly with Ragnar Frisch – to receive, in 1969, the Nobel Memorial Prize in Economics.

Main publications

1929. *Minimumproblemen in de natuurkunde en de ekonomie* [Minimum problems in physics and economics], Amsterdam, J.H. Paris.
1935. 'Annual Survey: Suggestions on Quantitative Business Cycle Theory', *Econometrica*, vol. 3, 241–308.
1936. 'Kan hier te lande, al dan niet na Overheidsingrijpen, een verbetering van de binnenlandse conjuctuur intreden, ook zonder verbeteing van onze exportpositie?', in *Prae-adviezen voor de Vereeniging voor de Staathuishoudkunde en de Statistiek*, 's-Gravenhage, 1936, 62–108; Engl. transl. 1959, 'An economic policy for 1936', in Tinbergen 1959, 37–84.
1939. *Statistical Testing of Business-Cycle Theories*, vol. 1 *A Method and its Application to Investment Activity*; vol. 2 *Business Cycles in the United States of America, 1919–32*, Geneva, League of Nations.
1942. 'Zur Theorie der Langnistigen Wirtschaftsentwicklung', *Weltwirtschaftliches Archiv*, vol. 55, 511–49; Engl. transl., 'On the Theory of Trend Movements', in Tinbergen 1959, 182–221.
1945. *International Economic Cooperation*, Amsterdam, Elsevier; revised edn 1954, *International Economic Integration*, Amsterdam, Elsevier.
1951. *Business Cycles in the United Kingdom, 1870–1914*, Amsterdam, North-Holland.
1951. *Econometrics*, London, George Allen & Unwin.
1952. *On the Theory of Economic Policy*, Amsterdam, North-Holland.
1954. *Centralization and Decentralization in Economic Policy*, Amsterdam, North-Holland.
1956. *Economic Policy: Principles and Design*, Amsterdam, North-Holland.
1958. *The Design of Development*, Baltimore, Johns Hopkins.
1959. *Selected Papers*, edited by L.H. Klaassen, L.M. Koyck and H.J. Witteveen, Amsterdam, North-Holland.
1962. *Shaping the World Economy: Suggestions for an International Economic Policy*, New York, Twentieth Century Fund.
1962. With Hendricus Cornelis Bos, *Mathematical Models of Economic Growth*, New York, McGraw-Hill.
1964. *Central Planning*, New Haven, Connecticut, Yale University Press.
1965. With Hendricus Cornelis Bos, *Econometric Models of Education*, Paris, OECD.
1967. *Development Planning*, New York, McGraw-Hill.
1972. *Politique économique et optimum social*, Paris, Economica.
1972. With Stefan Jensen and Barry Hake, *Possible Futures of European Education: Numerical and System's Forecasts*, The Hague, Martinus Nijhoff.
1975. *Income Distribution Analysis and Policies*, Amsterdam, Elsevier.
1976 (ed., with Anthony J. Dolman and Jan Van Ettinger). *Reshaping the International Order: A Report to the Club of Rome*, New York, E.P. Dutton.
1979. 'Recollections of Professional Experiences', *Quarterly Review, Banca Nazionale del Lavoro*, no. 131, 331–60; in Kregel 1988, 67–95.
1985. *Production, Income and Welfare: The Search for An Optimal Social Order*, Lincoln, University of Nebraska Press.
1990. *World Security and Equity*, Aldershot, Hants, Edward Elgar.
1992. 'Solving the Most Urgent Problems First', in Szenberg 1992, 275–82.

J. Tinbergen's work lends itself rather well to a presentation by period, but one should not forget its very deep unity. First, Tinbergen was not the man of any school and was attracted neither by academic debates nor by formal sophistications. He attached importance to observation of facts and to quantification (therefore to measurement), to formalization and to theoretical development (conditions of rigorous empirical work) and to the capacity to inform decision and action. And his scientific rigour was always prompted by the ideal of a less unequal and, if possible, better world.

In the 1930s and during the Second World War, he asserted himself as an econometrician, participating with Frisch in the creation of the Econometric Society. After work on the cycles in naval construction, he endeavoured to formalize the overall dynamics of the Dutch economy, with the intention of bringing out the main elements of a full employment policy (1936). He did this with a 24-equation model, in the context of which he extracted a first draft of the future Phillips curve; he did not find a satisfying verification of the acceleration principle but, agreeing with Kalecki, found a relation between profit and investment. One can therefore consider that, simultaneously with Keynes, Tinbergen was one of the founders of modern macroeconomics. It should also be pointed out that a part of that period's works, published in Dutch, was only to become available to the English-speaking economic community at the time of their publication in English in the 1959 book.

His work at the League of Nations, parallel with Haberler's but in the context of quantification, carried further the concern with formalization, with, for business cycle analysis, a model of 48 equations, which was to permit the bringing out of the explanatory weight of the different variables (1939). This process was severely criticized by Keynes (1939) and gave rise to a debate in which the principal founders of applied econometrics participated. Tinbergen continued his work on Great Britain (1951 *Business*) and broadened it to the study of long cycles (1942). From 1945, Tinbergen's new responsibilities led him to focus his work on economic policy (1952, 1954, 1956), first in the perspective of Dutch reconstruction, then in that of growth policy. In the tradition of the Swedish economists and of Frisch, he was one of the first theorists of economic policy. He developed a model of the Dutch economy (with 48 equations) whose quality would reveal itself both in forecasting and in the choice of economic policy. Against the coexistence of juxtaposed policies each aiming at an objective, he advocated a unique policy striving towards a range of objectives. He showed that, to be efficient, such a policy must give itself as many means (for example, taxation, the exchange rate or public spending) as it gives itself objectives (for example, full employment, price stability or equilibrium of the balance of payments). More generally, he considered that it is the government's responsibility to express objectives of social welfare (full employment, growth and fair distribution of wealth) and that those can be reached, in a free market economy, thanks to a level (which can be high) of public intervention (public sector, taxation, public investment and planning). This was the postwar social-democrat policy model, very close to Keynesian policies, and which would come up against the same limits and would sustain the same attacks.

From 1955, Tinbergen worked mainly on development issues. His experience of planning led him to suggest more simple and more robust methods, taking into account the nature of the problems and the means of each country (1958, 1967). In particular, he advocated the use of simplified interindustrial tables, but distinguishing the products which are the objects of foreign trade from the others. He pleaded for help from rich countries for developing countries, for the opening of industrialized countries to the products of these countries and, more broadly, for a new international order (1962 *Shaping*, 1976). He was also led to put more and more emphasis on problems of training and education (1965, 1972 *Possible Futures*).

Finally, Tinbergen took up, deepened and tied together the fundamental themes of his thinking (1975, 1985, 1990): how to reconcile equity, which implies a limitation of unequalities, with economic efficiency, which rests on income differentiation, or social welfare and individual happiness; how to hierarchize objectives and take emergencies into account; and how to do this, not only on the level of the national collectivity, but on a world scale.

It was 'for having developed and applied dynamic models for the analysis of economic processes' (*SJE* 1969, p. 300) that Tinbergen received, with Frisch, the first Nobel Memorial Prize in Economic Science. At the time, B. Hansen emphasized that Tinbergen would also have been deserving the Nobel Peace Prize (ibid., p. 336).

Main references

'The First Nobel Prize in Economics'. Official announcement and article by Bent Hansen, *Swedish Journal of Economics*, 1969, vol. 71, 300–301 and 325–36; article reprinted in Spiegel and Samuels 1984, 319–32 and in Sellekaerts 1974 *International Trade*, 1–16.

De Economist 1970, vol. 118, 112–72. Bibliography by J.P. Pronk and articles by H.C. Bos, P. de Wolff, F. Hartog.

KEYNES John Maynard 1939. 'Professor Tinbergen's Method', *Economic Journal*, vol. 49, 306–18; reply by Tinbergen, 1940, 'On a Method of Statistical Business-Cycle Research: A Reply', *Economic Journal*, vol. 50, 141–54; 'Comment' by Keynes, 154–60. See also J. M. Keynes, *Collected Writings*, vol. 14, 285–320.

SELLEKAERTS Willy 1974 (ed.). *Econometrics and Economic Theory: Essays in Honour of Jan Tinbergen*, Toronto, Macmillan of Canada.

SELLEKAERTS Willy 1974 (ed.). *Economic Development and Planning: Essays in Honour of Jan Tinbergen*, London, Macmillan.

SELLEKAERTS Willy 1974 (ed.). *International Trade and Finance: Essays in Honour of Jan Tinbergen*, London, Macmillan.

TINBERGEN 1979, 1992.

WOLFF Pieter de, LINNEMANN Hans and BOS Hendricus Cornelis 1973 (eds). *Economic Structure and Development: Essays in Honour of Jan Tinbergen*, Amsterdam, North-Holland.

BLAUG 1985, 244–6. MEIER and SEERS 1984, 315–31. MORGAN 1990, 101–30. *New Palgrave* 1987, vol. 4, 652–4. SILLS 1979, 766–70.

TOBIN James (born 1918)

James Tobin was born in Champaign, Illinois. He completed all his university studies at Harvard, from which he obtained successively a BA (1939), MA (1940) and PhD (1947). His studies were interrupted by his involvement in the US Navy between 1942 and 1946, immediately after which he began teaching at Harvard. He was named associate professor (1950), then professor (1955) at Yale University, where he remained throughout his career. He was director of the Cowles Foundation from 1955 (at which date the Cowles Commission moved from Chicago to Yale to become the Cowles Foundation) until 1961, and again in 1964–5. He was associate editor of *Econometrica* (1951–3) and American editor of *Review of Economic Studies* (1952–4). President of the Econometric Society in 1958 and of the American Economic Association in 1971, he received the latter's John Bates Clark Medal in 1955 and the Nobel Memorial Prize in Economics in 1981. Very active in a number of public and academic organizations, he was a member of President Kennedy's Council of Economic Advisers in 1961–2.

Main publications

1947. 'Liquidity Preference and Monetary Policy', *Review of Economics and Statistics*, vol. 29, 124–31.

1947. 'Money Wage Rates and Employment', in S. Harris (ed.), *The New Economics: Keynes' Influence on Theory and Public Policy*, New York, Alfred A. Knopf, 572–87.

1955. 'A Dynamic Aggregative Model', *Journal of Political Economy*, vol. 63, 103–15.

1956. 'The Interest Elasticity of Transactions Demand for Cash', *Review of Economics and Statistics*, vol. 38, 241–7.

1956. With Seymour E. Harris, Carl Kaysen and Francis X. Sutton, *The American Creed*, Cambridge, Massachusetts, Harvard University Press.

1958. 'Liquidity Preference as Behavior Towards Risk', *Review of Economic Studies*, vol. 25, 65–86.

1961. 'Money, Capital and Other Stores of Value', *American Economic Review*, vol. 51, *Papers and Proceedings*, 26–37.

1966. *National Economic Policy*, New Haven, Connecticut, Yale University Press.

1968. With William C. Brainard, 'Pitfalls in Financial Model Building', *American Economic Review*, vol. 58, *Papers and Proceedings*, 99–122.

1968. With W. Allen Wallis, *Welfare Programs: An Economic Appraisal*, Washington, DC, American Enterprise Institute for Public Policy Research.

1969. 'A General Equilibrium Approach to Monetary Theory', *Journal of Money, Credit and Banking*, vol. 1, 15–29.

1971. *Essays in Economics*, vol. 1, *Macroeconomics*, Chicago, Markham.

1972. 'Inflation and Unemployment', *American Economic Review*, vol. 62, 1–18.

1974. *The New Economics, One Decade Older*, Princeton University Press.

1975. *Essays in Economics*, vol. 2, *Consumption and Econometrics*, Amsterdam, North-Holland.

1980. *Asset Accumulation and Economic Activity: Reflections on Contemporary Macroeconomic Theory*, University of Chicago Press; Oxford, Basil Blackwell.

1981. 'The Monetarist Counter-Revolution Today: An Appraisal', *Economic Journal*, vol. 91, 29–42.

1982. *Essays in Economics*, vol. 3, *Theory and Policy*, Cambridge, Massachusetts, MIT Press.

1982. 'Money and Finance in The Macro-Economic Process', in *Les Prix Nobel 1981*, Stockholm, Nobel Foundation; *Journal of Money, Credit and Banking*, vol. 14, 171–204.
1983. Interview, in Klamer 1983, 97-113.
1983 (ed.). *Macroeconomics, Prices and Quantities: Essays in Memory of Arthur Okun*, Oxford, Basil Blackwell; Washington, DC, Brookings Institution.
1986. 'My Evolution as an Economist', in Breit and Spencer 1986, 113–35.
1987. *Policies for Prosperity: Essays in a Keynesian Mode*, edited by P.M. Jackson, Brighton, Wheatsheaf Books; Cambridge, Massachusetts, MIT Press.
1988 (ed., with Murray L. Weidenbaum). *Two Revolutions in Economic Policy: The First Economic Reports of Presidents Kennedy and Reagan*, Cambridge, Massachusetts, MIT Press.

James Tobin began his studies in economics by reading Keynes's *General Theory*, in 1936, on the recommendation of his tutor at Harvard. Fascinated by the work, he became, and has remained until today, a disciple of Keynes. Playing a key role in the creation of the neoclassical synthesis, he made himself the promoter of what became the 'new economics' when president John F. Kennedy appointed him to his Council of Economic Advisers in 1961. Of the Economic Report of the President, then written with Heller, Gordon, Solow and Okun, Tobin wrote that, even if this work does not appear in his bibliography, 'I am proud of it as a work of a professional economist as well as a public document' (1986, p. 132). Twenty years later, in 1981, the report written by President Reagan's economic advisers signalled again a big shift in US economic policy, with the end of Keynesian interventionism and the triumph of the principles of monetarism and supply-side economics (see 1988, in which the two reports are reproduced). Having already asserted himself as a principal critic of Friedman, Tobin then became a fervent opponent of what became known as Reaganomics (see the papers collected in 1987). Continuing to affirm, through thick and thin, the necessity of active state intervention to assure a high level of employment, associated with an incomes policy to combat inflation, Tobin is today, without doubt, among Keynesians, one of the most vigorous adversaries of the new classical macroeconomics.

A disciple of Keynes, Tobin is nevertheless no unconditional supporter. Beginning with his first articles, he has drawn attention to certain inadequacies and incoherences in *The General Theory*. In his doctoral thesis, and in several later works, he focused on the consumption function, drawing attention to the link between consumption and long-run income and to the wealth effect. He criticized Keynes's analysis of the determination of the money wage (1947 *Money*). He returned to this question several times, devoting articles to the Phillips curve and criticizing, in his presidential address to the American Economic Association (1972), the hypothesis of a natural rate of unemployment which Friedman had offered in his own address, four years earlier.

But it is his contributions to the study of liquidity preference which have had, without doubt, most influence. Affirming, in opposition to the monetarist-type theses of Fellner and Warburton, that the demand for money is sensitive to the rate of interest (1947), Tobin offered an analysis of this relationship which is much more elaborate than that of Keynes (1956, 1958). In the latter article, one of those most cited after the Second World War, Tobin developed an analysis of portfolio selection by economic agents, thereby creating the foundations of finance theory, parallel to the works of Markowitz, who won the Nobel prize in 1990. For Tobin, one must consider the agent to have a choice between a large number of financial instruments and not only, as in the simple Keynesian model, between money and bonds. He offered the 'separation' theorem, according to which portfolio choice is independent of the decision concerning the division of the investment between risky assets and the only sure one, money.

Beginning with these reflections, Tobin, continuing thereby the research programme begun by Hicks in 1935, devoted a good deal of his efforts to establishing the link between the financial and real sectors of the economy. He developed, in order to take account of this, his famous 'q' index (1968 *AER*, 1969), defined as the relationship between the market valuation of an asset and its real replacement cost. It is this relationship which links the financial markets and those for goods and services, and which determines, in particular, the rate of investment. Thus Tobin explains the recession of 1973–4 by a sharp fall of the coefficient q, provoked by a too strict anti-inflationary monetary policy. Preoccupied by the links between cyclical fluctuations and economic growth, Tobin also devoted several articles to this question, the first, and certainly the most influential, in 1955. Here he sought once again to integrate money into models at that time conceived as 'real' ones (1955).

Tobin is also the author of numerous empirical analyses. Finally, he has always been as interested in social problems as in economic policy, and in particular in inequality and in discrimination against blacks in the United States.

Main references

'The Nobel Memorial Prize in Economics 1981'. Official announcement, articles by Douglas D. Purvis and Johan Myhrman and bibliography, *Scandinavian Journal of Economics* 1982, vol. 84, 57–110.

HESTER D. 1977. 'Contributions and Growth in Tobin's Economic Essays: A Review Essay', *Journal of Economic Literature*, vol. 15, 486–94.

LUCAS Robert E., Jr. 1981. 'Tobin and Monetarism: A Review Article', *Journal of Economic Literature*, vol. 19, 558–67.

TOBIN 1983 *Interview*, 1986.

WEISMAN D.L. 1984. 'Tobin on Keynes: A Suggested Interpretation', *Journal of Post Keynesian Economics*, vol. 6, 411–20.

BLAUG 1985, 247–9.

TRIFFIN Robert (1911–1993)

Born in Flobecq, Belgium, R. Triffin studied at Louvain, then at Harvard (MA in 1936, PhD in 1938). A lecturer at Louvain (1938–9), then instructor at Harvard (1939–42), he was in charge of the Latin America section of the Board of the Governors of the Federal Reserve System (1942–6), worked at the International Monetary Fund in Washington and then in Paris (1946–9) and, still in Paris, at the European Recovery Administration (1949–51). He was then professor at Yale (1951–80) and at Louvain (1977–82), while working as a consultant for international organizations, governments and central banks.

Main publications

1940. *Monopolistic Competition and General Equilibrium Theory*, Cambridge, Massachusetts, Harvard University Press.

1957. *Europe and the Money Muddle: From Bilateralism to Near-Convertibility*, New Haven, Connecticut, Yale University Press.

1960. *Gold and the Dollar Crisis: The Future of Convertibility*, New Haven, Connecticut, Yale University Press.

1966. *The World Money Maze: National Currencies in International Payments*, New Haven, Connecticut, Yale University Press.

1981. 'An Economist's Career: What? Why? How?', *Quarterly Review, Banca Nazionale del Lavoro*, no. 138, 239–59; in Kregel 1988, 137–56.

1987. 'The IMS (International Monetary System ... or Scandal?) and the EMS (European Monetary System)', *Quarterly Review, Banca Nazionale del Lavoro*, no. 162, 239–63.

1987. 'The Paper Exchange Standard: 1971–19...', in Paul A. Volcker *et al.*, *International Monetary Cooperation: Essays in Honor of Henry C. Wallich*, Princeton University Press, 70–85.

1989. 'The Intermixture of Politics and Economics in World Monetary Scandal: Diagnosis and Prescription', *American Economist*, vol. 33, Spring, 5–15.

R. Triffin's thesis, presented in 1938 and published in 1940, devoted to monopolistic competition and the theory of general equilibrium, was extended in an article published in *Econometrica* in 1941 on monopoly in particular and general equilibrium analyses. From 1943 on, his publications were linked to his work as adviser and monetary expert: therefore they were first about politics and monetary reforms in different countries of Latin America (1940s), and then on European monetary issues (1950s). Triffin then became a specialist of national, regional (plurinational) and world monetary issues: a supporter and architect of the return to convertibility, he linked reform of the world monetary system to regional monetary integration. His writings accompanied, and often anticipated, the return to currency convertibility and the end of the dollar shortage (1957), the beginning of the dollars' glut and its associated difficulties (1960, 1966). A constant advocate of a system relying on the creation of a reserve instrument controlled by the IMF and on a new equilibrium between the United States and different regional groups, he followed, a perceptive spectator, the demolishing of the older international monetary system and its replacement by a new scenario, replete with multiple risks and serious world disorders (1987 and 1989 publications). But he saw, in the achievements of the European monetary system, at least in part, the fruits of his tireless persistence in analysing, diagnosing and suggesting, and found in them new reasons for hope.

Main references

Robert Triffin, 'San Paolo Prize for Economics' 1987, 1988, Torino, Istituto Bancario San Paolo di Torino (with a bibliography 1935–88, 43–112 and Triffin 1981).
TRIFFIN 1981.

BLAUG 1985, 250–51. *New Palgrave* 1987, vol. 4, 701–2.

TSURU Shigeto (born 1912)

Shigeto Tsuru was born in Oita, Japan. He went to the United States in 1931, where he studied at Harvard, from which he obtained a PhD in 1940. He returned to Japan in 1942 and worked, after the Second World War, for the minister of foreign affairs and the vice minister of the Economic Stabilization Board. In 1948, he was named professor at the University of Hitotsubashi, from which he retired in 1975 with the title of professor emeritus. He was also a professor at Meiji Gakuin University. He is now chairman of the Village Shonan Incorporated, a centre for international academic and cultural exchange.

Main publications

1941. 'Economic Fluctuations in Japan, 1868–1893', *Review of Economics and Statistics*, vol. 23, 176–86.
1942. 'On Reproduction Schemes', appendix A in Paul M. Sweezy, *The Theory of Capitalist Development*, New York, Oxford University Press.
1954. 'Keynes versus Marx: The Methodology of Aggregates', in Kenneth K. Kurihara (ed.), *Post Keynesian Economics*, New Brunswick, New Jersey, Rutgers University Press, 320–44.
1958. *Essays on Japanese Economy*, Tokyo, Kinokuniya.
1961. *Has Capitalism Changed?*, Tokyo, Iwanami Shoten.
1965. 'The Effects of Technology on Productivity', in E.A.G. Robinson (ed.), *Problems in Economic Development*, London, Macmillan.
1976. *Works of Shigeto Tsuru* [in Japanese], 13 vols, Tokyo, Kodanska; vol. 13, *Towards a New Political Economy*, in English.
1982. 'A Peripatetic Economist', *Quarterly Review, Banca Nazionale del Lavoro*, no. 142, 227–44; in Kregel 1988, 181–97.
1992. 'Scientific Humanism as an Ideal', in Szenberg 1992, 283–98.
1993. *Institutional Economics Revisited*, Cambridge, England, Cambridge University Press.
1993. *Japan's Capitalism: Creative Defeat and Beyond*, Cambridge, England, Cambridge University Press.

Shigeto Tsuru belongs to that group of Japanese economists who are as much at ease with Marx's analysis as with that of Keynes and with neoclassical theory. He attempted on several occasions to establish links between these diverse approaches, while clearly indicating the divergences which opposed them, in particular at the methodological level (1954). Earlier, in an appendix to a book by Sweezy (1942), Tsuru had suggested an original comparison between Quesnay's *Tableau économique*, Marx's schemes of reproduction and the system of Keynesian aggregates.

Inspired by the approach of Schumpeter, of whom he was a student at Harvard, Tsuru is the author of numerous works on economic growth and business cycles. In his doctoral thesis he studied the gestation of industrial capitalism and the emergence of the first modern crises in Japan of the Meiji restoration at the end of the nineteenth century (the 1941 article was based on this thesis). He wrote a good deal on Japan's economic problems and suggested analyses of the sources of Japanese growth, emphasizing, in particular, the importance of war and that of foreign trade in this process (1958, 1993 *Japan*). Tsuru also became interested in environmental issues, which were particularly important in his own country. It should be noted that the most important part of his work only exists in Japanese (1976).

Main references

TSURU 1982, 1992.

New Palgrave 1987, vol. 4, 704.

TULLOCK Gordon (born 1922)

Born in Rockford, Illinois, G. Tullock studied law at the University of Chicago, where he obtained, after his military service, his diploma (JD) in 1947. He worked in a law office, was vice consul in Tientsin (China), then learnt Chinese at Yale (1949–51) and at Cornell (1951–2), before working at the consulate generalcy in Hong Kong and at the American embassy in Korea. He left the diplomatic service in 1956, was a researcher at the University of Virginia (1958–9), assistant, then associate professor, at the University of South Carolina (1959–62), associate professor at the University of Virginia (1962–7), then professor at Rice University (1967–8), at Virginia State University (1968–83), at the George Mason University (1983–7) and, since 1987, at the University of Arizona.

Main publications

1962. With James Buchanan, *The Calculus of Consent: Logical Foundations of Constitutional Democracy*, Ann Arbor, University of Michigan Press.

1965. *The Politics of Bureaucracy*, Washington, DC, Public Affairs Press.
1967. *Toward a Mathematics of Politics*, Ann Arbor, University of Michigan Press.
1970. *Private Wants, Public Means: An Economic Analysis of the Desirable Scope of Government*, New York, Basic Books.
1971. *The Logic of the Law*, New York, Basic Books.
1974. *The Social Dilemma: The Economics of War and Revolution*, Blacksburg, Virginia, Center for Study of Public Choice.
1975. With Richard B. McKenzie, *The New World of Economics: Explorations into the Human Experience*, Homewood, Illinois, Richard D. Irwin; 5th edn 1989, *The Best of the New World of Economics... and then some.*
1976. *The Vote Motive*, London, Institute of Economic Affairs.
1978. With Richard B. McKenzie, *Modern Political Economy: An Introduction to Economics*, New York, McGraw-Hill.
1983. *Economics of Income Redistribution*, Boston, Kluwer-Nijhoff.
1986. *The Economics of Wealth and Poverty*, Brighton, Wheatsheaf.
1988. *Wealth, Poverty & Politics*, Oxford, Basil Blackwell.
1989. *The Economics of Special Privilege and Rent Seeking*, Boston and Dordrecht, Kluwer.

In the 1950s, G. Tullock's publications dealt with economic and monetary questions concerning China and Korea, and the problem of majority voting. Then he was co-author, with J. Buchanan, of their 1962 book, founded with him the Public Choice Society (of which he was president in 1965) and published in 1966–7 the *Papers on Non-Market Decision Making*, which became the journal *Public Choice*.

A believer in methodological individualism, he applied the microeconomic approach to the most varied domains: not only in the specific area of public choice, to the analysis of bureaucracy, of politics and of public activity (1965, 1967, 1970), but also, like Becker, in a profusion of books and articles, to the analysis of law, rights, judicial procedure, crime and punishment, biology, charity and altruism and pollution; and in textbooks intended for students he applied the analysis, in terms of individual choices, supply and demand, cost and marginal cost, to sex, marriage, crime and even to teaching (1975). In the fifth edition of this last book, McKenzie and Tullock devoted two pages to the 'limits of economic thinking': 'Although we consider many diverse dimensions of human experience in this book, we do not suggest that economic analysis can be used to explain all human behavior. The interaction of individuals in a social state, with each reacting to actions of the others, is indeed very complex.' And if they defended, against their critics, the interest of their 'scientific study', they agreed that it is necessary not to 'exaggerate the importance of the insights we gain from our study' ([1975] 1989, p. 23).

Tullock also studied income distribution, including charity (1983), poverty, wealth and the search for rents and privileges (1986, 1988, 1989).

Main reference

BLAUG 1985, 252–3.

VANEK Jaroslav (born 1930)

After going to high school in Prague, where he was born, J. Vanek began studies in Paris (certificate in statistics at the Sorbonne in 1952), continued them in Geneva (licence in economics in 1954), then emigrated to the United States in 1955 and obtained a PhD at MIT in 1957. He taught as instructor and assistant professor at Harvard University (1957–64) and was named professor at Cornell University in 1966.

Main publications

1960. *International Trade: Theory and Economic Policy*, Homewood, Illinois, Richard D. Irwin.

1962. *The Balance of Payments, Level of Economic Activity and the Value of Currency: Theory and Some Recent Experiences*, Geneva, Droz.

1963. *The Natural Resource Content of United States Foreign Trade: 1870–1955*, Cambridge, Massachusetts, MIT Press.

1965. *General Equilibrium of International Discrimination: The Case of Customs Unions*, Cambridge, Massachusetts, Harvard University Press.

1967. *Estimating Foreign Resource Needs for Economic Development: Theory, Method, and a Case Study of Colombia*, New York, McGraw-Hill.

1968. *Maximal Economic Growth: A Geometric Approach to Von Neumann's Growth Theory and the Turnpike Theorem*, Ithaca, New York, Cornell University Press.

1970. *The General Theory of Labor-Managed Market Economies*, Ithaca, New York, Cornell University Press.

1971. *The Participatory Economy: An Evolutionary Hypothesis and a Strategy for Development*, Ithaca, New York, Cornell University Press.

1977. *The Labor-Managed Economy: Essays*, Ithaca, New York, Cornell University Press.

J. Vanek began his career as an American academic economist with several books on international economics (1960, 1962, 1963, 1965) and a book on the theory of growth (1968). Then he worked on two areas: the economy of worker-managed firms which can, according to his theoretical demonstration, have the same qualities as the economy based on private property (1970) and economic development, which he tackled in his work on Peru and Colombia (1967). It was to these questions that, from then on – with less and less concern for academia – he devoted his work (1977): stressing the role which, in a 'participation economy', cooperatives in production and consumption could play (1971), emphasizing the contribution of popular participation to development, devoting himself to the needs of the poor populations of the planet, to solar energy and to less costly technologies. In 1984, he created a foundation, STEVEN (Solar Technology and Energy for Vital Economic Needs), published production manuals and conducted missions for the implementation of projects.

Main references

BLAUG 1985, 254–5. BLAUG *Who's Who*, 1986, 852–3.

VERNON Raymond (born 1913)

Born in New York, R. Vernon studied first at its City College (BA in 1933), then at Columbia University (PhD in 1941). He worked at the Securities and Exchange Commission (1935–46), at the Department of State, in particular as acting director of the Office of Economic Defense and Trade Policy (1946–54), in a private firm (1954–6), then as director of a New York Metropolitan Region Study (1956–9). He was then professor at Harvard: at the Harvard Business School (1959–80), at the Faculty of Arts and Sciences (1976–83) and at the Kennedy School of Government thereafter.

Main publications

1941. *The Regulation of Stock Exchange Members*, New York, Columbia University Press.
1960. With Edgar M. Hoover, *Anatomy of a Metropolis*, Cambridge, Massachusetts, Harvard University Press.
1963. *The Dilemma of Mexico's Development*, Cambridge, Massachusetts, Harvard University Press.
1966. *The Myth and Reality of our Urban Problems*, Cambridge, Massachusetts, Harvard University Press.
1968. *Manager in the International Economy*, New York, Prentice-Hall.
1971. *Sovereignty at Bay: The Multinational Spread of U.S. Enterprises*, New York, Basic Books.
1972. *The Economic and Political Consequences of Multinational Enterprises: An Anthology*, Cambridge, Massachusetts, Harvard University Press.
1977. *Storm Over the Multinationals: The Real Issues*, Cambridge, Massachusetts, Harvard University Press.
1983. *Two Hungry Giants: The United States and Japan in the Quest for Oil and Ores*, Cambridge, Massachusetts, Harvard University Press.
1985. *Exploring the Global Economy: Emerging Issues in Trade and Investment*, Cambridge, Massachusetts, Harvard University Press.
1989. With Debora L. Spar, *Beyond Globalism: Remaking American Foreign Economic Policy*, New York, The Free Press.
1991. With Debora L. Spar and Glen Tobin, *Iron Triangles and Revolving Doors*, New York, Praeger.

R. Vernon's first publications came with and extended his professional activities: they were about the regulation of stock exchange activities (1941), the problems and prospects of a large metropolis (1960, 1963, 1966), international trade and foreign investment (1968).

In the 1970s, Vernon published extensively on multinational firms: he analysed their strategies of multinationalization as a function of their mastering of certain activities (high standard of services, technical and organizational knowledge) and of the 'product cycle' which they control. He studied the choice of country of location in relation to characteristics of the different phases of that cycle, the relations of the multinational firms both with their own country's government and with those of the countries where the subsidiaries were located, international trade, technology transfer and division of labour between countries (1971, 1972, 1977).

In the 1980s, without losing interest in multinational firms, Vernon also wrote works devoted to state-controlled enterprises. He extended his analysis to East–West relations and to the role of the large industrialized countries, in short to the 'global economy' (1985). Comparing the responses to the threat of shortage of petrol and minerals, he demonstrated the superior efficiency of those of the government and firms of Japan, as compared to those of the United States (1983). More broadly, emphasizing the obsolescence of rules and institutions established in the nineteenth century, he demonstrated the incoherence and inefficiency of the contemporary economic foreign policy of the United States (1989, 1991).

Main references

BLAUG *Who's Who* 1986, 855–6. *New Palgrave* 1987, vol. 4, 806–7.

WEINTRAUB Sidney (1914–1983)

Sidney Weintraub was born in Brooklyn. He studied at the London School of Economics (1938–9) and at New York University, from which he received a doctorate in 1941. After holding several positions, including some in public organizations, in the 1940s, he began to teach at New York's New School for Social Research in 1950, and in 1952 became professor at the University of Pennsylvania, where he stayed until the end of his career, while teaching as an invited professor in universities throughout the world. He was founder (1978) and editor, with Paul Davidson, of the *Journal of Post Keynesian Economics*.

Main publications

1940. 'Inflation and Price Control', *Harvard Business Review*, vol. 18, 429–36.
1946. 'Monopoly Pricing and Unemployment', *Quarterly Journal of Economics*, vol. 61, 108–24.
1949. *Price Theory*, New York, Pitman.
1951. *Income and Employment Analysis*, New York, Pitman.
1956. 'A Macroeconomic Approach to the Theory of Wages', *American Economic Review*, vol. 46, 837–56.
1957. 'The Micro-Foundations of Aggregate Demand and Supply', *Economic Journal*, vol. 67, 455–70.
1958. *An Approach to the Theory of Income Distribution*, Philadelphia, Chilton.
1959. *A General Theory of the Price Level, Output, Income Distribution, and Economic Growth*, Philadelphia, Chilton.
1961. *Classical Keynesianism, Monetary Theory and the Price Level*, Philadelphia, Chilton.
1963. *Some Aspects of Wage Theory and Policy*, Philadelphia, Chilton.
1966. *A Keynesian Theory of Employment, Growth and Income Distribution*, Philadelphia, Chilton.
1966. *Trade Preferences for Less-Developed Countries: An Analysis of United States Policy*, New York, Praeger.
1971. With H.C. Wallich, 'A Tax-Based Incomes Policy', *Journal of Economic Issues*, vol. 5, 1–19.
1973. *Keynes, Keynesians and Monetarists*, Philadelphia, University of Pennsylvania Press.
1978. *Capitalism's Inflation and Unemployment Crisis: Beyond Monetarism and Keynesianism*, Reading, Massachusetts, Addison-Wesley.
1981. *Our Stagflation Malaise: Ending Inflation and Unemployment*, Westport, Connecticut, Quorum Books.
1983. 'A Jevonian Seditionist: A Mutiny to Enhance the Economic Bounty', *Quarterly Review, Banca Nazionale del Lavoro*, no. 146, 215–34; in Kregel 1988, 37–56.

Founder of the *Journal of Post Keynesian Economics*, Sidney Weintraub is associated with the post-Keynesian current, of which he is considered the principal initiator in the United States. But, perhaps more correctly, Paul Samuelson had already defined him as a 'lone-wolf Keynesian', following, since the early 1940s, a solitary and original route, which led him to foresee, before others, the coexistence of unemployment and inflation, which was to become the main difficulty for modern economies from the end of the 1960s.

Well before Leijonhufvud, Weintraub made the distinction between Keynes's contribution and that of his disciples, whom he called the classical Keynesians. As early as the 1950s, he criticized both Samuelson's Keynesianism, with his 45° graph, and the more sophisticated interpretation of Hicks, in terms of *IS–LM* (see, *inter alia,* the articles gathered in 1961), which he blamed for having no satisfactory explanation of price determination and distribution. Before the monetarists, he drew attention to the dangers of inflation, whose pernicious attack makes itself felt before the realization of full employment. But he nonetheless rejected the monetarist explanation of this phenomenon as well as the Phillips curve analysis, whose acceptance represents for him an abdication of Keynesianism in the face of inflation, henceforth considered as the inescapable price to be paid for the reduction of unemployment (see, among others, the texts collected in 1973).

Before it became fashionable in the 1980s, Weintraub suggested new microeconomic foundations compatible with the Keynesian theory of employment, a theory which he formulated in terms of aggregate supply and demand curves, integrating as parameters prices and the money wage (1956, 1957, 1958 and 1959). He himself described his analysis as the theory of wage cost mark-up. It is captured in his equation: $P = kw/A$, where P is the price level, k the average mark-up on unit wage costs, w the average money wage rate and A average productivity per worker. Weintraub estimated that the mark-up, k, is in the long run a fairly constant parameter, more stable, for example, than the propensity to consume, if Keynes is to be believed, or, looking to Friedman, than the velocity of money. A being determined by technological data, it emerges that the money wage, w, is the main causal variable in explaining the price level and, therefore, inflation. Far from being determined by the supply–demand nexus, under the form of Walrasian *tâtonnement,* w is the result of a power struggle between employers, unions and governments, and even constitutes, as Keynes had sensed, moreover, the true *numéraire* of modern economies.

On the basis of this analysis, Weintraub suggested adding to the traditional Keynesian policies of demand management an incomes policy to control inflation, of which he rejects the monetarist explanation based on the quantity of money, as well as the Keynesian explanation based on the pressure of demand. It is a question of linking the evolution of money wages to that of productivity. In fact, Weintraub suggested this measure from the beginning of his career (1940). In 1971, he put forward a policy of fiscal penalty for recalcitrant enterprises in order to achieve this objective, the incomes policy based on taxation, popularized under the initials TIP (Tax-based Income Policy). It was, for him, the only alternative to the monetarist policy of inflation management through the increase of unemployment, around which, furthermore, some 'Hicksian-oriented Phillips-curve-Keynesians' were rallying (1978, p. 208; see also 1981 and 1983).

Main references

KREGEL Jan 1989 (ed.). *Inflation and Income Distribution in Capitalist Crisis: Essays in Memory of Sidney Weintraub*, London, Macmillan.
WEINTRAUB 1983.

ARESTIS and SAWYER 1992, 608–15. BLAUG 1985, 257–60. *New Palgrave* 1987, vol. 4, 888. SPIEGEL and SAMUELS 1984, 201–13.

WILLIAMSON Oliver E. (born 1932)

Oliver E. Williamson was born in Superior, Wisconsin. He obtained an SB from the Massachusetts Institute of Technology in 1955, an MBA from Stanford in 1960 and a PhD from Carnegie-Mellon in 1963. He was assistant professor at the University of California at Berkeley (1963–5); associate professor (1965–8) and professor (1968–83) at the University of Pennsylvania; professor (1983–8) at Yale University. Since 1988 he has been a professor at the University of California at Berkeley. Williamson has also acted as a consultant to the Rand Corporation (1964–6), a special economic assistant to the Assistant Attorney General for Antitrust, US Department of Justice (1966–7), a consultant to the U.S. Department of Justice (1967–9) and a consultant to the Federal Trade Commission (1978–80).

Main publications

1963. 'Managerial Discretion and Business Behavior', *American Economic Review*, vol. 53, 1032–57.
1964. *The Economics of Discretionary Behavior: Managerial Objectives in a Theory of the Firm*, Englewood Cliffs, New Jersey, Prentice-Hall.
1966. 'Peak Load Pricing and Optimal Capacity under Indivisibility Constraints', *American Economic Review*, vol. 56, 810–27.
1968 (ed., with Almarin Phillips). *Prices: Issues in Theory, Practice and Public Policy*, Philadelphia, University of Pennsylvania Press.
1970. *Corporate Control and Business Behavior: An Inquiry into the Effects of Organization Form on Enterprise Behavior*, Englewood Cliffs, New Jersey, Prentice-Hall.
1974. 'The Economics of Antitrust: Transaction Cost Considerations', *University of Pennsylvania Law Review*, vol. 122, 1439–96.
1975. *Markets and Hierarchies: Analysis and Antitrust Implications*, New York, Free Press; new edn, 1983.
1979. 'Transaction Cost Economics: The Governance of Contractual Relations', *Journal of Law and Economics*, vol. 22, 233–61.
1980 (ed.). *Antitrust Law and Economics*, Houston, Dame Publishing.
1985. *The Economic Institutions of Capitalism: Firms, Markets, Relational Contracting*, New York, Free Press.
1986. 'An Autobiographical Sketch', in 1986 *Economic Organization*, xi–xviii.
1986. *Economic Organization: Firms, Markets and Policy Control*, New York University Press.

1989 (ed., with Masahiko Aoki and Bo Gustafson). *The Firm as a Nexus of Treaties*, London, Sage.
1990 (ed.). *Industrial Organization*, Aldershot, Hants, Edward Elgar.
1990 (ed.). *Organization Theory: From Chester Barnard to the Present and Beyond*, New York, Oxford University Press.
1991 (ed., with S.G. Winter). *The Nature of the Firm: Origins, Evolution, and Development*, New York, Oxford University Press.

Influenced by his behaviouralist training at Carnegie-Mellon, Williamson acknowledges a great debt to K. Arrow for his treatment of information, to Alfred Chandler for recognizing the importance of institutional innovation, to R. Coase for his transaction cost approach and to H. Simon for introducing a complex of behavioural assumptions into economics. The extensive knowledge of large firms acquired by Williamson, in particular in his early research on Antitrust, for the US Department of Justice, formed a basis for this significant contribution to the development of the new institutional economics, particularly his analysis of the firm from the perspective of managerial discretion and discretionary behaviour (1963, 1964), of price formation, which includes his concept of peak load pricing (1966, 1968) and of the effects of antitrust legislation on the behaviour of large firms and on vertical integration (1974, 1975, 1980).

In studying the firm as a governance structure, as distinct from a single production function, Williamson found in transaction costs a valuable tool. He used this tool first to analyse firms and the market, two different modes of coordination, each having its specific features, and also to understand institutional phenomena. In *Markets and Hierarchies* (1975), following the lead of Alfred Chandler, he explained the organizational structure of firms in terms of their strategic behaviour in the market, essentially as regards their degree of product diversification. In this analysis, Williamson presented a classification of firms. At one end of the spectrum is the 'unitary form enterprise' (U-form), characterized by weak diversification (either one main product or a group of very homogeneous products), high centralization, large organization functions and moderate organization costs. At the other end of the spectrum is the 'divisional structure' (M-form) characterized by a large diversification of products and a centralized direction, with decentralization into several operational divisions (corresponding to groups of homogeneous products). In addition, Williamson distinguished the holding form (H-form) and three hybrid forms.

Williamson has worked to develop a new analytical framework for organization theory on the basis of the minimization of transaction costs (1985, 1986), drawn partially from John R. Commons's simple view that 'the transaction is the ultimate unit of microeconomic analysis' ([1975] 1983, p. xi). Not only does this allow for a common framework with which to analyse firms and the market, relations inside firms and relations in the market, as contractual relations, but transaction costs analysis also permits the analysis of vertical integration, non-competitive behaviour (1974, 1975) and hierarchical relations within enterprises (1979, 1985). Finally, the firm, according to Williamson, may be treated as a nexus of treaties (1989).

From his initial association with the behaviouralist school and later with the law and economics approach, Williamson has become, after Coase, a common reference for those working in the new theoretical currents of institutionalism, industrial economics and the economics of convention, and for those neoclassical theorists increasingly concerned with the need to better understand the reality of firms and markets.

Main references

WILLIAMSON O.E. 1986 'An Autobiographical Sketch'.

BLAUG *Who's Who* 1986, 889–90.

ZELLNER Arnold (born 1927)

Arnold Zellner was born in Brooklyn. He obtained a Master's in physics from Harvard University (1949) and a PhD in economics from the University of California at Berkeley. He was assistant professor (1955–8), then associate professor (1959–60) at the University of Washington, and associate, then full, professor at the University of Wisconsin (1961–6). Since 1966 he has been professor at the University of Chicago. He was co-founder and editor, from 1973, of the *Journal of Econometrics*, founder and editor (1981–7) of the *Journal of Business and Economic Statistics* (1981–7) and president of the American Statistical Association (1989–91).

Main publications

1957. 'The Short-Run Consumption Function', *Econometrica*, vol. 25, 552–67.
1962. With H. Theil, 'Three-Stage Least Squares: Simultaneous Estimation of Simultaneous Equations', *Econometrica*, vol. 30, 54–78.
1963. 'Decision Rules for Economic Forecasting', *Econometrica*, vol. 31, 111–30.
1964. With G.C. Tiao, 'Bayes' Theorem and the Use of Prior Knowledge in Regression Analysis', *Biometrika*, vol. 65, 219–30.
1966. With J. Kmenta and J.H. Drèze, 'Specification and Estimation of Cobb–Douglas Production Function Models', *Econometrica*, vol. 34, 784–95.
1968 (ed.). *Readings in Economic Statistics and Econometrics*, Boston, Little, Brown.
1970. With T.C. Lee and George G. Judge, *Estimating the Parameters of the Markov Probability Model from Aggregate Time Series Data*, Amsterdam, North-Holland.
1971. *An Introduction to Bayesian Inference in Econometrics*, New York, John Wiley & Sons.
1974. With F. Palm, 'Time Series Analysis and Simultaneous Equation Models', *Journal of Econometrics*, vol. 2, 17–54.
1979. 'Statistical Analysis of Econometric Models', *Journal of the American Statistical Association*, vol. 74, 628–51.
1981. 'Philosophy and Objectives of Econometrics', in D. Currie, R. Nobay and D. Peel (eds), *Macroeconomic Analysis: Essays in Macroeconomics and Econometrics*, London, Croom Helm, 24–34.
1982. 'Basic Issues in Econometrics: Past and Present', *The American Economist*, vol. 26, 5–10.
1984. *Basic Issues in Econometrics*, University of Chicago Press.
1985. 'Bayesian Econometrics', *Econometrica*, vol. 53, 253–69.
1987. 'Bayesian Inference', *New Palgrave*, vol. 1, 208–18.
1988. 'Causality and Causal Laws in Economics', *Journal of Econometrics*, vol. 39, 7–21.

A physicist and economist by training, Arnold Zellner made contributions both to the techniques of modern econometrics, for example the method which he called SEMTSA (Structural Econometric Modeling Time Series Analysis, 1974, 1979) and to its applications, among others, to the analysis of consumption (1957) and production (1966), as well as to its epistemological and philosophical foundations (1981, 1982, 1988). For Zellner, who supports the principle of the unity of the scientific method enunciated by the statistician and philosopher Karl Pearson (*The Grammar of Science*, 1892), econometrics, which he identifies with modern quantitative economics, must be characterized by a close relationship between the collection of data, economic theory and its applications, and draw as much on intuition as from logic. An advocate of what he calls the principle of simplicity, he has criticized several economists for constructing complex models which have no hold upon reality. He has also blamed traditional econometrics for not having at its disposal methods for discovering and correcting the faults of the models. This was what led him to become one of the main promoters of Bayesian techniques of analysis (from the name of the English statistician who enunciated, in 1763, the principle of inverse probability). In this view, prior information must play an essential role in econometric analysis. It is a question of learning and modifying the theory in the light of the data and of the experience, in the way science progresses. Zellner associated this approach with reductive inference, which he opposed to purely deductive or inductive inference, and to a determinist and rationalist view of causality in which physicians no longer believe, whilst some economists continue to delude themselves on this subject: 'For example, it is impossible to *prove*, deductively or inductively that generalizations or laws, even the Chicago quantity theory of money, are absolutely true. … There is an unavoidable uncertainty associated with laws in all areas of science, including economics' (1984, p. 5).

Main reference

SPIEGEL and SAMUELS 1984, 423–40.

Bibliography

ADAMS J. 1980 (ed.). *Institutional Economics: Contributions to the Development of Holistic Economics. Essays in Honor of Allan G. Gruchy*, The Hague, Martinus Nijhoff.

AHMAD Syed 1990. *Capital in Economic Theory: Neoclassical, Cambridge and Chaos*, Aldershot, Hants, Edward Elgar.

AKERLOF George A. and YELLEN J.L. 1986 (eds). *Efficiency Wage Models of the Labor Market*, Cambridge, Massachusetts, Cambridge University Press.

ALBERTINI Jean-Marie and SILEM Albert 1983. *Comprendre les théories économiques*, 2 vols, Paris, Seuil.

ANDREFF Wladimir *et al.* 1982. *L'Économie fiction: Contre les nouveaux économistes*, Paris, François Maspero.

ARENA Richard and TORRE Dominique 1992 (eds). *Keynes et les nouveaux keynésiens*, Paris, Presses Universitaires de France.

ARESTIS Philip 1991. *The Post-Keynesian Revolution in Economics: An Alternative Analysis of Economic Theory and Policy*, Aldershot, Hants, Edward Elgar.

ARESTIS Philip and KITROMILIDES Yiannis 1989 (eds). *Theory and Policy in Political Economy: Essays in Pricing, Distribution and Growth*, Aldershot, Hants, Edward Elgar.

ARESTIS Philip and MINSKY Hyman P. 1989 (eds). *Post-Keynesian Monetary Economics*, Aldershot, Hants, Edward Elgar.

ARESTIS Philip and SAWYER Malcolm 1992 (eds). *A Biographical Dictionary of Dissenting Economists*, Aldershot, Hants, Edward Elgar.

ARESTIS Philip and SKOURAS Thanos 1985 (eds). *Post Keynesian Economic Theory*, Armonk, New York, M.E. Sharpe.

BACKHOUSE Roger. 1985. *A History of Modern Economic Analysis,* Oxford, Basil Blackwell.

BALL Laurence, MANKIW N. Gregory and ROMER David 1988. 'The New Keynesian Economics and the Output–Inflation Trade-Off', *Brookings Papers on Economic Activity*, no. 1, 1–82.

BARBER William J. 1991 (ed.). *Perspectives on the History of Economic Thought*, vol. 6, *Themes in Keynesian Criticism and Supplementary Modern Topics*, Aldershot, Hants, Edward Elgar.

BARRERE Alain 1974. *Histoire de la pensée économique et analyse contemporaine*, Paris, Les Cours de Droit.

BARRO Robert J. and FISCHER Stanley 1976. 'Recent Developments in Monetary Theory', *Journal of Monetary Economics*, vol. 2, 133–67.

BARRY N. 1987. *On Classical Liberalism and Libertarianism*, New York, St Martin's Press.

BARTOLI Henri 1977. *Economie et création collective*, Paris, Economica.

BASLE Maurice *et al.* 1988. *Histoire des pensées économiques, les contemporains*, Paris, Sirey.

BEGG David K.H. 1982. *The Rational Expectations Revolution in Macroeconomics: Theories and Evidence,* Oxford, Philip Allan; Baltimore, Johns Hopkins.

BELL D. and KRISTOL I. 1981. *The Crisis in Economic Theory,* New York, Basic Books.

BERG Maxine 1990 (ed.). *Political Economy in the Twentieth Century*, London, Philip Allan; Savage, Maryland, Barnes & Noble.

BLANCHARD Olivier J. and FISCHER Stanley 1989– (eds). *NBER Macroeconomics Annual*, Cambridge, Massachusetts, MIT Press.

BLAUG Mark 1962. *Economic Theory in Retrospect*, Homewood, Ill., Richard D. Irwin.

BLAUG Mark 1985. *Great Economists Since Keynes: An Introduction to the Lives & Works of One Hundred Modern Economists,* Brighton, Wheatsheaf.

BLAUG Mark 1989–90 (general ed.). *Schools of Thought in Economics*, Aldershot, Hants, Edward Elgar [11 titles and *Cumulative Index*].

BLAUG Mark 1990– (general ed.). *The International Library of Critical Writings in Economics*, Aldershot, Hants, Edward Elgar.

BLAUG Mark and STURGES Paul 1983 (eds). *Who's Who in Economics: A Biographical Dictionary, 1700–1981*, Brighton, Harvester Press; Cambridge, Massachusetts, MIT Press; 2nd edn 1986.

BODKIN R.G., KLEIN L.R. and MARWAH K. 1991. *A History of Macroeconomic Model-Building*, Aldershot, Hants, Edward Elgar.

BOWLES Samuel and EDWARDS Richard 1990 (eds). *Radical Political Economy*, 2 vols, Aldershot, Hants, Edward Elgar.

BREIT William and RANSOM Roger L. 1971. *The Academic Scribblers: American Economists in Collision*, New York, Holt, Rinehart and Winston.

BREIT William and SPENCER Roger W. 1986. *Lives of the Laureates: Seven Nobel Economists,* Cambridge, Massachusetts, MIT Press.

BREIT William and SPENCER Roger W. 1990. *Lives of the Laureates: Ten Nobel Economists*, Cambridge, Massachusetts, MIT Press.

BRONFENBRENNER Martin 1970. 'Radical Economics in America: A 1970 Survey', *Journal of Economic Literature*, vol. 8, 747–66.

BRUNNER Karl and MELTZER Allan H. 1976– (eds). *Carnegie-Rochester Conference Series on Public Policy*, A bi-annual Conference Proceedings, Amsterdam, North-Holland.

CALDWELL Bruce and BOEHM Stephan 1992 (eds). *Austrian Economics: Tensions and New Directions*, Boston, Kluwer Academic.

CAPIE Forrest and WOOD Geoffrey E. 1989 (eds). *Monetary Economics in the 1980s*, London, Macmillan.

CHRYSTAL K.A. 1979. *Controversies in Macroeconomics*, Oxford, Philip Allan; 2nd edn, 1983.

CHRYSTAL K. Alec. 1990 (ed.). *Monetarism*, 2 vols, Aldershot, Hants, Edward Elgar [Schools of Thought in Economics].

CUTHBERSON Keith 1979. *The New Cambridge, Keynesian and Monetarist Controversies*, London, Macmillan.

DASGUPTA A.K. 1985. *Epochs of Economic Theory*, Oxford, Basil Blackwell.

DEANE P. 1978. *The Evolution of Economic Ideas*, Cambridge, England, Cambridge University Press.

De MARCHI Neil and GILBERT Christopher 1989 (eds). *History and Methodology of Econometrics*, Oxford, Clarendon Press; New York, Oxford University Press.

DENIS Henri 1966. *Histoire de la pensée économique*, Paris, Presses Universitaires de France.

DESAI Meghnad 1981. *Testing Monetarism*, London, Frances Pinter.

DOLAN E.G. 1976 (ed.). *The Foundations of Modern Austrian Economics*, Kansas City, Sheed & Ward.

DORE Mohammed 1993. *The Macrodynamics of Business Cycles: A Comparative Evaluation*, Oxford, Basil Blackwell.

DOW Sheila C. 1985. *Macroeconomic Thought: A Methodological Approach*, Oxford, Basil Blackwell.

DRAZEN Allan 1980. 'Recent Developments in Macroeconomic Disequilibrium Theory', *Econometrica*, vol. 48, 283–306.

EARL Peter E. 1988 (ed.). *Behavioural Economics*, 2 vols, Aldershot, Hants, Edward Elgar [Schools of Thought in Economics].

EATWELL John, MILGATE Murray and NEWMAN Peter 1987 (eds). *The New Palgrave: A Dictionary of Economics*, 4 vols, London, Macmillan; New York, Stockton.

EGGERTSSON Thráinn 1990. *Economic Behavior and Institutions*, Cambridge, England, Cambridge University Press.

EICHNER A. 1978 (ed.). *A Guide to Post-Keynesian Economics*, Armonk, New York, M.E. Sharpe.

EICHNER A. and KREGEL J. 1975. 'An Essay on Post-Keynesian Theory: A New Paradigm in Economics', *Journal of Economic Literature*, vol.13, 1293–1314.

EKELUND R.B., Jr., FURUBOTN E.G. and GRAMM W.P. 1972 (eds). *The Evolution of Modern Demand Theory*, Lexington, Massachusetts.

EPSTEIN R.J. 1987. *A History of Econometrics*, Amsterdam, North-Holland.

FELLNER William 1976. 'Schools of Thought in the Mainstream of American Economics', *Acta Oekonomica*, vol. 18, 247–62.

FELS Rendigs and SIEGFRIED JOHN J. 1974. *Recent Advances in Economics. A Book of Readings*, Homewood, Illinois, Richard D. Irwin.

FINK Richard H. 1982 (ed.). *Supply-Side Economics: A Critical Appraisal*, University Publications of America.

FISCHER Stanley 1975. 'Recent Developments in Monetary Theory', *American Economic Review*, vol. 65, *Papers and Proceedings*, 157–66.

FISCHER Stanley 1980 (ed.). *Rational Expectations and Economic Policy*, University of Chicago Press.

FISCHER Stanley 1986–88 (ed.). *NBER Macroeconomics Annual*, Cambridge, Massachusetts, MIT Press.

FISCHER Stanley 1988. 'Recent Developments in Macroeconomics', *Economic Journal*, vol. 98, 294–339.

FRIEDMAN Benjamin and HAHN Frank 1987 (eds). *Handbook of Monetary Economics*, Amsterdam, North-Holland.

FRYDMAN Roman and PHELPS Edmund S. 1983 (eds). *Individual Forecasting and Aggregate Outcomes: 'Rational Expectations' Examined*, Cambridge, England, Cambridge University Press.

GIBSON William E. and KAUFMAN George G. 1971 (eds). *Monetary Economics: Readings on Current Issues*, New York, McGraw-Hill.

GORDON Robert J. 1976. 'Recent Developments in the Theory of Inflation and Unemployment', *Journal of Monetary Economics*, vol. 2, 185–219.

GORDON Robert J. 1990. 'What is New-Keynesian Economics?', *Journal of Economic Literature*, vol. 28, 1115–71.

GRANDMONT J.M. 1977. 'Temporary General Equilibrium Theory', *Econometrica*, vol. 43, 535–72.

GRASSL W. and SMITH B. 1986 (eds). *Austrian Economics: Historical and Philosophical Background*, London, Croom Helm.

GREENAWAY, David, BLEANEY Michael and STEWART Ian 1992 (eds). *Companion to Contemporary Economic Thought*, London, Routledge.

GREENAWAY David and PRESLEY John R. 1989. *Pioneers of Modern Economics in Britain*, vol. 2, London, Macmillan.

GREENWALD B. and STIGLITZ Joseph E. 1987. 'Keynesian, New Keynesian and New Classical Economics', *Oxford Economic Papers*, vol. 37, 119–32.

GRUCHY A.G. 1947. *Modern Economic Thought: The American Contribution*, New York, Prentice-Hall.

GRUCHY A.G. 1972. *Contemporary Economic Thought: The Contribution of Neo-Institutional Economics*, Clifton, New Jersey, Augustus M. Kelley.

HAHN F. and MATTHEWS R.C. 1964. 'The Theory of Economic Growth: A Survey', *Economic Journal*, vol. 74, 779–902.

HAILSTONES T.J. 1982 (ed.). *Viewpoints on Supply-Side Economics*, Richmond, Virginia, Robert F. Dame.

HALEY B.F. 1952 (ed.). *A Survey of Contemporary Economics*, Homewood, Illinois, Richard D. Irwin.

HARCOURT G.C. 1975. *Some Cambridge Controversies in the Theory of Capital,* Cambridge, England, University Press.

HARCOURT G.C. 1992. *Post-Keynesian Essays in Biography: Portraits of Twentieth Century Political Economists*, London, Macmillan.

HARGREAVES-HEAP S.P. 1991. *The New Keynesian Macroeconomics*, Aldershot, Hants, Edward Elgar.

HENIN Pierre-Yves and MICHEL Philippe 1982 (eds). *Croissance et accumulation en déséquilibre*, Paris, Economica.

HEY J.D. and LAMBERT P.J. 1987 (eds). *Survey in the Economics of Uncertainty*, New York, Basil Blackwell.

HILDRETH C. 1986. *The Cowles Commission in Chicago, 1939–1955*, Berlin, Springer-Verlag.

HONKAPOHJA Seppo 1990 (ed.). *The State of Macroeconomics*, Oxford, Basil Blackwell.

HOOVER Kevin D. 1984. 'Two Types of Monetarism', *Journal of Economic Literature*, vol. 22, 58–76.

HOOVER Kevin D. 1988. *The New Classical Macroeconomics: A Sceptical Enquiry*, Oxford, Basil Blackwell.

HOWARD M.C. and KING J.E. 1992. *A History of Marxian Economics*, vol. 2, *1929–1990*, London, Macmillan; Princeton University Press.

HSIEH Ching-Yao and MANGUM Stephen L. 1986. *A Search for Synthesis in Economic Theory*, Armonk, New York, M.E. Sharpe.

HUNT E.K. 1979. *History of Economic Thought: A Critical Perspective*, Belmont, California, Wadsworth.

HUTCHISON Terence W. 1978. *On Revolutions and Progress in Economic Knowledge,* Cambridge, England, Cambridge University Press.

HUTCHISON Terence W. 1981. *The Politics and Philosophy of Economics: Marxists, Keynesians, and Austrians,* Oxford, Basil Blackwell.

INGRAO Bruna and ISRAEL Giorgio 1987. *La mano invisibile*, Rome–Bari, Gius, Laterza & Figli Spa; Engl. transl. 1990. *The Invisible Hand. Economic Equilibrium in the History of Science*, Cambridge, Massachusetts, MIT Press.

International Bibliography of the Social Sciences, London, Routledge.

JOHNSON Harry G. 1962. 'Monetary Theory and Policy', *American Economic Review,* vol. 52, 335–84.

JOHNSON Harry G. 1971. 'The Keynesian Revolution and the Monetarist Counter-Revolution', *American Economic Review*, vol. 61, 1–14.

JOHNSON Harry G. and NOBAY A.R. 1977. 'Monetarism: A Historic–Theoretic Perspective', *Journal of Economic Literature*, vol. 15, 470–95.

KANTOR Brian1979. 'Rational Expectations and Economic Thought', *Journal of Economic Literature*, vol. 17, 1422–41.

KING J.E. 1990 (ed.). *Marxian Economics*, 3 vols, Aldershot, Hants, Edward Elgar [Schools of Thought in Economics].

KIRZNER Israel 1982 (ed.). *Method, Process and Austrian Economics: Essays in Honor of Ludwig von Mises*, Lexington, Massachusetts, Lexington Books.

KLAMER Arjo 1983. *Conversations with Economists: New Classical Economists and Opponents Speak out on the Current Controversy in Macroeconomics*, Towota, New Jersey, Rowman and Allenheld; UK edn, *The New Classical Macroeconomics: Conversations with New Classical Economists and their Opponents*, Brighton, Wheatsheaf.

KLAMER Arjo, McCLOSKEY Donald N. and SOLOW Robert M. 1988 (eds). *The Consequences of Economic Rhetoric*, Cambridge, England, Cambridge University Press.

KREGEL Jan A. 1988 (ed.). *Recollections of Eminent Economists*, vol. 1, London, Macmillan; US edn 1989, New York University Press.

KREGEL Jan A. 1989 (ed.). *Recollections of Eminent Economists*, vol. 2, London, Macmillan; US edn 1989, New York University Press.

KUPER Adam and KUPER Jessica 1985. *The Social Science Encyclopedia*, London, Routledge & Kegan Paul.

LAIDLER David 1981. 'Monetarism: An Interpretation and an Assessment', *Economic Journal,* vol. 91, 1–28.

LAIDLER David and PARKIN Michael 1975. 'Inflation – A Survey', *Economic Journal*, vol. 85, 741–97.

LAL Deepak 1992 (ed.). *Development Economics*, 4 vols, Aldershot, Hants, Edward Elgar.

LANGLOIS R.N. 1986 (ed.). *Economics as a Process. Essays in the New Institutional Economics*, Cambridge, England, Cambridge University Press.

LAVOIE Marc 1992. *Foundations of Post-Keynesian Economic Analysis*, Aldershot, Hants, Edward Elgar.

LINDBECK Assar 1985. 'The Prize in Economic Science in Memory of Alfred Nobel', *Journal of Economic Literature*, vol. 23, 37–56.

LITTLECHILD Stephen 1990 (ed.). *Austrian Economics*, 3 vols, Aldershot, Hants, Edward Elgar [Schools of Thought in Economics].

LOASBY Brian J. 1989. *The Mind and Method of the Economist: A Critical Appraisal of Major Economists in the Twentieth Century*, Aldershot, Hants, Edward Elgar.

MACESICH G. 1984. *The Politics of Monetarism: The Historical and Institutional Development*, Towota, New Jersey, Rowman & Allenheld.

MAIR Douglas and MILLER Anne G. 1991. *A Modern Guide to Economic*

Thought: An Introduction to Comparative Schools of Thought in Economics, Aldershot, Hants, Edward Elgar.

MANKIW N. Gregory 1990. 'A Quick Refresher Course in Macroeconomics', *Journal of Economic Literature*, vol. 28, 1645–60.

MANKIW N. Gregory and ROMER David 1991 (eds). *New Keynesian Economics*, vol. 1, *Imperfect Competition and Sticky Prices*; vol. 2, *Coordination Failures and Real Rigidities*, Cambridge, Massachusetts, MIT Press.

MARCHAL André 1953. *La Pensée économique en France depuis 1945*, Paris, Presses Universitaires de France.

MAYER Thomas 1990. *Monetarism and Macroeconomic Policy*, Aldershot, Hants, Edward Elgar.

MAYER, Thomas 1990 (ed.). *Monetary Theory*, Aldershot, Hants, Edward Elgar.

MAYER Thomas *et al.* 1978. *The Structure of Monetarism*, New York, W.W. Norton.

MEIDINGER C. 1983 (ed.). *La Nouvelle économie libérale*, Paris, Presses de la Fondation Nationale des Sciences Politiques.

MEIER Gerald M. and SEERS Dudley 1984 (eds). *Pioneers in Development*, New York, Oxford University Press.

MIROWSKI Philip 1989. *More Heat Than Light. Economics as Social Physics: Physics as Nature's Economics*, Cambridge, England, Cambridge University Press.

MOGGRIDGE Donald E. 1990 (ed.). *Perspectives on the History of Economic Thought*, vol. 4, *Keynes, Macroeconomics and Method*, Aldershot, Hants, Edward Elgar.

MORGAN Mary S. 1990. *The History of Econometric Ideas*, Cambridge, England, Cambridge University Press.

New Palgrave 1987, see EATWELL John, MILGATE Murray and NEWMAN Peter K. 1987 (eds).

O'BRIEN D.P. and PRESLEY J.R. 1981 (eds). *Pioneers of Modern Economics in Britain,* vol. 1, London, Macmillan.

OMMAN Charles P. and WIGNARAJA Ganeshan 1991. *The Postwar Evolution of Development Thinking*, London, Macmillan.

O'SULLIVAN P.J. *et al.* 1990. *Beyond the Austrian School*, London, Macmillan.

PESARAN M.H. 1987. *The Limits to Rational Expectations*, Oxford, Basil Blackwell.

PHEBY John 1989 (ed.). *New Directions in Post-Keynesian Economics*, Aldershot, Hants, Edward Elgar.

PHELPS Edmund S. 1990 (ed.). *Recent Development in Macroeconomics*, Aldershot, Hants, Edward Elgar.

QUANDT Richard E. 1976. 'Some Quantitative Aspects of the Economics Journal Literature', *Journal of Political Economy*, vol. 84, 741–55.

RABOY David 1982 (ed.). *Essays in Supply Side Economics*, Washington, Heritage Foundation.

REDER M.W. 1982. 'Chicago Economics: Permanence and Change', *Journal of Economic Literature*, vol. 20, no. 1, 1–38.

REDMAN Deborah A. 1992. *A Reader's Guide to Rational Expectations: A Survey and Comprehensive Annotated Bibliography*, Aldershot, Hants, Edward Elgar.

RICKETTS Martin I. 1989 (ed.). *Neoclassical Microeconomics*, 2 vols, Aldershot, Hants, Edward Elgar [Schools of Thought in Economics].

RIZZO, M. 1979 (ed.). *Time, Uncertainty and Disequilibrium: Exploration of Austrian Themes,* Lexington, Massachusetts, Lexington Books.

ROBBINS Lionel 1970. *The Evolution of Modern Economic Theory and Other Papers on the History of Economic Thought*, Chicago, Aldine.

ROSEN S. 1985. 'Implicit Contracts: A Survey', *Journal of Economic Literature*, vol. 23, 1144–75.

ROUSSEAS Stephen 1982. *The Political Economy of Reaganomics*, Armonk, New York, M.E. Sharpe.

ROUX Dominique and SOULIE Daniel 1991. *Les Prix Nobel de sciences économiques 1969–1990*, Paris, Economica.

SAMUELS Warren J. 1983– (ed.). *Research in the History of Economic Thought and Methodology*, A Research Annual, Greenwich, Conn. and London, JAI Press.

SAMUELS Warren J. 1989 (ed.). *Institutional Economics*, 3 vols, Aldershot, Hants, Edward Elgar [Schools of Thought in Economics].

SAMUELS Warren J. 1992 (ed.). *New Horizons in Economic Thought*, Aldershot, Hants, Edward Elgar.

SAMUELSON Alain 1985. *Les grands courants de la pensée économique*, Presses Universitaires de Grenoble.

SAWYER Malcolm C. 1989 (ed.). *Post-Keynesian Economics,* Aldershot, Hants, Edward Elgar [Schools of Thought in Economics].

SCHOTTER Andrew and SCHWODIAUER Gerhard 1980. 'Economics and the Theory of Games: A Survey', *Journal of Economic Literature*, vol. 18, 479–527.

SCHUMPETER Joseph A. 1954. *History of Economic Analysis*, London, George Allen & Unwin.

SELIGMAN Ben B. 1962. *Main Currents in Modern Economics: Economic Thought Since 1870*, New York, The Free Press of Glencoe.

SHACKLETON J.R. 1990 (ed.). *New Thinking in Economics*, Aldershot, Hants, Edward Elgar.

SHACKLETON J.R. and LOCKSLEY G. 1981 (eds). *Twelve Contemporary Economists*, London, Macmillan.

SHAND Alexander 1989. *Free Market Morality: The Political Economy of the Austrian School*, London, Routledge.

SHAW Graham K. 1988. *Keynesian Economics: The Permanent Revolution*, Aldershot, Hants, Edward Elgar.

SHAW Graham K. 1989 (ed.). *The Keynesian Heritage*, 2 vols, Aldershot, Hants, Edward Elgar [Schools of Thought in Economics].

SHEFFRIN Steven M. 1983. *Rational Expectations: An Elementary Exposition*, Cambridge, England, Cambridge University Press.

SHEPHERD William G. 1990. 'Mainstream Industrial Organization and "New Schools"', *Revue économique*, vol. 41, 453–80.

SHERMAN Howard J. 1987. *Foundations of Radical Political Economy*, Armonk, New York, M.E. Sharpe.

SHILLER Robert J. 1978. 'Rational Expectations and the Dynamic Structure of Macroeconomic Models: A Critical Review', *Journal of Monetary Economics*, vol. 4, 1–44.

SILK Leonard S. 1976. *The Economists,* New York, Basic Books.

SILLS David F. 1968 (ed.). *International Encyclopedia of the Social Sciences,* 17 vols, New York, The Free Press; London, Collier–Macmillan.

SILLS David F. 1979 (ed.). *International Encyclopedia of the Social Sciences, Biographical Supplement*, vol. 18, New York, The Free Press; London, Collier–Macmillan.

SMITH D. 1988. *The Chicago School: A Liberal Critique of Capitalism*, London, Macmillan.

SMITH Vernon L. 1990 (ed.). *Experimental Economics*, Aldershot, Hants, Edward Elgar [Schools of Thought in Economics].

SMITHIN John N. 1990. *Macroeconomics After Thatcher and Reagan: The Conservative Policy in Retrospect*, Aldershot, Hants, Edward Elgar.

SOBEL R. 1980. *The Worldly Economists*, New York, The Free Press.

SPIEGEL Henry William and SAMUELS Warren J. 1984 (eds). *Contemporary Economists in Perspective*, 2 vols, Greenwich, Connecticut and London, JAI Press.

STEEDMAN Ian 1989 (ed.). *Sraffian Economics*, 2 vols, Aldershot, Hants, Edward Elgar [Schools of Thought in Economics].

STEELE G.R. 1989. *Monetarism and the Demise of Keynesian Economics*, London, Macmillan.

STEIN Jerome L. 1976 (ed.). *Monetarism, Studies in Monetary Economy*, Amsterdam, North-Holland.

STEIN Jerome L. 1982. *Monetarism, Keynesian and New Classical Economics*, New York University Press.

STERN N. 1989. 'The Economics of Development', *Economic Journal*, vol. 99, 597–685.

STURGES Paul 1990 (ed.). *Who's Who in British Economics: A Directory of Economists in Higher Education, Business and Government*, Aldershot, Hants, Edward Elgar.

SZENBERG Michael 1992 (ed.). *Eminent Economists: Their Life Philosophies*, Cambridge, England, Cambridge University Press.

THYGESEN Niels and VELUPILLAI Kumaraswamy 1991 (eds). *Recent Development in Business Cycle Theory*, London, Macmillan.

TOOL Marc 1988 (ed.). *Evolutionary Economics: Foundations of Institutional Thought*, 2 vols, Armonk, New York, M.E. Sharpe.

WALKER Donald A. 1989 (ed.). *Perspectives on the History of Economic Thought*, vol. 2, *Twentieth-Century Economic Thought*, Aldershot, Hants, Edward Elgar.

WALLISER Bernard and PROU Charles 1988. *La Science économique*, Paris, Seuil.

WALSH V. and GRAM H. 1980. *Classical and Neo-Classical Theories of General Equilibrium*, Oxford University Press.

WARD B. 1979. *The Ideal Worlds of Economics. Liberal, Radical and Conservative World Views*, New York, Basic Books.

WARSH David 1993. *Economic Principals: Masters and Mavericks of Modern Economics*, New York, Free Press.

WEINTRAUB E.R. 1991. *Stabilizing Dynamics*, Cambridge, England, Cambridge University Press.

WEINTRAUB Sidney 1977 (ed.). *Modern Economic Thought*, Philadelphia, University of Pennsylvania Press.

WOOD Geoffrey 1989 (ed.). *Monetary Economics in the 1980s*, London, Macmillan.

WOOD John Cunningham 1989– (series ed.). *Critical Assessments of Contemporary Economists,* London, Routledge.

YOUNG Warren 1987. *Interpreting Mr Keynes: The IS/LM Enigma*, Boulder, Colorado, Westview Press; Oxford, Basil Blackwell.

ZARNOWITZ Victor 1985. 'Recent Work on Business Cycles in Historical Perspective: A Review of Theories and Evidence', *Journal of Economic Literature*, vol. 23, 523–80.

Name index

Subject index

4 3 3 9 5 0 1 0 0 3 0 9 8 4 4 2 7 7 2 6 0 1 2

CHARTERHOUSE LIBRARY
007002